Land Rover
One Ten
Parts Catalogue

Part No RTC9863CE

Covering Vehicles up to Aug. 1986

Whilst every effort is made to ensure the accuracy of the particulars contained in this Catalogue, modifications and vehicle specification changes may effect the information specified. No responsibility is accepted for the incorrect supply of parts or any other consequence that may arise as a result of information in this Catalogue not being in accord with modifications or vehicle specifications changes which are subsequent to the date of this Catalogue. Also no responsibility is accepted for the incorrect supply of parts or any other consequence that may arise as a result of any misinterpretation of information specified in this Catalogue.

LAND ROVER PARTS LTD

VEHICLE AND SERIAL COMMENCING NUMBERS
SERIE VEHICULE ET ORGANE NUMEROS DE DEBUT
SERIENANFANGSNUMMERN DER FAHRZEUGE UND ENHEITEN

10H00001A   2.25 Petrol 8:1 CR Non Detoxed
11H00001A   2.25 Petrol 8:1 CR Detoxed
13H00001A   2.25 Petrol 7:1 CR Low Compression

10J00001A   2.25 Diesel
12J00001C   2.5 Diesel

LAND ROVER PARTS LTD

VEHICLE AND SERIAL COMMENCING NUMBERS
SERIE VEHICULE ET ORGANE NUMEROS DE DEBUT
SERIENANFANGSNUMMERN DER FAHRZEUGE UND ENHEITEN

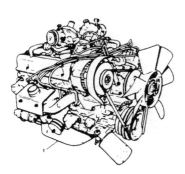

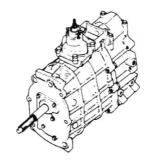

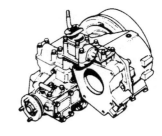

14G00001A   3.5 Litre V8 8.13:1 CR Non Detoxed
15G00001A   3.5 Litre V8 8.13:1 CR Detoxed
17G00001A   3.5 Litre V8   Detoxed
20G00001A   3.5 Litre V8   Non Detoxed
21G00001A   3.5 Litre V8   Detoxed
24G00001A   3.5 Litre V8   Detoxed

50A00001A Gearbox 2.25 Petrol and Diesel
                  2.5 Diesel

10D00001A   Transfer Box 2.25P&D 2.4 WD
                         2.5D 2/4 WD
12D00001A   Transfer Box 2.25P&D Perm 4 WD
                         2.5D   Perm 4 WD
20D00001A   Transfer Box 4 Cyl   Perm 4WD
25D00001A   Transfer Box V8   Perm 4WD

LAND ROVER PARTS LTD

VEHICLE AND SERIAL COMMENCING NUMBERS
SERIE VEHICULE ET ORGANE NUMEROS DE DEBUT
SERIENANFANGSNUMMERN DER FAHRZEUGE UND ENHEITEN

AXLE SERIAL NUMBERS

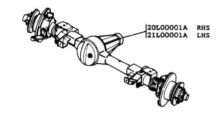

20L00001A   RHS
21L00001A   LHS

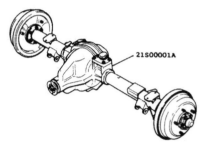

21S00001A

13C00001A   Gearbox 3.5 Litre V8 4 Speed
20C00001A   Gearbox 3.5 Litre V8 5 Speed
22C00001A   Gearbox 3.5 Litre V8 5 Speed

LAND ROVER PARTS LTD

EXTERIOR PAINT CODES

Paint colour codes are recorded on the Vehicle Identification Plate

Body Colour	Code
Russet	AAE
Sand	ACF
Masai Red	CCC
Bronze Green	HCC
Light Green	HCD
Marine Blue	JCC

Body Colour	Code
Mid Grey	LCB
Limestone	NCJ
Trident Green	HCN
Roan Brown	ACV
Stratos Blue	JCP

EXTERIOR PAINT - DIRECT SUPPLY

Supplies of re-finishing paints are available in one litre cans from International Pinchin Johnson outlets. To obtain details of the service and facilities offered, or in the event of any difficulties, please contact I.P.J. direct.

For Home and European
Markets:

International Pinchin Johnson
Transport Paints Division
PO Box 359
Rotton Park Street
Ladywood
Birmingham
B16 0AD

Telephone: 021-455-9866

Telex: 339266

For Overseas
Markets:

International Pinchin Johnson
Export Division
380 Richmond Road
Kingston-Upon-Thames
Surrey
England

Telephone: 01-546-1234

Telex: 27527

LAND ROVER UK LTD

1-
2-

PAINT   TRIM

LAND -
- ROVER

LAND ROVER PARTS LTD

VEHICLE IDENTIFICATION NUMBERING

VIN CODE	ENGINE	GEARBOX	STEERING
HIGH CAPACITY PICK-UP			
SALLDHHH7AA	2.25 Petrol	5 Speed	RH Stg
SALLDHHH7BA	2.25 Petrol	5 Speed	RH Stg
SALLDHHH8AA	2.25 Petrol	5 Speed	LH Stg
SALLDHHH8BA	2.25 Petrol	5 Speed	LH Stg
SALLDHHD7BA	2.5 Petrol	5 Speed	RH Stg
SALLDHHD8BA	2.5 Petrol	5 Speed	LH Stg
SALLDHHG7AA	2.25 Diesel	5 Speed	RH Stg
SALLDHHG8AA	2.25 Diesel	5 Speed	LH Stg
SALLDHHC7AA	2.5 Diesel	5 Speed	RH Stg
SALLDHHC7BA	2.5 Diesel	5 Speed	RH Stg
SALLDHHC8AA	2.5 Diesel	5 Speed	LH Stg
SALLDHHC8BA	2.5 Diesel	5 Speed	LH Stg
SALLDHHV1AA	3.5 Petrol	4 Speed	RH Speed
SALLDHHV1BA	3.5 Petrol	4 Speed	RH Stg
SALLDHHV7BA	3.5 Petrol	5 Speed	RH Stg
SALLDHHV2AA	3.5 Petrol	4 Speed	LH Stg
SALLDHHV2BA	3.5 Petrol	4 Speed	LH Stg
SALLDHHV8BA	3.5 Petrol	5 Speed	LH Stg

Note: In some instances the 7th digit in the VIN CODE for the High-Capacity Pick-Up will read 'A' instead of 'H'

VEHICLE IDENTIFICATION NUMBERING

VIN CODE	ENGINE	GEARBOX	STEERING
HOOD/CAB/HARDTOP			
SALLDHAH7AA	2.25 Petrol	5 Speed	RH Stg
SALLDHAH7BA	2.25 Petrol	5 Speed	RH Stg
SALLDHAH8AA	2.25 Petrol	5 Speed	LH Stg
SALLDHAH8BA	2.25 Petrol	5 Speed	LH Stg
SALLDHAD7BA	2.5 Petrol	5 Speed	RH Stg
SALLDHAD8BA	2.5 Petrol	5 Speed	LH Stg
SALLDHAG7AA	2.25 Diesel	5 Speed	RH Stg
SALLDHAG8AA	2.25 Diesel	5 Speed	LH Stg
SALLDHAC7AA	2.5 Diesel	5 Speed	RH Stg
SALLDHAC7BA	2.5 Diesel	5 Speed	RH Stg
SALLDHAC8AA	2.5 Diesel	5 Speed	LH Stg
SALLDHAC8BA	2.5 Diesel	5 Speed	LH Stg
SALLDHAV1AA	3.5 Petrol	4 Speed	RH Stg
SALLDHAV1BA	3.5 Petrol	4 Speed	RH Stg
SALLDHAV7BA	3.5 Petrol	5 Speed	RH Stg
SALLDHAV2AA	3.5 Petrol	4 Speed	LH Stg
SALLDHAV2BA	3.5 Petrol	4 Speed	LH Stg
SALLDHAV8BA	3.5 Petrol	5 Speed	LH Stg
STATION WAGON			
SALLDHMH7AA	2.25 Petrol	5 Speed	RH Stg
SALLDHMH7BA	2.25 Petrol	5 Speed	RH Stg
SALLDHMH8AA	2.25 Petrol	5 Speed	LH Stg
SALLDHMH8BA	2.25 Petrol	5 Speed	LH Stg
SALLDHMD7BA	2.5 Petrol	5 Speed	RH Stg
SALLDHMD8BA	2.5 Petrol	5 Speed	LH Stg
SALLDHMG7AA	2.25 Diesel	5 Speed	RH Stg
SALLDHMG8AA	2.25 Diesel	5 Speed	LH Stg
SALLDHMC7AA	2.5 Diesel	5 Speed	RH Stg
SALLDHMC7BA	2.5 Diesel	5 Speed	RH Stg
SALLDHMC8AA	2.5 Diesel	5 Speed	LH Stg
SALLDHMC8BA	2.5 Diesel	5 Speed	LH Stg
SALLDHMV1AA	3.5 Petrol	4 Speed	RH Stg
SALLDHMV1BA	3.5 Petrol	4 Speed	RH Stg
SALLDHMV7BA	3.5 Petrol	5 Speed	RH Stg
SALLDHMV2AA	3.5 Petrol	4 Speed	LH Stg
SALLDHMV2BA	3.5 Petrol	4 Speed	LH Stg
SALLDHMV8BA	3.5 Petrol	5 Speed	LH Stg

LAND ROVER PARTS LTD

6

FITTING INSTRUCTION FOR INTERMEDIATE SEAT BELT MOUNTINGS LOWER
  - LR110

1.0 Jack up rear of vehicle, support on stands, remove road wheels.

2.0 Fold intermediate seats forward (or remove) and remove rear load space mat or carpet.

3.0 Outer Lower Mounting:
    Remove existing bolt(A), floor to bodyframe and ensure a full 5/16" clearance.

3.1 Fit bracket (347844) under wheelarch and temporally secure at lower end using bolt (SH605081L) and nut (SH605041L). Ensure that the slots in the bracket are located over the outer pair of pop rivets.

3.2 Drill upper fixing hole 5/16" from under wheelarch and fit bolt (255227) to locate bracket.

3.3 Mark position of lower seat belt fixing point on the underside of the wheelarch. Remove bracket and drill seat belt fixing with 1/4" pilot hole and then open up to 5/8"

3.4 Refit bracket using bolt (SH605081L) 1 off at lower fixing and bolt (255227) 1 off at the upper fixing. Secure using plain washer (3830L) spring washer (WM600051L) and nut (NH605041L).

4.0 Floor Mounting.
    Locate step in wheelarch box and draw a vertical line down to floor. Find mid point between rivets in floor and draw a line across the floor.

4.1 Measure 6¹/₂" and 10¹/₄" from, either side of wheelarch and mark position. Drill 1/4" pilot holes through floor and crossmember.

4.2 On outer holes open up to 5/8" through floor skin only, open pilot holes to 5/16" in crossmember. On inner holes open up to 5/8" through floor and crossmember.

4.3 In outer holes fit spacers, screws, washers and nuts and tighten. Place anchor point tube in inner holes, drill holes 3/16" for rivets and rivet to floor.

4.4 From under vehicle fit screws, washers and tabwashers. Tighten screw and bend tabwasher over screws and crossmember.

5.0 Replace rear mat or carpet and replace seats.

6.0 Replace road wheels and remove vehicle from stands.

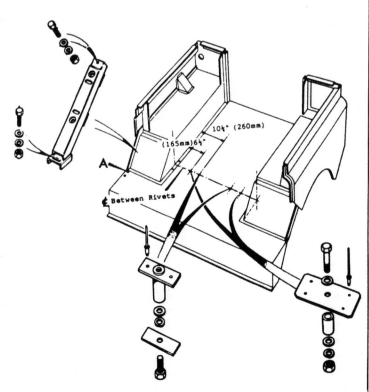

LAND ROVER PARTS LTD

7

FITTING INSTRUCTION FOR REAR INWARD FACING SEAT BELT MOUNTINGS - LR110

1.0 Remove inward facing seats.

2.0 Jack up vehicle, support on stands and remove rear road wheels.

3.0 Remove rear light covers and the rear tool retaining strap from wheelarch.

4.0 Check stiffeners and open holes for monobolts ref A on illustration to 17/64"

5.0 Mark position for stiffeners as follows:
Front Stiffener (B)
From step in wheelarch box measure 7 1/4", draw a line from wheelarch inner edge to bodyside. Measure 1.5/8" from bodyside and drill 1/4" pilot hole.

5.1 Centre Stiffener (C)
From step in wheelarch box measure 23.1/8" and 24.5/15", draw a line from wheelarch inner edge to bodyside. Measure 1.5/8" from bodyside and drill 1/4" pilot holes.

5.2 Rear Stiffener (C)
From step in wheelarch box measure 43.1/8", draw a line from whee-larch inner edge to bodyside. Measure 4.5/8" from bodyside and drill 1/4" pilot holes.

5.3 Open up pilot holes to 5/8" and deburr.

6.0 Front and Centre Stiffener

From under vehicle position stiffeners to wheelarch box, locate angel bracket and use 7/16" UNF bolt and washer to position stiffen-ers, tighten bolt, drill 3/16" holes for rivets ref E, deburr and rivet, drill holes 17/64" for monobolts Ref A, deburr and rivet up.

6.1 Rear Stiffener.

From under wheelarch at rear of vehicle remove rubber protector for rear lamp wiring, trim 1/4" to 1/2" from top of protector to allow stiffener to fit body. Remove excess sealer as required and refit rubber protector. Position stiffener to wheelarch box, use 7/16" UNF bolt and washer to position stiffener, drill 3/16" holes for rivets, deburr and rivet, drill holes 17/64" for monobolts deburr and rivet up.

7.0 Remove 7/16" bolts and repeat operations for opposite wheelarch.

8.0 Refit light covers and re position tool retaining strap to forward edge of centre angle bracket.

Fit seatbelts with long end of belt in centre fixings and tighten -

9.0 Refit seats - Road Wheels and remove vehicle from stands.

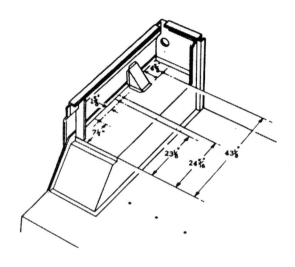

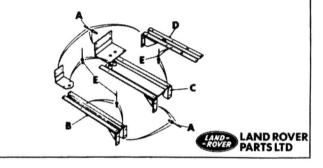

LAND ROVER PARTS LTD

MASTER INDEX

GROUP B

ENGINE

MODEL LR110 - UP TO AUGUST 1986
BLOCK VS 4134
PAGE B 2
GROUP B

ENGINE - 2.25 PETROL - ENGINE ASSEMBLY COMPLETE

ILL	PART NO	DESCRIPTION	QTY REMARKS
		NO FULL ASSEMBLIES AVAILABLE	

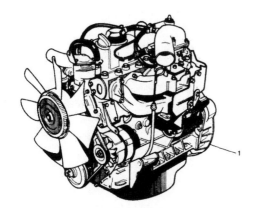

VS4134

MODEL LR110 - UP TO AUGUST 1986
BLOCK TS 6461
PAGE B 4
GROUP B

ENGINE - 2.25 PETROL - ENGINE ASSEMBLY STRIPPED

ILL	PART NO	DESCRIPTION	QTY	REMARKS
1	RTC2918N	Engine Assembly Stripped-New	1	
	RTC2918E	Engine Assembly Stripped-Exchange	1	

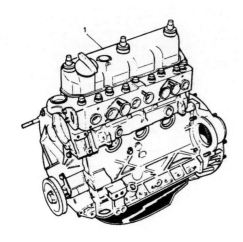

TS 6461

LAND ROVER PARTS LTD

18

MODEL LR110 - UP TO AUGUST 1986
BLOCK TS 6357
PAGE B 6
GROUP B

ENGINE - 2.25 PETROL - SHORT ENGINES

ILL	PART NO	DESCRIPTION	QTY	REMARKS
1	RTC2978	Short Engine Assembly	1	8:1C/R

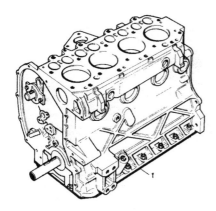

TS6357

LAND ROVER PARTS LTD

19

MODEL LR110 - UP TO AUGUST 1986
BLOCK VS 3736
PAGE B 8
GROUP B

ENGINE - 2.25 PETROL - CYLINDER BLOCK

ILL	PART NO	DESCRIPTION	QTY	REMARKS
1	RTC2926	CYLINDER BLOCK ASSEMBLY	1	
2	247965	+Plug-Tappet Feed Hole	1	
3	247127	+Plug-Oil Gallery	2	
4	213700	+Dowel-Chain Tensioner	2	
5	501593	+Dowel-Bearing Caps	10	
6	ERC4996	+Cup Plug-Side/Ends	6	
7	597586	+Cup Plug-Water Rail/Ends	3	
8	ERC4644	+Dowel-Flywheel Housing	2	
9	527269	+Plug-Immersion Heater	1	
10	243959	+Joint Washer-Gallery Pipe	2	
11	536577	+Plug-Gallery Pipe	2	
12	90519054	+Camshaft Bearing-Front	1	
13	90519055	+Camshaft Bearing-Inter/Rear	3	
14	ERC4995	+Cup Plug-Top Plug	2	
15	247755	+Bolt-Main Bearing Cap	10	
16	504006	+Washer	10	

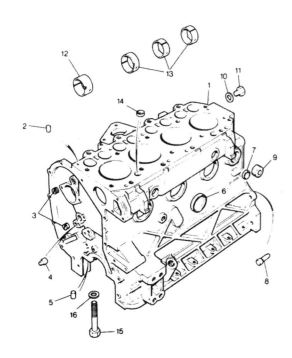

VS3736

LAND ROVER PARTS LTD

MODEL LR110 - UP TO AUGUST 1986
BLOCK TS 5766
PAGE B 10
GROUP B

ENGINE - 2.25 PETROL - ENGINE MOUNTINGS

ILL	PART NO	DESCRIPTION	QTY	REMARKS
1	NRC5434	Mounting Foot RH	1	
2	NRC9557	Mounting Foot LH	1	
3	SH112251L	Screw	4	
4	WL112001L	Spring Washer	4	
5	ERC9410	Drain Plug	1	
6	AFU1882L	Joint Washer-Drain Plug	1	
7	ERC5086	Packing Strip	2	
8	NRC9560	Rubber-Engine Mounting	2	
9	NH110041L	Nut-Rubber to Foot	4	
10	WC110061L	Washer-Rubber to Foot	2	
11	WL110001L	Washer Spring-Rubber to Foot	4	

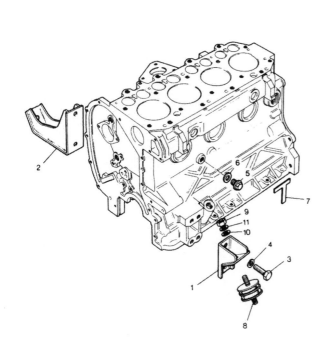

TS5766

LAND ROVER PARTS LTD

MODEL LR110 - UP TO AUGUST 1986
BLOCK 1RE 99
PAGE B 12
GROUP B

ENGINE - 2.25 PETROL - PISTONS

ILL	PART NO	DESCRIPTION	QTY	REMARKS
		PISTON ASSEMBLY		
1	RTC4188S	+Standard	4	)
	RTC418820	+0.020"(0.508mm) O/S	4	)8:1 CR
	RTC418840	+0.040"(1.016mm) O/S	4	)
		RING-PISTON-PISTON SET		
2	RTC4190S	+Standard	1	
	RTC419020	+0.020"(0.508mm) O/S	1	
	RTC419040	+0.040"(1.016mm) O/S	1	
3	265169	+Gudgeon Pin	4	
4	265175	+Circlip	8	
5	ETC5157	ROD ASSEMBLY CONNECTING	4	
6	528004	+Bush-Gudgeon Pin	4	
7	ERC8751	+Bolt-Conn Rod	8	
8	ETC5155	+Nut-Conn Rod	8	
		BEARING-CONNECTING ROD ENG SET		
9	RTC1730	+Standard	1	
	RTC173010	+0.010"(0.254mm) U/S	1	
	RTC173020	+0.020"(0.508mm) U/S	1	

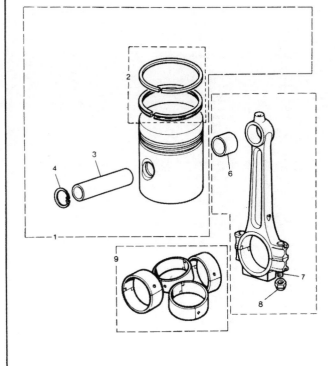

1RE99

MODEL LR110 - UP TO AUGUST 1986
BLOCK VS 3722
PAGE B 14
GROUP B

ENGINE - 2.25 PETROL - CRANKSHAFT

ILL	PART NO	DESCRIPTION	QTY	REMARKS
1	ERC5014	CRANKSHAFT ASSEMBLY	1	
2	ERC4650	+Dowel	1	
3	8566L	+Bush	1	
		KIT MAIN BEARINGS		
4	RTC2626	+Standard	1	
	RTC262610	+0.010"(0.254mm) U/S	1	
	RTC262620	+0.020"(0.508mm) U/S	1	
5	23577D	Key-Chainwheel	1	
6	568333	Chainwheel	1	
		KIT-THRUST WASHERS		
7	RTC2825	+Standard	1	
	538131	+0.0025" O/S	1	
	538132	+0.005" O/S	1	
	538133	+0.0075" O/S	1	
	538134	+0.010" O/S	1	
8	ERC5349	Crankshaft Pulley	1	)NLA Use RTC4817)Except PAS &)Air Con
	ERC5128	Crankshaft Pulley	1	Power Steering
	ERC5127	Crankshaft Pulley	1	)NLA Use RTC4815)Air Con
	ERC7089	Crankshaft Pulley	1	)NLA-Use RTC4816)Power Steering)& Air Con
	RTC4817	Crankshaft Pulley	1	)Except Power Stg)& Air Con
	RTC4815	Crankshaft Pulley	1	Air Con Only
	RTC4816	Crankshaft Pulley	1	)Power Stg &)Air Con
9	ERC4672	Starting Dog	1	)Alternative
	ETC7934	Bolt-Crankshaft	1	)
10	ETC5369	Oil Seal	1	

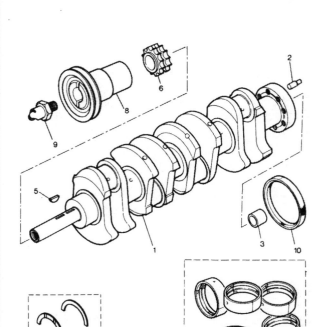

VS3722

MODEL LR110 - UP TO AUGUST 1986
BLOCK 1RE 106
PAGE B 16
GROUP B

ENGINE - 2.25 PETROL - OIL PUMP

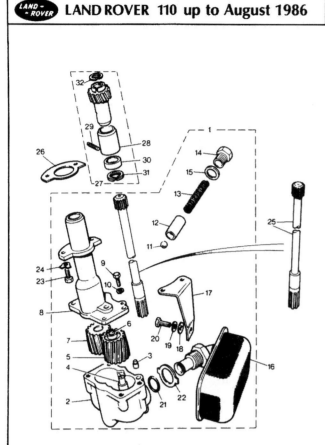

ILL	PART NO	DESCRIPTION	QTY	REMARKS
1	ETC7054	OIL PUMP ASSEMBLY	1	
2	513641	+Oil Pump Body-Note(1)	1	)Upto Suffix B)No Longer)Serviced
	ETC4464	+Oil Pump Body-Note(1)	1	)From Suffix C)No Longer)Serviced
	ETC5646	+Oil Pump Body-Note(2)	1	
3	236257	+Dowel	2	
4	90502209	+Idler Wheel Spindle	1	
5	278109	++Idler Wheel Assembly	1	)Note(1)
6	214995	++Bush	1	)
7	240555	+Driver Wheel	1	)
5	ERC9707	+Idler Wheel	1	)Note(2)
7	ERC9706	+Driver Wheel	1	)
8	513639	+Oil Pump Cover	1	)No Longer)Serviced
9	SH605071L	+Bolt	4	)To Suffix B
10	WM600051L	+Spring Washer	4	)
9	SH108201L	+Bolt	4	)From Suffix C
10	WL108001L	+Spring Washer	4	)
11	3748	+Ball-Oil Relief-Note(1)	1	
12	273111	+Plunger-Oil Relief-Note(1)	1	
	ETC4880	+Plunger-Oil Relief-Note(2)	1	)No Longer)Available
13	564456	+Spring-Oil Relief	1	
14	549909	+End Plug-Oil Relief	1	)Without Oil)Cooler
	564455	+End Plug-Oil Relief	1	)With Oil Cooler)& all Pumps)with Ten)Toothed Gears
15	232044	+Joint Washer-Oil Relief	1	

NOTE(1): For Pumps With Nine Toothed Gears

NOTE(2): For Pumps With Ten Toothed Gears

1RE106

LAND ROVER PARTS LTD

24

MODEL LR110 - UP TO AUGUST 1986
BLOCK 1RE 106
PAGE B 16.02
GROUP B

ENGINE - 2.25 PETROL - OIL PUMP CONTINUED

ILL	PART NO	DESCRIPTION	QTY	REMARKS
16	ERC7530	+Filter	1	
17	ERC7940	+Bracket-Support	1	
18	WA108051L	+Washer	1	
19	WL108001L	+Washer-Spring	1	
20	SH108201L	+Screw	1	
21	244488	+O Ring	1	
22	244487	+Lockwasher	1	
23	SH108251L	+Bolt	2	
24	247665	+Lockwasher	2	
25	ERC9669	Shaft	1	
26	ERC8408	Gasket-Pump Cover to Block	1	
27	ETC6139	DRIVE SHAFT GEAR & BUSH ASSY	1	
28	522745	+Bush	1	
29	ERC8976	+Locating Screw	1	)Earlier Type
30	530178	+Thrust Washer	1	)With Spring Ring
31	530179	+Retaining Ring	1	)Type of Retainer
29	ETC6142	+Locating Screw	1	)Later Type with
30	ETC6137	+Thrust Washer	1	)Locking Ring
31	ETC6138	+Locking Ring	1	)Type of)Retainer
32	247742	+Circlip	1	

1RE106

LAND ROVER PARTS LTD

25

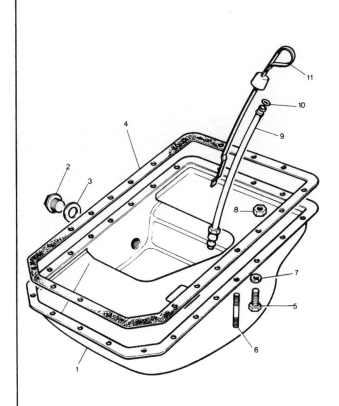

```
MODEL LR110 - UP TO AUGUST 1986
BLOCK 1RE 131
PAGE B 18
GROUP B

ENGINE - 2.25 PETROL - SUMP
```

ILL	PART NO	DESCRIPTION	QTY	REMARKS
1	RTC4841	Sump	1	
2	536577	Drain Plug	1	Upto Engine No 07464
	ETC5577	Drain Plug	1	From Engine No 07465
3	243959	Joint Washer-Plug	1	Upto Engine No 07464
	FRC4808	Joint Washer-Plug	1	From Engine No 07465
4	546841	Joint Washer-Sump	1	Note(1)
5	SH108251L	Screw	21	)Use with Earlier
6	TE108041L	Stud	1	)Type of Sump
7	WL108001L	Spring Washer	22	)that has
8	NH108041L	Nut	1	)Stiffeners
				)Welded to the
				)Flange
1	RTC4841	SUMP ASSEMBLY	1	Note(2)
2	ETC5577	+Plug	1	
3	FRC4808	+Joint Washer-Plug	1	
5	SH108161L	+Screw	21	
6	TE108031L	+Stud	1	
7	WL108001L	+Spring Washer	22	
8	NH108041L	+Nut	1	
9	ERC8980	Tube-Oil Level Rod	1	
10	532387	Sealing Ring-Tube	1	
11	ETC7867	Oil Level Rod	1	

```
NOTE(1):  Later Sump Is Sealed With Liquid Gasket Compound. The
          Sump Gasket 546841 Can Be Fitted As An Alternative
          For Service.

NOTE(2):  Latest Sump Has A Thinner Flange & Should Be Fitted
          Using The Fixings Enclosed With The Kit To Prevent
          The Screws Bottoming.
```

1RE131

 **LAND ROVER PARTS LTD**

```
MODEL 110 - UP TO AUGUST 1986
BLOCK 1RE 273
PAGE B 20
GROUP B

ENGINE - 2.25 PETROL - TIMING CHAIN
```

ILL	PART NO	DESCRIPTION	QTY	REMARKS
1	ETC4499	Timing Chain	1	
2	3739	Ball	1	
3	233328	Retaining Clip-Ball	1	
4	233326	Spring-Tensioner Cylinder	1	
5	267451	Spring-Ratchet	1	
6	ERC8975	Stepped Bolt	1	
7	247912	Piston Assembly-Timing Tensioner	1	
8	546026	Ratched & Bush Assembly	1	
9	236067	IDLER WHEEL & BUSH ASSEMBLY	1	
10	234124	+Bush	1	
11	277388	Cylinder Assembly-Chain Tensioner	1	
12	TE108051L	Stud	1	
13	BH108061L	Bolt	1	
14	WL108001L	Spring Washer	1	
15	NH108041L	Nut	1	
16	275234	Vibration Damper	1	
17	SH106121L	Screw	2	
18	557523	Lockwasher	2	

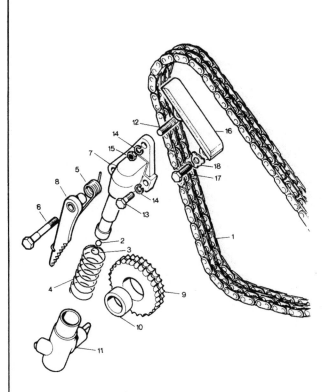

1RE273

LAND ROVER PARTS LTD

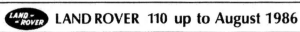
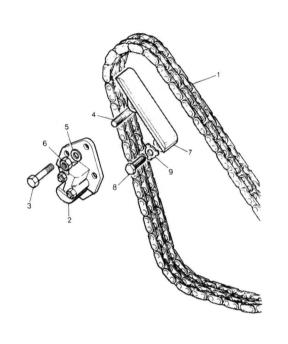

MODEL LR110 - UP TO AUGUST 1986
BLOCK TS 5365
PAGE B 20.02
GROUP B

ENGINE - 2.25 PETROL - TIMING CHAIN

ILL	PART NO	DESCRIPTION	QTY	REMARKS
1	ETC5191	Timing Chain	1	
2	ETC5190	Tensioner-Timing Chain	1	
3	SH108201L	Screw	2	
4	TE108051L	Stud	1	
5	WA108051L	Washer	3	
6	NH108041L	Nut	1	
7	275234	Vibration Damper	1	
8	SH106121L	Screw	2	
9	557523	Lock Washer	2	

TS5365

MODEL LR110 - UP TO AUGUST 1986
BLOCK VS 3734A
PAGE B 22
GROUP B

ENGINE - 2.25 PETROL - CAMSHAFT

ILL	PART NO	DESCRIPTION	QTY	REMARKS
1	ERC5475	Camshaft	1	)No Longer)Available)Use ETC7128
	ETC7128	Camshaft	1	
2	ERC1561	Thrust Plate	1	
3	SH106161L	Screw	2	
4	2995	Lockwasher	2	
5	230313	Woodruff Key	1	
6	ETC5551	Chainwheel-Camshaft	1	
7	ETC4140	Retaining Washer	1	
8	ETC4141	Retaining Bolt	1	)Use with)Camshaft ERC5475
	BH110071L	Retaining Bolt	1	)Use with)Camshaft)ETC7128

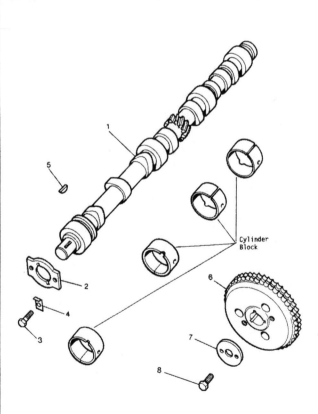

Cylinder Block

VS3734A

MODEL LR110 - UP TO AUGUST 1986
BLOCK 1RE 101
PAGE B 24
GROUP B

ENGINE - 2.25 PETROL - VALVES AND TAPPETS

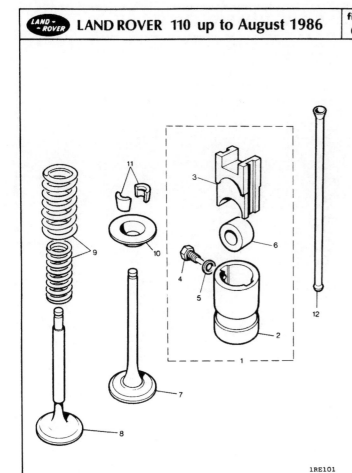

ILL	PART NO	DESCRIPTION	QTY	REMARKS
1	507829	TAPPET ASSEMBLY	8	
2	502473	+Tappet Guide	8	
3	ETC5057	+Tappet	8	
4	ETC4246	+Bolt	8	
5	273069	+Plain Washer	8	
6	90517429	+Roller Follower	8	
7	ERC7150	Inlet Valve	4	)Up to Engine
8	ERC7151	Exhaust Valve	4	)No 11H02983C
7	ETC4067	Inlet Valve	4	)From Engine
8	ETC4066	EXHAUST VALVE	4	)No 11H02984C
	ETC5866	EXHAUST VALVE	4	)For Use On)Cylinder Heads)with Exhaust)Valve Seat)Insert
9	ETC7203	+Valve Stem Protection Cap	8	See Note Below
9	568550	Valve Spring	8	
10	268292	Cup-Valve Spring	8	)Up to Engine
11	268293	Split Cotter Halves	16	)No 11H02983C
10	ETC4068	Cup-Valve Spring	8	)From Engine
11	ETC4069	Split Cotter Halves	16	)No 11H02984C
12	546798	Push Rod	8	

NOTE: Can Be Fitted If Suffering From Excessive Valve Stem
      Or Valve Rocker Wear.

1RE101

LAND ROVER PARTS LTD

30

MODEL LR110 - UP TO AUGUST 1986
BLOCK 1RE 102A
PAGE B 26
GROUP B

ENGINE - 2.25 PETROL - VALVE ROCKERS

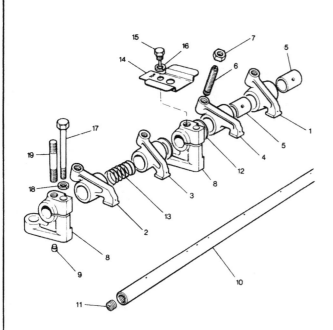

ILL	PART NO	DESCRIPTION	QTY	REMARKS
1	90512208	Valve Rocker Assy-Exhaust-RH	2	)
2	512207	Valve Rocker Assy-Exhaust-LH	2	)To Suffix B Inc
3	512206	Valve Rocker Assy-Inlet-RH	2	)
4	90512205	Valve Rocker Assy-Inlet-LH	2	)
1	ERC9103	Valve Rocker Assy-Exhaust-RH	2	)
2	ERC9102	Valve Rocker Assy-Exhaust-LH	2	)Suffix C Onward
3	ERC9107	Valve Rocker Assy-Inlet-RH	2	)
4	ERC9106	Valve Rocker Assy-Inlet-LH	2	)
5	247614	Bush	8	
6	506814	Adjusting Screw	8	)
7	NT605061L	Locknut	8	)To Suffix B Inc
8	554602	Pedestal Bracket	5	)
6	ERC9054	Adjusting Screw	8	)
7	NT108041L	Locknut	8	)Suffix C Onward
8	ERC9138	Pedestal Bracket	5	)
9	277956	Ring Dowel	3	
10	ERC6341	ROCKER SHAFT ASSEMBLY	1	
11	ERC6337	+Plug	2	
12	525389	Plain Washer	6	
13	247040	Spring	4	
14	ERC9278	Breather-Baffle Plate	1	
15	525390	Screw-Locating	1	)To Suffix B Inc
16	WM600051L	Spring-Washer	1	)
15	ETC4460	Screw-Locating	1	)Suffix C Onward
16	WL108001L	Spring Washer	1	)
17	BH108151L	Bolt	5	
18	WL108001L	Washer-Spring	5	
19	TE605211L	Stud	3	To Suffix B Inc
19	TE108111L	Stud	3	Suffix C Onward

1RE102A

LAND ROVER PARTS LTD

31

MODEL LR110 - UP TO AUGUST 1986
BLOCK VS 3739
PAGE B 28
GROUP B

ENGINE - 2.25 PETROL - ROCKER COVER

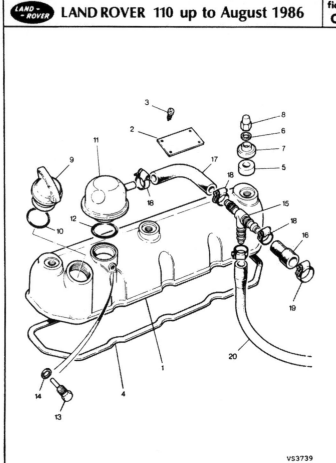

ILL	PART NO	DESCRIPTION	QTY	REMARKS
1	ERC2866	ROCKER COVER	1	)
2	247634	+Plate-Tappet Clearance	1	)Note(1)
3	AB606021L	+Screw-Plate to Cover	4	)
4	ETC6439	Joint Washer Cover to Head	1	
5	506069	Sealing Washer	3	Note(1)
6	273069	Sealing Washer	3	
7	247624	Cover for Washer	3	Note(1)
8	247121	Domed Nut	3	To Suffix B Only
	ERC9220	Domed Nut	3	Suffix C Onward
9	625038	Oil Filler Cap	1	)
10	564258	O Ring-Filler Cap	1	)
11	574658	Breather Silencer Assembly	1	)Note(1)
12	268887	O Ring-Breather	1	)
13	515291	Screw	1	)
14	232037	Joint Washer	1	)
15	ERC6200	Tee Piece	1	
16	ERC9032	Hose-Tee Piece to Elbow	1	
17	ERC9031	Hose-Rocker to Tee Piece	1	
18	CN100208L	Clip-Hose	4	Optional
19	CN100148L	Clip-Hose	1	
20	ERC9033	Hose-Tee Piece to Carb	1	
1	ETC5955	Rocker Cover	1	)
5	ETC5297	Breather Silencer Assembly	1	)Note(2)
6	ERC8049	O Ring-Breather	1	)

NOTE(1):   Use With Earlier Rocker Cover
           (ERC2866) Which Has Seperate Oil Filter &
           Breather Filter Holes.

NOTE(2):   Use With Latest Type Rocker Cover (ETC5955)
           Which Uses Breather Filter Hole As The Oil Filler.

VS3739

LAND ROVER PARTS LTD

MODEL LR110 - UP TO AUGUST 1986
BLOCK VS 3738A
PAGE B 30
GROUP B

ENGINE - 2.25 PETROL - SIDE COVERS

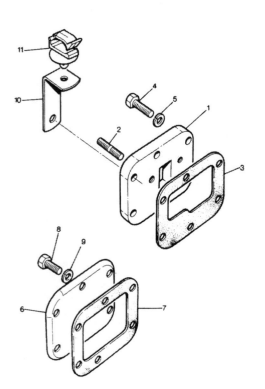

ILL	PART NO	DESCRIPTION	QTY	REMARKS
1	542600	SIDE COVER & STUD ASSEMBLY REAR	1	)To Suffix B)Only
	ERC9073	SIDE COVER & STUD ASSEMBLY REAR	1	)Suffix C Onward)
	ETC4799	SIDE COVER REAR	1	)Vehicles with)Electrical Fuel)Pump Only.
2	542601	+Stud	2	To Suffix B Only
	TE108041L	+Stud	2	Suffix C Onward
3	247554	Joint Washer-Cover to Block	1	
4	SH108251L	Screw	6	
5	WL108001L	Spring Washer	6	
6	ERC2869	Side Cover-Front	1	
7	247555	Joint Washer-Cover to Block	1	)Engines with)Mechanical Fuel)Pump Only
8	SH108251L	Screw	6	
	SH108201L	Screw	6	)Vehicles with)Electrical Fuel)Pump Only
9	WL108001L	Spring Washer	6	
10	ERC9480	Bracket-Clip to Side Cover	1	
11	AFU1090L	Clip	1	

VS3738A

LAND ROVER PARTS LTD

```
MODEL LR110 - UP TO AUGUST 1986
BLOCK VS 3740
PAGE B 32
GROUP B
```

ENGINE - 2.25 PETROL - FRONT COVER

ILL	PART NO	DESCRIPTION	QTY	REMARKS
1		Front Cover Assembly		
	ERC9519	-Single Lip Seal Type	1	Except Air Con
	ERC9528	-Single Lip Seal Type	1	Air Con Only
	ETC6081	-Twin Lip Seal Type	1	Except Air Con
	ETC6082	-Twin Lip Seal Type	1	Air Con Only
2	247766	+Mud Excluder	1	
3	AB606061L	+Screw	8	
4	6395L	+Dowel	2	
5	ERC7987	+Oil Seal-Single Lip	1	Except Air Con
	90516028	+Oil Seal-Single Lip	1	Air Con Only
	ETC5187	+Oil Seal-Twin Lip	1	
6	538038	Joint Washer-Water Inlet	1	
7	538039	Joint Washer-Front Cover	1	
8	ERC5361	Timing Pointer	1	
9	ERC6869	Spacer	1	
10	ERC8964	Bolt	1	
11	WL108001L	Spring Washer	1	
12	ERC8965	Bolt-Special-See Note(1)	1	)
	ETC4994	Bolt-Special-See Note(2)	1	)Except
	BH108151L	Bolt	1	)Air Con
	BH108101L	Bolt	6	)

NOTE(1):   Use With Fan Cowl Without Flexible Mountings.

NOTE(2):   Use With Fan Cowl With Flexible Mounting.

VS3740

34

```
MODEL LR110 - UP TO AUGUST 1986
BLOCK VS 3740
PAGE B 32.02
GROUP B
```

ENGINE - 2.25 PETROL - FRONT COVER CONTINUED

ILL	PART NO	DESCRIPTION	QTY	REMARKS
12	ERCB965	Bolt Special-Note(1)	1	)Vehicles Fitted
	ETC4944	Bolt Special-Note(2)	1	)With Split
	BH108101L	Bolt	5	)Charge Option
	ERC9468	Stud	1	)
14	NH108041L	Nut	1	)
12	ERC9467	Bolt-Special	1	)NLA Use ETC4995
	ETC4995	Bolt-Special	1	)
	ERC9468	Stud-Special	1	)
	BH108131L	Bolt	1	)
	BH108151L	Bolt	1	)
	BH108101L	Bolt	2	)Air Con Only
	ERC8964	Bolt	2	)
	BH108201L	Bolt	1	)
13	WL108001L	Washer Spring	9	)
	WL108001L	Washer Spring	8	Except Air Con
14	NH108041L	Nut	1	Air Con Only
	574469	Blanking Plate-Front Cover	1	)
16	542636	Gasket-Blanking Plate	1	)
17	SH106201L	Screw	3	)
18	WL106001L	spring Washer	3	)
19	ERC6479	Cowl Mounting Bracket	1	)Air Con Only
20	SH108201L	Screw	3	)
21	WL108001L	Spring Washer	3	)
	WA108051L	Plain Washer	1	)
	ERC9404	Bracket-Harness Clip	1	)
	AFU1090L	Clip	1	)Alternatives
	RTC3772	Cable Tie	1	)

NOTE(1):   Use With Fan Cowl Without Flexible Mounting

NOTE(2):   Use With Fan Cowl With Flexible Mounting.

VS3740

35

MODEL LR110 - UP TO AUGUST 1986
BLOCK VS 3745
PAGE B 34
GROUP B

ENGINE - 2.25 PETROL - WATER PUMP

ILL	PART NO	DESCRIPTION	QTY	REMARKS
1	RTC6333	WATER PUMP ASSEMBLY	1	Air Con Only
	RTC3644	WATER PUMP ASSEMBLY	1	)Except Air Con
2	ERC7313	+Stub-De Aerator	1	)
3	ERC7312	+Plug-De Aerator Boss	1	Air Con Only
4	232046	+Joint Washer	1	
5	ERC5600	+Special Screw	1	
6	WL106001L	+Spring Washer	1	
7	ERC5655	+Gasket	1	
8	ERC5578	Pulley-Single Groove	1	Except Air Con
9	ETC4785	Pulley-Twin Groove	1	Air Con Only
10	ERC7489	Spacer-Fan to Water Pump	1	)Except Air Con
11	ERC5545	Fan Assembly	1	)
	ETC7554	Fan Assembly	1	Air Con Only
12	BH108111L	Bolt-Pulley to Pump	4	)Except Air Con
13	WL108001L	Spring Washer-Pulley to Pump	4	)
14	BH106051L	Bolt-Pulley to Hub	4	)
15	WL106001L	Spring Washer-Pulley to Hub	4	)Air Con Only
16	SH108161L	Screw-Fan to Hub	4	)
17	WL108001L	Spring Washer-Fan to Hub	4	)
18	BH108161L	Bolt-Pump to Block	2	
19	WL108001L	Spring Washer-Pump to Block	4	
20	BH108171L	Bolt-Pump to Block	1	
21	BH108151L	Bolt-Pump to Block	1	
22	BH108061L	Bolt-Pump to Cover	3	
23	WL108001L	Spring Washer-Pump to Cover	3	
24	ERC5654	Hose-By Pass to Outlet	1	
25	CN100408L	Clip-Hose	2	
26	563132	Belt-Fan	1	Except Air Con
	ERC8938	Belt-Fan	1	Air Con Only
	ERC8938	Belt-Fan	1	Split Charge
	ERC5708	Viscous Unit	1	)
	ERC5709	Special Bolt	4	)Air Con Only
	4589L	Washer Plain	4	)

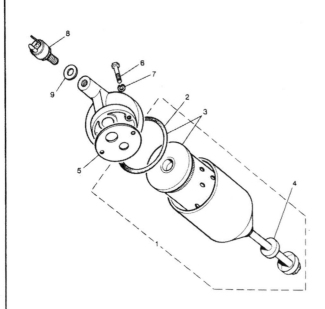

VS3745

36

MODEL LR110 - UP TO AUGUST 1986
BLOCK 1RE 132A
PAGE B 36
GROUP B

ENGINE - 2.25 PETROL - OIL FILTER

ILL	PART NO	DESCRIPTION	QTY	REMARKS
1	537229	OIL FILTER ASSEMBLY	1	
2	272539	+Sealing Ring	1	
3	RTC3184	+Filter Element	1	
4	269889	+Distance Washer	1	
5	ETC5276	Joint Washer	1	
6	SH110301L	Bolt-Filter to Block 1.25"	2	Except Oil Cooler
	ERC9499	Bolt-Filter to Block 2.875"	2	Oil Cooler Only
7	WL110001L	Spring Washer	2	
8	90519864	Oil Pressure Switch	1	
9	232039	Joint Washer-Switch	1	
	PRC2505	Transmitter-Oil Temperature	1	Optional

1RE132A

37

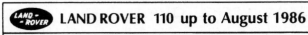
MODEL LR110 - UP TO AUGUST 1986
BLOCK TS 5000
PAGE B 36.02
GROUP B

ENGINE - 2.25 PETROL - OIL FILTER

ILL	PART NO	DESCRIPTION	QTY	REMARKS
1	ETC5347	OIL FILTER ADAPTOR ASSEMBLY	1	
2	10713	+Plug	1	
3	213961	+Washer	1	
4	ERC5913	+O Ring	1	
5	ERC9884	+End Plate	1	
6	ETC4021	+Plug	1	
7	SH106141L	+Screw	2	
8	WA106041L	+Washer-Plain	2	
9	ETC6599	Element-Oil Filter	1	
10	SH110301L	Screw-Filter to Block	2	
11	WL110001L	Washer-Spring-Filter to Block	2	
12	ETC5276	Gasket-Oil Filter	1	
13	PRC6387	Switch-Oil Pressure	1	

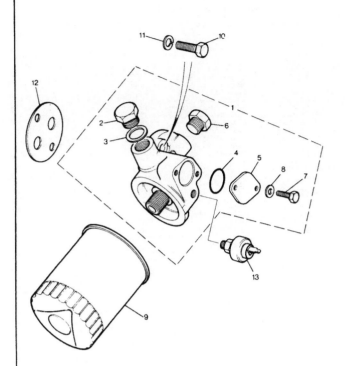

TS5000

MODEL LR110 - UP TO AUGUST 1986
BLOCK VS 4205A
PAGE B 36.04
GROUP B

ENGINE - 2.25 PETROL - OIL FILTER WITH OIL COOLER

ILL	PART NO	DESCRIPTION	QTY	REMARKS
1	ETC5348	OIL FILTER ADAPTOR ASSEMBLY	1	
2	ERC5923	+Thermostat Bulb	1	
3	ETC4022	+Adaptor	1	
4	ERC5913	+O Ring	1	
5	ETC4021	+Plug	1	
6	SH106141L	+Screw	2	
7	WA106041L	+Washer	2	
8	ETC6599	Element-Oil Filter	1	
9	SH110301L	Screw-Filter to Block	2	
10	WL110001L	Washer-Spring	2	
11	ETC5276	Gasket-Oil Filter	1	
12	PRC6387	Switch-Oil Pressure	1	

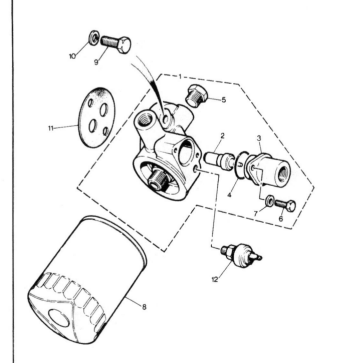

VS4205A

MODEL LR110 - UP TO AUGUST 1986
BLOCK VS 3755
PAGE B 38
GROUP B

ENGINE - 2.25 PETROL - THERMOSTAT HOUSING

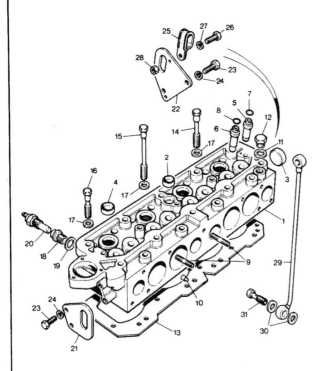

ILL	PART NO	DESCRIPTION	QTY	REMARKS
1	ERC8758	Thermostat Housing & By Pass	1	Note(3)
2	ETC4763	Thermostat 82 Degrees	1	
	ETC4761	Thermostat 74 Degrees	1	Option VE19A
3	ERC7951	Joint Washer	1	
4	247874	Joint Washer	1	
5	ERC7510	Hose-Thermo Housing to	1	Without Heater
		Adaptor		
6	CN100258	Clip-Hose	2	
7	ERC5314	Water Outlet Connector)	1	Except Air Con
	ERC8554	Water Outlet Connector)Note	1	Air Con Only
8	ERC6478	Cowl Mounting Bracket)(4)	1	
9	BH106131L	Bolt)	1	
10	BH106151L	Bolt)	2	
7	ETC5967	Water Outlet Connector)	1	Except Air Con
	ETC5958	Water Outlet Connector)Note	1	Air Con Only
8	ETC5965	Cowl Mounting Bracket)(5)	1	
10	BH106151L	Bolt)	3	
11	WL106001L	Spring Washer	3	
12	624091	Adaptor-Thermo Housing	1	
13	243959	Joint Washer	1	
14	ERC8758	Thermostat Housing & By Pass	1	Note(3)
15	90511958	Joint Washer	1	
16	SH108251L	Screw	2	
17	WL108001L	Spring Washer	2	
18	624091	Adaptor	1	
19	243959	Joint Washer	1	
	PRC3366	Switch-Temperature Sensor-Fan	1	)
		See Note(1)		)
	PRC3541	Switch-Temperature Sensor-	1	)Air Con Only
		Compressor-See Note(2)		)
	C457593	Washer	2	)

NOTE(1): Identified By Blue Paint
NOTE(2): Identified By Red Paint
NOTE(3): One Piece Thermostat Housing & Thermostat By Pass
NOTE(4): Earlier Condition Where The Water Outlet Connector
Points To The Right When Viewed From The Drivers Seat
NOTE(5): Later Condition Where The Water Outlet Connector
Points To the Left When Viewed From The Drivers Seat

VS3755

 **LAND ROVER PARTS LTD**

MODEL LR110 - UP TO AUGUST 1986
BLOCK VS 3827
PAGE B 40
GROUP B

ENGINE - 2.25 PETROL - CYLINDER HEAD

ILL	PART NO	DESCRIPTION	QTY	REMARKS
1	ETC5412	CYLINDER HEAD ASSEMBLY	1	
2	525497	+Cup Plug	1	
3	524765	+Cup Plug	1	
4	549702	+Cup Plug	4	
5	568686	+Valve Guide-Inlet	4	
6	568687	+Valve Guide-Exhaust	4	
	ETC6278	+Insert-Valve Seat-Exhaust	4	
7	ETC4709	Seal-Inlet Valve	4	
8	ETC4751	Seal-Exhaust Valve	4	
9	TE108051L	Stud	3	
10	213700	Dowel	2	
11	AFU1890L	Joint Washer	1	
12	ERC9448	Plug	1	
13	ERC6380	Gasket	1	
14	247051	Bolt-UNFx4.562"	9	
15	279648	Bolt-UNFx2.312"	4	
16	554621	Bolt-UNFx4.125"	5	
17	ERC6821	Washer	18	
18	ERC8973	Adaptor-Water Temp Trans	1	
19	AFU1890L	Joint Washer	1	
20	PRC2505	Water Temperature Transmitter	1	
21	ERC2254	Lifting Bracket-Front	1	
22	ETC7135	Lifting Bracket-Rear	1	
23	SH108201L	Screw	4	
24	WL108001L	Spring Washer	4	
25	543589	Clip	1	
26	SH104121L	Screw	1	
27	WA104001L	Washer	1	
28	NH104041L	Nut	1	
29	275679	Oil Feed Pipe-Rockers	1	
30	ETC6510	Joint Washer	4	
31	ERC8977	Banjo Bolt	2	

VS3827

 **LAND ROVER PARTS LTD**

MODEL LR110 - UP TO AUGUST 1986
BLOCK VS 3744
PAGE B 42
GROUP B

ENGINE - 2.25 PETROL - MANIFOLDS

ILL	PART NO	DESCRIPTION	QTY	REMARKS
1	ERC9069	Inlet Manifold	1	
2	90513171	Adaptor-Servo	1	
	587517	Adaptor-Servo	1	)Variant VE05B)ECE 15-04
3	243958	Joint Washer	1	
	243958	Joint Washer	2	)Variant VE05B
	ERC6691	Banjo	1	)ECE 15-04
4	TE108071L	Stud-Carb to Inlet Manifold	4	Without Hand Throttle Control
	TE108071L	Stud-Carb to Inlet Manifold	2	)With Hand
	TE108081L	Stud-Carb to Inlet Manifold	2	)Throttle Control
5	ERC86451	Joint Washer-Carb to Manifold	2	
6	564307	Joint Washer-Manifold to Head	2	
7	ERC8460	Packing Piece	1	
8	NH108041L	Nut-Manifold to Head	2	
9	BH108101L	Bolt-Manifold to Head	2	
10	587405	Washer-Manifold to Head	4	
11	WL108001L	Spring Washer	4	
12	NH108041L	Nut-Manifold to Manifold	4	
13	WA108051L	Washer-Manifold to Manifold	4	
14	ERC8124	Joint Washer-Mainfold to Manifold	1	
15	ERC9071	Exhaust Manifold	1	
16	TE108131L	Stud-Manifold to Manifold	2	
17	AFU1848L	Stud-Fixing Exhaust Pipe	3	
18	BH108141L	Bolt-Manifold to Head	2	
19	SH108301L	Screw-Manifold to Head	2	

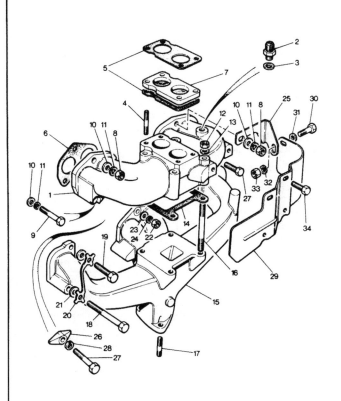

VS3744

LAND ROVER PARTS LTD

MODEL LR110 - UP TO AUGUST 1986
BLOCK VS 3744
PAGE B 42.02
GROUP B

ENGINE - 2.25 PETROL - MANIFOLDS CONTINUED

ILL	PART NO	DESCRIPTION	QTY	REMARKS
20	596490	Locking Plate-Manifold to Head	2	
21	587405	Washer-Manifold to Head	4	
22	NH108041L	Nut-Centre Flange to Head	1	
23	587405	Washer-Centre Flange to Head	1	
24	WL108001L	Spring Washer-Flange to Head	1	
25	ETC5040	Bracket-Heat Shield	1	
26	564308	Clamp-Manifold to Head	2	
27	BH108141L	Bolt-Manifolds to Head	2	
28	WL108001L	Spring Washer-Manifolds to Head	2	
29	ERC8712	Shield-Exhaust Manifold	1	
30	SH108201L	Bolt-Shield to Manifold	1	
31	WA108051L	Washer-Shield to Manifold	4	
32	WL108001L	Spring Washer-Shield to Manifold	3	
33	NH108041L	Nut-Shield to Manifold	1	
34	SH108141L	Screw-Shield to Manifold	2	
	ERC8722	Bolt-Special-Shield to Manifold	2	
	NH108041L	Nut-Manifold to Carb	4	
	WL108001L	Washer-Spring-Manifold to Carb	4	

VS3744

LAND ROVER PARTS LTD

MODEL LR110 - UP TO AUGUST 1986
BLOCK VS 3743
PAGE B 44
GROUP B

ENGINE - 2.25 PETROL - GASKET KITS

ILL	PART NO	DESCRIPTION	QTY	REMARKS
1	RTC2889	Gasket & Seals Kit-Decarbonising	1	
2	RTC2890	Gasket & Seal Kit-Overhaul	1	Use With RTC2889
	RTC3254	RTV Silicon Sealant 110 Gram Tube	1	

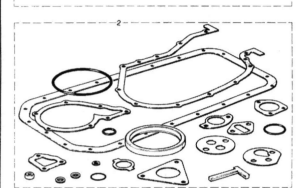

VS3743

LAND ROVER PARTS LTD

MASTER INDEX

GROUP B

ENGINE

LAND ROVER PARTS LTD

MODEL LR110 - UP TO AUGUST 1986
BLOCK VS 4134
PAGE B 44.02
GROUP B

ENGINE - 2.5 PETROL - ENGINE ASSEMBLY COMPLETE AND STRIPPED

ILL	PART NO	DESCRIPTION	QTY	REMARKS
1	ETC5900N	Engine & Clutch Complete Assy	1	
	RTC4595N	Engine Assembly Stripped-New	1	

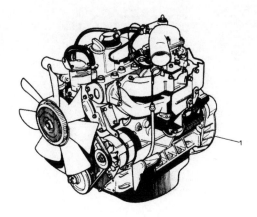

VS4134

46

MODEL LR110 - UP TO AUGUST 1986
BLOCK TS 6357
PAGE B 44.04
GROUP B

ENGINE - 2.5 PETROL - ENGINE CONTINUED

ILL	PART NO	DESCRIPTION	QTY	REMARKS
1	RTC4594	Engine Assembly-Short	1	

TS6357

MODEL LR110 - UP TO AUGUST 1986
BLOCK VS 3736B
PAGE B 44.06
GROUP B

ENGINE - 2.5 PETROL - CYLINDER BLOCK

ILL	PART NO	DESCRIPTION	QTY	REMARKS
1	RTC3985	CYLINDER BLOCK ASSEMBLY	1	
2	247965	+Plug-Tappet Hole Feed	1	
3	247127	+Plug-Oil Gallery	2	
4	501593	+Dowel-Bearing Cap	10	
5	ERC4996	+Cup Plug-Side/Ends	6	
6	597586	+Cup Plug-Water Rail	3	
7	ERC4644	+Dowel-Flywheel Housing	2	
8	527269	+Plug-Immersion Heater	1	
9	243959	+Joint Washer-Gallery Pipe	2	
10	ETC4922	+Plug-Gallery Pipe	2	
11	90519054	+Bearing-Camshaft-Front	1	
12	90519055	+Bearing-Camshaft-Inter/Rear	3	
13	ERC4995	+Cup Plug-Top	2	
14	247755	+Bolt-Main Bearing Cap	10	
15	504006	+Washer-Main Bearing Cap	10	
	ETC7708	+Plug-Camshaft Oil Feed	3	

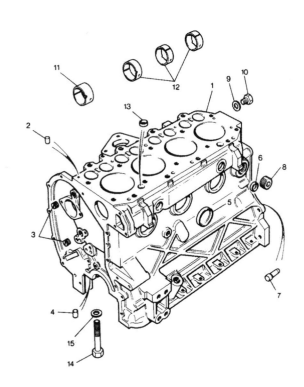

VS3736B

LAND ROVER PARTS LTD

48

MODEL LR110 - UP TO AUGUST 1986
BLOCK TS 5766
PAGE B 44.08
GROUP B

ENGINE - 2.5 PETROL - ENGINE MOUNTINGS

ILL	PART NO	DESCRIPTION	QTY	REMARKS
1	NRC5434	Mounting Foot-RH	1	
2	NRC9557	Mounting Foot-LH	1	
3	SH112251L	Screw	4	
4	WL112001L	Washer-Spring	4	
5	ERC9410	Drain Plug	1	
6	AFU1882L	Joint Washer-Plug	1	
7	ERC5086	Packing Strip	2	
8	NRC9560	Rubber-Engine Mounting	2	
9	NH110041L	Nut-Rubber to Foot	4	
10	WC110061L	Washer-Rubber to Foot	2	
11	WL110001L	Washer-Spring-Rubber to Foot	4	

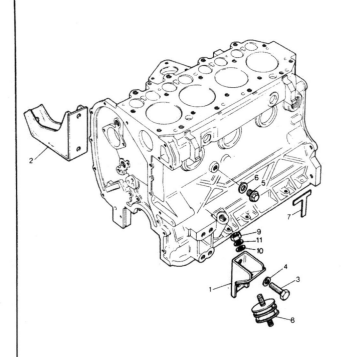

TS5766

LAND ROVER PARTS LTD

49

MODEL LR110 - UP TO AUGUST 1986
BLOCK 1RE 99
PAGE B 44.10
GROUP B

ENGINE - 2.5 PETROL - PISTON

ILL	PART NO	DESCRIPTION	QTY	REMARKS
		PISTON ASSEMBLY		
1	RTC4189S	+Standard	4	
	RTC418920	+0.020"(0.508mm) Oversize	4	
		PISTON RINGS (PISTON SET)		
2	RTC4374S	+Standard	4	
	RTC437420	+0.020"(0.508mm) Oversize	4	
3	ETC5994	Gudgeon Pin	4	
4	265175	Circlip	8	
5	ETC5959	CONNECTING ROD ASSEMBLY	4	
6	528004	+Bush	4	
7	ERC8751	+Bolt	8	
8	ETC5155	+Nut	8	
		BEARING-CONNECTING ROD-ENGINE SET		
9	RTC2993	+Standard	1	
	RTC299310	+0.10"(0.254mm) Undersize	1	

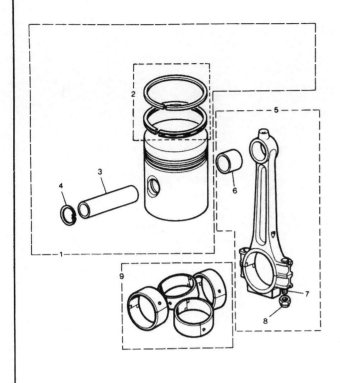

IRE99

MODEL LR110 - UP TO AUGUST 1986
BLOCK VS 3722A
PAGE B 44.12
GROUP B

ENGINE - 2.5 PETROL - CRANKSHAFT

ILL	PART NO	DESCRIPTION	QTY	REMARKS
1	ERC9000	Crankshaft	1	Upto 17H12320C
	ETC8829	Crankshaft	1	From 17H12321C
2	ERC4650	Dowel	1	
3	8566L	Bush	1	
4		KIT-MAIN BEARING		
	RTC2992	+Standard	1	
	RTC299210	+0.010"(0.254mm) Undersize	1	
	RTC299220	+0.020"(0.508mm) Undersize	1	
5	235770	Key-Chainwheel	1	
6	568333	Chainwheel	1	
7		THRUST WASHER-PAIRS		
	RTC2825	+Standard	A/R	
	538131	+0.0025" O/S	A/R	
	538132	+0.0050" O/S	A/R	
	538133	+0.0075" O/S	A/R	
	538134	+0.0100" O/S	A/R	
8	ERC5349	Crankshaft Pulley	1	)No Longer)Available)Use RTC4817
	ERC5128	Crankshaft Pulley	1	)With Power)Steering Only
	ERC5127	Crankshaft Pulley	1	)No Longer)Available)Use RTC4815)With Air Con)Only
	ERC7089	Crankshaft Pulley	1	)Power Steering)& Air Con Only
	RTC4817	Crankshaft Pulley	1	Basic
	RTC4815	Crankshaft Pulley	1	)With Air Con)Only
9	ETC7934	Bolt-Crankshaft Pulley	1	
10	ETC5369	Oil Seal Main	1	

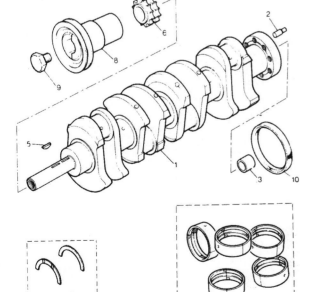

VS3722A

MODEL LR110 - UP TO AUGUST 1986
BLOCK 1RE 106X
PAGE B 44.14
GROUP B

ENGINE - 2.5 PETROL - OIL PUMP

ILL	PART NO	DESCRIPTION	QTY	REMARKS
1	ETC7054	OIL PUMP ASSEMBLY	1	
2	ETC5646	+Oil Pump Body	1	NLS Use ETC7054
3	236257	++Dowel	2	
4	90502209	++Idler Wheel Spindle	1	
5	ERC9707	+Idler Wheel	1	
6	ERC9706	+Driver Wheel	1	
7	513639	+Oil Pump Cover	1	NLS Use ETC7054
8	SH108201L	+Bolt	4	
9	WL108001L	+Spring Washer	4	
10	ETC4880	+Plunger-Oil Relief	1	
11	564456	+Spring-Oil Relief	1	
12	564455	+End Plug-Oil Relief	1	
13	232044	+Joint Washer-Oil Relief	1	
14	ERC7530	+Filter	1	
15	ERC7940	+Support Bracket	1	
16	WA108051L	+Washer-Filter to Support Bracket	1	
17	WL108001L	+Spring Washer-Filter to +Support Bracket	1	
18	SH108201L	+Screw-Filter to Support Brkt	1	
19	244488	+O Ring	1	
20	244487	+Lock Washer	1	
21	SH108251L	+Bolt	2	
22	247665	+Lockwasher	2	
23	ERC9669	Shaft	1	
24	ERC8408	Gasket-Pump Cover to Block	1	
25	ETC6139	DRIVE SHAFT-GEAR & BUSH ASSY	1	
26	522745	+Bush	1	
27	ERC8976	+Locating Screw	1	)Earlier Type
28	530178	+Thrust Washer	1	)With Spring)Ring Type
29	530179	+Retaining Ring	1	)Retaining Ring
27	ETC6142	+Locating Screw	1	)Later Type With
28	ETC6137	+Thrust Washer	1	)Locking Ring
29	ETC6138	+Locking Ring	1	)Type Of)Retainer
30	247742	+Circlip	1	

1RE106X

LAND ROVER PARTS LTD

52

MODEL LR110 - UP TO AUGUST 1986
BLOCK 1RE 131
PAGE B 44.16
GROUP B

ENGINE - 2.5 PETROL - SUMP

ILL	PART NO	DESCRIPTION	QTY	REMARKS
1	RTC3833	SUMP	1	)No Longer)Available-)Use RTC4841
2	ETC5577	+Drain Plug	1	
3	FRC4808	+Joint Washer-Plug	1	
4	546841	Joint Washer-Sump	1	Note(1)
5	SH108251L	Screw	21	
6	TE108041L	Stud	1	
7	WL108001L	Spring Washer	22	
8	NH108041L	Nut	1	
1	RTC4841	SUMP ASSEMBLY	1	)
2	ETC5577	+Plug	1	)
3	FRC4808	+Joint Washer-Plug	1	)
5	SH108161L	+Screw	21	)Note(2)
6	TE108031L	+Stud	1	)
7	WL108001L	+Spring Washer	22	)
8	NH108041L	+Nut	1	)
9	ERC8980	Tube-Oil Level Rod	1	
10	532387	Sealing Ring-Tube	1	
11	ETC7867	Oil Level Rod	1	

NOTE(1): Later Sump Is Sealed With Liquid Gasket Compound.
The Sump Gasket 546841 Can Be Fitted As An
Alternative For Service.

NOTE(2): Latest Sump Has A Thinner Flange & Should Be Fitted
Using The Fixings Enclosed With The Kit To Prevent
The Screws Bottoming.

1RE131

LAND ROVER PARTS LTD

53

MODEL LR110 - UP TO AUGUST 1986
BLOCK TS 5365
PAGE B 44.18
GROUP B

ENGINE 2.5 PETROL - TIMING CHAIN

ILL	PART NO	DESCRIPTION	QTY	REMARKS
1	ETC5191	Timing Chain	1	
2	ETC5190	Tensioner-Timing Chain	1	
3	SH108201L	Screw	2	
4	TE108051L	Stud	1	
5	WA108051L	Washer	3	
6	NH108041L	Nut	1	
7	275234	Vibration Damper	1	
8	SH106121L	Screw	2	
9	557523	Lock Washer	2	

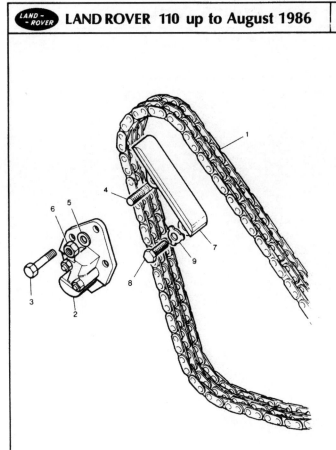

TS5365

LAND ROVER PARTS LTD

MODEL LR110 - UP TO AUGUST 1986
BLOCK VS 3734A
PAGE B 44.20
GROUP B

ENGINE - 2.5 PETROL - CAMSHAFT

ILL	PART NO	DESCRIPTION	QTY	REMARKS
1	ERC5475	Camshaft	1	NLA Use ETC7128
	ETC7128	Camshaft	1	
2	ERC1561	Thrust Plate	1	
3	SH106161L	Screw	2	
5	230313	Woodruff Key	1	
6	ETC5172	Chainwheel-Camshaft	1	
7	ETC4140	Retaining Washer	1	
8	ETC4141	Retaining Bolt	1	Use With ERC5475
	BH110071L	Retaining Bolt	1	Use With ETC7128

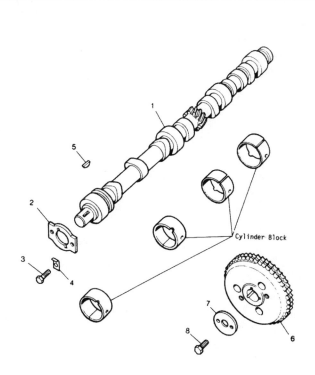

Cylinder Block

VS3734A

LAND ROVER PARTS LTD

MODEL LR110 - UP TO AUGUST 1986
BLOCK 1RE 101
PAGE B 44.22
GROUP B

ENGINE - 2.5 PETROL - VALVES AND TAPPET

ILL	PART NO	DESCRIPTION	QTY	REMARKS
1	507829	TAPPET ASSEMBLY	8	
2	502473	+Tappet Guide	8	
3	ETC5057	+Tappet	8	
4	ETC4246	+Bolt	8	
5	273069	+Plain Washer	8	
6	90517429	+Roller Follower	8	
7	ETC4067	Inlet Valve	4	
8	ETC5866	EXHAUST VALVE	4	
	ETC7203	+Valve Stem Protection Cap	8	Note(1)
9	568550	Valve Spring	8	
10	ETC4068	Cup-Valve Spring	8	
11	ETC4069	Split Cotter Halves	16	
12	546798	Push Rod	8	

NOTE(1):   Can Be Fitted If Suffering From Excessive Valve
Stem Or Valve Rocker Wear

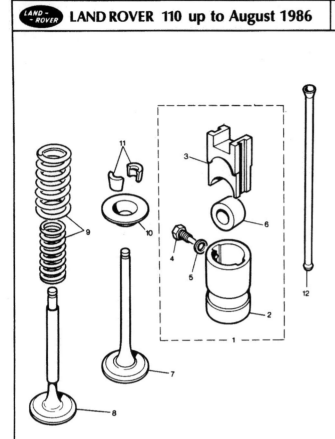

1RE101

MODEL LR110 - UP TO AUGUST 1986
BLOCK 1RE 102A
PAGE B 44.24A
GROUP B

ENGINE - 2.5 PETROL - VALVE ROCKERS

ILL	PART NO	DESCRIPTION	QTY	REMARKS
1	ERC9103	VALVE ROCKER ASSY-EXHAUST-RH	2	
2	ERC9102	VALVE ROCKER ASSY-EXHAUST-LH	2	
3	ERC9107	VALVE ROCKER ASSY-INLET-RH	2	
4	ERC9106	VALVE ROCKER ASSY-INLET-LH	2	
5	247614	+Bush	8	
6	ERC9054	Adjusting Screw	8	
7	NT108041L	Locknut	8	
8	ERC9138	Pedestal Bracket	5	
9	277956	Ring Dowel	3	
10	ERC6341	ROCKER SHAFT ASSEMBLY	1	
11	ERC6337	+Plug	2	
12	525389	Plain Washer	6	
13	247040	Spring	4	
14	ERC9278	Baffle Plate-Breather	1	
15	ETC4460	Screw-Locating	1	
16	WL108001L	Spring Washer	1	
17	BH108151L	Bolt	5	
18	WL108001L	Spring Washer	5	
19	TE108081L	Stud	3	

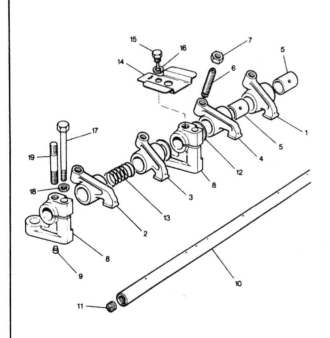

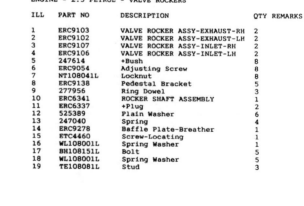

1RE102A

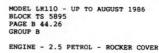
MODEL LR110 - UP TO AUGUST 1986
BLOCK TS 5895
PAGE B 44.26
GROUP B

ENGINE - 2.5 PETROL - ROCKER COVER

ILL	PART NO	DESCRIPTION	QTY	REMARKS
1	ETC5955	Rocker Cover	1	
2	ETC6439	Joint Washer-Cover to Head	1	
3	ERC9220	Domed Nut	3	
4	273069	Sealing Washer	3	
5	ETC5297	BREATHER SILENCER ASSEMBLY	1	
6	ERC8049	O Ring Breather	1	
7	ERC6200	Tee Piece	1	
8	ERC9032	Hose-Tee Piece to Elbow	1	
9	ERC9031	Hose-Rocker to Tee Piece	1	
10	CN100208L	Clip-Hose	4	
11	CN100148L	Clip-Hose	1	
12	ERC9033	Hose-Tee Piece to Carb	1	

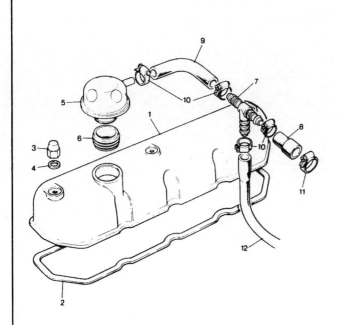

TS5895

LAND ROVER PARTS LTD

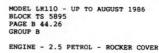
MODEL LR110 - UP TO AUGUST 1986
BLOCK VS 3738A
PAGE B 44.28
GROUP B

ENGINE - 2.5 PETROL - SIDE COVERS

ILL	PART NO	DESCRIPTION	QTY	REMARKS
1	ETC4799	SIDE COVER-REAR	1	
2	TE108041L	+Stud	2	
3	247554	Joint Washer-Cover to Block	1	
4	SH108201L	Screw	6	
5	WL108001L	Spring Washer	6	
6	ERC2869	Side Cover-Front	1	
7	247555	Joint Washer-Cover to Block	1	
8	SH108201L	Screw	6	
9	WL108001L	Spring Washer	6	
10	ERC9480	Bracket-Clip to Side Cover	1	
11	AFU1090L	Clip	1	

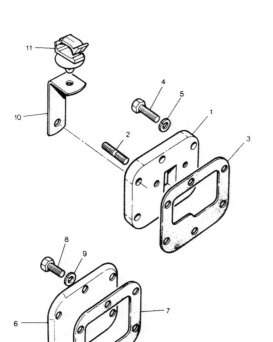

VS3738A

LAND ROVER PARTS LTD

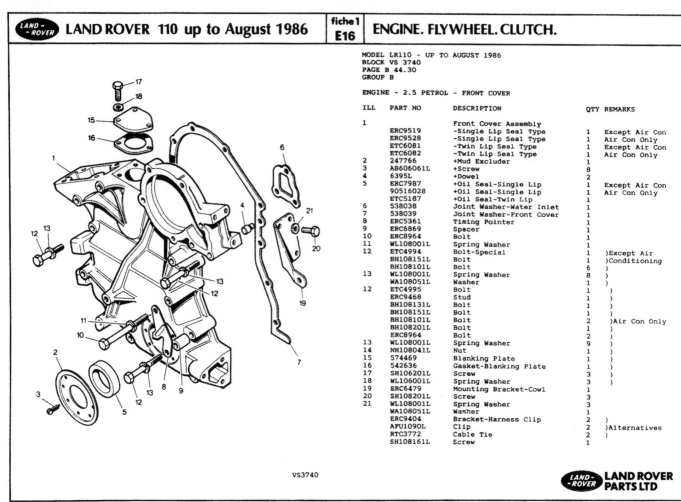

```
MODEL LR110 - UP TO AUGUST 1986
BLOCK VS 3740
PAGE B 44.30
GROUP B

ENGINE - 2.5 PETROL - FRONT COVER
```

ILL	PART NO	DESCRIPTION	QTY	REMARKS
1		Front Cover Assembly		
	ERC9519	-Single Lip Seal Type	1	Except Air Con
	ERC9528	-Single Lip Seal Type	1	Air Con Only
	ETC6081	-Twin Lip Seal Type	1	Except Air Con
	ETC6082	-Twin Lip Seal Type	1	Air Con Only
2	247766	+Mud Excluder	1	
3	AB606061L	+Screw	8	
4	6395L	+Dowel	2	
5	ERC7987	+Oil Seal-Single Lip	1	Except Air Con
	90516028	+Oil Seal-Single Lip	1	Air Con Only
	ETC5187	+Oil Seal-Twin Lip	1	
6	538038	Joint Washer-Water Inlet	1	
7	538039	Joint Washer-Front Cover	1	
8	ERC5361	Timing Pointer	1	
9	ERC6869	Spacer	1	
10	ERC8964	Bolt	1	
11	WL108001L	Spring Washer	1	
12	ETC4994	Bolt-Special	1	)Except Air
	BH108151L	Bolt	1	)Conditioning
	BH108101L	Bolt	6	)
13	WL108001L	Spring Washer	8	)
	WA108051L	Washer	1	)
12	ETC4995	Bolt	1	)
	ERC9468	Stud	1	)
	BH108131L	Bolt	1	)
	BH108151L	Bolt	1	)
	BH108101L	Bolt	2	)Air Con Only
	BH108201L	Bolt	1	)
	ERC8964	Bolt	2	)
13	WL108001L	Spring Washer	9	)
14	NH108041L	Nut	1	)
15	574469	Blanking Plate	1	)
16	542636	Gasket-Blanking Plate	1	)
17	SH106201L	Screw	3	)
18	WL106001L	Spring Washer	3	)
19	ERC6479	Mounting Bracket-Cowl	1	
20	SH108201L	Screw	3	
21	WL108001L	Spring Washer	3	
	WA108051L	Washer	1	
	ERC9404	Bracket-Harness Clip	2	)
	AFU1090L	Clip	2	)Alternatives
	RTC3772	Cable Tie	2	)
	SH108161L	Screw	1	

VS3740

LAND ROVER PARTS LTD

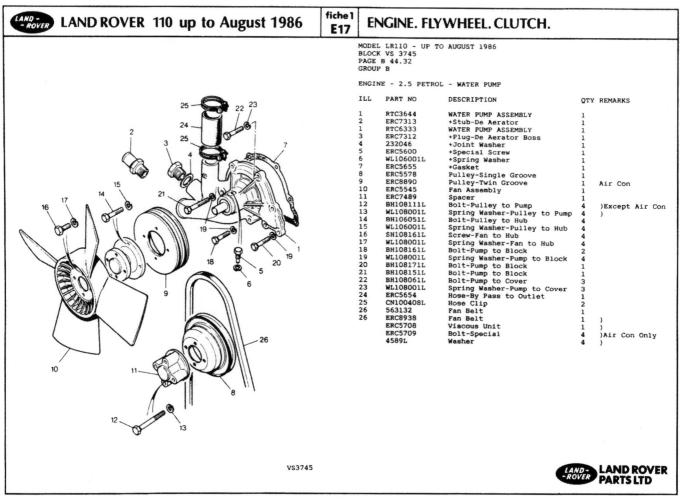

```
MODEL LR110 - UP TO AUGUST 1986
BLOCK VS 3745
PAGE B 44.32
GROUP B

ENGINE - 2.5 PETROL - WATER PUMP
```

ILL	PART NO	DESCRIPTION	QTY	REMARKS
1	RTC3644	WATER PUMP ASSEMBLY	1	
2	ERC7313	+Stub-De Aerator	1	
1	RTC6333	WATER PUMP ASSEMBLY	1	
3	ERC7312	+Plug-De Aerator Boss	1	
4	232046	+Joint Washer	1	
5	ERC5600	+Special Screw	1	
6	WL106001L	+Spring Washer	1	
7	ERC5655	+Gasket	1	
8	ERC5578	Pulley-Single Groove	1	
9	ERC8890	Pulley-Twin Groove	1	Air Con
10	ERC5545	Fan Assembly	1	
11	ERC7489	Spacer	1	
12	BH108111L	Bolt-Pulley to Pump	4	)Except Air Con
13	WL108001L	Spring Washer-Pulley to Pump	4	)
14	BH106051L	Bolt-Pulley to Hub	4	
15	WL106001L	Spring Washer-Pulley to Hub	4	
16	SH108161L	Screw-Fan to Hub	4	
17	WL108001L	Spring Washer-Fan to Hub	4	
18	BH108161L	Bolt-Pump to Block	2	
19	WL108001L	Spring Washer-Pump to Block	4	
20	BH108171L	Bolt-Pump to Block	1	
21	BH108151L	Bolt-Pump to Block	1	
22	BH108061L	Bolt-Pump to Cover	3	
23	WL108001L	Spring Washer-Pump to Cover	3	
24	ERC5654	Hose-By Pass to Outlet	1	
25	CN100408L	Hose Clip	2	
26	563132	Fan Belt	1	
26	ERC8938	Fan Belt	1	)
	ERC5708	Viscous Unit	1	)
	ERC5709	Bolt-Special	4	)Air Con Only
	4589L	Washer	4	)

VS3745

LAND ROVER PARTS LTD

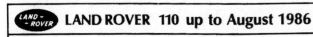

MODEL LR110 - UP TO AUGUST 1986
BLOCK TS 5000
PAGE B 44.34
GROUP B

ENGINE - 2.5 PETROL - OIL FILTER

ILL	PART NO	DESCRIPTION	QTY	REMARKS
1	ETC5347	OIL FILTER ADAPTOR ASSEMBLY	1	
2	10713	+Plug	1	
3	213961	+Washer	1	
4	ERC5913	+O Ring	1	
5	ERC9884	+End Plate	1	
6	ETC4021	+Plug	1	
7	SH106141L	+Screw	2	
8	WA106041L	+Washer-Plain	2	
9	ETC6599	Element-Oil Filter	1	
10	SH110301L	Screw-Filter to Block	2	
11	WL110001L	Washer-Spring-Filter to Block	2	
12	ETC5276	Gasket-Oil Filter	1	
13	PRC4044	Switch-Oil Pressure	1	NLA-Use PRC6387
	PRC6387	Switch-Oil Pressure	1	
	PRC2505	Transmitter-Oil Temperature	1	

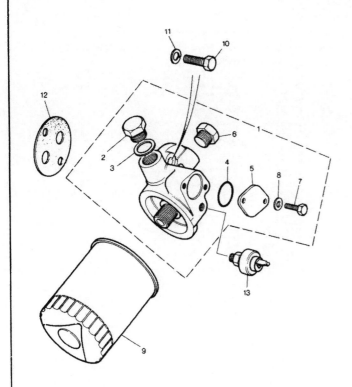

TS5000

62

MODEL LR110 - UP TO AUGUST 1986
BLOCK VS 4205A
PAGE B 44.36
GROUP B

ENGINE - 2.5 PETROL - OIL FILTER WITH OIL COOLER

ILL	PART NO	DESCRIPTION	QTY	REMARKS
1	ETC5348	OIL FILTER ADAPTOR ASSEMBLY	1	
2	ERC5923	+Thermostat Bulb	1	
3	ETC4022	+Adaptor	1	
4	ERC5913	+O Ring	1	
5	ETC4021	+Plug	1	
6	SH106141L	+Screw	2	
7	WA106041L	Washer	2	
8	ETC6599	Element-Oil Filter	1	
9	SH110301L	Screw-Filter to Block	2	
10	WL110301L	Washer-Filter to Block	2	
11	ETC5276	Gasket-Oil Filter	1	
12	PRC4044	Switch-Oil Pressure	1	NLA-Use PRC6387
	PRC6387	Switch-Oil Pressure	1	
	PRC2505	Transmitter-Oil Temperature	1	

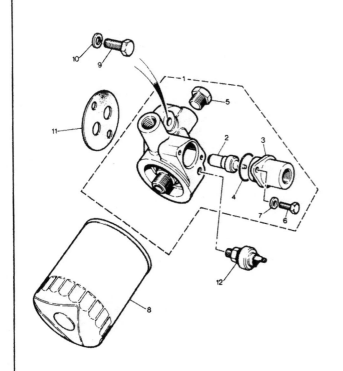

VS4205A

63

MODEL LR110 - UP TO AUGUST 1986
BLOCK VS 3755
PAGE B 44.38
GROUP B

ENGINE - 2.5 PETROL - THERMOSTAT HOUSING

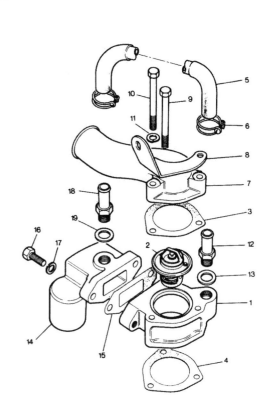

ILL	PART NO	DESCRIPTION	QTY	REMARKS
1	ERC7642	Thermostat Housing	1	NLA-Use ERC8758
	ERC8758	Thermostat Housing & By Pass	1	Note(3)
2	ETC4763	Thermostat 82 Degrees	1	
	ETC4761	Thermostat 74 Degrees	1	Optional
3	ERC7951	Joint Washer	1	
4	247874	Joint Washer	1	
5	ERC7510	Hose-Thermo Housing to Adaptor	1	
6	CN100258	Clip-Hose	2	
7	ERC5314	Water Outlet Connector)	1	Except Air Con
	ERC8554	Water Outlet Connector)Note	1	Air Con Only
8	ERC6478	Cowl Mounting Bracket)(4)	1	
9	BH106131L	Bolt)	1	
10	BH106151L	Bolt)	2	
7	ETC5967	Water Outlet Connector)	1	Except Air Con
	ETC5958	Water Outlet Connector)Note	1	Air Con Only
8	ETC5965	Bracket-Cowl Mounting)(5)	1	
10	BH106151L	Bolt)	3	
11	WL106001L	Spring Washer	3	
12	624091	Adaptor-Thermo Housing	1	
13	243959	Joint Washer	1	
14	530476	Pipe-Thermostat By Pass	1	NLA-Use ERC8758
	ERC8758	Thermostat Housing & By Pass	1	Note(3)
15	90511958	Joint Washer	1	
16	SH108251L	Screw	2	
17	WL108001L	Spring Washer	2	
18	624091	Adaptor	1	
19	243959	Joint Washer	1	
	PRC3366	Switch-Temperature Sensor-Fan See Note(1)	1	))
	PRC3541	Switch-Temperature Sensor-Compressor-See Note(2)	1	)Air Con Only)
	C457593L	Washer	2	)

NOTE(1): Identified By Blue Paint
NOTE(2): Identified By Red Paint
NOTE(3): One Piece Thermostat Housing & Thermostat By Pass
NOTE(4): Earlier Condition Where The Water Outlet Connector
Points To The Right When Viewed From The Drivers Seat
NOTE(5): Later Condition Where The Water Outlet Connector
Points To the Left When Viewed From The Drivers Seat

VS3755

LAND ROVER PARTS LTD

MODEL LR110 - UP TO AUGUST 1986
BLOCK VS 3827/A
PAGE B 44.40
GROUP B

ENGINE - 2.5 PETROL - CYLINDER HEAD

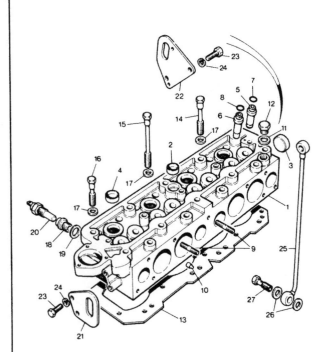

ILL	PART NO	DESCRIPTION	QTY	REMARKS
1	ETC5412	CYLINDER HEAD ASSEMBLY	1	
2	525497	+Cup Plug	1	
3	524765	+Cup Plug	1	
4	549702	+Cup Plug	4	
5	568686	+Valve Guide-Inlet	4	
6	568687	+Valve Guide-Exhaust	4	
	ETC6278	+Insert-Valve Seat-Exhaust	4	
7	ETC4709	Seal-Inlet Valve	4	
8	ETC4751	Seal-Exhaust Valve	4	
9	TE108051L	Stud	3	
10	213700	Dowel	2	
11	AFU1890L	Joint Washer	1	
12	ERC9448	Plug	1	
13	ERC6380	Gasket	1	
14	247051	Bolt-4.562"	9	
15	279648	Bolt-2.312"	4	
16	554621	Bolt-4.125"	5	
17	ERC6821	Washer	18	
18	ERC8973	Adaptor-Water Temp	1	
19	AFU1890L	Joint Washer	1	
20	PRC2505	Water Temperature Transmitter	1	
21	ERC2254	Lifting Bracket-Front	1	
22	ETC7135	Lifting Bracket-Rear	1	
23	SH108201L	Screw-Brackets to Head	4	
24	WL108001L	Spring Washer-Brackets to Head	4	
25	275679	Oil Feed Pipe-Rockers	1	
26	ETC6510	Joint Washer	4	
27	ETC4498	Banjo Bolt	2	

VS3827A

LAND ROVER PARTS LTD

MODEL LR110 - UP TO AUGUST 1986
BLOCK VS 3744
PAGE B 44.42
GROUP B

ENGINE - 2.5 PETROL - MANIFOLDS

ILL	PART NO	DESCRIPTION	QTY	REMARKS
1	ERC9069	Inlet Manifold	1	
2	513171	Adaptor-Servo	1	
	ETC6929	Banjo Assembly	1	)Vehicles with
				)Charcoal
				)Canisters Only
3	243958	Joint Washer	1	
4	TE108081L	Stud-Carb to Inlet Manifold	4	
	NH108041L	Nut-Carb to Inlet Manifold	4	
	WL108001L	Spring Washer-Carb to Inlet Manifold	4	
5	ERC8645	Joint Washer-Carb to Manifold	2	
6	564307	Joint Washer-Manifold to Head	2	
7	ERC8460	Packing Piece	1	
8	NH108041L	Nut-Manifold to Head	2	
9	BH108101L	Bolt-Manifold to Head	2	
10	587405	Washer-Manifold to Head	4	
11	WL108001L	Spring Washer-Manifold to Head	4	
12	NH108041L	Nut-Manifold to Manifold	4	
13	WA108051L	Washer-Manifold to Manifold	4	
14	ERC8124	Joint Washer-Manifold to Manifold	1	
15	ERC9071	Exhaust Manifold	1	Note(1)
	ETC5330	Exhaust Manifold	1	Note(2) From 17H05171C

NOTE(1): Optional Check Before Ordering. With Conical Bore To Take Downpipe With Welded Olive End.

NOTE(2): Optional Check Before Ordering. With Parallel Sided Bore To Take Copper/Asbestos 'O' Ring

VS3744

LAND ROVER PARTS LTD

66

MODEL LR110 - UP TO AUGUST 1986
BLOCK VS 3744
PAGE B 44.44
GROUP B

ENGINE - 2.5 PETROL - MANIFOLDS CONTINUED

ILL	PART NO	DESCRIPTION	QTY	REMARKS
16	TE108131L	Stud-Manifold to Manifold	4	
17	AFU1848L	Stud-Exhaust Pipe	3	
18	BH108141L	Bolt-Manifold to Head	2	
19	SH108301L	Screw-Manifold to Head	2	
20	596490	Locking Plate-Manifold to Head	2	
21	587405	Washer-Manifold to Head	4	
22	NH108041L	Nut-Centre Flange to Head	1	
23	587405	Washer-Centre Flange to Head	1	
24	WL108001L	Spring Washer-Centre Flange to Head	1	
25	ETC5040	Bracket-Heat Shield	1	
26	564308	Clamp-Manifold to Head	2	
27	BH108141L	Bolt-Manifold to Head	2	
28	WL108001L	Spring Washer-Manifold to Head	2	
29	ERC8712	Shield-Exhaust Manifold	1	
30	SH108201L	Bolt-Shield to Manifold	1	
31	WA108051L	Washer-Shield to Manifold	4	
32	WL108001L	Spring Washer-Shield to Manifold	3	
33	NH108041L	Nut-Shield to Manifold	1	
34	SH108141L	Screw-Shield to Manifold	2	
	ERC8722	Bolt-Shield to Manifold	2	

NOTE(1): Optional Check Before Ordering. With Conical Bore To Take Downpipe With Welded Olive End.

NOTE(2): Optional Check Before Ordering. With Parallel Sided Bore To Take Copper/Asbestos 'O' Ring.

VS3744

67

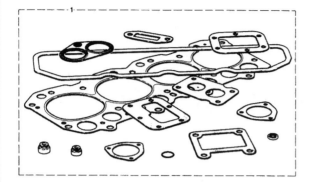

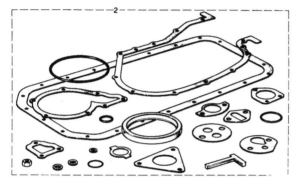

MODEL LR110 - UP TO AUGUST 1986
BLOCK VS 3743
PAGE B 44.46
GROUP B

ENGINE - 2.5 PETROL - GASKET KITS

ILL	PART NO	DESCRIPTION	QTY	REMARKS
1	RTC2889	Gasket & Seals Kit-Decarbonising	1	
2	RTC2890	Gasket & Seals Kit-Overhaul	1	Use With RTC2889
	RTC3254	RTV Silicon Sealant 110Gram Tube	1	

VS3743

68

MASTER INDEX

GROUP B

ENGINE

69

MODEL LR110 - UP TO AUGUST 1986
BLOCK VS 1329
PAGE B 46
GROUP B

ENGINE - 2.25 DIESEL - ENGINE

ILL	PART NO	DESCRIPTION	QTY	REMARKS
1	RTC2977N	Engine Assembly Stripped-New	1	
	RTC2977R	Engine Assembly Stripped-Rebuilt	1	

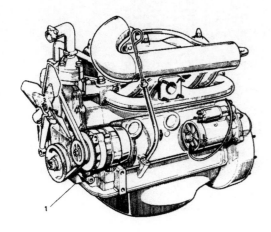

VS1329

LAND ROVER PARTS LTD

70

MODEL LR110 - UP TO AUGUST 1986
BLOCK TS 6357
PAGE B 48
GROUP B

ENGINE - 2.25 DIESEL - ENGINE CONTINUED

ILL	PART NO	DESCRIPTION	QTY	REMARKS
1	RTC2920	Short Engine Assembly	1	

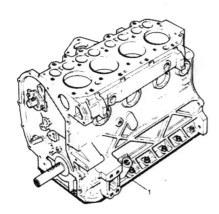

TS6357

LAND ROVER PARTS LTD

MODEL LR110 - UP TO AUGUST 1986
BLOCK VS 3736
PAGE B 50
GROUP B

ENGINE - 2.25 DIESEL - CYLINDER BLOCK

ILL	PART NO	DESCRIPTION	QTY	REMARKS
1	RTC2926	CYLINDER BLOCK ASSEMBLY	1	
2	247965	+Plug-Tappet Feed Hole	1	
3	247127	+Plug-Oil Gallery	2	
4	213700	+Dowel-Chain Tensioner	1	
5	501593	+Dowel-Main Bearing Cap	10	
6	ERC4996	+Plug-Cup Side/Ends	6	
7	597586	+Plug-Cup Water Rail End	3	
8	ERC4644	+Dowel-Flywheel Housing	2	
9	527269	+Plug-Immersion Heater	1	
10	243959	+Washer-Joint Rear Plug	2	
11	536577	+Plug-Oil Gallery Rear	2	
12	90519054	+Bearing-Camshaft Front	1	
13	90519055	+Bearing-Camshaft Inter/Rear	3	
14	ERC4995	+Plug-Cup Top	2	
15	247755	+Bolt-Main Bearing Cap	10	
16	504006	+Washer	10	

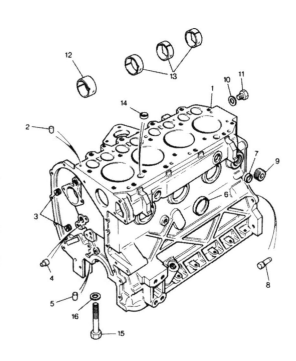

VS3736

LAND ROVER PARTS LTD

72

MODEL LR110 - UP TO AUGUST 1986
BLOCK TS 6444
PAGE B 52
GROUP B

ENGINE - 2.25 DIESEL - ENGINE MOUNTINGS

ILL	PART NO	DESCRIPTION	QTY	REMARKS
1	NRC5434	Mounting Foot-RH	1	
2	NRC4340	Mounting Foot-LH	1	
	NRC9557	Mounting Foot-LH	1	NLA-Use NRC9557
3	SH112251L	Screw	4	
4	WL112001L	Washer-Spring	4	
5	ERC9410	Drain Plug	1	
6	AFU1882	Joint Washer-Drain Plug	1	
7	ERC5086	Packing Strip	2	
8	TE108061L	Stud-Distributor Pump	3	
9	NRC9560	Rubber-Engine Mounting	2	
10	NH110041L	Nut	4	
11	WC110061L	Plain Washer	2	
12	WL110001L	Spring Washer	2	

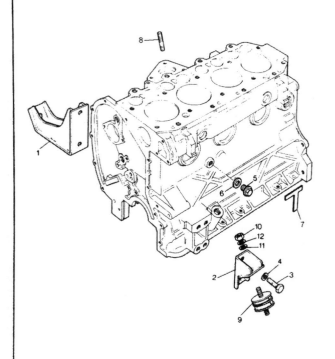

TS6444

LAND ROVER PARTS LTD

73

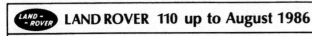
MODEL LR110 - UP TO AUGUST 1986
BLOCK 1RE 283
PAGE B 54
GROUP B

ENGINE - 2.25 DIESEL - PISTONS

ILL	PART NO	DESCRIPTION	QTY	REMARKS
1	RTC4191S	PISTON & RINGS ASSY-STD	4	
	RTC419120	PISTON & RINGS ASSY-0.020"O/S	4	
	RTC419140	PISTON & RINGS ASSY-0.040"O/S	4	
2	RTC4193S	+Kit-Piston Rings-Std	4	
	RTC419320	+Kit-Piston Rings-0.020"O/S	4	
	RTC419340	+Kit-Piston Rings-0.040"O/S	4	
3	502029	+Gudgeon Pin	4	
4	266945	+Circlip	8	
5	ETC5156	CONNECTING ROD ASSEMBLY	4	
6	247583	+Bush-Gudgeon Pin	4	
7	ERC8751	+Bolt-Conn Rod	8	
8	ETC5155	+Nut-Conn Rod	8	
9	RTC1730	Kit-Connecting Rod-Bearings	1	

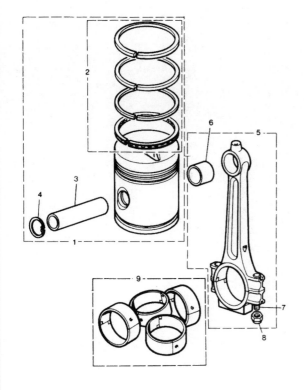

1RE283

MODEL LR110 - UP TO AUGUST 1986
BLOCK VS 3722A
PAGE B 56
GROUP B

ENGINE - 2.25 DIESEL - CRANKSHAFT

ILL	PART NO	DESCRIPTION	QTY	REMARKS
1	ERC5014	CRANKSHAFT ASSEMBLY	1	
2	ERC4650	+Dowel	1	
3	8566L	+Bush	1	
4	RTC2626	KIT MAIN BEARING	1	
5	235770	Key-Chainwheel	1	
6	568333	Chainwheel	1	
		KIT-THRUST WASHER		
7	RTC2825	+Standard	1	
	538131	+0.0025" O/S	1	
	538132	+0.005" O/S	1	
	538133	+0.0075" O/S	1	
	538134	+0.010" O/S	1	
8	ERC3600	Torsional Vibration Damper & Pulley	1	)
	ERC6630	Torsional Vibration Damper-Air Con & PAS	1	)Damper & Pulley)are Supplied
	ERC6859	Pulley-TV Damper-Air Con with PAS Only	1	)Seperately
	ERC6860	Pulley-TV Damper-Air Con Only	1	)
	ERC6861	Pulley-TV Damper-PAS Only	1	)
9	SH108251L	Screw-Pulley TV Damper	4	)Air Con & PAS
10	WL108001L	Washer Spring-Pulley TV Damper	4	)
11	ERC4672	Starting Dog	1	)Alternative
	ETC7934	Bolt-Crankshaft	1	)
12	ETC4969	Oil Seal	1	NLA-Use ETC5369
	ETC5369	Oil Seal	1	

VS3722A

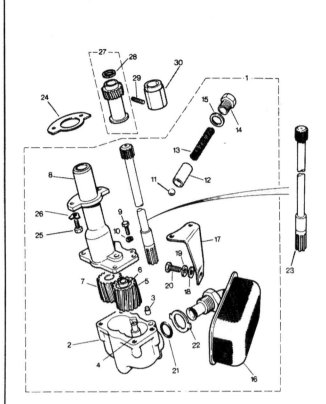

MODEL LR110 - UP TO AUGUST 1986
BLOCK 1RE 279A
PAGE B 58
GROUP B

ENGINE - 2.25 DIESEL - OIL PUMP

ILL	PART NO	DESCRIPTION	QTY	REMARKS
1	ETC7054	OIL PUMP ASSEMBLY	1	
2	513641	+Oil Pump Body-Note(1)	1	)Upto Suffix B)No Longer)Serviced
	ETC4464	+Oil Pump Body-Note(1)	1	)From Suffix C)No Longer)Serviced
	ETC5646	+Oil Pump Body-Note(2)	1	
3	236257	+Dowel	2	
4	90502209	+Spindle-Idler Wheel	1	
5	278109	+IDLER WHEEL ASSEMBLY	1	)Note(1)
6	214995	++Bush	1	)
7	240555	+Drive Wheel	1	)
5	ERC9707	+Idler Wheel	1	)Note(2)
7	ERC9706	+Driver Wheel	1	)
8	513639	+Cover	1	
9	SH605071L	+Screw	4	)To Suffix B Only
10	WM600051L	+Spring Washer	4	)
9	SH108201L	+Screw	4	)Suffix C Onward
10	WL108001L	+Spring Washer	4	)
11	3748	+Ball	1	)Note(1)
12	273711	+Plunger	1	)
	ETC4880	+Plunger	1	Note(2)
13	564456	+Spring	1	
14	549909	+Plug	1	)Without Oil)Cooler
	564455	+Plug	1	)With Oil)Cooler & all)Pumps with Ten)Toothed Gears
15	232044	+Joint Washer	1	
16	ERC7530	+Filter	1	
17	ERC7940	+Bracket-Support	1	
18	WA108051L	+Washer	1	
19	WL108001L	+Washer-Spring	1	
20	SH108201L	+Screw	1	
21	244488	+O Ring	1	
22	244487	+Lockwasher	1	
23	ERC9669	Drive Shaft	1	
24	ERC8408	Gasket	1	
25	SH108251L	Screw	2	
26	247665	Lockwasher	2	

NOTE(1): For Pumps With Nine Toothed Gears

NOTE(2): For Pumps With Ten Toothed Gears

1RE279A

LAND ROVER PARTS LTD

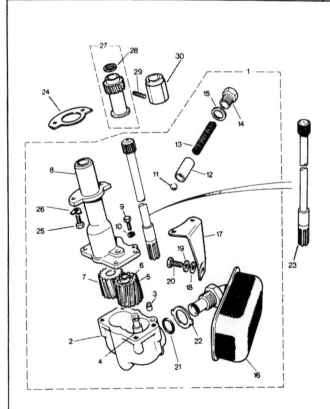

MODEL LR110 - UP TO AUGUST 1986
BLOCK 1RE 279A
PAGE B 58.02
GROUP B

ENGINE - 2.25 DIESEL - OIL PUMP CONTINUED

ILL	PART NO	DESCRIPTION	QTY	REMARKS
27	ETC6139	VERTICAL DRIVE SHAFT ASSY	1	
28	247742	+Circlip	1	
29	524769	Screw-Locating	1	)Old type of)Drive Shaft with)Flange Retaining)the Bush
30	247653	Bush-Split	1	
	522745	Bush	1	)Later type of)Drive Shaft)with Locking)Ring Retaining)the Bush
	ETC6142	Locating Screw	1	
	ETC6137	Thrust Washer	1	
	ETC6138	Locking Ring	1	

1RE279A

LAND ROVER PARTS LTD

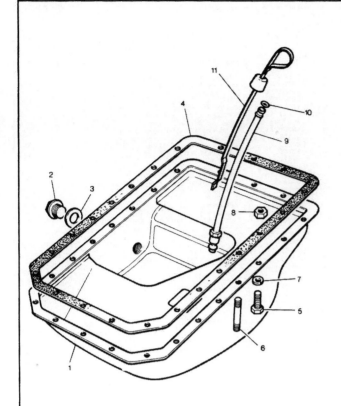

MODEL LR110 - UP TO AUGUST 1986
BLOCK 1RE 276
PAGE B 60
GROUP B

ENGINE - 2.25 DIESEL - SUMP

ILL	PART NO	DESCRIPTION	QTY	REMARKS
1	RTC4841	Sump-Crankcase	1	
2	536577	Drain Plug	1	
	ETC5577	Drain Plug	1	
3	243959	Joint Washer-Plug	1	
	FRC4808	Joint Washer-Plug	1	
4	546841	Joint Washer-Sump to Block	1	Note(1)
5	SH108251L	Screw	21	
6	TE108041L	Stud	1	
7	WL108001L	Spring Washer	22	
8	NH108041L	Nut	1	
1	RTC4841	SUMP ASSEMBLY	1	)
2	ETC5577	+Plug	1	)
3	FRC4808	+Joint Washer-Plug	1	)
5	SH108161L	+Screw	21	)Note(2)
6	TE108031L	+Stud	1	)
7	WL108001L	+Spring Washer	22	)
8	NH108041L	+Nut	1	)
9	ERC8980	Tube-Dipstick	1	
10	532387	Sealing Ring	1	
11	ETC7867	Dipstick	1	

NOTE(1): Later Sump Is Sealed With Liquid Gasket Compound.
          The Sump Gasket 546841 Can Be Fitted As An Alternative
          For Service.

NOTE(2): Latest Sump Has A Thinner Flange & Should Be Fitted
          Using The Fixings Enclosed With The Kit To Prevent
          The Screws Bottoming.

1RE276

 **LAND ROVER PARTS LTD**

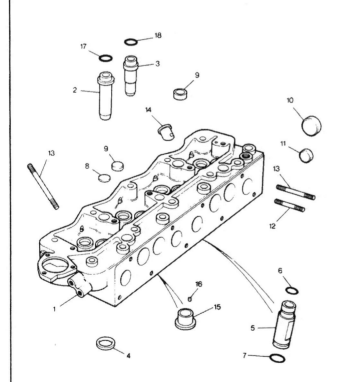

MODEL LR110 - UP TO AUGUST 1986
BLOCK VS 3990
PAGE B 62
GROUP B

ENGINE - 2.25 DIESEL - CYLINDER HEAD

ILL	PART NO	DESCRIPTION	QTY	REMARKS
1	ERC9359	CYLINDER HEAD ASSEMBLY	1	Note(1)
	ETC4301	CYLINDER HEAD ASSEMBLY	1	Note(2)
2	568688	+Valve Guide-Inlet	4	
3	568689	+Valve-Guide-Exhaust	4	
4	512828	+Insert-Valve Seat	4	Note(1)
	ERC9631	+Insert-Valve Seat	4	Note(2)
5	ERC8663	+Tube-Push Rod	8	
6	TRS1013L	+O Ring-Tube	8	Note(1)
7	TRS1114L	+O Ring-Tube	8	Note(1)
8	250830	+Plug-Welch	2	
9	525497	+Plug-Cup	9	
10	524765	+Plug-Cup	1	
11	602289	+Plug-Cup	1	
12	TE108051L	Stud-Manifold Fixing	5	
13	TE108071L	Stud	12	
14	524680	Shroud-Injection Bore	4	
15	558168	Hot Plug	4	
16	PA105101L	Locating Peg-Hot Plug	4	
17	ETC4709	Seal-Inlet Valve	4	
18	ETC4751	Seal-Exhaust Valve	4	

NOTE(1): Up To Engine Number 10J001364

NOTE(2): From Engine Number 10J001365

VS3990

 **LAND ROVER PARTS LTD**

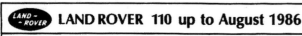
MODEL LR110 - UP TO AUGUST 1986
BLOCK VS 3822
PAGE B 64
GROUP B

ENGINE - 2.25 DIESEL - CYLINDER HEAD CONTINUED

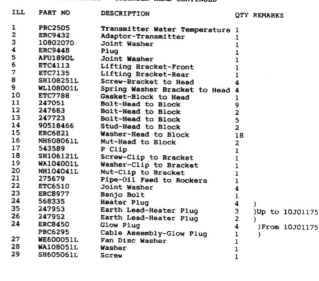

ILL	PART NO	DESCRIPTION	QTY	REMARKS
1	PRC2505	Transmitter Water Temperature	1	
2	ERC9432	Adaptor-Transmitter	1	
3	10802070	Joint Washer	1	
4	ERC9448	Plug	1	
5	AFU1890L	Joint Washer	1	
6	ETC4113	Lifting Bracket-Front	1	
7	ETC7135	Lifting Bracket-Rear	1	
8	SH108251L	Screw-Bracket to Head	4	
9	WL108001L	Spring Washer Bracket to Head	4	
10	ETC7788	Gasket-Block to Head	1	
11	247051	Bolt-Head to Block	9	
12	247683	Bolt-Head to Block	2	
13	247723	Bolt-Head to Block	5	
14	90518466	Stud-Head to Block	2	
15	ERC6821	Washer-Head to Block	18	
16	NH608061L	Nut-Head to Block	2	
17	543589	P Clip	1	
18	SH106121L	Screw-Clip to Bracket	1	
19	WA104001L	Washer-Clip to Bracket	1	
20	NH104041L	Nut-Clip to Bracket	1	
21	275679	Pipe-Oil Feed to Rockers	1	
22	ETC6510	Joint Washer	4	
23	ERC8977	Banjo Bolt	1	
24	568335	Heater Plug	4	)
35	247953	Earth Lead-Heater Plug	3	)Up to 10J01175
26	247952	Earth Lead-Heater Plug	2	)
24	ERC8450	Glow Plug	4	)From 10J01175
	PRC6295	Cable Assembly-Glow Plug	1	)
27	WE600051L	Fan Disc Washer	1	
28	WA108051L	Washer	1	
29	SH605061L	Screw	1	

VS3822

LAND ROVER PARTS LTD

MODEL LR110 - UP TO AUGUST 1986
BLOCK VS 3755A
PAGE B 66
GROUP B

ENGINE - 2.25 DIESEL - THERMOSTAT HOUSING

ILL	PART NO	DESCRIPTION	QTY	REMARKS
1	ERC8758	Thermostat Housing & By Pass	1	
2	ETC4763	Thermostat	1	
3	ERC7951	Joint Washer	1	
4	247874	Joint Washer	1	
5	ERC7510	Hose-Thermo Housing to Adaptor	1	
6	CN100258	Clip-Hose	2	
7	ERC5314	Connector-Water Outlet	1	
	ERC8554	Connector-Water Outlet	1	)Air Con & Air)Con with PAS)Only
8	ERC6478	Bracket-Cowl Mounting	1	
9	BH106131L	Bolt	1	
10	BH106151L	Bolt	2	
11	WL106001L	Spring Washer	3	
12	624091	Adaptor	1	
13	243959	Joint Washer	1	
14	ERC8758	Thermostat Housing & By Pass	1	
15	90511958	Joint Washer	1	
16	SH108251L	Screw	2	
17	WL108001L	Spring Washer	2	
18	624091	Adaptor	1	
19	243959	Joint Washer	1	
20	PRC3366	Switch-Temperature Sensor-Fan-See Note(1)	1	)Air Con & Air)Con with PAS
21	PRC3541	Switch-Temperature Sensor-Compressor-See Note(2)	1	)Only)
22	C457593	Washer Copper	2	)

NOTE(1): Identified By Blue Paint

NOTE(2): Identified By Red Paint

VS3755A

LAND ROVER PARTS LTD

MODEL LR110 - UP TO AUGUST 1986
BLOCK VS 3734A
PAGE B 68
GROUP B

ENGINE - 2.25 DIESEL - CAMSHAFT

ILL	PART NO	DESCRIPTION	QTY	REMARKS
1	ERC5475	Camshaft	1	)No Longer)Available)Use ETC7128
	ETC7128	Camshaft	1	
2	ERC1561	Thrust Plate-Camshaft	1	
3	SH106161L	Screw	2	
4	2995	Lockwasher	2	
5	230313	Woodruff Key-Chainwheel to Shaft	1	
6	ETC5551	Chainwheel	1	
7	ETC4140	Retaining Washer	1	
8	ETC4141	Retaining Bolt	1	)Use with)Camshaft ERC5475
	BH110071L	Retaining Bolt	1	)Use with)Camshaft)ETC7128

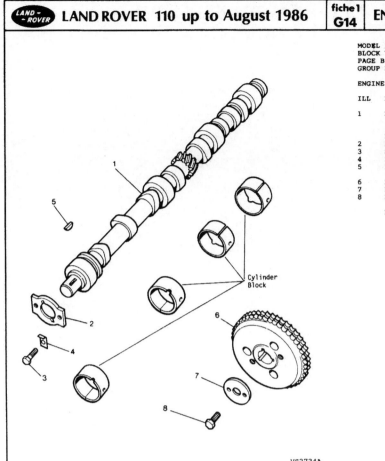

Cylinder Block

VS3734A

LAND ROVER PARTS LTD

MODEL LR110 - UP TO AUGUST 1986
BLOCK 1RE 273
PAGE B 70
GROUP B

ENGINE - 2.25 DIESEL - TIMING CHAIN

ILL	PART NO	DESCRIPTION	QTY	REMARKS
1	ETC4499	Timing Chain	1	
2	3739	Ball	1	
3	233328	Retaining Clip-Ball	1	
4	233326	Spring-Tension Cylinder	1	
5	267451	Spring-Ratchet	1	
6	ERC8975	Stepped Bolt	1	
7	247912	Piston Assy-Timing Tensioner	1	
8	546026	Ratchet and Bush Assy	1	
9	236067	IDLER WHEEL AND BUSH ASSY	1	
10	234124	+Bush	1	
11	277388	Cylinder Assembly-Chain Tensioner	1	
12	TE108051L	Stud	1	
13	BH108061L	Bolt	1	
14	WL108001L	Spring Washer	1	
15	NH108041L	Nut	1	
16	275234	Vibration Damper	1	
17	SH106121L	Screw	2	
18	557523	Lockwasher	2	

1RE273

LAND ROVER PARTS LTD

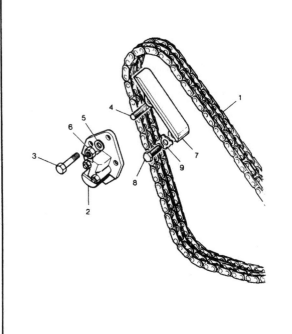

MODEL LR110 - UP TO AUGUST 1986
BLOCK TS 5365
PAGE B 70.02
GROUP B

ENGINE - 2.25 DIESEL - TIMING CHAIN

ILL	PART NO	DESCRIPTION	QTY	REMARKS
1	ETC5191	Timing Chain	1	
2	ETC5190	Tensioner-Timing Chain	1	
3	SH108201L	Screw	2	
4	TE108051L	Stud	1	
5	WA108051L	Washer	3	
6	NH108041L	Nut	1	
7	275234	Vibration Damper	1	
8	SH106121L	Screw	2	
9	557523	Lock Washer	2	

TS5365

LAND ROVER PARTS LTD

MODEL LR110 - UP TO AUGUST 1986
BLOCK 1RE 280
PAGE B 72
GROUP B

ENGINE - 2.25 DIESEL - VALVES AND TAPPETS

ILL	PART NO	DESCRIPTION	QTY	REMARKS
1	507829	TAPPET ASSEMBLY	8	
2	502473	+Tappet Guide	8	
3	ETC4246	+Bolt-Set	8	
4	273069	+Washer	8	
5	90517429	+Roller Follower	8	
6	ETC5057	+Tappet	8	
7	ETC5739	Valve-Inlet	4	
8	ERC9738	Valve-Exhaust	4	
	ETC7203	+Valve Stem Protection Cap	8	Note(1)
9	568550	Spring-Valves	8	
10	ETC4068	Cup-Valve Spring	8	
11	ETC4069	Split Cotter	16	
12	546799	Push Rod	8	

NOTE(1): Can Be Fitted If Suffering From Excessive Valve Stem
Or Valve Rocker Wear.

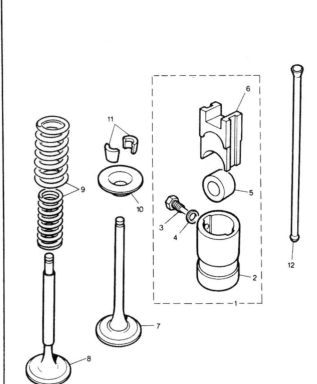

1RE280

LAND ROVER PARTS LTD

MODEL LR110 - UP TO AUGUST 1986
BLOCK 1RE 278
PAGE B 74
GROUP B

ENGINE - 2.25 DIESEL - ROCKER SHAFT

ILL	PART NO	DESCRIPTION	QTY	REMARKS
1	274773	Valve Rocker Assy-Exhaust-RH	2	)
2	274772	Valve Rocker Assy-Exhaust-LH	2	)To Suffix B Only
3	274775	Valve Rocker Assy-Inlet-RH	2	)
4	274774	Valve Rocker Assy-Inlet-LH	2	)
1	ERC9060	Valve Rocker Assy-Exhaust-RH	2	)
2	ERC9059	Valve Rocker Assy-Exhaust-LH	2	)Suffix C Onward
3	ERC9056	Valve Rocker Assy-Inlet-RH	2	)
4	ERC9055	Valve Rocker Assy-Inlet-LH	2	)
5	247738	Bush	4	
6	247737	Bush	4	
7	ERC6341	SHAFT-VALVE ROCKERS	1	
8	ERC6337	+Plug-Shaft	2	
9	506814	Screw-Tappet Adjusting	8	)To Suffix B Only
10	NT605061L	Locknut-Screw	8	)
9	ERC9054	Screw-Tappet Adjusting	8	)Suffix C Onward
10	NT108041L	Locknut-Screw	8	)
11	247040	Spring	4	
12	523181	Bracket-Rocker Shaft	5	To Suffix B Only
12	ERC9137	Bracket-Rocker Shaft	5	Suffix C Onward
13	WL108001L	Spring Washer	5	
14	BH108111L	Bolt	5	
15	247153	Washer	8	
16	525390	Screw-Shaft Locating	1	To Suffix B Only
	ETC4460	Screw-Shaft Locating	1	Suffix C Onward
17	WL108001L	Spring Washer	1	
18	247607	Stud	3	To Suffix B Only
	TD108091L	Stud	3	Suffix C Onward
19	277956	Dowel-Rocker Shaft Bracket	3	

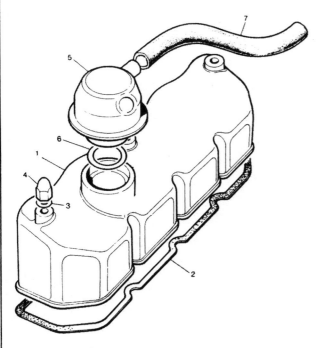

1RE278

MODEL LR110 - UP TO AUGUST 1986
BLOCK 1RE 266
PAGE B 74.02
GROUP B

ENGINE - 2.25 DIESEL - ROCKER COVER ASSEMBLY

ILL	PART NO	DESCRIPTION	QTY	REMARKS
1	ERC8051	Rocker Cover Assembly	1	
2	247606	Gasket-Cover to Cylinder Head	1	NLA-Use ETC6438
	ETC6438	Gasket-Cover to Cylinder Head	1	
3	273069	Washer-Sealing	3	
4	247121	Nut-Dome	3	To Suffix B Only
	ERC9220	Nut-Dome	3	Suffix C Onward
5	ETC5297	Breather Filter	1	
6	ERC8049	O Ring	1	
7	ERC9728	Hose	1	
	ETC5588	Bracket-Compressor Supply Pipe	1	Air Con Only

1RE266

BLANK

BLANK

LAND ROVER PARTS LTD

88

MODEL LR110 - UP TO AUGUST 1986
BLOCK VS 3854
PAGE B 78
GROUP B

ENGINE - 2.25 DIESEL - FRONT COVER - EXCEPT AIR CON

ILL	PART NO	DESCRIPTION	QTY	REMARKS
1	ERC9519	FRONT COVER ASSEMBLY	1	
2	247766	+Mud Excluder	1	
3	AB606021L	+Screw	8	
4	6395L	+Dowel	2	
5	ERC7987	+Oil Seal	1	
6	538038	Washer-Joint-Water Inlet	1	
7	538039	Washer-Joint-Front Cover	1	
8	ERC8965	Bolt-Stud	1	)Use wtih Fan)Cowl without)Flexible Mtg
	ETC4994	Bolt-Stud	1	)Use with Fan)Cowl with)Flexible Mtg
9	BH108151L	Bolt	1	
10	BH108101L	Bolt	6	
11	WL108001L	Washer-Spring	8	

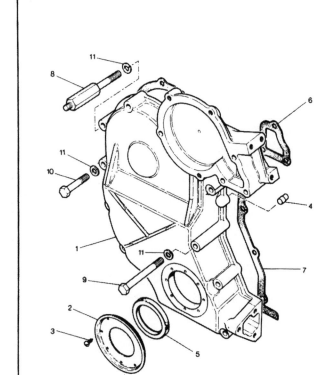

VS3854

 LAND ROVER PARTS LTD

89

MODEL LR110 - UP TO AUGUST 1986
BLOCK VS 3927A
PAGE B 78.02
GROUP B

ENGINE - 2.25 DIESEL - FRONT COVER - AIR CON

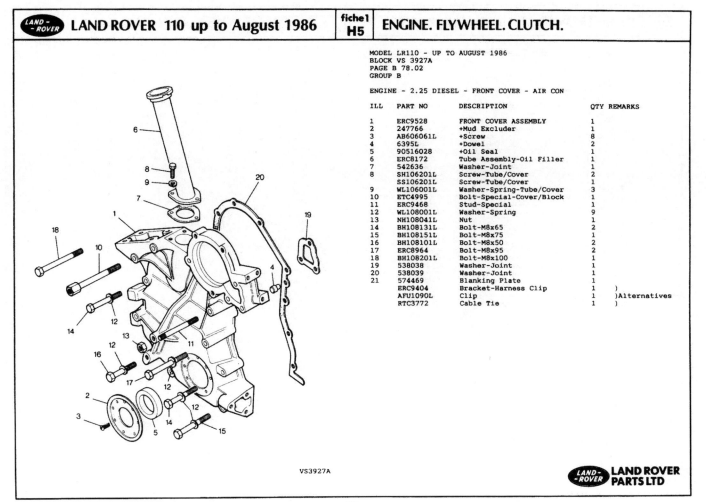

ILL	PART NO	DESCRIPTION	QTY	REMARKS
1	ERC9528	FRONT COVER ASSEMBLY	1	
2	247766	+Mud Excluder	1	
3	AB606061L	+Screw	8	
4	6395L	+Dowel	2	
5	90516028	+Oil Seal	1	
6	ERC8172	Tube Assembly-Oil Filler	1	
7	542636	Washer-Joint	1	
8	SH106201L	Screw-Tube/Cover	2	
	SS106201L	Screw-Tube/Cover		
9	WL106001L	Washer-Spring-Tube/Cover	3	
10	ETC4995	Bolt-Special-Cover/Block	1	
11	ERC9468	Stud-Special	1	
12	WL108001L	Washer-Spring	9	
13	NH108041L	Nut	1	
14	BH108131L	Bolt-M8x65	2	
15	BH108151L	Bolt-M8x75	1	
16	BH108101L	Bolt-M8x50	2	
17	ERC8964	Bolt-M8x95	2	
18	BH108201L	Bolt-M8x100	1	
19	538038	Washer-Joint	1	
20	538039	Washer-Joint	1	
21	574469	Blanking Plate	1	
	ERC9404	Bracket-Harness Clip	1	)
	AFU1090L	Clip	1	)Alternatives
	RTC3772	Cable Tie	1	)

VS3927A

LAND ROVER PARTS LTD

MODEL LR110 - UP TO AUGUST 1986
BLOCK VS 3789
PAGE B 80
GROUP B

ENGINE - 2.25 DIESEL - WATER PUMP

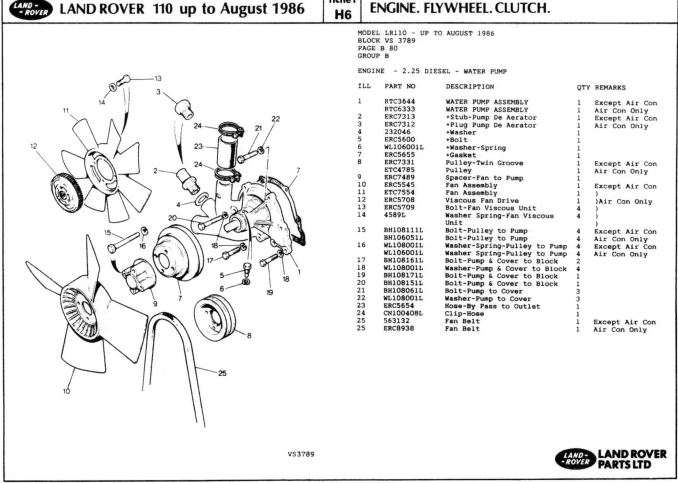

ILL	PART NO	DESCRIPTION	QTY	REMARKS
1	RTC3644	WATER PUMP ASSEMBLY	1	Except Air Con
	RTC6333	WATER PUMP ASSEMBLY	1	Air Con Only
2	ERC7313	+Stub-Pump De Aerator	1	Except Air Con
3	ERC7312	+Plug Pump De Aerator	1	Air Con Only
4	232046	+Washer	1	
5	ERC5600	+Bolt	1	
6	WL106001L	+Washer-Spring	1	
7	ERC5655	+Gasket	1	
8	ERC7331	Pulley-Twin Groove	1	Except Air Con
	ETC4785	Pulley	1	Air Con Only
9	ERC7489	Spacer-Fan to Pump	1	
10	ERC5545	Fan Assembly	1	Except Air Con
11	ETC7554	Fan Assembly	1	)
12	ERC5708	Viscous Fan Drive	1	)Air Con Only
13	ERC5709	Bolt-Fan Viscous Unit	4	)
14	4589L	Washer Spring-Fan Viscous Unit	4	)
15	BH108111L	Bolt-Pulley to Pump	4	Except Air Con
	BH106051L	Bolt-Pulley to Pump	4	Air Con Only
16	WL108001L	Washer-Spring-Pulley to Pump	4	Except Air Con
	WL106001L	Washer Spring-Pulley to Pump	4	Air Con Only
17	BH108161L	Bolt-Pump & Cover to Block	2	
18	WL108001L	Washer-Pump & Cover to Block	4	
19	BH108171L	Bolt-Pump & Cover to Block	1	
20	BH108151L	Bolt-Pump & Cover to Block	1	
21	BH108061L	Bolt-Pump to Cover	3	
22	WL108001L	Washer-Pump to Cover	3	
23	ERC5654	Hose-By Pass to Outlet	1	
24	CN100408L	Clip-Hose	1	
25	563132	Fan Belt	1	Except Air Con
25	ERC8938	Fan Belt	1	Air Con Only

VS3789

LAND ROVER PARTS LTD

MODEL LR110 - UP TO AUGUST 1986
BLOCK TS 5011
PAGE B 82
GROUP B

ENGINE - 2.25 DIESEL - SIDE COVER

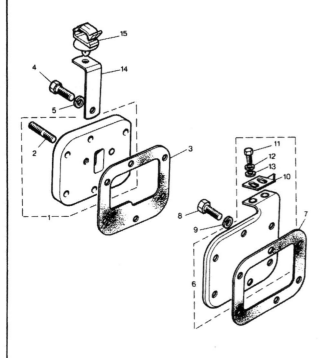

ILL	PART NO	DESCRIPTION	QTY	REMARKS
1	542600	SIDE COVER & STUD ASSEMBLY	1	To Suffix B Only
	ERC9073	SIDE COVER & STUD ASSEMBLY	1	Suffix C Onward
2	542601	+Stud	2	To Suffix B Only
	TE108041L	+Stud	2	Suffix C Onward
	247554	Joint Washer	1	
4	SH108251L	Screw	6	
5	WL108001L	Washer-Spring	6	
6	ERC9727	Side Cover Assembly	1	
7	247555	Joint Washer	1	
8	SH108161L	Screw	6	
9	WL108001L	Washer-Spring	6	
10	564470	Pointer-Timing-Distributor Pump	1	
11	SH104121L	Screw	2	
12	WL104001L	Washer-Spring	2	
13	WA104041L	Washer	2	
14	ERC9480	Bracket	1	
15	AFU1090L	Cable Clip	1	

TS5011

MODEL LR110 - UP TO AUGUST 1986
BLOCK 1RE 132A
PAGE B 84
GROUP B

ENGINE - 2.25 DIESEL - OIL FILTER

ILL	PART NO	DESCRIPTION	QTY	REMARKS
1	537229	OIL FILTER ASSEMBLY	1	
2	272539	+Sealing Ring	1	
3	RTC3184	+Filter Element	1	
4	269889	+Distance Washer	1	
5	ETC5276	Joint Washer	1	
6	SH110301L	Bolt-Filter to Block 1.25"	2	Except Oil Cooler
	ERC9499	Bolt-Filter to Block 2.875"	2	Oil Cooler Only
7	WL110001L	Spring Washer	2	
8	90519864	Oil Pressure Switch	1	
9	232039	Joint Washer-Switch	1	

1RE132A

MODEL LR110 - UP TO AUGUST 1986
BLOCK VS 3831
PAGE B 86
GROUP B

ENGINE - 2.25 DIESEL - MANIFOLDS

ILL	PART NO	DESCRIPTION	QTY	REMARKS
1	ERC6939	Inlet-Manifold	1	
2	525428	Plug-Cup	1	
3	ERC6047	Tube	1	
4	ETC5312	Joint Washer	1	
5	564308	Clamp	4	
6	WL108001L	Spring Washer	9	
7	NH108041L	Nut	9	
8	WA108051L	Washer	5	
9	574654	Clip-Manifold Clamp	1	
10	598104	Exhaust Manifold	1	
11	568664	Stud	3	

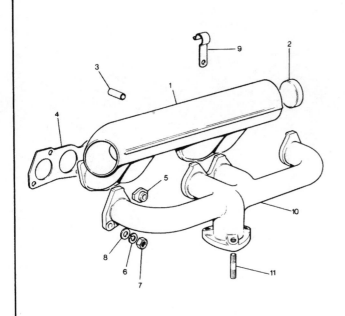

VS3831

LAND ROVER PARTS LTD

MODEL LR110 - UP TO AUGUST 1986
BLOCK VS 3824
PAGE B 88
GROUP B

ENGINE - 2.25 DIESEL - VACUUM PUMP

ILL	PART NO	DESCRIPTION	QTY	REMARKS
1	ERC9639	Vacuum Pump	1	
2	ERC7338	Pulley	1	Except Air Con & PAS
	ERC8982	Pulley	1	)Air Con & PAS)Only
3	SH106161L	Screw-Pulley to Pump	4	
4	WM600041L	Spring Washer-Pulley to Pump	4	
5	ERC6518	Bracket-Vacuum Pipe	1	
6	BH108151L	Bolt-Bracket to Pump	1	
7	WC108051L	Washer-Bracket to Pump	2	
8	NY108041L	Nut-Nyloc-Bracket to Pump	1	
9	ERC6520	Adjusting Link	1	
10	ERC6517	Spacer-Link to Bracket	1	
11	SH108141L	Screw-Link to Pump	2	
12	WM600051L	Spring Washer-Link to Pump	2	
13	ETC4267	Belt-Vacuum Pump	1	Except Air Con & PAS
13	ETC4266	Belt-Vacuum Pump	1	Air Con & PAS Only
14	BH108071L	Bolt-Bracket to Front Cover	2	
15	BH108081L	Bolt-Bracket to Front Cover	1	
16	WM600051L	Spring Washer-Bracket to Front Cover	3	
17	SH108251L	Screw-Link to Bracket	1	
18	WM600051L	Spring Washer-Link to Bracket	1	
19	WC108051L	Washer-Link to Bracket	1	
	BAU2325	Kit-Gasket	1	
	BAU2326	Kit-Diaphragm	1	

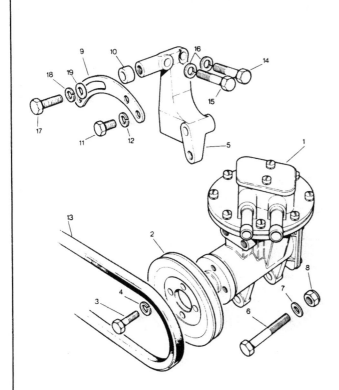

VS3824

LAND ROVER PARTS LTD

MODEL LR110 - UP TO AUGUST 1986
BLOCK VS 3996
PAGE B 92
GROUP B

ENGINE - 2.25 DIESEL - GASKET KITS

ILL	PART NO	DESCRIPTION	QTY	REMARKS
1	RTC3336	Gasket/Seal Kit-Decarbonising	1	
2	RTC2916	Gasket/Seal Kit-Overhaul	1	Use with RTC3336
	RTC3254	RTV Silicon Sealant-110 Gram Tube	1	

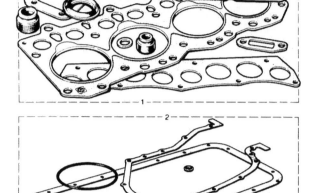

VS3996

MASTER INDEX

GROUP B

ENGINE

MODEL LR110 - UP TO AUGUST 1986
BLOCK TS 5787
PAGE B 94
GROUP B

ENGINE - 2.5 DIESEL - ENGINE ASSEMBLY

ILL	PART NO	DESCRIPTION	QTY	REMARKS
1	ERC9476N	Engine-Complete with Clutch And Flywheel	1	

Serial No.12J00001C

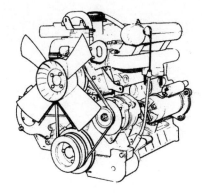

TS5787

MODEL LR110 - UP TO AUGUST 1986
BLOCK TS 6462
PAGE B 96
GROUP B

ENGINE - STRIPPED - 2.5 DIESEL

ILL	PART NO	DESCRIPTION	QTY	REMARKS
1	RTC4059N	Engine Assembly-Stripped-New	1	
	RTC4059E	Engine Assembly-Stripped-Exchange	1	

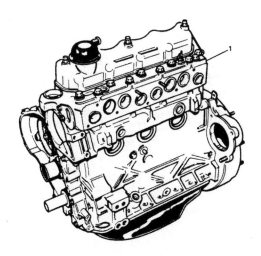

TS 6462

MODEL LR110 - UP TO AUGUST 1986
BLOCK TS 6357
PAGE B 98
GROUP B

ENGINE - 2.5 DIESEL - SHORT ENGINE

ILL	PART NO	DESCRIPTION	QTY	REMARKS
1	RTC3033N	Short Engine Assembly	1	

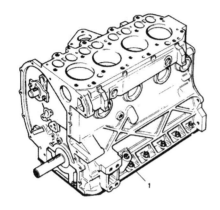

TS6357

MODEL LR110 - UP TO AUGUST 1986
BLOCK VS 4190B
PAGE B 100
GROUP B

ENGINE - 2.5 DIESEL - CYLINDER BLOCK

ILL	PART NO	DESCRIPTION	QTY	REMARKS
1	RTC2991	CYLINDER BLOCK ASSEMBLY	1	
2	247965	+Plug-Tappet Feed Hole	1	
3	247127	+Plug-Oil Gallery	2	
4	ETC4529	+Cup Plug-Oil Feed Tensioner	1	
5	501593	+Dowel-Bearing Caps	10	
6	ERC4996	+Cup Plug Side/Ends	6	
7	597586	+Cup Plug Water Rail/Ends	3	
8	ERC4644	+Dowel-Flywheel Housing	2	
9	527269	+Plug-Immersion Heater	1	
10	243959	+Joint Washer-Gallery Pipe	2	
11	536577	+Plug-Gallery Pipe	2	
12	90519054	+Bearing-Camshaft Front	1	
13	90519055	+Bearing-Camshaft Inter/Rear	3	
14	ERC4995	+Cup Plug-Top	2	
15	247755	+Bolt-Main Bearing Cap	10	
16	504006	+Washer Main Bearing Cap	10	
17	TE108031L	+Stud-Starter Motor Bracket	1	
	ETC7708	+Plug-Camshaft Oil Feed	3	

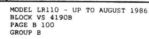

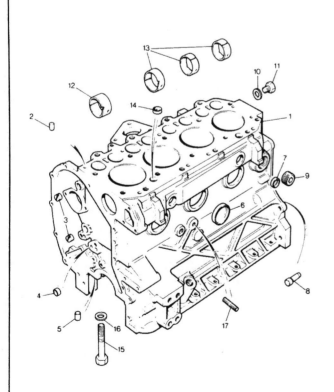

VS4190B

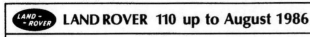

MODEL LR110 - UP TO AUGUST 1986
BLOCK TS 6443
PAGE B 102
GROUP B

ENGINE - 2.5 DIESEL - CYLINDER BLOCK/ENGINE MOUNTINGS

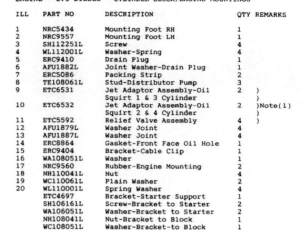

ILL	PART NO	DESCRIPTION	QTY	REMARKS
1	NRC5434	Mounting Foot RH	1	
2	NRC9557	Mounting Foot LH	1	
3	SH112251L	Screw	4	
4	WL112001L	Washer-Spring	4	
5	ERC9410	Drain Plug	1	
6	AFU1882L	Joint Washer-Drain Plug	1	
7	ERC5086	Packing Strip	2	
8	TE108061L	Stud-Distributor Pump	3	
9	ETC6531	Jet Adaptor Assembly-Oil Squirt 1 & 3 Cylinder	2	)
10	ETC6532	Jet Adaptor Assembly-Oil Squirt 2 & 4 Cylinder	2	)Note(1)
11	ETC5592	Relief Valve Assembly	4	)
12	AFU1879L	Washer Joint	4	
13	AFU1887L	Washer Joint	4	
14	ERC8864	Gasket-Front Face Oil Hole	1	
15	ERC9404	Bracket-Cable Clip	1	
16	WA108051L	Washer	1	
17	NRC9560	Rubber-Engine Mounting	2	
18	NH110041L	Nut	4	
19	WC110061L	Plain Washer	2	
20	WL110001L	Spring Washer	4	
	ETC4697	Bracket-Starter Support	1	
	SH106161L	Screw-Bracket to Starter	2	
	WA106051L	Washer-Bracket to Starter	2	
	NH108041L	Nut-Bracket to Block	1	
	WC108051L	Washer-Bracket-to Block	1	

NOTE(1):   When Fitting New Jet Adaptor Assembly Also Fit
A New Relief Valve Assembly.

TS6443

LAND ROVER PARTS LTD

MODEL LR110 - UP TO AUGUST 1986
BLOCK 1RE 99A
PAGE B 104
GROUP B

ENGINE - 2.5 DIESEL - PISTONS

ILL	PART NO	DESCRIPTION	QTY	REMARKS
		PISTON & RINGS ASSEMBLY		
1	ETC6835	Piston & Ring Assy-Standard	4	Note(2)
	RTC473320	Piston & Ring Assy-0.020" O/S	4	
		+KIT PISTON RING		
2	RTC3053S	Standard	4	)Alternative
	RTC305320	0.020" O/S	4	)Note(1)
	RTC305340	0.040" O/S	4	)GKN Manufacture
	RTC4778S	+Kit-Piston Ring Std	4	)Alternative
	RTC477820	+Kit-Piston Ring 0.020" O/S	4	)Note(1)
				)Hepolite
				)Manufacture
3	266945	+Circlip	8	
4	ETC5158	CONNECTING ROD ASSEMBLY	4	
5	247583	+Bush-Gudgeon Pin	4	
6	ETC5155	+Nut-Conn Rod	8	
7	ERC8751	+Bolt-Conn Rod	8	
8	RTC2993	Kit-Connecting Rod Bearing	1	

NOTE(1):   Piston Ring Sets Are Not Interchangeable-Fit Hepolite
Rings Only To Hepolite Pistons & GKN Rings to GKN
Pistons.

NOTE(2):   Hepolite & GKN Piston & Ring Sets Are Interchangeable
As A Set.

1RE99A

LAND ROVER PARTS LTD

MODEL LR110 - UP TO AUGUST 1986
BLOCK VS 4260
PAGE B 106
GROUP B

ENGINE - 2.5 DIESEL - CRANKSHAFT

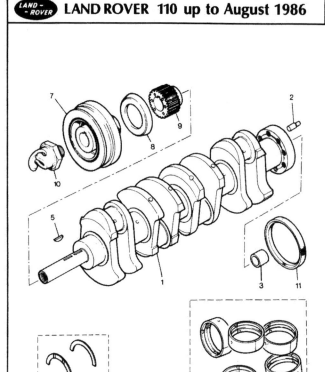

ILL	PART NO	DESCRIPTION	QTY	REMARKS
1	ERC9000	Crankshaft	1	Upto 12J39677C
	ETC8829	Crankshaft	1	From 12J39678C
2	ERC4650	Dowel-Crankshaft	1	
3	8566L	Bush-Crankshaft	1	
4	RTC2992	Kit-Main Bearing	1	
5	235770	Key	2	
		KIT-THRUST WASHER		
6	RTC2825	Standard	1	
	538131	0.0025" O/S	1	
	538132	0.005" O/S	1	
	538133	0.0075" O/S	1	
	538134	0.010" O/S	1	
7	ETC4077	TORSIONAL VIBRATION DAMPER	1	Except Air Con & PAS
	ETC4105	TORSIONAL VIBRATION DAMPER	1	All Air Con & PAS
	ERC6860	+Pulley-TV Damper-Crankshaft	1	Air Con Only
	ERC6859	+Pulley-TV Damper-Crankshaft	1	Air Con With PAS Only
	ERC6861	+Pulley-TV Damper-Crankshaft	1	Power Assisted Steering Only
	SH108251L	Screw Fixing Pulley to Damper	4	
	WL108001L	Washer Spring Fixing Pulley to Damper	4	
8	ETC4390	Flinger-TV Damper	1	
9	ERC9765	Pulley-Crankshaft	1	
10	ERC4672	Starting Dog	1	Alternative
	ETC7934	Bolt-Crankshaft	1	Alternative
11	ETC5369	Oil Seal	1	

VS4260

LAND ROVER PARTS LTD

104

MODEL LR110 - UP TO AUGUST 1986
BLOCK TS 6274A
PAGE B 108
GROUP B

ENGINE - 2.5 DIESEL - OIL PUMP

ILL	PART NO	DESCRIPTION	QTY	REMARKS
1	ETC7054	OIL PUMP ASSEMBLY	1	
2	236257	++Dowel	2	
3	90502209	++Spindle-Idler Wheel	1	
4	ERC9707	+Idler Wheel Assembly	1	
5	ERC9706	+Drive Wheel	1	
6	SH108201L	+Screw	4	
7	WL108001L	+Spring Washer	4	
8	ETC4880	+Plunger-Oil Relief	1	
9	564456	+Spring-Oil Relief	1	
10	564455	+Plug-Oil Relief	1	
11	232044	+Joint Washer	1	
12	ERC7530	+Filter	1	
13	ERC7940	+Bracket-Support	1	
14	WA108051L	+Washer	1	
15	WL108001L	+Spring Washer	1	
16	SH108201L	+Screw	1	
17	244488	+O Ring	1	
18	244487	+Lockwasher	1	
19	ERC9669	Drive Shaft	1	
20	SH108251L	Screw	2	
21	247665	Lockwasher	2	
22	ERC8408	Gasket	1	
23	ETC6139	DRIVE SHAFT	1	See Note
24	522745	+Bush	1	
25	530178	+Thrust Washer	1	)Earlier Type of
26	530179	+Retaining Ring	1	)Shaft with
27	ERC8976	Screw-Locating Shaft	1	)Spring Ring Type)of Retainer
25	ETC6137	+Thrust washer	1	)Later Type of
26	ETC6138	+Locking Ring	1	)Shaft with
27	ETC6142	Screw-Locating Shaft	1	)Locking Ring)Type of)Retainer
28	ETC4706	Coupling-Drive Shaft to Vacuum Pump	1	
29	RTC6167	+O Ring-Inner	1	
30	RTC6168	+O Ring-Outer	1	

NOTE: Before Assembling Drive Shaft & Coupling,
      The Plug Must Be Removed From The Drive Shaft

TS6274/A

LAND ROVER PARTS LTD

105

MODEL LR110 - UP TO AUGUST 1986
BLOCK 1RE 276
PAGE B 110
GROUP B

ENGINE - 2.5 DIESEL - SUMP

ILL	PART NO	DESCRIPTION	QTY	REMARKS
1	RTC3833	Sump-Crankcase	1	NLA Use RTC4841
2	536577	Drain Plug	1	Upto Engine No. 09893
	ETC5577	Drain Plug	1	From Engine No. 09894
3	243959	Joint Washer-Plug	1	Upto Engine No. 09893
	FRC4808	Joint Washer	1	From Engine No. 09894
4	546841	Joint Washer-Sump to Block	1	Note(1)
5	SH108251L	Screw	21	
6	TE108041L	Stud	1	
7	WL108001L	Spring Washer	22	
8	NH108041L	Nut	1	
1	RTC4841	SUMP ASSEMBLY	1	)
2	ETC5577	+Plug	1	)
3	FRC4808	+Joint Washer-Plug	1	)
5	SH108161L	+Screw	21	)Note(2)
6	TE108031L	+Stud	1	)
7	WL108001L	+Spring Washer	22	)
8	NH108041L	+Nut	1	)
9	ERC8980	Tube-Dipstick	1	
10	532387	Sealing Ring	1	
11	ETC7867	Dipstick	1	

NOTE(1): Later Sump Is Sealed With Liquid Gasket Compound. The
Sump Gasket 546841 Can Be Fitted As An Alternative For
Service.

NOTE(2): Latest Sump Has A Thinner Flange And Should Be Fitted
Using The Fixings Enclosed With The Kit To Prevent The
Screws Bottoming.

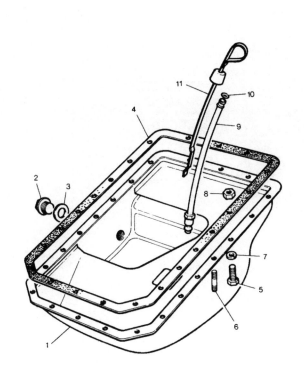

1RE276

LAND ROVER PARTS LTD

MODEL LR110 - UP TO AUGUST 1986
BLOCK VS 4198
PAGE B 112
GROUP B

ENGINE - 2.5 DIESEL - CYLINDER HEAD

ILL	PART NO	DESCRIPTION	QTY	REMARKS
1	ETC4649	CYLINDER HEAD ASSEMBLY	1	
2	568688	+Valve Guide-Inlet	4	
3	568689	+Valve Guide-Exhaust	4	
4	ERC9631	+Insert-Valve Seat-Exhaust	4	
	ETC4643	+Insert-Valve Seat-Inlet	4	
5	ERC8663	+Tube-Push Rod	8	
6	250830	+Plug-Welch	2	
7	525497	+Plug-Cup	9	
8	524765	+Plug-Cup	1	
9	602289	+Plug-Cup	2	
10	TE108051L	Stud-Manifold Fixing	5	
11	TE108071L	Stud	12	
12	ERC9501	Shroud-Injector	4	
13	ETC8620	Hot Plug	4	
14	PA105101L	Locating Peg-Hot Plug	4	
15	ETC4709	Seal-Inlet Valve	4	
16	ETC4751	Seal-Exhaust Valve	4	

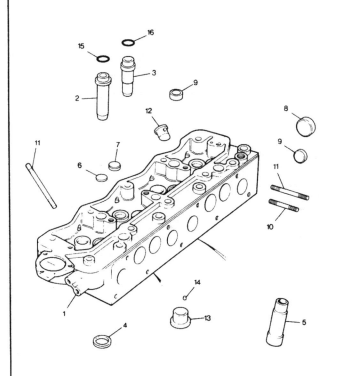

VS4198

LAND ROVER PARTS LTD

MODEL LR110 - UP TO AUGUST 1986
BLOCK VS 4192A
PAGE B 114
GROUP B

ENGINE - 2.5 DIESEL - CYLINDER HEAD CONTINUED

ILL	PART NO	DESCRIPTION	QTY	REMARKS
I	PRC2505	Transmitter-Water Temperature	1	
2	ERC9432	Adaptor-Transmitter	1	
3	10802070	Washer-Adaptor	1	
4	ERC9448	Plug-Rear Heater Hole	1	
5	AFU1890L	Joint Washer-Plug	1	
6	ERC2254	Lifting-Bracket-Front	1	
7	ETC7135	Lifting Bracket-Rear	1	
8	SH108201L	Screw-Bracket to Head	4	
9	WL108001L	Spring Washer Bracket to Head	4	
10	ETC7788	Gasket-Block to Head	1	
11	247051	Bolt-Head to Block	9	
12	247683	Bolt-Head to Block	2	
13	247723	Bolt-Head to Block	5	
14	90518466	Stud-Head to Block	2	
15	ERC6821	Washer-Head to Block	18	
16	NH608061L	Nut-Head to Block	2	
17	275679	Pipe-Oil Feed to Rockers	1	
18	ETC6510	Washer Joint	4	
19	ETC4498	Banjo Bolt	2	
20	ERC8450	Glow Plug	4	
21	PRC6295	Cable Assembly-Glow Plugs	1	

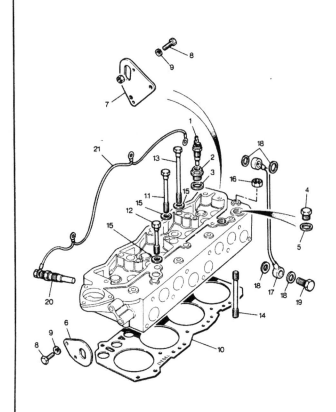

VS4192A

LAND ROVER PARTS LTD

108

MODEL LR110 - UP TO AUGUST 1986
BLOCK VS 4259
PAGE B 116
GROUP B

ENGINE - 2.5 DIESEL - THERMOSTAT HOUSING

ILL	PART NO	DESCRIPTION	QTY	REMARKS
1	ERC8758	Thermostat Housing	1	
2	ETC4763	Thermostat 82°	1	
	ETC4761	Thermostat 74°	1	Optional
3	ERC7951	Gasket-Outlet Pipe Thermo Hsg	1	
4	247874	Gasket-Thermo Housing to Head	1	
5	ERC7510	Hose-Connecting Adaptors	1	
6	CN100258	Clip Hose	2	
7	ERC8757	Cover-Water Outlet-Thermo-	1	)Earlier
		Except Air Con		)Condition Where
	ETC4217	Cover-Water Outlet-Thermo-	1	)the Water Outlet
		Air Con Only		)Connector Points
8	ERC6478	Bracket-Cowl Mounting	1	)to the Right
9	BH106131L	Bolt-Cover to Head	1	)when Viewed from
	BH106151L	Bolt-Cover to Head	2	)the Drivers Seat
7	ETC5967	Water Outlet Connector-	1	)Latest
		Except Air Con		)Condition where
	ETC5958	Water Outlet Connector-	1	)the Water
		Air Con Only		)Outlet
8	ETC5965	Bracket-Cowl Mounting	1	)Connector
9	BH106151L	Bolt	3	)Points to the
				)Left when
				)Viewed from the
				)Drivers Seat
10	WL106001L	Spring Washer-Cover to Head	3	
11	624091	Adaptor-Housing/By Pass Pipe	2	
12	243959	Joint Washer	2	
	PRC3366	Switch-Temperature Sensor-	1	)
		Fan-See Note(1)		)
	PRC3541	Switch-Temperature Sensor-	1	)Air Con Only
		Compressor-See Note(2)		)
	C457593	Washer-Copper	2	)

NOTE(1): Identified By Blue Paint

NOTE(2): Identified By Red Paint

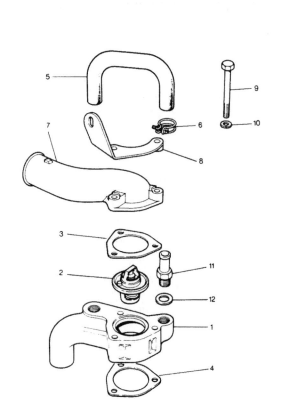

VS4259

LAND ROVER PARTS LTD

109

MODEL LR110 - UP TO AUGUST 1986
BLOCK VS 4193
PAGE B 118
GROUP B

ENGINE - 2.5 DIESEL - CAMSHAFT

ILL	PART NO	DESCRIPTION	QTY	REMARKS
1	ETC7128	Camshaft	1	
2	ERC1561	Thrust Plate-Camshaft	1	
3	SH106161L	Screw-Plate to Block	2	
4	WL106001L	Spring Washer-Plate to Block	2	
5	ETC4014	Pulley	1	
6	230313	Woodruff Key-Chainwheel to Shaft	1	
7	ERC8847	Plate Retaining	1	
8	ERC8849	O Ring	1	
9	ETC4076	O Ring	1	
10	BH110071L	Bolt	1	Use with ETC7128
11	ETC4670	Washer-Plain	1	

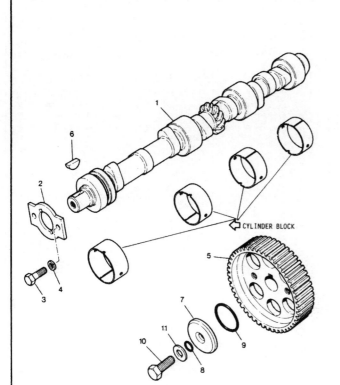

CYLINDER BLOCK

VS4193

110

MODEL LR110 - UP TO AUGUST 1986
BLOCK VS 4258A
PAGE B 120
GROUP B

ENGINE - 2.5 DIESEL - TIMING BELT

ILL	PART NO	DESCRIPTION	QTY	REMARKS
1	ERC7763	Belt Timing-Super Torque	1	
2	ERC8861	Tensioner Assembly-Timing Belt	1	
3	ERC7768	Support Plate	1	NLA Use 4594L
	4594L	Washer-Support	2	
4	TE108061L	Stud	2	
5	NY108041L	Nut	2	

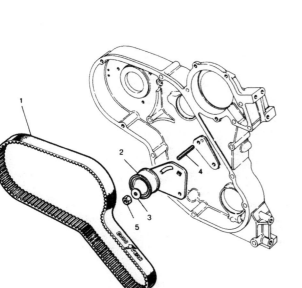

VS4258A

111

MODEL LR110 - UP TO AUGUST 1986
BLOCK 1RE 280
PAGE B 122
GROUP B

ENGINE - 2.5 DIESEL - VALVES AND TAPPETS

ILL	PART NO	DESCRIPTION	QTY	REMARKS
1	507829	TAPPET	8	
2	502473	+Tappet Guide	8	
3	ETC4246	+Bolt-Set	8	
4	273069	+Washer-Tappet Guide	8	
5	90517429	+Roller Follower	8	
6	ETC5057	+Tappet Slide	8	
7	ETC5739	VALVE-INLET	4	
8	ERC9738	VALVE-EXHAUST	4	
	ETC7203	+Valve Stem Protection Cap	8	Note(1)
9	568550	Spring-Valves	8	
10	ETC4068	Cup-Valve Spring	8	
11	ETC4069	Split Cotter-Valve Spring	16	
12	546799	Push Rod	8	

NOTE(1):   Can Be Fitted If Suffering From Excessive
           Valve Stem Or Valve Rocker Wear

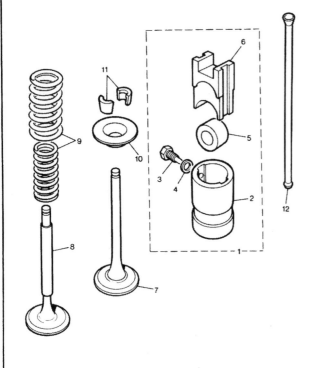

1RE280

LAND ROVER PARTS LTD

112

MODEL LR110 - UP TO AUGUST 1986
BLOCK 1RE 278
PAGE B 124
GROUP B

ENGINE - 2.5 DIESEL - ROCKER SHAFT

ILL	PART NO	DESCRIPTION	QTY	REMARKS
1	ERC9060	Valve Rocker Assy-Exhaust-RH	2	
2	ERC9059	Valve Rocker Assy-Exhaust-LH	2	
3	ERC9056	Valve Rocker Assy-Inlet-RH	2	
4	ERC9055	Valve Rocker Assy-Inlet-LH	2	
5	247738	Bush-Valve Rockers	4	
6	247737	Bush-Valve Rockers	4	
7	ERC6341	SHAFT-VALVE ROCKERS	1	
8	ERC6337	+Plug-Shaft	2	
9	ERC9054	Screw-Tappet Adjusting	8	
10	NT108041L	Locknut-Screw	8	
11	247040	Spring	4	
12	ERC9137	Bracket-Rocker Shaft	5	
13	WL108001L	Washer-Spring	5	
14	BH108111L	Bolt	5	
15	247153	Washer-Rocker Shaft	8	
16	ETC4460	Screw-Shaft Location	1	
18	TD108091L	Stud	3	
19	277956	Dowel-Rocker Shaft Bracket	3	

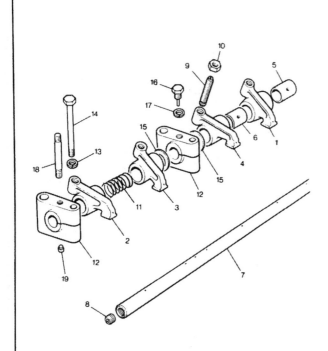

1RE278

LAND ROVER PARTS LTD

113

MODEL LR110 - UP TO AUGUST 1986
BLOCK 1RE 266
PAGE B 126
GROUP B

ENGINE - 2.5 DIESEL - ROCKER COVER ASSEMBLY

ILL	PART NO	DESCRIPTION	QTY	REMARKS
1	ETC6924	Rocker Cover Assembly	1	
2	ETC6438	Gasket-Cover to Cylinder Head	1	
3	273069	Washer Joint	3	
4	ERC9220	Nut-Dome	3	
5	ETC5297	Breather Filter	1	
6	ERC8049	O Ring	1	
7	ERC9728	Hose-Breather to Manifold	1	
	ETC5588	Bracket-Compressor Supply Pipe	1	Air Con Only

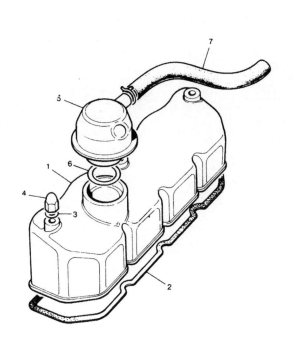

1RE266

LAND ROVER PARTS LTD

114

MODEL LR110 - UP TO AUGUST 1986
BLOCK TS 5001
PAGE B 128
GROUP B

ENGINE - 2.5 DIESEL - FRONT COVER

ILL	PART NO	DESCRIPTION	QTY	REMARKS
1	ETC4421	Front Cover	1	Except Air Con
	ETC5672	Front Cover	1	Air Con Only
2	6395L	Dowel-Front Cover	5	
3	ETC5064	Oil Seal-Camshaft	1	
4	ETC5065	Oil Seal-Crankshaft	1	
5	538038	Gasket-Front Cover and Water Inlet	1	
6	538039	Gasket-Front Cover	1	
7	BH108111L	Bolt-Cover to Block	1	
8	BH108121L	Bolt-Cover to Block	4	
9	SH108201L	Screw-Cover to Block	2	
10	SH108251L	Screw-Cover to Block	1	
11	WA108051L	Washer-Plain Cover to Block	8	
12	ETC4422	Plate-Front Cover	1	Except Air Con
	ETC5675	Plate-Front Cover	1	Air Con Only
13	ETC4154	Seal-Cover Plate	1	
14	BH108131L	Bolt-Plate to Block	1	
15	WA108051L	Washer-Plain-Plate to Block	1	
16	SH108251L	Screw-Cover Plate to Front Cover	7	
17	WA108051L	Washer-Plain-Plate to Cover	7	

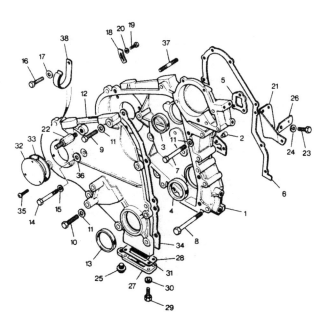

TS5001

LAND ROVER PARTS LTD

115

MODEL LR110 - UP TO AUGUST 1986
BLOCK TS 5001
PAGE B 128.02
GROUP B

ENGINE - 2.5 DIESEL - FRONT COVER - CONTINUED

ILL	PART NO	DESCRIPTION	QTY	REMARKS
18	ERC9819	Timing Point	1	
19	SH105121L	Screw-Pointer to Cover	2	
20	WA702101L	Washer-Plain-Pointer to Cover	2	
21	ERC6479	Bracket-Cowl Mounting	1	
22	ETC4996	Bolt-Special-Bracket to Cover	1	
23	SH108201L	Screw-Bracket to Cover	3	
24	WL108001L	Washer-Spring-Bracket to Cover	3	
25	ERC7295	Plug	1	
26	ERC9404	Bracket-Harness Clip	1	)
	AFU1090L	Clip	1	)Alternatives
	RTC3772	Cable Tie	1	)
27	ETC4058	Drain Plate	1	
28	ETC4122	Gasket-Drain Plate	1	
29	SH106201L	Screw-Plate to Cover	4	
30	WA106041L	Washer-Plate to Cover	4	
31	ETC4063	Strainer	1	
32	ERC9199	Cover Plate	1	
33	ERC9201	Gasket-Cover Plate	1	
34	ETC4420	Gasket-Cover Plate to Front Cover	1	
35	SE106121L	Screw-Plate to Cover Plate	3	
36	ETC4124	Joint Washer-Bolt	1	
37	ETC4873	Stud-DPS to Front Cover	3	
38	ETC4630	Clip-Bottom Hose	1	
	ETC4218	DAMPER PULLEY ASSEMBLY	1	)
	4095	+Plain Washer	1	)Air Con Only
	WB108051L	+Plain Washer	1	)
	SH108161L	Screw M8x16	1	)

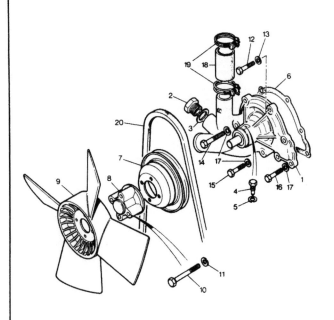

TS5001

LAND ROVER PARTS LTD

116

MODEL LR110 - UP TO AUGUST 1986
BLOCK TS 5010
PAGE B 130
GROUP B

ENGINE - 2.5 DIESEL - WATER PUMP

ILL	PART NO	DESCRIPTION	QTY	REMARKS
1	RTC6331	WATER PUMP ASSEMBLY	1	
2	ERC7312	+Plug	1	
3	232046	+Washer Joint	1	
4	ERC5600	+Bolt-Special	1	
5	WL106001L	+Washer-Spring	1	
6	ERC5655	+Gasket	1	
7	ERC5578	Pulley	1	
8	ERC7489	Spacer-Fan to Pump	1	
9	ERC5545	Fan Assembly	1	
10	BH108111L	Bolt	4	
11	WL108001L	Washer-Spring	4	
12	BH108061L	Bolt-Pump to Cover	3	
13	WL108001L	Washer-Spring-Pump to Cover	3	
14	BH108151L	Bolt-Pump to Block	1	
15	BH108161L	Bolt-Pump to Block	2	
16	BH108171L	Bolt-Pump to Block	1	
17	WL108001L	Washer-Spring	4	
18	ERC5654	Hose-By Pass Water Outlet	1	
19	CN100408L	Clip-Hose	2	
20	563132	Fan Belt	1	

TS5010

LAND ROVER PARTS LTD

117

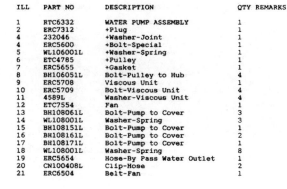

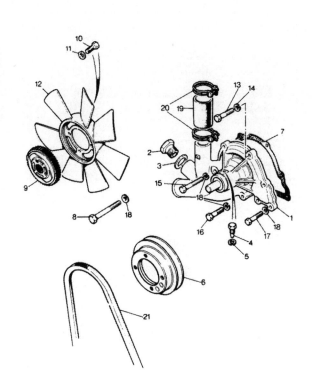

MODEL LR110 - UP TO AUGUST 1986
BLOCK TS 5888
PAGE B 130.02
GROUP B

ENGINE - 2.5 DIESEL - WATER PUMP - AIR CONDITIONING

ILL	PART NO	DESCRIPTION	QTY	REMARKS
1	RTC6332	WATER PUMP ASSEMBLY	1	
2	ERC7312	+Plug	1	
4	232046	+Washer-Joint	1	
4	ERC5600	+Bolt-Special	1	
5	WL106001L	+Washer-Spring	1	
6	ETC4785	+Pulley	1	
7	ERC5655	+Gasket	1	
8	BH106051L	Bolt-Pulley to Hub	4	
9	ERC5708	Viscous Unit	1	
10	ERC5709	Bolt-Viscous Unit	4	
11	4589L	Washer-Viscous Unit	4	
12	ETC7554	Fan	1	
13	BH108061L	Bolt-Pump to Cover	3	
14	WL108001L	Washer-Spring	3	
15	BH108151L	Bolt-Pump to Cover	1	
16	BH108161L	Bolt-Pump to Cover	2	
17	BH108171L	Bolt-Pump to Cover	1	
18	WL108001L	Washer-Spring	8	
19	ERC5654	Hose-By Pass Water Outlet	1	
20	CN100408L	Clip-Hose	2	
21	ERC6504	Belt-Fan	1	

TS5888

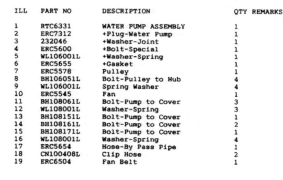

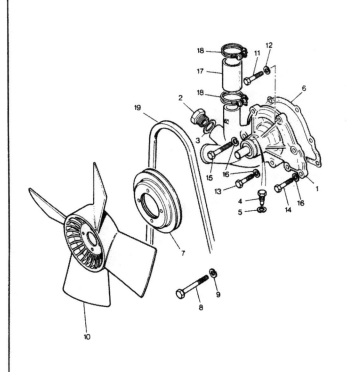

MODEL LR110 - UP TO AUGUST 1986
BLOCK TS 5890
PAGE B 130.04
GROUP B

ENGINE - 2.5 DIESEL - WATER PUMP - 65 AMP ALTERNATOR

ILL	PART NO	DESCRIPTION	QTY	REMARKS
1	RTC6331	WATER PUMP ASSEMBLY	1	
2	ERC7312	+Plug-Water Pump	1	
3	232046	+Washer-Joint	1	
4	ERC5600	+Bolt-Special	1	
5	WL106001L	+Washer-Spring	1	
6	ERC5655	+Gasket	1	
7	ERC5578	Pulley	1	
8	BH106051L	Bolt-Pulley to Hub	4	
9	WL106001L	Spring Washer	4	
10	ERC5545	Fan	1	
11	BH108061L	Bolt-Pump to Cover	3	
12	WL108001L	Washer-Spring	3	
13	BH108151L	Bolt-Pump to Cover	1	
14	BH108161L	Bolt-Pump to Cover	2	
15	BH108171L	Bolt-Pump to Cover	1	
16	WL108001L	Washer-Spring	4	
17	ERC5654	Hose-By Pass Pipe	1	
18	CN100408L	Clip Hose	2	
19	ERC6504	Fan Belt	1	

TS5890

MODEL LR110 - UP TO AUGUST 1986
BLOCK TS 5887
PAGE B 130.06
GROUP B

ENGINE - 2.5 DIESEL - WATER PUMP - NOISE REDUCTION PACKAGE

ILL	PART NO	DESCRIPTION	QTY	REMARKS
1	RTC6332	WATER PUMP ASSEMBLY	1	
2	ERC7312	+Plug-Water Pump	1	
3	232046	+Washer-joint	1	
4	ERC5600	+Bolt-Special	1	
5	WL106001L	+Washer-Spring	1	
6	ERC5655	+Gasket	1	
7	ETC4785	Pulley	1	
8	BH106051L	Bolt-Pulley to Hub	4	
9	ERC5708	Viscous Unit	1	
10	ERC5709	Bolt-Viscous Unit	4	
11	4589L	Washer-Viscous Unit	4	
12	ETC7554	Fan	1	
13	BH108061L	Bolt-Pump to Cover	3	
14	WL108001L	Washer-Spring	3	
15	BH108151L	Bolt-Pump to Cover	1	
16	BH108161L	Bolt-Pump to Cover	2	
17	BH108171L	Bolt-Pump to Cover	1	
18	WL108001L	Washer-Spring	8	
19	ERC5654	Hose-By Pass	1	
20	CN100408L	Clip-Hose	2	
21	ERC6886	Belt-Fan	1	

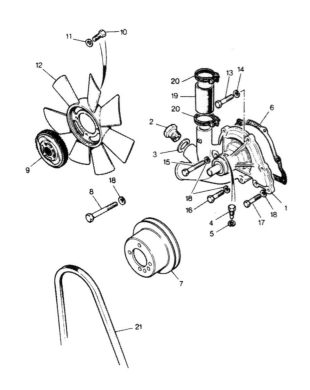

TS5887

MODEL LR110 - UP TO AUGUST 1986
BLOCK VS 4196
PAGE B 132
GROUP B

ENGINE -2.5 DIESEL - SIDE COVER

ILL	PART NO	DESCRIPTION	QTY	REMARKS
1	ERC9073	SIDE COVER & STUD ASSEMBLY	1	
2	TE108041L	+Stud	2	
3	247554	Joint Washer	1	
4	SH108251L	Screw-Cover to Block	6	
5	WL108001L	Washer-Spring-Cover to Block	6	
6	541010	Cover Side	1	
7	ERC9480	Bracket-Harness Clip	1	
8	SH108201L	Screw	3	
	SH108251L	Screw	3	
9	WA108051L	Washer-Plain	3	
10	WL108001L	Washer-Spring	6	
11	247555	Gasket-Side Cover	1	

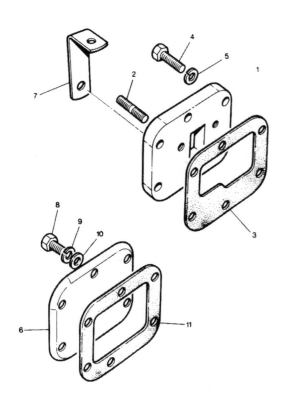

VS4196

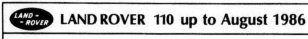
MODEL LR110 - UP TO AUGUST 1986
BLOCK TS 5000
PAGE B 134
GROUP B

ENGINE - 2.5 DIESEL - OIL FILTER - WITHOUT OIL COOLER

ILL	PART NO	DESCRIPTION	QTY	REMARKS
1	ETC5347	OIL FILTER ADAPTOR ASSEMBLY	1	
2	10713	+Plug	1	
3	213961	+Washer	1	
4	ERC5913	+O Ring-Oil Filter Adaptor	1	
5	ERC9884	+End Plate	1	
6	ETC4021	+Plug	1	
7	SH106141L	+Screw	2	
8	WA106041L	+Washer-Plain	2	
9	ETC6599	Oil Filter-Element	1	
10	SH110301L	Screw-Filter to Block	2	
11	WL110001L	Washer-Spring-Filter to Block	2	
12	ETC5276	Gasket-Oil Filter	1	
13	PRC6387	Oil Pressure Switch	1	
	PRC4043	Oil Pressure Transmitter	1	)
	AFU1887L	Washer-Joint	2	)Optional
	ETC4033	Adaptor-OP Switch	1	)
	ETC4034	Banjo-OP Switch	1	)
	PRC4372	Temperature Transmitter	1	)

TS5000

LAND ROVER PARTS LTD

122

MODEL LR110 - UP TO AUGUST 1986
BLOCK VS 4205A
PAGE B 134.02
GROUP B

ENGINE - 2.5 DIESEL - OIL FILTER WITH OIL COOLER

ILL	PART NO	DESCRIPTION	QTY	REMARKS
1	ETC5348	OIL FILTER ADAPTOR ASSEMBLY	1	
2	ERC5923	+Thermostat Bulb	1	
3	ETC4022	+Adaptor	1	
4	ERC5913	+O Ring	1	
5	ETC4021	+Plug	1	
6	SH106141L	+Screw	2	
7	WA106041L	+Washer Plain	2	
8	ETC6599	Element-Oil Filter	1	
9	SH110301L	Screw-Filter to Block	2	
10	WL110001L	Washer-Spring	2	
11	ETC5276	Gasket-Oil Filter	1	
12	PRC6387	Switch-Oil Pressure	1	
	PRC4043	Oil Pressure Transmitter	1	)
	AFU1887L	Washer Joint	2	)Optional
	ETC4033	Adaptor-OP Switch	1	)
	ETC4034	Banjo-OP Switch	1	)
	PRC4372	Temperature Transmitter	1	)

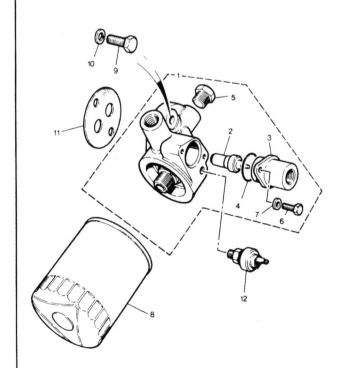

VS4205A

LAND ROVER PARTS LTD

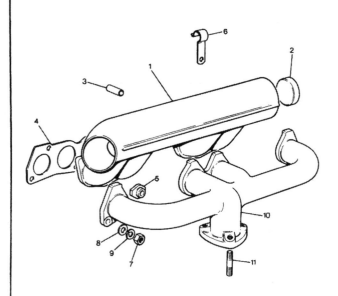

MODEL LR110 - UP TO AUGUST 1986
BLOCK VS 3831
PAGE B 136
GROUP B

ENGINE - 2.5 DIESEL - MANIFOLDS

ILL	PART NO	DESCRIPTION	QTY	REMARKS
1	ERC6939	Inlet Manifold	1	
2	525428	Plug-Cup	1	
3	ERC6047	Tube	1	
4	ETC5312	Gasket-Manifold to Head	1	
5	564308	Clamp-Manifold to Head	4	
6	574654	Clip-Manifold Clamp	1	
7	NH108041L	Nut	9	
8	WA108051L	Washer-Plain	9	
9	WL108001L	Washer-Spring	9	
10	ERC9688	Exhaust Manifold	1	Upto VIN 266789
	ETC5331	Exhaust Manifold	1	From VIN 266790
11	AFU1848L	Stud	3	

VS3831

MODEL LR110 - UP TO AUGUST 1986
BLOCK VS 4291
PAGE B 138
GROUP B

ENGINE - 2.5 DIESEL - VACUUM PUMP

ILL	PART NO	DESCRIPTION	QTY	REMARKS
1	ETC7405	VACUUM PUMP	1	
2	AEU2717	+End Plate Assembly	1	
3	AEU2720	+Bolt-End Plate to Body	4	
4	WL106001L	+Washer-Spring-End Plate to Body	4	
5	AEU2718	+Rotor Blade	4	
6	AEU2719L	+O Ring-End Plate to Body	1	
7	ETC4616	Gasket	2	
8	SS108301L	Bolt-Pump to Bracket	3	
9	WM600051L	Washer-Spring-Pump to Bracket	3	

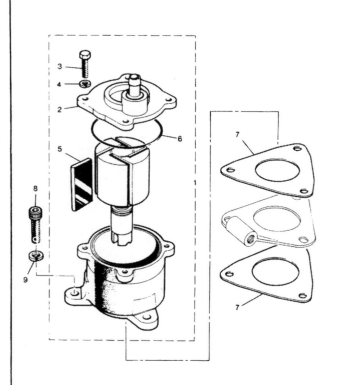

VS4291

MODEL LR110 - UP TO AUGUST 1986
BLOCK VS 3996
PAGE B 140
GROUP B

ENGINE - 2.5 DIESEL - GASKET KITS

ILL	PART NO	DESCRIPTION	QTY	REMARKS
1	RTC3037	Kit-Gasket-Decarbonising	1	
2	RTC3038	Kit-Gasket-Overhaul	1	Use with RTC3037
	RTC3254	RTV Silicon Sealant-110 Gram Tube	1	

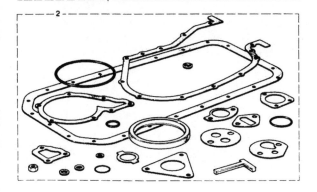

VS3996

MASTER INDEX

GROUP B

ENGINE

MODEL LR110 - UP TO AUGUST 1986
BLOCK VS 3099
PAGE B 148
GROUP B

ENGINE - 3.5 LITRE V8 PETROL - ENGINE ASSEMBLIES COMPLETE

ILL	PART NO	DESCRIPTION	QTY	REMARKS
1	ETC8445	Engine and Clutch Assembly-Non Detoxed	1	Engine Prefix 20G Only
	ETC6589	Engine and Clutch Assembly-Detoxed	1	Engine Prefix 21G and 24G

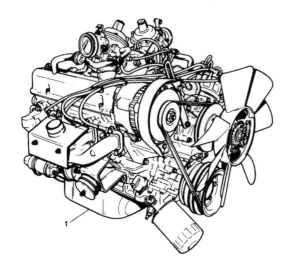

VS3099

MODEL LR110 - UP TO AUGUST 1986
BLOCK VS 1247
PAGE B 150
GROUP B

ENGINE - 3.5 LITRE V8 PETROL - ENGINE ASSEMBLIES STRIPPED, 8.13:1 CR

ILL	PART NO	DESCRIPTION	QTY	REMARKS
1	RTC2972N	Engine Assembly Stripped-New Non Detoxed	1	)Engine Prefix)14G & 20G
	RTC2972R	Engine Assembly Stripped-Rebuilt-Non Detoxed	1	))
	RTC2973N	Engine Assembly Stripped-New Detoxed	1	)Engine Prefix)15G & 21G
	RTC4608N	Engine Assembly Stripped-New	1	)Engine Prefix)24G

NOTE: Stripped Engines For Service Are Supplied Less Water
       Pump, Manifolds, Carburetters, Electrics, Clutch,
       Flywheel, Mountings Etc.

VS1247

MODEL LR110 - UP TO AUGUST 1986
BLOCK VS 3762
PAGE B 152
GROUP B

ENGINE - 3.5 LITRE V8 PETROL - ENGINE ASSEMBLIES SHORT (BLOCK,
                                       CRANKSHAFT AND PISTONS)

ILL	PART NO	DESCRIPTION	QTY	REMARKS
1	ETC7714	Short Engine Assembly	1	8.13:1 CR
	RTC2372	Short Engine Assembly	1	9.34:1 CR Australia

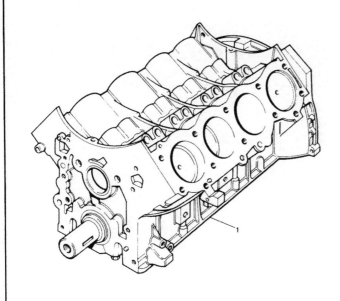

VS3762

MODEL LR110 - UP TO AUGUST 1986
BLOCK VS 1644
PAGE B 154
GROUP B

ENGINE - 3.5 LITRE V8 PETROL - CYLINDER BLOCK

ILL	PART NO	DESCRIPTION	QTY	REMARKS
1	ERC6934	CYLINDER BLOCK ASSEMBLY	1	
2	252513	+Stud-Timing Cover	1	
3	602152	+Plug	8	
4	602147	+Plug-Tappet/Angular Holes	4	
5	602146	+Plug-Cam Bore	1	
6	602212	+Plug-Tappet Line Rear	2	
7	602141	+Dowel-Flywheel Housing	2	
8	3290	+Taper Plug	2	
9	ERC5761	+Pipe Assembly-Crankcase Breather	1	
9	603143	+Pipe Assembly-Crankcase Breather	1	Engine 17G Only
10	602130	+Bolt-Main Bearing Cap	10	
11	612898	Plug-Rear Block	2	
12	NRC1302	Mounting Foot-RH	1	
13	NRC3314	Mounting Foot-LH	1	
14	SH507091	Screw-Feet/Engine	4	
15	WM600071L	Spring Washer	4	
16	SH505071L	Screw	2	
17	WM600051L	Spring Washer	2	
18	566222	Mounting Rubber	2	)
19	WD110061L	Plain Washer-Rubbers/Body	2	)
20	WM600061L	Spring Washer	2	)Imperial
21	611409	Oil Seal-Crankshaft	1	)*See Note(1)
22	611089	Packing-Oil Seal	2	)*
23	NH606041L	Nut	2	)
	RTC6115	Engine Mtg Kit	2	)
	NH110041LD	+Nut	2	)Metric
	WC110061LD	+Washer	1	)
	WL110001LD	+Spring Washer	2	)

*NOTE(1): Part of Engine Gaskets/Seals Kit RTC2104

VS1644

MODEL LR110 - UP TO AUGUST 1986
BLOCK VS 1644
PAGE B 156
GROUP B

ENGINE - 3.5 LITRE V8 PETROL - CYLINDER BLOCK - CONTINUED

ILL	PART NO	DESCRIPTION	QTY	REMARKS
24	ERC2690	Tube-Dipstick	1	)Alternatives-
25	532319	'O' Ring See Note(1)	1	)Interchangeable
26	ERC4558	Dipstick	1	)As A Set
24	ERC6437	Tube-Dipstick	1	)
25	602545	'O' Ring	1	)
26	ERC8545	Dipstick	1	)
27	614585	Clamp Bracket	1	
28	SH604031L	Screw-Bracket/Head	1	
29	610489	Clip	1	
30	78862	Screw-10UNCx0.5"-Clip-Rocker Cover	1	
31	ERC2973	Support Bracket	1	)
32	257017	Screw-10UNFx0.5"-Clip to Support Bracket	1	)Engines 15G
33	WA702101L	Plain Washer	1	)& 21G
34	WM702001L	Spring Washer	1	)
35	HN2005L	Nut-10UNF	1	)
36	NRC3301	Heatshield-LH	1	
	577846	Heatshield-RH	1	
37	BH106051L	Bolt	4	
38	WA106041L	Washer-Plain	4	
39	WL106001L	Washer-Lock	4	
40	NH106041L	Nut	4	

NOTE(1):   Part Of Engine Gaskets/Seals Kit RTC2104

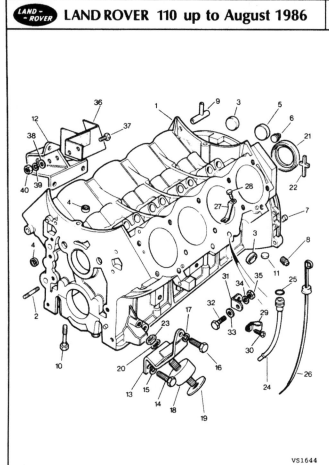

VS1644

LAND ROVER PARTS LTD

132

MODEL LR110 - UP TO AUGUST 1986
BLOCK 4RE 170
PAGE B 158
GROUP B

ENGINE - 3.5 LITRE V8 PETROL - PISTON & CONNECTING ROD ASSY

ILL	PART NO	DESCRIPTION	QTY	REMARKS
1	RTC2186S	KIT-PISTON & RINGS-STD	8	)8.13:1 CR
	RTC218620	KIT-PISTON & RINGS-0.020" O/S	8	)
	RTC2295S	KIT-PISTON & RINGS-STD	8	)9.35:1 CR
	RTC229520	KIT-PISTON & RINGS-0.020" O/S	8	)
2	RTC2408	+Kit-Piston Rings-STD	8	
	RTC240820	+Kit-Piston Rings-0.020" O/S	8	
3	602082	CONNECTING ROD ASSEMBLY	8	
4	602609	+Bolt	16	
5	602061	+Nut	16	
6	RTC2117	Kit-Conn Rod Bearings-STD	1	
	RTC211710	Kit-Conn Rod Bearings-0.010"	1	
	RTC211720	Kit-Conn Rod Bearings-0.020" O/S	1	

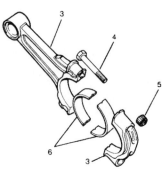

4RE170

LAND ROVER PARTS LTD

133

MODEL LR110 - UP TO AUGUST 1986
BLOCK VS 1632A
PAGE B 160
GROUP B

ENGINE - 3.5 LITRE V8 PETROL - CRANKSHAFT

ILL	PART NO	DESCRIPTION	QTY	REMARKS
1	612989	CRANKSHAFT	1	
2	549911	Spigot Bush	1	
3	90602372	Sprocket	1	
4	90602025	Key-Sprocket-Crankshaft	1	
5	ERC5462	Vibration Damper	1	
6	603535	Spring Dowel Pin	1	
7	611019	Pulley-Fan/Alternator	1	Basic
7	ETC4369	Pulley-C/Shaft-Front	1	)Power Steering
7	ETC4330	Pulley-C/Shaft to P.A.S. Pump	1	)Except Air Con)
7	ETC4354	Pulley-C/Shaft-Front	1	)All Air Con
7	ETC4330	Pulley-C/Shaft-Rear	1	)
8	602587	Reinforcing Plate	1	
9	603301	Balancing Rim	1	
10	613671	Mud Deflector	1	
11	BH605121L	Bolt-Pulley/Damper	6	Basic And Air Con Only
11	BH605131L	Bolt-Pulley to Damper	6	Power Steering Only
12	NH605041L	Nut	3	
13	602411	Washer-Damper/Crankshaft	1	
14	610178	Starting Dog	1	
15		BALANCE WEIGHT-DAMPER		
	ERC4877	0.180 OZ	2	
	ERC4878	0.360 OZ	2	
	ERC4879	0.540 OZ	2	
	ERC4880	0.720 OZ	2	
16	RTC1718	Kit-Main Bearing Std	1	)See Note
	RTC171810	Kit-Main Bearing 0.010" U/S	1	)
	RTC171820	Kit-Main Bearing 0.020" U/S	1	)
17	ERC416	Washer-Damper to Crankshaft	1	
18	ERC417	Bolt-Damper to Crankshaft	1	

NOTE: Latest Condition Does Not Have Thrust Plate On Bottom
Half Of Centre Bearing.

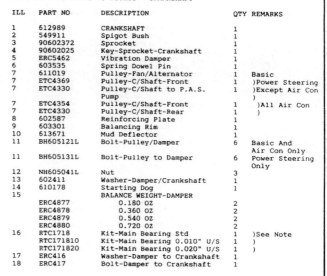

VS1632A

LAND ROVER PARTS LTD

134

MODEL LR110 - UP TO AUGUST 1986
BLOCK M 876
PAGE B 162
GROUP B

ENGINE - 3.5 LITRE V8 PETROL - SUMP

ILL	PART NO	DESCRIPTION	QTY	REMARKS
1	612710	Oil Screen Housing	1	
2	90602068	Gasket-Housing/Block	1	See Note(1)
3	SH506081L	Screw	2	
4	WM600041L	Spring Washer	2	
5	602070	Oil Screen	1	
6	612980	Sump Assembly	1	)No Longer)Available-Use)ETC6290)Use With Gasket)602087
6	ETC6290	Sump Assembly	1	)No Gasket)Required-Seal)With RTV)Hylosil 102
7	603659	Drain Plug	1	
8	213961	Joint Washer	1	)See Note(1)
9	602087	Gasket-Sump/Block	1	)
10	602199	Sems-Screw	16	

NOTE(1): Part Of Engine Gaskets/Seals Kit RTC2104

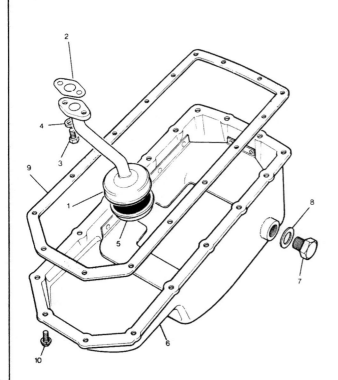

M876

LAND ROVER PARTS LTD

135

MODEL LR110 - UP TO AUGUST 1986
BLOCK VS 1633
PAGE B 164
GROUP B

ENGINE - 3.5 LITRE V8 PETROL - OIL PUMP

ILL	PART NO	DESCRIPTION	QTY	REMARKS
1	ERC1351	Oil Pump Shaft and Gear	1	
2	614037	Driven Gear	1	
3	ERC7787	Oil Pump Cover Assembly	1	)No Longer)Available-Use)ETC4276
	ETC4276	OIL PUMP COVER ASSEMBLY	1	
4	614202	+Strainer	1	)Part of ERC7787)Only
5	90602064	+Relief Valve	1	
6	602067	+Spring	1	
7	602071	+Cap	1	
8	603521	+Joint Washer-Note(1)	1	)
9	DRC2479	+Oil Pressure Transducer	1	)
10	243967	+Joint Washer-Note(1)	1	)Part of ERC7787
11	PRC2507	+Oil Temperature Transmitter	1	)But Not of
12	243968	+Joint Washer-Note(1)	1	)ETC4276
13	611514	+Adaptor-Transmitter	1	)
14	PRC7204	+Oil Pressure Switch	1	
15	243968	+Joint Washer-Note(1)	1	
16	90602072	Gasket-Pump/Timing Cover	1	Note(1)
17	602912	Bolt	2	
	602910	Bolt	3	
	602913	Bolt	1	
18	ETC6599	Oil Filter Cartridge	1	
	RTC4477	Repair Kit-Oil Pump	1	

NOTE(1): Part OF Engine Gasket/Seals Kit RTC2104

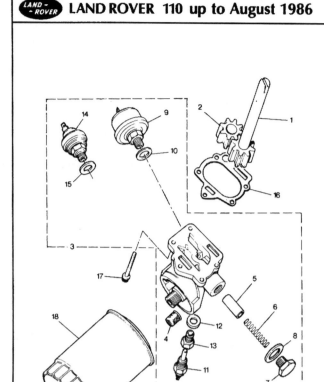

VS1633

LAND ROVER PARTS LTD

136

MODEL LR110 - UP TO AUGUST 1986
BLOCK VS 1635
PAGE B 166
GROUP B

ENGINE - 3.5 LITRE V8 PETROL - CAMSHAFT

ILL	PART NO	DESCRIPTION	QTY	REMARKS
1	ETC6849	Camshaft	1	
	ERC2003	Camshaft-High Lift	1	NLA Use ETC6850 Note(1)
	ETC6850	Camshaft-High Lift	1	Note(1)
2	ERC2838	Key-Camshaft	1	
3	610289	Chainwheel	1	
4	ERC2839	Spacer	1	
5	614188	Gear-Distributor Drive	1	
6	ERC6552	Plain Washer	1	
7	ERC5749	Bolt-M12-Camshaft Sprocket	1	
8	ERC7929	Timing Chain	1	
	RTC5918	Camshaft Bearings Set	1	)Upto Engine)Suffix E
	RTC5919	Camshaft Bearings Set	1	)From Engine)Suffix F

NOTE(1): Engine Prefix 19G And 20G Only

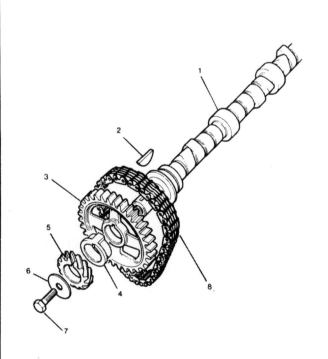

VS1635

LAND ROVER PARTS LTD

137

MODEL LR110 - UP TO AUGUST 1986
BLOCK VS 1636A
PAGE B 168
GROUP B

ENGINE - 3.5 LITRE V8 PETROL - CYLINDER HEAD

ILL	PART NO	DESCRIPTION	QTY	REMARKS
1	ERC215	CYLINDER HEAD ASSEMBLY	2	Eng.14G & 20G
	ERC676	CYLINDER HEAD ASSEMBLY	2	Eng.15G,17G & 21G
	ETC6471	CYLINDER HEAD ASSEMBLY	2	Eng.24G
2	603554	+Valve Guide	16	
3	ERC224	+Insert-Inlet Valve Seat-Std	8	
	ERC225	+Insert-Inlet Valve Seat-0.010" O/S	8	
4	ERC210	+Insert-Exhaust Valve Seat-Std	8	
	ERC211	+Insert-Exhaust Valve Seat-0.010" O/S	8	
5	602123	+Core Plug	4	
6	602289	+Cup Plug	4	
7	614089	Exhaust Valve	8	
8	614088	Inlet Valve	8	
9	ERC7865	Seal-Inlet Valve	8	)Note(1)
10	603796	Gasket-Head/Block	2	)
11	602040	Dowel	4	
12	90614584	Bolt	1	
13	602191	Bolt	7	
14	602192	Bolt	14	Except Air Con
	602192	Bolt	13	Air Con
15	602193	Bolt	6	
16	602098	Plain Washer	28	
17	603031	Lifting Bracket-Front LH	1	)Except P/Stg)& Air Con
	90611812	Lifting Bracket-Front LH	1	)With P/Stg)Note(2)
18	SF506071L	Screw	2	)Except Power
19	WM600061L	Spring Washer	2	)Steering
	SH506071L	Screw	3	)With P/Stg
	WM600061L	Spring Washer	3	)& Air Con
	SA506081L	Screw	1	)
20	ERC2920	Bracket-to Lifting Brkt Front	1	)Except Air Con
21	DRC1538	Strap	2	)

NOTE(1): Part Of Engine Gasket/Seals Kit
RTC2913

NOTE(2): For Air Conditioning Lifting Bracket See
Alternator Mountings

VS1636A

LAND ROVER PARTS LTD

MODEL LR110 - UP TO AUGUST 1986
BLOCK VS 1634
PAGE B 170
GROUP B

ENGINE - 3.5 LITRE V8 PETROL - VALVE GEAR

ILL	PART NO	DESCRIPTION	QTY	REMARKS
1	606661	ROCKER SHAFT ASSEMBLY	2	
2	154545	+Plug	4	
3	603734	Pedestal Bracket	8	
4	602142	Spring	6	
5	602148	Spring-Shafts Ends	4	
6	602186	Washer	4	
7	PS606101L	Split Pin	4	
8	602153	Valve Rocker Assy R Handed	8	
9	602154	Valve Rocker Assy L Handed	8	
10	602097	Bolt-UNF	8	
11	602172	Oil Baffle	2	Upto 24G0388B
	ETC8633	Oil Baffle Breather RH	1	)From 24G03884B
	ETC8658	Oil Baffle Breather LH	1	)
12	UKC8137L	Valve Spring	16	
13	ERC573	Cap Valve Spring	16	
14	ERC1637	Split Cotter	32	
15	603378	Push Rod-Valves	16	
16	ERC4949	Hydraulic Tappet Complete	16	

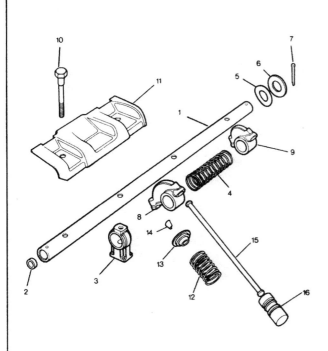

VS1634

LAND ROVER PARTS LTD

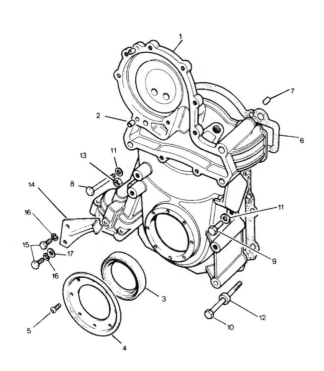

MODEL LR110 - UP TO AUGUST 1986
BLOCK VS 1630
PAGE B 172
GROUP B

ENGINE - 3.5 LITRE V8 PETROL - VALVE ROCKER COVERS

ILL	PART NO	DESCRIPTION	QTY	REMARKS
1	RTC2348	Rocker Cover-RH	1	
2	RTC2349	Rocker Cover-LH	1	
3	ERC3179	Oil Filler Neck	1	
4	ERC5512	Retainer-HT Cables	1	
5	78862	Screw-10 UNC X 0.562"	1	
6	603675	Retainer-HT Cables	1	
7	78861	Screw-10 UNC x 0.625"	1	
8	602512	Gasket-Cover/Head	2	NOTE(1)
9	603127	Bolt	4	
	SY504072L	Bolt	4	
10	WM600041L	Spring Washer	8	
11	WB106041L	Plain Washer	8	
12	625038	Filler Cap	1	
13	564258	'O' Ring Cap	1	NOTE(1)
14	ERC614	Lifting Bracket-Rear	1	
15	WM600061L	Spring Washer	2	
16	SH506071L	Screw	2	
17	586440	Cable Clip	1	
18	WM600041L	Spring Washer	1	
19	WB106041L	Plain Washer	1	
20	SH604041L	Screw	1	
21	ERC2144	Spacer-H.T./L.T. Leads	1	
22	603184	Clip,Leads to Filler Neck	1	
23	78593	Screw 10UNF x 0.5"	2	
24	WA702101L	Washer Plain	2	
25	HN2005L	Nut	2	
	ETC5594	Bracket-Plug Leads	2	
	78861	Screw For Bracket	2	

NOTE(1):   Part of Engine Gaskets/Seals Kit RTC2913

VS1630

MODEL LR110 - UP TO AUGUST 1986
BLOCK 2RE 287
PAGE B 174
GROUP B

ENGINE - 3.5 LITRE V8 PETROL - TIMING CHAIN COVER

ILL	PART NO	DESCRIPTION	QTY	REMARKS
1	ETC7385	TIMING CHAIN COVER ASSY	1	
2	602201	+Dowel-Water Pump	2	
3	ERC7987	+Oil Seal	1	NOTE(1)
4	247766	+Mud Excluder	1	
5	78782	+Screw-No6 x 0.25" Excluder/ Cover	8	
	154545	+Cup Plug	1	
6	603775	Gasket-Cover/Block	1	NOTE(1)
7	90602202	Dowel	2	
8	BH505241L	Bolt	1	
9	SH505091L	Screw	2	
10	602388	Bolt	1	
11	WA108051L	Plain Washer	4	
12	4075L	Plain Washer	1	
13	NH605041L	Nut	1	
14	ETC7345	Timing Pointer	1	
15	SH504051L	Screw-Pointer/Block	2	
16	WM600041L	Spring Washer	2	
17	RTC609	Plain Washer	1	

NOTE(1):   Part of Engine Gasket/Seals Kit RTC2104

2RE287

MODEL LR110 - UP TO AUGUST 1986
BLOCK 2RE 71
PAGE B 176
GROUP B

ENGINE - 3.5 LITRE V8 PETROL - WATER PUMP - NON VISCOUS DRIVE

ILL	PART NO	DESCRIPTION	QTY	REMARKS
1	RTC3661	Water Pump Assembly	1	
2	612326	Gasket-Cover-Pump	1	NOTE(1)
3	BH505401L	Bolt-Pump and Timing Cover to Cyl Block	3	
4	BH505381L	Bolt	1	
5	WA108051L	Washer-Plain	4	
6	BH504101L	Bolt	6	
7	BH504151L	Bolt	2	
8	BH504161L	Bolt	1	
9	WC106041L	Washer-Plain	9	
10	252516	Stud-Water Pump to Timing Cover	1	
11	4421	Washer Plain	1	
12	WM600051L	Washer Spring	1	
13	NT605041L	Locknut	1	
14	BH505121L	Bolt-Water Pump to Timing Cover	1	
15	WM600051L	Washer Spring	1	

NOTE(1):   Part of Engine Gasket/Seals Kit RTC2104

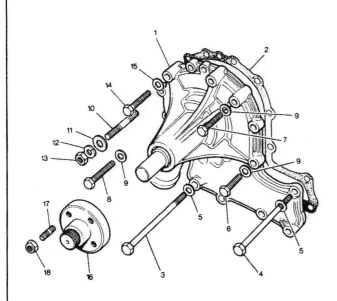

2RE71

 **LAND ROVER PARTS LTD**

142

MODEL LR110 - UP TO AUGUST 1986
BLOCK VS 3778
PAGE B 178
GROUP B

ENGINE - 3.5 LITRE V8 PETROL - WATER PUMP - WITH VISCOUS DRIVE

ILL	PART NO	DESCRIPTION	QTY	REMARKS
1	RTC6337	Water Pump Assembly	1	
	RTC6338	Water Pump Assembly	1	All Air Con
2	612326	Gasket-Cover-Pump	1	Note(1)
3	BH505401L	Bolt-Pump & Timing Cover to Cylinder Block	3	
	BH505401L	Bolt	1	Air Con
4	BH505381L	Bolt	1	
5	WA108051L	Washer Plain	4	
6	BH504101L	Bolt	6	)
7	BH504151L	Bolt	2	)Except Air Con
8	BH504161L	Bolt	1	)Power Stg
9	WC106041L	Washer Plain	9	)
	BH504101L	Bolt-Pump-Timing Cover	2	)
	BH505121L	Bolt	2	)Air Con
	WM600051L	Washer-Spring	2	)
	WC106041L	Washer-Plain	3	)
	BH504101L	Bolt-Pump-Timing Cover	4	)
	BH504151L	Bolt	2	)Power Steering
	BH504161L	Bolt	1	)
	WC106041L	Washer Plain	7	)
10	252516	Stud-Water Pump to Timing Cover	1	)
11	4421	Washer-Plain	1	)
12	WM600051L	Washer Spring	1	)Except Air Con
13	NT605041L	Locknut	1	)
14	BH505121L	Bolt-Water Pump to Timing Cover	1	)
15	WM600051L	Washer spring	1	)
16	ERC5705	Hub Assembly Pulley to Pump	1	
17	TE108041L	Stud-M8x20mm	1	
18	NY108041L	Nut-Nyloc-M8-Pulley to Pump	4	

NOTE(1):   Part Of Engine Gasket/Seals Kit RTC2104

VS3778

 **LAND ROVER PARTS LTD**

143

MODEL LR110 - UP TO AUGUST 1986
BLOCK M 877A
PAGE B 180
GROUP B

ENGINE - 3.5 LITRE V8 PETROL - COOLING FAN - ENGINE 14G AND 20G
(NON DETOXED) LESS AIR CON AND POWER STEERING

ILL	PART NO	DESCRIPTION	QTY	REMARKS
1	613087	Fan Assembly-5 Blades (Non-Viscous Type)	1	
	ERC8164	Fan Assembly-11 Blades	1	Optional
2	602582	Pulley	1	
3	SH504051L	Screw-Pulley/Hub	3	
4	WM600041L	Spring Washer	3	
5	SH505061L	Screw-Fan/Pump	4	
6	WM600051L	Spring Washer	4	
7	610578	Hub Assembly	1	
8	603428	Spring Pin	1	

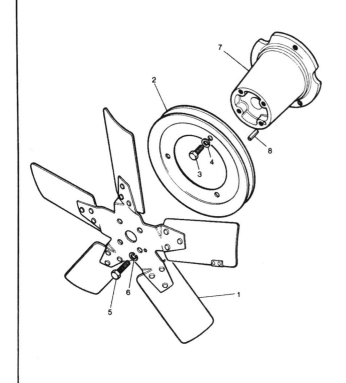

M877A

LAND ROVER PARTS LTD

144

MODEL LR110 - UP TO AUGUST 1986
BLOCK VS 3775A
PAGE B 182
GROUP B

ENGINE - 3.5 LITRE V8 PETROL - COOLING FAN - ENGINE - 15G 17G
19G AND 21G AND ALL AIR CON WITH POWER STEERING

ILL	PART NO	DESCRIPTION	QTY	REMARKS
1	ETC7553	Fan Assy-7 Blades	1	
2	ERC5707	Pulley-Single Groove	1	
3	ERC6540	Pulley-Twin Groove	1	)Air Con and
				)Power Steering
4	ERC5708	Viscous Drive	1	
5	ERC5709	Bolt-M6 x 14mm Fan/Viscous Drive	4	
6	4589L	Plain Washer-M6	4	

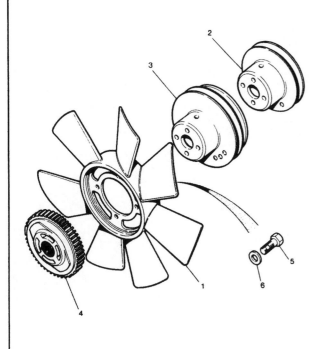

VS3775A

LAND ROVER PARTS LTD

145

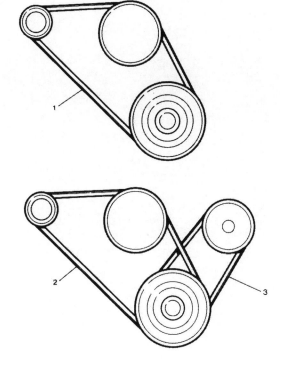

MODEL LR110 - UP TO AUGUST 1986
BLOCK VS 4009
PAGE B 184
GROUP B

ENGINE - 3.5 LITRE V8 PETROL - DRIVING BELTS

ILL	PART NO	DESCRIPTION	QTY REMARKS
		LESS POWER STEERING AND AIR CONDITIONING	
1	613602	Belt-Driving-Fan & Alternator	1
		WITH POWER STEERING-LESS AIR CONDITIONING	
2	613602	Belt-Driving-Fan & Alternator	1
3	ERC675	Belt-Driving-Pump-Power Steering	1

VS4009

LAND ROVER PARTS LTD

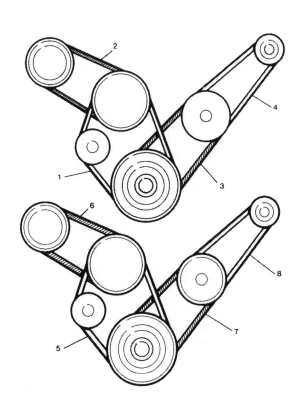

MODEL LR110 - UP TO AUGUST 1986
BLOCK VS 4008
PAGE B 186
GROUP B

ENGINE - 3.5 LITRE V8 PETROL - DRIVING BELTS

ILL	PART NO	DESCRIPTION	QTY REMARKS
		WITH AIR CONDITIONING, LESS POWER STEERING	
1	614670	Belt-Driving-Fan	1
2	603713	Belt-Driving-Compressor-Air Conditioning	1
3	ERC675	Belt-Driving-Idler	1
4	ERC8852	Belt-Driving-Alternator	1
		WITH AIR CONDITIONING AND POWER STEERING	
5	614670	Belt-Driving-Fan	1
6	603713	Belt-Driving-Compressor-Air Conditioning	1
7	ERC675	Belt-Driving-Pump-Power Stg	1
8	ERC8852	Belt-Driving-Alternator	1

VS4008

LAND ROVER PARTS LTD

MODEL LR110 - UP TO AUGUST 1986
BLOCK VS 3614A
PAGE B 188
GROUP B

ENGINE - 3.5 LITRE V8 PETROL - INLET MANIFOLD

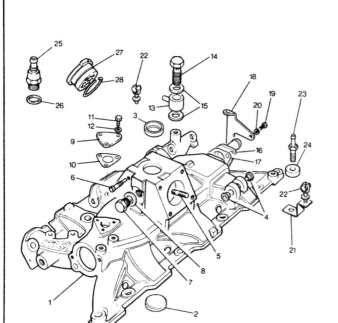

ILL	PART NO	DESCRIPTION	QTY	REMARKS
1	ETC7915	INLET MANIFOLD ASSEMBLY	1	
2	602152	+Cup Plug	1	
3	ERC256	+Cup Plug	2	
4	522932	+Oilite Bush-Accelerator	2	
5	252514	+Stud-Carburetters	8	
6	ERC4820	+Adaptor-Air Bleed	1	
7	603224	+Blanking Plug	1	
8	232043	+Joint Washer	1	NOTE(1)
9	598006	Blanking Plate	1	
10	236022	Joint Washer-Switch/Manifold	1	NOTE(1)
11	257064	Screw-10UNC x 0.437	3	
12	WM702001L	Spring Washer	3	
13	603277	Banjo-Vacuum Signal	1	Engine 14G,17G & 20G
	610246	Banjo-Vacuum Signal	1	Engine 15G & 21G
14	534897	Banjo Bolt	1	
15	267604	Joint Washer	2	Note(1)
16	ERC3561	Water Outlet Pipe	1	
17	603441	Gasket	1	Note(1)
18	603561	Spring Anchor Bracket-Accelerator	1	
19	SH504061L	Screw	2	
20	WM600041L	Spring Washer	2	
21	NRC2864	Bracket-Pipe Clip	2	
22	CRC1226	Clip-Fuel Pipe	A/R	
23	ERC2297	Peg-Air Cleaner Mounting	2	
24	4594L	Washer Plain	2	
25	ADU1402L	Valve-Non Return-Brake-Servo	1	
26	232043	Joint Washer	1	NOTE(1)
27	ERC3493	Restrictor	2	
28	ERC3729	Spring Ring	2	

NOTE(1): Part of Engine Gaskets/Seals Kit RTC2913

VS3614A

LAND ROVER PARTS LTD

MODEL LR110 - UP TO AUGUST 1986
BLOCK VS 4097
PAGE B 190
GROUP B

ENGINE - 3.5 LITRE V8 PETROL - INLET MANIFOLD PIPES ELBOWS & HOSES

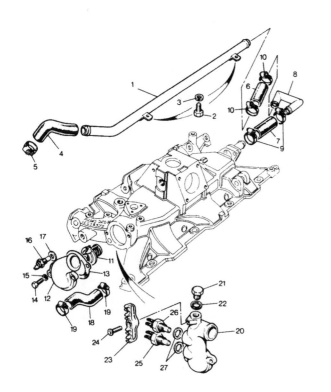

ILL	PART NO	DESCRIPTION	QTY	REMARKS
1	ERC2143	Water Outlet Pipe	1	
2	SH504041L	Screw	2	
3	WM600041L	Washer Spring	2	
4	ERC2320	Hose-Heater Return	1	
5	RTC3497	Clip	2	
6	ERC3489	Hose-Outlet Pipe	1	
7	ERC3562	Hose-Return Pipe	1	
8	ERC3563	Adaptor-Manifold Outlet	1	
9	CJ600144L	Clip	2	
10	RTC3497	Clip	2	
11	ETC4763	Thermostat-82 Degrees	1	)Engines 14G,15G,)20G and 21G
	ETC4765	Thermostat-88 Degrees	1	Engines 17G
12	ERC2139	Water Outlet Elbow	1	Except Air Con
13	611786	Gasket-Elbow to Manifold	1	See Note(1)
14	SH505091L	Screw	2	
15	WM600051L	Washer Spring	2	
16	PRC2506	Transmitter-Water-Temp	1	
	PRC4430	Transmitter-Water-Temp	1	Variant VD75E Hot Climate Vehs Only
17	90568054	Sealing Washer	1	See Note(1)
18	ERC2319	Hose By-Pass Thermostat	1	
19	RTC3497	Clip	2	
20	ERC8639	Elbow-Water Outlet	1	)
21	603224	Plug-Blanking	1	)
22	232043	Washer	1	)
23	603672	Retainer-Spark Plug Cables	1	)Air Conditioning
24	AB610031L	Screw	1	)Only
25	PRC3505	Switch-Temp-Sensor-Fan	1	)
26	PRC3359	Switch-Temp-Sensor-Cut-Out	1	)
27	C457593	Washer	2	)

NOTE(1): Part Of Engine Gasket/Seals Kit RTC2913.

VS4097

LAND ROVER PARTS LTD

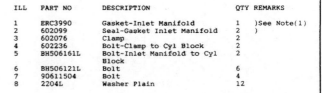
MODEL LR110 - UP TO AUGUST 1986
BLOCK VS 4096
PAGE B 192
GROUP B

ENGINE - 3.5 LITRE V8 PETROL - INLET MANIFOLD FIXINGS & GASKET

ILL	PART NO	DESCRIPTION	QTY	REMARKS
1	ERC3990	Gasket-Inlet Manifold	1	)See Note(1)
2	602099	Seal-Gasket Inlet Manifold	2	)
3	602076	Clamp	2	
4	602236	Bolt-Clamp to Cyl Block	2	
5	BH506161L	Bolt-Inlet Manifold to Cyl Block	2	
6	BH506121L	Bolt	6	
7	90611504	Bolt	4	
8	2204L	Washer Plain	12	

NOTE(1):   Part Of Engine Gasket/Seals Kit RTC2913.

VS4096

150

MODEL LR110 - UP TO AUGUST 1986
BLOCK VS 3850A
PAGE B 194
GROUP B

ENGINE - 3.5 LITRE V8 PETROL - EXHAUST MANIFOLDS

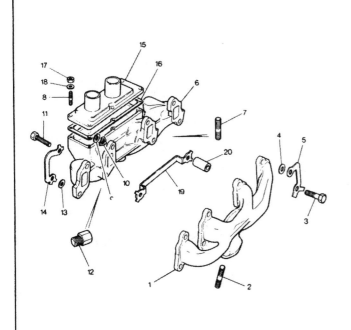

ILL	PART NO	DESCRIPTION	QTY	REMARKS
1	ERC5069	EXHAUST MANIFOLD ASSEMBLY-LH	1	Note(1)
	ETC6538	EXHAUST MANIFOLD ASSEMBLY-LH	1	Note(2)
2	252623	+Stud-Flange	3	
3	SH506101L	Screw-LH Manifold/Block	8	
4	3036L	Plain Washer	8	
5	ERC7321	Locking Washer	4	
6	ERC3101	EXHAUST MANIFOLD ASSEMBLY-RH	1	Note(3)
	ERC5925	EXHAUST MANIFOLD ASSEMBLY-RH	1	Note(4)
	ETC6634	EXHAUST MANIFOLD ASSEMBLY-RH	1	Note(2)
7	252623	+Stud-Flange	3	
11	SH506101L	Screw	7	)Engines 14G,
12	614443	Bolt	1	)17G & 20G
13	3036L	Plain Washer	8	)
14	ERC7321	Lockwasher	4	)
7	252623	+Stud-Flange	3	)
8	ERC3690	+Stud-Heat Cover	6	)
9	ERC3699	Plain Washer	2	)
10	612689	Lockwasher	2	)
11	SH506101L	Screw	5	)
	BH506441	Bolt	2	)Engines 15G &
12	614443	Bolt	1	)21G, 24G.
13	3036L	Plain Washer	4	)
14	ERC7321	Lockwasher	2	)
15	ERC7611	Cover-Heat Transfer Assembly	1	)
16	ERC4989	Gasket	1	)
17	RTC609	Washer-Plain	6	)
18	NR604090	Nut	6	)
19	ERC7896	Washer	1	)
20	ERC7897	Distance Tube	2	)

NOTE(1):   All 14G, 15G, 17G, 21G & Up To
           20G01428A & 24G00048A

NOTE(2):   From 20G01429A & 24G00049A

NOTE(3):   All 14G, 17G, & Up To 20G01428A

NOTE(4):   All 15G & 21G & Up To 24G00048A

VS3850A

151

MODEL LR110 - UP TO AUGUST 1986
BLOCK VS 1696A
PAGE B 196
GROUP B

ENGINE - 3.5 LITRE V8 PETROL - HEATSHIELDS

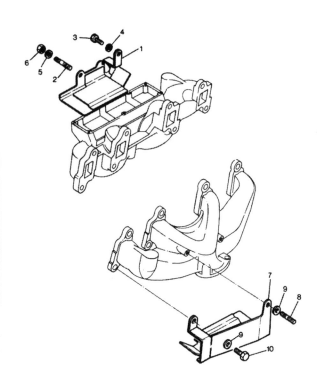

ILL	PART NO	DESCRIPTION	QTY	REMARKS
1	ERC5875	Heatshield Assembly-Solenoid	1	Engines 15G & 21G
2	ERC3690	Stud-Starter Motor-Solenoid Heatshield	1	
3	SH605051L	Screw-Shield/Manifold	1	
4	RTC609	Plain Washer	1	
5	RTC609	Plain Washer	1	
6	NR604090L	Nut	1	
7	ERC5786	Heatshield Assembly-Solenoid	1	Engines 14G,17G & 20G
8	ERC3458	Stud	1	
9	RTC613	Plain Washer	2	
10	SH605051L	Screw	1	

VS1696A

LAND ROVER PARTS LTD

MODEL LR110 - UP TO AUGUST 1986
BLOCK 6RE 40
PAGE B 198
GROUP B

ENGINE - 3.5 LITRE V8 PETROL - GASKET KITS

ILL	PART NO	DESCRIPTION	QTY	REMARKS
1	RTC2104	Gasket Kit-Engine Overhaul	1	)Note(1)
2	RTC2913	Gasket Kit-Engine Decarbonising	1	)

NOTE(1): For A Complete Engine Build Both Gasket Kits
          Will Be Required.

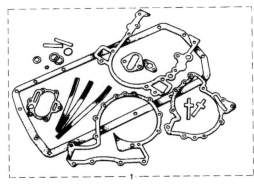

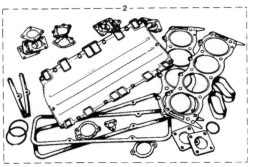

6RE40

LAND ROVER PARTS LTD

MASTER INDEX

GROUP C

CLUTCH

MODEL LR110 - UP TO AUGUST 1986
BLOCK VS 3826A
PAGE C 2
GROUP C

ENGINE - 4 CYLINDER PETROL - FLYWHEEL CLUTCH HOUSING

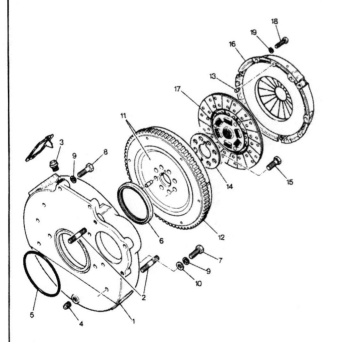

ILL	PART NO	DESCRIPTION	QTY	REMARKS
1	ETC6394	FLYWHEEL HOUSING ASSEMBLY	1	
2	TE110061L	+Stud-Bell Housing	13	
3	ERC7295	+Plug	1	
	NH110041L	Nut	11	
4	3290	Drain Plug-Flywheel Housing	1	
5	ERC6432	O Ring	1	Upto Engine 11H08034C
6	ETC5369	Oil Seal-Main	1	
7	SH110301L	Bolt	6	
8	BH110071L	Bolt	2	
9	WL110001L	Spring Washer	2	
10	WA110061L	Plain Washer	6	
11	ERC6408	FLYWHEEL & STARTER RING ASSY	1	
12	ERC5293	+Starter Ring	1	
13	502116	+Dowel-Clutch	3	
14	ERC4658	Reinforcing Plate	1	
15	ERC6551	Bolt-Flywheel to Crankshaft	8	
16	576557	Clutch Cover	1	
17	FRC2671	Clutch Plate	1	
	FTC159	Clutch Plate	1	Asbestos Free
18	SX108201L	Set Bolt	6	
19	WL108001L	Spring Washer	6	
20	ERC9404	Bracket-Clip to Housing	2	
21	AFU1090L	Clip	2	

VS3826A

MODEL LR110 - UP TO AUGUST 1986
BLOCK VS 4046
PAGE C 4
GROUP C

ENGINE - 2.25 DIESEL - FLYWHEEL AND CLUTCH

ILL	PART NO	DESCRIPTION	QTY	REMARKS
1	ETC7336	Flywheel Housing Assembly	1	
2	TE110061L	Stud-Bell Housing	11	
3	ERC9240	Stud-Starter Motor	1	
4	TE106041L	Stud-Inspection Cover	2	Note(1)
5	ERC7295	Plug	1	
6	ERC6432	O Ring	1	
	NH110041L	Nut	11	
7	3290	Plug-Flywheel Housing	1	
8	SH110301L	Screw-Housing to Block	6	
9	BH110091L	Bolt-Housing to Block	2	
10	WL110001L	Washer-Spring-Housing to Block	2	
11	WA110061L	Washer-Housing to Block	6	
12	ERC9404	Bracket-Harness Clip	2	
13	ETC5780	FLYWHEEL ASSEMBLY	1	
14	568431	+Starter Ring	1	
15	502116	+Dowel	3	
16	ERC4658	Reinforcing Plate	1	
17	ERC6551	Bolt-Flywheel to Crankshaft	8	
18	56140	Cover Plate	1	)
19	50216	Joint Washer	1	)
20	WL106001L	Washer-Spring	2	)Note(1)
21	WA106041L	Washer-Plain	2	)
22	NH106041L	Nut	2	)
23	FRC8573	Clutch Cover	1	
24	FRC8574	Clutch Plate	1	
	FTC148	Clutch Plate	1	Asbestos Free
25	SX108201L	Bolt-Set	6	
26	WL108001L	Spring Washer	6	

NOTE(1): Only Fitted To Earlier Engines (Before July 1986).

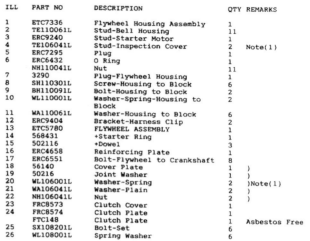

VS4046

LAND ROVER PARTS LTD

MODEL LR110 - UP TO AUGUST 1986
BLOCK VS 4217
PAGE C 4.02
GROUP C

ENGINE - 2.5 DIESEL - FLYWHEEL AND CLUTCH

ILL	PART NO	DESCRIPTION	QTY	REMARKS
1	ETC7336	Flywheel Housing Assembly	1	
2	TE110061L	Stud-Bell Housing	11	
3	ERC9240	Stud-Starter Motor	1	
4	TE106041L	Stud-Inspection Cover	2	Note(1)
5	ERC7295	Plug	1	
6	ERC6432	O Ring-Flywheel Housing	1	Upto Engine 12J10960C Only
	NH110041L	Nut	11	
7	SH110301L	Screw-Housing to Block	6	
8	BH110091L	Bolt-Housing to Block	2	
9	WL110001L	Washer-Spring-Housing to Block	2	
10	WA110061L	Washer-Housing to Block	6	
11	ERC9404	Bracket-Harness Clip	2	
12	ETC5780	FLYWHEEL ASSEMBLY	1	
13	568431	+Starter Ring	1	
14	502116	+Dowel	3	
15	ERC4658	Reinforcing Plate	1	
16	ERC6551	Bolt-Flywheel to Crankshaft	8	
17	56140	Cover Plate	1	)
18	50216	Joint Washer	1	)
19	WL106001L	Washer-Spring	2	)Note(1)
20	WA106041L	Washer-Plain	2	)
21	NH106041L	Nut	2	)
22	FRC8573	Clutch Cover	1	
23	FRC8574	Clutch Plate	1	
	FTC148	Clutch Plate	1	Asbestos Free
24	SX108201L	Bolt-Set	6	
25	WL108001L	Spring Washer	6	

NOTE(1): Only Fitted To Early Engines (Before July 1986).

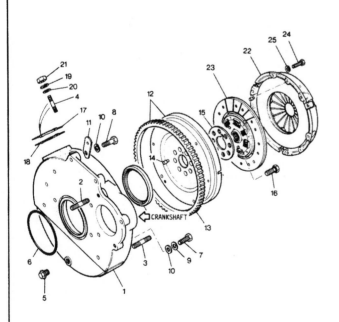

VS4217

LAND ROVER PARTS LTD

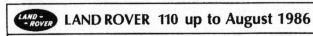
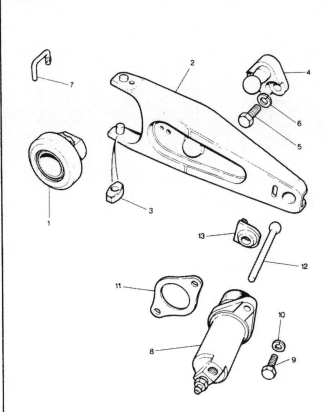

MODEL LR110 - UP TO AUGUST 1986
BLOCK VS 3855
PAGE C 6
GROUP C

ENGINE - 4 CYLINDER PETROL & DIESEL - CLUTCH RELEASE MECHANISM

ILL	PART NO	DESCRIPTION	QTY	REMARKS
1	FRC9568	Bearing & Sleeve-Clutch Release	1	
2	FRC3326	Operating Lever Assy Clutch	1	
3	FRC5255	Slipper Pad-Clutch Lever	2	
4	FRC5180	Pivot Plate Assembly-Clutch Release Lever	1	
5	BH108061L	Bolt-Fixing Pivot Plate	2	
6	WL108001L	Spring-Washer-Fixing Pivot Plate	2	
7	FRC3416	Staple-Release Lever to Sleeve	1	
8	591231	Clutch Slave Cylinder	1	
	8G8600L	Overhaul Kit-Slave Cylinder	1	
9	SH108251L	Screw	2	
10	WL108001L	Spring Washer	2	
11	591988	Backing Plate-Slave Cylinder	1	
12	FRC3417	Push Rod-Slave Cylinder	1	
13	FRC3327	Clip-Push Rod to Lever	1	

VS3855

BLANK   **BLANK**

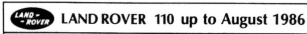
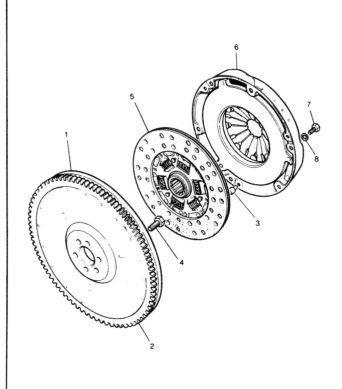

MODEL LR110 - UP TO AUGUST 1986
BLOCK M 671
PAGE C 10
GROUP C

ENGINE - 3.5 LITRE V8 PETROL - CLUTCH - FLYWHEEL

ILL	PART NO	DESCRIPTION	QTY	REMARKS
1	611324	FLYWHEEL AND STARTER RING ASSEMBLY	1	
2	611323	+Starter Ring	1	
3	6395L	+Dowel-Clutch	3	
4	SH607081L	Screw-Flywheel/Crankshaft	6	
5	FRC6631	Clutch Plate	1	
	FRC6685	Clutch Plate	1	Prefix 20C Only
	FTC160	Clutch Plate	1	Asbestos Free
6	576476	Clutch Cover	1	
7	SH606061L	Screw-Clutch/Flywheel	6	
8	WM600041L	Spring Washer	6	
	AEU1750	Lining Package-Clutch Plate	1	

M671

 **LAND ROVER PARTS LTD**

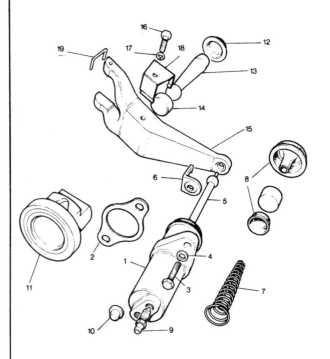

MODEL LR110 - UP TO AUGUST 1986
BLOCK VS 1697
PAGE C 12
GROUP C

ENGINE - 3.5 LITRE V8 PETROL - CLUTCH RELEASE MECHANISM
                  GEARBOX PREFIX 13C

ILL	PART NO	DESCRIPTION	QTY	REMARKS
1	UKC8677L	Slave Cylinder-Clutch	1	
2	FRC2402	Backing Plate	1	
3	SH108251L	Bolt-Slave Cyl to Bell Hsg-M8x25mm	2	
4	WL108001L	Washer Spring-Slave Cyl to Bell Housing	2	
5	571160	Push Rod	1	
6	576723	Clip-Push Rod to Release Lever	1	
7	606731	Spring-Slave Cylinder	1	
8	BHM7063L	Repair Kit-Slave Cylinder	1	
9	606733	Bleed Screw	1	
10	594091	Cap	1	
11	FRC9568	Bearing & Sleeve-Clutch Release	1	
12	571164	Cap-Pivot Lever	1	
13	594176	Pivot Pin	1	
14	571161	Insert-Clutch Release Lever	1	
15	576137	Lever-Clutch Release Assy	1	
16	SH106101L	Bolt M6x10mm Clutch Release Lever to Pivot	1	
17	WL106001L	Washer Spring	1	
18	571163	Clip	1	
19	576203	Staple-Clutch Lever to Bearing Sleeve	1	
	NRC3947	Pipe Clutch-Hose to Slave Cylinder	1	

VS1697

 **LAND ROVER PARTS LTD**

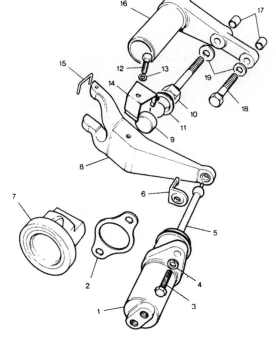

MODEL LR110 - UP TO AUGUST 1986
BLOCK TS 5780
PAGE C 12.02
GROUP C

ENGINE - 3.5 LITRE PETROL - CLUTCH RELEASE MECHANISM
GEARBOX PREFIX 20C

ILL	PART NO	DESCRIPTION	QTY	REMARKS
1	UKC8677L	Slave Cylinder-Clutch	1	
	BHM7063L	Repair Kit-Slave Cylinder	1	
2	FRC2402	Backing Plate-Slave Cylinder	1	
3	SH108251L	Screw-Slave Cylinder to Bell Housing	2	
4	WL108001L	Washer-Spring-Slave Cylinder to Bell Housing	2	
5	571160	Push Rod-Slave Cylinder	1	
6	576723	Clip-Push Rod to Release Lever	1	
7	FRC9568	Clutch Release Bearing & Sleeve	1	
8	576137	Clutch Release Lever Assembly	1	
9	FRC2975	Cap-Pivot Lever	1	
10	FRC2528	Pivot-Release Lever	1	
11	571161	Insert-Clutch Release Lever	1	
12	SH106101L	Screw-Clutch Release Lever to Pivot	1	
13	WM106001L	Washer-Spring	1	
14	571163	Clip-Clutch Release Lever	1	
15	576203	Staple-Clutch Lever to Bearing Sleeve	1	
16	FRC4803	Guide-Clutch Release Bearing	1	
17	FRC2481	Dowel-Guide	2	
18	SH108401L	Screw	1	
19	WL108001L	Washer-Spring	2	

TS5780

LAND ROVER PARTS LTD

162

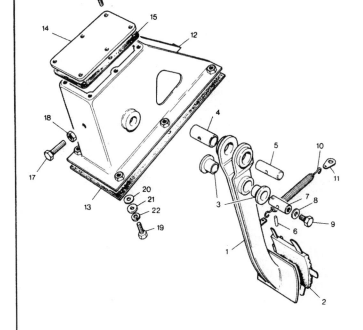

MODEL LR110 - UP TO AUGUST 1986
BLOCK VS 3977
PAGE C 14
GROUP C

CLUTCH - PEDAL AND PEDAL BOX

ILL	PART NO	DESCRIPTION	QTY	REMAKRS
1	568895	Clutch Pedal-RHS	1	)To VIN 234135
	NRC9217	Clutch Pedal-LHS	1	)
	NTC1112	Clutch Pedal	1	From VIN 234136
2	278166	Rubber-Clutch Pedal	1	)To VIN 234135)Optional
	61K738	Rubber-Clutch Pedal	1	From VIN 234136
3	272714	Bush-Clutch Pedal	2	
4	269783	Bush	1	
5	568883	Trunnion	1	
6	50446	Mills Pin	1	
7	272712	Pivot Pin	1	
8	3052	Joint Washer	1	
9	SH604031L	Bolt	1	
10	569701	Return spring	1	
	NRC7869	Sleeve-Return Spring	1	
11	240708	Anchor Plate-Spring	1	
12	272632	Pedal Box Assembly	1	
13	NRC8885	Gasket-Pedal Box to Dash	1	To VIN 234805
	MUC7505	Gasket-Pedal Box to Dash	1	From VIN 234806
14	272713	Top Cover-Pedal Box	1	
15	272819	Gasket-Top Cover	1	
16	78227	Drive Screw-Top Cover	6	
17	SH604081L	Bolt-Pedal Stop	1	
18	NH604041L	Nut-Pedal Stop	1	
129	GG605081	Bolt-Pedal Box to Dash	6	
20	RTC610	Plain Washer-Thin	5	
21	5494	Plain Washer-Thick	1	
22	WM600051L	Spring-Washer	6	
23	FH506165	Bolt	2	
24	WM600061L	Washer-Spring	2	

VS3977

LAND ROVER PARTS LTD

163

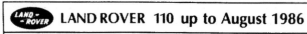
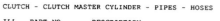

MODEL LR110 - UP TO AUGUST 1986
BLOCK VS 3975
PAGE C 16
GROUP C

CLUTCH - CLUTCH MASTER CYLINDER - PIPES - HOSES

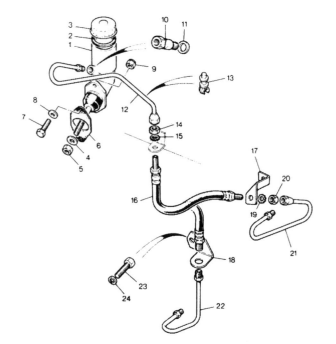

ILL	PART NO	DESCRIPTION	QTY	REMARKS
1	550732	CLUTCH MASTER CYLINDER	1	
2	264767	+Sealing Washer	1	
3	500201	+Cap-Master Cylinder	1	
	8G8837L	Repair Kit-Master Cylinder	1	
4	RTC626	Washer-Push Rod to Pedal	2	
5	NH605041L	Nut-Push Rod to Pedal	2	
6	592358	Gasket-Cylinder to Dash	1	
7	BH108061L	Bolt	2	
8	WA108051L	Washer	2	
9	NY108041L	Nut	2	
10	139082	Adaptor	1	
11	233220	Gasket-Adaptor	1	
12	NRC8330	Pipe-Master Cylinder to Hose	1	RHS
	NRC8329	Pipe-Master Cylinder to Hose	1	LHS
13	79123	Pipe Clip	2	RHS
14	NT607041L	Nut-Bracket to Hose	2	4 Cylinder
	NT604041L	Nut-Bracket to Hose	1	V8
15	WF600071L	Washer-Bracket to Hose	2	4 Cylinder
	WE600071L	Washer-Bracket to Hose	1	V8
16	RTC4425	Clutch Hose	1	4 Cylinder
	NRC2211	Clutch Hose	1	V8
17	NRC7441	Bracket	1	4 Cylinder
18	90577642	Bracket	1	)
19	WE600101L	Washer	1	)V8
20	2K8686L	Nut	1	)
21	NRC9595	Pipe-Hose to Slave Cylinder	1	4 Cylinder
22	577643	Pipe-Hose to Slave Cylinder	1	V8
23	BH506165	Bolt	2	
24	WM600061L	Spring Washer	2	

VS3995

 **LAND ROVER PARTS LTD**

MODEL LR110 - UP TO AUGUST 1986
BLOCK TS 5039
PAGE D 2
GROUP D

GEARBOX - 4 CYLINDER MODELS - GEARBOX ASSEMBLY

ILL	PART NO	DESCRIPTION	QTY	REMARKS
1	FRC5928R	Gearbox Assembly-Exchange	1	Upto Suffix E
	RTC6082N	Gearbox Assembly-New	1	From Suffix F

Serial No.50A00001A On.

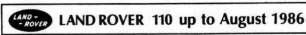

TS5039

MODEL LR110 - UP TO AUGUST 1986
BLOCK VS 3852
PAGE D 4
GROUP D

GEARBOX - 4 CYLINDER MODELS - CLUTCH HOUSING

ILL	PART NO	DESCRIPTION	QTY	REMARKS
1	FRC9865	Clutch Housing	1	
2	BH112091L	Bolt-Housing to Gearbox	2	
3	SH112301L	Screw-Housing to Gearbox	4	
4	WL112001L	Spring Washer-Housing to Gearbox	6	
5	WA112081L	Washer-Housing to Gearbox	2	
6	UKC25L	Dowel-Housing to Gearbox	2	
7	FRC6375	Breather Assembly	1	

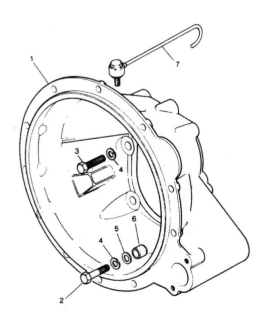

VS3852

MODEL LR110 - UP TO AUGUST 1986
BLOCK VS 3880A
PAGE D 6
GROUP D

GEARBOX - 4 CYLINDER MODELS - GEARCASE

ILL	PART NO	DESCRIPTION	QTY	REMARKS
	FRC7713	GEARCASE-DOWELS-CENTRE PLATE ASSEMBLY	1	Upto 0173664
	FRC9827	GEARCASE-DOWELS-CENTRE PLATE ASSEMBLY	1	From 0173665
1	FRC6950	+Pin-Reverse Lever Mounting	1	Upto 0173664
	FRC8383	+Pin-Reverse Lever Fixing	1	From 0173665
2	WA110061L	+Washer	1	
3	WL110001L	+Spring Washer	1	
4	NH110041L	+Nut	1	
5	UKC170L	+Hollow Dowel	2	
6	FRC6145	Drain Plug	1	
7	FRC7064	Joint Washer	1	
8	TKC1229L	Gasket-Gearcase to Centre Plate	1	
9	TKC1235L	Gasket-Centre Plate to Extension Housing	1	
10	3292	Plug-Oil Level	1	
11	UKC24L	Plug-Core	1	
12	UKC30L	Plug-Core	1	
13	TKC5779L	Oil Catcher	1	

VS3880A

MODEL LR110 - UP TO AUGUST 1986
BLOCK VS 3883
PAGE D 8
GROUP D

GEARBOX - 4 CYLINDER MODELS - EXTENSION CASE

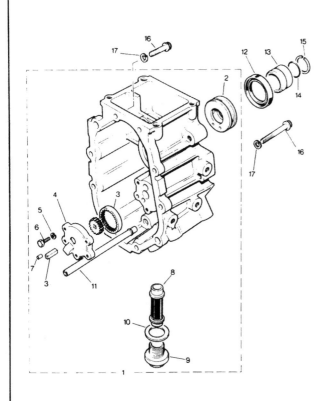

ILL	PART NO	DESCRIPTION	QTY	REMARKS
1	FRC8105	EXTENSION CASE AND OIL PUMP ASSEMBLY	1	See Note(1)
	FRC9562	EXTENSION CASE AND OIL PUMP ASSEMBLY	1	See Note(2)
2	FRC4449	+Oil Feed Ring	1	
3	RTC2057	+Kit-Pump Gears and Shaft	1	
4	FRC6246	+Body-Oil Pump	1	
5	WL106001L	+Spring Washer	3	
6	SH106201L	+Screw	4	
7	UKC2738L	+Dowel	2	
8	FRC6244	+Filter	1	
9	90571104	+Plug-Filter	1	
10	FRC4810	+Washer-Plug	1	
11	FRC8104	+Inlet Pipe-Pump	1	
12	FRC2365	Oil Seal-Extension Case	1	
13	FRC4493	Collar-Oil Seal	1	
14	FRC4501	'O' Ring-Collar	1	
15	FRC4494	Spring Ring-Collar	1	
16	BH108101L	Bolt-Extension to Gearbox	2	
	FRC4282	Bolt-Extension to Gearbox	8	
17	WL108001L	Spring Washer-Extension to Gearbox	10	

NOTE(1): Early Type With Pivot Bracket And Cross Lever Mechanism On The Diff Lock.

NOTE(2): Latest Type With The Connecting Rod Going Direct Between The Selector Finger And The Operating Arm On The Transfer Gear Change.

VS3883

MODEL LR110 - UP TO AUGUST 1986
BLOCK VS 3877
PAGE D 10
GROUP D

GEARBOX - 4 CYLINDER MODELS - MAINSHAFT

ILL	PART NO	DESCRIPTION	QTY	REMARKS
1	FRC4856	COVER ASSEMBLY-GEARBOX FRONT	1	
2	UKC1060L	+Oil Seal-Front Cover	1	
3	SH108251L	Screw	6	
4	WA108051L	Washer	6	
5	FRC4873	Gasket-Front Cover to Gearcase	1	
6		SELECTIVE WASHER CONSTANT PINION		
	FRC4327	1.51mm		A/R
	FRC4329	1.57mm		A/R
	FRC4331	1.63mm		A/R
	FRC4333	1.69mm		A/R
	FRC4335	1.75mm		A/R
	FRC4337	1.81mm		A/R
	FRC4339	1.87mm		A/R
	FRC4341	1.93mm		A/R
	FRC4343	1.99mm		A/R
	FRC4345	2.05mm		A/R
	FRC4347	2.11mm		A/R
	FRC4349	2.17mm		A/R
	FRC4351	2.23mm		A/R
	FRC4353	2.29mm		A/R
	FRC4355	2.35mm		A/R
	FRC4357	2.41mm		A/R
	FRC4359	2.47mm		A/R
	FRC4361	2.53mm		A/R
	FRC4363	2.59mm		A/R
	FRC4365	2.65mm		A/R
	FRC4367	2.71mm		A/R
	FRC4369	2.77mm		A/R

VS3877

MODEL LR110 - UP TO AUGUST 1986
BLOCK VS 3877
PAGE D 10.02
GROUP D

GEARBOX - 4 CYLINDER MODELS - MAINSHAFT - CONTINUED

ILL	PART NO	DESCRIPTION	QTY	REMARKS
7	FRC7145	Bearing	1	
8	FRC4845	Shaft-Constant Pinion	1	
9	UKC8L	Bearing-Constant Pinion-Rear	1	
10	UKC37L	Spacer-Synchro Hub to Pilot Bearing	1	
11	FRC9387	Synchromesh Assembly 3rd/4th Gears	1	
12	FRC8232	Baulk Ring 3rd/4th Gears	2	
13	UKC31L	Spring-Synchromesh	2	
14	UKC3530L	Shifting Plate	3	
15	TKC6962L	Mainshaft Gear 3rd Speed	1	
16	FRC5305	Mainshaft Assembly	1	

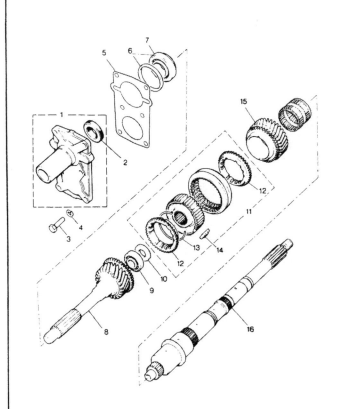

VS3877

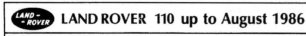
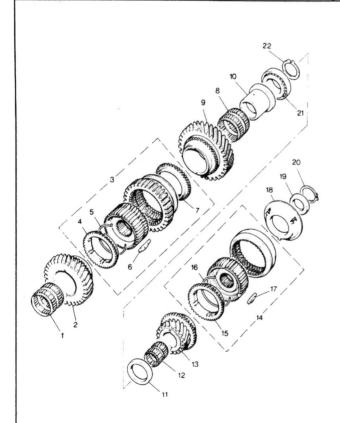

```
MODEL LR110 - UP TO AUGUST 1986
BLOCK VS 3881
PAGE D 12
GROUP D
```

GEARBOX - 4 CYLINDER MODELS - MAINSHAFT GEARS

ILL	PART NO	DESCRIPTION	QTY	REMARKS
1	FRC5678	BEARING-NEEDLE ROLLER 2ND/3RD GEARS	2	
2	FRC5279	GEAR-2ND SPEED	1	
3	FRC6670	SYNCHROMESH ASSEMBLY-1ST/2ND GEAR	1	Upto 0173664
	FRC9386	SYNCHROMESH ASSEMBLY-1ST/2ND GEAR	1	From 0173665
4	FRC8232	+Baulk Ring-2nd Gear	1	
5	UKC31L	+Spring	2	
6	UKC3531L	+Shifting Plate 1st/2nd	3	
7	FRC8232	+Baulk Ring-1st Gear	1	
8	FRC5679	Bearing-Needle Roller 1st Gear	1	
9	FRC5253	GEAR-1ST SPEED	1	
10		BUSH-1ST SPEED		
	FRC5243	40.16 to 40.21mm	A/R	
	FRC5244	40.21 to 40.26mm	A/R	
	FRC5245	40.26 to 40.31mm	A/R	
	FRC5246	40.31 to 40.36mm	A/R	
	FRC5247	40.36 to 40.41mm	A/R	
11	FRC4321	Collar-5th Gear	1	
12	FRC5280	Needle Bearing-5th Gear	1	
13	RKC5098L	Gear-5th	1	
14	FRC9389	Synchromesh Assembly-5th Gear	1	
15	FRC8232	+Baulk Ring-5th Speed Gear	1	
16	UKC31L	+Spring	2	
17	UKC3530L	+Shifting Plate	3	

VS3881

 **LAND ROVER PARTS LTD**

```
MODEL LR110 - UP TO AUGUST 1986
BLOCK VS 3881
PAGE D 12.02
GROUP D
```

GEARBOX - 4 CYLINDER MODELS - MAINSHAFT GEARS - CONTINUED

ILL	PART NO	DESCRIPTION	QTY	REMARKS
18	FRC5235	Support Plate Assembly-Synchro Hub	1	
19		WASHER-SUPPORT PLATE		
	FRC5284	5.10mm	A/R	
	FRC5286	5.16mm	A/R	
	FRC5288	5.22mm	A/R	
	FRC5290	5.28mm	A/R	
	FRC5292	5.34mm	A/R	
	FRC5294	5.40mm	A/R	
	FRC5296	5.46mm	A/R	
	FRC5298	5.52mm	A/R	
	FRC5300	5.58mm	A/R	
	FRC5302	5.64mm	A/R	
20	FRC9526	Circlip-5th Synchro Hub	1	
21	RTC2914	Bearing-Mainshaft-Rear	1	
22	FRC9812	Circlip-Bearing to Mainshaft	1	

VS3881

 **LAND ROVER PARTS LTD**

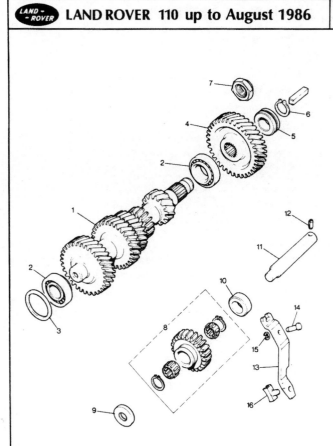

MODEL LR110 - UP TO AUGUST 1986
BLOCK VS 3878A
PAGE D 14
GROUP D

GEARBOX - 4 CYLINDER MODELS - LAYSHAFT

ILL	PART NO	DESCRIPTION	QTY	REMARKS
1	FRC7575	Layshaft Cluster Assembly	1	Upto 0173664
	FRC8141	Layshaft Cluster Assembly	1	From 0173665
2	ULC1796L	Bearing-Layshaft	2	
3		SELECTIVE WASHER-LAYSHAFT		
	TKC4633L	1.69mm	A/R	
	TKC4635L	1.75mm	A/R	
	TKC4637L	1.81mm	A/R	
	TKC4639L	1.87mm	A/R	
	TKC4641L	1.93mm	A/R	
	TKC4643L	1.99mm	A/R	
	TKC4645L	2.05mm	A/R	
	TKC4647L	2.11mm	A/R	
	TKC4649L	2.17mm	A/R	
	TKC4651L	2.23mm	A/R	
	TKC4653L	2.29mm	A/R	
	TKC4655L	2.35mm	A/R	
	TKC4657L	2.41mm	A/R	
	TKC4659L	2.47mm	A/R	
	TKC4661L	2.53mm	A/R	
	TKC4663L	2.59mm	A/R	
4	FRC5162	Layshaft Gear-5th Speed	1	
5	UKC1689L	Washer-5th Speed L/shaft Gear	1	
6	UKC1690L	Circlip-Gear/Layshaft	1	
7	FRC7214	Nut-Fixing Fifth Gear to Layshaft	1	
8	FRC7602	Gear Assembly-Reverse Idler	1	Upto 0173664
	FRC8285	Gear Assembly-Reverse Idler	1	From 0173665
9	FRC4947	Spacer-Reverse Idler Shaft Front	1	
10	FRC5186	Spacer-Reverse Idler Shaft Rear	1	
11	FRC5095	Shaft-Reverse Idler	1	
12	UKC18L	Roll Pin-Reverse Idler Shaft	1	
13	TKC1428L	Lever-Reverse Operating	1	)Upto 0173664
14	UKC2662L	Pivot-Reverse Lever	1	)
	FRC8246	Lever-Reverse Operating	1	)
	FRC8382	Pivot-Reverse Lever	1	)From 0173665
	FRC8383	Pivot Post-Reverse Lever	1	)
15	13H2023L	Circlip-Pin to Mounting Pin	1	
16	FRC4946	Slipper Pad-Reverse Gear	1	Upto 0173664
	FRC8384	Slipper Pad-Reverse Gear	1	From 0173665

VS3878A

LAND ROVER PARTS LTD

MODEL LR110 - UP TO AUGUST 1986
BLOCK VS 3882
PAGE D 16
GROUP D

GEARBOX - 4 CYLINDER MODELS - SELECTORS AND SHAFTS

ILL	PART NO	DESCRIPTION	QTY	REMARKS
1	FRC7194	SHAFT ASSEMBLY-C/W SELECTOR FORK 1ST/2ND GEAR	1	)Upto Gearbox)0063205D)No Longer)Available)See Note(1)
	FRC8126	SHAFT ASSEMBLY-C/W SELECTOR FORK 1ST/2ND GEAR	1	)From Gearbox)0063206D
2	FRC4940	+Fork-Selector-1st/2nd Gear	1	)No Longer)Available Use)FRC9548
	FRC9548	+Fork-Selector Gears	1	
3	BLS112L	Ball-Detent	1	
4	FRC7195	Spring-Detent	1	
5	UKC75L	Plug-Spring Retaining	1	
6	UKC73L	Circlip-Selector Shaft	1	
7	FRC4890	Quadrant-Main Selector Shaft	1	)Upto Gearbox)0063205D)No Longer)Available)See Note(1)
8	FRC7335	Spring Pin-Quadrant to Shaft	1	)Upto Gearbox)0063205D
	FRC7330	Quadrant-Main Selector Shaft	1	)From Gearbox
	FRC7332	Spring Pin-Quadrant to Shaft	1	)No. 0063206D
9	FRC7334	Shaft Selector	1	
10	FRC7333	Quadrant-Remote Selector Shaft	1	
11	FRC7335	Spring Pin-Quadrant to Shaft	1	
12	FRC4435	Roller-Quadrant Shaft	1	
13	FRC4434	Shaft-Quadrant Roller	1	
14	CR120105L	Circlip-Quadrant Shaft	1	
15	FRC4951	'O' Ring-Remote Selector Shaft	1	
16	FRC5864	Yoke-Shaft to Gear Lever	1	
17	UKC3058L	Screw	1	No Longer Available Use FRC7018
	FRC7018	Screw	1	
18	FRC5859	Seat-Ball End	1	
19	CR120335L	Circlip-Seat to Yoke	1	

NOTE(1): Use FRC8126 & FRC7330 & FRC7332

VS3882

LAND ROVER PARTS LTD

MODEL LR110 - UP TO AUGUST 1986
BLOCK VS 3882
PAGE D 16.02
GROUP D

GEARBOX - **4** CYLINDER MODELS - SELECTORS AND SHAFTS - CONTINUED

ILL	PART NO	DESCRIPTION	QTY	REMARKS
20	FRC4882	Fork-Selector-3rd/4th Gear	1	)No Longer)Available Use)FRC9547
	FRC9547	Fork-Selector-3rd/4th Gear	1	
21	TKC290L	Spool-Interlock-1st/2nd/3rd/ 4th Gear	1	
22	UKC3660L	Plate Assembly-Interlock Attachment	1	
23	WL106001L	Washer-Spring	2	
24	SH106161L	Screw-Interlock/Blanking Plate	2	
25	RTC2058	FORK-SELECTOR AND SUPPORT BRACKET ASSEMBLY-5TH GEAR	1	
26	532943	+Pad-Selector-5th Gear Fork	2	
27	UKC2089L	+Pin-Pivot 5th Gear Fork	2	
28	UKC2105L	+Circlip-Pivot Pin Locating	2	
29	SH108251L	+Screw-Support Bracket to Fork	2	
30	WL108001L	+Washer Spring	2	
31	FRC7192	Spool-Interlock-5th Gear	1	
32	FRC4905	Plate Assembly-Interlock Attachment 5th Gear	1	
33	WL106001L	Washer-Spring Interlock Plate	2	
34	SH106161L	Screw Interlock Plate	2	

VS3882

MODEL LR110 - UP TO AUGUST 1986
BLOCK VS 4130
PAGE D 18
GROUP D

GEARBOX - **4** CYLINDER MODELS - GEAR LEVER

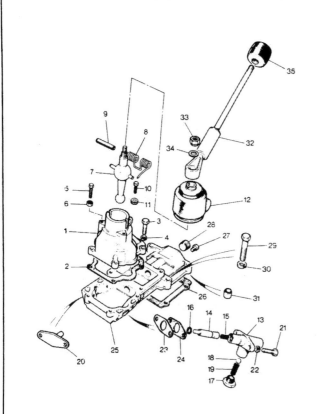

ILL	PART NO	DESCRIPTION	QTY	REMARKS
1	FRC7155	Housing-Gear Lever	1	
2	FRC4490	Joint Washer-Housing	1	
3	BH108061L	Bolt-Housing to Remote Hsg	4	
4	WL108001L	Spring Washer	4	
5	SH106201L	Set Screw	2	
6	NH106041L	Nut	2	
7	FRC8025	GEAR LEVER LOWER ASSY	1	No Longer Available Use FRC8724
	FRC8724	GEAR LEVER LOWER ASSEMBLY	1	
	UKC3092	+Pin-Gear Lever-Locating	2	
	22G1988L	+Plunger-Lower Gear Lever	1	
	22G1989L	+Spring-Lower Gear Lever	1	
8	FRC7414	Spring-Torsion	1	
9	PA120751L	Spring Pin	1	)Alternatives
	PA120801L	Spring Pin	1	)
10	SH106161L	Set Screw-Clamping Plate	1	
11	FRC7158	Clamping Plate-Damping Washer	1	No Longer Available Use FRC7886
	FRC7886	Clamping Plate-Damping Washer	1	
12	FRC7160	Grommet-Gear Lever	1	
	AFU4173	Tie-Securing Grommet	1	
		PLUNGER UNIT-REVERSE BAULK		
13	FRC6316	+Housing-Plunger Unit	1	
14	FRC8119	+Plunger-Reverse Baulk	1	
15	FRC6318	+Spring-Plunger Return	1	
16	FRC5596	+Spring Clip-Plunger Housing	1	Not Required with Adjustable Plug
17	FRC8120	+Plug-Detent	1	
	FRC8773	+Locknut	1	
18	571146	+Ball-Detent	1	
19	571439	+Spring-Detent	1	

VS4130

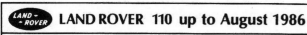
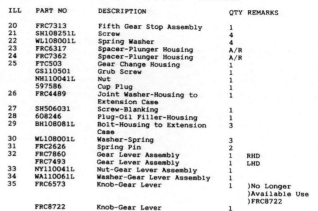

MODEL LR110 - UP TO AUGUST 1986
BLOCK VS 4130
PAGE D 18.02
GROUP D

GEARBOX - 4 CYLINDER MODELS - GEAR LEVER - CONTINUED

ILL	PART NO	DESCRIPTION	QTY	REMARKS
20	FRC7313	Fifth Gear Stop Assembly	1	
21	SH108251L	Screw	4	
22	WL108001L	Spring Washer	4	
23	FRC6317	Spacer-Plunger Housing	A/R	
24	FRC7362	Spacer-Plunger Housing	A/R	
25	FTC503	Gear Change Housing	1	
	GS110501	Grub Screw	1	
	NH110041L	Nut	1	
	597586	Cup Plug	1	
26	FRC4489	Joint Washer-Housing to Extension Case	1	
27	SH506031	Screw-Blanking	1	
28	608246	Plug-Oil Filler-Housing	1	
29	BH108081L	Bolt-Housing to Extension Case	3	
30	WL108001L	Washer-Spring	3	
31	FRC2626	Spring Pin	2	
32	FRC7860	Gear Lever Assembly	1	RHD
	FRC7493	Gear Lever Assembly	1	LHD
33	NY110041L	Nut-Gear Lever Assembly	1	
34	WA110061L	Washer-Gear Lever Assembly	1	
35	FRC6573	Knob-Gear Lever	1	)No Longer)Available Use)FRC8722
	FRC8722	Knob-Gear Lever	1	

VS4130

LAND ROVER PARTS LTD

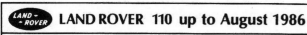
MODEL LR110 - UP TO AUGUST 1986
BLOCK VS 3201
PAGE D 18.04
GROUP D

GEARBOX - 4 CYLINDER MODELS - GASKET & SEAL KIT

ILL	PART NO	DESCRIPTION	QTY	REMARKS
1	RTC3889	GASKET & SEAL KIT	1	
	FRC7064	+Joint Washer-Drain Plug	1	
	TKC1229	+Gasket-Gearcase to Centre Plate	1	
	TKC1235	+Gasket-Centre Plate to Extension Housing	1	
	FRC4810	+Joint Washer Plug	1	
	FRC2365	+Oil Seal-Extension Case	1	
	FRC4501	+O Ring-Oil Seal Collar	1	
	UKC1060	+Oil Seal-Front Cover	1	
	FRC4873	+Gasket-Front Cover to Gearcase	1	
	FRC4490	+Joint Washer-Housing	1	
	FRC4489	+Joint Washer-Housing to Extn	1	

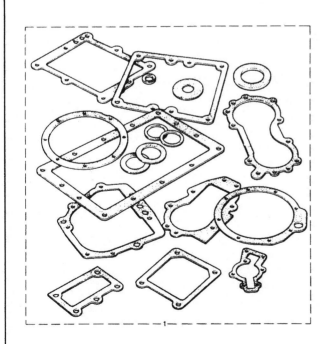

VS3201

LAND ROVER PARTS LTD

MODEL LR110 - UP TO AUGUST 1986
BLOCK VS 3742
PAGE D 20
GROUP D

GEARBOX - 4 CYLINDER MODELS - TRANSFER BOX LT230R

ILL	PART NO	DESCRIPTION	QTY	REMARKS
1	FRC9469N	Transfer Box Assembly-New	1	
	FRC7944	Gate Plate	1	Note(1)

NOTE(1): When Fitting New Transfer Gearbox Assembly
(LT230T Type) To Replace LT230R Type Transfer Gearbox
(Prefix 10D & 12D) Also Change The Gate Plate In The
Transfer Gear Change Assembly.

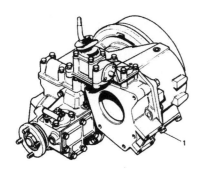

VS3742

180

MODEL LR110 - UP TO AUGUST 1986
BLOCK VS 3892
PAGE D 22
GROUP D

GEARBOX - 2.25 PETROL/DIESEL AND 2.5 DIESEL - TRANSFER BOX LT230R
SERIAL PREFIX 10D/12D

ILL	PART NO	DESCRIPTION	QTY	REMARKS
1	FRC7869	TRANSFER GEAR CHANGE ASSEMBLY 2/4 WHEEL DRIVE	1	)Note(1)
	FRC7870	TRANSFER GEAR CHANGE ASSEMBLY PERMANENT 4 WHEEL DRIVE	1	)
2	FRC6873	+Plate	1	
3	FRC6872	+Grommet	1	
4	SH106201L	+Screw	4	
5	WA108051L	+Washer	4	
6	FRC5483	+Gate Plate	1	2/4 Wheel Drive
	FRC5482	+Gate Plate	1	Permanent 4 Wheel Drive
7	FRC5486	+Gasket	1	
8	FRC5478	+Operating Arm	1	
9	BH106051L	+Bolt	1	
10	WL106001L	+Washer	1	
11	SH108251L	+Screw	2	
12	BH108111L	+Bolt	2	
13	WL108001L	+Washer	4	
14	RTC1956	+Detent Spring	1	
15	FRC6125	+Retainer-Spring	1	
16	WA105001L	+Washer	2	
17	NY105041L	+Nut	2	

NOTE(1): Both Of These Parts Are Now Obsolete. If They Are
Ordered We Will Supply The LT230T Type Transfer
Gear Change & The Appropriate Gate Plate Which Need
To Be Fitted In Place Of The One Supplied In the
Assembly.

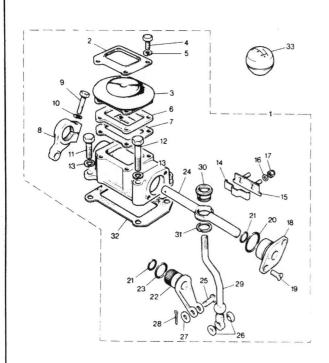

VS3892

181

MODEL LR110 - UP TO AUGUST 1986
BLOCK VS 3892
PAGE D 22.02
GROUP D

GEARBOX - 2.25 PETROL/DIESEL AND 2.5 DIESEL - TRANSFER BOX LT230R
               SERIAL PREFIX 10D/12D

ILL	PART NO	DESCRIPTION	QTY	REMARKS
18	FRC5574	+End Cover	1	
19	SF106201L	+Screw	2	
20	FRC4565	+O Ring	1	
21	FRC4509	+O Ring	2	
22	FRC5480	+Crank Arm	1	
23	FRC5479	+O Ring	1	
24	FRC6117	+Cross Shaft	1	
25	PC108321L	+Clevis Pin	1	
26	FRC4499	+Bush	2	
27	WA108051L	+Washer	1	
28	PS104121L	+Split Pin	1	
29	FRC7487	+Lever	1	
30	FRC5076	+Seat	1	
31	CR120215L	+Circlip	1	
32	FRC6306	+Gasket	1	
33	FRC6593	Knob	1	2/4 Wheel Drive
	FRC6595	Knob	1	Permanent 4 Wheel Drive

VS3892

LAND ROVER PARTS LTD

182

MODEL LR110 - UP TO AUGUST 1986
BLOCK TS 5012
PAGE D 24
GROUP D

GEARBOX - 2.25 PETROL/DIESEL AND 2.5 DIESEL - TRANSFER BOX LT230R
               SERIAL PREFIX 10D/12D

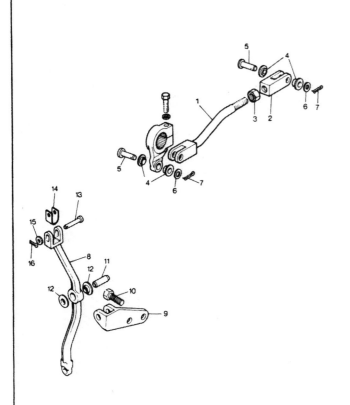

ILL	PART NO	DESCRIPTION	QTY	REMARKS
		TRANSFER GEAR CHANGE-CONTINUED		
1	FRC6000	Connecting Rod Assembly	1	
2	FRC5998	Clevis-High/Low Lever	1	
3	NY108041L	Locknut-Conn Rod	1	
4	FRC4499	Bush	4	
5	PC108321L	Clevis Pin	2	
6	WA108051L	Washer	2	
7	PS104127L	Split Pin	2	
8	FRC7315	Lever-Cross Shaft/Diff Lock	1	
9	FRC6066	Pivot Bracket-Lever	1	
10	SH108251L	Screw	2	
11	FRC7325	Pin-Spiral Roll	1	
12	FRC4499	Bush	2	
13	PC105401L	Clevis Pin	1	
14	FRC4505	Nylon Strip	1	
15	WA105001L	Washer	1	
16	PS103101L	Split Pin	1	

TS5012

LAND ROVER PARTS LTD

183

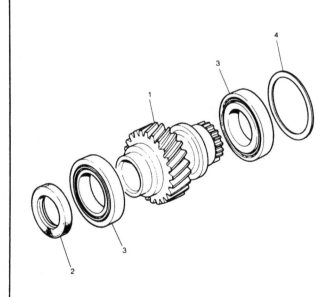

MODEL LR110 - UP TO AUGUST 1986
BLOCK VS 3891
PAGE D 26
GROUP D

GEARBOX - 2.25 PETROL/DIESEL AND 2.5 DIESEL - TRANSFER BOX LT230R
SERIAL PREFIX 10D/12D

ILL	PART NO	DESCRIPTION	QTY	REMARKS
		TRANSFER CASING		
1	FRC7026	TRANSFER CASING ASSEMBLY	1	
2	UKC24L	+Cup Plug	1	
3	FRC5595	+Stud	2	
4	608246	Plug-Oil Filler	2	
5	FRC6578	Speedo Housing Assembly	1	
6	FRC5409	Joint Washer-Speedo Housing	1	
7	SH110301L	Screw-Housing to Transfer Casing	5	
8	BH110091L	Screw	1	
9	WA110061L	Spring Washer	6	
10	FRC5594	Dowel-Output Housing to Transfer Casing	1	
11	FRC6943	Housing-Mainshaft Transfer Bearing	1	
12	FRC5413	Joint Washer	2	
13	FRC5668	Cover Power Take Off	1	
14	SF108251L	Screw-Countersunk	2	
15	BH110071L	Bolt	6	
16	WA110061L	Washer	6	
17	599552	Drain Plug	1	
18	FRC4808	Washer-Drain Plug	1	
19	FRC5415	Cover-Bottom-Transfer Casing	1	
20	FRC5416	Joint Washer-Bottom Cover	1	
21	BH108061L	Bolt	10	
22	WA108051L	Joint Washer	10	
23	FRC5419	O Ring-Intermediate Shaft	1	
24	FRC2482	Dowel-Hollow	1	
25	BH110081L	Bolt	3	
26	BH110091L	Bolt	1	
27	WL110001L	Washer	6	
28	NH110041L	Nut	2	
29	571134	Dowel	1	

VS3891

 **LAND ROVER PARTS LTD**

MODEL LR110 - UP TO AUGUST 1986
BLOCK VS 3729
PAGE D 28
GROUP D

GEARBOX - 2.25 PETROL/DIESEL AND 2.5 DIESEL - TRANSFER BOX LT230R
PREFIX 10D/12D

ILL	PART NO	DESCRIPTION	QTY	REMARKS
		TRANSFER GEAR-MAINSHAFT		
1	FRC5428	Gear-Mainshaft Transfer	1	
2	FRC2365	Oil Seal	1	
3	FRC5564	Bearing	2	
4		SELECTIVE SHIM-MAINSHAFT BEARING HOUSING		
	FRC9928	3.20mm	A/R	
	FRC9930	3.25mm	A/R	
	FRC9932	3.30mm	A/R	
	FRC9934	3.35mm	A/R	
	FRC9936	3.40mm	A/R	
	FRC9938	3.45mm	A/R	
	FRC9940	3.50mm	A/R	
	FRC9942	3.55mm	A/R	
	FRC9944	3.60mm	A/R	
	FRC9946	3.65mm	A/R	
	FRC9948	3.70mm	A/R	
	FRC9950	3.75mm	A/R	
	FRC9952	3.80mm	A/R	
	FRC9954	3.85mm	A/R	
	FRC9956	3.90mm	A/R	
	FRC9958	3.95mm	A/R	
	FRC9960	4.00mm	A/R	

VS3729

 **LAND ROVER PARTS LTD**

MODEL LR110 - UP TO AUGUST 1986
BLOCK VS 3680
PAGE D 30
GROUP D

GEARBOX - 2.25 PETROL/DIESEL AND 2.5 DIESEL - TRANSFER BOX LT230R
         PREFIX 10D/12D

ILL	PART NO	DESCRIPTION	QTY	REMARKS
		TRANSFER INTERMEDIATE SHAFT		
1	FRC5454	INTERMEDIATE SHAFT	1	
	FRC3196	+Plug	2	
2	532323	O Ring Shaft	1	
3	FRC5420	Gear-Intermediate Cluster	1	
4	594290	Bearing-Needle	2	
5	FRC2317	Spacer	1	
6	FRC6861	Thrust Washer	2	
7	FRC5494	Plate Retaining Inter Shaft	1	
8	WA108051L	Washer	1	
9	SH108201L	Bolt	1	

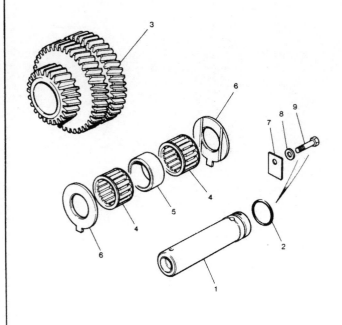

VS3680

LAND ROVER PARTS LTD

186

MODEL LR110 - UP TO AUGUST 1986
BLOCK VS 3728
PAGE D 32
GROUP D

GEARBOX - 2.25 PETROL/DIESEL AND 2.5 DIESEL - TRANSFER BOX LT230R
         SERIAL PREFIX 10D/12D

ILL	PART NO	DESCRIPTION	QTY	REMARKS
		TRANSFER FRONT HOUSING		
1	FRC6865	Housing-Front Output	1	
2	FRC6103	Joint Washer-Front Output Housing	1	
3	BH108061L	Bolt	7	
4	BH108181L	Bolt	1	
5	WA108051L	Spring Washer	8	
6	FRC6104	Cover-Front Output Housing	1	
7	FRC6105	Joint Washer	1	
8	SH108251L	Screw	7	
9	WA108051L	Spring Washer	7	
10	FRC6106	Housing-Cross Shaft-High/Low	1	
11	FRC7998	Joint Washer-Housing	1	
12	BH108111L	Bolt	6	
13	WA108051L	Washer	6	
14	FRC168	Breather Pipe	1	

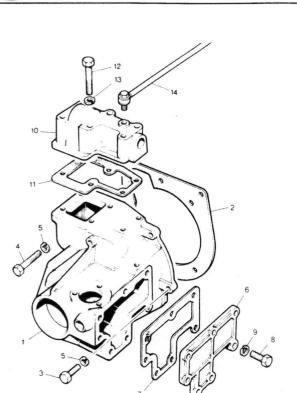

VS3728

LAND ROVER PARTS LTD

187

MODEL LR110 - UP TO AUGUST 1986
BLOCK VS 3893A
PAGE D 34
GROUP D

GEARBOX - 2.25 PETROL/DIESEL AND 2.5 DIESEL - TRANSFER BOX LT230R
SERIAL PREFIX 10D/12D

ILL	PART NO	DESCRIPTION	QTY	REMARKS
		TRANSFER DIFF LOCK		
1	FRC5500	Shaft-Front Output	1	2/4 Wheel Drive Prefix 10D Only
	FRC5449	Shaft-Front Output	1	Permanent 4 Wheel Drive
2	FRC5440	Dog Clutch-Front Drive Lock Up	1	
3		SELECTIVE SHIM-FRONT OUTPUT TAPER BEARING		
	FTC726	+2.00mm		
	FTC728	+2.05mm	1	
	FTC730	+2.10mm	1	
	FTC732	+2.15mm	1	
	FTC734	+2.20mm	1	
	FTC736	+2.25mm	1	
	FTC738	+2.30mm	1	
	FTC740	+2.35mm	1	
	FTC742	+2.40mm	1	
	FTC744	+2.45mm	1	
	FTC746	+2.50mm	1	
	FTC748	+2.55mm	1	
	FTC750	+2.60mm	1	
	FTC752	+2.65mm	1	
	FTC754	+2.70mm	1	
	FTC756	+2.75mm	1	
	FTC758	+2.80mm	1	
	FTC760	+2.85mm	1	
	FTC762	+2.90mm	1	
	FTC764	+2.95mm	1	
	FTC766	+3.00mm	1	
	FTC768	+3.05mm	1	
	FTC770	+3.10mm	1	
	FTC772	+3.15mm	1	
	FTC774	+3.20mm	1	
	FTC776	+3.25mm	1	
4	FRC7871	Bearing-Taper	1	)2/4 Wheel Drive
5	FRC5498	Bearing-Roller	1	)Only Prefix 10D)Only

VS3893A

LAND ROVER PARTS LTD

188

MODEL LR110 - UP TO AUGUST 1986
BLOCK VS 3893A
PAGE D 34.02
GROUP D

GEARBOX - 2.25 PETROL/DIESEL AND 2.5 DIESEL - TRANSFER BOX LT230R
SERIAL PREFIX 10D/12D - CONTINUED

ILL	PART NO	DESCRIPTION	QTY	REMARKS
6	FRC6069	Shaft-Main Drive	1	
7	FRC6109	Selector Fork-Diff Lock	1	
8	FRC6030	Selector Shaft-Diff Lock	1	
9	FRC6110	Plug-Selector Shaft	1	
10	FRC5468	Spring-Diff Lock	1	
11	FRC5469	Clip	2	
12	FRC7686	HOUSING ASSY-SELECTOR FINGER	1	
13	FRC7652	Connecting Link	1	
14	NY108051L	+Nut	1	
15	WA108051L	+Washer-Plain	1	
16	FRC5473	O Ring	1	
17	FRC5576	+O Ring	1	
18	SH108251L	Screw	3	
19	WA108051L	Washer	3	
20	SU112101L	Plug-Detent	1	
21	FRC5562	Spring-Detent	1	
22	571146	Ball-Detent	1	
23	PRC2911	Switch-Diff Lock	1	
24	22A1613L	Locknut-Switch	1	

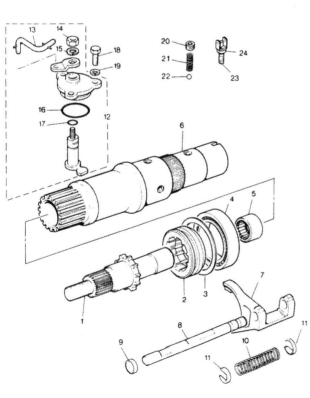

VS3893A

LAND ROVER PARTS LTD

189

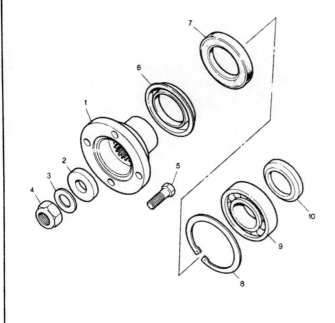

MODEL LR110 - UP TO AUGUST 1986
BLOCK VS 3725
PAGE D 36
GROUP D

GEARBOX - 2.25 PETROL/DIESEL AND 2.5 DIESEL - TRANSFER BOX LT230R
        PREFIX 10D/12D

ILL	PART NO	DESCRIPTION	QTY	REMARKS
		TRANSFER FRONT FLANGE		
1	FRC5442	Flange-Front Output	1	
2	FRC2464	Sealing Washer	1	
3	571468	Washer-Shaft	1	
4	NY120041L	Nut-Shaft	1	
5	BT606101L	Bolt-Flange	4	
6	FRC6121	Mudshield	1	
7	FRC7043	Oil Seal	1	
8	216962	Circlip	1	
9	RTC3406	Bearing	1	
10	FRC5439	Spacer	1	

VS3725

190

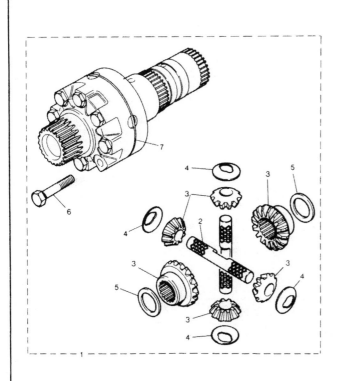

MODEL LR110 - UP TO AUGUST 1986
BLOCK TS 5703
PAGE D 38
GROUP D

GEARBOX - 2.25 PETROL/DIESEL AND 2.5 DIESEL - TRANSFER BOX LT230R
        PREFIX 12D

ILL	PART NO	DESCRIPTION	QTY	REMARKS
		TRANSFER DIFFERENTIAL		
1	FRC7569	DIFFERENTIAL ASSEMBLY	1	
2	RTC3397	+Cross Shaft Kit	1	Matched Pair
3	RTC4490	+Differential Gears & Thrust	1	Matched Set
		Washer Kit		
4	FRC6968	++Thrust Washer	4	
5		+SELECTIVE THRUST WASHER		
		DIFF WHEEL		
	FRC6956	1.05mm	A/R	
	FRC6958	1.15mm	A/R	
	FRC6960	1.25mm	A/R	
	FRC6962	1.35mm	A/R	
	FRC6964	1.45mm	A/R	
6	BH110121L	+Bolt-Diff Case	8	
7	FRC7499	+Retaining Ring	1	

TS5703

191

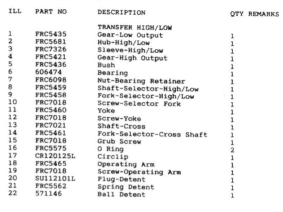

MODEL LR110 - UP TO AUGUST 1986
BLOCK VS 3758A
PAGE D 38.02
GROUP D

GEARBOX - 2.25 PETROL/DIESEL AND 2.5 DIESEL - TRANSFER BOX LT230R
PREFIX 10D/12D

ILL	PART NO	DESCRIPTION	QTY REMARKS
		TRANSFER HIGH/LOW	
1	FRC5435	Gear-Low Output	1
2	FRC5681	Hub-High/Low	1
3	FRC7326	Sleeve-High/Low	1
4	FRC5421	Gear-High Output	1
5	FRC5436	Bush	1
6	606474	Bearing	1
7	FRC6098	Nut-Bearing Retainer	1
8	FRC5459	Shaft-Selector-High/Low	1
9	FRC5458	Fork-Selector-High/Low	1
10	FRC7018	Screw-Selector Fork	1
11	FRC5460	Yoke	1
12	FRC7018	Screw-Yoke	1
13	FRC7021	Shaft-Cross	1
14	FRC5461	Fork-Selector-Cross Shaft	1
15	FRC7018	Grub Screw	1
16	FRC5575	O Ring	2
17	CR120125L	Circlip	1
18	FRC5465	Operating Arm	1
19	FRC7018	Screw-Operating Arm	1
20	SU112101L	Plug-Detent	1
21	FRC5562	Spring Detent	1
22	571146	Ball Detent	1

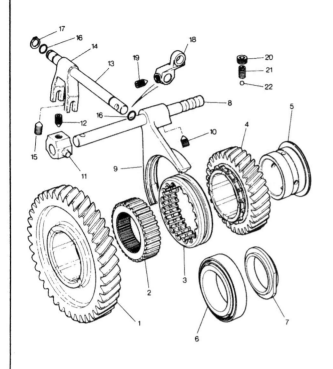

VS3758A

 **LAND ROVER PARTS LTD**

MODEL LR110 - UP TO AUGUST 1986
BLOCK VS 3730A
PAGE D 38.04
GROUP D

GEARBOX - 2.25 PETROL/DIESEL AND 2.5 DIESEL - TRANSFER BOX LT230R
SERIAL PREFIX 10D/12D

ILL	PART NO	DESCRIPTION	QTY REMARKS
		TRANSFER REAR FLANGE	
1	FRC5450	Shaft-Rear Output	1
2	FRC3162	Speedo Worm	1
3	FRC5446	Spacer-Speedo Worm	1
4	RTC3406	Bearing	1
5	216962	Circlip	1
6	FRC7043	Oil Seal	1
7	571970	Oil Shield	1
8	571682	Circlip	1
9	FRC3602	Bolt	4
10	FRC5438	Flange-Rear-Output	1
11	FRC2464	Sealing Washer	1
12	571468	Washer	1
13	NY120041L	Nut	1
14	FRC3310	Speedo Drive Gear & Spindle	1
15	571665	O Ring	1
16	FRC3286	Housing-Speedo Spindle	1
17	AAU2304	Oil Seal	1
18	533765	Plate-Retaining Speedo Cable	1
19	571536	Stud	1
20	WA106041L	Washer	1
21	NY106041L	Nut	1

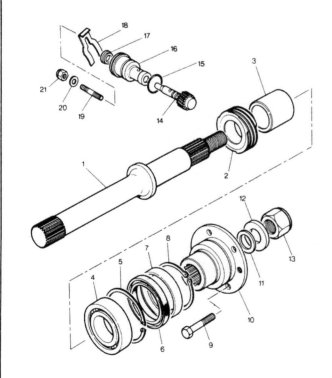

VS3730A

 **LAND ROVER PARTS LTD**

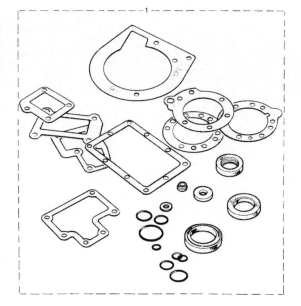

TS6373

MODEL LR110 - UP TO AUGUST 1986
BLOCK TS 6373
PAGE D 38.08
GROUP D

GEARBOX - 2.25 PETROL/DIESEL AND 2.5 DIESEL - TRANSFER BOX LT230R
          SERIAL PREFIX 10D/12D

ILL	PART NO	DESCRIPTION	QTY	REMARKS
1	RTC3890	GASKET & SEAL KIT	1	
	FRC5486	+Gasket-Gearchange Housing	1	
	FRC6306	+Gasket-Gearchange Housing	1	
	FRC4565	+O Ring-Transfer Gearchange	1	
	FRC5479	+O Ring-Transfer Gearchange	1	
	FRC4509	+O Ring-Transfer Gearchange	2	
	FRC5416	+Joint Washer-Bottom Cover	1	
	FRC5409	+Joint Washer-Speedo Housing	1	
	FRC5413	+Joint Washer-Housing	2	
	FRC4808	+Joint Washer-Drain Plug	1	
	FRC5419	+O Ring-Intershaft	1	
	FRC2365	+Oil Seal-Mainshaft	1	
	532323	+O Ring-Shaft	1	
	FRC6103	+Joint Washer-Frt Output Hsg	1	
	FRC6105	+Joint Washer-Frt Output Hsg	1	
	FRC7998	+Joint Washer-Frt Output Hsg	1	
	FRC2464	+Sealing Washer-Output Flange	2	
	FRC7043	+Oil Seal-Selector Finger	1	
	FRC5473	+O Ring-Selector Finger	1	
	FRC5576	+O Ring-Selector Finger	1	
	FRC7043	+Oil Seal-Rear Output Shaft	1	
	571665	+O Ring-Speedo Spindle	1	
	AAU2304	+Oil Seal-Speedo Spindle	1	

 LAND ROVER PARTS LTD

194

BLANK   **BLANK**

 LAND ROVER PARTS LTD

195

MODEL LR110 - UP TO AUGUST 1986
BLOCK VS 3742
PAGE D 38.12
GROUP D

GEARBOX - 4 CYLINDER MODELS - TRANSFER BOX LT230T

ILL	PART NO	DESCRIPTION	QTY	REMARKS
1	FRC9469N	Transfer Box Assembly-New	1	Prefix 20D

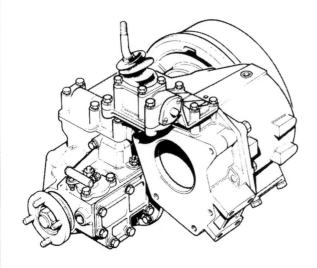

VS3742

196

MODEL LR110 - UP TO AUGUST 1986
BLOCK VS 3892
PAGE D 38.14
GROUP D

GEARBOX - 4 CYLINDER MODELS - TRANSFER BOX LT230T - PREFIX 20D

ILL	PART NO	DESCRIPTION	QTY	REMARKS
1	FRC7941	TRANSFER GEARCHANGE ASSY	1	Note(1)
	FRC9555	TRANSFER GEARCHANGE ASSY	1	Note(2)
2	FRC6873	+Plate	1	
3	FRC6872	+Grommet	1	
4	SH106201L	+Screw	4	
5	WA106041L	+Washer-Plain	4	
6	FRC7944	+Gateplate	1	Note(1)
	FRC8561	+Gateplate	1	Note(2)
7	FRC5486	+Gasket	1	
8	FRC5478	+Operating Arm	1	
9	BH106051L	+Bolt	1	
10	WA106041L	+Washer-Plain	1	
11	SH108251L	+Screw	2	
12	BH108111L	+Bolt	2	
13	WL108001L	+Washer-Spring	4	
14	RTC1956	+Detent Spring	1	
15	FRC6125	+Retainer-Spring	1	
16	WA105001L	+Washer	2	
17	NY105041L	+Nut	2	

NOTE(1): Earlier Type With Cross Shaft Lever And Pivot Bracket

NOTE(2): For Use With Later Type of LT230T Transfer Gearbox
Where The Connecting Rod Joins the Operating Arm On
The Gear Change & The Operating Arm For The Selector
Finger.

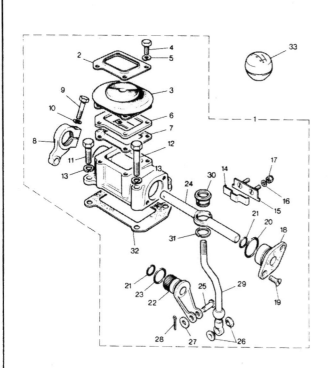

VS3892

197

MODEL LR110 - UP TO AUGUST 1986
BLOCK VS 3892
PAGE D 38.16
GROUP D

GEARBOX - 4 CYLINDER MODELS - TRANSFER BOX LT230T - PREFIX 20D

ILL	PART NO	DESCRIPTION	QTY	REMARKS
		TRANSFER GEARCHANGE ASSY		
18	FRC5574	+End Cover	1	
19	SF106201L	+Screw	2	
20	FRC4565	+O Ring	1	
21	FRC4509	+O Ring	2	
22	FRC5480	+Crank Arm	1	
23	FRC5479	+O Ring	1	
24	FRC6117	+Cross-Shaft	1	Note(1)
	FRC8203	+Cross-Shaft	1	Note(2)
25	PC108321L	+Clevis Pin	1	Note(1)
	FRC8766	+Clevis Pin	1	Note(2)
26	FRC4499	+Bush	2	
27	WA108051L	+Washer	1	
28	PS104127L	+Split Pin	1	Note(1)
	FRC8548	+Clip-Clevis	1	Note(2)
29	FRC8560	+Lever	1	Note(1)
	FRC7487	+Lever-Gearchange	1	Note(2)
30	FRC5076	+Seat-Gear Lever	1	
31	CR120215L	+Circlip	1	
32	FRC6306	+Gasket	1	
	FRC7930	+Plug-Housing	1	
33	FRC6595	Knob	1	

NOTE(1): Earlier Type With Cross Shaft Lever And Pivot Bracket

NOTE(2): For Use With Later Type Of LT230T Transfer Gearbox
Where The Connecting Rod Joins The Operating Arm On the
Gearchange & The Operating Arm For The Selector Finger.

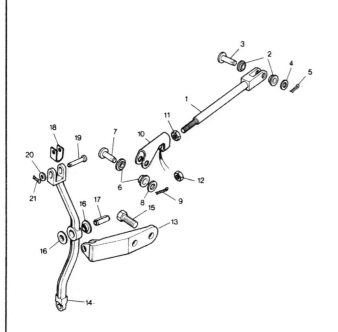

VS3892

LAND ROVER PARTS LTD

MODEL LR110 - UP TO AUGUST 1986
BLOCK TS 5351
PAGE D 38.18
GROUP D

GEARBOX - 4 CYLINDER MODELS - TRANSFER BOX LT230T - PREFIX 20D

ILL	PART NO	DESCRIPTION	QTY	REMARKS
		TRANSFER GEARCHANGE		
1	FRC6000	Connecting Rod Assembly	1	
2	FRC4499	Bush	2	
3	PC108321L	Clevis Pin	1	
4	WA108051L	Washer	1	
5	PS104127L	Split Pin	1	
6	FRC4499	Bush	2	
7	PC108321L	Clevis Pin	1	
8	WA108051L	Washer	1	
9	PS104127L	Split Pin	1	
10	FRC8075	Clevis-High/Low	1	
11	NY108041L	Nut	1	
12	NT108041L	Nut	1	
13	FRC6066	Pivot Bracket-Lever	1	
14	FRC7315	Lever-Cross Shaft/Diff Lock	1	
15	SH108251L	Screw	2	
16	FRC4499	Bush	2	
17	FRC7325	Pin-Spirol Roll	1	
18	FRC4505	Nylon Strip	1	
19	PC105401L	Clevis Pin	1	
20	WA105001L	Washer	1	
21	PS103101L	Split Pin	1	

TS5351

LAND ROVER PARTS LTD

MODEL LR110 - UP TO AUGUST 1986
BLOCK TS 6125
PAGE D 38.20
GROUP D

GEARBOX - **4** CYLINDER MODELS - TRANSFER BOX LT230T - PREFIX 20D

ILL	PART NO	DESCRIPTION	QTY	REMARKS
		TRANSFER GEARCHANGE - ALTERNATIVE TYPE		
1	FRC6000	Connecting Rod Assembly	1	
2	FRC4499	Bush	4	
3	FRC8075	Clevis-Connecting Rod	1	
4	FRC8767	Clevis Pin	2	
5	FRC8548	Safety Clip-Clevis	2	
6	FRC8204	Diff Lock Arm	1	
7	FRC8202	Pivot Pin	1	
8	NH108041L	Nut	1	
9	FRC8548	Safety Clip	2	
10	FRC8547	Clevis Pin	1	
11	NY108041L	Nut	1	
12	NT108041L	Nut	1	
13	FRC8768	Clevis Pin	1	
14	FRC8769	Safety Clip	1	

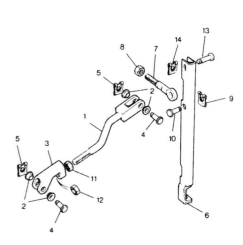

TS6125

MODEL LR110 - UP TO AUGUST 1986
BLOCK TS 5308A
PAGE D 38.22A
GROUP D

GEARBOX - **4** CYLINDER MODELS - TRANSFER BOX LT230T - PREFIX 20D

ILL	PART NO	DESCRIPTION	QTY	REMARKS
		TRANSFER CASING		
1	FRC8293	TRANSFER CASING ASSEMBLY	1	
2	FRC5595	+Stud	2	
3	608246	Plug-Oil Filter	2	
4	FRC7447	Speedo Housing Assembly	1	
5	FRC5409	Joint Washer-Speedo Housing	1	
6	SH110301L	Screw-Housing to Transfer	5	
7	BH110091L	Screw-Housing to Transfer	1	
8	WA110061L	Washer-Housing to Transfer	6	
9	FRC5594	Dowel-Housing to Transfer	1	
10	FRC6943	Housing-Mainshaft Transfer Bearing	1	
11	FRC5668	Cover-Power Take Off	1	
12	FRC5413	Joint Washer	2	
13	SF108251L	Screw	2	
14	BH110071L	Bolt	6	
15	WA110061L	Washer	6	
16	599552	Drain Plug	1	
17	FRC4808	Washer-Drain Plug	1	
18	FRC5415	Cover-Bottom-Transfer Case	1	
19	FRC5416	Joint Washer-Bottom Cover	1	
20	BH108061L	Bolt	10	
21	WA108051L	Washer	10	
22	FRC8292	O Ring	1	
23	FRC2482	Dowel-Hollow	1	
24	BH110081L	Bolt	3	
25	BH110091L	Bolt	1	
26	WL110001L	Washer	6	
27	571536	Stud-Cable Retainer	1	

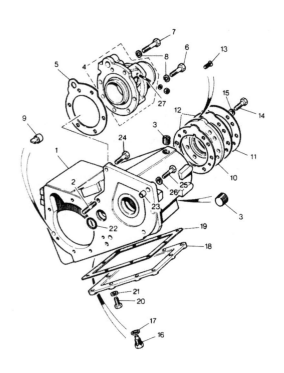

TS5308A

MODEL LR110 - UP TO AUGUST 1986
BLOCK VS 3729
PAGE D 38.24
GROUP D

GEARBOX - 4 CYLINDER MODELS - TRANSFER BOX LT230T - PREFIX 20D

ILL	PART NO	DESCRIPTION	QTY	REMARKS
		TRANSFER GEAR-MAINSHAFT		
1	FRC5428	Gear-Mainshaft Transfer	1	Suffix B Only
	FRC8917	Gear-Mainshaft Transfer	1	Suffix C Only
2	FRC2365	Oil Seal	1	
3	FRC5564	Bearing	2	
4		SELECTIVE SHIM-MAINSHAFT BEARING HOUSING		
	FRC6537	3.25mm	A/R	
	FRC6539	3.35mm	A/R	
	FRC6541	3.45mm	A/R	
	FRC6543	3.55mm	A/R	
	FRC6545	3.65mm	A/R	
	FRC6547	3.75mm	A/R	
	FRC6549	3.85mm	A/R	
	FRC6551	3.95mm	A/R	
	FRC9928	3.20mm	A/R	
	FRC9930	3.25mm	A/R	
	FRC9932	3.30mm	A/R	
	FRC9934	3.35mm	A/R	
	FRC9936	3.40mm	A/R	
	FRC9938	3.45mm	A/R	
	FRC9940	3.50mm	A/R	
	FRC9942	3.55mm	A/R	
	FRC9944	3.60mm	A/R	
	FRC9946	3.65mm	A/R	
	FRC9948	3.70mm	A/R	
	FRC9950	3.75mm	A/R	
	FRC9952	3.80mm	A/R	
	FRC9954	3.85mm	A/R	
	FRC9956	3.90mm	A/R	
	FRC9958	3.95mm	A/R	
	FRC9960	4.00mm	A/R	

VS3729

LAND ROVER PARTS LTD

MODEL LR110 - UP TO AUGUST 1986
BLOCK TS 5368
PAGE D 38.26
GROUP D

GEARBOX - 4 CYLINDER MODELS - TRANSFER BOX LT230T - PREFIX 20D

ILL	PART NO	DESCRIPTION	QTY	REMARKS
		TRANSFER INTERMEDIATE SHAFT		
1	FRC8291	Intermediate Shaft	1	
2	FRC7439	O Ring-Shaft	1	
3	FRC7426	Gear-Intermediate Cluster	1	Suffix B Only
	FRC9462	Gear-Intermediate Cluster	1	Suffix C Only
4	FRC7810	Bearing	2	
5	FRC7437	Spacer-Collapsible	1	
6	FRC7454	Circlip	2	
7	FRC7452	Plate-Anti Rotation-Int/Shaft	1	
8	FRC7453	Nut-Intermediate Shaft	1	
9	SH108201L	Screw	1	
10	WA108051L	Washer	1	

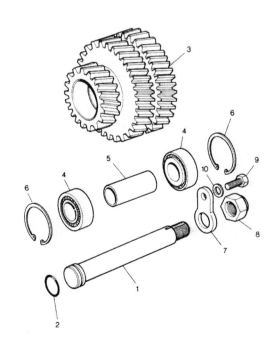

TS5368

LAND ROVER PARTS LTD

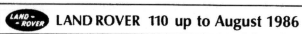
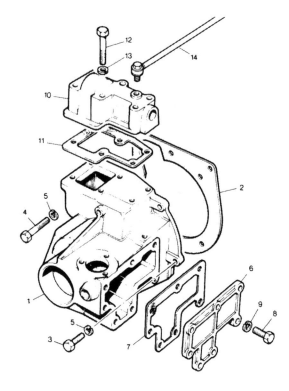

MODEL LR110 - UP TO AUGUST 1986
BLOCK VS 3728
PAGE D 38.28
GROUP D

GEARBOX - 4 CYLINDER MODELS - TRANSFER BOX LT230T - PREFIX 20D

ILL	PART NO	DESCRIPTION	QTY	REMARKS
		TRANSFER-FRONT HOUSING		
1	FRC8299	Housing-Front Output	1	
2	FRC6103	Joint Washer-Output Housing	1	
3	BH108061L	Bolt	7	
4	BH108181L	Bolt	1	
5	WA108051L	Washer	8	
6	FRC6104	Cover-Front Output Housing	1	
7	FRC6105	Joint Washer	1	
8	SH108251L	Screw	7	
9	WA108051L	Washer	7	
10	FRC6106	Housing-Cross Shaft-High/Low	1	
11	FRC7998	Joint Washer-Housing	1	
12	BH108111L	Bolt	6	
13	WA108051L	Washer	6	
14	FRC167	Breather Pipe	1	
	219676	Clip-Pipe-Single	1	

VS3728

 LAND ROVER PARTS LTD

MODEL LR110 - UP TO AUGUST 1986
BLOCK VS 3735C
PAGE D 38.30
GROUP D

GEARBOX - 4 CYLINDER MODELS - TRANSFER BOX LT230T - PREFIX 20D

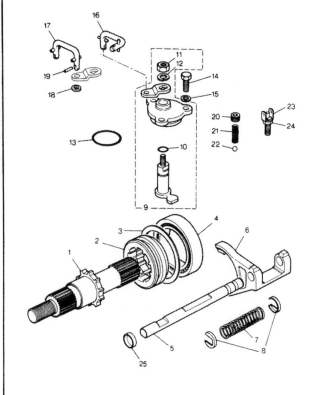

ILL	PART NO	DESCRIPTION	QTY	REMARKS
		TRANSFER DIFF LOCK		
1	FRC5449	Shaft-Front Output	1	
2	FRC5440	Dog Clutch-Front Drive Lock Up	1	
	FRC5575	O Ring-Dog Clutch	1	
3		SELECTIVE SHIM-FRONT OUTPUT TAPER BEARING		
	FTC726	+2.00mm		
	FTC728	+2.05mm	1	
	FTC730	+2.10mm	1	
	FTC732	+2.15mm	1	
	FTC734	+2.20mm	1	
	FTC736	+2.25mm	1	
	FTC738	+2.30mm	1	
	FTC740	+2.35mm	1	
	FTC742	+2.40mm	1	
	FTC744	+2.45mm	1	
	FTC746	+2.50mm	1	
	FTC748	+2.55mm	1	
	FTC750	+2.60mm	1	
	FTC752	+2.65mm	1	
	FTC754	+2.70mm	1	
	FTC756	+2.75mm	1	
	FTC758	+2.80mm	1	
	FTC760	+2.85mm	1	
	FTC762	+2.90mm	1	
	FTC764	+2.95mm	1	
	FTC766	+3.00mm	1	
	FTC768	+3.05mm	1	
	FTC770	+3.10mm	1	
	FTC772	+3.15mm	1	
	FTC774	+3.20mm	1	
	FTC776	+3.25mm	1	
4	FRC7871	Bearing-Taper	1	
5	FRC6030	Selector Shaft-Diff Lock	1	
6	FRC6109	Selector Fork-Diff Lock	1	
7	FRC5468	Spring-Diff Lock	1	
8	FRC5469	Clip-Spring	2	

VS3735C

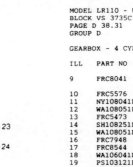

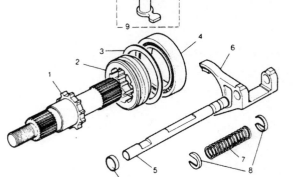

MODEL LR110 - UP TO AUGUST 1986
BLOCK VS 3735C
PAGE D 38.31
GROUP D

GEARBOX - 4 CYLINDER MODELS - TRANSFER BOX LT230T - PREFIX 20D

ILL	PART NO	DESCRIPTION	QTY	REMARKS
9	FRC8041	HOUSING ASSEMBLY-SELECTOR FINGER	1	
10	FRC5576	+O Ring	1	
11	NY108041L	+Nut	1	
12	WA108051L	+Washer	1	
13	FRC5473	O Ring	1	
14	SH108251L	Screw	3	
15	WA108051L	Washer	3	
16	FRC7948	Connecting Link Assembly	1	Note(1)
17	FRC8544	Connecting Link Assembly	1	)
18	WA106041L	Washer	2	)Note(2)
19	PS103121L	Split Pin	2	)
20	SU112101L	Plug-Detent	1	
21	FRC5562	Spring-Detent	1	
22	571146	Ball-Detent	1	
23	PRC2911	Switch-Diff Lock	1	
24	22A1613L	Locknut-Switch	1	
25	FRC6110	Plug-Selector Shaft	1	

NOTE(1):   Early Type With 'Dog Leg'Shape Link

NOTE(2):   Late Type With 'Horse Shoe' Shape Link.

VS3735C

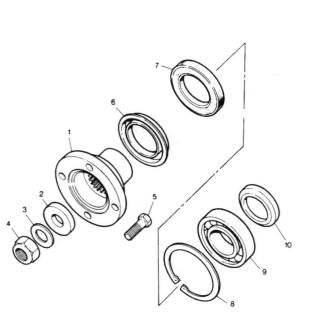

MODEL LR110 - UP TO AUGUST 1986
BLOCK VS 3725
PAGE D 38.32
GROUP D

GEARBOX - 4 CYLINDER MODELS - TRANSFER BOX LT230T - PREFIX 20D

ILL	PART NO	DESCRIPTION	QTY	REMARKS
		TRANSFER FRONT FLANGE		
1	FRC5442	Flange-Front Output	1	
2	FRC2464	Sealing Washer	1	
3	571468	Washer-Shaft	1	
4	NY120041L	Nut-Shaft	1	
5	BT606101L	Bolt-Flange	4	
6	FRC6121	Mudshield	1	
7	FRC7043	Oil Seal	1	
8	216962	Circlip	1	
9	RTC3406	Bearing	1	
10	FRC5439	Spacer	1	

VS3725

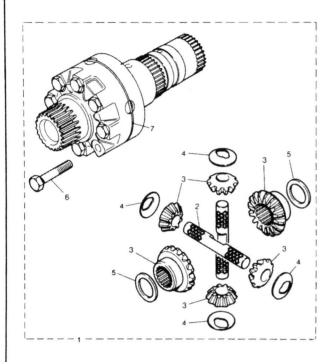

MODEL LR110 - UP TO AUGUST 1986
BLOCK TS 5703
PAGE D 38.34
GROUP D

GEARBOX - 4 CYLINDER MODELS - TRANSFER BOX LT230T - PREFIX 20D

ILL	PART NO	DESCRIPTION	QTY	REMARKS
		TRANSFER DIFFERENTIAL		
1	FRC7926	Differential Assembly	1	
2	FRC6674	Cross Shaft	1	NLS-Use RTC3397
	RTC3397	Cross Shaft Kit	1	Matched Pair
3	RTC4490	DIFFERENTIAL GEARS-BALANCED SET	1	
4	FRC6968	+Thrust Washer	4	
5		SELECTIVE THRUST WASHER-DIFF WHEEL		
	FRC9845	1.05mm	A/R	
	FRC9847	1.15mm	A/R	
	FRC9849	1.25mm	A/R	
	FRC9851	1.35mm	A/R	
	FRC9853	1.45mm	A/R	
6	BH110121L	Bolt-Diff Case	8	
7	FRC7499	Retaining Ring	1	

TS5703

 **LAND ROVER PARTS LTD**

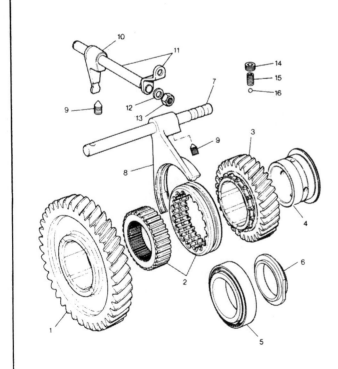

MODEL LR110 - UP TO AUGUST 1986
BLOCK TS 5762
PAGE D 38.36
GROUP D

GEARBOX - 4 CYLINDER MODELS - TRANSFER BOX LT230T - PREFIX 20D

ILL	PART NO	DESCRIPTION	QTY	REMARKS
		TRANSFER HIGH/LOW		
1	FRC7434	Gear-Low Output	1	Suffix B Only
	FRC9531	Gear-Low Output	1	Suffix C Only
2	RTC5064	Hub & Sleeve Assy-High/Low	1	Matched Pair
3	FRC7427	Gear-High Output	1	Suffix B Only
	FRC9532	Gear-High Output	1	Suffix C Only
4	FRC7441	Bush	1	
5	606474	Bearing	1	
6	FRC7970	Nut-Bearing Retainer	1	
7	FRC7457	Shaft-Selector-High/Low	1	Suffix B Only
	FRC9513	Shaft-Selector-High/Low	1	Suffix C Only
8	FRC5458	Fork-Selector High/Low	1	
9	FRC7018	Screw-Selector Fork	1	
10	FRC7929	Selector Finger	1	
11	FRC8091	Operating Arm-High/Low	1	NLS-Use FRC8900
	FRC8900	Operating Arm-High/Low	1	
12	WA108051L	Washer	1	)Only Needed with
13	NY108041L	Nut	1	)FRC8091
14	SU112101L	Plug-Detent	1	)Suffix B Only
15	FRC5562	Spring-Detent	1	)
14	FRC9549	Plug-Detent	1	)Suffix C Only
15	FRC9546	Spring-Detent	1	)
16	571146	Ball-Detent	1	

TS5762

 **LAND ROVER PARTS LTD**

MODEL LR110 - UP TO AUGUST 1986
BLOCK TS 5307
PAGE D 38.38
GROUP D

GEARBOX - 4 CYLINDER MODELS - TRANSFER BOX LT230T - PREFIX 20D

ILL	PART NO	DESCRIPTION	QTY	REMARKS
		TRANSFER REAR FLANGE		
1	FRC5450	Shaft-Rear Output	1	
2	FRC3162	Speedo Worm	1	
3	FRC5446	Spacer-Speedo Worm	1	
4	RTC3406	Bearing	1	
5	216962	Circlip	1	
6	FRC7043	Oil Seal	1	
7	571970	Oil Shield	1	
8	571682	Circlip	1	
9	FRC3602	Bolt	1	
10	FRC5438	Flange-Rear Output	1	
11	FRC2464	Sealing Washer	1	
12	571468	Washer	1	
13	NY120041L	Nut	1	
14	FRC3310	Speedo Drive Gear & Spindle	1	
15	571665	O Ring	1	
16	FRC3286	Housing Speedo Spindle	1	
17	AAU2304	Oil Seal	1	
18	533765	Plate-Retaining Speedo Cable	1	

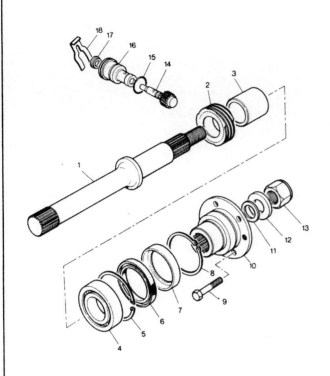

TS5307

LAND ROVER PARTS LTD

210

MODEL LR110 - UP TO AUGUST 1986
BLOCK TS 6373
PAGE D 38.40
GROUP D

GEARBOX - 4 CYLINDER MODELS - TRANSFER BOX LT230T - PREFIX 20D

ILL	PART NO	DESCRIPTION	QTY	REMARKS
1	RTC3890	GASKET & SEALS KIT	1	
	FRC5486	+Gasket-Gearchange Housing	1	
	FRC6306	+Gasket-Gearchange Housing	1	
	FRC4565	+O Ring-Transfer Gearchange	1	
	FRC5479	+O Ring-Transfer Gearchange	1	
	FRC4509	+O Ring-Transfer Gearchange	2	
	FRC5416	+Joint Washer-Bottom Cover	1	
	FRC5409	+joint Washer-Speedo Housing	1	
	FRC5413	+Joint Washer-Housing	2	
	FRC4808	+Joint Washer-Drain Plug	1	
	FRC5419	+O Ring-Intershaft	1	
	FRC2365	+Oil Seal-Mainshaft	1	
	532323	+O Ring-Shaft	1	
	FRC6103	+Joint Washer-Frt Output Hsg	1	
	FRC6105	+Joint Washer-Frt Output Hsg	1	
	FRC7998	+Joint Washer-Frt Output Hsg	1	
	FRC2464	+Sealing Washer-Output Flange	2	
	FRC7043	+Oil Seal-Output Flange	1	
	FRC5473	+O Ring-Selector Finger	1	
	FRC5576	+O Ring-Selector Finger	1	
	FRC7043	+Oil Seal-Rear Output Shaft	1	
	571665	+O Ring-Speedo Spindle	1	
	AAU2304	+Oil Seal-Speedo Spindle	1	

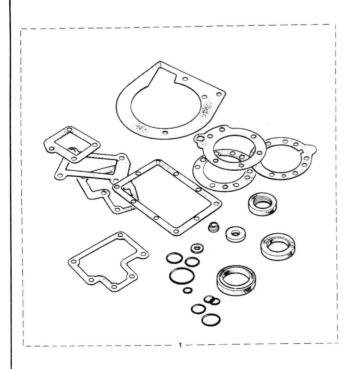

1

TS6373

LAND ROVER PARTS LTD

211

MODEL LR110 - UP TO AUGUST 1986
BLOCK VS 4011
PAGE D 38.42
GROUP D

GEARBOX - GEARBOX MOUNTINGS - 4 CYLINDER

ILL	PART NO	DESCRIPTION	QTY	REMARKS
1	NRC5742	Mounting Bracket-RH	1	
2	NRC5743	Mounting Bracket-LH	1	
3	BH108201	Bolt	6	
4	WP185	Washer	6	
5	WA108051L	Plain Washer	6	
6	WL108001L	Spring Washer	6	
7	NH108041L	Nut	6	
8	NRC7603	Mounting Rubber	2	2.25 Litre
	NRC9560	Mounting Rubber	2	2.5 Litre
9	WA110061L	Plain Washer	4	
10	WL110001	Spring Washer	4	
11	NH110041L	Nut	4	
12	NRC8204	Mounting Plate	2	
13	SH112201	Screw	8	
14	NRC9561	Tab Washer	4	

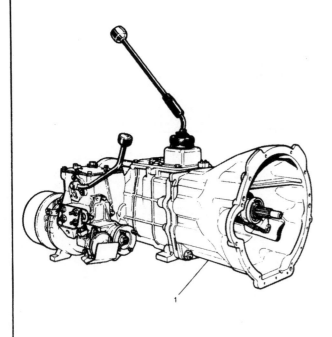

VS4011

LAND ROVER PARTS LTD

212

MODEL LR110 - UP TO AUGUST 1986
BLOCK VS 3101
PAGE D 40
GROUP D

GEARBOX - V8 - 4 SPEED - SERVICE GEARBOX ASSEMBLY

ILL	PART NO	DESCRIPTION	QTY	
1	FRC3133N	Gearbox Assembly New	1	)Prefix 13C
	FRC3133R	Gearbox Assembly Rebuilt	1	)

VS3101

LAND ROVER PARTS LTD

MODEL LR110 - UP TO AUGUST 1986
BLOCK M 953
PAGE D 42
GROUP D

GEARBOX - V8 - 4 SPEED - BELL HOUSING

ILL	PART NO	DESCRIPTION	QTY	REMARKS
1	FRC2858	Bell Housing	1	
2	BH112121L	Bolt M12 x 60mm-Gearbox Casing to Bell Housing	2	
3	WM112001L	Spring-Washer	4	
4	NH112041L	Nut	2	
5	BH116161L	Bolt M16 x 80mm-Gearbox Casing to Bell Housing	2	
6	WM116001L	Washer-Spring	4	
7	NH116041L	Nut	2	
8	3290	Plug Wading	1	
9	BH506161L	Bolt-Bell Housing to Cylinder Block	8	
10	WM600061L	Washer-Spring	8	

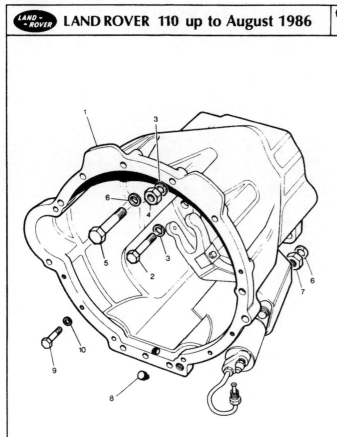

M953

LAND ROVER PARTS LTD

214

MODEL LR110 - UP TO AUGUST 1986
BLOCK VS 1637
PAGE D 44
GROUP D

GEARBOX - V8 - 4 SPEED - BOTTOM COVER FOR BELL HOUSING

ILL	PART NO	DESCRIPTION	QTY	REMARKS
1	FRC2859	Cover-Bottom Bell Housing	1	
2	594087	Seal-Cover to Bell Housing	1	
3	SH106451L	Bolt-Bottom Cover to Bell Housing	5	
4	WM106001L	Washer-Bottom Cover to Bell Housing	5	
5	NH106041L	Nut	5	
6	SH106251L	Bolt-Bottom Cover to Bell Housing	2	
7	WM106001L	Washer Spring-Bottom Cover to Bell Housing	2	
8	594134	Bolt	2	
9	WM108001L	Washer Spring	2	
10	SH504041L	Bolt	2	
11	232038	Washer	2	

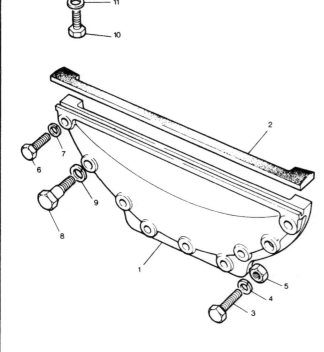

VS1637

LAND ROVER PARTS LTD

215

MODEL LR110 - UP TO AUGUST 1986
BLOCK M 968
PAGE D 46
GROUP D

GEARBOX - V8 - 4 SPEED - FRONT COVER AND OIL PUMP

ILL	PART NO	DESCRIPTION	QTY	REMARKS
1	576340	FRONT COVER AND PUMP ASSY	1	
2	571059	+Oil Seal-Front Cover	1	
3	591394	+Ring-Oil Pick-Up	1	
4	576342	+Gear-Oil Pump External	1	
5	90571086	+Gear-Oil Pump Internal	1	
6	BLS108L	+Ball-Oil Pressure Relief Valve	1	
7	556239	+Spring	1	
8	571168	+Screwed Plug	1	
9	90571105	Cover-Oil Pump	1	
10	90571106	Joint Washer-Oil Pump Cover	1	Note(1)
11	571134	Dowel-Oil Pump Cover to Front Cover	1	
12	SH106161L	Bolt-M6 x 16mm Oil Pump Cover to Front Cover	7	
13	571732	Sleeve-Extension-Front Cover	1	
14	571137	Joint Washer-Cover to Bearing Plate	1	Note(1)
15	BH108061L	Bolt-M8 x 30mm Front Cover and Bearing Plate	5	
16	WM108001L	Washer Spring	9	
17	NH108041L	Nut	4	
18	571139	Retaining Plate-Bearing	1	

NOTE(1): Also Part of Gasket Set 606754

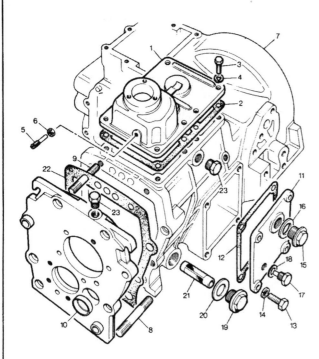
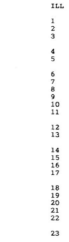

M968

LAND ROVER PARTS LTD

MODEL LR110 - UP TO AUGUST 1986
BLOCK VS 1638
PAGE D 48
GROUP D

GEARBOX - V8 - 4 SPEED - MAIN AND TRANSFER CASING - FRONT

ILL	PART NO	DESCRIPTION	QTY	REMARKS
1	FRC5629	Top Cover	1	
2	576195	Joint Washer-Top Cover	1	Note(1)
3	SH108251L	Screw-Top Cover to Gearbox Casing	8	
4	WM108001L	Washer Spring	8	
5	FRC5801	Grub Screw-Top Cover Reverse Stop	1	
6	NT108041L	Locknut-For Grub Screw	1	
7	FRC1778	Casing Gearbox-Complete Assy	1	
8	TE116155L	Stud-M16 x 100mm Front Face	2	
9	TE112115L	Stud-M12 x 17mm Front Face	2	
10	591290	Cup Plug Bearing Plate	1	
11	594320	Cover Plate-Reverse Idler Access	1	
12	571841	Joint Washer	1	Note(1)
13	SH110351L	Setscrew-Reverse Idler Cover Plate to Casing	4	
14	WM110001L	Washer Spring	4	
15	533358	Plug-Oil Filler Level	1	
16	FRC4835	Washer-Spring-Plug	1	Note(1)
17	599552	Plug Magnetic-Reverse Idler Access Plate	1	
18	FRC4808	Washer-Sealing Plug	1	Note(1)
19	90571104	Plug Oil Drain	1	
20	FRC4810	Washer-Sealing Plug	1	Note(1)
21	576220	Filter Oil-Drain Plug	1	
22	571837	Joint Washer-Bearing Plate to Gearbox	1	Note(1)
23	571944	Plug	2	

NOTE(1): Also Part of Gasket Set 606754

VS1638

LAND ROVER PARTS LTD

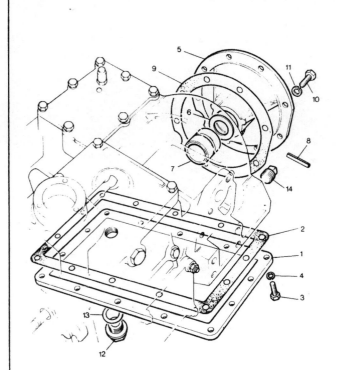

MODEL LR110 - UP TO AUGUST 1986
BLOCK M 951
PAGE D 50
GROUP D

GEARBOX - V8 - 4 SPEED - MAIN AND TRANSFER CASING - REAR

ILL	PART NO	DESCRIPTION	QTY	REMARKS
1	571977	Cover Bottom-Transfer Casing	1	
2	FRC7104	Joint Washer-Bottom Cover	1	Note(1)
3	SH108251L	Screw-M8 x 25mm Bottom Cover to Gearbox Casing	14	
4	WM108001L	Washer Spring	14	
5	FRC3515	BEARING HOUSING ASSEMBLY MAINSHAFT REAR	1	
6	571723	+Thrust Washer	1	
7	FRC3517	+Bearing-Outer Race	1	
8	PA108361L	+Spring Pin-4mm x 36mm	1	
9	571846	Joint Washer	1	Note(1)
10	SH108251L	Screw-M8 x 25mm Bearing Housing to Gear Case	6	
	SH108301L	Bolt M7 x 30mm	2	
11	WM108001L	Washer Spring	8	
12	90571104	Plug Drain-Transfer Gearbox	1	
13	FRC4810	Washer Sealing-Plug Drain	1	Note(1)
14	3292	Plug-Oil Level	1	

NOTE(1): Also Part of Gasket Set 606754

M951

LAND ROVER PARTS LTD

MODEL LR110 - UP TO AUGUST 1986
BLOCK VS 1645A
PAGE D 52
GROUP D

GEARBOX - V8 - 4 SPEED - MAIN AND TRANSFER CASING - TRANSFER PORTION PREFIX 13C

ILL	PART NO	DESCRIPTION	QTY	REMARKS
1	FRC5370	Housing Assembly Speedometer Drive	1	
2	571940	Joint Washer	1	Note(1)
3	SH108251L	Screw-M8 x 25-Speedo Housing to Main Case	8	
4	WL108001L	Washer Spring-Speedo Housing to Main Case	8	
5	FRC3508	TOP COVER ASSEMBLY-TRANSFER CASING	1	
6	FRC3355	+Baffle Assembly-Top Cover	1	
7	2982	+Rivet-Baffle to Cover	3	
8	576843	+Breather Baffle	1	
9	RTC616	+Rivet Baffle to Cover	1	
10	571979	Joint Washer	1	Note(1)
11	SH108251L	Screw-M8 x 25mm Top Cover and Detent to Casing	8	
12	WL108001L	Washer Spring	8	
13	591603	Pad-Sound Deadening	1	
14	571959	Housing-Vacuum Actuator	1	
15	571947	Joint Washer	1	
16	WL108001L	Washer Spring	4	
17	SH108251L	Screw-M8 x 25mm Actuator Hsg Hsg to Lock Up Dog Clutch Hsg	4	
18	FRC2257	Hsg Assy-Lock Up Dog Clutch	1	
19	571876	Joint Washer Dog Clutch Housing	1	Note(1)
20	WL108001L	Washer Spring	6	
21	SH108251L	Screw-M8 x 25mm Dog Clutch Assembly to Main Casing	6	
22	FRC6751	Plug-Sealing-Transfer Case	1	)No Longer)Serviced-Use)3290
	3290	Plug-Sealing-Transfer Box	1	
23	533358	Plug-Oil Filler Level	1	
24	FRC4835	Sealing Washer	1	
25	FRC167	Pipe-Breather	1	)
26	FRC168	Pipe-Breather	1	)
27	595478	Banjo Bolt	1	)Not Part of
28	599575	Washer	1	)Gearbox Assy
29	219676	Clip	1	)
30	622324	Clip	1	)

NOTE(1): Also Part of Gasket Set 606754

VS1645A

LAND ROVER PARTS LTD

MODEL LR110 - UP TO AUGUST 1986
BLOCK VS 1639
PAGE D 54
GROUP D

GEARBOX - V8 - 4 SPEED - GEARBOX MOUNTINGS

ILL	PART NO	DESCRIPTION	QTY	REMARKS
1	595119	Bracket Mounting RH-Engine Rear	1	
2	575651	Bracket Mounting LH-Engine Rear	1	
3	SH112251L	Setscrew-M12 x 25mm Rear Mounting Bracket	6	
4	WL112001L	Washer Spring-Rear Mounting Bracket	8	
5	566222	Rubber-Engine Mounting Rear	2	
6	WA110061L	Washer-Plain-Mounting Rubbers	2	
7	WM600061L	Washer-Spring	4	
8	NH606041L	Nut	4	
9	90575585	Mounting Bracket-Engine Rear	2	
10	BH108201L	Bolt-Mounting Bracket	6	
11	WA108051L	Washer-Plain	6	
12	WL108001L	Washer-Spring	6	
13	NH108041L	Nut	6	
14	WP185L	Plain Washer	6	

NOTE: Suspension Rubbers and Fixings Are
Not Part of Gearbox Assembly.

VS1639

220

MODEL LR110 - UP TO AUGUST 1986
BLOCK M 963
PAGE D 56
GROUP D

GEARBOX - V8 - 4 SPEED - PRIMARY PINION - 2ND AND 3RD MAINSHAFT GEARS

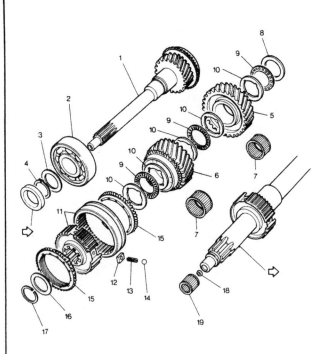

ILL	PART NO	DESCRIPTION	QTY	REMARKS
1	FRC1339	Primary Pinion And Tube Assy	1	
2	593619	Bearing Ball-Primary Pinion	1	
3		SHIM-PRIMARY PINION BEARING		
	594024	1.85mm	A/R	
	594023	1.90mm	A/R	
	594022	1.95mm	A/R	
	594021	2.00mm	A/R	
	594020	2.05mm	A/R	
	594019	2.10mm	A/R	
	594018	2.15mm	A/R	
4	214795	Circlip-Primary Pinion Bearing	1	
5	FRC1343	Gear 2nd Speed Mainshaft	1	
6	FRC1185	Gear 3rd Speed Mainshaft	1	
7	594292	Bearing-Needle Roller	2	
8	571931	Thrust Washer 2nd Mainshaft Gear	1	
9	571067	Thrust Needle Bearing 2nd/3rd Mainshaft Gears	3	
10	571066	Thrust Washer 2nd/3rd Main-Shaft Gears	5	
11	RTC2149	Synchro Pair 3rd/4th Gear	1	
12	FRC1337	Sliding Block 3rd/4th Gear	3	
13	503805	Spring-Synchromesh	3	
14	BLS108L	Ball-Synchromesh	3	
15	FRC5931	Baulk Ring	2	
16		SHIM-3RD/4TH GEAR		
	90571451	1.85mm	A/R	
	571452	2.00mm	A/R	
	571453	2.15mm	A/R	
	571454	2.30mm	A/R	
	571455	2.45mm	A/R	
17	571090	Snap Ring	1	
18	571142	Oil Seal-Mainshaft Front	1	
19	571062	Bearing Needle Roller Mainshaft	1	

M963

221

MODEL LR110 - UP TO AUGUST 1986
BLOCK VS 1656
PAGE D 58
GROUP D

GEARBOX - V8 - 4 SPEED - 1ST SPEED MAINSHAFT GEAR AND TRANSFER GEAR

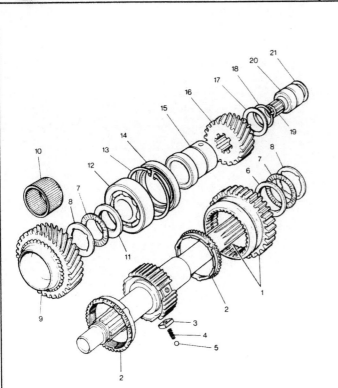

ILL	PART NO	DESCRIPTION	QTY	REMARKS
1	RTC2150	Mainshaft and Synchro Outer Member with Spacer	1	
2	FRC5931	Baulk Ring	2	
3	FRC1336	Sliding Block 1st/2nd Gear	3	
4	503805	Spring Synchromesh	3	
5	BLS108L	Ball Synchromesh	3	
6	571930	Thrust Washer-Front Mainshaft Gear	1	
7	571064	Thrust Washer Bearing Mainshaft Gear	2	
8	571065	Thrust Washer 1st Mainshaft Gear	2	
9	FRC1344	Gear 1st Speed Mainshaft	1	
10	594291	Needle Bearing 1st Mainshaft Gear	1	
11	571063	Thrust Washer-Rear Bearing to 1st Mainshaft Gear	1	
12	593619	Ball Bearing Mainshaft Rear	1	
13	CCN260	Circlip-Rear Bearing Mainshaft	1	
14	571838	Oil Seal-Mainshaft Rear	1	
15	622538	Spacer Mainshaft	1	
16	90571010	Gear Transfer-Mainshaft	1	
17		SHIM-MAINSHAFT TRANSFER GEAR		
	593814	1.65mm	A/R	
	593815	1.70mm	A/R	
	593816	1.75mm	A/R	
	593817	1.80mm	A/R	
	593818	1.85mm	A/R	
	593819	1.90mm	A/R	
	593820	1.95mm	A/R	
	593821	2.00mm	A/R	
18	90571091	Snap Ring Transfer Gear to Mainshaft	1	
19	571187	Roller Bearing-Solid-Mainshaft Transfer Gear	1	
20	FRC3517	Bearing-Outer Race-Mainshaft Rear	1	
21	571723	Thrust Washer-Mainshaft Rear	1	

VS1656

MODEL LR110 - UP TO AUGUST 1986
BLOCK VS 1640
PAGE D 60
GROUP D

GEARBOX - V8 - 4 SPEED - LAYSHAFT GEARS AND REVERSE

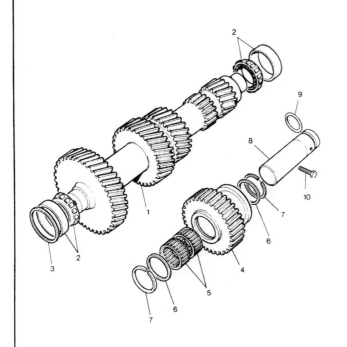

ILL	PART NO	DESCRIPTION	QTY	REMARKS
1	576343	Gear-Layshaft Cluster	1	
2	RTC3413	Bearing-Taper Roller-Layshaft	2	
3		SHIM-FRONT BEARING-LAYSHAFT		
	576351	1.550mm	A/R	
	FRC3642	1.575mm	A/R	
	576352	1.600mm	A/R	
	FRC3643	1.625mm	A/R	
	576353	1.650mm	A/R	
	FRC3644	1.675mm	A/R	
	576354	1.700mm	A/R	
	FRC3645	1.725mm	A/R	
	576355	1.750mm	A/R	
	FRC3646	1.775mm	A/R	
	576356	1.800mm	A/R	
	FRC3647	1.825mm	A/R	
	576357	1.850mm	A/R	
	FRC3648	1.875mm	A/R	
	576358	1.900mm	A/R	
	FRC3649	1.925mm	A/R	
	576359	1.950mm	A/R	
	FRC3650	1.975mm	A/R	
	576360	2.000mm	A/R	
	FRC3651	2.025mm	A/R	
	576361	2.050mm	A/R	
	FRC3652	2.075mm	A/R	
	576362	2.100mm	A/R	
	FRC3653	2.125mm	A/R	
	576363	2.150mm	A/R	
	FRC3654	2.175mm	A/R	
	576364	2.200mm	A/R	
	FRC3655	2.225mm	A/R	
	576365	2.250mm	A/R	
	FRC3656	2.275mm	A/R	
	576366	2.300mm	A/R	
	FRC3657	2.325mm	A/R	
	576367	2.350mm	A/R	
	FRC3658	2.375mm	A/R	
	576368	2.400mm	A/R	
	FRC3659	2.425mm	A/R	
	576369	2.450mm	A/R	
	FRC3660	2.475mm	A/R	
	576370	2.500mm	A/R	

VS1640

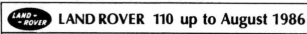
MODEL LR110 - UP TO AUGUST 1986
BLOCK VS 1640
PAGE D 62
GROUP D

GEARBOX - V8 - 4 SPEED - LAYSHAFT GEARS AND REVERSE - CONTINUED

ILL	PART NO	DESCRIPTION	QTY	REMARKS
4	594244	Gear Reverse Idler	1	
5	594389	Bearing-Needle Roller	2	
6	571885	Washer-Needle Bearing	2	
7	571144	Circlip-Retaining Bearing To Reverse Gear	2	
8	FRC1743	Shaft-Reverse Idler	1	
9	561699	Sealing Ring-Reverse Idler Shaft	1	
10	SH106351L	Bolt-Shaft to Casing	1	

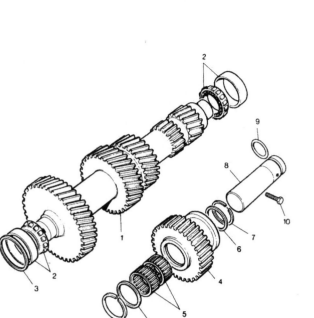

VS1640

 **LAND ROVER PARTS LTD**

224

MODEL LR110 - UP TO AUGUST 1986
BLOCK M 966
PAGE D 64
GROUP D

GEARBOX - V8 - 4 SPEED - INTERMEDIATE GEARS

ILL	PART NO	DESCRIPTION	QTY	REMARKS
1	FRC2963	Gear-Input and Outer Member Assy	1	
2	FRC2240	Gear-High Range	1	
3	591891	Gear-Low Range	1	
4	576683	Spacer-Shaft Intermediate	2	
5	591900	Ring Inner-Thrust Bearing	2	
6		THRUST WASHER AND PIN ASSY		
	FRC6284	3.55mm	A/R	
	FRC6285	3.59mm	A/R	
	FRC6286	3.67mm	A/R	
	FRC6287	3.75mm	A/R	
	FRC6288	3.79mm	A/R	
7	FRC3507	Shaft Assembly-Intermediate Gear	1	
8	532323	'O' Ring-Inter-Shaft	1	
9	594290	Bearing-Needle Roller Inter-Shaft	3	
10	FRC3500	Thrust Washer-Inter-Shaft	4	

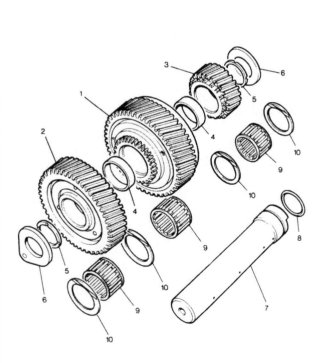

M966

 **LAND ROVER PARTS LTD**

225

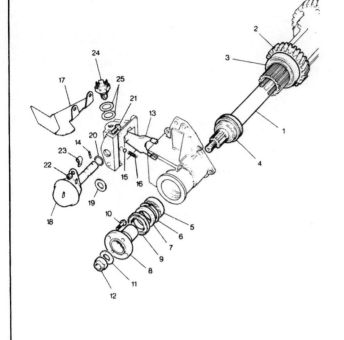

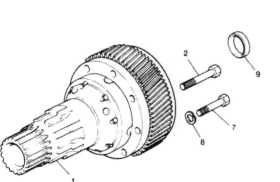

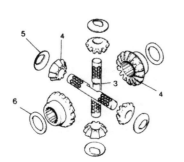

VS1641

MODEL LR110 - UP TO AUGUST 1986
BLOCK VS 1641
PAGE D 66
GROUP D

GEARBOX - V8 - 4 SPEED - FRONT OUTPUT SHAFT AND VACUUM ACTUATOR

ILL	PART NO	DESCRIPTION	QTY	REMARKS
1	594337	Shaft Output Front	1	
2	FRC2241	Gear-Output-High Range	1	
3	606473	Bearing Tapper Roller Diff-Case Front	1	
4	571875	Dog Clutch-Transfer Lock Up	1	
5	217325	Bearing Ball-Output Shaft Front	1	
6	90217526	Circlip-Bearing to Housing	1	
7	571175	Oil Seal-Output Shaft Front	1	
8	FRC2256	Flange Coupling-Front	1	
9	571177	Mudshield-Coupling Flange	1	
10	509045	Bolt	4	
11	571174	Washer Plain	1	
12	NY116041L	Nut Coupling Flange to Output Shaft	1	
13	571956	Fork-Lock Up Dog Clutch	1	
14	571158	Spring Pin-Fork to Actuator Shaft	1	
15	571146	Ball-Actuator Shaft Detent	1	
16	593802	Spring-Detent	1	
17	FRC2258	Heatshield Vacuum Actuator	1	
18	571957	Vacuum Actuator and Shaft Complete	1	
19	591345	Washer Joint	1	Note(1)
20	571991	'O' Ring	1	
21	SF108201L	Bolt M8 x 20mm	2	
22	NY108041L	Nut M8	2	
23	523203	Cable Clip	1	
24	PRC1039	Switch-Warning Light Diff Lock	1	
25	FRC5674	Shim-Switch Diff Lock	A/R	

NOTE(1): Also Part of Gasket Set 606754

MODEL LR110 - UP TO AUGUST 1986
BLOCK TS 5163
PAGE D 68
GROUP D

GEARBOX - V8 - 4 SPEED - DIFFERENTIAL

ILL	PART NO	DESCRIPTION	QTY	REMARKS
1	594340	DIFFERENTIAL COMPLETE ASSY	1	)No Longer)Available-Use)FRC7740
	FRC7740	DIFFERENTIAL COMPLETE ASSY	1	
2	BH110121L	+Bolt M10 x 60mm	8	
3	RTC3397	+Pinion Shafts (Matched Pair)	1	
4	608142	+Bevel Pinion-Side Gears and Thrust Washers-Set	1	)Upto Gearbox)13C03480A
5	556633	++Thrust Washer	4	)
4	608142	+Bevel Pinon-Side Gears and Thrust Washers-Set	1	
5	FRC6956	++Thrust Washer 1.05mm	A/R	)
	FRC6958	++Thrust Washer 1.15mm	A/R	)From Gearbox
	FRC6960	++Thrust Washer 1.25mm	A/R	)13C03481A
	FRC6962	++Thrust Washer 1.35mm	A/R	)
	FRC6964	++Thrust Washer 1.45mm	A/R	)
6	FRC6968	++Thrust Washer	4	)
7	BH110071L	+Bolt-M10 x 35mm	8	
8	WL110001L	+Washer-Spring	8	
9	FRC7745	+Ring-Oil Retaining	1	)From Gearbox)13C03481A

NOTE: Differential Includes Low Range Gear and Fixings as a Balanced Set.

TS5163

MODEL LR110 - UP TO AUGUST 1986
BLOCK M 976
PAGE D 70
GROUP D

GEARBOX - V8 - 4 SPEED - REAR OUTPUT SHAFT - GEARS AND SPEEDO
       WORM DRIVE

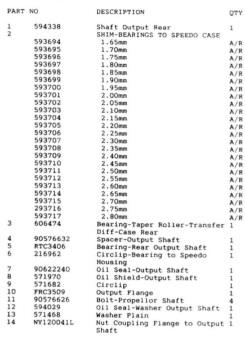

ILL	PART NO	DESCRIPTION	QTY	REMARKS
1	594338	Shaft Output Rear	1	
2		SHIM-BEARINGS TO SPEEDO CASE		
	593694	1.65mm	A/R	
	593695	1.70mm	A/R	
	593696	1.75mm	A/R	
	593697	1.80mm	A/R	
	593698	1.85mm	A/R	
	593699	1.90mm	A/R	
	593700	1.95mm	A/R	
	593701	2.00mm	A/R	
	593702	2.05mm	A/R	
	593703	2.10mm	A/R	
	593704	2.15mm	A/R	
	593705	2.20mm	A/R	
	593706	2.25mm	A/R	
	593707	2.30mm	A/R	
	593708	2.35mm	A/R	
	593709	2.40mm	A/R	
	593710	2.45mm	A/R	
	593711	2.50mm	A/R	
	593712	2.55mm	A/R	
	593713	2.60mm	A/R	
	593714	2.65mm	A/R	
	593715	2.70mm	A/R	
	293716	2.75mm	A/R	
	593717	2.80mm	A/R	
3	606474	Bearing-Taper Roller-Transfer Diff-Case Rear	1	
4	90576632	Spacer-Output Shaft	1	
5	RTC3406	Bearing-Rear Output Shaft	1	
6	216962	Circlip-Bearing to Speedo Housing	1	
7	90622240	Oil Seal-Output Shaft	1	
8	571970	Oil Shield-Output Shaft	1	
9	571682	Circlip	1	
10	FRC3509	Output Flange	1	
11	90576626	Bolt-Propellor Shaft	4	
12	594029	Oil Seal-Washer Output Shaft	1	
13	571468	Washer Plain	1	
14	NY120041L	Nut Coupling Flange to Output Shaft	1	

M976

LAND ROVER PARTS LTD

MODEL LR110 - UP TO AUGUST 1986
BLOCK M 976
PAGE D 72
GROUP D

GEARBOX - V8 - 4 SPEED - REAR OUTPUT SHAFT - GEARS AND SPEEDO
       WORM DRIVE - CONTINUED

ILL	PART NO	DESCRIPTION	QTY	REMARKS
15	FRC3162	Worm Speedometer	1	
16	FRC3310	Drivengear and Spindle	1	
17	FRC3286	Housing Speedo Spindle	1	
18	571665	'O' Ring-Spindle to Gear Hsg	1	
19	AAU2304	Oil Seal-Speedo-Spindle Hsg	1	
20	533765	Retaining Plate-Speedo Cable	1	
21	WA106041L	Washer Plain	1	
22	NY106041L	Nut-Retaining Plate to Stud	1	
23	571536	Stud	1	

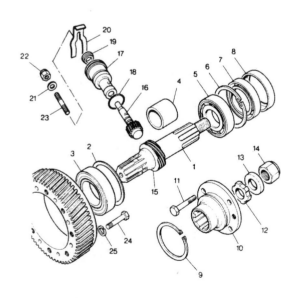

M976

LAND ROVER PARTS LTD

MODEL LR110 - UP TO AUGUST 1986
BLOCK VS 1699
PAGE D 74
GROUP D

GEARBOX - V8 - 4 SPEED - SELECTOR SHAFTS AND LEVERS

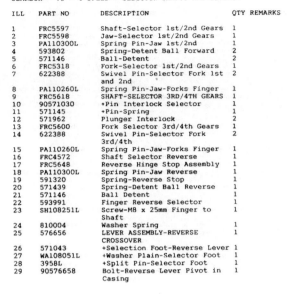

ILL	PART NO	DESCRIPTION	QTY	REMARKS
1	FRC5597	Shaft-Selector 1st/2nd Gears	1	
2	FRC5598	Jaw-Selector 1st/2nd Gears	1	
3	PA110300L	Spring Pin-Jaw 1st/2nd	1	
4	593802	Spring-Detent Ball Forward	2	
5	571146	Ball-Detent	2	
6	FRC5318	Fork-Selector 1st/2nd Gears	1	
7	622388	Swivel Pin-Selector Fork 1st and 2nd	2	
8	PA110260L	Spring Pin-Jaw-Forks Finger	1	
9	FRC5618	SHAFT-SELECTOR 3RD/4TH GEARS	1	
10	90571030	+Pin Interlock Selector	1	
11	571145	+Pin-Spring	1	
12	571962	Plunger Interlock	2	
13	FRC5600	Fork Selector 3rd/4th Gears	1	
14	622388	Swivel Pin-Selector Fork 3rd/4th	2	
15	PA110260L	Spring Pin-Jaw-Forks Finger	1	
16	FRC4572	Shaft Selector Reverse	1	
17	FRC5648	Reverse Hinge Stop Assembly	1	
18	PA110300L	Spring Pin-Jaw Reverse	1	
19	591320	Spring-Reverse Stop	1	
20	571439	Spring-Detent Ball Reverse	1	
21	571146	Ball Detent	1	
22	593991	Finger Reverse Selector	1	
23	SH108251L	Screw-M8 x 25mm Finger to Shaft	1	
24	810004	Washer Spring	1	
25	576656	LEVER ASSEMBLY-REVERSE CROSSOVER	1	
26	571043	+Selection Foot-Reverse Lever	1	
27	WA108051L	+Washer Plain-Selector Foot	1	
28	3958L	+Split Pin-Selector Foot	1	
29	90576658	Bolt-Reverse Lever Pivot in Casing	1	

VS1699

LAND ROVER PARTS LTD

MODEL LR110 - UP TO AUGUST 1986
BLOCK VS 1642
PAGE D 76
GROUP D

GEARBOX - V8 - 4 SPEED - SELECTOR SHAFTS AND LEVERS TRANSFER GEARBOX

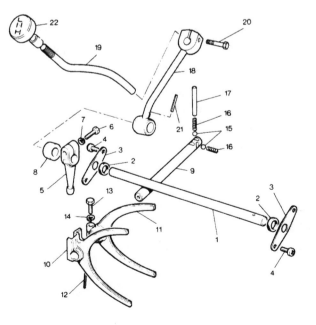

ILL	PART NO	DESCRIPTION	QTY	REMARKS
1	FRC5882	Cross Shaft-Gearchange	1	
2	FRC6468	'O' Ring-Cross Shaft	2	
3	576149	Plate Retaining-Sealing Ring	2	
4	SP108161L	Screw-Retaining Plate to Casing	4	
5	593981	Finger Selector-Complete	1	
6	SH108251L	Screw-M8 x 25mm Selector Finger to Cross Shaft	1	
7	WM108001L	Washer Spring	1	
8	593983	Spacer-Transfer Cross Shaft	1	
9	571981	Shaft Selector-High/Low Transfer	1	
10	571982	Fork-Jaw Selector High/Low Transfer	1	
11	571983	Fork Selector High/Low Transfer	1	
12	571158	Spring Pin-Jaw and Fork to Selector Shaft	1	
13	BH108061L	Bolt M8 x 30mm Fork to Selector Shaft	1	
14	WM108001L	Washer Spring	1	
15	571146	Ball Selector Shaft and Cross Hole Detent	2	
16	593802	Spring-Selector Shaft and Cross Hole Dent	2	
17	571980	Rod-Spacing Detent Spring	1	
18	FRC3570	Gear Lever High/Low Transfer RHD	1	
	FRC3571	Gear Lever High/Low Transfer LHD	1	
19	FRC2718	Gear Lever Extension-RHD	1	
	FRC2719	Gear Lever Extension-LHD	1	
20	SH108301L	Screw-Extension to Lower Lever	1	
21	576779	Spring-Gear Lever to Cross Shaft	1	
22	FRC6126	Knob and Sleeve Assembly Gear Lever-Transfer Box	1	

NOTE: Transfer Gear Lever, Knob & Fixings Are Not Part Of Gearbox Assembly.

VS1642

LAND ROVER PARTS LTD

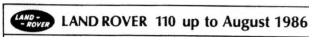
MODEL LR110 - UP TO AUGUST 1986
BLOCK VS 1643
PAGE D 78
GROUP D

GEARBOX - V8 - 4 SPEED - MAIN GEAR LEVER

ILL	PART NO	DESCRIPTION	QTY REMARKS
1	FRC4754	Gear Lever Assembly-RHD	1
	FRC4755	Gear Lever Assembly-LHD	1
2	591562	Knob & Sleeve Assembly Gear Lever	1
3	576319	Bolt-Gear Lever Assy-To Top Cover	1
4	576320	Pin Operating-Gear Lever	1

NOTE: All Items On This Page Are Not Part Of The Gearbox Assembly.

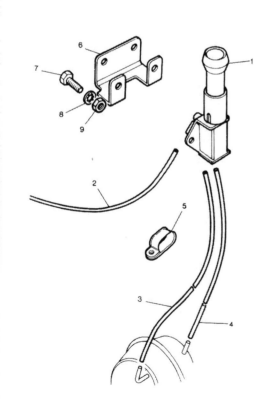

VS643

LAND ROVER PARTS LTD

MODEL LR110 - UP TO AUGUST 1986
BLOCK VS 3821
PAGE D 80
GROUP D

GEARBOX - V8 - 4 SPEED - VACUUM CONTROL VALVE

ILL	PART NO	DESCRIPTION	QTY REMARKS
1	FRC5656	Valve-Vacuum Co trol Transfer Box-Diff-Lock	1
2	FRC2273	Pipe-Vacuum Valve to Engine	1
3	FRC2274	Pipe-Vacuum Valve to Actuator Front	1
4	FRC2275	Pipe-Vacuum Valve to Actuator Rear	1
5	622324	Clip-Vacuum Pipes	2
6	392811	Bracket-Vacuum Control Valve	1
7	257017	Screw Bracket to Tunnel Inspection Cover	4
8	WF702101L	Washer	4
9	257011	Nut	4

NOTE: All The Above Items Are Not Part Of The Gearbox Assembly.

VS3821

LAND ROVER PARTS LTD

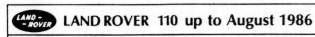

```
MODEL LR110 - UP TO AUGUST 1986
BLOCK VS 3201
PAGE D 82
GROUP D

GEARBOX - V8 - 4 SPEED - GASKET KIT

ILL   PART NO     DESCRIPTION              QTY REMARKS

1     606754      Gasket Kit               1
```

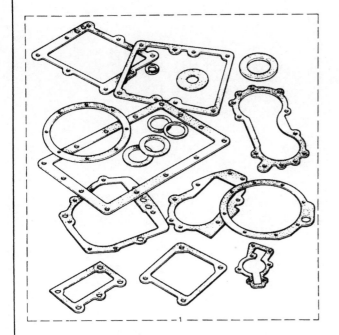

VS3201

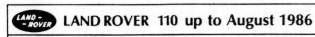

```
MODEL LR110 - UP TO AUGUST 1986
BLOCK TS 6465
PAGE D 84
GROUP D

GEARBOX - V8 - 5 SPEED - GEARBOX

ILL   PART NO     DESCRIPTION              QTY REMARKS

1     FRC7904N    Gearbox Assembly         1   Prefix 20C
      FRC9525N    Gearbox Assembly         1   Prefix 22C
```

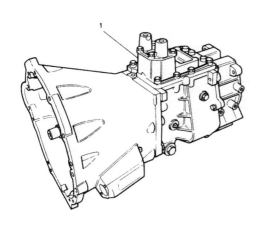

TS 6465

MODEL LR110 - UP TO AUGUST 1986
BLOCK TS 5918
PAGE D 86
GROUP D

GEARBOX - V8 - 5 SPEED - BELL HOUSING

ILL	PART NO	DESCRIPTION	QTY	REMARKS
1	FRC8529	Bell Housing	1	
2	BH112141L	Bolt M12x70-Bell Housing to Gearbox	6	
3	WL112001L	Washer-Spring-Bell Housing to Gearbox	6	
4	SH106301L	Screw M6x30	1	
5	NH106041L	Nut	1	
	3290	Plug-Wading	1	

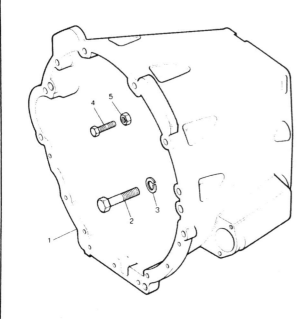

TS5918

MODEL LR110 - UP TO AUGUST 1986
BLOCK TS 5954
PAGE D 88
GROUP D

GEARBOX - V8 - 5 SPEED - GEARBOX & EXTENSION CASE

ILL	PART NO	DESCRIPTION	QTY	REMARKS
1	FRC3731	GEARBOX CASING ASSEMBLY	1	Prefix 20C
	FRC8397	GEARBOX CASING ASSEMBLY	1	Prefix 22C
2	FRC2309	+Dowel	2	
3	FRC5306	Extension Case-Gearbox	1	
4	FRC2365	Oil Seal-Extension Case	1	
5	FRC2465	Joint Washer-Extension Case to Gearbox	1	
6	FRC2482	Dowel-Extension Case to Gearbox	2	
7	BH110091L	Bolt-M10x45	3	
8	BH110101L	Bolt-M10x50	3	
9	BH110121L	Bolt-M10x60	2	
10	WL110001L	Washer-Spring	8	
11	NH110041L	Nut	1	
12	FRC3073	Washer-Joint-Clutch Housing to Bearing Plate	2	
13	FRC2542	Blanking Plate-Front Cover	1	
14	FRC3166	Grub Screw-Extension Casing to 3rd Speed	1	
15	90571086	Gear-Internal-Oil Pump	1	)
16	591227	Gear-External-Oil Pump	1	)Prefix 20C Only
17	576220	Filter	1	)
18	FRC2468	O Ring	1	)
19	90571104	Plug	1	
20	FRC4810	Washer-Drain Plug	1	
	608246	Drain Plug	1	
	571944	Plug-Reverse Switch Hole	1	
	PRC1039	Switch-Reverse Light	1	Optional
	FRC5674	Washer-Reverse Switch or Plug	1	
21	FRC2370	Bolt-Reverse Level	1	
22	3292	Plug-Oil Level	1	

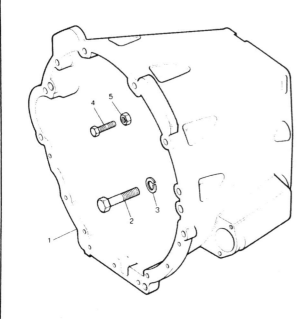

TS5954

MODEL LR110 - UP TO AUGUST 1986
BLOCK TS 5953
PAGE D 90
GROUP D

GEARBOX - V8 - 5 SPEED - GEARBOX FRONT COVER

ILL	PART NO	DESCRIPTION	QTY	REMARKS
1	FRC4875	FRONT COVER ASSEMBLY	1	Prefix 20C
	FRC9620	FRONT COVER ASSEMBLY	1	Prefix 22C
2	FRC2361	+Oil Seal	1	
3	591394	+Oil Pick Up Ring	1	
4	GS108081L	+Grub Screw	1	
5	SH108401L	Screw M8x40	8	
6	WL108001L	Washer-Spring	8	
7	571134	Dowel-Front Cover	2	
8	FRC3072	Joint Washer-Front Cover	1	Prefix 20C
	FRC8215	Joint Washer-Front Cover	1	Prefix 22C

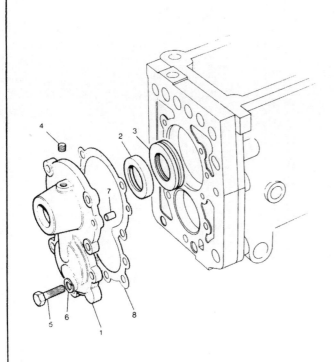

TS5953

LAND ROVER PARTS LTD

238

MODEL LR110 - UP TO AUGUST 1986
BLOCK TS 5961
PAGE D 92
GROUP D

GEARBOX - V8 - 5 SPEED - MAINSHAFT

ILL	PART NO	DESCRIPTION	QTY	REMARKS
1	FRC4714	Mainshaft	1	Prefix 20C
	FRC8214	Mainshaft	1	Prefix 22C
2	FRC7852	Constant Pinion Assembly	1	Prefix 20C
	FRC9621	Constant Pinion Assembly	1	Prefix 22C
3	FRC2301	Ball Bearing	1	
4		SHIMS-CONSTANT PINION		
	FRC2445	3.07	A/R	
	FRC2446	3.02	A/R	
	FRC2447	2.97	A/R	
	FRC2448	2.92	A/R	
	FRC2449	2.87	A/R	
5	FRC2488	Circlip	2	
6	571142	Oil Seal	1	
7	6397	Bearing	1	
8		SHIMS-3RD AND 4TH HUB		
	FRC2554	3.48	A/R	
	FRC2555	3.43	A/R	
	FRC2556	3.38	A/R	
9	FRC8139	SYNCHROMESH ASSEMBLY-3RD/4TH	1	
		MATCHED PAIR		
10	FRC8777	+Baulk Ring	2	
11	FRC7752	+Sliding Block	3	
12	503805	+Spring	3	
13	BLS108L	+Ball	3	
14	FRC3898	Spacer-3rd Gear	1	
15	FRC7764	Gear-3rd Speed-Mainshaft	1	Prefix 20C
	FRC8210	Gear-3rd Speed-Mainshaft	1	Prefix 22C
16	FRC2334	Needle Bearing	1	

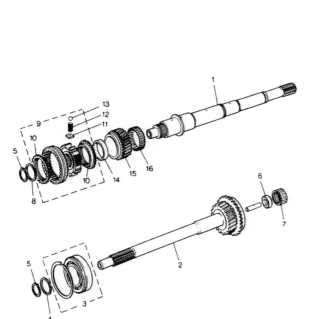

TS5961

LAND ROVER PARTS LTD

239

MODEL LR110 - UP TO AUGUST 1986
BLOCK TS 5965
PAGE D 94
GROUP D

GEARBOX - V8 - 5 SPEED - MAINSHAFT GEARS

ILL	PART NO	DESCRIPTION	QTY	REMARKS
1	FRC7763	Gear-2nd Speed-Mainshaft	1	Prefix 20C
	FRC8209	Gear-2nd Speed-Mainshaft	1	Prefix 22C
2	FRC8129	SYNCHROMESH ASSEMBLY-1ST/2ND MATCHED PAIR	1	NLA-Use FRC9556
	FRC9556	SYNCHROMESH ASSEMBLY-1ST/2ND MATCHED PAIR	1	
5	FRC8777	+Baulk Ring	2	
6	FRC7752	+Sliding Block-Synchro	3	
7	503805	+Spring	3	
8	BLS108L	+Ball	3	
3	FRC2334	Needle Bearing	1	
4	FRC3898	Spacer-2nd Speed	1	
9	FRC7761	Gear-1st Speed-Mainshaft	1	Prefix 20C
	FRC8208	Gear-1st Speed-Mainshaft	1	Prefix 22C
10	FRC3897	Spacer-1st Speed	1	
11	FRC2334	Needle Bearing	1	
12	FRC8422	Bush-1st Speed	1	
13		SHIM-1ST SPEED BUSH		
	FRC8400	1.15mm	A/R	
	FRC8401	1.20mm	A/R	
	FRC8402	1.25mm	A/R	
	FRC8403	1.30mm	A/R	
	FRC8404	1.35mm	A/R	
	FRC8405	1.40mm	A/R	
	FRC8406	1.45mm	A/R	
15	FRC2301	Ball-Bearing	1	
15	FRC2488	Circlip	1	
16	FRC5978	Thrust Washer-5th Gear	1	
17	FRC2479	Needle Bearing	1	
18	FRC3896	Spacer-5th Gear	1	
19	FRC7757	Gear-5th Speed	1	Prefix 20C
	FRC8211	Gear-5th Speed	1	Prefix 22C

TS5965

 LAND ROVER PARTS LTD

MODEL LR110 - UP TO AUGUST 1986
BLOCK TS 5965
PAGE D 96
GROUP D

GEARBOX - V8 - 5 SPEED - MAINSHAFT GEARS - CONTINUED

ILL	PART NO	DESCRIPTION	QTY	REMARKS
20	FRC8176	SYNCHROMESH ASSEMBLY-5TH SPEED	1	
21	FRC8777	+Baulk Ring	1	
22	BLS108L	+Ball	3	
23	503805	+Spring	3	
24	FRC7752	+Sliding Block	3	
25	FRC7753	Stop Plate 5th Speed Hub	1	
26	FRC8409	Anti Rotation Pin	1	
27	FRC2457	O Ring-Collar	1	
28	FRC5317	Collar-Oil Seal	1	
29		SUPPORT WASHER		
	FRC5602	4.25	A/R	
	FRC5603	4.30	A/R	
	FRC5604	4.35	A/R	
	FRC5605	4.40	A/R	
	FRC5606	4.45	A/R	
	FRC5607	4.50	A/R	
	FRC5608	4.55	A/R	
	FRC5609	4.60	A/R	
	FRC5610	4.65	A/R	
	FRC5611	4.70	A/R	
	FRC5612	4.75	A/R	
	FRC5613	4.80	A/R	
	FRC5614	4.85	A/R	
	FRC5615	4.90	A/R	
	FRC5616	4.95	A/R	
30	FRC4494	Snap Ring-Collar	1	

TS5965

 LAND ROVER PARTS LTD

MODEL LR110 - UP TO AUGUST 1986
BLOCK TS 5917
PAGE D 98
GROUP D

GEARBOX - V8 - 5 SPEED - LAYSHAFT

ILL	PART NO	DESCRIPTION	QTY	REMARKS
1	FRC3732	Layshaft Cluster Gear	1	Prefix 20C
	FRC8213	Layshaft Cluster Gear	1	Prefix 22C
2	FRC3795	Gear-5th Speed	1	
3	FRC3806	Nut-5th Gear to Layshaft	1	
4	FRC2578	Bearing-Roller-Layshaft Front	1	
5	FRC2470	Bearing-Ball-Layshaft Rear	1	
6	FRC8380	Retaining Plate-Rear Bearing	1	
7	SB108201L	Screw-Plate	2	
8	FRC3987	Spacer-Bearing Roller	1	
9	FRC3319	REVERSE IDLER ASSEMBLY	1	
10	FRC1032	+Bearing-Needle Roller	2	
11	FRC1034	+Washer	2	
12	FRC1035	+Circlip	2	
13	FRC3112	Shaft-Reverse Idler	1	
14	FRC8421	Washer-Thrust-Shaft	1	
15	591519	Spring Pin-Reverse Idler Shaft	1	

TS5917

MODEL LR110 - UP TO AUGUST 1986
BLOCK TS 5952
PAGE D 100
GROUP D

GEARBOX - V8 - 5 SPEED - SELECTORS AND SHAFTS

ILL	PART NO	DESCRIPTION	QTY	REMARKS
1	FRC2381	Selector Shaft-1st/2nd Gear	1	
2	FRC7769	Selector Fork-1st/2nd Gear	1	
3	FRC8452	Selector Jaw-1st/2nd Gear	1	
4	SX108351L	Bolt-1st/2nd Fork to Shaft	1	
5	FRC3118	Selector Shaft-3rd/4th Gear	1	
6	FRC7754	Selector Fork-3rd/4th Gear	1	
7	FRC8452	Selector Jaw-3rd/4th Gear	1	
8	FRC3282	Selector Shaft	1	
9	FRC7767	Selector Fork-5th Gear	1	
10	FRC8454	Selector Jaw-5th Gear	1	
11	622388	Swivel Pad-5th Fork	2	
12	FRC7766	Pivot Bracket-5th Fork	1	
13	FRC2481	Dowel-Bracket	2	
14	SH108301L	Screw M8x30	2	
15	WA108051L	Washer-Plain	2	
16	UKC2089L	Pivot Pin-5th Fork	2	
17	UKC2105L	Circlip-Pivot Pin	2	
18	WA106041L	Washer-Plain-Pivot Pin	1	
19	PC106561L	Clevis Pin-5th Fork to Selector	1	
20	FRC8270	Selector Shaft-Reverse	1	
21	FRC8455	Reverse Hinge & Jaw Assembly	1	
22	FRC3481	Spring-Reverse Hinge	1	
23	571158	Spring Pin-Jaws to Shaft	4	
24	PS103121L	Split Pin	1	
25	SH108301L	Screw M8x30	2	
26	FRC2577	Interlock Plunger-Cross Holes	3	
27	FRC3117	Interlock Pin-Selector Shaft	2	
28	FRC2390	Reverse Lever Assembly	1	
29	571043	+Selector Foot	1	
30	PS103121L	+Split Pin	1	
31	WA108051L	+Washer	1	
32	FRC2368	Reverse Beam	1	
33	FRC2370	Bolt-Reverse Lever Pivot	1	
	571146	Detent Ball	4	
35	593802	Detent Spring	4	
36	PS103121L	Split Pin-5th Speed Fork	1	

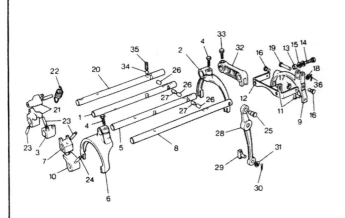

TS5952

MODEL LR110 - UP TO AUGUST 1986
BLOCK TS 5966
PAGE D 102
GROUP D

GEARBOX - V8 - 5 SPEED - GEAR LEVER

ILL	PART NO	DESCRIPTION	QTY	REMARKS
1	FRC8250	GEAR LEVER LOWER ASSEMBLY	1	
2	FRC2622	+Locating Pin-Gear Lever	2	
3	FRC2612	Seat-Gear Lever Lower	1	
4	FRC2583	Spring Housing-Gearchange	1	
5	FRC2587	Spring-Bias-Inner	2	
6	FRC2623	Disc-Bias Springs	4	
7	FRC3146	Spring-Bias-Outer	2	
8	GS112141L	Grub Screw-Bias Adjusting	2	
9	FRC2648	Joint Washer	1	
10	FRC5698	Top Cover-Gearbox	1	
11	FRC8271	Grommet Gear Lever Lower	1	
12	SH106251L	Screw M6x25	4	
13	WL106001L	Spring Washer	4	
14	3292	Plug-Filler-Top Cover	1	
15	BAU1689	Clip-Single-Breather Pipe	1	
16	622324	Clip-Double-Breather Pipe	1	
17	FRC4062	BREATHER ASSEMBLY	1	
18	FRC8863	Gear Lever-Upper	1	
19	WA110061L	Washer	1	
20	NY110041L	Nut	1	
21	FRC8722	Knob-Gear Lever	1	
22	FRC2487	Joint Washer-Top Cover	1	
23	FRC2626	Spring Pin-Top Cover	1	
24	FRC6306	Gasket-Gearchange Housing	1	

TS5966

MODEL LR110 - UP TO AUGUST 1986
BLOCK VS 3742
PAGE D 104
GROUP D

GEARBOX - V8 - TRANSFER BOX LT230T

ILL	PART NO	DESCRIPTION	QTY	REMARKS
1	FRC9468N	Transfer Box Assembly-New	1	Prefix 25D

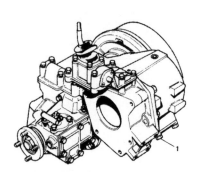

VS3742

MODEL LR110 - UP TO AUGUST 1986
BLOCK TS 5308A
PAGE D 106
GROUP D

GEARBOX - V8 - TRANSFER BOX LT230T - TRANSFER CASING

ILL	PART NO	DESCRIPTION	QTY	REMARKS
1	FRC8293	TRANSFER CASING ASSEMBLY	1	
2	FRC5595	+Stud	2	
3	608246	Plug-Oil Filler	2	
4	FRC7447	SPEEDO HOUSING ASSEMBLY	1	
5	FRC5409	Joint Washer-Speedo Housing	1	
6	SH110301L	Screw-Housing to Transfer	5	
7	BH110091L	Screw-Housing to Transfer	1	
8	WA110061L	Washer-Housing to Transfer	6	
9	FRC5594	Dowel-Housing to Transfer	1	
10	FRC6943	Housing-Mainshaft Transfer Bearing	1	
11	FRC5668	Cover-Power Take-Off	1	
12	FRC5413	Joint Washer	2	
13	SF108251L	Screw	2	
14	BH110071L	Bolt	6	
15	WA110061L	Washer	6	
16	599552	Drain Plug	1	
17	FRC4808	Washer-Drain Plug	1	
18	FRC5415	Bottom Cover-Transfer Case	1	
19	FRC5416	Joint Washer-Bottom Cover	1	
20	BH108061L	Bolt	10	
21	WA108051L	Washer	10	
22	FRC8292	O Ring	1	
23	FRC2482	Dowel-Hollow	1	
24	BH110081L	Bolt	3	
25	BH110091L	Bolt	1	
26	WL110001L	Washer	6	
27	571536	Stud-Cable Retainer	1	

TS5308A

MODEL LR110 - UP TO AUGUST 1986
BLOCK VS 3729
PAGE D 108
GROUP D

GEARBOX - V8 - TRANSFER BOX LT230T - TRANSFER GEAR - MAINSHAFT

ILL	PART NO	DESCRIPTION	QTY	REMARKS
1	FRC5428	Gear-Mainshaft-Transfer	1	Suffix B Only
	FRC8917	Gear-Mainshaft-Transfer	1	Suffix C Only
2	FRC2365	Oil Seal	1	
3	FRC5564	Bearing	2	
4		SELECTIVE SHIM-MAINSHAFT BEARING HOUSING		
	FRC9928	3.20mm	A/R	
	FRC9930	3.25mm	A/R	
	FRC9932	3.30mm	A/R	
	FRC9934	3.35mm	A/R	
	FRC9936	3.40mm	A/R	
	FRC9938	3.45mm	A/R	
	FRC9940	3.50mm	A/R	
	FRC9942	3.55mm	A/R	
	FRC9944	3.60mm	A/R	
	FRC9946	3.65mm	A/R	
	FRC9948	3.70mm	A/R	
	FRC9950	3.75mm	A/R	
	FRC9952	3.80mm	A/R	
	FRC9954	3.85mm	A/R	
	FRC9956	3.90mm	A/R	
	FRC9958	3.95mm	A/R	
	FRC9960	4.00mm	A/R	

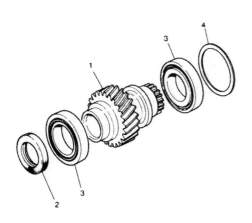

VS3729

MODEL LR110 - UP TO AUGUST 1986
BLOCK TS 5368
PAGE D 110
GROUP D

GEARBOX - V8 - TRANSFER BOX LT230T - TRANSFER INTERMEDIATE SHAFT

ILL	PART NO	DESCRIPTION	QTY	REMARKS
1	FRC8291	Intermediate Shaft	1	
2	FRC7439	O Ring-Shaft	1	
3	FRC7884	Gear-Intermediate Cluster	1	Suffix B Only
	FRC9460	Gear-Intermediate Cluster	1	Suffix C Only
4	FRC7810	Bearing	2	
5	FRC7437	Spacer-Collapsible	1	
6	FRC7454	Circlip	2	
7	FRC7452	Plate-Anti Rotation	1	
8	FRC7453	Nut-Intermediate Shaft	1	
9	SH108201L	Screw	1	
10	WA108051L	Washer	1	

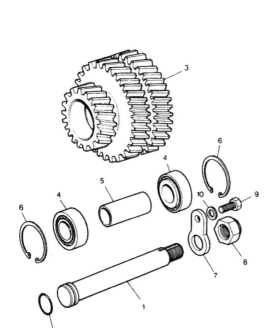

TS5368

LAND ROVER PARTS LTD

MODEL LR110 - UP TO AUGUST 1986
BLOCK VS 3728
PAGE D 112
GROUP D

GEARBOX - V8 - TRANSFER BOX LT230T - FRONT HOUSING

ILL	PART NO	DESCRIPTION	QTY	REMARKS
1	FRC8299	Housing-Front Output	1	
2	FRC6103	Joint Washer-Output Housing	1	
3	BH108061L	Bolt	7	
4	BH108181L	Bolt	1	
5	WA108051L	Washer	8	
6	FRC6104	Cover-Front Output Housing	1	
7	FRC6105	Joint Washer	1	
8	SH108251L	Screw	7	
9	WA108051L	Washer	7	
10	FRC6106	Housing-Cross Shaft-Hi/Low	1	
11	FRC7998	Joint Washer-Housing	1	
12	BH108111L	Bolt	6	
13	WA108051L	Washer	6	
14	FRC167	Breather Pipe	1	
	219676	Clip-Pipe	1	

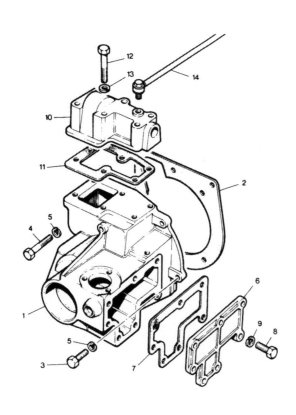

VSS3728

LAND ROVER PARTS LTD

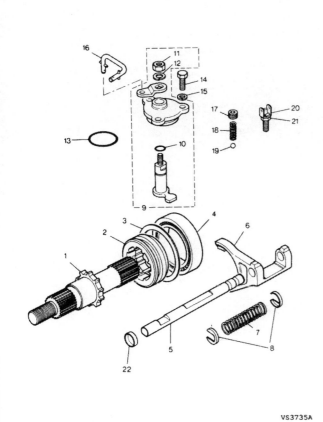

MODEL LR110 - UP TO AUGUST 1986
BLOCK VS 3735A
PAGE D 114
GROUP D

GEARBOX - V8 - TRANSFER BOX LT230T - DIFF LOCK

ILL	PART NO	DESCRIPTION	QTY	REMARKS
1	FRC5449	Shaft-Front Output	1	
2	FRC5440	Dog Clutch-Front Drive Lock Up	1	
	FRC5575	O Ring-Dog Clutch	1	
3		SELECTIVE SHIM-FRONT OUTPUT TAPER BEARING		
	FTC726	+2.00mm	1	
	FTC728	+2.05mm	1	
	FTC730	+2.10mm	1	
	FTC732	+2.15mm	1	
	FTC734	+2.20mm	1	
	FTC736	+2.25mm	1	
	FTC738	+2.30mm	1	
	FTC740	+2.35mm	1	
	FTC742	+2.40mm	1	
	FTC744	+2.45mm	1	
	FTC746	+2.50mm	1	
	FTC748	+2.55mm	1	
	FTC750	+2.60mm	1	
	FTC752	+2.65mm	1	
	FTC754	+2.70mm	1	
	FTC756	+2.75mm	1	
	FTC758	+2.80mm	1	
	FTC760	+2.85mm	1	
	FTC762	+2.90mm	1	
	FTC764	+2.95mm	1	
	FTC766	+3.00mm	1	
	FTC768	+3.05mm	1	
	FTC770	+3.10mm	1	
	FTC772	+3.15mm	1	
	FTC774	+3.20mm	1	
	FTC776	+3.25mm	1	
4	FRC7871	Bearing-Taper	1	
5	FRC6030	Selector Shaft-Diff Lock	1	
6	FRC6109	Selector Fork-Diff Lock	1	
7	FRC5468	Spring-Diff Lock	1	
8	FRC5469	Clip-Spring	2	

VS3735A

LAND ROVER PARTS LTD

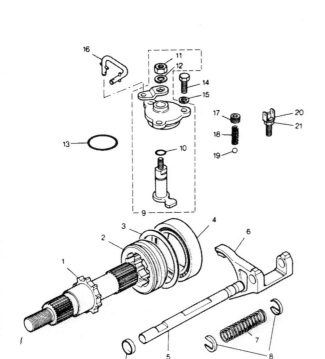

MODEL LR110 - UP TO AUGUST 1986
BLOCK VS 3735A
PAGE D 114.02
GROUP D

GEARBOX - V8 - TRANSFER BOX LT230T - DIFF LOCK - CONTINUED

ILL	PART NO	DESCRIPTION	QTY	REMARKS
9	FRC8041	HOUSING ASSEMBLY-SELECTOR FINGER	1	
10	FRC5576	+O Ring	1	
11	NY108041L	+Nut	1	
12	WA108051L	Washer	1	
13	FRC5473	O Ring	1	
14	SH108251L	Screw	3	
15	WA108051L	Washer	3	
16	FRC7948	Connecting Link Assembly	1	
17	SU112101L	Plug-Detent	1	
18	FRC5562	Spring-Detent	1	
19	571146	Ball-Detent	1	
20	PRC2911	Switch-Diff Lock	1	
21	22A1613L	Locknut-Switch	1	
22	FRC6110	Plug-Selection Shaft	1	

VS 3735A

LAND ROVER PARTS LTD

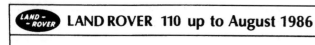
MODEL LR110 - UP TO AUGUST 1986
BLOCK VS 3725
PAGE D 116
GROUP D

GEARBOX - V8 - TRANSFER BOX LT230T - FRONT FLANGE

ILL	PART NO	DESCRIPTION	QTY	REMARKS
1	FRC5442	Flange-Front Output	1	
2	FRC2464	Sealing Washer	1	
3	571468	Washer-Shaft	1	
4	NY120041L	Nut-Shaft	1	
5	BT606101L	Bolt-Flange	4	
6	FRC6121	Mudshield	1	
7	FRC7043	Oil Seal	1	
8	216962	Circlip	1	
9	RTC3406	Bearing	1	
10	FRC5439	Spacer	1	

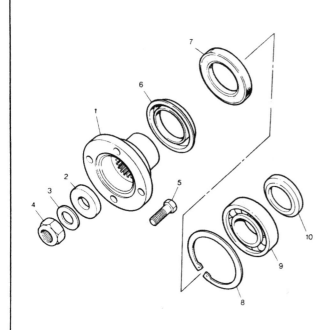

VS3725

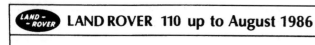
MODEL LR110 - UP TO AUGUST 1986
BLOCK TS 5703
PAGE D 118
GROUP D

GEARBOX - V8 - TRANSFER BOX LT230T - DIFFERENTIAL

ILL	PART NO	DESCRIPTION	QTY	REMARKS
1	FRC7926	Differential Assembly	1	
2	FRC6674	Cross Shaft	2	NLS-Use RTC3397
	RTC3397	Cross Shaft Kit	1	Matched Pair
3	RTC4490	DIFF GEARS-BALANCED SET	1	
4	FRC6968	+Thrust Washer	4	
5		SELECTIVE THRUST WASHER		
		DIFF WHEEL		
	FRC6956	1.05mm	A/R	
	FRC6958	1.15mm	A/R	
	FRC6960	1.25mm	A/R	
	FRC6962	1.35mm	A/R	
	FRC6964	1.45mm	A/R	
6	BH110121L	Bolt-Diff Case	8	
7	FRC7499	Retaining Ring	1	

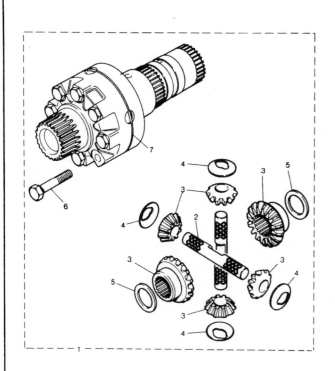

TS5703

MODEL LR110 - UP TO AUGUST 1986
BLOCK TS 5762
PAGE D 120
GROUP D

GEARBOX - V8 - TRANSFER BOX LT230T - TRANSFER - HIGH/LOW

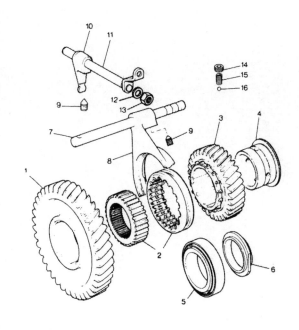

ILL	PART NO	DESCRIPTION	QTY	REMARKS
1	FRC7434	Gear-Low Output	1	)
2	RTC4373	Hub & Sleeve Assy-High/Low	1	)Suffix B Only
3	FRC7885	Gear-High Output	1	)
1	FRC9531	Gear-Low Output	1	)
2	RTC5064	Hub & Sleeve Assy-High/Low	1	)Suffix C Only
3	FRC9533	Gear-High Output	1	)
4	FRC7441	Bush	1	
5	606474	Bearing	1	
6	FRC7970	Nut-Bearing Retainer	1	
7	FRC7457	Shaft-High/Low Selector	1	Suffix B Only
	FRC9513	Selector Shaft-High/Low	1	Suffix C Only
8	FRC5458	Fork-High/Low Selector	1	
9	FRC7018	Screw-Selector Fork	1	
10	FRC7929	Selector Finger	1	
11	FRC8899	Operating Arm-High/Low	1	
12	WA108051L	Washer	1	
13	NY108041L	Nut	1	
14	SU112101L	Plug-Detent	1	)Suffix B Only
15	FRC5562	Spring-Detent	1	)
14	FRC9549	Plug-Detent	1	)Suffix C Only
15	FRC9546	Spring-Detent	1	)
16	571146	Ball-Detent	1	

TS5762

MODEL LR110 - UP TO AUGUST 1986
BLOCK TS 5307
PAGE D 122
GROUP D

GEARBOX - V8 - TRANSFER BOX LT230T - REAR FLANGE

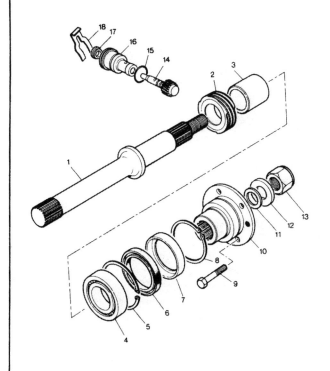

ILL	PART NO	DESCRIPTION	QTY	REMARKS
1	FRC5450	Shaft-Rear Output	1	
2	FRC3162	Speedo Worm	1	
3	FRC5446	Spacer-Speedo Worm	1	
4	RTC3406	Bearing	1	
5	216962	Circlip	1	
6	FRC7043	Oil Seal	1	
8	571682	Circlip	1	
9	FRC3602	Bolt	1	
10	FRC5438	Flange-Rear Output	1	
11	FRC2464	Sealing Washer	1	
12	571468	Washer	1	
13	NY120041L	Nut	1	
14	FRC3310	Speedo Drive Gear & Spindle	1	
15	571665	O Ring	1	
16	FRC3286	Housing-Speedo Spindle	1	
17	AAU2304	Oil Seal	1	
18	533765	Plate-Retaining Speedo Cable	1	

TS5307

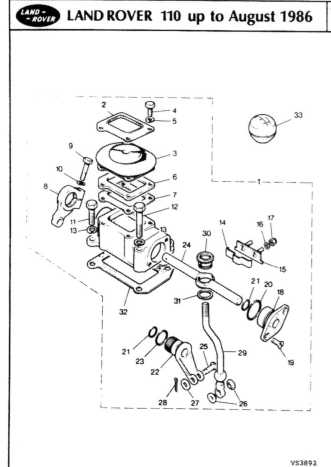

MODEL LR110 - UP TO AUGUST 1986
BLOCK VS 3892
PAGE D 124
GROUP D

GEARBOX - V8 - TRANSFER BOX LT230T - TRANSFER GEAR CHANGE

ILL	PART NO	DESCRIPTION	QTY	REMARKS
1	FRC7941	TRANSFER GEAR CHANGE ASSY	1	
2	FRC6873	+Plate	1	
3	FRC6872	+Grommet	1	
4	SH106201L	+Screw	4	
5	WA106041L	+Washer	4	
6	FRC7944	+Gate Plate	1	
7	FRC5486	+Gasket	1	
8	FRC5478	+Operating Arm	1	
9	BH106051L	+Bolt	1	
10	WA106041L	+Washer	1	
11	SH108251L	+Screw	2	
12	BH108111L	+Bolt	2	
13	WL108001L	+Washer-Spring	4	
14	RTC1956	+Detent Spring	1	
15	FRC6125	+Retainer-Spring	1	
16	WA105001L	+Washer	2	
17	NY105041L	+Nut	2	

VS3892

LAND ROVER PARTS LTD

MODEL LR110 - UP TO AUGUST 1986
BLOCK VS 3892
PAGE D 126
GROUP D

GEARBOX - V8 - TRANSFER BOX LT230T - TRANSFER GEAR CHANGE - CONTINUED

ILL	PART NO	DESCRIPTION	QTY	REMARKS
18	FRC5574	+End Cover	1	
19	SF106201L	+Screw	2	
20	FRC4565	+O Ring	1	
21	FRC4509	+O Ring	2	
22	FRC5480	+Crank Arm	1	
23	FRC5479	+O Ring	1	
24	FRC6117	+Cross Shaft	1	
25	PC108321L	+Clevis Pin	1	
26	FRC4499	+Bush	2	
27	WA108051L	+Washer	1	
28	PS104121L	+Split Pin	1	
29	FRC8560	+Lever	1	
30	FRC5076	+Seat-Gear Lever	1	
31	CR120215L	+Circlip	1	
32	FRC6306	+Gasket	1	
	FRC7930	+Plug-Housing	1	
33	FRC6595	Knob	1	

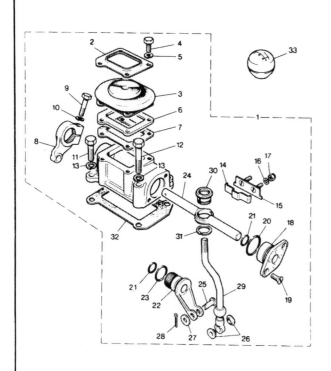

VS3892

LAND ROVER PARTS LTD

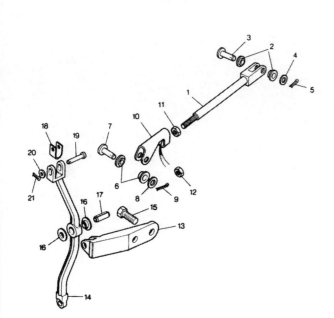

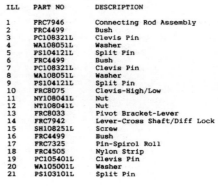

MODEL LR110 - UP TO AUGUST 1986
BLOCK TS 5351
PAGE D 128
GROUP D

GEARBOX - V8 - TRANSFER BOX LT230T - GEAR CHANGE

ILL	PART NO	DESCRIPTION	QTY	REMARKS
1	FRC7946	Connecting Rod Assembly	1	
2	FRC4499	Bush	2	
3	PC108321L	Clevis Pin	1	
4	WA108051L	Washer	1	
5	PS104121L	Split Pin	1	
6	FRC4499	Bush	2	
7	PC108321L	Clevis Pin	1	
8	WA108051L	Washer	1	
9	PS104121L	Split Pin	1	
10	FRC8075	Clevis-High/Low	1	
11	NY108041L	Nut	1	
12	NT108041L	Nut	1	
13	FRC8033	Pivot Bracket-Lever	1	
14	FRC7942	Lever-Cross Shaft/Diff Lock	1	
15	SH108251L	Screw	2	
16	FRC4499	Bush	2	
17	FRC7325	Pin-Spirol Roll	1	
18	FRC4505	Nylon Strip	1	
19	PC105401L	Clevis Pin	1	
20	WA105001L	Washer	1	
21	PS103101L	Split Pin	1	

TS5351

LAND ROVER PARTS LTD

258

MODEL LR110 - UP TO AUGUST 1986
BLOCK TS 5761
PAGE D 130
GROUP D

GEARBOX - V8 - GEARBOX MOUNTINGS

ILL	PART NO	DESCRIPTION	QTY	REMARKS
1	NRC9501	Mounting Bracket-LH	1	
2	SH112251L	Screw Fixing Bracket to Gearbox	4	
3	WL112001L	Washer Spring Fixing Bracket to Gearbox	4	
4	NTC1201	Mounting Bracket-RH	1	
5	90575585	Mounting Bracket	2	
6	566222	Mounting Rubber	2	Imperial
	RTC6115	Engine Mtg Kit	2	)
	NH110041LD	+Nut	2	)Metric
	WC110061LD	+Washer	1	)
	WL110001LD	+Spring Washer	2	)
7	2251L	Washer Rubber to Bracket	2	
8	WL600061L	Washer Spring Rubber to Bracket	2	
9	NH606041L	Nut Rubber to Bracket	2	
10	WL600061L	Washer Rubber to Bracket	2	
11	NH606041L	Nut Rubber to Bracket	2	

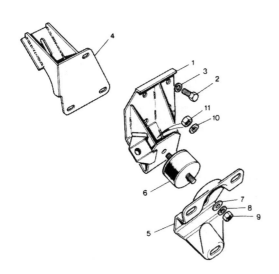

TS5761

LAND ROVER PARTS LTD

259

MASTER INDEX

GROUP E

AXLES AND SUSPENSION

MODEL LR110 - UP TO AUGUST 1986
BLOCK VS 3766
PAGE E 2
GROUP E

FRONT AXLE

ILL	PART NO	DESCRIPTION	QTY	REMARKS
		FRONT AXLE COMPLETE ASSY		
	FRC8782	-RHD	1	
	FRC8783	-LHD	1	

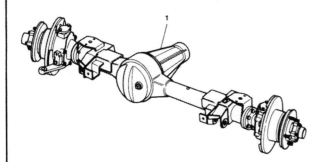

VS3766

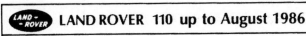
MODEL LR110 - UP TO AUGUST 1986
BLOCK VS 3765
PAGE E 4
GROUP E

FRONT AXLE - AXLE CASE

ILL	PART NO	DESCRIPTION	QTY	REMARKS
1	FRC4307	AXLE CASE AND STUD ASSY	1	
2	561195	+Stud	4	
3	561196	+Stud	6	
4	608246	+Filler/Drain Plug	2	

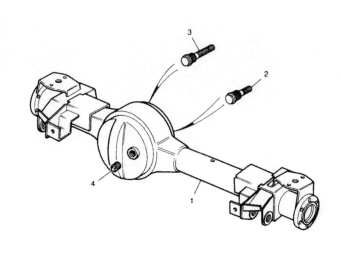

VS3765

LAND ROVER PARTS LTD

262

MODEL LR110 - UP TO AUGUST 1986
BLOCK TS 5546
PAGE E 6
GROUP E

FRONT AXLE - DIFFERENTIAL

ILL	PART NO	DESCRIPTION	QTY	REMARKS
	FRC5688	DIFFERENTIAL ASSEMBLY	1	To Note(1)
	FRC8521	DIFFERENTIAL ASSEMBLY	1	From Note(2)
1	FRC5690	+Pinion Housing	1	
2	BH112101L	++Set-Bolt	4	
3	608246	+Filler Plug	1	
4	FRC5204	+Locking Ring	2	
5	FRC5661	+Locking Tab	2	
6	576159	+Spring Pin	2	
7	NY606041L	+Self Locking Nut	10	
8	FRC1193	+Shim 0.060"	2	
	FRC1195	+Shim 0.062"	2	
	FRC1197	+Shim 0.064"	2	
	FRC1199	+Shim 0.066"	2	
	FRC1201	+Shim 0.068"	2	
	FRC1203	+Shim 0.070"	2	
	539718	+Shim 0.072"	2	
	539720	+Shim 0.074"	2	
	539722	+Shim 0.076"	2	
	539724	+Shim 0.078"	2	
9	539707	+Pinion Bearing Outer	1	
10	539745	+Spacer	1	
11	FRC4586	+Oil Seal	1	To Note(1)
	FRC8220	+Oil Seal	1	From Note(2)
12	236072	+Mud Shield	1	To Note(1)
	FRC8154	+Mud Shield	1	From Note(2)
13	236632	+Flange	1	
14	90513454	+Plain Washer	1	
15	3259	+Castle Nut	1	
16	PS608101L	+Split Pin	1	
17	NRC9713	Bracket-Track Rod Protection	1	
18	SH406061	Bolt	2	
19	WM600061	Spring Washer	2	

NOTE(1): Axle No.20L13358B-RHS, 21L10631B-LHS

NOTE(2): Axle No.20L13359B-RHS, 21L10632B-LHS

TS5546

 LAND ROVER PARTS LTD

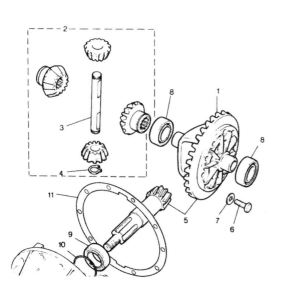

MODEL LR110 - UP TO AUGUST 1986
BLOCK 3RE 376A
PAGE E 8
GROUP E

FRONT AXLE - DIFFERENTIAL CONTINUED

ILL	PART NO	DESCRIPTION	QTY	REMARKS
1	FRC2933	Differential Case	1	
2	RTC4486	Differential Gear Kit	1	
3	599945	+Cross Shaft	1	
4	CCN110L	+Circlip	2	
5	594493	Crownwheel & Pinion	1	
6	593692	Bolt	10	
7	593693	Plain Washer	10	
8	RTC2726	Differential Bearing	2	
9	539706	Pinion Bearing-Inner	1	
10	549230	Shim 0.038"	1	
	549232	Shim 0.040"	1	
	549234	Shim 0.042"	1	
	549236	Shim 0.044"	1	
	549238	Shim 0.046"	1	
	549240	Shim 0.048"	1	
	549242	Shim 0.050"	1	
	549244	Shim 0.052"	1	
	549246	Shim 0.054"	1	
	549248	Shim 0.056"	1	
	549250	Shim 0.058"	1	
	549252	Shim 0.060"	1	
	576236	Shim 0.062"	1	
	576237	Shim 0.063"	1	
	576238	Shim 0.064"	1	
	576239	Shim 0.065"	1	
11	7316	Joint Washer	1	

3RE376A

 **LAND ROVER PARTS LTD**

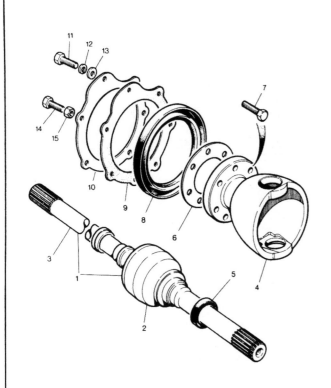

MODEL LR110 - UP TO AUGUST 1986
BLOCK VS 3764/A
PAGE E 10
GROUP E

FRONT AXLE - SHAFT & CV JOINT ASSEMBLY

ILL	PART NO	DESCRIPTION	QTY	REMARKS
	FRC3890	SHAFT & CV JOINT ASSY-RH	1	
1	FRC3891	SHAFT & CV JOINT ASSY-LH	1	
2	AEU2522	+CV Joint	2	
	AEU2520	+Shaft RH	1	
3	AEU2521	+Shaft LH	1	
4	FRC2644	S.P Bearing Housing	2	
5	571718	Oil Seal	2	
6	FRC2349	Joint Washer	2	
7	AFU1030	Bolt-Housing to Axle Case	14	
	FRC8528	Bolt-Housing to Axle Case	14	)Note(1)
	FRC8530	Washer	14	)
8	FRC2889	Oil Seal	2	
9	FRC4206	Joint Washer	2	
10	FRC4142	Retaining Plate	2	
11	SH106121	Bolt-Plate to Housing	14	
12	WL106001	Spring Washer	14	
13	WA106001L	Plain Washer	14	
14	AFU1234	Lock Stop Bolt	2	
15	NT112041	Locknut	2	

NOTE(1): FRC8528, FRC8530 Are Alternatives To AFU1030.

VS3764A

 **LAND ROVER PARTS LTD**

MODEL LR110 - UP TO AUGUST 1986
BLOCK VS 3767
PAGE E 12
GROUP E

FRONT AXLE - SWIVEL PIN HOUSING

ILL	PART NO	DESCRIPTION	QTY	REMARKS
		SWIVEL PIN HOUSING		
	FRC4838	RH-RHD	1	
1	FRC4839	LH-RHD	1	
	FRC4840	RH-LHD	1	
	FRC4841	LH-LHD	1	
2	3291	Filler Plug	2	
3	3290	Drain Plug	2	
4	FRC2916	Housing and Bush	2	
5	FRC2906	Thrust Washer	2	
6	FRC3511	Swivel Pin Upper	2	
7	FRC2883	Shim 0.075mm	2	
	FRC2884	Shim 0.130mm	2	
	FRC2885	Shim 0.250mm	2	
	FRC2886	Shim 0.750mm	2	
8	BX110071L	Bolt	4	
9	WL110001	Spring Washer	4	
10	FRC2894	Swivel Pin Lower	2	
11	FRC2897	Joint Washer	2	
12	606666	Bearing	2	
13	BH108061L	Bolt	4	
14	WL108001L	Spring Washer	4	
15	FRC3725	Retaining Bracket	2	

VS3767

266

MODEL LR110 - UP TO AUGUST 1986
BLOCK VS 3768
PAGE E 14
GROUP E

FRONT AXLE - FRONT HUBS

ILL	PART NO	DESCRIPTION	QTY	REMARKS
1	FRC4320	STUB AXLE ASSEMBLY	2	
2	FRC3099	+Oil Seal	2	
3	FRC4319	+Bush	2	
4	FRC3205	Joint Washer	2	
5	FRC2310	Mudshield	2	
6	SX110251	Bolt-Stub Axle to SP Housing	12	
7	WL110001L	Spring Washer	12	
8	RTC3511	Oil Seal	2	To Note(1)
	FRC8221	Oil Seal	2	From Note(2)
9	RTC3429	Bearing Inner and Outer	4	
10	FRC6139	HUB AND STUD ASSEMBLY	2	
11	FRC6137	+Stud	10	
12	217352	Key Washer	2	
13	90217355	Locknut	4	To Note(1)
	FRC8700	Locknut	4	From Note(2)
14	217353	Locker	2	
15	FRC3988	Joint Washer	2	
16	FRC5806	Hub Driving Member	2	
17	AFU1181	Bolt	10	
18	WL110001L	Spring Washer	10	
19	FRC6782	Shim 0.45mm	4	
	FRC6783	Shim 0.60mm	4	
	FRC6784	Shim 0.75mm	4	
	FRC6785	Shim 0.90mm	4	
	FRC6786	Shim 1.05mm	4	
	FRC6787	Shim 1.20mm	4	
	FRC6788	Shim 1.35mm	4	
	FRC6789	Shim 1.50mm	4	
	FRC6790	Shim 1.65mm	4	
20	549473	Circlip	2	
21	FRC4377	Hub Cap	2	

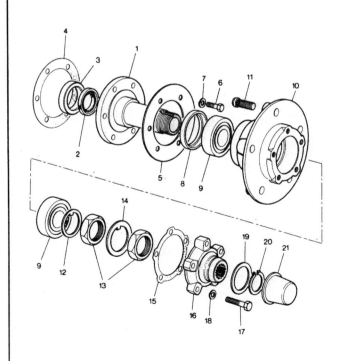

NOTE(1): Axle No.20L13358B-RHS, 21L10631B-LHS

NOTE(2): Axle No.20L13359B-RHS, 21L10632B-LHS

VS3768

MODEL LR110 - UP TO AUGUST 1986
BLOCK TS 6592
PAGE E 14.02
GROUP E

FRONT AXLE - FREE WHEELING HUB KIT - 4 CYLINDER

ILL	PART NO	DESCRIPTION	QTY	REMARKS
1	RTC8063	KIT-FREE WHEELING HUBS	1	
2	549473	+Circlip	2	
3	RTC7131	+Main Spring	2	
4	RTC7132	+Actuator Assy	2	
5	RTC7133	+Hub Cover	2	
6	RTC7136	+Service Kit	2	
7	WE110001L	+Shakeproof Washer	10	
8	FRC3988	+Gasket	2	
9	RTC7137	+Bearing Kit	2	

NOTE: For Use On Vehicles to Selectable 2 And
      4 Wheel Drive.

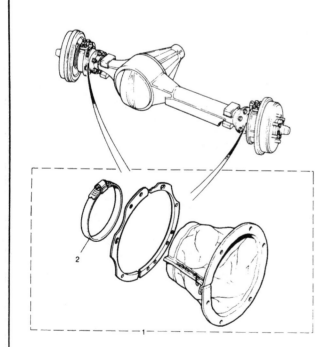

TS 6592

LAND ROVER PARTS LTD

MODEL LR110 - UP TO AUGUST 1986
BLOCK TS 5339
PAGE E 14.04
GROUP E

FRONT AXLE - GAITER KIT

ILL	PART NO	DESCRIPTION	QTY	REMARKS
1	RTC3826	GAITER KIT	1	
2	RTC3519	+Hose Clip	2	

TS5339

LAND ROVER PARTS LTD

MODEL LR110 - UP TO AUGUST 1986
BLOCK VS 3769
PAGE E 16
GROUP E

REAR AXLE - REAR AXLE COMPLETE ASSEMBLY

ILL	PART NO	DESCRIPTION	QTY	REMARKS
1	FRC9995	REAR AXLE COMPLETE ASSEMBLY	1	
2	FRC9991	+Rear Axle Housing Assembly	1	

VS3769

MODEL LR110 - UP TO AUGUST 1986
BLOCK VS 3770
PAGE E 18
GROUP E

REAR AXLE - AXLE CASE

ILL	PART NO	DESCRIPTION	QTY	REMARKS
1	AEU2536	Axle Casing	1	)No Longer)Serviced
2	607163	Bolt-Diff Bearing Cap	4	
3	RTC1139	Gasket	1	
4	RTC844	Cover	1	
5	607173	Bolt	10	
6	AAU2825	Lock Washer	10	
7	608246	Filler/Drain Plug	2	
8	RTC845	Flitch Plate	1	
9	NRC8024	Bracket-3 Way	1	
10	NRC5346	Plate-Brake Pipe	1	
11	FRC6249	Bracket-Ball Joint	1	
12	AEU2508	Special Bolt	4	
13	607181	Pinion Bearing-Outer	1	
14	607182	Oil Thrower	1	
15	607183	Gasket	1	
16	AEU2515	Oil Seal	1	
17	607185	Flange	1	
18	607357	Washer	1	
19	90608545	Locknut	1	

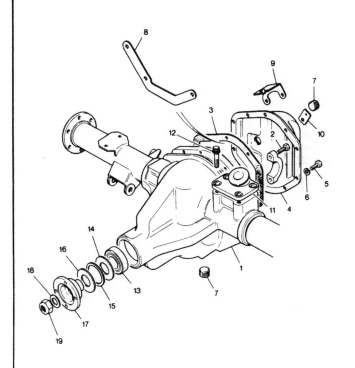

VS3770

MODEL LR110 - UP TO AUGUST 1986
BLOCK 1RE 169
PAGE E 20
GROUP E

REAR AXLE - DIFFERENTIAL

ILL	PART NO	DESCRIPTION	QTY	REMARKS
1	AEU1489	Differential Case	1	
2	607165	Bolt-Diff Case	8	
	RTC4488	Differential Gear Kit	1	
3	607166	+Differential Gear	2	
4	607169	+Thrust Washer	2	
5	607167	+Differential Wheel	4	
6	607168	+Thrust Washer	4	
7	90607170	Cross Shaft	1	
8	AEU1488	Crown Wheel & Pinion	1	
9	RTC773	Bolt-Crown Wheel	12	
10	607187	Bearing-Differential	2	
11		Shim-Diff Bearing	A/R	
	607188	0.003"	2	
	607189	0.005"	2	
	607190	0.010"	2	
	607191	0.030"	2	
12	607180	Pinion Bearing-Inner	1	
13		Shim-Pinion Bearing	A/R	
	607177	0.003"	2	
	607178	0.005"	2	
	607179	0.010"	2	
14	607197	Collapsible Spacer	1	

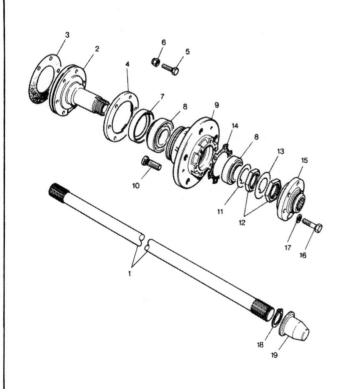

IRE169

LAND ROVER PARTS LTD

MODEL LR110 - UP TO AUGUST 1986
BLOCK VS 3771
PAGE E 22
GROUP E

REAR AXLE - AXLE SHAFTS AND HUBS

ILL	PART NO	DESCRIPTION	QTY	REMARKS
1	FRC2454	Rear Axle Shaft RH	1	
	FRC2455	Rear Axle Shaft LH	1	
2	FRC3132	Hub Bearing Sleeve	2	Note(1)
	FRC8540	Hub Bearing Sleeve	2	Note(2)
3	FRC3136	Joint Washer	2	
4	FRC3147	Oil Catcher	2	)Note(1)
5	AFU1032	Bolt Sleeve to Axle Case	12	)
	FRC7257	Bolt Sleeve to Axle	12	Note(2)
6	NY110041L	Nyloc Nut Sleeve to Axle Case	12	
7	RTC3511	Oil Seal	2	Note(1)
	FRC8221	Oil Seal	2	Note(2)
8	RTC3429	Bearing-Inner & Outer	4	
9	FRC6141	HUB & STUD ASSEMBLY	2	Note(1)
	FRC8555	HUB & STUD ASSEMBLY	2	Note(2)
10	FRC6137	+Stud	10	
11	217352	Key Washer	2	Note(1)
	FRC8227	Spacer	2	Note(2)
12	90217355	Locknut	4	Note(1)
	FRC8700	Locknut	4	Note(2)
13	217353	Locker	2	Note(1)
	FRC8002	Locker	2	)Note(2)
	FRC8222	Oil Seal-Outer	2	)
14	FRC3988	Joint Washer	2	
15	FRC5806	Hub Driving Member	2	
16	AFU1181	Bolt	10	
17	WL110001L	Spring Washer	10	
18	549473	Circlip	2	
19	FRC4377	Hub Cap	2	

NOTE(1): To Axle No. 21S22954B

NOTE(2): From Axle No. 21S22955B.

VS3771

LAND ROVER PARTS LTD

MODEL LR110 - UP TO AUGUST 1986
BLOCK VS 3772A
PAGE E 24
GROUP E

AXLES - FRONT AND REAR - REMOTE BREATHERS

ILL	PART NO	DESCRIPTION	QTY	REMARKS
1	FRC4718	Remote Breather-Front	1	To VIN 189380
	FRC7229	Remote Breather-Front	1	From VIN 189381
2	FRC4719	Remote Breather-Rear	1	To VIN 189380
	FRC7230	Remote Breather-Rear	1	From VIN 189381
3	589806	P Clip-Front Breather	1	
4	6860	Grommet-Front Breather	1	
5	568680	Tie-Front Breather	6	
6	589806	P Clip Rear Breather	2	
7	6860	Grommet-Rear Breather	2	
8	NH110041L	Nut	1	From VIN 189381
9	568680	Tie-Rear Breather	4	)
10	AEU1449	P Clip-Rear Breather	1	)To VIN 189380
11	79123	Pipe Clip-Rear Breather	2	)
12	622324	Pipe Clip	2	From VIN 189381
	NRC9246	Pipe Clip	7	

VS3772A

LAND ROVER PARTS LTD

274

MODEL LR110 - UP TO AUGUST 1986
BLOCK VS 4010
PAGE E 26
GROUP E

PROPSHAFT

ILL	PART NO	DESCRIPTION	QTY	REMARKS
1	FRC5566	Front Propshaft-4 Cylinder	1	To VIN 252442
	FRC4799	Front Propshaft-V8-4 Speed	1	To VIN 252257
	FRC6243	Front Propshaft-V8-5 Speed	1	To VIN 252257
	FRC8390	Front Propshaft-4 Cylinder	1	From VIN 252443
	FRC8388	Front Propshaft-V8-4 Speed	1	From VIN 252258
	FRC8386	Front Propshaft-V8-5 Speed	1	From VIN 252258
2	RTC3346	+Universal Joint	2	Note(1)
	RTC3458	+Universal Joint	2	Note(2)
3	591279	Rear Propshaft-4 Cylinder	1	To VIN 252442
	FRC2980	Rear Propshaft-V8	1	To VIN 252442
	FRC8391	Rear Propshaft-4 Cylinder	1	From VIN 252443
	FRC8389	Rear Propshaft-V8	1	From VIN 252258
	RTC3346	+Universal Joint	2	Note(1)
	RTC3458	+Universal Joint	2	Note(2)
4	509045	Bolt	8	
5	NZ606041L	Nut	16	
6	549229	Grease Nipple	2	
7	234532	Grease Nipple	1	
8	276484	Grommet Assy-Front Propshaft	1	

NOTE(1): RTC3346 For Use With FRC5566,
FRC4799, FRC6243, FRC2980, 591279

NOTE(2): RTC3458 For Use With FRC8386,
FRC8388, FRC8389, FRC8390, FRC8391

VS4010

LAND ROVER PARTS LTD

275

MODEL LR110 - UP TO AUGUST 1986
BLOCK VS 3951A
PAGE E 28
GROUP E

SUSPENSION - RADIUS ARM AND PANHARD ROD

ILL	PART NO	DESCRIPTION	QTY	REMARKS
1	NTC2705	Radius Arm	2	
2	NTC1774	+Bush	4	
3	BH610281L	Bolt-Arm to Axle	4	
4	NY610041	Nyloc Nut	4	
5	NRC4514	Bush-Arm to Chassis	4	
6	NRC4515	Dished Washer	2	
7	NRC4516	Plain Washer	2	
8	NY120041	Nyloc Nut	2	
9	575707	Rubber-Front Bump Stop	2	
10	SH108251L	Screw-Fixing Bump Stop	4	
11	WA108051L	Plain Washer	4	
12	WL108001L	Spring Washer	4	
13	NH108041L	Nut	4	
14	NRC9729	Panhard Rod	1	
15	NRC9728	+Bush	2	
16	BH114161	Bolt-Rod to Mounting Arm	1	
17	BH114151	Bolt-Rod to Axle Bracket	1	
18	NY114041	Nyloc Nut	2	
19	NRC5764	Mounting Arm-RHD	1	
	NRC5765	Mounting Arm-LHD	1	
20	253952	Bolt-Arm to Chassis	1	
21	BH608461	Bolt-Arm to Chassis	1	
22	WC112081L	Plain Washer	2	
23	252164	Nut	2	

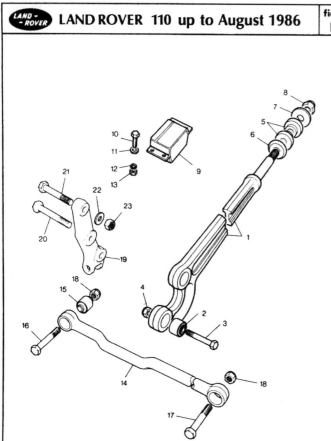

VS3951A

LAND ROVER PARTS LTD

276

MODEL LR110 - UP TO AUGUST 1986
BLOCK VS 3950
PAGE E 30
GROUP E

SUSPENSION - FRONT SPRING AND SHOCK ABSORBER

ILL	PART NO	DESCRIPTION	QTY	REMARKS
1	RTC4637	Shock Absorber Kit	2	
2	552818	+Cushion Rubber	8	
3	500746	+Retaining Washer	8	
4	NRC4365	+Guide Washer	8	
5	NY608041L	+Nut	2	)Alternatives
	NV608041	+Nut	2	)
6	NT608041L	+Locknut	4	)
7	NRC6372	Bracket-Shock Absorber	2	
8	572087	Securing Ring-Bracket	2	
9	WM600051L	Spring Washer	8	
10	NH605041L	Nut	8	
11		Front Spring		
	NRC8044	-Drivers	1	
	NRC8045	-Passengers	1	
	NRC9448	-Drivers-Heavy Duty	1	
	NRC9449	-Passengers-Heavy Duty	1	
12	575579	Spring Seat-Lower	2	
13	SH606061L	Bolt-Seat to Axle	4	
14	WM600061L	Spring Washer-Seat to Axle	4	

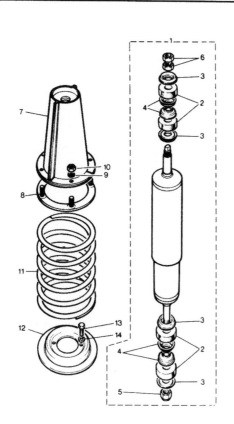

VS3950

LAND ROVER PARTS LTD

277

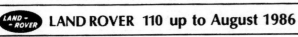

MODEL LR110 - UP TO AUGUST 1986
BLOCK VS 3942
PAGE E 32
GROUP E

SUSPENSION - ANTI ROLL BAR

ILL	PART NO	DESCRIPTION	QTY	REMARKS
1	NRC6221	Anti Roll Bar	1	
2	NRC5674	Bush-Anti Roll Bar	2	
3	592773	Strap	2	
4	SH108251L	Screw	8	
5	WA108051L	Plain Washer	8	
6	WL108001L	Spring Washer	8	
7	NH108041L	Nut	8	
8	NRC7101	Ball Joint & Link Assembly	2	
9	WC112081	Washer	2	
10	NC112041	Nut	2	
11	PS105251	Split Pin	2	
12	NRC6658	Pin-Anti Roll Bar	2	
13	264024	Washer	2	
14	552819	Bush	2	
15	WC116101	Plain Washer	2	
16	NY116041	Nut	2	

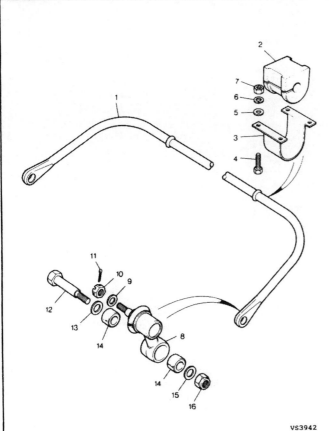

VS3942

LAND ROVER PARTS LTD

278

MODEL LR110 - UP TO AUGUST 1986
BLOCK VS 3949
PAGE E 34
GROUP E

SUSPENSION - BOTTOM LINK

ILL	PART NO	DESCRIPTION	QTY	REMARKS
1	NTC2708	Bottom Link Assembly	2	
2	NTC1772	+Bush-Bottom Link	2	
3	BH610321L	Bolt-Link to Axle	2	
4	252166	Nut-Link to Axle	2	
5	NRC7491	Mounting Rubber-Link to Frame	2	
6	WA120001	Plain Washer	2	
7	NY120041	Nut	2	
8	SH110301	Bolt-Mounting Rubber to Frame	6	
9	NY110041	Nut-Mounting Rubber to Frame	6	
10	90575789	Bump Rubber	2	
11	SH108251L	Screw	4	
12	WA108051L	Plain Washer	4	
13	WL108001L	Spring Washer	4	
14	NH108041L	Nut	4	

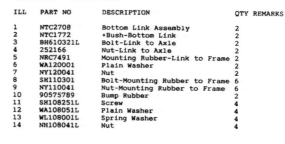
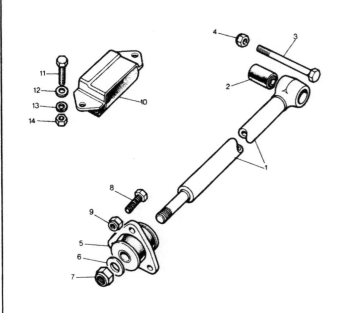

VS3949

LAND ROVER PARTS LTD

279

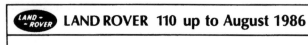

MODEL LR110 - UP TO AUGUST 1986
BLOCK VS 3947
PAGE E 36
GROUP E

SUSPENSION - TOP LINK AND BUSH

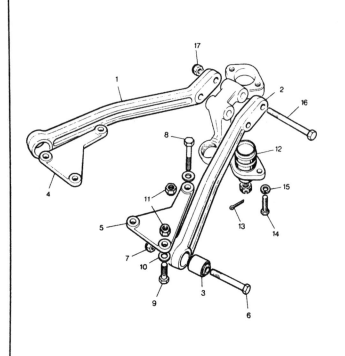

ILL	PART NO	DESCRIPTION	QTY	REMARKS
1	90575627	TOP LINK & BUSH ASSY-RH	1	
2	575628	TOP LINK & BUSH ASSY-LH	1	
3	90575626	+Bush	2	
4	575615	Bracket-Top Link Mounting-RH	1	
5	575616	Bracket-Top Link Mounting-LH	1	
6	BH612321	Bolt-Link to Mounting Bracket	2	
7	NY612041	Nut	2	
8	BX110111L	Bolt-Bracket to Chassis	2	
9	BX110091L	Bolt-Bracket to Chassis	4	
10	WC110061L	Plain Washer	6	
11	NY110051L	Nut	6	
12	NRC7661	Ball-Joint	1	
	NRC6631	Dust Cover	1	
	NRC6632	Spring Ring	1	
	592445	Spring Ring	1	
13	PS608101L	Split Pin	1	
14	SH605081L	Bolt	2	
15	WM600051L	Spring Washer	2	
16	253948	Bolt	2	
17	NY608041L	Nut	2	

VS3947

MODEL LR110 - UP TO AUGUST 1986
BLOCK VS 3948
PAGE E 38
GROUP E

SUSPENSION - LEVELLING UNIT - OPTIONAL

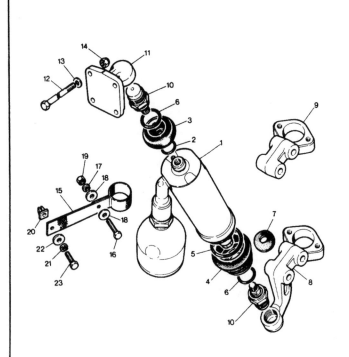

ILL	PART NO	DESCRIPTION	QTY	REMARKS
1	NRC7050	Levelling Unit	1	)
2	NRC7066	Spring Ring	1	)
3	NRC5707	Upper Gaiter	1	)
4	NRC6561	Lower Gaiter	1	)Note(1)
5	577703	Spring Ring-Large	1	)
6	90577704	Spring Ring-Small	2	)
7	NRC8007	Dirt Seal	1	)
8	90575878	Bracket	1	)
9	NRC3923	Bracket	1	
10	575882	Ball Joint	2	)
11	NRC8375	Upper Housing	1	)
12	BH110351	Bolt-Housing to Frame	4	)
13	NRC5758	Washer	4	)
14	NY110041L	Nut	4	)
15	NRC6320	Retaining Strap	1	)Note(1)
	NRC8518	Retaining Strap-Additional	1	)Heavy Duty
16	SH106301	Screw-Strap to Unit	1	)
17	WL106001L	Spring Washer	1	)
18	2215L	Plain Washer	1	)
19	NH106041L	Nut	1	)
20	NN106011	Nutsert-Strap to Crossmember	1	)
21	WL106001L	Spring Washer	1	)
11	2215L	Plain Washer	1	)
23	SH106201L	Screw	1	)

NOTE(1): Fitted On Vehicles With Levelled Suspension.

VS3948

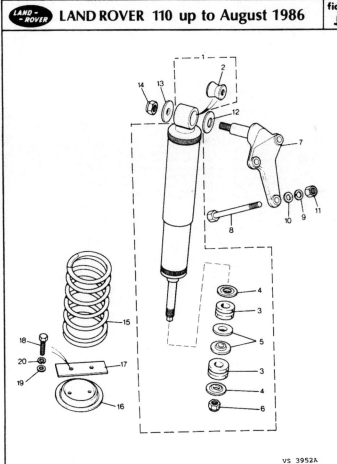

MODEL LR110 - UP TO AUGUST 1986
BLOCK VS 3952A
PAGE E 40
GROUP E

SUSPENSION - REAR SPRING AND SHOCK ABSORBER

ILL	PART NO	DESCRIPTION	QTY	REMARKS
1	RTC4638	Shock Absorber Kit	2	Note(1)
	RTC4639	Shock Absorber Kit	2	
2	NRC5593	+Rubber Bush-Upper	2	
3	552818	+Cushion Rubber	4	
4	500746	+Retainer Washer	4	
5	NRC6235	+Guide Washer	4	
6	NY608041L	+Nut	2	)Alternatives
	NV608041L	+Nut	2	)
7	NRC7981	Bracket Shock Absorber	2	
8	BH110221L	Bolt-Bracket to Frame	6	
9	WM110001L	Spring Washer	6	
10	WC110061L	Plain Washer	6	
11	NH110061	Nut	6	
12	NRC5602	Inner Retainer	2	
13	NRC5603	Outer Retainer	2	
14	NY110041L	Nut	2	
15	NRC6388	Rear Spring-Drivers	1	Note(1)
	NRC6389	Rear Spring-Drivers	1	
	NRC7000	Rear Spring-Passengers	1	Note(1)
	NRC6904	Rear Spring-Passengers	1	
16	NRC4317	Spring Seat Lower	2	
17	NRC4318	Spring Retainer	2	
18	SH110251L	Screw	4	
19	WA110061L	Plain Washer	8	
20	WM110001L	Spring Washer	4	

NOTE(1): Fitted On Vehicles With Levelled Suspension.

VS 3952A

MODEL LR110 - UP TO AUGUST 1986
BLOCK VS 3946
PAGE E 42
GROUP E

SUSPENSION - ROAD WHEEL

ILL	PART NO	DESCRIPTION	QTY	REMARKS
1	NRC7578PM	Road Wheel	5	
2	90577473	Nut-Road Wheel	20	

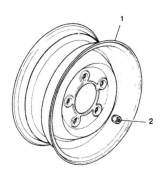

VS3946

MASTER INDEX

GROUP F

STEERING

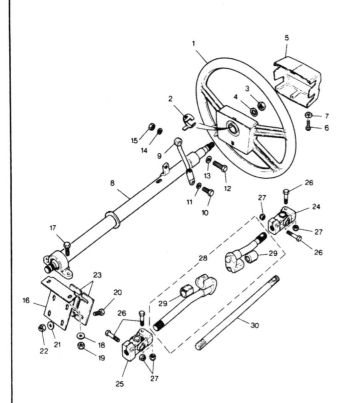

MODEL LR110 - UP TO AUGUST 1986
BLOCK TS 5547B
PAGE F 2
GROUP F

STEERING - STEERING WHEEL AND COLUMN

ILL	PART NO	DESCRIPTION	QTY	REMARKS
1	NRC5281	Steering Wheel	1	
2	NRC7636	Striker Ring	1	
3	CRC2015	Nut	1	
4	WE600081	Shakeproof Washer	1	
5	NRC6747	Hub Moulding	1	
6	SE106121L	Screw-Hub Moulding	1	
7	NK106081	Grip Nut	1	
8	NRC7635	Steering Column-Upper	1	
9	NRC7451	Tie Rod Assy-Column to Dash	1	)Alternatives
	NRC9711	Tie Rod-Fixed	1	)
10	SH110161L	Screw-Tie Rod to Column	1	
11	WL110001L	Spring Washer	1	
12	SH110301L	Screw-Tie Rod to Dash	1	
13	WA110061L	Plain Washer	1	
14	WL110001L	Spring Washer	1	
15	NH110041L	Nut	1	
16	NRC7127	Support-Steering Column	1	
17	BH108251L	Bolt-Column to Support	2	
18	WC108051L	Plain Washer	2	
19	NY108041L	Nyloc Nut	2	
20	BH108251L	Bolt-Support to Toe Box	4	
21	WC108051L	Plain Washer	4	
22	NY108041L	Nyloc Nut	4	
23	569522	Packer Piece	4	
24	NRC7387	Universal Joint	1	
25	NRC7704	Universal Joint	1	
26	BH108091L	Bolt	4	
27	NY108041L	Nyloc Nut	4	
28	RTC4738	Steering Shaft Assembly	1	Collapsible
29	NRC8367	+Reinforced Sleeve	2	)No Longer)Serviced
30	NTC1731	Steering Shaft	1	)Non Collapsible)No Longer)Available Use)RTC4738

TS5547 B

MODEL LR110 - UP TO AUGUST 1986
BLOCK VS 4021
PAGE F 4
GROUP F

STEERING - STEERING COLUMN SHROUD

ILL	PART NO	DESCRIPTION	QTY	REMARKS
1	MTC3499	Shroud-Upper	1	
2	MTC3801	Shroud-Lower	1	
3	SE105401	Screw-Upper to Lower Shroud	2	
4	AR608031	Screw-Lower Shroud to Switch Plate	2	
5	SE105161	Screw-Lower Shroud to Ignition Switch	1	
6	NRC7836	Clamp-Shroud Support	1	
7	NRC7835	Bracket-Ignition Switch	1	
8	SH105121	Screw-Clamp to Bracket	2	
9	WA105001	Spring Washer	2	
10	NH105041	Nut	2	
	331083	Grommet-Blanking	1	Diesel

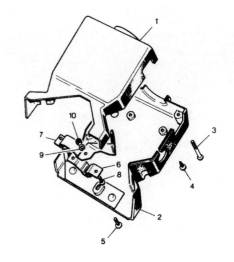

VS4021

286

MODEL LR110 - UP TO AUGUST 1986
BLOCK VS 4022
PAGE F 6
GROUP F

STEERING - COLUMN TOP SUPPORT

ILL	PART NO	DESCRIPTION	QTY	REMARKS
1	MTC1382	Support Bracket Assembly	1	
2	MUC7000	Seal-Steering Column	1	
3	346722	Clamp-Top-Steering Column	1	
4	MTC1078	Clamp-Lower-Steering Column	1	
5	348747	Rubber Strip	1	
6	SH108251L	Screw-Support Bracket to Dash	2	
7	WA108051L	Plain Washer	1	
8	MTC4771	Bracket-Dash Cable	1	
9	WL108001L	Spring Washer	2	
	NN108021	Nutsert-Bracket to Dash	2	
10	GG108251L	Screw-Clamp Bracket to Support Bracket	2	
11	WA108051L	Plain Washer	2	
12	WL108001L	Spring Washer	2	
13	GG106251L	Screw-Top Clamp to Lower Clamp	2	
14	WL106001L	Spring Washer	2	
15	WA106041L	Plain Washer	2	

VS4022

287

MODEL LR110 - UP TO AUGUST 1986
BLOCK TS 6226B
PAGE F 8
GROUP F

STEERING - STEERING BOX - MANUAL - GEMMER

ILL	PART NO	DESCRIPTION	QTY	REMARKS
1	NRC8588	Steering Box-RHS	1	NLA-Use NTC2590
	NRC8589	Steering Box-LHS	1	NLA-Use NTC2591
2	600265	+Washer	1	
3	NTC614041	+Nut	1	
4	NRC8556	Drop Arm-RHS	1	)NLA-Use RTC6398)Note(1)
	NRC8557	Drop Arm-LHS	1	)NLA-Use RTC6399)Note(1)
5	AEU2761	Ball Joint Kit	1	Note(2)
	RTC4198	Ball Joint Kit	1	Note(3)
6	BH607381	Bolt-Steering Box to Chassis	4	Note(2)
	BX112201	Bolt-Steering Box to Chassis	4	Note(3)
7	572077	Tab Washer	2	
8	WA600071	Plain Washer	8	Note(2)
	WA112081L	Plain Washer	4	Note(3)
9	NY607041	Nut	4	Note(2)
10	594947	Tie Bar-RHS	1	
	594946	Tie Bar-LHS	1	
11	4905	Plain Washer)Tie Bar to	1	
12	252164	Nut)Panhard Rod	1	
13	253963	Bolt)	2	
14	217245	Plain Washer)Tie Bar to	2	
15	3261	Plain Washer)Steering Box	2	
16	NY607041L	Nut)	2	

NOTE(1): Use RTC4198 Ball Joint Kit When Fitting Replacement
          Drop Arm RTC6398/RTC6399

NOTE(2): For Steering Box NRC8588/NRC8589

NOTE(3): For Steering Box NTC2590/NTC2591

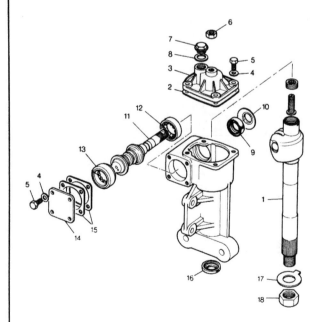

TS 6226B

LAND ROVER PARTS LTD

288

MODEL LR110 - UP TO AUGUST 1986
BLOCK TS 5005
PAGE F 8.04
GROUP F

STEERING - MANUAL STEERING - GEMMER

ILL	PART NO	DESCRIPTION	QTY	REMARKS
1	AEU4011	Rockershaft-LHS	1	
	AEU4012	Rockershaft-RHS	1	
2	BAU4865	Seal-Cover Plate	1	
3	AEU4013	Cover Plate	1	
4	AEU4014	Screw	8	
5	AEU4015	Washer	8	
6	AEU4016	Nut	1	
7	AEU4017	Filler Plug	1	
8	AEU4018	Seal-Filler Plug	1	
9	BAU4870	Seal-Wormshaft	1	
10	AEU4019	Dust Seal	1	
11	AEU4020	Wormshaft-LHS	1	
	AEU4021	Wormshaft-RHS	1	
12	RTC6130	Bearing	2	
13	RTC6129	Bearing	1	
14	AEU4023	Cover Plate	1	
15	BAU4871	Shim	A/R	
16	AEU4024	Seal	1	
17	AEU4025	Tab Washer	1	
18	AEU4026	Nut	1	

TS5005

LAND ROVER PARTS LTD

289

MODEL LR110 - UP TO AUGUST 1986
BLOCK VS 4025B
PAGE F 10
GROUP F

STEERING - STEERING BOX - POWER - TO VIN 243977 RHS, VIN 244542 LHS

ILL	PART NO	DESCRIPTION	QTY	REMARKS
1	NRC6051	STEERING BOX-RHS	1	)Adwest
	NRC6052	STEERING BOX-LHS	1	)Heavyweight
2	600265	+Washer-Drop Arm to Box	1	
3	NH614041	+Nut-Drop Arm to Box	1	
4	NRC8556	Drop Arm-RHS	1	
	NRC8557	Drop Arm-LHS	1	
5	AEU2761	Ball Joint Kit	1	
6	NRC7616	Bolt-Steering Box to Chassis	4	
7	572077	Tab Washer	2	
8	WA600071L	Plain Washer	4	
9	594947	Tie Bar-RHS	1	
	594946	Tie Bar-LHS	1	
10	4905	Plain Washer) Tie Bar to	1	
11	252164	Nut) Panhard Rod	1	
12	BH607161L	Bolt)	2	
13	3261L	Plain Washer) Tie Bar to	2	
14	217245	Plain Washer) Steering Box	2	
15	NY607041L	Nut)	2	

VS 4025B

290

MODEL LR110 - UP TO AUGUST 1986
BLOCK VS 4105
PAGE F 10.02
GROUP F

STEERING - HOUSING AND SECTOR SHAFT P.A.S - TO VIN 243977 RHS, VIN 244542 LHS

ILL	PART NO	DESCRIPTION	QTY	REMARKS
1	AEU1358	HOUSING ASSY-RHS	1	
	AEU1359	HOUSING ASSY-LHS	1	
2	606564	+Plug	1	
3	608066	+Seal	1	)
4	608068	+Back Up Washer	1	)NOTE(1)
5	608067	+Back Up Seal	1	)
6	606551	+Circlip	1	
7	11987L	+Seat	3	
8	11988L	+Seat	1	
9	606563	+Steel Ball	1	
10	RTC297	+Stud	3	
	RTC6110	Dust Seal	1	
11	RTC294	Cover Plate and Bush	1	
12	11015L	Bleed Screw	1	
13	608069	Seal	1	NOTE(1)
14	RTC298	Washer	3	
15	RTC299	Nut	3	
16	RTC295	Seal	1	NOTE(1)
17	AEU1029	Pipe-RHS	1	
	RTC307	Pipe-LHS	1	
18	11011L	Screw	1	
19	606544	Pad-Rack	1	
20	608065	Seal	1	NOTE(1)
21	606545	Screw-Rack Adjusting	1	
22	RTC300	SECTOR SHAFT AND NUT-RHS	1	
	RTC301	SECTOR SHAFT AND NUT-LHS	1	
23	606566	+Nut	1	

NOTE(1): Part of RTC308 Seal Kit

VS4105

291

MODEL R110 - UP TO AUGUST 1986
BLOCK 3RE 333
PAGE F 10.04
GROUP F

STEERING - PISTON AND VALVE - P.A.S - TO VIN 243977 RHS, VIN 244542 LHS

ILL	PART NO	DESCRIPTION	QTY	REMARKS
1	606542	Piston	1	
2	RTC305	Teflon Ring	1	)NOTE(1)
3	90608071	O Ring	1	)
4	606543	Cover	1	
5	608064	Seal	1	NOTE(1)
6	11009L	Retaining Ring	1	
7	RTC4411	Circlip	1	
8	RTC304	Washer-Seal	1	)NOTE(1)
9	AEU1248	Seal-Rotor	1	)
10	606561	Needle Bearing	1	
11	RTC2762	Shim Set	1	
12	606538	Bearing Race Assembly	2	
13	608000	Teflon Ring	4	
14	606567	Circlip	1	
15	AEU1356	Worm and Valve Assy-RHS	1	
	AEU1357	Worm and Valve Assy-LHS	1	
16	608073	Seal	1	NOTE(1)
17	RTC306	Screw-Worm Adjusting	1	
18	606553	Locknut	1	

NOTE(1):   Part of RTC308 Seal Kit

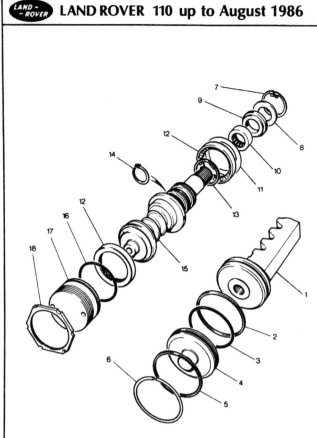

3RE333

LAND ROVER PARTS LTD

292

MODEL LR110 - UP TO AUGUST 1986
BLOCK TS 5695A
PAGE F 10.06
BLOCK F

STEERING - STEERING BOX - POWER - FROM VIN 243978 RHS, VIN 244543 LHS
                                    TO SEE NOTE(1)

ILL	PART NO	DESCRIPTION	QTY	REMARKS
1	NTC1580	STEERING BOX-RHS	1	)Adwest
	NTC1581	STEERING BOX-LHS	1	)Lightweight
2	RTC6396	+Drop Arm-RHS	1	
	RTC6397	+Drop Arm-LHS	1	
3	600265	+Washer	1	
4	NT614041L	+Nut	1	
5	RTC4198	+Ball Joint Kit	1	
6	BX112201	Bolt	4	
7	572077	Tab Washer	2	
8	WA112081L	Plain Washer	4	
9	594947	Tiebar-RHS	1	
	594946	Tiebar-LHS	1	
10	4905	Plain Washer) Tie Bar to	1	
11	252164	Nut) Panhard Rod	1	
12	BH607161L	Bolt)	2	
13	3261L	Plain Washer) Tiebar to	2	
14	217245	Plain Washer) Steering Box	2	
15	NY607041L	Nyloc Nut)	2	

NOTE(1): To VIN 256704 RHS VIN 257104
          LHS-V8 Only

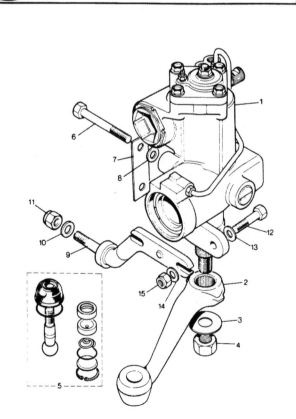

TS5695

LAND ROVER PARTS LTD

293

MODEL LR110 - UP TO AUGUST 1986
BLOCK TS 5694
PAGE F 10.08
GROUP F

STEERING - HOUSING AND SECTOR SHAFT P.A.S. - FROM VIN 243978 RHS,
                                              VIN 244543 LHS TO NOTE(2)

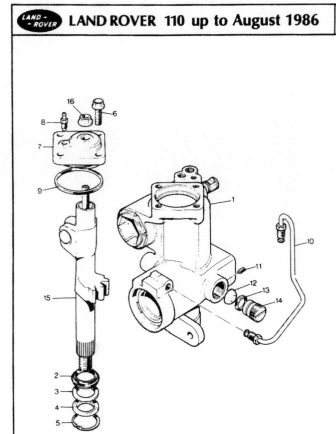

ILL	PART NO	DESCRIPTION	QTY	REMARKS
1	RTC4391	HOUSING ASSEMBLY-RHS	1	
	RTC4392	HOUSING ASSEMBLY-LHS	1	
2	608066	+Seal	1	)
3	608068	+Back Up Washer	1	) Note(1)
4	608067	+Back Up Seal	1	)
5	606551	+Circlip	1	
	RTC6110	Dust Seal	1	
6	RTC4393	Screw	4	
7	RTC4396	Cover Plate And Bush	1	
8	RTC4395	Bleed Screw	1	
9	RTC4397	Seal	1	Note(1)
10	RTC4400	Pipe-RHS	1	
	RTC4401	Pipe-LHS	1	
11	11011L	Screw	1	
12	606544	Pad-Rack	1	
13	608065	Seal	1	Note(1)
14	606545	Screw-Adjusting	1	
15	RTC4398	Sector Shaft And Nut-RHS	1	
	RTC4399	Sector Shaft And Nut-LHS	1	
16	RTC4394	+Nut	1	

NOTES(1): Seal Kit RTC4412
     (2): TO VIN 256704 RHS VIN 257104
           LHS-V8 Only

TS5694

LAND ROVER PARTS LTD

294

MODEL LR110 - UP TO AUGUST 1986
BLOCK VS 4025B
PAGE F 10
GROUP F

STEERING - STEERING BOX - POWER - TO VIN 243977 RHS, VIN 244542 LHS

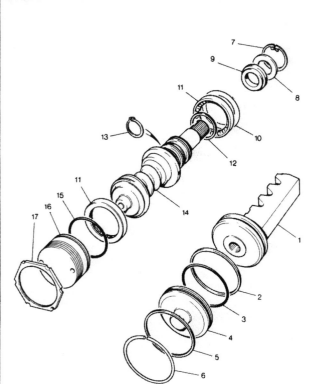

ILL	PART NO	DESCRIPTION	QTY	REMARKS
1	NRC6051	STEERING BOX-RHS	1	)Adwest
	NRC6052	STEERING BOX-LHS	1	)Heavyweight
2	600265	+Washer	1	
3	NH614041	+Nut	1	
4	NRC8556	Drop Arm-RHS	1	NLA-Use RTC6396 Note(1)
	NRC8557	Drop Arm-LHS	1	NLA-Use RTC6397 Note(1)
5	AEU2761	Ball Joint Kit	1	
	RTC4198	Ball Joint Kit	1	Note(1)
6	NRC7616	Bolt	4	
7	572077	Tab Washer	2	
8	WA600071L	Plain Washer	4	
9	594947	Tie Bar-RHS	1	
	594946	Tie Bar-LHS	1	
10	4905	Plain Washer) Tie Bar to	1	
11	252164	Nut) Panhard Rod	1	
12	BH607161L	Bolt)	2	
13	3261L	Plain Washer) Tie Bar to	2	
14	217245	Plain Washer) Steering Box	2	
15	NY607041L	Nyloc Nut)	2	

Note(1)   Use RTC4198 Ball Joint Kit When Fitting
          Replacement Drop Arm RTC6396/RTC6397

TS5696

LAND ROVER PARTS LTD

295

MODEL LR110 - UP TO AUGUST 1986
BLOCK TS 6330A
PAGE F 10.12
GROUP F

STEERING - STEERING BOX - POWER - FROM VIN 256705 RHS
                                   VIN 257105 LHS V8 ONLY

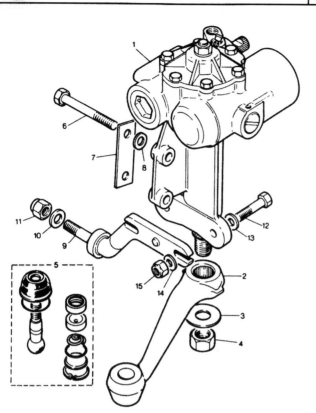

ILL	PART NO	DESCRIPTION	QTY	REMARKS
1	NTC1582	STEERING BOX-RHS	1	)Gemmer
	NTC1583	STEERING BOX-LHS	1	)
2	RTC6398	+Drop Arm-RHS	1	
	RTC6399	+Drop Arm-LHS	1	
3	600265	+Washer	1	
4	NT614041	+Nut	1	
5	RTC4198	+Ball Joint Kit	1	
6	BX112201	Bolt	4	
7	572077	Tab Washer	2	
8	WA112081L	Plain Washer	4	
9	594947	Tiebar-RHS	1	
	594946	Tiebar-LHS	1	
10	4905	Plain Washer	1	
11	252164	Nut	1	
12	BH607161L	Bolt	2	
13	3261	Plain Washer	2	
14	217245	Plain Washer	2	
15	NY607041L	Nyloc Nut	2	
	RTC5068	Valve Assembly-LHD	1	)
	RTC5069	Output Shaft-LHD	1	)No Longer)Available
	RTC5070	Output Shaft-RHD	1	)
	RTC5071	Seal Kit	1	
	RTC5072	Piston Rack Kit	1	
	RTC5073	Cover Assy-Output Shaft	1	No Longer Available
	RTC5074	Bearing Kit-Housing	1	

TS 6330A

LAND ROVER PARTS LTD

MODEL LR110 - UP TO AUGUST 1986
BLOCK VS 4036B
PAGE F 12
GROUP F

STEERING - TRACK RODS

ILL	PART NO	DESCRIPTION		QTY	REMARKS
1	NRC8231	Crossrod Eye End-RHS		1	
	NRC8232	Crossrod Eye End-LHS		1	
2	NRC5582	Crossrod Tube		1	
3	RTC5869	BALL JOINT KIT RH		1	
4	WC112081L	+Plain Washer		1	
5	NC112041L	+Castle Nut		1	
6	PS105321L	+Split Pin		1	
7	577898	Clamp		2	
8	BH604151L	Bolt-Clamp		4	
9	WA106041L	Plain Washer		8	
10	NY604041L	Nyloc Nut		4	
11	NRC9743	Track Rod Assembly		1	
12	NRC9742	+Track Rod Tube		1	
13	RTC5869	+BALL JOINT KIT RH		1	
14	WC112081L	++Plain Washer		1	
15	NC112041L	++Castle Nut		1	
16	PS105321L	++Split Pin		1	
17	RTC5870	+BALL JOINT KIT LH		1	
18	WC112081L	++Plain Washer		1	
19	NC112041L	++Castle Nut		1	
20	PS105321L	++Split Pin		1	
21	577898	+Clamp		2	
22	B604151L	+Bolt-Clamp		4	
23	WA106041L	+Plain Washer		8	
24	NY604041L	+Nyloc Nut		4	
25	RTC4472	STEERING DAMPER KIT		1	
26	595199	+Plain Washer	)	1	
27	568858	+Rubber	)Steering	2	
28	543819	+Washer-Intermediate	)Damper	2	
29	90575597	+Washer-Stem	)to	2	
30	WJ110001	+Plain Washer	)Chassis	1	
31	AFU4214	+Nut-Thin M10	)	2	
32	NTC1775	+Bush-Steering Damper		1	
33	BH110121L	Bolt-Damper to Crossrod		1	
34	WA110061L	Plain Washer		1	
35	NY110041L	Nyloc Nut		1	

VS 4036B

LAND ROVER PARTS LTD

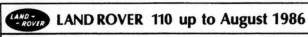
MODEL LR110 - UP TO AUGUST 1986
BLOCK VS 3746B
PAGE F 20
GROUP F

STEERING - 4 CYLINDER POWER STEERING PUMP

ILL	PART NO	DESCRIPTION	QTY	REMARKS
1	ERC8447	PUMP-POWER STEERING	1	)No Longer)Available Use)ETC9077
1	ETC9077	PUMP-POWER STEERING	1	
	RTC4485	+Banjo	1	
2	ERC6974	Bracket-Mounting Pump & Alt	1	
3	SH108251L	Screw-Bracket to Front Cover	3	
4	WL108001L	Spring Washer-Bracket to Cover	3	
5	SH108301L	Screw	1	
6	WL108001L	Spring Washer	1	
7	BH108181L	Bolt-Bracket to Block	1	
8	WL108001L	Spring Washer-Bracket to Block	1	
9	ERC6976	Spigot-Idler Arm Mounting	1	
10	ERC6977	Special Nut-Spigot	1	
11	ERC5145	Pulley-Power Steering Pump	1	
12	ERC6975	Mounting Plate-Pump	1	
13	SH108141L	Screw-Pulley to Pump	3	
14	WL108001L	Spring Washer-Pulley to Pump	3	
15	SH106201L	Screw-Pump to Plate	4	
16	WL106001L	Spring Washer-Pump to Plate	4	
17	SH108251L	Screw-Plate to Bracket	3	
18	WL108001L	Spring Washer-Plate to Bracket	3	
19	ETC4153	IDLER ARM AND PULLEY ASSY	1	
20	SH108401L	+Screw-Idler Arm Clamp	1	
21	WL108001L	+Spring Washer-Idler Arm Clamp	1	
22	CR120195L	Circlip	2	
23	ERC5146	Driving Belt	1	)Except Air)Conditioning
23	ETC4272	Driving Belt	1	)With Air)Conditioning
	AEU4119	Washer Special-Banjo	2	

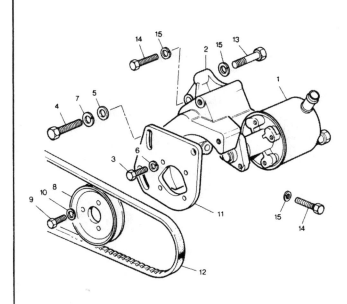

VS3746B

LAND ROVER PARTS LTD

MODEL LR110 - UP TO AUGUST 1986
BLOCK TS 6347
PAGE F 20.02
GROUP F

STEERING -4 CYLINDER POWER STEERING PUMP

ILL	PART NO	DESCRIPTION	QTY	REMARKS
1	ETC9077	POWER STEERING PUMP	1	
	RTC5674	+Banjo	1	
	RTC5675	+Sealing Washer	1	
2	ETC5792	Bracket-Mounting Pump And Alternator	1	
3	SH106201L	Screw-Pump to Bracket	4	
4	SH108251L	Screw-Pump to Bracket	3	
5	WA108051L	Washer-Pump to Bracket	2	
6	WL106001L	Spring Washer-Pump to Bracket	4	
7	WL108001L	Spring Washer-Pump to Bracket	3	
8	ETC5783	Pulley-Power Steering Pump	1	
9	SH108141L	Screw-Pulley to Pump	3	
10	WL108001L	Spring Washer-Pulley to Pump	3	
11	ETC5944	Mounting Plate-P.A.S Pump	1	
12	ETC5815	Belt-Power Steering Pump	1	
13	BH108181L	Bolt-P.A.S Mounting Bracket to Front	1	)
14	SH108251L	Screw-P.A.S Mounting Bracket to Front	3	))Petrol
	SH108301L	Screw-P.A.S Mounting Bracket to Front	1	)
15	WL108001L	Spring Washer-P.A.S Mounting Bracket to Front	5	)
13	BH108181L	Bolt-P.A.S Mounting Bracket to Front	1	)
14	SH108251L	Screw-P.A.S Mounting Bracket to Front	2	))Diesel
14	SH108301L	Screw-P.A.S Mounting Bracket to Front	1	)
15	WL108001L	Spring Washer-P.A.S Mounting Bracket to Front	4	)

TS6347

LAND ROVER PARTS LTD

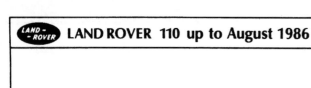

MODEL LR110 - UP TO AUGUST 1986
BLOCK 3RE 336A
PAGE F 22
GROUP F

STEERING - POWER STEERING - PUMP - 3.5 LITRE V8 PETROL

ILL	PART NO	DESCRIPTION	QTY	
1	610020	PUMP-POWER STEERING	1	Upto VIN 243977 (RHS)244542(LHS)
2	605181	+Bearing	1	
3	536373	+Spring	1	
4	RTC327	+Valve Assembly	1	
5	605180	+Shaft	1	
6	605174	+Valve Carrier & Rollers Assembly	1	
7	536382	Banjo Bolt	1	
8	ABU7142	Kit-Oil Seals	1	
9	ABU7145	Kit-Gaskets	1	
1	ETC5689	Pump-Power Steering-30 Series	1	From VIN 243978 (RHS)244542 (LHS) Eng No.19G00008 20G00504,21G01043 22G00326
1	ETC6496	Pump-Power Steering-200 Series	1	From Engine No 19G00043,20G01145 21G02210,22G00356

3RE336A

LAND ROVER PARTS LTD

300

MODEL LR110 - UP TO AUGUST 1986
BLOCK VS 4014A
PAGE F 24
GROUP F

STEERING - POWER STEERING - PUMP - 3.5 LITRE V8 PETROL
EXCEPT AIR CONDITIONING=30 SERIES

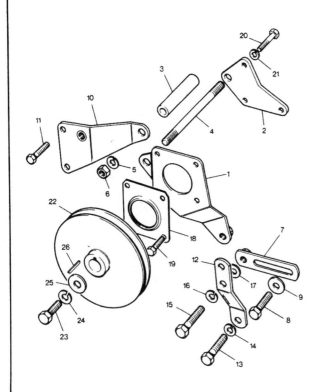

	PART NO	DESCRIPTION	QTY REMARKS
1	90611439	Mounting Bracket-Front	1
2	603972	Mounting Bracket-Rear	1
3	611215	Distance Tube	1
4	610789	Stud	1
5	WM600061L	Spring Washer	1
6	NH606041L	Nut	1
7	611440	Adjusting Link	1
8	SH605061L	Screw Link/Bracket	1
9	4478	Plain Washer	1
10	90610796	Support Bracket-Pump	1
11	BH504121L	Bolt-Bracket/Water Pump	2
12	611213	Link-Pump/Bracket	1
13	SH506071L	Screw Bracket/Chain Cover	1
14	WM600061L	Spring Washer	1
15	SH605081L	Screw Support Bracket/Link	1
16	WM600051L	Spring Washer	1
17	4581	Plain Washer	1
18	611212	Bearing Retainer	1
19	SH604061L	Screw Pump/Bracket	4
20	SH604061L	Screw Pump/Rear Bracket	3
21	WM600041L	Spring Washer	3
22	611379	Pulley-Single Groove	1
23	SH505071L	Screw Pulley/Pump	1
24	WM600051L	Spring Washer	1
25	2217L	Plain Washer	1
26	554880	Key	1

VS4104A

LAND ROVER PARTS LTD

MODEL LR110 - UP TO AUGUST 1986
BLOCK VS 4013
PAGE F 26
GROUP F

STEERING - POWER STEERING - PUMP - 3.5 LITRE V8 PETROL WITH
            AIR CONDITIONING-30 SERIES

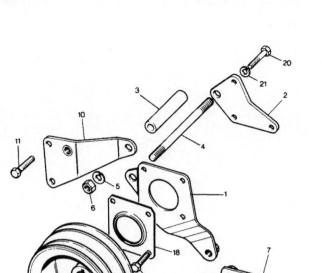

ILL	PART NO	DESCRIPTION	QTY	REMARKS
1	614743	Mounting Bracket-Front	1	
2	603972	Mounting Bracket-Rear	1	
3	611215	Distance Tube	1	
4	610789	Stud	1	
5	WM600061L	Spring Washer	1	
6	NH606041L	Nut	1	
7	611440	Adjusting Link	1	
8	SH605061L	Screw Link/Bracket	1	
9	4478	Plain Washer	1	
10	90610796	Support Bracket-Pump	1	
11	BH504121L	Bolt-Bracket/Water Pump	2	
12	611213	Link-Pump/Bracket	1	
13	SH506071L	Screw Bracket/Chain Cover	1	
14	WM600061L	Spring Washer	1	
15	SH605081L	Screw Support Bracket/Link	1	
16	WM600051L	Spring Washer	1	
17	4581	Plain Washer	1	
18	611212	Bearing Retainer	1	
19	SH604061L	Screw Pump/Bracket	4	
20	SH604061L	Screw Pump/Rear Bracket	3	
21	WM600041L	Spring Washer	3	
22	610792	Pulley-Twin Groove	1	
23	SH505071L	Screw Pulley/Pump	1	
24	WM600051L	Spring Washer	1	
25	2217L	Plain Washer	1	

VS4103

302

MODEL LR110 - UP TO AUGUST 1986
BLOCK TS 5008
PAGE F 28
GROUP F

STEERING - POWER STEERING RESERVOIR - TO VIN 264696 RHS, 271354 LHS

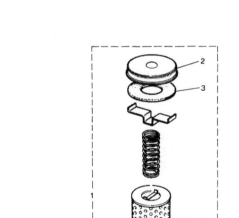

ILL	PART NO	DESCRIPTION	QTY	REMARKS
1	NRC9551	Reservoir-Power Steering	1	Note(1)
	NRC9552	Reservoir-Power Steering	1	)Note(2) and)Note(3)
2	RTC3056	Cap	1	
3	RTC3962	Seal	1	
4	RTC3058	Filter	1	
5	NRC5982	Bracket	1	
6	SH106167	Screw-Bracket to Wing	1	
7	NH106047	Nut	4	
8	WA106047L	Plain Washer	4	
9	WL106007L	Spring Washer	4	

NOTE(1):   Upto VIN 243977 RHS VIN 244542 LHS - Except Air Con

NOTE(2):   Air Con Vehicles Also Non Air Con From
           VIN 243978 RHS And VIN 244543 LHS

NOTE(3):   No Longer Available -
           Use NTC1791 and NTC2749 See Following Page

TS5008

303

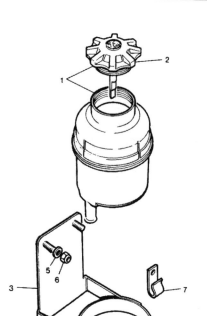

MODEL LR110 - UP TO AUGUST 1986
BLOCK TS 6227
PAGE F 28.02
GROUP F

STEERING - POWER STEERING RESERVOIR FROM VIN 264697 RHS, 271355 LHS

ILL	PART NO	DESCRIPTION	QTY	REMARKS
1	NTC1791	RESERVOIR-POWER STEERING	1	
2	NTC2723	+Cap-PAS Reservoir	1	
3	NTC2749	Carrier Bracket Assembly	1	
4	SH106251L	Screw	1	
5	WA106041L	Plain Washer	4	
6	NY106041	Nut	3	
7	NRC2383	P Clip	1	

TS6227

 LAND ROVER PARTS LTD

304

MODEL LR110 - UP TO AUGUST 1986
BLOCK VS 4133A
PAGE F 30
GROUP F

STEERING - POWER STEERING PIPES TO VIN 243977 RHS, VIN 244542 LHS

ILL	PART NO	DESCRIPTION	QTY	REMARKS
1	NRC8286	Pipe-Reservoir to Pump	1	4 Cyl
	NRC5975	Pipe-Reservoir to Pump	1	V8
2	NRC8290	Pipe-Pump to Steering Box-RHS	1	4 Cyl
	NRC7988	Pipe-Pump to Steering Box-RHS	1	V8
	NRC8291	Pipe-Pump to Steering Box-LHS	1	4 Cyl
	NRC8292	Pipe-Pump to Steering Box-LHS	1	V8
3	NRC7987	Pipe-Stg Box to Reservoir-RHS	1	4 Cyl
	NRC5976	Pipe-Stg Box to Reservoir-RHS	1	V8
	NRC8287	Pipe-Stg Box to Reservoir-LHS	1	4 Cyl
	NRC5977	Pipe-Stg Box to Reservoir-LHS	1	V8
4	NRC6302	Pipe Clip-Air Cleaner-RHS	1	)4 Cyl
5	NRC8408	Pipe Clip-Air Cleaner-LHS	1	)Petrol
	NRC9492	Support Clip	1	2.5 Diesel
6	NN106011	Nutsert	2	
7	NRC6302	Pipe Clip-Crossmember-LHS	2	
	NRC8404	Pipe Clip-Crossmember-RHS	2	
8	NRC8404	Pipe Clip	1	
9	NRC8405	Plate-Pipe Clip	1	
10	SH106121L	Screw-Clip to Crossmember-RHS	3	4 Cyl
	SH106161L	Screw-Clip to Crossmember-RHS	2	V8
	SH106121L	Screw-Clip to Crossmember-LHS	4	4 Cyl
	SH106161L	Screw-Clip to Crossmember-LHS	3	V8
11	WA106041L	Plain Washer	A/R	
12	WL106001L	Spring Washer	A/R	
13	NH106041L	Nut	A/R	
14	ADU9081L	Pipe Clip	1	

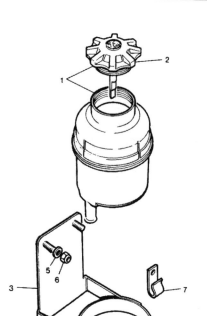

VS4133A

 LAND ROVER PARTS LTD

305

MODEL LR110 - UP TO AUGUST 1986
BLOCK VS 4133B
PAGE F 30.02
GROUP F

STEERING - POWER STEERING PIPES FROM VIN 243978 RHS, VIN 244543 LHS

ILL	PART NO	DESCRIPTION	QTY	REMARKS
1		Pipe-Reservoir to Pump		
	NTC1691	-4 Cylinder	1	
	NTC1685	-V8	1	)To VIN
				)262292 RHS
				)VIN 263156 LHS
	NTC2595	-V8	1	)From VIN
				)262293 RHS
				)VIN 263157 LHS
2		Pipe-Pump to Steering Box		
	NTC1682	-RHS-4 Cylinder	1	
	NTC1687	-RHS-V8	1	To VIN 262292
	NTC2597	-RHS-V8	1	From VIN 262293
	NTC1681	-LHS-4 Cylinder	1	
	NTC1686	-LHS-V8	1	To VIN 263156
	NTC4165	-LHS-V8	1	From VIN 263157
	RTC4826	O Ring-Pipe	1	
3	NTC1684	Pipe-Stg Box to Reservoir-RHS	1	
	NTC1683	Pipe-Stg Box to Reservoir-LHS	1	
	RTC4825	O Ring-Pipe	1	
4	NRC6302	Pipe Clip-Air Cleaner-RHS	1	)4 Cyl
5	NRC8408	Pipe Clip-Air Cleaner-LHS	1	)Petrol
	NRC9492	Support Clip	1	2.5 Diesel
6	NN106011	Nutsert	2	
7	NRC6302	Pipe Clip-Crossmember-RHS	2	
	NRC8404	Pipe Clip-Crossmember-LHS	2	
8	NRC8404	Pipe Clip	1	
9	NRC8405	Plate-Pipe Clip	1	
10	SH106121L	Screw-Clip to Crossmember-RHS	3	4 Cyl
	SH106161L	Screw-Clip to Crossmember-RHS	2	V8
	SH106121L	Screw-Clip to Crossmember-LHS	4	4 Cyl
	SH106161L	Screw-Clip to Crossmember-LHS	3	V8
11	WA106041L	Plain Washer	A/R	
12	WL106001L	Spring Washer	A/R	
13	NH106041L	Nut	A/R	
14	ADU9081L	Pipe Clip	1	
15	CN100208L	Jubilee Clip	2	

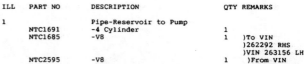

VS4133B

LAND ROVER PARTS LTD

MASTER INDEX

GROUP G

BRAKES

 **LAND ROVER PARTS LTD**

MODEL LR110 - UP TO AUGUST 1986
BLOCK VS 3967/A
PAGE G 2
GROUP G

BRAKES - FRONT BRAKES

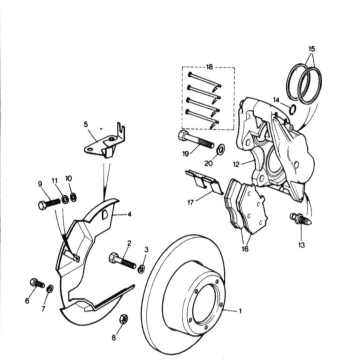

ILL	PART NO	DESCRIPTION	QTY	REMARKS
1	FRC7329	Brake Disc	2	
2	AFU1180	Bolt-Disc to Hub	10	
3	WL110001L	Spring Washer	10	
4	FRC6402	Mudshield-RH	1	
	FRC6403	Mudshield-LH	1	
5	FRC7202	Retaining Bracket-RH	1	)Jump Hose &
	FRC7201	Retaining Bracket-LH	1	)Mudshield
6	SH106121L	Screw-Mudshield to Bracket	2	
7	WL106001L	Spring Washer	2	
8	NH106041L	Nut	2	
9	SH106121L	Screw)Mudshield to	2	
10	WL106001L	Spring Washer)Swivel Housing	2	
11	WA106041L	Plain Washer)	2	
12	AEU2537	Brake Caliper RH-Less Pads	1	To Note(1)
	AEU2538	Brake Caliper LH-Less Pads	1	To Note(1)
	RTC5572	Brake Caliper RH-Less Pads	1	From Note(2)
	RTC5573	Brake Caliper LH-Less Pads	1	From Note(2)
13	RTC1526	+Bleed Screw	2	
14	17H8764L	+Fluid Channel Seal	4	
15	AEU2539	Repair Kit	2	
16	RTC3348	Brake Pad-Axle Set	1	To Note(1)
17	606688	+Anti Rattle Spring	4	To Note(1)
	RTC5574	Brake Pad-Axle Set	1	From Note(2)
18	RTC5001	Retention Kit-Brake Pad	1	From Note(2)
19	AFU1031	Bolt-Caliper to Housing	4	
20	WL112001L	Spring Washer	4	

NOTE(1): Axle No 20L21632B-RHS, 21L18648B-LHS

NOTE(2): Axle No 20L21633B-RHS, 21L18649B-LHS

VS 3967/A

LAND ROVER PARTS LTD

308

MODEL LR110 - UP TO AUGUST 1986
BLOCK VS 3968
PAGE G 4
GROUP G

BRAKES - REAR BRAKES

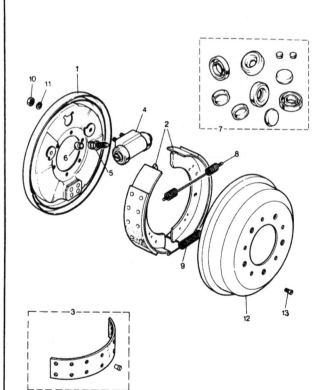

ILL	PART NO	DESCRIPTION	QTY	REMARKS
1	AEU2496	Backplate-RH	1	
	AEU2497	Backplate-LH	1	
2	RTC3418	BRAKESHOE- AXLE SET	1	
3	AEU1880	+Linings & Rivets-Axle Set	1	
4	RTC3626	WHEEL CYLINDER-RH	1	
	RTC3627	WHEEL CYLINDER-LH	1	
5	608400	+Bleed Screw	2	
6	234957	+Dust Cap	2	
7	AEU2498	Wheel Cylinder Repair Kit	2	
8	548169	Return Spring-Top	2	
9	531893	Return Spring-Bottom	2	
10	NH605041L	Nut-Wheel Cyl to Backplate	4	
11	WM600051L	Spring Washer	4	
12	576973	Brake Drum	2	
13	SA108161	Screw	2	
	RTC3176	Brake Adjuster Kit	1	

VS3968

LAND ROVER PARTS LTD

309

MODEL LR110 - UP TO AUGUST 1986
BLOCK VS 3957
PAGE G 6
GROUP G

BRAKES - TRANSMISSION BRAKE

ILL	PART NO	DESCRIPTION	QTY	REMARKS
1	AEU2733	Backplate	1	
2	RTC3403	Brake Shoe Set	1	
3	37H4558L	ADJUSTER ASSEMBLY	1	
	8G7019L	Service Kit-Adjuster	1	
4	AEU2734	EXPANDER ASSEMBLY	1	
	AEU2735	Service Kit-Expander	1	
5	AEU2736	Drawlink	1	
6	FRC3234	Spring-Shoe Return	2	
7	515466	Dust Cover	1	
8	515467	Plate-Locking	1	
9	515470	Plate-Packing	1	
10	515468	Plate-Spring	1	
11	AEU2737	Bolt	2	
12	AEU2738	Washer	2	
13	FRC3502	Brake Drum	1	
14	SA108201L	Screw-Fixing Drum	2	
15	FRC8093	Oil Catcher	1	
16	AFU1400	Bolt-Transmission Brake	4	

VS3957

310

MODEL LR110 - UP TO AUGUST 1986
BLOCK VS 3969A
PAGE G 8
GROUP G

BRAKES - BRAKE PEDAL

ILL	PART NO	DESCRIPTION	QTY	REMARKS
1	NRC9183	Brake Pedal	1	To VIN 234135
	NTC1077	Brake Pedal	1	From VIN 234136
2	NRC9224	Rubber-Brake Pedal	1	)To VIN 234135)Optional
	61K738	Pedal Pad-Rubber	1	From VIN 234136
3	564816	Bush-Brake Pedal	2	
4	564813	Pedal Shaft	1	
5	50446	Pin	1	
6	NRC6058	Pedal Box Assembly	1	
7	GG108251L	Screw	6	
8	WL108001L	Spring Washer	6	
9	WA108051L	Plain Washer	6	
10	MUC7506	Gasket-Pedal Box to Dash	1	
11	AFU2627	Plug-Sealing	1	
12	338029	Plug-Sealing	2	
13	569291	Spring-Pedal Return	2	
	NRC7869	Sleeve-Return Spring	1	
14	NRC4665	Clevis Pin-Pedal to Servo	1	
15	WA112081L	Plain Washer-Pedal to Servo	1	
16	PS106201	Split Pin-Pedal to Servo	1	
17	PRC4297	Switch-Brake Lamps	1	
18	BMK1903	Nut	1	
	NRC9169	Sealing Strip-Servo to Pedal Box	1	
	NRC9233	Sealant Ring-Servo to Pedal Box	1	

VS3939A

311

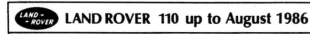

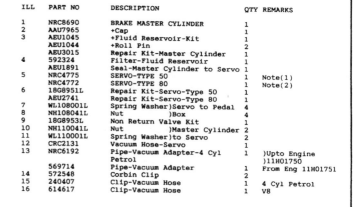

MODEL LR110 - UP TO AUGUST 1986
BLOCK VS 4037
PAGE G 10
GROUP G

BRAKES - BRAKE MASTER CYLINDER AND SERVO

ILL	PART NO	DESCRIPTION	QTY	REMARKS
1	NRC8690	BRAKE MASTER CYLINDER	1	
2	AAU7965	+Cap	1	
3	AEU1045	+Fluid Reservoir-Kit	1	
	AEU1044	+Roll Pin	2	
	AEU3015	Repair Kit-Master Cylinder	1	
4	592324	Filter-Fluid Reservoir	1	
	AEU1891	Seal-Master Cylinder to Servo	1	
5	NRC4775	SERVO-TYPE 50	1	Note(1)
	NRC4772	SERVO-TYPE 80	1	Note(2)
6	18G8951L	Repair Kit-Servo-Type 50	1	
	AEU2741	Repair Kit-Servo-Type 80	1	
7	WL108001L	Spring Washer)Servo to Pedal	4	
8	NH108041L	Nut)Box	4	
9	18G8953L	Non Return Valve Kit	1	
10	NH110041L	Nut)Master Cylinder	2	
11	WL110001L	Spring Washer)to Servo	2	
12	CRC2131	Vacuum Hose-Servo	1	
13	NRC6192	Pipe-Vacuum Adapter-4 Cyl Petrol	1	)Upto Engine)11H01750
	569714	Pipe-Vacuum Adapter	1	From Eng 11H01751
14	572548	Corbin Clip	2	
15	240407	Clip-Vacuum Hose	1	4 Cyl Petrol
16	614617	Clip-Vacuum Hose	1	V8

NOTE(1):   Type 50 - 227mm Diameter
           Non Return Valve Aperture At Bottom, Right of Centre

NOTE(2):   Type 80 - 276mm Diameter
           Non Return Valve Aperture At Top, Left of Centre

VS4037

LAND ROVER PARTS LTD

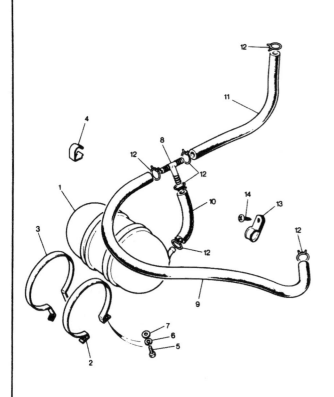

MODEL LR110 - UP TO AUGUST 1986
BLOCK VS 4085
PAGE G 12
GROUP G

BRAKES - VACUUM TANK - HOSE - 2.25 DIESEL AND 2.5 DIESEL

ILL	PART NO	DESCRIPTION	QTY	REMARKS
1	C36471L	Vacuum Tank	1	
2	NRC7357	Front Clip	1	
3	NRC7358	Rear Clip	1	
4	NRC7551	Spring Clip	2	
5	SE106201L	Screw	4	
6	WL106001L	Spring Washer	4	
7	WA106041L	Plain Washer	4	
8	592443	Tee Piece	1	
9	CRC2135	Hose-Pump to Tee Piece-RHS	1	1092mm Required
	CRC2131	Hose-Pump to Tee Piece-LHS	1	76mm Required
10	CRC2131	Hose-Tank to Tee Piece-RHS	1	115mm Required
	CRC2131	Hose-Tank to Tee Piece-LHS	1	457mm Required
11	CRC2131	Hose-Servo to Tee Piece-RHS	1	508mm Required
	CRC2135	Hose-Servo to Tee Piece-LHS	1	991mm Required
12	CS600244	Corbin Clip	6	
13	CP105191	Clip-Hose to Turret	1	
14	AR608021L	Drive Screw	1	
		VACUUM HOSE-2.5 DIESEL		
	CRC2131	Vacuum Hose	1	
	NRC9338	Clip	1	
	NRC7551	Spring-Clip	2	

VS4085

LAND ROVER PARTS LTD

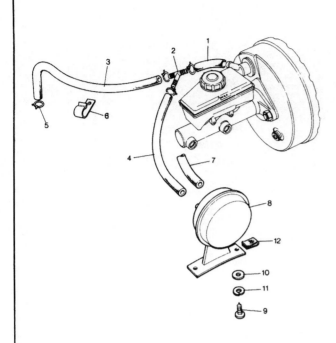

MODEL LR110 - UP TO AUGUST 1986
BLOCK TS 6225
PAGE G 12.02
GROUP G

BRAKES - VACUUM HOSE - AIR CONDITIONING - LHD AND RHD

ILL	PART NO	DESCRIPTION	QTY	REMARKS
1	CRC2131	Hose-Servo to T Piece	1	Diesel
	NRC8349	Hose-Servo to T Piece	1	Petrol
2	592443	T Piece	1	
3	CRC2131	Hose-Engine to T Piece	1	Diesel
	NRC8352	Hose-Engine to T Piece	1	Petrol
4	CRC2134	Hose-T Piece to Valve	1	Diesel
	NRC8629	Hose-T Piece to Valve	1	Petrol
	NRC8593	Valve-One Way	1	
	NRC8352	Hose-Valve to Vacuum Manifold	1	
5	CS600244	Corbin Clip	6	
6	NRC9338	Clip-Rocker Box	1	Diesel
7	RTC4199	Vacuum Hose	A/R	
		VACUUM HOSE-AIR CONDITIONING RHD		
	CRC2131	Hose-Servo to Manifold	1	
	575548	Corbin Clip	1	

TS6225

LAND ROVER PARTS LTD

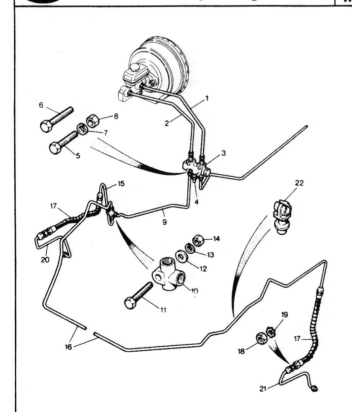

MODEL LR110 - UP TO AUGUST 1986
BLOCK VS 3962
PAGE G 14
GROUP G

BRAKES - BRAKE PIPES - FRONT

ILL	PART NO	DESCRIPTION	QTY	REMARKS
1	NRC7901	Pipe-Primary-Master Cyl to PDWA	1	RHS
	NRC7902	Pipe-Primary-Master Cyl to PDWA	1	LHS
2	NRC7903	Pipe-Secondary-Master Cyl to PDWA	1	RHS
	NRC7904	Pipe-Secondary-Master Cyl to PDWA	1	LHS
3	NRC7871	Valve-PDWA	1	Note(1)
	NRC6515	Valve-PDWA/PCR	1	Note(2)
4	AAU1700	+Switch	1	
5	BH106091L	Bolt	1	
6	BH106111L	Bolt-Dual Brakes	1	
7	WL106001L	Spring Washer	1	
8	NH106041L	Nut	1	
9	NRC9731	Pipe-PDWA to Tee Piece	1	
10	NRC4251	Tee Piece	1	
11	BH106061L	Bolt	1	
12	WC106041L	Plain Washer	1	
13	WL106001L	Spring Washer	1	
14	NH106041L	Nut	1	
15	NRC8721	Pipe-Tee Piece to Hose-RH	1	
16	NRC7801	Pipe-Tee Piece to Hose-LH	1	
17	NRC7874	Front Brake Hose	2	
18	CRC1487	Nut	4	
19	WF110001L	Lock Washer	4	
20	NRC9575	Pipe-Hose to Caliper-RH	1	
21	NRC7799	Pipe-Hose to Caliper-LH	1	
22	CRC1250	Pipe Clip	8	

NOTE(1): PDWA = Pressure Differential Warning Actuator (Single Barrel)

NOTE(2): PDWA/PCR = Pressure Differential Warning Actuator Combined With Pressure Concious Reduction (Double Barrel)

VS3962

LAND ROVER PARTS LTD

MODEL LR110 - UP TO AUGUST 1986
BLOCK VS 3763A
PAGE G 16
GROUP G

BRAKES - BRAKE PIPES - REAR

ILL	PART NO	DESCRIPTION	QTY	REMARKS
1	NTC1792	Pipe-PDWA to Rear Hose	1	
2	NRC9456	Rear Brake Hose	1	
3	NRC4251	Tee Piece	1	
4	BH106061L	Bolt	1	
5	WC106041L	Plain Washer	1	
6	WL106041L	Spring Washer	1	
7	NH106041L	Nut	1	
8	CRC1487	Nut	1	
9	WF110001L	Lock Washer	1	
10	NRC7905	Pipe-to RH Brake	1	
11	NRC7906	Pipe-to LH Brake	1	
12	CRC1250	Pipe Clip	5	
13	79127	Pipe Clip-Double	1	
14	AFU1217	Pipe Clip-Triple	2	
15	11820L	Clip-Pipe to Axle	3	
16	NRC8215	G Valve	1	)
17	NRC8213	Pipe-PDWA to G Valve	1	)
18	NRC8214	Pipe-G Valve to Rear Hose	1	)
19	NRC9035	Bracket-G Valve	1	)Note(1)
20	BH108091L	Bolt-G Valve to Bracket	1	)
21	WA108051L	Washer	1	)
22	NY108041L	Nut	1	)
23	SH106251L	Screw	1	)
24	WA106041L	Washer	1	)
25	NY106041L	Nut	1	)

NOTE(1):   For Use On Hard Top Vehicles With Extra
           Seats Fitted In The Rear.

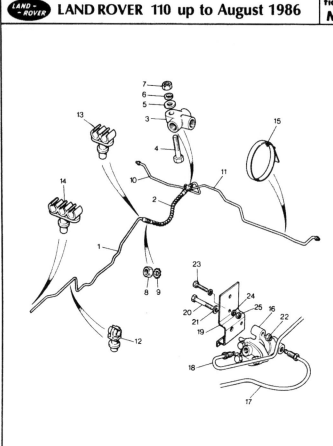

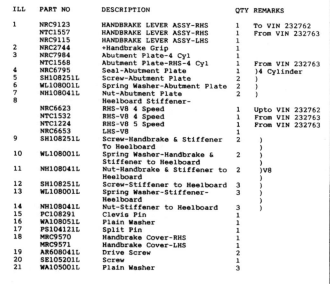

VS3763A

MODEL LR110 - UP TO AUGUST 1986
BLOCK VS 3970
PAGE G 18
GROUP G

BRAKES - HANDBRAKE LEVER AND COVER

ILL	PART NO	DESCRIPTION	QTY	REMARKS
1	NRC9123	HANDBRAKE LEVER ASSY-RHS	1	To VIN 232762
	NTC1557	HANDBRAKE LEVER ASSY-RHS	1	From VIN 232763
	NRC9115	HANDBRAKE LEVER ASSY-LHS	1	
2	NRC2744	+Handbrake Grip	1	
3	NRC7984	Abutment Plate-4 Cyl	1	
	NTC1568	Abutment Plate-RHS-4 Cyl	1	From VIN 232763
4	NRC6795	Seal-Abutment Plate	1	)4 Cylinder
5	SH108251L	Screw-Abutment Plate	2	)
6	WL108001L	Spring Washer-Abutment Plate	2	)
7	NH108041L	Nut-Abutment Plate	2	)
8		Heelboard Stiffener-		
	NRC6623	RHS-V8 4 Speed	1	Upto VIN 232762
	NTC1532	RHS-V8 4 Speed	1	From VIN 232763
	NTC1224	RHS-V8 5 Speed	1	From VIN 232763
	NRC6653	LHS-V8	1	
9	SH108251L	Screw-Handbrake & Stiffener To Heelboard	2	)
10	WL108001L	Spring Washer-Handbrake & Stiffener to Heelboard	2	)
11	NH108041L	Nut-Handbrake & Stiffener to Heelboard	2	)V8
12	SH108251L	Screw-Stiffener to Heelboard	3	)
13	WL108001L	Spring Washer-Stiffener-Heelboard	3	)
14	NH108041L	Nut-Stiffener to Heelboard	3	)
15	PC108291	Clevis Pin	1	
16	WA108051L	Plain Washer	1	
17	PS104121L	Split Pin	1	
18	MRC9570	Handbrake Cover-RHS	1	
	MRC9571	Handbrake Cover-LHS	1	
19	AR608041L	Drive Screw	2	
20	SE105201L	Screw	1	
21	WA105001L	Plain Washer	3	

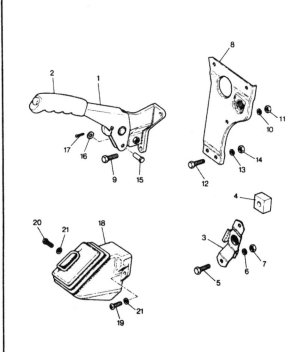

VS3970

MODEL LR110 - UP TO AUGUST 1986
BLOCK TS 5132
PAGE G 18.02
GROUP G

BRAKES - HANDBRAKE LEVER - AUSTRALIA

ILL	PART NO	DESCRIPTION	QTY	REMARKS
1	NRC9123	HANDBRAKE ASSEMBLY	1	To VIN 232762
	NTC1563	HANDBRAKE ASSEMBLY	1	From VIN 232763
2	NRC2744	+Handbrake Grip	1	
3	ADU2888L	Switch-Handbrake	1	
4	SE104121L	Screw	2	
5	WF104001L	Shakeproof Washer	2	
6	PRC4442	Lead Assembly	1	
7	DRC1538	Cable Tie	4	
8	PRC3353	Cable Assembly	1	
9	NRC6623	Heelboard Stiffener	1	To VIN 232762
	NTC1532	Heelboard Stiffener	1	From VIN 232763
10	SH108251L	Screw-Handbrake & Stiffener to Heelboard	2	
11	WL108001L	Spring-Washer	2	
12	NH108041L	Nut	2	
13	SH108251L	Screw-Stiffener to Heelboard	3	
14	WL108001L	Spring Washer	3	
15	NH108041L	Nut	3	
16	PC108291	Clevis Pin	1	
17	WA108051L	Plain Washer	1	
18	PS104121L	Split Pin	1	
19	MRC9570	Handbrake Cover	1	
20	AR608041L	Drive Screw	2	
21	SE105201L	Screw	1	
22	WA105001L	Plain Washer	3	

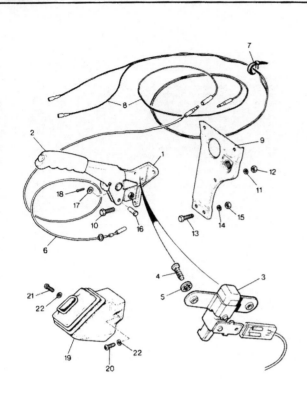

TS5132

318

MODEL LR110 - UP TO AUGUST 1986
BLOCK VS 3971
PAGE G 20
GROUP G

BRAKES - HANDBRAKE CABLE

ILL	PART NO	DESCRIPTION	QTY	REMARKS
1	NRC5088	Handbrake Cable-RHS	1	
	NRC5089	Handbrake Cable-LHS	1	
2	WF116001L	Shakeproof Washer	1	
3	NRC8059	Carrier-4 Cylinder	1	
4	NRC5110	Carrier-V8	1	To VIN 232762
	NTC1643	Carrier-V8	1	From VIN 232763
5	NRC7044	Lever	1	
6	PS104161	Split Pin	1	
7	NRC5104	Pin	1	
8	SH108251L	Screw-Carrier to Housing	2	)
9	BH108091L	Bolt-Carrier to Housing	2	)4 Cylinder
10	WL108001L	Spring Washer	4	)
11	NRC7124	Spacer	2	)
12	SH606061L	Screw-Carrier to Pillar	2	)V8
13	WM600061L	Spring Washer	2	)
14	PC108291	Clevis Pin-Cable to Lever	1	
15	PS104121L	Split Pin	1	
16	NRC7648	Clevis-Lever to Push Rod	1	
17	WA108051L	Plain Washer	2	
18	PS104121L	Split Pin	2	
	NRC9461	Clip-Anti Rattle	1	)RHS
	AFU1350	Mononbolt	1	)
	AEU1446	Clip-Anti Rattle	1	)
	SE105161	Screw	1	)LHS
	WL105001L	Spring Washer	1	)
	NH105041	Nut	1	)

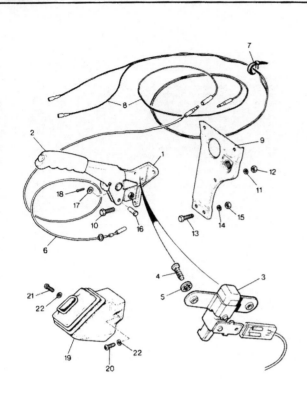

VS3971

319

MASTER INDEX

GROUP H

FUEL

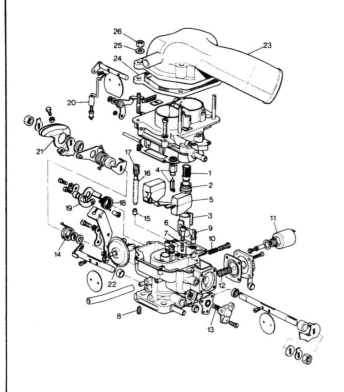

MODEL LR110 - UP TO AUGUST 1986
BLOCK VS 3994
PAGE H 2
GROUP H

FUEL SYSTEM - 2.25 PETROL - CARBURETTER - MECHANICAL FUEL PUMP

ILL	PART NO	DESCRIPTION	QTY	REMARKS
	ERC9713	CARBURETTER (Single Solenoid) With Hand Throttle Control	1	
	ERC8410	CARBURETTER (Single Solenoid) Without Hand Throttle Control	1	Note(1)
	ERC9894	CARBURETTER (Single Solenoid) Variant VE05B European Detox Regulations ECE 15-04	1	Note(2)
1	AEU2587	+Element Filter	1	
2	AEU2586	+Cap-Filter Element	1	
3	AEU2585	+Centring Device Primary/ Secondary	2	
4	AEU2584	+Valve Needle	1	
5	AEU2583	+Float	1	
6	AEU2582	+Holder-Idling Jet	2	
7	AEU2581	+Jet-Primary-Idling	1	
	AEU2580	+Jet-Secondary-Idling	1	
8	AEU2579	+Screw-Adjusting	2	
9	AEU2578	+Pump Jet	1	

NOTE(1): No Longer Available -
          Use ETC5305 Carburetter (Twin Solenoid)
          Plus RTC3948 Conversion Kit

NOTE(2): No Longer Available -
          Use ETC5306 Carburetter (Twin Solenoid)
          Plus RTC3948 Conversion Kit

VS3994

MODEL LR110 - UP TO AUGUST 1986
BLOCK VS 3994
PAGE H 2.02
GROUP H

FUEL SYSTEM - 2.25 PETROL - CARBURETTER - MECHANICAL FUEL PUMP
            CONTINUED

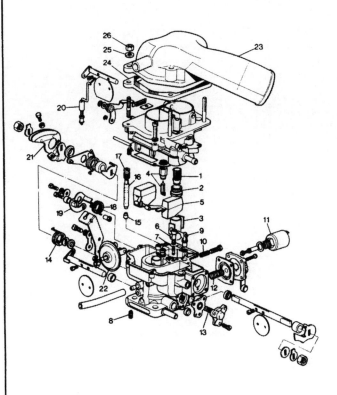

ILL	PART NO	DESCRIPTION	QTY	REMARKS
10	AEU2577	Spring-Primary Butterfly-Adjusting Screw	1	
11	RTC4850	Solenoid-Idle Cut Off	1	
12	AEU2575	Spring-Preload-Pump	1	
13	AEU2572	Spring-Fuel Power Valve	1	
14	AEU2569	Spring-Spindle Return	1	
15	AEU2568	Jet-Primary-Main	1	
	AEU2567	Jet-Secondary-Main	1	
16	AEU2566	Tube-Mixer-Primary/Secondary	2	
17	AEU2565	Jet-Air-Brake Primary/Secondary	2	
18	AEU2564	Spring-Starting Lever-Return	1	
19	AEU2563	Lever-Starting Control	1	
20	AEU2562	Rod-Starting	1	
21	AEU2561	Lever Butterfly Valve Control	1	
22	AEU2560	Throttle	1	

VS3994

LAND ROVER PARTS LTD

322

MODEL LR110 - UP TO AUGUST 1986
BLOCK TS 6591
PAGE H 2.04
GROUP H

FUEL SYSTEM - 2.25 PETROL - CARBURETTER - CONTINUED

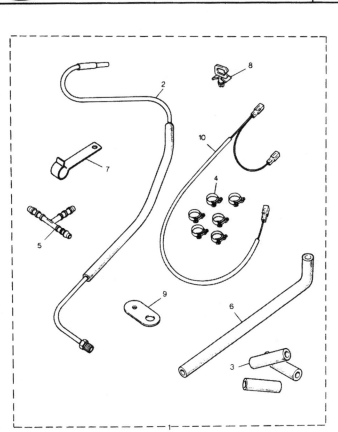

ILL	PART NO	DESCRIPTION	QTY	REMARKS
1	RTC3948	CONVERSION KIT-CARBURETTER	1	See Note(1)
2	ETC5603	+Fuel Pipe Sub Assembly	1	
3	ETC5605	+Connector	3	
4	C435996L	+Clip	6	
5	RTC3949	+Tee Piece	1	
6	ERC298	+Hose	1	
7	ETC4959	+Clip-Carb Breather	1	
8	PRC3702	+Clip	1	
9	PRC3494	+Mounting Plate	1	
10	PRC4376	+Lead-Coil to Solenoids	1	

NOTE(1): For Use On Early Carburetters With A Hot
         Start Problem. Also Use Carburetter ETC5305 Or
         ETC5306.

TS 6591

LAND ROVER PARTS LTD

323

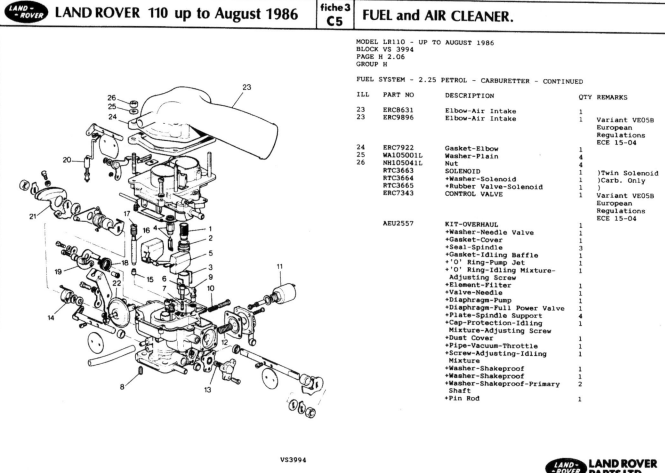

MODEL LR110 - UP TO AUGUST 1986
BLOCK VS 3994
PAGE H 2.06
GROUP H

FUEL SYSTEM - 2.25 PETROL - CARBURETTER - CONTINUED

ILL	PART NO	DESCRIPTION	QTY	REMARKS
23	ERC8631	Elbow-Air Intake	1	
23	ERC9896	Elbow-Air Intake	1	Variant VE05B European Regulations ECE 15-04
24	ERC7922	Gasket-Elbow	1	
25	WA105001L	Washer-Plain	4	
26	NH105041L	Nut	4	
	RTC3663	SOLENOID	1	)Twin Solenoid
	RTC3664	+Washer-Solenoid	1	)Carb. Only
	RTC3665	+Rubber Valve-Solenoid	1	)
	ERC7343	CONTROL VALVE	1	Variant VE05B European Regulations ECE 15-04
	AEU2557	KIT-OVERHAUL	1	
		+Washer-Needle Valve	1	
		+Gasket-Cover	1	
		+Seal-Spindle	3	
		+Gasket-Idling Baffle	1	
		+'O' Ring-Pump Jet	1	
		+'O' Ring-Idling Mixture-Adjusting Screw	1	
		+Element-Filter	1	
		+Valve-Needle	1	
		+Diaphragm-Pump	1	
		+Diaphragm-Full Power Valve	1	
		+Plate-Spindle Support	4	
		+Cap-Protection-Idling Mixture-Adjusting Screw	1	
		+Dust Cover	1	
		+Pipe-Vacuum-Throttle	1	
		+Screw-Adjusting-Idling Mixture	1	
		+Washer-Shakeproof	1	
		+Washer-Shakeproof	1	
		+Washer-Shakeproof-Primary Shaft	2	
		+Pin Rod	1	

VS3994

LAND ROVER PARTS LTD

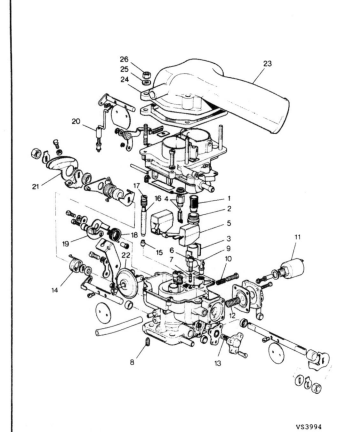

MODEL LR110 - UP TO AUGUST 1986
BLOCK VS 3994
PAGE H 4.02
GROUP H

FUEL SYSTEM - 2.25 PETROL - CARBURETTER - ELECTRIC FUEL PUMP

ILL	PART NO	DESCRIPTION	QTY	REMARKS
	ETC4928	CARBURETTER-TWIN CHOKE	1	)No Longer)Available Use)ETC5305)See Note(1)
	ETC5305	CARBURETTER-TWIN CHOKE	1	
	ETC4929	CARBURETTER-TWIN CHOKE	1	)No Longer)Available Use)ETC5306)See Note(1)
	ETC5306	CARBURETTER-TWIN CHOKE	1	Variant VE05B European Detox To ECE 15-04
1	RTC4421	+Element Filter	1	Horizontal Fitting
	RTC4420	+Washer	1	
	RTC4419	+Inlet Pipe	1	Screw In Type
3	AEU2585	+Centring Device-Primary/Secondary	2	
4	AEU2584	+Valve Needle	1	
5	AEU2583	+Float	1	
6	AEU2582	+Holder-Idling Jet	2	
7	AEU2581	+Jet-Primary-Idling	1	
7	AEU2580	+Jet-Secondary-Idling	1	
8	AEU2579	+Screw-Adjusting	2	
9	AEU2578	+Pump Jet	1	

NOTE(1): Carburetters Identified By Part Number Stamped
          On Metal Tag Attached To The Carburetter Body.

VS3994

LAND ROVER PARTS LTD

MODEL LR110 - UP TO AUGUST 1986
BLOCK VS 3994
PAGE H 4.04
GROUP H

FUEL SYSTEM - 2.25 PETROL - CARBURETTER - ELECTRIC FUEL PUMP -
          CONTINUED.

ILL	PART NO	DESCRIPTION	QTY	REMARKS
10	AEU2577	Spring-Primary Butterfly-Adjusting Screw	1	
11	RTC4850	Solenoid-Idle Cut Off	1	
12	AEU2575	Spring-Preload-Pump	1	
13	AEU2572	Spring-Full Power Valve	1	
14	AEU2569	Spring-Spindle Return	1	
15	AEU2568	Jet-Primary-Main	1	
15	AEU2567	Jet-Secondary-Main	1	
16	AEU2566	Tube-Mixer-Primary/Secondary	2	
17	AEU2565	Jet-Air-Brake-Primary/Secondary	2	
18	AEU2564	Spring-Starting Lever-Return	1	
19	AEU2563	Lever-Starting Control	1	
20	AEU2562	Rod-Starting	1	
21	AEU2561	Lever-Butterfly Valve Control	1	
22	AEU2560	Throttle	1	

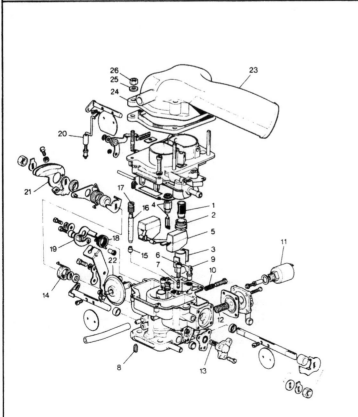

VS3994

LAND ROVER PARTS LTD

MODEL LR110 - UP TO AUGUST 1986
BLOCK VS 3994
PAGE H 4.06
GROUP H

FUEL SYSTEM - 2.25 PETROL - CARBURETTER - ELECTRIC FUEL PUMP
          CONTINUED

ILL	PART NO	DESCRIPTION	QTY	REMARKS
23	ERC8631	Elbow-Air Intake	1	
23	ERC9896	Elbow-Air Intake	1	Variant VE05B European Regulation ECE 15-04
24	ERC7922	Gasket-Elbow	1	
25	WA105001L	Washer-Plain	4	
26	NH105041L	Nut	4	
	RTC3663	SOLENOID	1	
	RTC3664	+Washer-Solenoid	1	
	RTC3665	+Valve-Solenoid	1	
	ERC7343	CONTROL VALVE	1	Variant VE05B European Detox Regulation ECE 15-04
	AEU2557	KIT-OVERHAUL	1	
		+Washer-Needle Valve	1	
		+Gasket-Cover	1	
		+Seal-Spindle	3	
		+Gasket-Idling Baffle	1	
		+'O' Ring-Pump Jet	1	
		+'O' Ring-Idling Mixture-Adjusting Screw	1	
		+Element-Filter	1	
		+Valve-Needle	1	
		DIAPHRAGM-PUMP	1	
		DIAPHRAGM-FULL POWER VALVE	1	
		+Plate-Spindle Support	4	
		+Cap-Protection-Idling Mixture-Adjusting Screw	1	
		+Dust Cover	1	
		+Pipe-Vacuum-Throttle	1	
		+Screw-Adjusting-Idling Mixture	1	
		+Washer-Shakeproof	1	
		+Washer-Shakeproof	1	
		+Washer-Shakeproof-Primary Shaft	2	
		+Pin Rod	1	

VS3994

LAND ROVER PARTS LTD

MODEL LR110 - UP TO AUGUST 1986
BLOCK VS 3777
PAGE H 4.08
GROUP H

FUEL SYSTEM - 4 CYLINDER PETROL - VACUUM PIPES

ILL	PART NO	DESCRIPTION	QTY	REMARKS
1	ERC9294	Pipe Assembly-Vacuum Advance	1	
2	ERC8119	Valve-Vacuum Delay	1	
3	ERC6996	Hose-Dist to Delay Valve	1	
4	512646	Clip-Vacuum Pipe	1	
5	214228	Clip-Vacuum Pipe	1	
6	214229	Grommet-Clip	2	
7	SH604051L	Screw	1	
8	RTC609	Washer-Plain	1	
9	WM600041L	Washer-Spring	1	
10	NH604041L	Nut	1	
	RTC3942	Pipe-Vacuum Unit to Control Valve	1	)Variant VE05B)European
	RTC3942	Pipe-Control Valve to Air Intake Elbow.	1	)Detoxed)ECE 15.04
	ERC7085	Pipe-Control Valve to Servo Adaptor	1	)

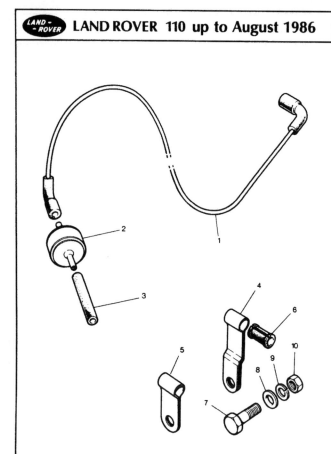

VS3777

MODEL LR110 - UP TO AUGUST 1986
BLOCK VS 3985A
PAGE H 4.10
GROUP H

FUEL SYSTEM - 4 CYLINDER - HAND THROTTLE CONTROL

ILL	PART NO	DESCRIPTION	QTY	REMARKS
1	ERC9708	Hand Throttle Bracket Assy	1	
2	ERC9693	+Lever	1	
3	ERC9704	+Spring	1	
4	WB600071L	+Washer-Plain	1	
5	CR120115L	+Circlip	1	

VS3985A

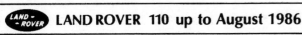

LAND ROVER 110 up to August 1986 | fiche 3 C11 | FUEL and AIR CLEANER.

MODEL LR110 - UP TO AUGUST 1986
BLOCK TS 6344
PAGE H 4.12
GROUP H

FUEL SYSTEM - 2.5 PETROL - CARBURETTER FIXINGS

ILL	PART NO	DESCRIPTION		QTY	REMARKS
1	ERC8631	Air-Inlet Elbow		1	
2	ERC7922	Gasket-Elbow		1	
3	ERC298	Hose-Carb Vent		1	
4	AAU1979	Clip-Hose		1	
5	ETC4959	Clip-Hose		1	
6	NH108041L	Nut	)Carb to Inlet	4	
7	WL108001L	Spring Washer	)Manifold	4	

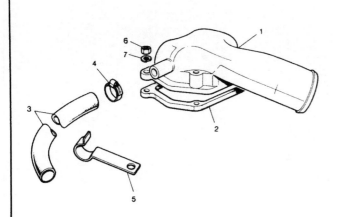

TS6344

LAND ROVER PARTS LTD

330

MODEL LR110 - UP TO AUGUST 1986
BLOCK TS 5899
PAGE H 4.14
GROUP H

FUEL SYSTEM - 2.5 PETROL - CARBURETTERS - WEBER

ILL	PART NO	DESCRIPTION	QTY	REMARKS
1	ETC6350	CARBURETTER-TWIN CHOKE	1	
2	RTC4421	+Filter	1	
3	RTC4420	+Washer	1	
4	RTC4419	+Fuel-Inlet	1	
5	AEU2583	+Float	1	
6	RTC4896	+Gasket-Needle Valve	1	
7	AEU2584	+Needle Valve	1	
8	AEU2565	+Air Correction Jet-Primary	1	
8	AEU4858	+Air Correction Jet-Secondary	1	
9	AEU2566	+Emulsion Tube-Primary	1	
9	RTC4857	+Emulsion Tube-Secondary	1	
10	RTC4852	+Main Jet-Primary & Secondary	2	
11	AEU2582	+Idle Jet Holder	1	
12	RTC4849	+Idle Jet-Primary	1	
12	AEU2580	+Idle Jet-Secondary	1	
13	RTC4897	+'O' Ring	1	
14	RTC4578	+Pump Jet	1	
15	AEU2585	+Auxiliary Venturi(Pri)	1	
15	RTC4859	+Auxiliary Venturi(Sec)	1	
16	AEU2577	+Spring-Idle Speed Screw	1	
17	RTC4898	+Idle Speed Screw	1	
18	RTC4899	+Idle Mixture Screw	1	
19	RTC4900	+'O' Ring-Mixture Screw	1	
20	RTC4850	+Solenoid-Idle Cut Off	1	
21	AEU2575	+Pump Spring	1	
22	RTC4901	+Pump Diaphragm	1	
23	RTC4902	+Top Cover Gasket	1	
24	RTC4903	+Shaft Seal	3	

TS5899

LAND ROVER PARTS LTD

331

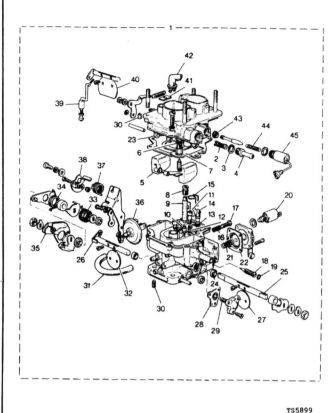

MODEL LR110 - UP TO AUGUST 1986
BLOCK TS 5899
PAGE H 4.16
GROUP H

FUEL SYSTEM - 2.5 PETROL CARBURETTER - WEBER - CONTINUED

ILL	PART NO	DESCRIPTION	QTY	REMARKS
25	AEU2573	Primary Shaft	1	
26	AEU2570	Secondary Shaft	1	
27	AEU2574	Throttle Plate	1	
28	RTC4860	Power Valve Diaphragm	1	
29	RTC4851	Power Valve Spring	1	
30	AEU2579	Screw-Secondary Adjusting	1	
30	AEU2579	Screw- Choke Setting	1	
31	RTC4904	Tube	1	
32	AEU2571	Throttle Plate	1	
33	AEU2569	Spring	1	
34	AEU2564	Spring	1	
35	RTC4853	Throttle Lever	1	
36	AEU2560	Pull Down Capsule	1	
37	AEU2564	Spring-Fast Idle Cam	1	
38	AEU2563	Fast Idle Cam	1	
39	AEU2562	Choke Link	1	
40	AEU2558	Choke Plate	1	
41	RTC4906	Dust Seal	1	
42	RTC4861	Vent Elbow	1	
43	RTC3665	Valve Seal	1	
44	RTC4908	Spring	1	
45	RTC3663	Solenoid	1	
	RTC5970	Gasket Kit	1	
	RTC5863	Overhaul Kit	1	

TS5899

 **LAND ROVER PARTS LTD**

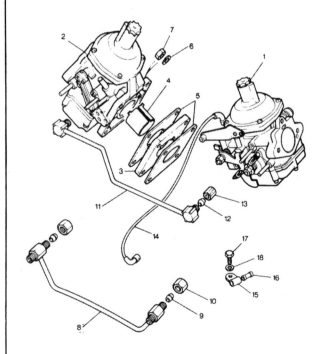

MODEL LR110 - UP TO AUGUST 1986
BLOCK VS 3621
PAGE H 6
GROUP H

FUEL SYSTEM - 3.5 LITRE V8 PETROL - CARBURETTERS (SOLEX)

ILL	PART NO	DESCRIPTION	QTY	REMARKS
1	ERC6364	Carburetter Assembly-LH	1	)Engine 14G Only
2	ERC6365	Carburetter Assembly-RH	1	)
1	ERC5870	Carburetter Assembly-LH	1	)Engine 20G
2	ERC5871	Carburetter Assembly-RH	1	)Only
3	610849	Insulator	2	
4	611026	Liner	2	
5	ERC2154	Joint Washer	4	See Note(1)
6	WM600051L	Spring Washer	8	
7	NH605041L	Nut	8	
8	612505	FUEL FEED PIPE ASSEMBLY	1	
9	614555	+Olive	2	
10	534790	+Nut	2	
11	613514	Choke Connecting Pipe	1	
12	611015	+Olive	2	
13	90611014	+Nut	2	
14	614891	Vacuum Advance Pipe	A/R	See Note(2)
15	AEU1449	Clip Pipe to Manifold	1	
16	541215	Grommet	1	
17	SH504051L	Screw	1	
18	WM600041L	Washer Spring	1	

NOTE(1): Part of Engine Gasket/Seals Kit RTC2913.

NOTE(2): Supplied as 31" Length Cut Off As Required.

VS3621

LAND ROVER PARTS LTD

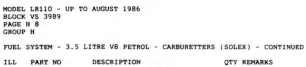

MODEL LR110 - UP TO AUGUST 1986
BLOCK VS 3989
PAGE H 8
GROUP H

FUEL SYSTEM - 3.5 LITRE V8 PETROL - CARBURETTERS (SOLEX) - CONTINUED

ILL	PART NO	DESCRIPTION	QTY	REMARKS
1	ERC6362	Carburetter Assembly-LH	1	)Engines 15G Only
2	ERC6363	Carburetter Assembly-RH	1	)& 21G Only
1	ERC7109	Carburetter Assembly-LH	1	)Engine 17G
2	ERC7110	Carburetter Assembly-RH	1	)& 22G Only
1	ERC6329	Carburetter Assembly-LH	1	)Engine 19G Only
2	ERC6330	Carburetter Assembly-RH	1	)
3	610833	Insulator	2	
4	566737	Saw Tooth Deflector	2	
5	ERC2154	Joint Washer	6	See Note(1)
6	WM600051L	Spring Washer	8	
7	NH605041L	Nut	8	
8	ERC6997	Vacuum Delay Unit	1	
9	614891	Vacuum Pipe	A/R	See Note(2)
9	ERC6995	Vacuum Pipe	1	)Engines 17G
	ERC6996	Vacuum Pipe	1	)Only
10	612505	FUEL FEED PIPE ASSEMBLY	1	
11	614555	+Olive	2	
12	534790	+Nut	2	
13	613514	Choke Connecting Pipe	1	
14	611015	+Olive	2	
15	90611014	+Nut	2	

NOTE(1): Part of Engine Gasket/Seals Kit RTC2913.

NOTE(2): Supplied as 31" Length Cut Off As Required.

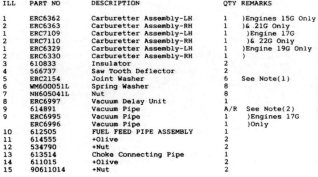

VS3989

LAND ROVER PARTS LTD

MODEL LR110 - UP TO AUGUST 1986
BLOCK TS 6360
PAGE H 8.02
GROUP H

FUEL SYSTEM - 3.5 LITRE V8 PETROL - CARBURETTERS - (S.U.)

ILL	PART NO	DESCRIPTION	QTY	REMARKS
1	ETC7122	CARBURETTER ASSEMBLY-LH	1	
	ETC7123	CARBURETTER ASSEMBLY-RH	1	
2	LZX2107L	+Throttle Lever Assembly	1	
3	JZX1303L	+Screw-Fast Idle	2	
4	AUD4771L	+Clip-Fast Idle	2	
5	JZX1181L	+Screw-Slow Run	2	
6	LZX1540L	+Valve Body Assembly-LH Carb	1	
	LZX1545L	+Valve Body Assembly-RH Carb	1	
7	LZX1988L	+Cam Lever Assembly-LH Carb	1	
	LZX1989L	+Cam Lever Assembly-RH Carb	1	
8	AUD4398	+Spring-Piston (Yellow)	2	
9	NZX8076L	+Needle Assembly	2	
10	AUD3306	+Spring-Needle	2	
11	JZX1039	+Guide-Needle	2	
12	JZX1394L	+Screw-Needle	6	
13	LZX1505	+Damper Assembly	2	
14	CUD2788L	+Jet Assembly-LH Carb	1	
	CUD2785L	+Jet Assembly-RH Carb	1	
15	LZX1600L	+Float Assembly-LH Carb	1	
	RTC3566	+Float Assembly-RH Carb	1	
16	CUD2399L	+BI Metal Assembly	2	
17	ETC7127	FUEL FEED PIPE ASSEMBLY	1	
18	612064	+Olive	2	
19	534790	+Nut	2	
	RTC6072	Seal Kit	1	

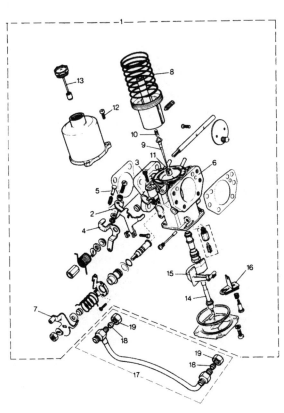

TS 6360

LAND ROVER PARTS LTD

MODEL LR110 - UP TO AUGUST 1986
BLOCK 6RE 33
PAGE H 10
GROUP H

FUEL SYSTEM - 3.5 LITRE V8 PETROL - CARBURETTER COMPONENTS - SOLEX

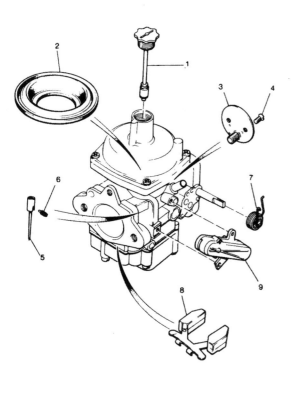

ILL	PART NO	DESCRIPTION	QTY	REMARKS
1	605848	Damper	2	
2	JS499L	Diaphragm	2	
3	605800	Throttle	2	)Engines 14G &)20G Only
	AAU7604	Throttle-With Valve	2	)Engines 15G,19G)& 21G Only
	AEU1848	Throttle-With Valve	2	)Engines 17G &)22G Only
4	601845	Screw-Throttle Valve	2	
5	AEU3077	Metering Needle	2	)Engines 15G,19G)& 21G Only
	AEU3078	Metering Needle	2	Engines 14G Only
	AEU1851	Metering Needle	2	)Engines 17G &)22G Only
	AEU2462	Metering Needle	2	Engines 20G Only
6	518653	Grub Screw	2	
7	516951	Spring-Throttle Return	2	
8	605833	Float	2	
9	AAU7899	Temperature Compensator	2	)Engines 15G,19G)& 21G Only
	AAU7900	Temperature Compensator	2	)Engines 17G &)22G Only

6RE33

LAND ROVER PARTS LTD

336

MODEL LR110 - UP TO AUGUST 1986
BLOCK VS 3491
PAGE H 12
GROUP H

FUEL SYSTEM - 3.5 LITRE V8 PETROL - CARBURETTER SERVICE KITS - SOLEX

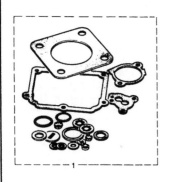

ILL	PART NO	DESCRIPTION	QTY	REMARKS
1	RTC1481	Gasket Kit	2	
2	AAU7219L	Emission Pack-12000 Miles Service	2	
3	RTC1482L	Needle Valve Pack	2	)No Longer)Serviced)Use BHM1079L
	BHM1079L	Needle Valve Pack	2	
4	AAU2967	Emission Pack-24000 Miles Service	2	

VS3491

LAND ROVER PARTS LTD

MODEL LR110 - UP TO AUGUST 1986
BLOCK VS 3874
PAGE H 16
GROUP H

FUEL SYSTEM - 3.5 LITRE V8 PETROL - FUEL TRAP ASSEMBLY
                ENGINE PREFIX 15G AND 17G

ILL	PART NO	DESCRIPTION	QTY	REMARKS
1	ERC2042	Fuel Trap Assembly	1	
2	ERC4193	Support and Clamp	1	
3	253942	Bolt-Clamp to Trap	1	
4	WA702101L	Washer Plain	2	
5	257071	Nut	1	
6	614891	Vacuum Pipe	A/R	
7	SH504041L	Screw-Pipe to Manifold	2	
8	WM600041L	Washer Spring	2	

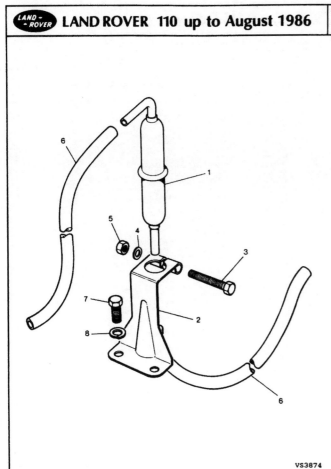

VS3874

LAND ROVER PARTS LTD

338

MODEL LR110 - UP TO AUGUST 1986
BLOCK VS 3953A
PAGE H 18
GROUP H

FUEL SYSTEM - 3.5 LITRE V8 PETROL - AIR INTAKE ADAPTORS

ILL	PART NO	DESCRIPTION	QTY	REMARKS
1	ERC9213	Air Intake Adaptor	2	)Note(2)
2	610327	Joint Washer-See Note(1)	2	)
1	ETC7216	Air Intake Adaptor	2	)Note(3)
2	612435	Joint Washer-See Note(1)	2	)
3	602634	O Ring-See Note(1)	2	
4	TE505105L	Stud Adaptor to Carburetter	4	
5	BH505111L	Bolt	2	
6	WM600051L	Spring Washer	6	
7	NH605041L	Nut	4	
8	239600	Clip-LH Adaptor	1	
	523203	Clip-RH Adaptor	1	
9	273370	Grommet-LH Adaptor	1	
10	NRC223	Elbow-Vent Pipe to Intake Adaptor	2	))
11	ERC8906	Vent Pipe-LH	1	)Note(2)
12	ERC8907	Vent Pipe-RH	1	)
10	577458	Elbow-Vent Pipe to Intake Adaptor	2	))
11	NTC3793	Vent Pipe-LH	1	)Note(3)
12	NTC3794	Vent Pipe-RH	1	)
13	UKC3803L	Hose Band	2	
14	AFU1342L	Clip	1	)
15	573256	Cable Tie-Vent Pipes	1	)Note(2)
	568680	Cable Tie	1	)
14	50641	P Clip	1	)
	589254	Grommet	1	)Note(3)
15	NTC2292	Pipe Clip	1	)
	594594	Cable Tie	1	)

NOTE(1): Part Of Engine Gasket And Seals Kit RTC2913

NOTE(2): Use Only With Solex Carburetters

NOTE(3): Use Only With SU Carburetters.

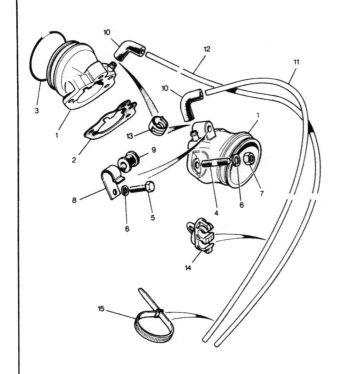

VS3953A

LAND ROVER PARTS LTD

339

MODEL LR110 - UP TO AUGUST 1986
BLOCK VS 3825B
PAGE H 20
GROUP H

FUEL SYSTEM - 2.25 DIESEL - DISTRIBUTOR PUMP/INJECTORS AND PIPES

ILL	PART NO	DESCRIPTION	QTY	REMARKS
1	ERC7329	Distributor Pump	1	
	ERC7329E	Distributor Pump	1	Exchange
2	247212	Joint Washer	1	
3	2920	Washer-Pump to Block	3	
4	WL108001L	Spring Washer-Pump to Block	3	
5	NH108041L	Nut-Pump to Block	3	
6	546282	Sealing Sleeve	1	
7	ETC4335	Mounting Bracket	1	
8	ERC9859	Lever-Accelerator Cable	1	
9	ETC4338	Countershaft Lever	1	
10	NRC5792	+Bush	2	
11	ETC4341	Lever-Hand Throttle	1	
12	NRC5792	+Bush	2	
13	ETC4020	Control Rod	1	
14	564332	Injector	4	
	564332E	Injector	4	Exchange
15	247726	+Nozzle	4	
16	12H220L	Washer-Sealing	4	
17	247179	Joint Washer-Injector to Head	4	
18	273069	Joint Washer-Leak Off Pipe	8	
19	WL108001L	Spring Washer-Injector to Head	8	
20	NH108041L	Nut-Injector to Head	8	
21	541229	Plate-Clamping	4	
22	272512	Grommet	4	
23	SH106161L	Screw-Clamping Plate	2	
24	WL106001L	Spring Washer	2	
25	NH106041L	Nut	2	
26	563165	Injector Pipe-No.1 Cylinder	1	
	ERC7673	Injector Pipe-No.2 Cylinder	1	
	ERC5681	Injector Pipe-No.3 Cylinder	1	
	563168	Injector Pipe-No.4 Cylinder	1	
27	ERC4480	Spill Rail	1	
28	563195	Banjo-Pipe to No.4 Injector	1	
29	273521	Banjo-Pipe to No.1,2,3 Injector	3	
30	ERC9808	Shaft-Hand Throttle	1	
31	ERC9871	Spring-Hand Throttle	1	
32	CR120061L	Circlip	3	
	BAU4611	Switch-Fuel Cut-Off	1	

VS3825B

LAND ROVER PARTS LTD

340

MODEL LR110 - UP TO AUGUST 1986
BLOCK TS 5773
PAGE H 20.02
GROUP H

FUEL SYSTEM - 2.5 DIESEL - DISTRIBUTOR PUMP

ILL	PART NO	DESCRIPTION	QTY	REMARKS
1	ERC6761	Distributor Pump	1	
	ERC6761E	Distributor Pump	1	Exchange
2	ETC4070	Bracket-Support-Pump	1	
3	WA108051L	Washer-Pump to Bracket	2	
4	SH108251L	Screw-Pump to Bracket	1	
5	NY108041L	Nut-Pump to Bracket	1	
6	NY108041L	Nut	3	
7	WA108051L	Washer	3	
8	ERC7766	Pulley	1	No Longer Serviced Use ETC5717
	ETC5717	Pulley	1	
9	RTC5077	Key-Pulley	1	
10	NH112041L	Nut-Fixing Pulley	1	
11	ETC4755	Throttle Lever & Bracket Assy	1	No Longer Serviced Use ETC6675
	ETC6675	Throttle Lever & Bracket Assy	1	
12	ETC4417	Throttle Link Assembly	1	
13	NH105041L	Nut	2	
14	WA105001L	Washer	2	
15	ETC4440	Gasket-Pump to Cover	1	
16	BAU4611L	Switch-Fuel-Cut Off	1	
17	ETC4752	Sleeve-Locking Speed Stop	1	
18	RTC5891	Spring-Throttle Return	1	

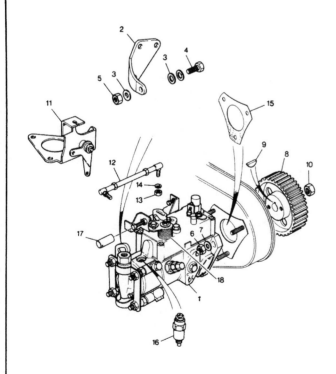

TS5773

LAND ROVER PARTS LTD

341

MODEL LR110 - UP TO AUGUST 1986
BLOCK TS 5763
PAGE H 20.04
GROUP H

FUEL SYSTEM - 2.5 DIESEL - INJECTORS AND PIPES

ILL	PART NO	DESCRIPTION	QTY	REMARKS
1	ERC4480	Spill Rail Assembly	1	
2	ETC4291	Pipe-Injector No.1	1	
3	ETC4292	Pipe-Injector No.2	1	
4	ETC4293	Pipe-Injector No.3	1	
5	ETC4294	Pipe-Injector No.4	1	
6	564332	Injector	4	
	564332E	Injector	4	Exchange
	247726	+Nozzle	4	
7	NH108041L	Nut-Injector to Head	8	
8	WL108001L	Washer-Injector to Head	8	
9	247179	Washer Joint-Injector	4	
10	12H220L	Washer-Spring-Injector	4	
11	ETC4156	Clip-Injector Pipes	2	
12	ETC4308	Clip-Injector Pipes	1	
13	273069	Washer-Joint-Leak Off Pipe	8	
14	273521	Banjo-1,2,3 Injectors	3	
	563195	Banjo-4 Injector	1	

TS5763

LAND ROVER PARTS LTD

342

MODEL LR110 - UP TO AUGUST 1986
BLOCK TS 5690
PAGE H 20.06
GROUP H

FUEL SYSTEM 2.5 DIESEL - HAND THROTTLE CONTROL

ILL	PART NO	DESCRIPTION	QTY	REMARKS
	ETC5181	HAND THROTTLE CONTROL ASSY	1	)No Longer)Serviced Use)ETC6630
	ETC4677	+Bracket-Throttle-Linkage	1	)No Longer)Serviced
1	ETC6630	HAND THROTTLE CONTROL ASSY	1	
2	ETC4678	+Relay Lever Assy	1	
3	613915	++Bush-Relay Lever	2	
4	ETC4686	+Pivot Pin	1	
5	CR120081L	+Circlip	1	
6	WA108051L	+Plain Washer	1	
7	ETC5182	+Throttle Lever Assy	1	
8	522932	++Bush	1	
9	ETC5183	+Hand Throttle Lever Assy	1	
10	522932	++Bush	1	

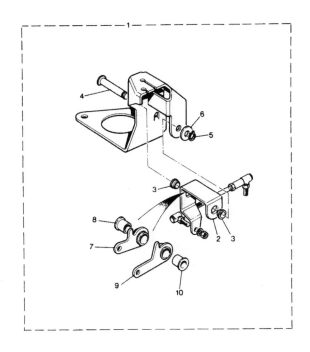

TS 5690

LAND ROVER PARTS LTD

343

MODEL LR110 - UP TO AUGUST 1986
BLOCK VS 4034A
PAGE H 22
GROUP H

FUEL SYSTEM - AIR CLEANER - 4 CYLINDER - OIL BATH TYPE

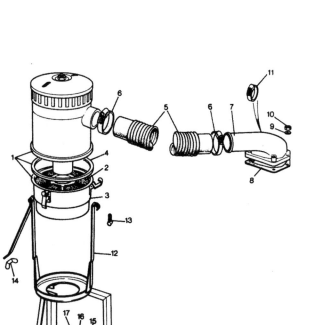

ILL	PART NO	DESCRIPTION	QTY	REMARKS
1	279652	AIR CLEANER	1	
2	600613	+Element	1	
3	90600400	+Oil Container	1	
4	261414	+Seal	1	
5	517903	Hose	1	
6	594753	Hose Clip	2	
7	ERC8631	Air Inlet Elbow	1	)
8	ERC7922	Gasket-Inlet Elbow	1	)
9	WA105001L	Plain Washer-Elbow to Carb	4	)4 Cyl Petrol
10	NH105041L	Nut-Elbow to Carb	4	)
11	CN100258	Hose-Clip	1	)
12	NRC6046	Air Cleaner Support	1	
	NRC8413	Air Cleaner Support	1	PAS Option
13	232538	Tee Bolt	1	
14	250431	Wing Nut	1	
15	SH106121L	Screw	3	
16	WL106001L	Spring Washer	3	
17	NH106041L	Nut	3	

VS4034A

LAND ROVER PARTS LTD

344

MODEL LR110 - UP TO AUGUST 1986
BLOCK TS 5024
PAGE H 22.02
GROUP H

FUEL SYSTEM - AIR CLEANER - 4 CYLINDER - PAPER ELEMENT TYPE

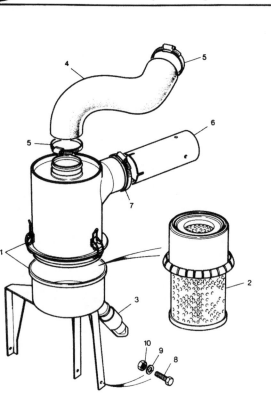

ILL	PART NO	DESCRIPTION	QTY	REMARKS
1	NRC8683	AIR CLEANER	1	
2	NRC9238	+Element	1	
3	NRC8955	+Dump Valve	1	
4	NRC8962	Hose-Cleaner to Manifold	1	Diesel
	NTC1650	Hose-Cleaner to Carburetter	1	Petrol
5	CJ600504L	Hose-Clip	2	
6	NRC8987	Resonator	1	)Diesel Only
7	CJ600504L	Clip-Resonator to Cleaner	1	)
8	SH106121L	Screw	3	
9	WL106001L	Spring Washer	3	
10	NH106041L	Nut	3	

TS5024

LAND ROVER PARTS LTD

345

MODEL LR110 - UP TO AUGUST 1986
BLOCK VS 3945
PAGE H 24
GROUP H

FUEL SYSTEM - RAISED AIR INTAKE - 4 CYLINDER

ILL	PART NO	DESCRIPTION	QTY	REMARKS
1	NRC6920	Air Cleaner-Centrifugal	1	
2	NRC6919	Clip-Air Cleaner	1	
3	SH106201L	Screw	1	
4	WL106001L	Spring Washer	1	
5	NH106041L	Nut	1	
6	NRC7457	Air Intake Pipe	1	
7	NRC6917	Bracket-Air Intake Pipe	1	
8	SH106141L	Screw Bracket to Screen	2	
9	WL106001L	Spring Washer	2	
10	NN106021L	Nutsert	2	
11	NRC7154	Clip-Pipe to Bracket	2	
12	276426	Seal	2	
13	SH108251L	Screw-Clip to Bracket	1	
14	WA108051L	Plain Washer	1	
15	WL108001L	Spring Washer	1	
16	NH108041L	Nut	1	
17	SH108251L	Screw-Pipe to Hinge Bracket	1	
18	WA108051L	Plain Washer	1	
19	WL108001L	Spring Washer	1	
20	NRC6254	Hose	1	
21	CJ600504L	Hose Clip	2	
22	NRC7490	Pipe and Bracket Assembly	1	
23	SH106201L	Screw	2	
24	WA106041L	Plain Washer	2	
25	WL106001L	Spring Washer	2	
26	NH106041L	Nut	2	

NOTE: For Use With Oil Bath Air Cleaner.

VS3945

LAND ROVER PARTS LTD

MODEL LR110 - UP TO AUGUST 1986
BLOCK VS 3944
PAGE H 26
GROUP H

FUEL SYSTEM - RAISED AIR INTAKE - 4 CYLINDER CONTINUED - OIL BATH TYPE

ILL	PART NO	DESCRIPTION	QTY	REMARKS
1	NRC7086	Elbow-Wing Mounting	1	
2	276426	Seal-Pipe to Elbow	1	
3	CJ600504L	Clip	2	
4	SH106161L	Screw-Elbow to Wing	3	
5	WA106041L	Plain Washer	6	
6	WL106001L	Spring Washer	3	
7	NH106041L	Nut	3	
8	347641	Protection Strip-Front Wing	1	
9	NRC6257	Hose-Elbow to Air Cleaner	1	
10	CA600404	Hose Clip	2	
11	NRC7524	Packing Piece	1	
12	NRC7039	Air Cleaner	1	
13	261414	Gasket	1	
14	90600400	Oil Container	1	
15	509510	Packing Piece	1	

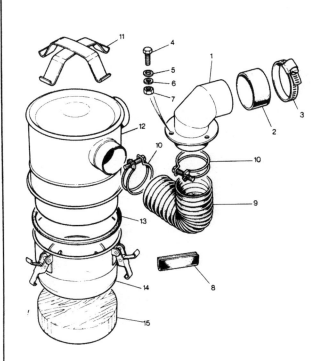

VS3944

LAND ROVER PARTS LTD

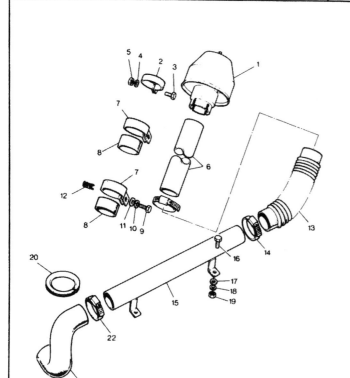

MODEL LR110 - UP TO AUGUST 1986
BLOCK TS 5025
PAGE H 26.02
GROUP H

FUEL SYSTEM - RAISED AIR CLEANER - 4 CYLINDER - 2.5 LITRE
PAPER ELEMENT TYPE

ILL	PART NO	DESCRIPTION	QTY	REMARKS
1	NRC6920	Air Cleaner-Centrifugal	1	
2	NRC6919	Clip-Air Cleaner	1	
3	SH106201L	Screw	1	
4	WL106001L	Spring Washer	1	
5	NH106041L	Nut	1	
6	NRC7457	Air Intake Pipe	1	
7	NRC7154	Clip	2	
8	276426	Seal	2	
9	SH108251L	Screw)Clip to	2	
10	WA108051L	Plain Washer)Windscreen	2	
11	WL108001L	Spring Washer)Frame	2	
12	ML106015	Insert	2	
13	NRC6254	Hose	1	
14	CJ600504L	Hose-Clip	2	
15	NRC9107	Pipe & Bracket Assembly	1	
16	SH106201L	Screw	4	
17	WA106041L	Plain Washer	4	
18	WL106001L	Spring Washer	4	
19	NH106041L	Nut	4	
20	MTC7513	Edging Strip	A/R	
21	NRC8984	Hose-Pipe to Air Cleaner	1	
22	RTC3511	Hose Clip	1	

TS5025

LAND ROVER PARTS LTD

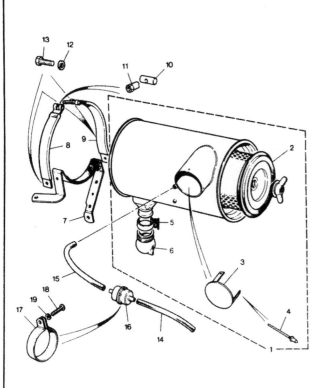

MODEL LR110 - UP TO AUGUST 1986
BLOCK VS 4055
PAGE H 26.10
GROUP H

FUEL SYSTEM - AIR CLEANER - V8

ILL	PART NO	DESCRIPTION	QTY	REMARKS
1	ERC8505	AIR CLEANER	1	
2	RTC3479	+Element	1	
3	ERC3896	+Baffle	1	
4	78704	+Pop Rivet	3	
5	606247	+Clip	1	
6	606248	+Dust Valve	1	
7	ERC3892	Support Bracket-LH	1	
	ERC3893	Support Bracket-RH	1	
8	ERC3946	Retaining Strap-Front	2	
9	ERC3897	Retaining Strap-Rear	2	
10	572994	Trunnion Pin	2	
11	578023	Tension Nut	2	
12	SH505051	Screw	4	
13	WM600051L	Spring Washer	4	
14	ERC3955	Hose-Filter to Air Cleaner	1	
15	ERC3954	Hose-Filter to Block	1	
16	606168	Filter	1	
17	613805	Clip-Filter	1	
18	79134	Screw	1	
19	WL700101	Spring Washer	1	

VS4055

LAND ROVER PARTS LTD

MODEL LR110 - UP TO AUGUST 1986
BLOCK VS 4056
PAGE H 26.12
GROUP H

FUEL SYSTEM - AIR-INLET ELBOWS - NON DETOXED

ILL	PART NO	DESCRIPTION	QTY	REMARKS
1	ERC5247	Air-Inlet Elbow	2	
2	ERC5453	Air-Inlet Duct	1	
3	ERC5052	Hose-Duct to Elbow	2	
4	RTC3518	Hose Clip	4	
5	4594	Spacer	2	
6	603851	Grommet	2	
7	ERC3956	Connecting Tube	1	
8	CA600424	Clip	2	
9	ERC3899	Air Seal	1	
10	ERC5400	Adaptor	1	
11	RTC3502	Hose Clip	1	

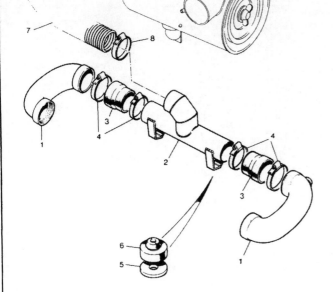

VS4056

LAND ROVER PARTS LTD

MODEL LR110 - UP TO AUGUST 1986
BLOCK TS 6084
PAGE H 28
GROUP H

ENGINE - AIR INLETS - SU CARBURETTER - NON DETOXED - 3.5 V8 PETROL

ILL	PART NO	DESCRIPTION	QTY	REMARKS
1	ETC7193	Air Inlet Duct Assembly	1	
2	ERC3956	Hose-Air Duct to Air Cleaner	1	
3	ERC5247	Elbows-Carburetter	2	
4	ERC3915	Hose-Air Inlet Duct to Elbow	2	
5	RTC3518	Hose Clip	4	
6	ETC7199	Breather Hose	1	
7	UKC3799L	Hose Clamp	2	
8	ETC7201	Adaptor Assembly	1	
9	ERC6878	Check Valve	1	
10	ETC7189	Breather Hose	1	
11	ETC7188	Flamp Trap	1	
12	611092	Hose to Rocker Cover	1	
13	611097	Hose to Carburetter	1	
14	594594	Cable Tie-Retaining Breather Hose	1	

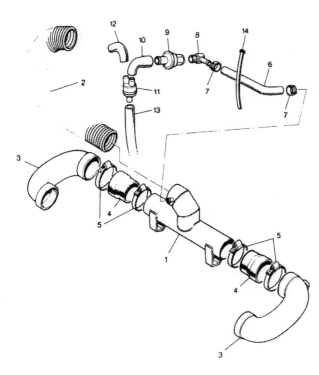

TS6084

LAND ROVER PARTS LTD

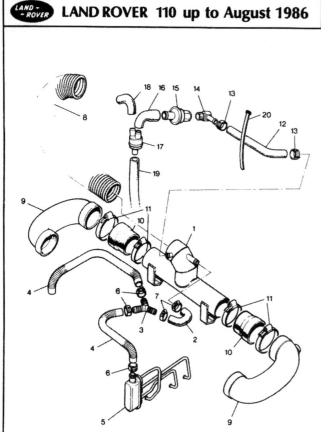

MODEL LR110 - UP TO AUGUST 1986
BLOCK TS 6041
PAGE H 28.02
GROUP H

ENGINE - AIR INLETS - SU CARBURETTER - DETOXED - 3.5 V8 PETROL

ILL	PART NO	DESCRIPTION	QTY	REMARKS
1	ETC7195	Air Inlet Duct Assy	1	
2	ERC9398	Connection Hose	1	
3	ETC6579	Y Connection	1	
4	ETC6581	Air Hose-Flexible	2	
5	ETC5989	Pulsair Box Assembly-LH	1	
	ETC5990	Pulsair Box Assembly-RH	1	Except Air Con
	ETC6912	Pulsair Box Assembly-RH	1	Air Con Only
	ETC6550	Steady-Pulsair Box LH	1	
	ETC6549	Steady-Pulsair Box RH	1	Except Air Con
	ETC6249	Steady-Pulsair Box RH	1	)Air Con Only
	ETC7012	Steady-Pulsair Box RH	1	)
6	UKC3802L	Hose Clamp	4	
7	CN100308L	Hose Clip	2	
8	ERC3956	Air Hose-Air Duct to Air Cleaner	1	
9	ERC5247	Elbow-Carburetter	2	
10	ERC3915	Hose-Air Inlet Duct to Elbow	2	
11	RTC3518	Hose Clip	4	
12	ETC7199	Breather Hose	1	
13	UKC3799L	Hose Clamp	2	
14	ETC7201	Adaptor Assembly	1	
15	ERC6878	Check Valve	1	
16	ETC7189	Breather Hose	1	
17	ETC7188	Flame Trap	1	
18	611092	Hose to Rocker Cover	1	
19	611097	Hose to Carburetter	1	
20	594594	Cable Tie-Retaining Breather Hose	1	
	ETC5918	Injection Tube	2	

TS6041

LAND ROVER PARTS LTD

MODEL LR110 - UP TO AUGUST 1986
BLOCK VS 4057
PAGE H 28.04
GROUP H

FUEL SYSTEM - AIR INLET ELBOWS - DETOXED

ILL	PART NO	DESCRIPTION	QTY	REMARKS
1	ERC9037	Air-Inlet Elbow	2	
2	ERC7144	Air-Inlet Duct	1	
3	ERC6399	Sensor	1	
4	614892	Hose	2	
5	614866	Non Return Valve	1	
6	614891	Hose-Sensor to Valve	1	
7	ERC5052	Hose-Duct to Elbow	2	
8	RTC3518	Hose Clip	4	
9	ERC3890	Mounting Bracket	1	
10	SH108121L	Screw	2	
11	WL108001L	Spring Washer	2	
12	ERC4591	ATC Valve	1	
13	ETC4639	Adaptor	1	
	ETC5147	Adaptor	1	Air Con
14	AB600031	Drive Screw	4	
15	216708	Clip-Choke Cable	1	
16	ERC3884	Adaptor-ATC Valve to Duct	1	
17	ERC4293	Hose	1	
18	ERC4294	Hose	1	
19	CN100508	Hose Clip	4	
20	ERC3891	Clip-ATC Valve	2	
21	WL600041L	Spring Washer	2	
22	NH604041L	Nut	2	
23	ERC3899	Air Seal	1	
24	ERC5400	Adaptor	1	
25	RTC3502	Hose Clip	1	
26	ERC4074	Connection Hose	1	
27	600424	Clip	2	

VS4057

LAND ROVER PARTS LTD

MODEL LR110 - UP TO AUGUST 1986
BLOCK VS 4057A
PAGE H 28.06
GROUP H

FUEL SYSTEM - EVAPORATIVE LOSS - V8 - AUSTRALIA, SAUDI ARABIA

ILL	PART NO	DESCRIPTION	QTY	REMARKS
1	ERC7882	Air Inlet Elbow-RH	1	
2	ERC7881	Air Inlet Elbow-LH	1	
3	ERC7144	Air Inlet Duct	1	
4	ERC7879	Sensor	1	
5	613601	Hose	1	
6	614866	Non Return Valve	1	
7	614891	Hose-Valve to Manifold	1	
8	ERC5052	Hose-Duct to Elbow	2	
9	RTC3518	Hose Clip	4	
10	ERC3890	Mounting Bracket	1	
11	SH505041L	Screw	2	
12	WL108001L	Washer-Spring	2	
13	ERC4591	Air Temperature Control Valve	1	
14	ETC5147	Adaptor	1	
15	AB610031L	Drive Screw	4	
16	ERC3884	Adaptor-ATC Valve to Duct	1	
17	ERC4293	Hose	1	
18	ERC4294	Hose	1	
19	CN100508	Hose Clip	4	
20	ERC3891	Clip-ATC Valve	2	
21	WM600041L	Washer Spring	2	
22	NH604041L	Nut	2	
23	ERC3889	Air Seal	1	
24	ERC5400	Adaptor	1	
25	RTC3502	Hose-Clip	1	
26	ERC3956	Hose-Connection	1	
27	CA600424	Clip	2	

VS4057A

LAND ROVER PARTS LTD

MODEL LR110 - UP TO AUGUST 1986
BLOCK TS 6590
PAGE H 28.08
GROUP H

FUEL SYSTEM - EVAPORATIVE LOSS - V8 - AUSTRALIA, SAUDI ARABIA

ILL	PART NO	DESCRIPTION	QTY	REMARKS
1	606168	Breather Filter	1	
2	613805	Clip	1	
3	AB610041L	Drive Screw	1	
4	RTC3725	Spire Nut	1	
5	ERC5958	Mounting Bracket-Filter	1	
6	ERC8874	Hose-Filter to Crankcase	1	Upto VIN 232762
	ETC5398	Hose-Filter to Crankcase	1	From VIN 232763
7	ERC4176	Hose-Filter to Cannister-RHS	1	
	ERC4176	Hose-Filter to Cannister-LHS	1	Upto VIN 232762
	ETC5397	Hose-Filter to Cannister-LHS	1	From VIN 232763
8	ERC5550	Pipe-Cannister to Y Piece	1	Upto VIN 232762
	ETC5379	Pipe-Cannister to Y Piece-RHS	1	)From VIN 232763
	ETC5378	Pipe-Cannister to Y Piece-LHS	1	)
9	154503	Y Piece	1	
10	ERC8877	Pipe-Y Piece to Carb-RH	1	Upto VIN 232762
	ETC5376	Pipe-Y Piece to Carb-RH	1	From VIN 232763
11	ERC8876	Pipe-Y Piece to Carb-LH	1	Upto VIN 232762
	ETC5377	Pipe-Y Piece to Carb-LH	1	From VIN 232763
12	614617	Clip-Pipe to Intake-LH	1	
13	UKC3794L	Hose-Clip	3	
14	UKC3803	Hose-Clip	2	
	UKC3798L	Hose-Clip	2	
	ERC8873	Plug-Blanking Air Cleaner	1	

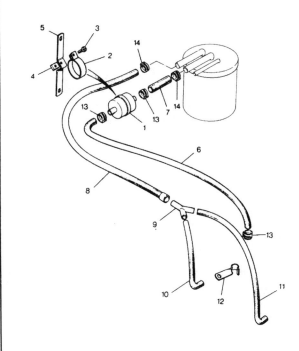

TS 6590

LAND ROVER PARTS LTD

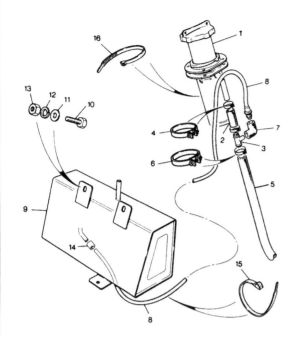

MODEL LR110 - UP TO AUGUST 1986
BLOCK TS 5713
PAGE H 28.10
GROUP H

FUEL SYSTEM - EVAPORATIVE LOSS - V8 - HCPU - SAUDI ARABIA, AUSTRALIA

ILL	PART NO	DESCRIPTION	QTY	REMARKS
1	NRC2536	Fuel Filler Assembly	1	
2	NRC2159	Connection-Rubber	1	
3	NRC2652	Tee Piece	1	
4	572839	Clip	2	
5	NRC2214	Breather Hose	1	To VIN 232762
	NRC9508	Breather Pipe	1	From VIN 232763
				Australia
6	603887	Hose Clip	1	
7	577548	Rubber Elbow	2	
8	NRC9508	Pipe-Tank to Elbow	1	
9	NRC9472	Petrol Catch Tank	1	
10	SH108251L	Screw-Tank Mounting	2	
11	WA108001	Washer-Plain	2	
12	WC108001	Washer-Spring	2	
13	NH108041L	Nut	2	
14	577549	Connector	1	
15	C45099L	Cable Tie-Pipe to Tie Bar	1	
16	UKC6683L	Cable Tie-Fuel Filler Neck	1	

TS5713

LAND ROVER PARTS LTD

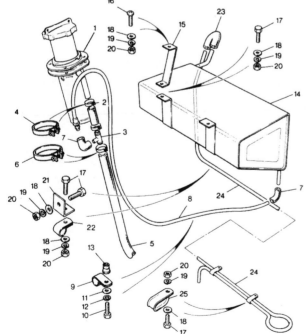

MODEL LR110 - UP TO AUGUST 1986
BLOCK TS 5714
PAGE H 28.12
GROUP H

FUEL SYSTEM - EVAPORATIVE LOSS - V8 - STATION WAGON
                AUSTRALIA, SAUDI ARABIA

ILL	PART NO	DESCRIPTION	QTY	REMARKS
1	NRC2536	Fuel Filler Assembly	1	
2	NRC2159	Rubber Connection	1	
3	NRC2652	Tee Piece	1	
4	572839	Clip	2	
5	NRC2214	Breather Hose	1	
6	603887	Clip	1	
7	577548	Rubber Elbow	3	
8	NRC2195	Pipe	1	
9	CP105081	P-Clip	2	
10	SH105121	Screw	3	
11	WA105001	Washer-Plain	3	
12	WL105001	Washer-Spring	3	
13	NN105011	Nutsert	3	
14	592326	Petrol Catch Tank	1	
15	NRC2087	Mounting Bracket-Front	2	
16	SE106161	Screw	2	
17	SH106161	Screw	6	
18	MRC5695	Plain Washer	6	
19	WL106001	Washer-Spring	8	
20	NH106041L	Nut	8	
21	NRC2089	Mounting Bracket-Rear	2	
22	CP106081	P-Clip	2	
23	611110	Connector	1	
24	NRC2015	Pipe-Tank to Elbow	1	
25	543589	Clip	2	

TS5714

LAND ROVER PARTS LTD

MODEL LR110 - UP TO AUGUST 1986
BLOCK TS 5712
PAGE H 28.14
GROUP H

FUEL SYSTEM - EVAPORATIVE LOSS - V8 - HCPU - SAUDI ARABIA, AUSTRALIA

ILL	PART NO	DESCRIPTION	QTY	REMARKS
1	AFU1085L	Charcoal Cannister	1	
2	NRC4776	Bracket-Charcoal Cannister	1	
3	NRC9865	Support Bracket Assembly	1	Saudi Arabia
4	NRC5844	Support Bracket Assembly	1	Australia
5	SH106141L	Screw	2	
6	SH106351L	Screw	1	
7	WL106001L	Washer-Spring	2	
8	NY106041L	Nut	1	
9	79122	Pipe Clip	4	
10	NTC1048	Pipe-Cannister to Catch Tank	1	Saudi Arabia
11	NRC9507	Pipe-Cannister to Catch Tank	1	Australia
12	577548	Elbow	2	
13	AFU1077L	Swivel Clip	7	
14	NRC5415	Pipe Clip	2	
15	79158	Pipe Clip	3	

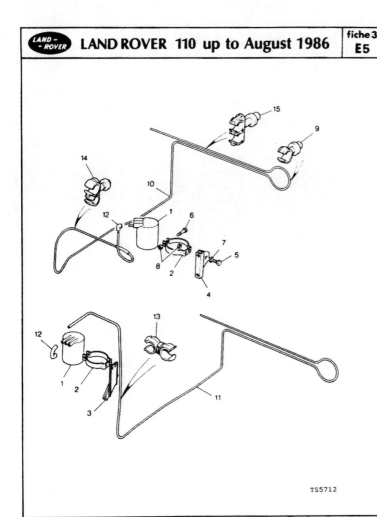

TS5712

LAND ROVER PARTS LTD

MODEL LR110 - UP TO AUGUST 1986
BLOCK TS 5715
PAGE H 28.16
GROUP H

FUEL SYSTEM - EVAPORATIVE LOSS - V8 - STATION WAGON

ILL	PART NO	DESCRIPTION	QTY	REMARKS
1	AFU1085L	Charcoal Cannister	1	
2	NRC4776	Bracket-Charcoal Cannister	1	
3	NRC5844	Support Bracket Assembly	1	Australia
4	NRC9865	Support Bracket Assembly	1	Saudi Arabia
5	SH106141L	Screw	2	
6	SH106351L	Screw	1	
7	WL106001L	Washer Spring	2	
8	NY106041L	Nut	1	
9	CP108081L	P-Clip	1	Australia
10	79122	Pipe Clip	3	
11	NRC5818	Pipe-Cannister to Rear	1	Australia
12	NRC9862	Pipe-Cannister to Rear Pipe	1	)Saudi Arabia
13	NRC9863	Pipe-Front Pipe to Rear Elbow	1	)
14	577548	Elbow	2	
15	AFU1077L	Swivel Clip	6	
16	NRC4515	Pipe Clip	3	)Saudi Arabia
17	79158	Pipe Clip	1	)

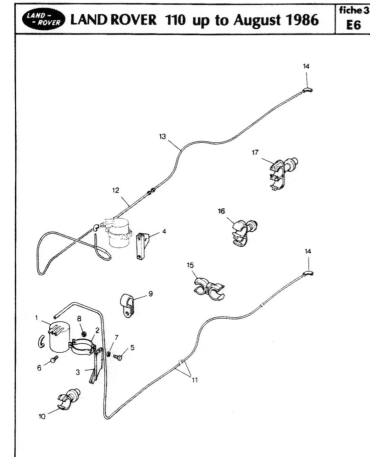

TS5715

LAND ROVER PARTS LTD

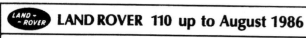
MODEL LR110 - UP TO AUGUST 1986
BLOCK M 890
PAGE H 30
GROUP H

FUEL SYSTEM 3.5 V8 PETROL - ENGINE BREATHER

ILL	PART NO	DESCRIPTION	QTY	REMARKS
1	603330	Flame Trap	2	
2	603376	Clip	2	)Use with Solex
				)Carburetter
	90513220	Clip	1	)Use with SU
				)Carburetters
3	611351	Bracket	1	
4	AB610031L	Screw	2	
5	611114	Hose-Breather to LH Rocker Cover	1	)Use with Solex
				)Carburetter
6	90611112	Hose-Flame Trap to LH Carb	1	)
5	613718	Hose-Breather to LH Rocker Cover	1	)Use with SU
				)Carburetters
6	613402	Hose-Flame Trap to LH Carb	1	)
7	ERC3930	Hose-Breather to RH Rocker Cover	1	
8	ERC3931	Hose-Flame Trap to RH Carb	1	
9	ERC4670	Bracket-Clip/Penthouse	1	

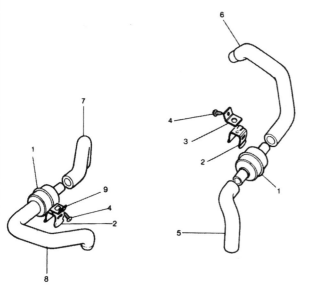

M890

LAND ROVER PARTS LTD

MODEL LR110 - UP TO AUGUST 1986
BLOCK VS 3088
PAGE H 32
GROUP H

FUEL SYSTEM - 3.5 LITRE V8 PETROL - AIR MANIFOLD ENGINES

ILL	PART NO	DESCRIPTION	QTY	REMARKS
1	ERC9035	Air Manifold Assembly	2	)
2	ERC3588	Tube	4	)
3	ERC4204	Tube-LH	2	)
4	ERC4203	Tube-RH	2	)
5	ERC6878	Check Valve Assembly	2	)
6	ERC7629	Pipe Connection-LH	1	)15G, 17G, 21G
7	ERC7630	Pipe Connection-RH	1	)Engines
8	ERC9039	Hose-to Check Valve	2	)
9	ERC7631	Hose-to Intake Elbow	2	)
10	RTC3499	Clip-Hose to Intake Elbow	4	)
11	CN100308L	Clip-Hose to Check Valve	4	)
	ETC5989	Pulsair Box Assy LH	1	)
	ETC5990	Pulsair Box Assy RH	1	)24G Engine
	ETC6474	Plug-Cylinder Head	2	)
	ETC6549	Steady-Pulsair Box RH	1	)
	ETC6550	Steady-Pulsair Box LH	1	)
	ETC5918	Injection Tube	2	)

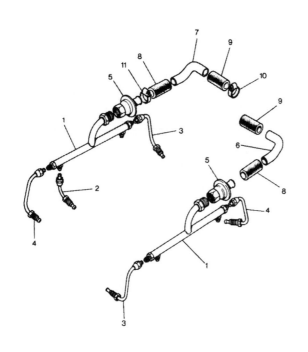

VS3088

LAND ROVER PARTS LTD

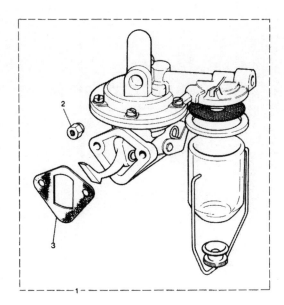

MODEL LR110 - UP TO AUGUST 1986
BLOCK 1RE 108A
PAGE H 34
GROUP H

FUEL SYSTEM - FUEL PUMP - 2.25 PETROL

ILL	PART NO	DESCRIPTION	QTY	REMARKS
1	ERC9594	Fuel Pump-Mechanical	1	
2	NV605041L	+Nut	2	Upto Suffix B
	NY108041L	+Nut-Nyloc	2	From Suffix C
3	275565	Gasket-Pump to Block	1	
	AEU2760	Repair/Overhaul Kit-Fuel Pump	1	

1RE108A

MODEL LR110 - UP TO AUGUST 1986
BLOCK VS 3829A
PAGE H 36
GROUP H

FUEL SYSTEM - FUEL PUMP AND FUEL FILTER - 4 CYLINDER DIESEL

ILL	PART NO	DESCRIPTION	QTY	REMARKS
1	563190	FUEL FILTER	1	
2	90517711	+Element	1	
3	AAU9903	+Seal-Element-Top	1	
4	AAU9902	+Seal-Element-Bottom	1	
5	37H575L	+Seal-Element-Small	1	
6	605013	+Seal-Drain Plug	1	
7	605012	+Drain Plug	1	
8	37H8119L	+Bolt-Centre	1	
9	522940	+Washer-Centre Bolt	1	
10	37H770L	+O Ring-Centre Bolt	1	
11	517689	Plug-Blanking	1	
12	517706	Washer-Plug	1	
13	13H1515L	Bolt-Banjo	1	
14	517976	Washer-Joint	1	
15	SH108301L	Bolt) Filter	2	
16	WL108001L	Washer-Spring) to	2	
17	WA108051L	Washer-Plain) Dash	2	
18	NN108021	Rivnut)	1	
19	RTC6180	Fuel Pump-Mechanical	1	
20	275565	Gasket-Pump to Block	1	
21	NV605041L	Nut-UNF-Philidas	2	
	AEU2760	Repair /Overhaul Kit-Fuel Pump	1	

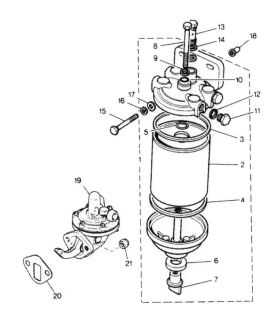

VS3829

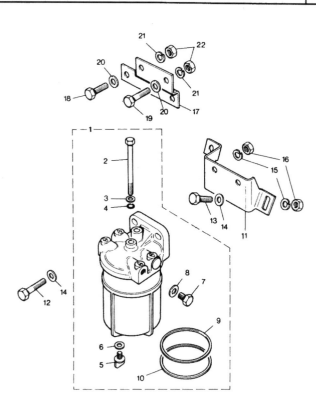

MODEL LR110 - UP TO AUGUST 1986
BLOCK VS 3993
PAGE H 38
GROUP H

FUEL SYSTEM - SEDIMENTORS - 4 CYLINDER DIESEL

ILL	PART NO	DESCRIPTION	QTY	REMARKS
1	562748	SEDIMENTOR	1	See Note(1)
2	37H8119	+Bolt-Centre	1	
3	522940	+Washer-Centre Bolt	1	
4	37H770	+O Ring-Centre Bolt	1	
5	37H7920	+Drain Plug	1	
6	605011	+Seal-Drain Plug	1	
7	517689	+Plug-Blanking	1	
8	517706	+Joint Washer	1	
9	AAU9903	+Seal-Sedimentor-Top	1	
10	AAU9902	+Seal-Sedimentor-Bottom	1	
11	NRC5623	Bracket-Rear Sedimentor	1	)
12	BH108061L	Bolt-Sedimentor to Bracket	2	))Fixing
13	SH108201	Bolt-Bracket to Chassis	2	)Sedimentor
14	WA108051L	Washer-Plain	4	)For Rear Tank
15	WL108001L	Washer-Spring	4	)
16	NH108041L	Nut	4	)
17	NRC7372	Bracket-Sedimentor-Side Fuel Tank	1	)
18	SH108251L	Bolt-Sedimentor to Bracket	2	)Fixing)Sedimentor
19	SH108201	Bolt-Bracket to Chassis	2	)For Side Fuel
20	WA108051L	Washer-Plain	4	)Tank
21	WL108001L	Washer-Spring	4	)
22	NH108041L	Nut	4	)

NOTE(1): 562748 Sedimentor Is Used For Rear & Side
          Tank But Alter Blanking Plugs As Required.

VS3993

364

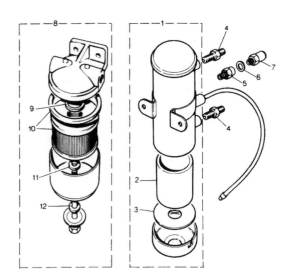

MODEL LR110 - UP TO AUGUST 1986
BLOCK VS 3790A
PAGE H 40
GROUP H

FUEL SYSTEM - FUEL PUMP AND FUEL FILTER - SEE NOTE(1)

ILL	PART NO	DESCRIPTION	QTY	REMARKS
1	PRC3343	FUEL PUMP-ELECTRIC	1	
2	90606262	+Filter-Pump	1	
3	90606261	+Gasket-Bottom Cover	1	
4	572535	Adaptor-Upper and Lower	2	Except Note(2)
	572535	Adaptor-Lower	1	)
5	NRC9621	Adaptor-Upper	1	)Note(2)
6	517706	Joint Washer	1	)
7	ERC3788	Non Return Valve	1	)
8	90577064	Fuel Filter	1	
9	JS657L	+Gasket-Seating	1	
10	JS660L	+Element	1	
11	AEU1147	+Seal-Centre Bolt	1	
12	606207	+Seal-Centre Bolt	1	

NOTE(1): Fitted To V8 & 4 Cyl Petrol From
          VIN203223 Up To Introduction Of In
          Tank Fuel Pumps.

NOTE(2): When Additional Fuel Pump Is Fitted
          - Twin Tanks

VS 3790A

MODEL LR110 - UP TO AUGUST 1986
BLOCK TS 6595
PAGE H 40.02
GROUP H

FUEL SYSTEM - ADDITIONAL FUEL PUMP - 4 CYL PETROL - TWIN PUMPS
            SEE NOTE(1)

ILL	PART NO	DESCRIPTION	QTY	REMARKS
1	PRC3901	FUEL PUMP-ELECTRIC	1	
2	90606262	+Filter-Pump	1	
3	90606261	+Gasket-Bottom Cover	1	
4	572535	Adaptor-Lower	1	
5	NRC9621	Adaptor-Upper	1	
6	517706	Joint-Washer	1	
7	564909	Non Return Valve	1	

NOTE(1): Fitted Up To Introduction Of In Tank Pumps.

TS 6595

366

MODEL LR110 - UP TO AUGUST 1986
BLOCK VS 3828
PAGE H 42
GROUP H

FUEL SYSTEM - PUMP & FILTER MOUNTINGS - PETROL - SEE NOTE(1) & NOTE(3)

ILL	PART NO	DESCRIPTION	QTY	REMARKS
1	NRC7284	Mounting Plate	1	
2	SH106201L	Screw	2	
3	WA106041L	Washer-Plain	2	
4	WL106001L	Washer-Spring	2	
5	NH106041L	Nut	2	
6	NRC7135	Rubber Mount	3	
7	WM600041L	Washer-Spring	3	
8	NH604041L	Nut	3	
9	568244	Earth Braid	1	
10	SH106201L	Screw	2	
11	WA106041L	Washer-Plain	3	
12	WL106001L	Washer-Spring	2	
13	NH106041L	Nut	2	
14	NRC7930	Pipe-Pump to Filter	1	
15	NRC7454	Cover-Pump and Filter	1	See Note(2)
16	SH106121L	Screw	2	
17	WA106041L	Washer-Plain	2	
18	WL106001L	Washer-Spring	2	
19	NH106041L	Nut	2	
20	SH106121L	Screw	1	
21	WA106041L	Washer-Plain	1	
22	WL106001L	Washer-Spring	1	
23	NH106041L	Nut	1	

NOTES:
(1): Fitted on V8 & 4 Cylinder Petrol
      From VIN203223
(2): Item 15 Cover-Pump & Filter, Also Used
      To Cover Sedimentors on Diesel Vehicles
(3): Fitted Up To Introduction Of In Tank Pumps.

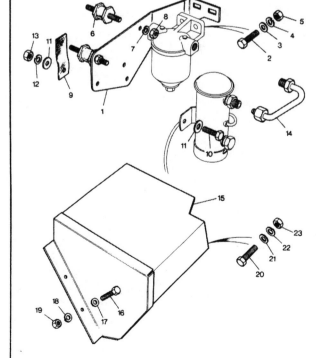

VS3828

367

MODEL LR110 - UP TO AUGUST 1986
BLOCK TS 6594
PAGE H 42.02
GROUP H

FUEL SYSTEM - MOUNTINGS - ADDITIONAL FUEL PUMP - 4 CYLINDER PETROL
               - TWIN PUMPS - SEE NOTE(1)

ILL	PART NO	DESCRIPTION	QTY	REMARKS
1	NTC1043	Mounting Plate	1	
2	NRC7135	Rubber Mount	2	
3	WM600041L	Spring Washer	4	
4	NH604041L	Nut	4	
5	568244	Earth Braid	1	
6	NTC1044	Stay Bracket	1	
7	SH104141L	Screw	1	
8	WL104041	Spring Washer	1	
9	NH104041L	Nut	1	
10	BH106141L	Bolt	2	
11	WL106041L	Spring Washer	2	
12	NH106041L	Nut	2	

NOTE(1): Fitted Up To Introduction Of In Tank Pumps.

TS 6594

 **LAND ROVER PARTS LTD**

368

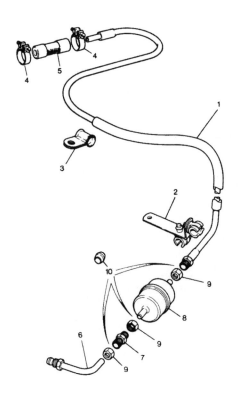

MODEL LR110 - UP TO AUGUST 1986
BLOCK VS 3776
PAGE H 44
GROUP H

FUEL SYSTEM - FUEL CONNECTIONS - 2.25 PETROL

ILL	PART NO	DESCRIPTION	QTY	REMARKS
1	ETC4925	Pipe-Fuel	1	)Note(1)
	ETC5027	Pipe Assembly-Fuel	1	)
	ETC4999	Connector-Fuel Pipe	1	)
	CC600084L	Hose Clip	2	)Note(2)
	ETC5021	Connector-Fuel Pipe	1	)
	CC600094L	Hose Clip	2	)
	ERC9522	Pipe Assembly-Fuel	1	)
2	ETC4098	Bracket & Clips Assembly	1	)
3	ERC9336	Clip-Rocker Cover Stud	1	)
4	572839	Clip-Hose	2	)
5	587684	Connection Assembly-Petrolflex	1	)Note(3))
6	ERC9526	Fuel Pipe Assembly	1	)
7	ERC9525	Adaptor-Fuel Filter to Pipe	1	))
8	606188	Filter	1	)
9	603431	Union Nut	3	)
10	542846	Olive	3	)

NOTE(1): Vehicles with Electric Fuel Pump
          Upto Engine No. 11H01749.
NOTE(2): Vehicles with Electric Fuel Pump
          From Engine No. 11H01750.
NOTE(3): Vehicles with Mechanical Fuel Pump

VS3776

 **LAND ROVER PARTS LTD**

369

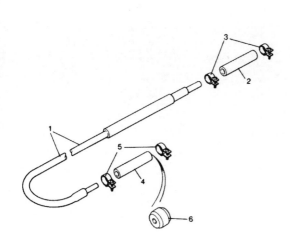

MODEL LR110 - UP TO AUGUST 1986
BLOCK TS 6324
PAGE H 44.02
GROUP H

FUEL SYSTEM - FUEL CONNECTION - 2.5 PETROL

ILL	PART NO	DESCRIPTION	QTY	REMARKS
1	ETC5027	Fuel Pipe Assembly	1	
2	ETC6155	Connector Hose-Fuel Pipe	1	
3	EAC32151	Hose Clip-Connector	2	
4	ETC6156	Connector Hose-Fuel Pipe	1	
5	EAC32151	Hose Clip-Connector	2	
6	ETC6243	Restrictor	1	

TS 6324

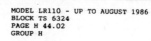
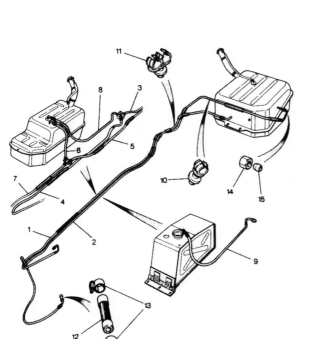

MODEL LR110 - UPTO AUGUST 1986
BLOCK VS 3913
PAGE H 46
GROUP H

FUEL SYSTEM - FUEL PIPES - 4 CYLINDER PETROL - UP TO VIN 203222

ILL	PART NO	DESCRIPTION	QTY	REMARKS
		Fuel Pipe		
1	NRC7979	-Tank to Pump-Feed	1	
2	NRC8111	-Spill to Tank	1	
		ADDITIONAL FUEL TANK		Optional
		Fuel Pipe		
3	NRC7893	-Tank to Tap-Feed	1	)
4	NRC8107	-Tap to Pump-Feed	1	)Pick-Up &
5	NRC7308	-Tap to Tank-Spill	1	)Station Wagon
6	NRC7310	-Side Tank to Tap-Spill	1	)
7	NRC8114	-Spill Outlet-Carb to Tap	1	)
8	NRC7303	-Side Tank to Tap-Feed	1	Pick-Up
9	NRC8087	-Side Tank to Tap-Feed	1	Station Wagon
10	79121	Clip-Single	3	
	79122	Clip-Single	3	
11	NRC5415	Clip-Double	7	
12	587684	Flexible Coupling	1	
13	572839	Clip	2	
14	603431	Nut	A/R	
15	542846	Olive	A/R	

VS3913

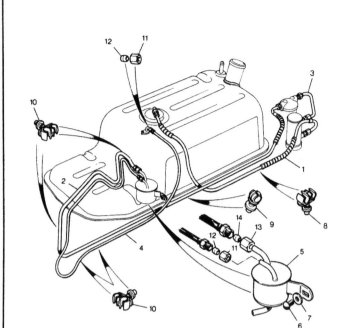

```
MODEL LR110 - UP TO AUGUST 1986
BLOCK TS 5167A
PAGE H 46.02
GROUP H
```

FUEL SYSTEM - FUEL PIPES - **4** CYLINDER PETROL - FROM VIN 203223
SEE NOTE(1)

ILL	PART NO	DESCRIPTION	QTY	REMARKS
		Fuel Pipe		
1	NRC7886	-Tank to Pump-Feed	1	
2	NRC9536	-Filter to Separator	1	
3	NRC7930	-Pump to Filter	1	
4	NRC9540	-Spill Return to Tank	1	
5	NRC9526	Vapour Separator	1	
6	72628	Screw	2	
7	WJ106001L	Washer	2	
8	AFU1077L	Swivel Clip	1	
9	79121	Clip-Single	7	
	79122	Clip-Single	2	
10	NRC5415	Clip-Double	10	
11	603431	Nut	A/R	
12	542846	Olive	A/R	
13	534790	Nut	1	
14	534797	Olive	1	

NOTE(1): Fitted Up To Introduction Of In Tank Pumps.
VIN 243343

TS 5167A

```
MODEL LR110 - UP TO AUGUST 1986
BLOCK TS 5520
PAGE H 46.04
GROUP H
```

FUEL SYSTEM - FUEL PIPES - **4** CYLINDER PETROL - TWIN PUMPS - SEE NOTE(1)

ILL	PART NO	DESCRIPTION	QTY	REMARKS
		Fuel Pipe		
1	NTC1008	-Rear Tank to Rear Pump	1	
2	NTC1011	-Rear Pump to Tee Piece	1	
3	NRC9620	Tee Piece	1	
		Fuel Pipe		
4	NTC1014	-Tee Piece to Filter	1	
5	NTC1016	-Front Pump to Tee Piece	1	
6	NTC1005	-Front Tank to Front Pump	1	
7	NTC1004	-Tap to Rear Tank-Spill	1	
8	NRC7310	-Tap to Front Tank-Spill	1	
9	NTC1003	-Tap to Vapour Separator	1	
10	79121	Pipe Clip	4	
	79122	Pipe Clip	2	
11	NRC5415	Pipe Clip	8	
12	AFU1077L	Swivel Clip	1	

NOTE(1): Fitted Up To Introduction Of In Tank Pumps.
VIN 243343

TS5520

MODEL LR110 - UP TO AUGUST 1986
BLOCK TS 5737
PAGE H 46.06
GROUP H

FUEL SYSTEM - VAPOUR SEPARATOR, FUEL FILTER, FUEL PIPES - FRONT
             - 4 CYLINDER PETROL - WITH IN TANK PUMP

ILL	PART NO	DESCRIPTION	QTY	REMARKS
1	NRC9772	Vapour Separator	1	
2	72628	Screw	2	)Separator
3	WJ106001L	Washer	2	)to Dash
4	NRC9771	Olive	1	
5	NRC9770	Nut	1	
6	NTC2223	Restrictor	1	)
7	NTC2876	Hose	2	)See Note(1)
8	NTC2224	Fuel Feed Pipe-Metal	1	)
	NTC3866	Fuel Feed Pipe-Plastic	1	
9	NTC2073	Spill Pipe-Metal	1	See Note(1)
	NTC3867	Spill Pipe-Plastic	1	
10	CN100708L	Hose Clip	2	See Note(1)
11	NTC2876	Hose	2	
12	CN100708L	Hose Clip	4	
13	NTC2069	Fuel Feed Pipe	1	See Note(1)
14	NRC9786	Fuel Filter	1	
15	SH106201L	Screw	2	
16	WA106041L	Plain Washer	2	
17	WL106001L	Spring Washer	2	
18	NH106041L	Nut	2	
19	79158	Pipe Clip-Double	4	
20	NTC2072	Spill Pipe	1	
21	NTC2096	Spill Pipe	1	)
22	NTC2876	Hose	1	)Extra Tank
23	CN100708L	Hose Clip	2	)

NOTE(1): Fitted Up To Introduction Of Plastic Pipes

TS5737

LAND ROVER PARTS LTD

MODEL LR110 - UP TO AUGUST 1986
BLOCK VS 3915
PAGE H 48
GROUP H

FUEL SYSTEM - FUEL PIPES - 4 CYLINDER DIESEL - WITHOUT SEDIMENTORS

ILL	PART NO	DESCRIPTION	QTY	REMARKS
		Fuel Pipe		
1	NRC7979	-Tank to Pump-Feed	1	
2	NRC3848	-Spill Outlet to Tank	1	To Note(1)
	NTC2157	-Spill Outlet to Tank	1	From Note(1)
		ADDITIONAL FUEL TANK		Optional
		Fuel Pipe		
3	NRC7893	-Tank to Tap-Feed	1	)
4	NRC8104	-Tap to Pump-Feed	1	)Pick-Up &
5	NRC7308	-Tap to Tank-Spill	1	)Station Wagon
		(To Note(1))		)
	NTC2179	-Tap to Tank-Spill	1	)
		(From Note(1))		)
6	NRC7310	-Side Tank to Tap-Sill	1	)
7	NRC7351	-Spill Rail to Tap	1	)
8	NRC7303	-Side Tank to Tap-Feed	1	Pick-Up
9	NRC8087	-Side Tank to Tap-Feed	1	Station Wagon
10	79121	Clip-Single	4	
	78122	Clip-Single	1	
11	NRC5415	Clip-Double	7	
12	603431	Nut	A/R	
13	542846	Olive	A/R	

NOTE(1):   VIN 243343

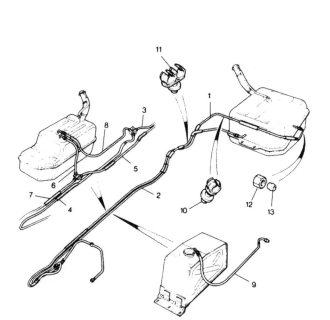

VS3915

LAND ROVER PARTS LTD

MODEL LR110 - UP TO AUGUST 1986
BLOCK VS 3916
PAGE H 50
GROUP H

FUEL SYSTEM - FUEL PIPES - 4 CYLINDER DIESEL-WITH SEDIMENTORS

ILL	PART NO	DESCRIPTION	QTY	REMARKS
		Fuel Pipe		
1	NRC8462	-Tank to Sedimentors	1	
2	NRC8103	-Sedimentor to Pump	1	
3	NRC3848	-Spill Rail to Tank	1	To Note(1)
	NTC2157	-Spill Rail to tank	1	From Note(1)
		ADDITIONAL FUEL TANK		Optional
		Fuel Pipe		
4	NRC7318	-Rear Sedimentor to Tap	1	)
5	NRC7319	-Front Sedimentor to Tap	1	)
6	NRC8108	-Side Tank to Front	1	)Pick-Up &
		-Sedimentor		)Station Wagon
7	NRC8104	-Tap to Pump	1	)
8	NRC7308	-Tap to Tank-Spill	1	)
		(To Note(1))		)
	NTC2179	-Tap to Tank-Spill	1	)
		(From Note(1))		)
9	NRC7310	-Side Tank to Tap-Spill	1	)
10	NRC7351	-Spill Rail to Tap	1	)
11	79121	Clip-Single	4	
	79122	Clip-Single	1	
12	NRC5415	Clip-Double	7	
13	603431	Nut	A/R	
14	542846	Olive	A/R	

NOTE(1):   VIN 243343

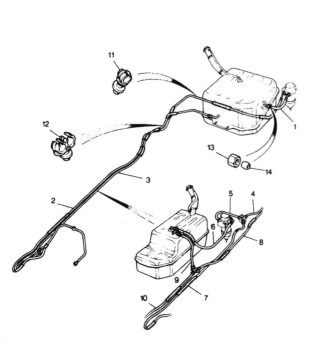

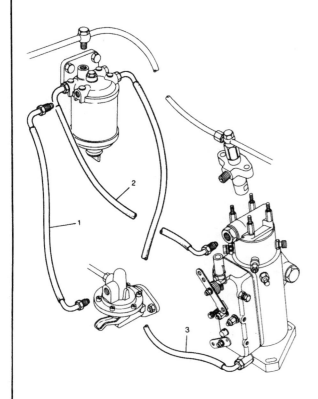

VS3916

LAND ROVER PARTS LTD

MODEL LR110 - UP TO AUGUST 1986
BLOCK VS 3830
PAGE H 52
GROUP H

FUEL SYSTEM - FUEL PIPES - 2.25 DIESEL

ILL	PART NO	DESCRIPTION	QTY	REMARKS
		Fuel Pipe		
1	ERR244	-Pump to Filter	1	
2	NRC7976	-Top DPA Pump to Filter	1	
3	NRC7977	-Bottom DPA Pump to	1	
		Filter		

VS3830

LAND ROVER PARTS LTD

MODEL LR110 - UP TO AUGUST 1986
BLOCK TS 5156
PAGE H 52.02
GROUP H

FUEL SYSTEM - FUEL PIPES - 2.5 DIESEL

ILL	PART NO	DESCRIPTION	QTY	REMARKS
		Fuel Pipe		
1	ETC6903	-Fuel Pump to Filter	1	
2	ETC6901	-DPA Pump to Filter	1	
3	ETC6902	-DPA Pump to Filter-Spill	1	
4	AAU3509	Non Return Valve	1	
5	517706	Joint Washer	1	
6	578293	Hose Clip	6	Sweden

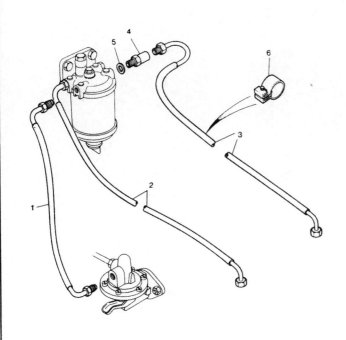

TS5156

LAND ROVER PARTS LTD

MODEL LR110 - UP TO AUGUST 1986
BLOCK VS 3914
PAGE H 54
GROUP H

FUEL SYSTEM - FUEL PIPES - V8 PETROL - NOTE(1)

ILL	PART NO	DESCRIPTION	QTY	REMARKS
		Fuel Pipe		
1	NRC7886	-Tank to Pump-Feed	1	
2	NRC8018	-Filter to Feed	1	
3	NRC7930	-Pump to Filter	1	
4	NRC8017	-Spill Outlet to Tank	1	
		ADDITIONAL FUEL TANK		OPTIONAL
		Fuel Pipe		
5	NRC7893	-Tank to Tap-Feed	1	)
6	NRC7894	-Tap to Pump-Feed	1	)
7	NRC7930	-Pump to Filter-Feed	1	)Pick-Up &
8	NRC8018	-Filter to Feed	1	)Station Wagon
9	NRC7308	-Tap to Tank-Spill	1	)
10	NRC7310	-Side Tank to Tap-Spill	1	)
11	NRC7312	-Tap to Spill	1	)
12	NRC7303	-Side Tank to Tap-Feed	1	Pick-Up
13	NRC8087	-Side Tank to Tap-Feed	1	Station Wagon
14	AFU1077L	Clip-Swivel	1	
15	79121	Clip-Single	7	
	79122	Clip-Single	2	
16	NRC5415	Clip-Double	7	
17	603431	Nut	A/R	
18	542846	Olive	A/R	

NOTE(1): Up To Introduction Of In Tank Pumps
          VIN 243343

          For Vent Pipes-See Carburettor Air Intake Adaptors.

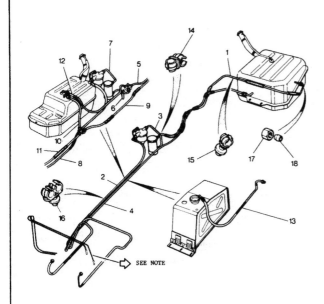

SEE NOTE

VS3914

LAND ROVER PARTS LTD

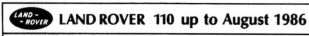
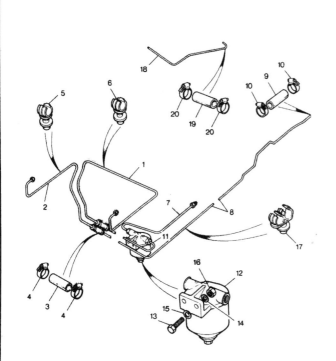

```
MODEL LR110 - UP TO AUGUST 1986
BLOCK TS 5736
PAGE H 54.02
GROUP H

FUEL SYSTEM - FUEL FILTER - FUEL PIPES - FRONT
              - V8 PETROL - WITH IN TANK PUMP
```

ILL	PART NO	DESCRIPTION	QTY	REMARKS
1	NTC2120	Fuel Feed Pipe	1	To VIN267579
	NTC3692	Fuel Feed Pipe	1	From VIN267580
2	NTC2122	Spill Pipe	1	
3	NTC2876	Hose	2	
4	CN100708L	Hose Clip	2	
5	79122	Pipe Clip	1	
6	79121	Pipe Clip	3	
7	NTC2224	Fuel Feed Pipe	1	
8	NTC2073	Spill Pipe	1	
9	NTC2876	Hose	2	
10	CN100708L	Hose Clip	4	
11	NTC2069	Fuel Feed Pipe	1	
12	NRC9786	Fuel Filter	1	
	JS660L	+Element	1	
13	SH106201L	Screw	2	
14	WA106041L	Plain Washer	2	
15	WL106001L	Spring Washer	2	
16	NH106041L	Nut	2	
17	79158	Pipe Clip-Double	4	
18	NTC2096	Spill Pipe	1	)
19	NTC2876	Hose	1	)Extra Tank
20	CN100708L	Hose Clip	2	)

TS5736

LAND ROVER PARTS LTD

```
MODEL LR110 - UP TO AUGUST 1986
BLOCK TS 5735
PAGE H 54.06
GROUP H

FUEL SYSTEM - FUEL PIPES - REAR - SINGLE TANK - WITH IN TANK PUMP
                         PETROL
```

ILL	PART NO	DESCRIPTION	QTY	REMARKS
1	NTC2225	Fuel Pipe	1	
2	NTC2227	Connection	1	
3	NTC2263	Fuel Pipe	1	
4	NTC2064	Fuel Pipe	1	
5	NTC2876	Hose	1	
6	CN100708L	Hose Clip	2	
7	ETC5340	Rubber Elbow	1	
8	CN100708L	Hose Clip	2	
9	79122	Pipe Clip	4	
10	79158	Pipe Clip-Double	5	

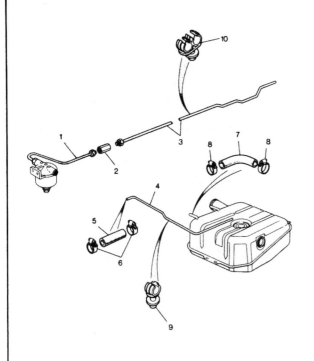

TS5735

LAND ROVER PARTS LTD

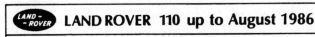
MODEL LR110 - UP TO AUGUST 1986
BLOCK TS 5734A
PAGE H 54.08
GROUP H

FUEL SYSTEM - FUEL PIPES - REAR - TWIN TANKS - WITH IN TANK PUMP
              PETROL

ILL	PART NO	DESCRIPTION	QTY	REMARKS
1	NTC2225	Fuel Pipe-Filter to T Piece	1	
2	NTC2093	T Piece	1	
3	NTC2263	Fuel Pipe	1	
4	NTC2878	Fuel Pipe-T Piece to Connection	1	)Non Station)Wagon
	NTC2879	Fuel Pipe-T Piece to Connection	1	)Station Wagon)
5	CN100708L	Hose Clip	2	
6	NTC2880	Fuel Pipe, Non Return Valve and Hose Assy	1	
7	NTC2876	Hose	2	
8	CN100708L	Hose Clip	4	
9	PRC5543	Solenoid	1	
10	SH104201L	Screw	2	
11	WA104001L	Plain Washer	2	
12	WL104001L	Spring Washer	2	
13	NH104041L	Nut	2	
14	NTC2876	Hose	1	
15	CN100708L	Hose Clip	2	
16	NTC2099	Spill Pipe	1	
17	ETC5340	Rubber Elbow	1	
18	CN100708L	Hose Clip	2	
19	NTC2097	Hose	1	
20	CN100708L	Hose Clip	2	
21	79122	Pipe Clip	4	
22	79158	Pipe Clip-Double	6	

TS5734/A

 **LAND ROVER PARTS LTD**

382

MODEL LR110 - UP TO AUGUST 1986
BLOCK VS 3791
PAGE H 56
GROUP H

FUEL SYSTEM - FUEL CHANGEOVER TAPS FOR EXTRA TANK - OPTIONAL

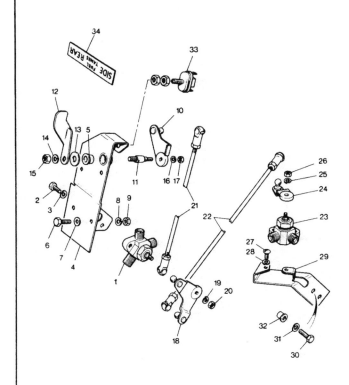

ILL	PART NO	DESCRIPTION	QTY	REMARKS
1	NRC7249	Fuel Tap-Heelboard	1	
2	SH105101	Screw	2	)Tap to Bracket
3	WL105001	Washer-Spring	2	)
4	NRC7230	Bracket & Sleeve	1	
5	NRC6339	Bush-Bracket	1	
6	SH105121	Screw	4	)
7	WA105001	Washer-Plain	4	)Bracket to
8	WL105001	Washer-Spring	4	)Heelboard
9	NH105041	Nut	4	)
10	NRC7235	Lever and Ball Assembly	1	
11	NRC7238	Pin-Lever	1	
12	NRC7311	Hand Lever	1	
13	WA108051L	Washer-Plain	1	)
14	WL106001	Washer-Spring	1	)Lever to Pin
15	NH106041L	Nut	1	)
16	WL105001	Washer-Spring	1	)Lever to Ball
17	NH105041	Nut	1	)to Pin
18	NRC7240	Lever and Ball Assembly	1	
19	WL105001	Washer-Spring	1	)Lever to Tap
20	NH105041	Nut	1	)
21	NTC3455	Control Rod-Short	1	
22	NTC3457	Control Rod-Long	1	
23	NRC7249	Fuel Tap-Rear Tank	1	
24	NRC7232	Lever and Ball Assembly	1	
25	WL105001	Washer-Spring	1	)Lever to Tap
26	NH105041	Nut	1	)
27	SP105121	Screw	2	)Tap to Bracket
28	WL105001	Washer-Spring	2	)
29	NRC7880	Bracket-Mounting Tap	1	
20	SH106141	Screw	2	)
31	WL106001	Washer-Spring	2	)Bracket to Body
32	NN106021	Nutsert	2	)
33	510267	Switch-Fuel Changeover	1	
34	559625	Label-2 Way Tap	1	

VS3791

 **LAND ROVER PARTS LTD**

383

MODEL LR110 - UP TO AUGUST 1986
BLOCK TS 5521
PAGE H 56.02
GROUP H

FUEL SYSTEM - FUEL CHANGEOVER TAP - TWIN TANKS - TWIN PUMPS

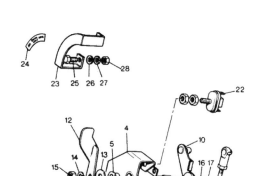

ILL	PART NO	DESCRIPTION	QTY	REMARKS
1	NRC7249	Fuel Tap-Heelboard	1	
2	SH105101L	Screw	2	)Tap to Bracket
3	WL105001L	Washer-Spring	2	)
4	NRC9812	Bracket and Sleeve	1	
5	NRC6339	Bush	1	
6	SH105121L	Screw	4	)
7	WA105001L	Washer-Plain	4	)Bracket to
8	WL105001L	Washer-Spring	4	)Heelboard
9	NH105041L	Nut	4	)
10	NTC1144	Lever and Ball Assembly	1	
11	NRC7283	Pin-Lever	1	
12	NRC7311	Hand Lever	1	
13	WA108051L	Washer-Plain	1	)
14	WL106001L	Washer-Spring	1	)Lever to Pin
15	NH106041L	Nut	1	)
16	WL105001L	Washer-Spring	1	)Lever and Ball
17	NH105041L	Nut	1	)to Pin
18	NRC7240	Lever and Ball Assembly	1	
19	WL105001L	Washer-Spring	1	)Lever to Tap
20	NH105041L	Nut	1	)
21	NRC7243	Control Rod	1	
22	510267	Switch-Fuel Changeover	1	
23	NRC9379	GUARD ASSEMBLY	1	
24	NTC1091	+Label	1	
25	BH106031	Bolt	2	
26	WA106001L	Washer-Plain	2	
27	WL106001L	Washer-Spring	2	
28	NH106041L	Nut	2	

TS5521

LAND ROVER PARTS LTD

MODEL LR110 - UP TO AUGUST 1986
BLOCK VS 3823A
PAGE H 58
GROUP H

FUEL SYSTEM - FUEL FILLER - MAIN TANK & PICK-UP SIDE TANK
- UP TO VIN 254502

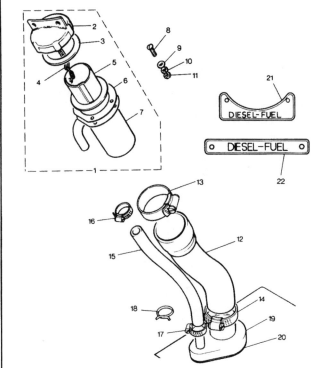

DIESEL-FUEL

DIESEL-FUEL

ILL	PART NO	DESCRIPTION	QTY	REMARKS
1	277259	FUEL FILLER COMPLETE	1	
2	277260	+Cap-3 Lug Fixing	1	Note(1)
	504655	+Cap-2 Lug Fixing	1	Note(2)
3	505244	+Washer-Cap	1	
4	231190	+Retaining Chain	1	
5	504656	+Extension Tube	1	
6	500710	+Seal	1	
7	504657	+Filler Tube	1	
8	77941	Screw	4	
9	WC702101L	Washer-Plain	4	
10	WL700101L	Washer-Spring	4	
11	RTC608	Nut	4	
12	NRC3753	Hose-Main Tank	1	
	MTC1507	Hose-Main Tank	1	HCPU
	NRC3659	Hose-Side Tank	1	
13	594753	Clip-Hose-Main Tank	2	
	594753	Clip-Hose-Side Tank	1	)Pick-Up
14	CN100508	Clip-Hose-Side Tank	1	)
15	543767	Hose-Breather-Main Tank	1	
	543765	Hose-Breather-Side Tank	1	
16	572839	Clip-Hose-Filler End	1	
17	572839	Clip-Hose-Tank End	1	Main Tank
18	546211	Clip-Hose-Tank End	1	Side Tank
19	504233	Seal-Filler Pipe	1	
20	504673	Joint Washer-Filler Seal	2	
21	502951	Label-Diesel Fuel	1	
22	MTC4320	Label-Diesel Fuel	1	HCPU
	RU612503	Pop Rivet	2	
	RRC3683	Catch Plate Assy	1	)Fuel
	RRC3684	Hasp Assy	1	)Filler
	RU612183	Pop Rivet	4	)Lock

NOTE(1): Required When 'Stepped' Filler Tube Is Fitted

NOTE(2): Required When 'Plain' Filler Tube Is Fitted.

VS3823A

LAND ROVER PARTS LTD

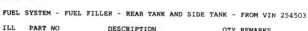
MODEL LR110 - UP TO AUGUST 1986
BLOCK TS 5768
PAGE H 58.02
GROUP H

FUEL SYSTEM - FUEL FILLER - REAR TANK AND SIDE TANK - FROM VIN 254503

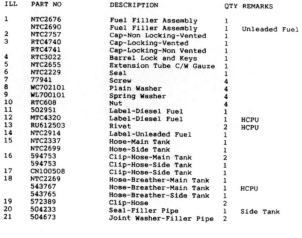

ILL	PART NO	DESCRIPTION	QTY	REMARKS
1	NTC2676	Fuel Filler Assembly	1	
	NTC2690	Fuel Filler Assembly	1	Unleaded Fuel
2	NTC2757	Cap-Non Locking-Vented	1	
3	RTC4740	Cap-Locking-Vented	1	
	RTC4741	Cap-Locking-Non Vented	1	
4	RTC3022	Barrel Lock and Keys	1	
5	NTC2655	Extension Tube C/W Gauze	1	
6	NTC2229	Seal	1	
7	77941	Screw	4	
8	WC702101	Plain Washer	4	
9	WL700101	Spring Washer	4	
10	RTC608	Nut	4	
11	502951	Label-Diesel Fuel	1	
12	MTC4320	Label-Diesel Fuel	1	HCPU
13	RU612503	Rivet	2	HCPU
14	NTC2914	Label-Unleaded Fuel	1	
15	NTC2337	Hose-Main Tank	1	
	NTC2699	Hose-Side Tank	1	
16	594753	Clip-Hose-Main Tank	2	
	594753	Clip-Hose-Side Tank	1	
17	CN100508	Clip-Hose-Side Tank	1	
18	NTC2269	Hose-Breather-Main Tank	1	
	543767	Hose-Breather-Main Tank	1	HCPU
	543765	Hose-Breather-Side Tank	1	
19	572389	Clip-Hose	2	
20	504233	Seal-Filler Pipe	1	Side Tank
21	504673	Joint Washer-Filler Pipe	2	

TS5768

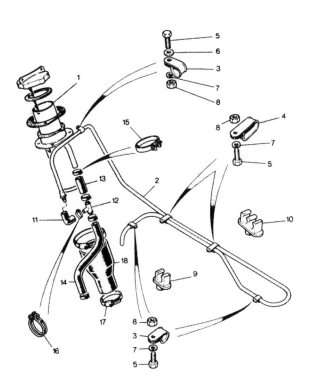

LAND ROVER PARTS LTD

MODEL LR110 - UP TO AUGUST 1986
BLOCK VS 3889
PAGE H 60
GROUP H

FUEL SYSTEM - ROLL OVER ANTI-SPILL SYSTEM

ILL	PART NO	DESCRIPTION	QTY	REMARKS
1	NRC2536	Fuel Filler	2	Rear & Side Tank
	NRC2538	Cap-Fuel Filler	1	
2	NRC2570	Pipe Assembly	1	Rear Tank
	NRC2572	Pipe Assembly	1	Side Tank
	NRC7730	Pipe Assembly	1	HCPU
3	CP105061	Clip-Single	3	)
	AEU1448	Clip-Single	1	)HCPU
4	543589	Clip-Double	2	)Fixing Spill
5	SH105121	Screw	5	)Pipe On Pick Up
6	WA105001	Washer-Plain	5	)Side Tank
7	WL105001	Washer-Spring	5	)
8	NH105041	Nut	5	)
9	79123	Clip-Single	2	)Fixing Rear
10	AFU1008	Clip-Double	2	)Tank Spill
				)Pipe
11	577458	Elbow-Rubber	1	
12	NRC2652	Tee Piece	1	
13	NRC2159	Pipe-Connection	1	
14	NRC2214	Hose-Breather	1	Rear Tank
	NRC2160	Hose-Breather	1	Side Tank
	543767	Hose-Breather	1	HCPU
15	572839	Clip-Hose	4	
16	565656	Clip-Hose-Elbow to Tee	1	
17	594753	Clip-Hose	2	
18	NRC3753	Hose-Filler	1	Rear Tank
	NRC3659	Hose-Filler	1	Side Tank

VS3889

LAND ROVER PARTS LTD

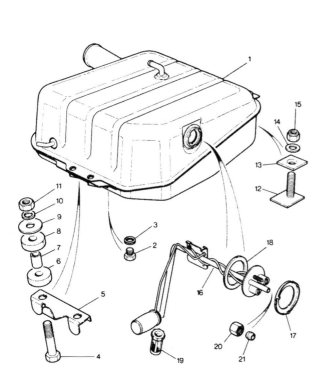

MODEL LR110 - UP TO AUGUST 1986
BLOCK VS 3885
PAGE H 62

FUEL SYSTEM - FUEL TANK - REAR - TO VIN 243342

ILL	PART NO	DESCRIPTION		QTY	REMARKS
1	NRC7570	FUEL TANK ASSEMBLY		1	Note(1)
	NRC9515	FUEL TANK ASSEMBLY		1	Note(2)
	NRC7570	FUEL TANK ASSEMBLY		1	Diesel
	NRC7570	FUEL TANK ASSEMBLY		1	V8
2	NRC62	+Drain Plug		1	
3	243958	+Washer-Copper		1	
4	BH110091L	Bolt	)	2	
	NRC6097	Tab Washer	)	1	
6	500447	Mounting Rubber	)Rear	2	
7	NRC4757	Distance Tube	)Tank	2	
8	500447	Mounting Rubber	)Front	2	
9	850641	Washer-Plain	)Fixings	2	
10	WL110001L	Washer-Spring	)	2	
11	NH110041L	Nut	)	2	
12	NRC6234	Bolt Plate	)Rear	2	
13	NRC4759	Bolt Retainer	)Tank	2	
14	WA108051L	Washer-Plain	)Rear	2	
15	NY108041L	Nut-Nyloc	)Fixings	2	
16	PRC3268	FUEL LEVEL UNIT		1	
17	ARA1501L	Locking Ring		1	
18	ARA1502L	Rubber Sealing Ring		1	
19	PRC2475	Filter-Petrol		1	
20	603431	Union Nut	)Pipe to	1	
21	542846	Olive	)Tank	1	

NOTE(1): 4 Cyl Petrol-Upto VIN 203222.
NOTE(2): 4 Cyl Petrol-From VIN 203222.

VS3885

MODEL LR110 - UP TO AUGUST 1986
BLOCK TS 5733
PAGE H 62.02
GROUP H

FUEL SYSTEM - FUEL TANK - REAR - WITH IN TANK PUMP - FROM VIN 243343

ILL	PART NO	DESCRIPTION	QTY	REMARKS
1	NTC2017	FUEL TANK-18 GALLON	1	
2	NRC62	+Drain Plug	1	
3	243958	+Washer	1	
4	BH110091L	Bolt	2	
5	NRC6097	Tab Washer	1	
6	500447	Mounting Rubber	2	
7	NRC4757	Distance Piece	2	
8	500447	Mounting Rubber	2	
9	850641	Washer	2	
10	WL110001L	Spring Washer	2	
11	NH110041L	Nut	2	
12	NTC2681	Bolt Plate	2	
13	NTC2837	Bolt Retainer	2	
14	WA108051L	Plain Washer	2	
15	NY108041L	Nyloc Nut	2	
16	PRC4972	FUEL LEVEL UNIT	1	Petrol
	PRC3268	FUEL LEVEL UNIT	1	Diesel
17	ARA1501L	Locking Ring	1	
18	ARA1502L	Sealing Ring	1	
19	PRC7020	FUEL PUMP	1	Petrol
	RTC6545	Connector	1	Petrol
20	NTC2156	SPILL RETURN ELBOW	1	Diesel
21	PRC5852	Sealing Ring	1	
22	SE105121L	Screw	5	
23	WL105001L	Spring Washer	5	
24	WA105001L	Plain Washer	5	
25	NTC1612	Plug	1	)
26	NRC9770	Nut	1	)Diesel
27	NRC9771	Olive	1	)

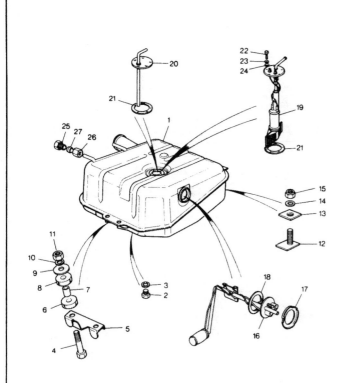

TS5733

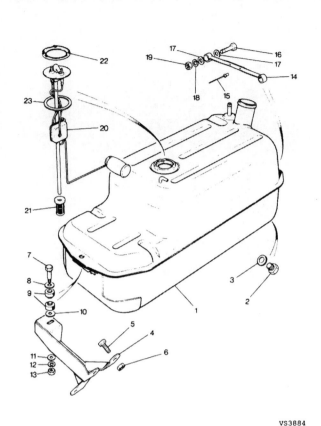

MODEL LR110 - UP TO AUGUST 1986
BLOCK VS 3884
PAGE H 64
GROUP H

FUEL SYSTEM - EXTRA FUEL TANK - PICK UP - TO VIN 243342

ILL	PART NO	DESCRIPTION	QTY	REMARKS
1	NRC7040	FUEL TANK-15 GALLON	1	
2	NRC62	+Drain Plug	1	
3	243958	+Washer-Copper	1	
4	NRC6829	Mounting Plate-Front Fixing	1	
5	SH108251L	Bolt	3	
6	NY108041L	Nut-Nyloc	3	
7	NRC4765	Bolt	1	
8	2265L	Washer-Plain	1	
9	90508545	Rubber Bush	2	
10	WP185L	Washer-Plain	1	
11	WA108051L	Washer-Plain	1	
12	WL108001L	Washer-Spring	1	
13	NH108041L	Nut	1	
14	NRC6526	Spacer Tube-Rear Fixing	1	
15	RA608177L	Rivet-Spacer Tube	2	
16	SH108351L	Bolt	2	
17	WC108051L	Washer-Plain	4	
18	WL108001L	Washer-Spring	2	
19	NH108041L	Nut	2	
20	PRC3196	FUEL LEVEL UNIT	1	
21	PRC2475	+Filter-Petrol	1	
22	ARA1501L	Locking Ring	1	
23	ARA1502L	Rubber Sealing Ring	1	

VS3884

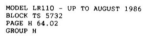

MODEL LR110 - UP TO AUGUST 1986
BLOCK TS 5732
PAGE H 64.02
GROUP H

FUEL SYSTEM - EXTRA FUEL TANK - PICK UP - FROM VIN 243343

ILL	PART NO	DESCRIPTION	QTY	REMARKS
1	NTC2089	FUEL TANK-15 GALLON	1	
2	NRC62	+Drain Plug	1	
3	243958	+Washer	1	
4	NRC6829	Mounting Plate-Front Fixing	1	
5	SH108251L	Bolt	3	
6	NY108041L	Nyloc Nut	3	
7	NRC4765	Bolt	1	
8	2265L	Plain Washer	1	
9	90508545	Rubber Bush	2	
10	WP185L	Plain Washer	1	
11	WA108051L	Plain Washer	1	
12	WL108001L	Spring Washer	1	
13	NH108041L	Nut	1	
14	NRC6526	Spacer Tube-Rear Fixing	1	
15	RA608177L	Rivet	2	
16	SH108351L	Bolt	2	
17	WL108001L	Spring Washer	2	
18	WC108051L	Plain Washer	4	
19	NH108041L	Nut	2	
20	PRC4975	FUEL LEVEL UNIT	1	
21	ARA1501L	Locking Ring	1	
22	ARA1502L	Sealing Ring	1	
23	PRC7018	FUEL PUMP	1	Petrol
	RTC6545	Connector	1	Petrol
24	NTC2180	FUEL FEED ELBOW	1	Diesel
25	PRC5852	Sealing Ring	1	
26	SE105121L	Screw	5	
27	WL105001L	Spring Washer	5	
28	WA105001L	Plain Washer	5	
29	NRC9543	Spill Return Elbow	1	Petrol
30	NRC9562	Spill Return Elbow	1	Diesel
31	267837	Joint Washer	1	
32	3890	Screw	2	
33	3101	Plain Washer	2	

TS5732

MODEL LR110 – UP TO AUGUST 1986
BLOCK VS 3871
PAGE H 66
GROUP H

FUEL SYSTEM – EXTRA FUEL TANK – STATION WAGON – UP TO VIN 243342

ILL	PART NO	DESCRIPTION	QTY	REMARKS
1	NRC5622	FUEL TANK-10 GALLON	1	
2	NRC62	+Drain Plug	1	
3	243958	+Washer-Copper	1	
4	NRC9138	Mounting Bracket-Front Fixing	1	
5	SH108251L	Bolt	3	
6	WA108051L	Washer-Plain	3	
7	WL108001L	Washer-Spring	3	
8	NH108041L	Nut	3	
9	NRC6558	Mounting Bracket-Rear Fixing	1	
10	NRC4765	Bolt	1	
11	2265L	Washer-Plain	1	
12	90508545	Rubber Bush	2	
13	WC108051L	Washer-Plain	1	
14	WL108001L	Washer-Spring	1	
15	NH108041L	Nut	1	
16	SH108251L	Bolt	2	
17	WL108001L	Washer-Spring	2	
18	NH108041L	Nut	2	
19	569006	Filler Cap	1	
20	NRC6836	Washer-Filler Cap	1	
21	NRC7118	Elbow and Pipe-Feed	1	Petrol
	NRC5414	Elbow and Pipe-Feed	1	Diesel
22	NRC5416	Elbow and Pipe-Spill	1	
23	267837	Joint Washer	2	
24	3972	Screw	4	
25	3101	Washer-Spring	4	
26	PRC3098	FUEL LEVEL UNIT	1	
27	RTC1148	Washer-Level Unit	1	
28	3890	Screw	6	
29	3101	Washer-Spring	6	

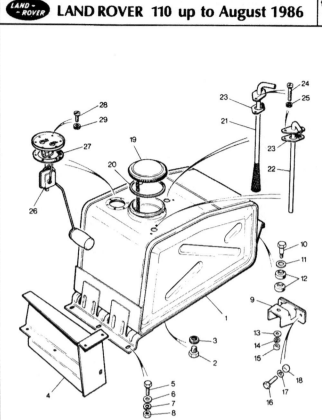

VS3871

LAND ROVER PARTS LTD

392

MODEL LR110 – UP TO AUGUST 1986
BLOCK TS 5731
PAGE H 66.02
GROUP H

FUEL SYSTEM – EXTRA FUEL TANK – STATION WAGON – FROM VIN 243343

ILL	PART NO	DESCRIPTION	QTY	REMARKS
1	NTC2110	FUEL TANK-10 GALLON	1	
2	NRC62	+Drain Plug	1	
3	243958	+Washer	1	
4	NRC9138	Mounting Bracket-Front Fixing	1	
5	SH108251L	Bolt	3	
6	WL108001L	Spring Washer	3	
7	WA108051L	Plain Washer	3	
8	NH108041L	Nut	3	
9	NRC6558	Mounting Bracket-Rear Fixing	1	
10	NRC4765	Bolt	1	
11	2265L	Plain Washer	1	
12	90508545	Rubber Bush	2	
13	WC108051L	Plain Washer	1	
14	WL108001L	Spring Washer	1	
15	NH108041L	Nut	1	
16	SH108251L	Bolt	2	
17	WL108001L	Spring Washer	2	
18	NH108041L	Nut	2	
19	569006	Filler Cap	1	
20	NRC6836	Washer-Filler Cap	1	
21	NRC9543	Elbow And Pipe-Spill	1	Petrol
22	NRC5414	Elbow And Pipe-Feed	1	)Diesel
23	NRC9678	Elbow And Pipe-Spill	1	)
24	NTC2334	Blanking Plate	1	Petrol
25	267837	Joint Washer	2	
26	3972	Screw	4	
27	3101	Spring Washer	4	
28	PRC3098	FUEL LEVEL UNIT	1	
29	RTC1148	Washer	1	
30	3890	Screw	6	
31	3101	Spring Washer	6	
32	PRC7019	FUEL PUMP	1	)
	RTC6545	Connector	1	)
33	PRC5852	Sealing Ring	1	)
34	SE105121L	Screw	5	)Petrol
35	WL105001L	Spring Washer	5	)
36	WA105001L	Plain Washer	5	)
37	NTC2333	Blanking Plate	1	Diesel

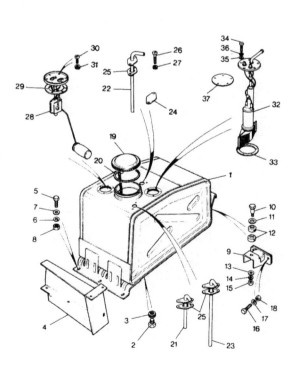

TS5731

LAND ROVER PARTS LTD

MODEL LR110 - UP TO AUGUST 1986
BLOCK VS 4035
PAGE H 68
GROUP H

FUEL SYSTEM - ACCELERATOR PEDAL AND CABLE

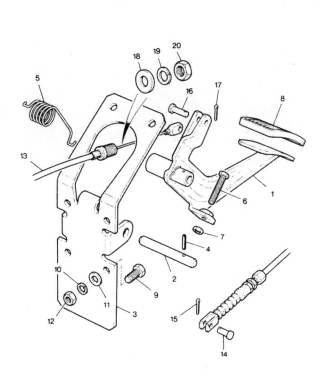

ILL	PART NO	DESCRIPTION	QTY	REMARKS
1	NRC7827	Accelerator Pedal	1	
2	NRC4475	Shaft-Accelerator Pedal	1	
3	NRC5220	Mounting Bracket	1	
4	PA105161	Spring Pin	1	
5	NRC9121	Spring-Accelerator Pedal	1	
6	SH106451	Screw-Pedal Stop	1	
7	NH605041L	Nut-Pedal Stop	1	
8	11H1781L	Rubber Pad-Pedal	1	
9	SH106161L	Screw-Pedal to Dash	6	
10	WL106001L	Spring Washer-Pedal to Dash	6	
11	WA106041L	Plain Washer-Pedal to Dash	6	
12	NH106041L	Nut-Pedal to Dash	6	
13		ACCELERATOR CABLE		
	NRC8116	RHS)2.25 Petrol	1	
	NRC8117	LHS)	1	
	NTC2086	RHS)2.5 Petrol	1	
	NTC2087	LHS)	1	
	NRC7606	RHS)2.25 Diesel	1	
	NRC7607	LHS)	1	
	NRC7605	RHS 2.5 Diesel	1	Upto VIN 267364 NLA-Use NTC2743 Note(1)
	NRC7606	LHS 2.5 Diesel	1	Upto VIN 267364
	NTC2743	RHS)2.5 Diesel	1	)From
	NTC3396	LHS)	1	)VIN 267365
	NRC5494	RHS/LHS-V8	1	
	6860L	Rubber Grommet	2	
14	562481	Clevis Pin-Cable to D.P.A	1	)4 Cyl Diesel
15	PS103081L	Split Pin-Cable to D.P.A	1	)
16	NRC5502	Clevis Pin-Cable to Pedal	1	
17	PS102081L	Split Pin-Cable to Pedal	1	
18	WA112081L	Plain Washer-Cable to Dash	1	
19	WF112001L	Spring Washer-Cable to Dash	1	
20	NT112041L	Nut-Cable to Dash	1	

NOTE(1): When Replacing NRC7605 With
NTC2743 Fit Also Abutment Bracket
ETC6675, Or ETC6630 If Hand Throttle
Is Also Fitted

VS4035

MODEL LR110 - UP TO AUGUST 1986
BLOCK VS 3984
PAGE H 70
GROUP H

FUEL SYSTEM - ACCELERATOR LINKAGE (SOLEX CARBURETTERS) - 3.5 LITRE
V8 PETROL

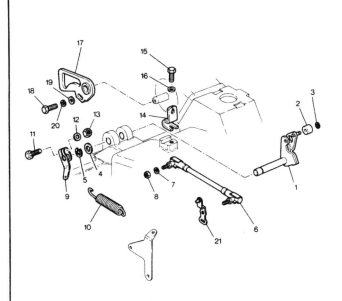

ILL	PART NO	DESCRIPTION	QTY	REMARKS
1	ERC2446	Countershaft Assembly	1	Except Hand Throttle
2	603237	Roller-Countershaft	1	
3	521452	Circlip	1	
4	WA108051L	Plain Washer-Countershaft/ Manifold	1	
5	521453	Circlip	1	
6	ERC7744	Throttle Link-Carburetters	1	
7	WM702001L	Spring Washer-Link/Levers	2	
8	257011	Nut	2	
9	AUD2437L	Lever-Throttle Spring	1	
10	603622	Return Spring	1	
11	257020	Screw-Lever/Shaft	1	
12	WA702101L	Plain Washer	1	
13	HN2005L	Nut	1	
14	ERC3163	Anchor Bracket-Throttle Cable	1	Except Hand Throttle
15	SH504051L	Screw-Bracket/Manifold	1	
16	WA106041L	Plain Washer	1	
17	610333	Throttle Lever-LH	1	
18	257123	Setscrew	1	
19	WA702101L	Plain Washer	1	
20	WM702001L	Spring Washer	1	
21	612320	Adjusting Lever-RH	1	

VS3984

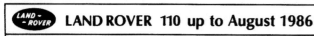
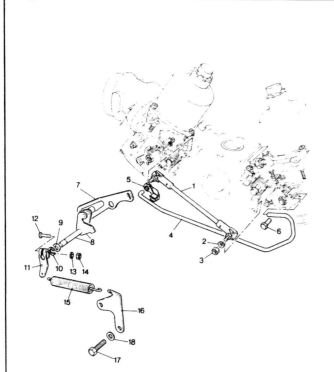

MODEL LR110 - UP TO AUGUST 1986
BLOCK TS 5986
PAGE H 70.02
GROUP H

FUEL SYSTEM - THROTTLE LINKAGE (SU CARBURETTERS) - 3.5 LITRE
V8 PETROL

ILL	PART NO	DESCRIPTION	QTY	REMARKS
1	ETC4728	Throttle Link-Carburetters	1	
2	WM702001L	Spring Washer	2	
3	NH910011L	Nut-10 UNF	2	
4	ERC1161	Rod-Choke Lever	1	
5	614538	Linkage Clip	1	
6	257014	Screw	1	
7	ETC7061	Throttle Cam Lever	1	
8	ERC2446	Countershaft Assembly	1	
9	WA108051L	Washer	1	
10	521453	Circlip	1	
11	AUD2437L	Lever-Throttle Spring	1	
12	SH910241L	Screw	1	
13	WA702101L	Washer	1	
14	NH910241L	Nut	1	
15	603622	Spring-Countershaft Return	1	
16	ERC8626	Bracket-Spring Anchor	1	
17	SH504041L	Screw-Fixing Bracket	3	
18	WA106041L	Washer-Fixing Bracket	3	

TS5986

LAND ROVER PARTS LTD

MODEL LR110 - UP TO AUGUST 1986
BLOCK VS 3981
PAGE H 72
GROUP H

FUEL SYSTEM - ACCELERATOR LINKAGE-HAND THROTTLE-SOLEX - 3.5 LITRE
V8 PETROL

ILL	PART NO	DESCRIPTION	QTY	REMARKS
1	613910	Countershaft Assembly	1	
2	613916	Cable Lever Assembly	1	
3	613915	Bush	1	
4	AAU1053	Swivel Clamp	1	
5	SH105201L	Screw	1	
6	WL105001L	Washer Spring	1	
7	NH105041L	Nut	1	
8	90613913	Lever Assembly-Accelerator	1	
9	613915	+Bush	1	
10	239673	Clip-Throttle Cable	1	
11	ETC4006	Anchor Bracket-Cable	1	
12	SH504051L	Screw-Bracket to Manifold	1	
13	WA106041L	Washer Plain	1	

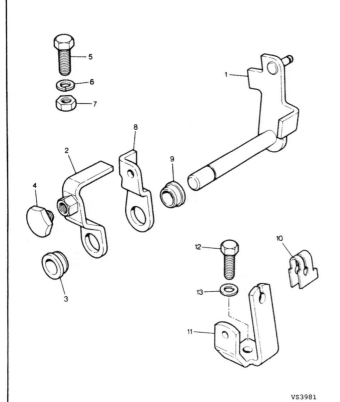

VS3981

LAND ROVER PARTS LTD

MODEL LR110 - UP TO AUGUST 1986
BLOCK VS 4033
PAGE H 74
GROUP H

FUEL SYSTEM - HAND THROTTLE AND CHOKE CABLE

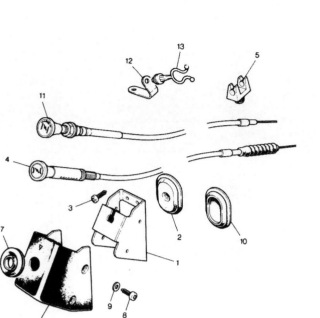

ILL	PART NO	DESCRIPTION	QTY	REMARKS
1	NRC8734	Mounting Bracket	1	
2	NRC6799	Grommet-Cable	1	
3	AB610041L	Screw-Mounting Bracket	4	
4		Hand Throttle Control Cable		
	NRC8560	4 Cyl Petrol	1	
	NRC8063	RHS-2.25 Diesel	1	
	NRC8062	LHS-2.25 Diesel	1	
	NRC8502	RHS-2.5 Diesel	1	
	NRC8503	LHS-2.5 Diesel	1	
	NRC9284	RHS-V8	1	
	NRC9285	LHS-V8	1	
	562481	Pin-Clevis	1	)2.5 Diesel
	PS102081	Pin-Split	1	)
5	NRC8206	Cable Clip-LHS	1	)V8
6	MTC3611	Cover-Hand Throttle	1	
7	531689	Grommet-Hand Throttle Cover	1	
8	AB608041L	Screw-Cover to Bracket	2	
9	WC105001L	Plain Washer	2	
10	MTC1650	Blanking Plug-When Hand Throttle Not Fitted	2	
11		CHOKE CONTROL CABLE		
	NRC8626	RHS) 4 Cylinder	1	)
	NRC8627	LHS) Petrol	1	)Upto VIN 270139
	NTC1384	RHS) 4 Cylinder	1	)From VIN
	NTC1385	LHS) Petrol	1	)270140
	NRC7792	RHS) V8	1	)
	NRC7791	LHS)	1	)Upto VIN 267729
	NTC3686	RHS)V8-With	1	)
	NTC3687	LHS)SU Carbs	1	)
	538890	Cable Clip)	1	)From VIN
	594594	Cable Tie)	1	)267730
12	NRC8333	Bracket-Cable Clip	1	
13	NRC8332	Cable Clip	1	

VS4033

MASTER INDEX

GROUP H

EXHAUST

MODEL LR110 - UP TO AUGUST 1986
BLOCK TS 5518
PAGE H 76
GROUP H

EXHAUST SYSTEM - FRONT EXHAUST - 4 CYLINDER - UP TO VIN 266789

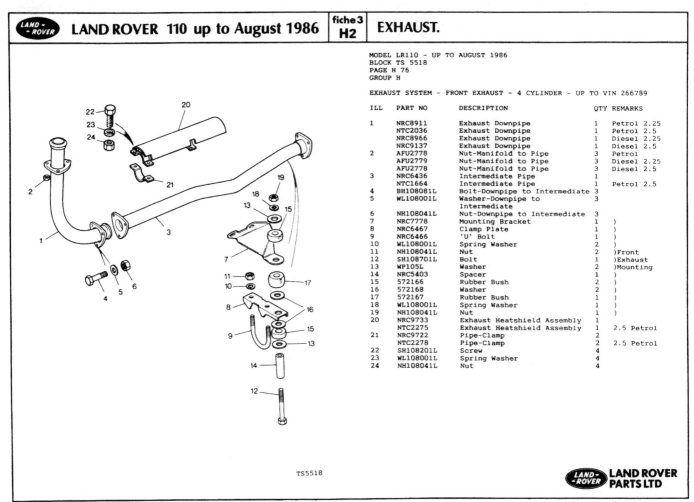

ILL	PART NO	DESCRIPTION	QTY	REMARKS
1	NRC8911	Exhaust Downpipe	1	Petrol 2.25
	NTC2036	Exhaust Downpipe	1	Petrol 2.5
	NRC8966	Exhaust Downpipe	1	Diesel 2.25
	NRC9137	Exhaust Downpipe	1	Diesel 2.5
2	AFU2778	Nut-Manifold to Pipe	3	Petrol
	AFU2779	Nut-Manifold to Pipe	3	Diesel 2.25
	AFU2778	Nut-Manifold to Pipe	3	Diesel 2.5
3	NRC6436	Intermediate Pipe	1	
	NTC1664	Intermediate Pipe	1	Petrol 2.5
4	BH108081L	Bolt-Downpipe to Intermediate	3	
5	WL108001L	Washer-Downpipe to Intermediate	3	
6	NH108041L	Nut-Downpipe to Intermediate	3	
7	NRC7778	Mounting Bracket	1	)
8	NRC6467	Clamp Plate	1	)
9	NRC6466	'U' Bolt	1	)
10	WL108001L	Spring Washer	2	)
11	NH108041L	Nut	2	)Front
12	SH108701L	Bolt	1	)Exhaust
13	WP105L	Washer	2	)Mounting
14	NRC5403	Spacer	1	)
15	572166	Rubber Bush	2	)
16	572168	Washer	2	)
17	572167	Rubber Bush	1	)
18	WL108001L	Spring Washer	1	)
19	NH108041L	Nut	1	)
20	NRC9733	Exhaust Heatshield Assembly	1	
	NTC2275	Exhaust Heatshield Assembly	1	2.5 Petrol
21	NRC9722	Pipe-Clamp	2	
	NTC2278	Pipe-Clamp	2	2.5 Petrol
22	SH108201L	Screw	4	
23	WL108001L	Spring Washer	4	
24	NH108041L	Nut	4	

TS5518

LAND ROVER PARTS LTD

MODEL LR110 - UP TO AUGUST 1986
BLOCK TS 5769A
PAGE H 76.02
GROUP H

EXHAUST SYSTEM - FRONT EXHAUST - 4 CYLINDER - FROM VIN 266790

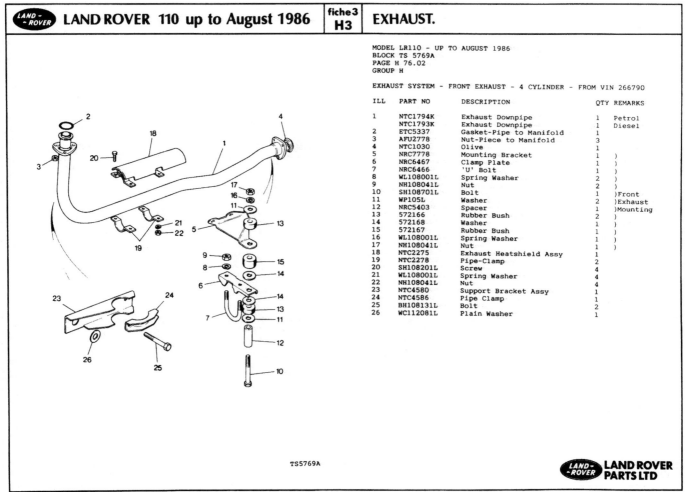

ILL	PART NO	DESCRIPTION	QTY	REMARKS
1	NTC1794K	Exhaust Downpipe	1	Petrol
	NTC1793K	Exhaust Downpipe	1	Diesel
2	ETC5337	Gasket-Pipe to Manifold	1	
3	AFU2778	Nut-Piece to Manifold	3	
4	NTC1030	Olive	1	
5	NRC7778	Mounting Bracket	1	)
6	NRC6467	Clamp Plate	1	)
7	NRC6466	'U' Bolt	1	)
8	WL108001L	Spring Washer	2	)
9	NH108041L	Nut	2	)
10	SH108701L	Bolt	1	)Front
11	WP105L	Washer	2	)Exhaust
12	NRC5403	Spacer	1	)Mounting
13	572166	Rubber Bush	2	)
14	572168	Washer	1	)
15	572167	Rubber Bush	1	)
16	WL108001L	Spring Washer	1	)
17	NH108041L	Nut	1	)
18	NTC2275	Exhaust Heatshield Assy	1	
19	NTC2278	Pipe-Clamp	2	
20	SH108201L	Screw	4	
21	WL108001L	Spring Washer	4	
22	NH108041L	Nut	4	
23	NTC4580	Support Bracket Assy	1	
24	NTC4586	Pipe Clamp	1	
25	BH108131L	Bolt	2	
26	WC112081L	Plain Washer	1	

TS5769A

LAND ROVER PARTS LTD

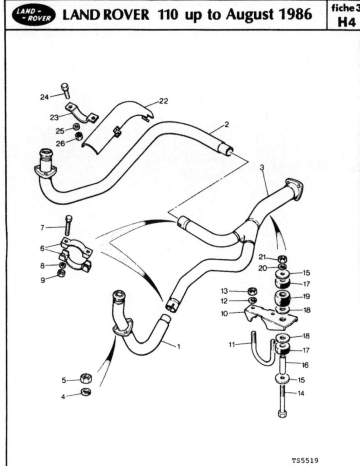

MODEL LR110 - UP TO AUGUST 1986
BLOCK TS 5519
PAGE H 78
GROUP H

EXHAUST SYSTEM - FRONT EXHAUST - V8 - UP TO VIN267907

ILL	PART NO	DESCRIPTION	QTY	REMARKS
1	NRC4219	Downpipe-LH	1	
2	NRC6432	Downpipe-RH	1	
3	NRC4218	'Y' Piece	1	
4	WM600051L	Spring Washer	6	)Pipe to Manifold
5	NH605041L	Nut	6	)
6	90575511	Clamp	4	)
7	BH108091L	Bolt	4	)Downpipe to 'Y'
8	WL108001L	Spring Washer	4	)Piece
9	NH108041L	Nut	4	)
10	90575748	Clamp Plate	1	)
11	NRC6374	'U' Bolt	1	)
12	WL108001L	Spring Washer	2	)
13	NH108041L	Nut	2	)
14	SH108701L	Bolt	1	)
15	WP105L	Washer	2	)Front Exhaust
16	NRC5403	Spacer	1	)Mounting
17	572166	Rubber Bush	2	)
18	572168	Washer	2	)
19	572167	Rubber Bush	1	)
20	WL108001L	Spring Washer	1	)
21	NH108041L	Nut	1	)
22	NRC9724	Exhaust Heatshield Assembly	2	
23	NRC9722	Pipe Clip	4	
24	SH108201L	Screw	8	
25	WL108001L	Spring Washer	8	
26	NH108041L	Nut	8	

TS5519

402

MODEL LR110 - UP TO AUGUST 1986
BLOCK TS 5770
PAGE H 78.02
GROUP H

EXHAUST SYSTEM - FRONT EXHAUST - V8 - FROM VIN 267908

ILL	PART NO	DESCRIPTION	QTY	REMARKS
1	NTC1133K	Downpipe-LH	1	
2	NTC1136K	Downpipe-RH	1	
3	ERC2734	Gasket-Pipe to Manifold	2	
4	NTC2726	'Y' Piece	1	
5	NTC1030	Olive	1	
6	WM600051L	Spring Washer	6	)Pipe to
7	NH605041L	Nut	6	)Manifold
8	90575511	Clamp	4	)
9	BH108091L	Bolt	4	)Downpipe to
10	WL108001L	Spring Washer	4	)'Y' Piece
11	NH108041L	Nut	4	)
12	90575748	Clamp Plate	1	)
13	NRC6374	'U' Bolt	1	)
14	WL108001L	Spring Washer	2	)
15	NH108041L	Nut	2	)Front
16	SH108701L	Bolt	1	)Exhaust
17	WP105L	Washer	2	)Mounting
18	NRC5403	Spacer	1	)
19	572166	Rubber Bush	2	)
20	572168	Washer	2	)
21	572167	Rubber Bush	1	)
22	WL108001L	Spring Washer	1	)
23	NH108041L	Nut	1	)
24	NRC9724	Exhaust Heatshield	2	
25	NRC9722	Pipe Clip	4	
26	SH108201L	Screw	8	
27	WL108001L	Spring Washer	8	
28	NH108041L	Nut	8	

TS5770

MODEL LR110 - UP TO AUGUST 1986
BLOCK VS 4030
PAGE H 80
GROUP H

EXHAUST SYSTEM - SILENCERS - UP TO VIN 266789

ILL	PART NO	DESCRIPTION	QTY	REMARKS
1	NRC6433	Front Silencer	1	
2	NRC7842	Rear Silencer-Single Can	1	
	NRC8369	Rear Silencer-Twin Can	1	Option
	NRC8369	Rear Silencer-Twin Can	1	Switzerland
	NRC8238	Finisher-Tailpipe	1	HCPU & Germany
3	BH108081L	Bolt	6	
4	WL108001L	Spring Washer	6	
5	NH108041L	Nut	6	
6	NRC7608	Clamp Plate	2	
7	NRC7609	'U' Bolt	2	
8	WL108001L	Spring Washer	4	
9	NH108041L	Nut	2	
10	SH108701L	Bolt	2	
11	WP105L	Washer	4	
12	NRC5403	Spacer	2	
13	572166	Rubber Bush-Thin	4	
14	572168	Washer	4	
15	572167	Rubber Bush-Thick	2	
16	WL108001L	Spring Washer	2	
17	NH108041L	Nut	2	

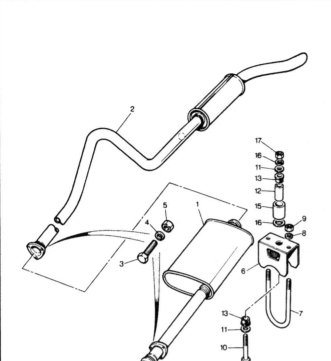

VS4030

 **LAND ROVER PARTS LTD**

404

MODEL LR110 - UP TO AUGUST 1986
BLOCK TS 5771
PAGE H 80.02
GROUP H

EXHAUST SYSTEM - SILENCERS - FROM VIN 266790

ILL	PART NO	DESCRIPTION	QTY	REMARKS
1	NTC1797	Front Silencers	1	
2	NTC2731	Olive	1	
3	NTC1800K	Rear Silencer-Single Can	1	
	NTC2701	Rear Silencer-Twin Can	1	Option
	NTC2701	Rear Silencer-Twin Can	1	Switzerland
4	NRC8238	Finisher-Tailpipe	1	HCPU & Germany
5	BH108081L	Bolt	6	
6	WL108001L	Spring Washer	6	
7	NH108041L	Nut	6	
8	NRC7608	Clamp Plate	2	
9	NRC7609	'U' Bolt	2	
10	WL108001L	Spring Washer	4	
11	NH108041L	Nut	4	
12	SH108701L	Bolt	2	
13	WP105L	Washer	4	
14	NRC5403	Spacer	2	
15	572166	Rubber Bush-Thin	4	
16	572168	Washer	4	
17	572167	Rubber Bush-Thick	2	
18	WL108001L	Spring Washer	2	
19	NH108041L	Nut	2	

TS5771

 **LAND ROVER PARTS LTD**

405

MASTER INDEX

GROUP J

COOLING, HEATING, AIR CONDITIONING

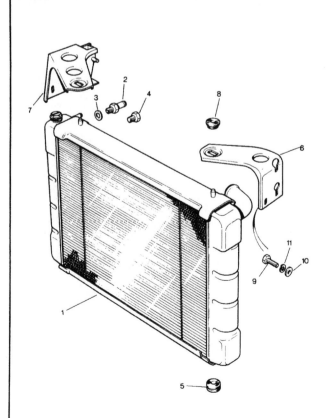

MODEL LR110 - UP TO AUGUST 1986
BLOCK VS 3964
PAGE J 2
GROUP J

COOLING SYSTEM - RADIATOR

	PART NO	DESCRIPTION	QTY	REMARKS
1	NRC6888	Radiator	1	2.25L Petrol
	NRC6889	Radiator	1	)2.25L Petrol)Heavy Duty)Option
	NRC6889	Radiator	1	)2.5L Petrol/)Diesel & V8
	NRC6889	Radiator	1	Air Con
	NTC5002	+Filler Plug	1	)Alternatives
	NTC4609	+Filler Plug	1	)
	NTC5171	+Sealing Washer	1	
2	KTP9024	Penthouse Vent	1	V8
3	RRO2125L	Washer	1	Diesel, V8
4	RRO2126L	Plug	1	Diesel
5	572312	Bush-Radiator Lower	2	
6	NRC4839	Upper Mounting Bracket-LH	1	
7	NRC8609	Upper Mounting Bracket-RH	1	
8	NRC5544	Bush-Radiator-Upper	2	
9	SH106201L	Bolt)Mounting	6	
10	WC106041L	Plain Washer)Bracket to	6	
11	WL106001L	Spring Washer)Body	6	

VS3964

MODEL LR110 - UP TO AUGUST 1986
BLOCK VS 3761
PAGE J 4
GROUP J

COOLING SYSTEM - FAN COWL

ILL	PART NO	DESCRIPTION	QTY	REMARKS
1	NRC3662	Fan Cowl-Radiator	1	4 Cyl Petrol
	NRC3977	Fan Cowl-Radiator	1	)4 Cyl Petrol)Heavy Duty)Option Diesel
	NRC3977	Fan Cowl-Radiator		
	NRC3406	Fan Cowl-Radiator	1	V8
2	562979	Screw-Fan Cowl	5	
3	WS600041L	Spring Washer	5	
4	NRC7227	Ducting	1	)4 Cylinder
5	NRC6430	Clip-Ducting to Cowl	2	)
6	ERC8536	Engine Fan Cowl-4 Cyl (To 209042 LHS, 209072 RHS Diesel)	1	
7	WL108001L	Spring Washer)Cowl to	1	
8	NH108041L	Nut)Front Cover	1	
9	SH108251L	Screw)Cowl to	1	
10	WL108001L	Spring Washer)LH Bracket	1	
11	SH108251L	Screw)	1	
12	WA108051L	Plain Washer)Fan Cowl to	1	
13	WL108001L	Spring Washer)Water Outlet	1	
14	NH108041L	Nut)Connection	1	
	ETC4989	Engine Fan Cowl-4 Cyl (From 209043 LHS) (209074 RHS Diesel)	1	See Note(1)
	ETC4993	Flexible Mounting	3	
	WA108051L	Plain Washer	2	
	WL108001L	Spring Washer	6	
	NH108041L	Nut	5	

NOTE(1): Fitted On 4 Cylinder Petrol From Engine No 11H03634.

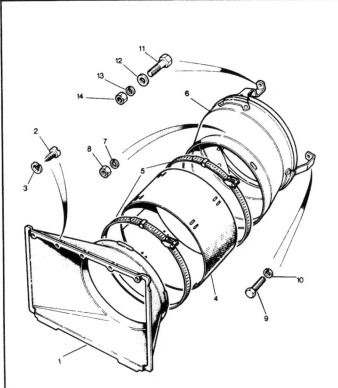

VS3761

LAND ROVER PARTS LTD

MODEL LR110 - UP TO AUGUST 1986
BLOCK VS 3966
PAGE J 6
GROUP J

COOLING SYSTEM - RADIATOR HOSES

ILL	PART NO	DESCRIPTION	QTY	REMARKS
1	NRC6403	Radiator Top Hose	1	4 Cylinder Petrol
	NRC6404	Radiator Top Hose	1	4 Cyl Petrol Heavy Duty Option
	NRC6404	Radiator Top Hose	1	2.25 Diesel
	NRC5985	Radiator Top Hose	1	V8
	NRC9710	Radiator Top Hose	1	V8-Air Con
2	NRC7448	Clip-Top Hose	1	4 Cylinder
3	NRC3664	Radiator Bottom Hose	1	4 Cylinder Petrol
	NRC3976	Radiator Bottom Hose	1	4 Cyl Petrol Heavy Duty Option
	NRC3976	Radiator Bottom Hose	1	2.25 Diesel
	NRC3405	Radiator Bottom Hose-Note(1)	1	)
	NTC3543	Radiator Bottom Hose-Note(2)	1	)V8
4	CN100508	Hose Clip	4	
5	NRC4852	Hose-Radiator to Exp. Tank	1	Heavy Duty
	NRC9726	Hose-Radiator to Exp. Tank	1	
6	AAU1979	Hose Clip	2	
7	NRC4850	Hose-Expansion Tank to Pump	1	)2.25 Cylinder
8	CN100408	Hose Clip	2	)
9	90575977	Hose-Penthouse Bleed	1	)
10	AAU1979	Hose Clip-Penthouse Bleed	2	)
11	NRC2383	Cable Clip	1	)
12	SH106201L	Screw	1	)V8
13	WA106041L	Plain Washer	1	)
14	WM106001L	Spring Washer	1	)
15	NH106041L	Nut	1	)
	239600	Clip-Penthouse Bleed Pipe	1	)
	SH108201L	Screw	1	)V8 Not Air
	WA108051L	Plain Washer	1	)Con
	WL108001L	Spring Washer	1	)
	NH108041L	Nut	1	)

NOTE(1): Up To VIN 256704 RHS, VIN 257104 LHS

NOTE(2): From VIN 256705 RHS, VIN 257105 LHS

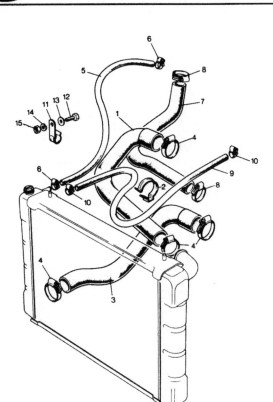

VS3966

LAND ROVER PARTS LTD

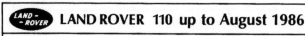

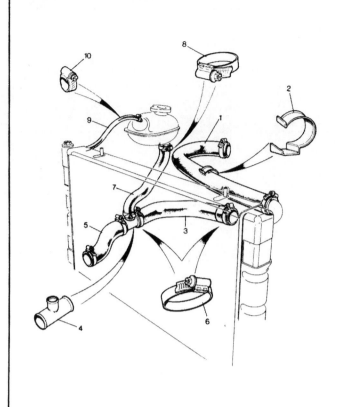

MODEL LR110 - UP TO AUGUST 1986
BLOCK TS 5195
PAGE J 6.02
GROUP J

COOLING SYSTEM - RADIATOR HOSES - 2.5 LITRE - SEE NOTE (1)

ILL	PART NO	DESCRIPTION	QTY	REMARKS
1	NRC6404	Top Hose	1	Upto VIN 263904
	NTC2029	Top Hose	1	From VIN 263905
2	NRC7448	Clip-Hose Retaining	1	
3	NRC4842	Hose-Engine to Connector	1	)
4	NRC4843	Connector	1	)
5	NRC4844	Hose-Connector to Radiator	1	)Upto VIN 263904
6	CN100508	Hose Clip	4	)
7	NRC4837	Hose-Tube to Expansion Tank Diesel	1	)
	NRC5503	Hose-Tube to Expansion Tank Petrol	1	)
8	CN100408	Hose Clip	2	)
	NTC1707	Bottom Hose	1	)From VIN 236905
6	CN100508	Hose Clip	2	)
8	CN100408	Hose Clip	1	)
9	NRC4852	Hose-Radiator to Tank	1	
10	AAU1979	Hose Clip	2	

NOTE(1):   Also used on all 4 Cylinder Air Con Vehicles.

TS5195

MODEL LR110 - UP TO AUGUST 1986
BLOCK VS 3965
PAGE J 8
GROUP J

COOLING SYSTEM - EXPANSION TANK

ILL	PART NO	DESCRIPTION	QTY	REMARKS
1	NRC7583	Expansion Tank-4 Cyl	1	To VIN 263904
	NTC2737	Expansion Tank-4 Cyl	1	From VIN 263905
	NRC7582	Expansion Tank-V8	1	
2	RTC3607	Cap-Expansion Tank-91b	1	4 Cylinder
	565540	Cap-Expansion Tank-151b	1	V8
3	NRC6692	Carrier-Expansion Tank	1	
4	NRC5294	+Polyurethane Strip	2	
5	NRC5295	+Polyurethane Strip	2	
6	SH106207	Screw-Carrier to Tank	1	
7	NY106041L	Nut-Carrier to Tank	1	
8	SH106207	Screw)	3	
9	WC106047	Plain Washer)Carrier	5	
10	WL106007L	Spring Washer)to Body	3	
11	NH106047	Nut)	2	
12	NRC7133	Nut Plate)	1	
13	564724	Hose-Overflow	1	
14	NRC1360	Clip-Overflow Hose	1	
15	CP106121	'P' Clip-Hose to Wing	1	

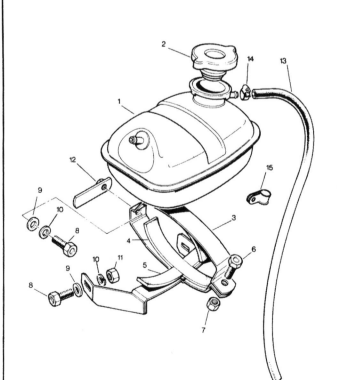

VS3965

MODEL LR110 - UP TO AUGUST 1986
BLOCK VS 4070
PAGE J 10
GROUP J

HEATING SYSTEM - HEATER

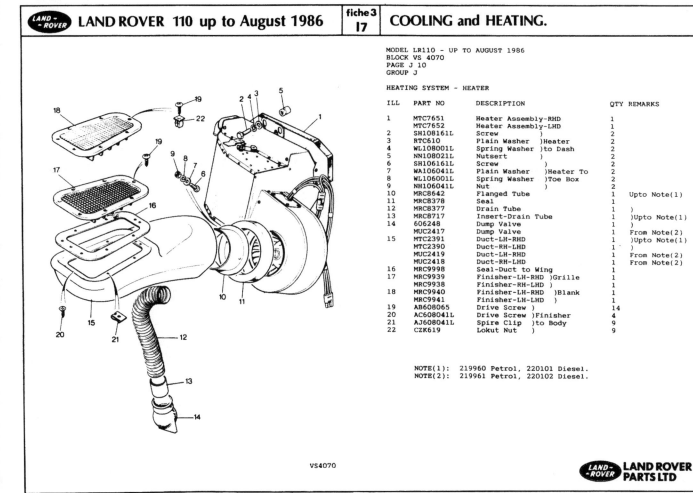

ILL	PART NO	DESCRIPTION	QTY	REMARKS
1	MTC7651	Heater Assembly-RHD	1	
	MTC7652	Heater Assembly-LHD	1	
2	SH108161L	Screw)	2	
3	RTC610	Plain Washer)Heater	2	
4	WL108001L	Spring Washer)to Dash	2	
5	NN108021L	Nutsert)	2	
6	SH106161L	Screw)	2	
7	WA106041L	Plain Washer)Heater To	2	
8	WL106001L	Spring Washer)Toe Box	2	
9	NH106041L	Nut)	2	
10	MRC8642	Flanged Tube	1	Upto Note(1)
11	MRC8378	Seal	1	
12	MRC8377	Drain Tube	1	)
13	MRC8717	Insert-Drain Tube	1	)Upto Note(1)
14	606248	Dump Valve	1	)
	MUC2417	Dump Valve	1	From Note(2)
15	MTC2391	Duct-LH-RHD	1	)Upto Note(1)
	MTC2390	Duct-RH-LHD	1	)
	MUC2419	Duct-LH-RHD	1	From Note(2)
	MUC2418	Duct-RH-LHD	1	From Note(2)
16	MRC9998	Seal-Duct to Wing	1	
17	MRC9939	Finisher-LH-RHD)Grille	1	
	MRC9938	Finisher-RH-LHD)	1	
18	MRC9940	Finisher-LH-RHD)Blank	1	
	MRC9941	Finisher-LH-LHD)	1	
19	AB608065	Drive Screw)	14	
20	AC608041L	Drive Screw)Finisher	4	
21	AJ608041L	Spire Clip)to Body	9	
22	CZK619	Lokut Nut)	9	

NOTE(1): 219960 Petrol, 220101 Diesel.
NOTE(2): 219961 Petrol, 220102 Diesel.

VS4070

LAND ROVER PARTS LTD

412

MODEL LR110 - UP TO AUGUST 1986
BLOCK VS 4072A
PAGE J 12
GROUP J

HEATING SYSTEM - HEATER - CONTINUED

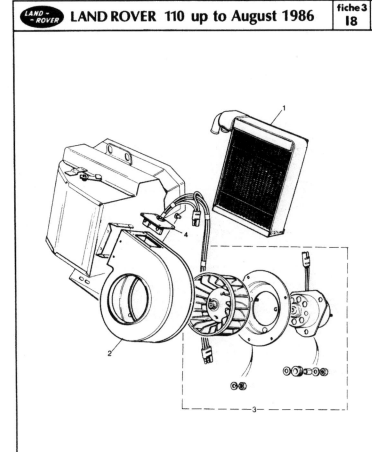

ILL	PART NO	DESCRIPTION	QTY	REMARKS
1	AAP817	Radiator-Heater	1	
2	AAP810	Volute-Heater-RHS	1	
	AAP811	Volute-Heater-LHS	1	
4	AAP888	Harness and Resistor-RHS	1	
	AAP889	Harness and Resistor-LHS	1	
3	RTC4200	Motor and Rotor-RHS	1	
3	RTC4201	Motor and Rotor-LHS	1	

NOTE: See LRPE Parts Bulletin Section 3 Number 1.

VS4072A

LAND ROVER PARTS LTD

413

MODEL LR110 - UP TO AUGUST 1986
BLOCK VS 4075A
PAGE J 14
GROUP J

HEATING SYSTEM - HEATER CONTROLS

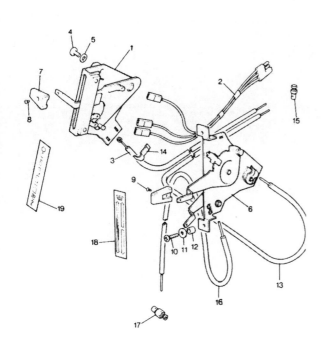

ILL	PART NO	DESCRIPTION	QTY	REMARKS
1	UTP1126	Control Assembly-Outlet-RHS	1	
	UTP1125	Control Assembly-Outlet-LHS	1	
2	AAP890	Wiring Harness	1	
3	AAP876	Control Cable-Outlet	1	
4	SE105161L	Screw-Control to Cowl	2	
5	WA105001L	Plain Washer-Control to Cowl	2	
6	346924	Mounting Plate and Levers-RHS	1	
	347586	Mounting Plate and Levers-LHS	1	
7	MTC2805	Knob-Lever	3	
8	SG103084	Screw-Knob Fixing	1	
9	MTC7737	Screw-Knob Fixing	2	
10	SE808244	Screw)Mounting Plate	2	
11	WA105004L	Plain Washer)to Dash	2	
12	MRC9922	Spacer)	2	
13	MTC6194	Control Cable-Blend	1	
14	13H7343L	Cable Clip)Blend and	2	
15	RTC5978	Trunnion Kit)Outlet Cables	2	
16	347939	Control Cable-Distribution	1	
17	566902	Trunnion-Distribution Cable	1	
18	MTC6006	Label-Heater	1	
19	MTC6007	Label-Fan	1	

VS4075

414

MODEL LR110 - UP TO AUGUST 1986
BLOCK VS 4071
PAGE J 16
GROUP J

HEATING SYSTEM - DEMISTER AND FLAPS

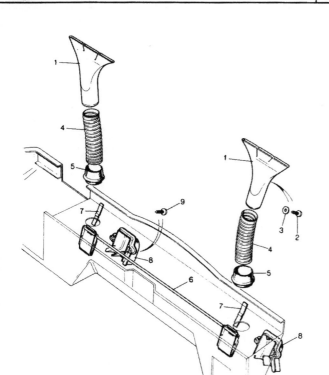

ILL	PART NO	DESCRIPTION	QTY	REMARKS
1	MRC9668	Demister Outlet-RH	1	
	MRC9669	Demister Outlet-LH	1	
2	AB608041L	Screw	2	
3	WA105001	Plain Washer	2	
4	MTC6382	Flexible Tube-Demister	2	
5	MRC7281	Grommet-Flexible Tube	2	
6	346894	Outlet Flaps Complete	1	
7	346976	Spring-Outlet Flaps	2	
8	395829	Heater Duct-Outlet Grille-RH	1	
	395830	Heater Duct-Outlet Grille-LH	1	
9	MRC1525	Screw-Grille to Duct	4	

VS4071

415

MODEL LR110 - UP TO AUGUST 1986
BLOCK VS 4071A
PAGE J 16.02
GROUP J

AIR CONDITIONING - DEMISTER AND FLAPS

ILL	PART NO	DESCRIPTION	QTY	REMARKS
1	NRC9668	Demister Outlet-RH	1	)
	NRC9669	Demister Outlet-LH	1	)
2	AB608041L	Screw	2	)LHS
3	WA105001	Plain Washer	2	)
4	MRC7279	Flexible Tube Demister	2	)
5	MRC7281	Grommet-Flexible Tube	2	)
6	MUC1139	Outlet-Flaps Assembly-LHS	1	
	MUC3278	Outlet-Flaps Assembly-RHS	1	
7	MTC5578	Actuating Bar	1	
8	346976	Spring-Outlet Flaps	2	
9	395829	Heater Duct Outlet Grille-RH	1	
	395830	Heater Duct Outlet Grille-LH	1	
10	MRC1525	Screw-Grille to Duct	4	

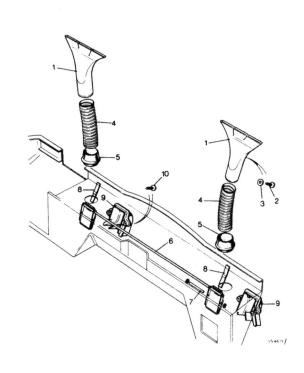

VS 4071A

LAND ROVER PARTS LTD

416

MODEL LR110 - UP TO AUGUST 1986
BLOCK VS 4073
PAGE J 18
GROUP J

HEATING SYSTEM - HEATER PIPES 4 CYLINDER

ILL	PART NO	DESCRIPTION	QTY	REMARKS
1	NRC6306	Hose-Engine Feed & Return	2	
2	NRC6307	Pipe-Heater Feed-RHS	1	
	NRC6422	Pipe-Heater Feed-LHS	1	
3	NRC6420	Pipe-Heater Return-RHS	1	
	NRC6421	Pipe-Heater Return-LHS	1	
4	NRC6308	Hose-Heater Feed & Return-RHS	2	
	NRC6309	Hose-Heater Feed & Return-LHS	2	
5	CN100258	Hose Clip	8	
6	NRC6417	Clip-Pipes to Engine-Petrol	1	
	NRC6418	Clip-Pipes to Engine-Diesel	1	
7	NRC6419	Saddle Clip	3	
8	SH106251L	Screw	2	
9	WL106001L	Spring Washer	2	
10	NH106041L	Nut	2	

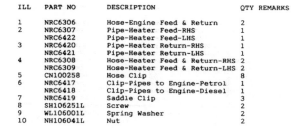
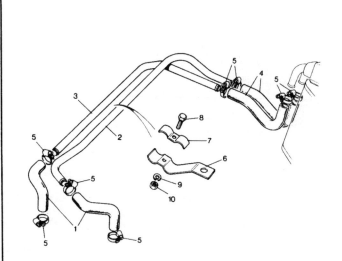

VS4073

LAND ROVER PARTS LTD

417

```
MODEL LR110 - UP TO AUGUST 1986
BLOCK TS 5549
PAGE J 18.02
GROUP J
```

AIR CONDITIONING - HEATER PIPES 4 CYLINDER - RHS

ILL	PART NO	DESCRIPTION	QTY	REMARKS
1	NRC6306	Hose-Heater Feed & Return	2	
2	CN100308	Hose-Clip	2	
3	NRC6307	Pipe-Heater Feed	1	
4	NRC6420	Pipe-Heater Return	1	
5	CN100258	Hose-Clip	8	
6	NTC1571	Hose-Pipe to Water Control	1	
7	NRC8346	Water Control Valve	1	
8	ERC3964	Hose-Water Control Valve	1	
9	NTC1570	Hose-Heater Return	1	
10	NRC6417	Mounting Clip	1	Petrol
	NRC6418	Mounting Clip	1	Diesel
11	NRC6419	Saddle Clip	1	
12	SH106251L	Screw	1	
13	WL106001L	Spring Washer	1	
14	NH106041L	Nut	1	

TS5549

```
MODEL LR110 - UP TO AUGUST 1986
BLOCK TS 5548
PAGE J 18.04
GROUP J
```

AIR CONDITIONING - HEATER PIPES - 4 CYLINDER - LHS

ILL	PART NO	DESCRIPTION	QTY	REMARKS
1	NRC6306	Hose-Heater Feed & Return	2	
2	CN100304	Hose-Clip	2	
3	NRC8245	Pipe-Heater Feed & Return	2	
4	CN100258	Hose-Clip	9	
5	ERC3964	Hose-Water Control Valve	1	
6	NRC8346	Water Control Valve	1	
7	NRC8347	Hose-Water Control Valve	1	
8	NRC8247	Hose-Engine to Heater	1	
9	NRC8248	Mounting Bracket	1	
10	594637	Saddle Clip	1	
11	SH106201L	Screw	1	
12	WL106001L	Spring Washer	1	
13	NH106041L	Nut	1	

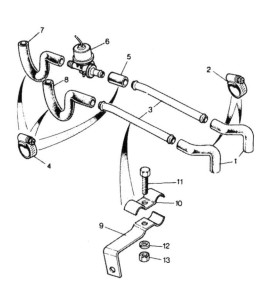

TS5548

MODEL LR110 - UP TO AUGUST 1986
BLOCK VS 4074
PAGE J 20
GROUP J

HEATING SYSTEM - HEATER PIPES - V8

ILL	PART NO	DESCRIPTION	QTY	REMARKS
1	NRC6311	Hose-Engine Feed-RHS	1	
	NRC6352	Hose-Engine Feed-LHS	1	
2	NRC6314	Hose-Engine Return-RHS	1	
	NRC6353	Hose-Engine Return-LHS	1	
3	NRC6902	Pipe-Heater Feed & Return-RHS	2	
	NRC6312	Pipe-Heater Feed & Return-LHS	2	
4	NRC6313	Hose-Heater Feed & Return	4	
5	CN100308	Hose Clip	8	
6	NRC8707	Support Brkt-Heater Pipes-RHS	1	
7	SH605071	Screw-Bracket to Engine	1	
8	WM600051L	Spring Washer	1	
9	NRC6419	Saddle Clip-RHS	1	
10	SH106301	Screw-Saddle Clip	1	
11	WL106001	Spring Washer-Saddle Clip	1	
12	NH106041L	Nut-Saddle Clip	1	

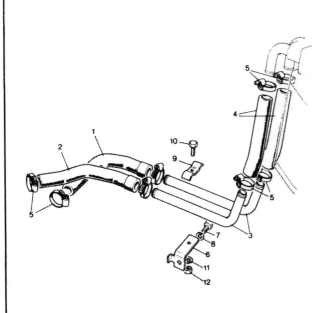

VS4074

LAND ROVER PARTS LTD

MODEL LR110 - UP TO AUGUST 1986
BLOCK TS 5551
PAGE J 20.02
GROUP J

AIR CONDITIONING - HEATER PIPES - V8 - RHS

ILL	PART NO	DESCRIPTION	QTY	REMARKS
1	NRC6314	Hose-Heater Feed & Return	2	
2	CN100308	Hose Clip	4	
3	NRC6902	Pipe-Heater Feed & Return	2	
4	ERC3964	Hose-Water Control Valve	1	
5	CN100258	Hose-Clip	10	
6	NRC8346	Water-Control Valve	1	
7	NTC1212	Hose-Valve to Heater	1	
8	NRC6308	Hose-Pipe to Heater	1	
9	NRC6903	Support Bracket	1	
10	NRC6419	Saddle Clip	1	
11	SH106301L	Screw	1	
12	WL106001L	Spring Washer	1	
13	NH106041L	Nut	1	

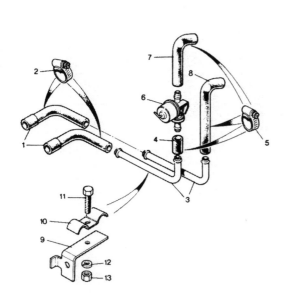

TS5551

LAND ROVER PARTS LTD

MODEL LR110 - UP TO AUGUST 1986
BLOCK TS 5550
PAGE J 20.04
GROUP J

AIR CONDITIONING - HEATER PIPES - V8 - LHS

ILL	PART NO	DESCRIPTION	QTY	REMARKS
1	NRC9098	Hose-Heater Feed	1	
2	NRC6353	Hose-Heater Return	1	
3	CN100308	Hose Clip	4	
4	NRC9091	Pipe-Heater Feed	1	
5	NTC1090	Pipe-Heater Return	1	
6	ERC3964	Hose-Water Control Valve	1	
7	CN100258	Hose-Clip	7	
8	NRC8346	Water Control Valve	1	
9	NTC1089	Hose-Valve to Heater	1	
10	NTC1088	Hose-Pipe to Heater	1	
11	NRC8620	Support Bracket	1	
12	594637	Saddle Clip	1	
13	SH106301L	Screw	1	
14	WL106001L	Spring Washer	1	
15	NH106041L	Nut	1	

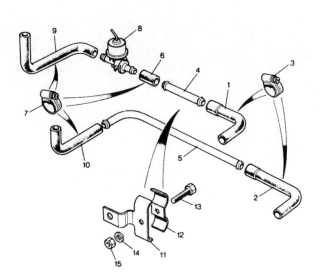

TS5550

422

MODEL LR110 - UP TO AUGUST 1986
BLOCK VS 4040
PAGE J 40
GROUP J

COOLING SYSTEM - AIR CONDITIONING - COMPRESSOR

ILL	PART NO	DESCRIPTION	QTY	REMARKS
	ERC6480	COMPRESSOR ASSEMBLY	1	
1	AEU1782	+Pulley Rim	1	
2	AEU1694	+Key-Clutch Hub	1	
3	AEU1780	+Screw-Rim Mounting	6	
4	AEU1779	+Washer-Rim Mounting	6	
5	AEU1784	+Screw and Washer Assembly-Front Head	4	
6	AEU1775	+Nut-Shaft	1	
7	AEU1778	+Coil and Housing Assembly	1	
8	AEU1777	+Rotor and Bearing Assembly	1	
9	AEU1785	+Front Head and Bearing Assembly	1	
10	AEU1776	+Clutch Assembly	1	

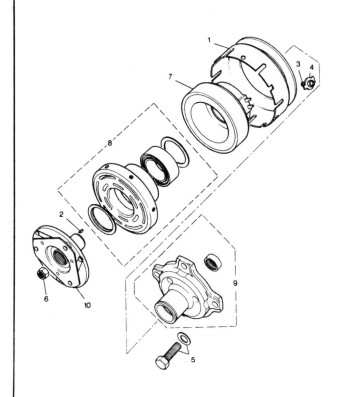

VS4040

423

MODEL LR110 - UP TO AUGUST 1986
BLOCK VS 4108
PAGE J 40.02
GROUP J

COOLING SYSTEM - AIR CONDITIONING - COMPRESSOR

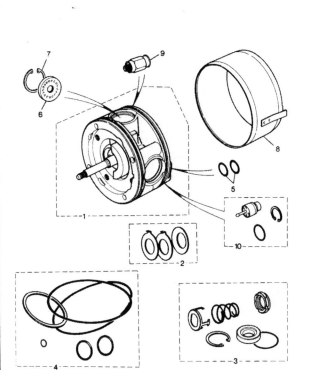

ILL	PART NO	DESCRIPTION	QTY	REMARKS
	ERC6480	COMPRESSOR ASSEMBLY	1	
1	AEU1792	+Kit-Cylinder and Shaft Assy	1	
2	AEU1791	++Kit-Thrust Washers	1	
3	AEU1790	++Kit-Shaft Seal	1	
4	AEU1192	++Kit-'O' Rings	1	
5	AEU1690	+++'O' Ring-Ports	2	
6	AEU1788	+Valve Plate Assembly	4	
7	AEU1787	+Retaining Ring-Valve Plate	4	
8	AEU1786	+Shell Assembly	1	
9	AEU1689	+Pressure Release Valve	1	
10	AEU1688	+Kit-Superheat Switch	1	
	ERC6072	Belt-Driving	2	)4 Cyl.Pet with)Twin Belts &)2.25 Dies.Only
	ETC4371	Belt-Driving	1	)2.5 Diesel &)2.5 Pet with)Single Belt
	603713	Belt-Driving	1	3.5 Petrol
	AEU1691	Oil-525 Viscosity-2PT(1136ML)	A/R	

MODEL LR110 - UP TO AUGUST 1986
BLOCK VS 3747
PAGE J 42
GROUP J

AIR CONDITIONING - COMPRESSOR - 4 CYLINDER

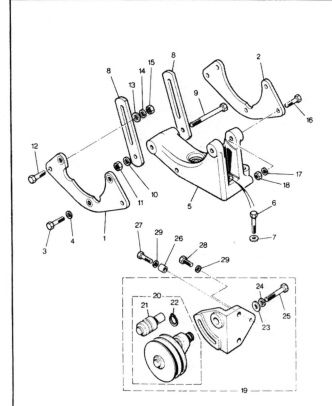

ILL	PART NO	DESCRIPTION	QTY	REMARKS
1	ERC7082	Mounting Plate-Front	1	
2	ERC5152	Mounting Plate-Rear	1	
3	BH110201L	Bolt-Compressor to Plate	3	
4	WL110001L	Spring Washer	3	
5	ERC5151	Bracket-Mounting Compressor	1	)2.25 Petrol)2.25 Diesel)2.5 Petrol-Twin)Belts
	ETC4882	Bracket-Mounting Compressor	1	2.5 Diesel & 2.5
	ETC4197	Adaptor Plate-Bracket	1	Petrol with Single Belt Only
	ETC4218	Belt Damper Assembly	1	
6	BH110101L	Bolt-Bracket to Cover	4	
7	WA110061L	Plain-Washer	8	
8	ERC5155	Link-Adjusting	2	
9	BH108181L	Bolt-Link to Bracket	1	
10	WL108001L	Spring Washer	1	
11	NH108041L	Nut	1	
12	SH108251L	Screw-Link to Plate	2	
13	WA108051L	Washer	2	
14	WL108001L	Spring Washer	2	
15	NH108041L	Nut	2	
16	BH108081L	Bolt-Bracket to Plates	2	
17	WL108001L	Spring Washer	2	
18	NH108041L	Nut	2	
19	ERC5386	Idler Pulley Bracket Assy	1	)
20	ERC5387	+Idler Arm Assembly	1	)
21	90613049	++Idler Pulley Bearing	1	)Use with Twin
22	CR120171L	++Circlip	1	)Belt System Only
23	WC108051L	+Washer-Idler Arm Clamp	1	)
24	WL108001L	+Spring Washer-Idler Arm Clamp	1	)
25	BH108081L	+Bolt-Idler Arm Clamp	1	)
26	ERC6071	Hollow Dowel	2	)
27	BH108061L	Bolt	2	)
28	SH108251L	Screw	1	)
29	WL108001L	Spring Washer	3	)

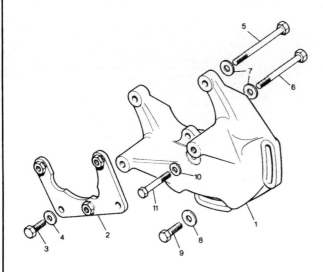

MODEL LR110 - UP TO AUGUST 1986
BLOCK VS 4041
PAGE J 44
GROUP J

AIR CONDITIONING - 3.5 V8 PETROL

ILL	PART NO	DESCRIPTION	QTY	REMARKS
		MOUNTING BRACKETS FOR COMPRESSOR AND IDLER PULLEY		
1	ERC7494	Mounting Bracket-Compressor	1	
2	ERC6545	Mounting Bracket-Front	1	
3	SH110301L	Screw-Front Mounting Bracket To Compressor Mounting Bracket	2	
4	WA110061L	Washer Plain	2	
5	BH110241L	Bolt	2	
6	BH110221L	Bolt	2	
7	WA110061L	Washer Plain	3	
8	4067	Washer Plain	2	
9	BH506111L	Bolt	2	
10	4866	Washer Plain	1	
11	BH505201L	Bolt	1	

VS4041

MODEL LR110 - UP TO AUGUST 1986
BLOCK VS 4042
PAGE J 46
GROUP J

AIR CONDITIONING - 4 CYLINDER

ILL	PART NO	DESCRIPTION	QTY	REMARKS
		MOUNTING BRACKETS-IDLER (TENSIONER) PULLEY		
1	613540	Mounting Brackets-Pulley	1	
2	BH505441L	Bolt-Tension Pulley Bracket to Timing Cover	2	
3	BH504151L	Bolt	1	
4	614718	Bearing Arm Assembly	1	
5	BH605101L	Bolt-Tensioning	1	
6	WM600051L	Washer-Spring	1	

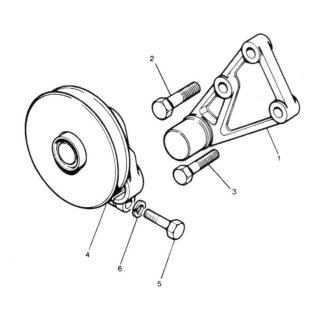

VS4042

MODEL LR110 - UP TO AUGUST 1986
BLOCK VS 4015
PAGE J 48
GROUP J

AIR CONDITIONING - 3.5 LITRE - V8 PETROL - LESS POWER STEERING

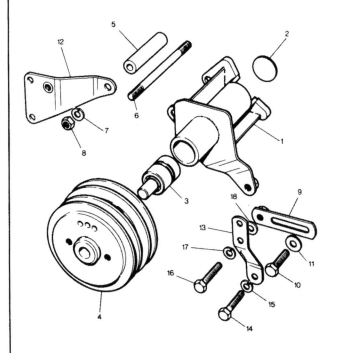

ILL	PART NO	DESCRIPTION	QTY	REMARKS
		IDLER PULLEY AND FIXINGS		
1	ERC758	Bracket Assembly Idler Pulley	1	
2	250836	Expansion Plug	1	
3	90613049	Bearing Spindle	1	
4	ERC865	Pulley-Idler	1	
5	611215	Distance Tube Pivot Pump & Pump Support Bracket	1	
6	610789	Stud	1	
7	WM600061L	Washer-Spring	1	
8	NH606041L	Nut	1	
9	611440	Adjusting Link	1	
10	SH605061L	Screw Link to Support Bracket	1	
11	4478	Washer Plain	1	
12	90610796	Support Bracket-Pump	1	
13	611213	Adjusting Link-Pump Support Bracket	1	
14	SH506071L	Screw-Link Bracket to Timing Chain Cover	1	
15	WM600061L	Washer Spring	1	
16	SH605081L	Screw-Support Bracket to Adjusting Link	1	
17	WM600051L	Washer-Spring	1	
18	4581	Washer-Plain	1	

VS4015

428

MODEL LR110 - UP TO AUGUST 1986
BLOCK TS 5531
PAGE J 60
GROUP J

AIR CONDITIONING - CONDENSER - LHD/RHD

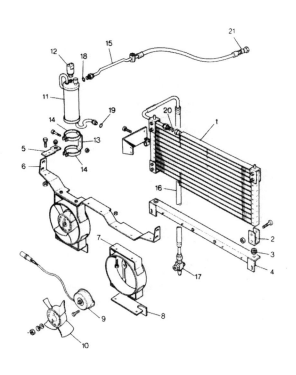

ILL	PART NO	DESCRIPTION	QTY	REMARKS
1	RTC7416	Condenser	1	
2	RTC7417	Support Bracket	4	
3	RTC7418	Grommet	4	
4	RTC7419	Lower Mounting Bracket	1	
5	RTC7420	Pilot Bracket	2	
6	RTC7421	Upper Mounting Bracket	1	
7	RTC7422	Fan Shroud	2	
8	RTC7423	Fan Shroud Support	2	
9	RTC7424	Motor Condenser	2	
10	RTC7425	Fan Condenser	2	
11	RTC7426	Receiver Drier	1	
12	AEU3068	Hi Pressure Switch	1	
13	RTC7427	Receiver Drier Bracket	1	
14	RTC7428	Clamp Bracket	2	
15	RTC7429	Hose Assembly	1	
16	RTC7430	Discharge Hose	1	
17	AEU3067	Discharge Valve	1	
18	AEU3056	'O' Ring	1	
19	AEU1626	'O' Ring (0.3125 Dia)	2	
20	AEU1627	'O' Ring (0.406 Dia)	2	
21	MTC8500	Coupling	1	

TS5531

429

MODEL LR110 - UP TO AUGUST 1986
BLOCK TS 5532A
PAGE J 62
GROUP J

AIR CONDITIONING - HEATER/COOLER ASSEMBLY - LHD

ILL	PART NO	DESCRIPTION	QTY	REMARKS
1	MTC5559	Heater/Cooler Assembly	1	See Note(1)
	RTC7431	Heater/Cooler Assembly	1	See Note(2)
2	AEU1747	Resistor	1	See Note(1)
	RTC7456	Resistor	1	See Note(2)
3	RTC7432	Heater Core	1	See Note(2)
	RTC7433	Heater Core	1	See Note(1)
4	RTC7434	Thermostat	1	
5	RTC7435	Evaporator	1	See Note(1)
	RTC7436	Evaporator	1	See Note(2)
6	RTC7437	Expansion Valve	1	See Note(1)
	AEU1213	Expansion Valve	1	)
7	AEU1214	Clamp-Expansion Valve	1	See Note(2)
8	RTC7458	Pipe Assembly	1	)
9	RTC7457	Pipe Coupling	1	
10	AEU3055	Service Valve	1	
11	RTC7439	Hose	1	
12	RTC7454	Relay	1	
13	RTC7455	Harness-Blower	1	
14	MUC4375	Vacuum Switch	1	See Note(2)
	RTC7414	Vacuum Switch	1	See Note(1)
15	RTC7471	Seal-Heater Core	2	See Note(2)
16	RTC7472	Seal-Heater	1	
17	RTC7473	Cover-Heater	1	
18	RTC7453	Seal-Evaporator to Duct	1	
19	MUC4358	Adaptor R4 Comp/Rotolock	1	
	RTC7452	Ring-Rotolock	2	
	MUC1661	Seal-Evaporator to Dash	1	

NOTE(1): Phase 1 Air Con-Early Vehicles.
NOTE(2): Phase 2 Air Con-Late Vehicles.

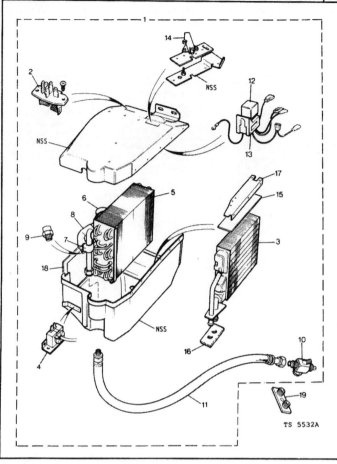

TS 5532A

LAND ROVER PARTS LTD

MODEL LR110 - UP TO AUGUST 1986
BLOCK TS 5568
PAGE J 62.10
GROUP J

AIR CONDITIONING - HEATER/COOLER ASSEMBLY - LHD - CONTINUED

ILL	PART NO	DESCRIPTION	QTY	REMARKS
1	RTC7440	Blower Motor	1	
2	RTC7468	Mount for Motor	1	
3	RTC7441	Blower Fan	1	
4	RTC7442	Motor Housing	1	
5	RTC7469	Brace	3	
6	RTC7470	Clamp	1	
7	RTC7446	Seal-Bulkhead	1	
	RTC7474	Seal-Firewall	1	

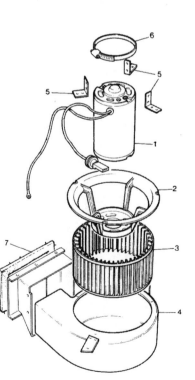

TS5568

LAND ROVER PARTS LTD

MODEL LR110 - UP TO AUGUST 1986
BLOCK TS 5533
PAGE J 64
GROUP J

AIR CONDITIONING - INTAKE/RECIRCULATION DUCT - LHD

ILL	PART NO	DESCRIPTION	QTY	REMARKS
1	MTC5571	Intake/Recirculation Duct	1	
2	RTC7461	Gasket	1	
3	RTC7460	Seal-Duct to Evaporator	1	
4	RTC7459	Seal-Duct to Dash	1	
5	AEU4002	Vacuum Motor	1	See Note(2)
	RTC7467	Vacuum Motor	1	See Note(3)
6		Vacuum Hose-5" Long	1	)
7		Vacuum Hose-12" Long	1	)See Note(1)
8		Vacuum Hose-9" Long	1	)
9	MUC4455	Vacuum Tee	1	
10	RTC7470	Drain Clamp	1	

NOTE(1):   Use MUC4878.
NOTE(2):   Phase 1 Air Con-Early Vehicles.
NOTE(3):   Phase 2 Air Con-Late Vehicles.

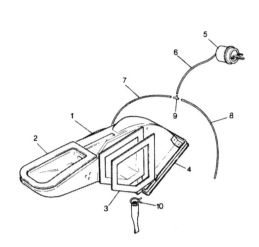

TS5533

432

MODEL LR110 - UP TO AUGUST 1986
BLOCK TS 5534
PAGE J 66
GROUP J

AIR CONDITIONING - INSULATION - LHD

ILL	PART NO	DESCRIPTION	QTY	REMARKS
		DUCT INSULATION		
1	MUC1657	-Top	1	
2	MUC1658	-Bottom	1	
3	MUC1659	-Outer	1	
4	MUC1660	-Inner	1	

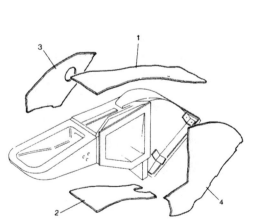

TS5534

433

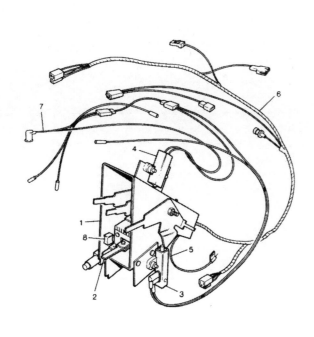

MODEL LR110 - UP TO AUGUST 1986
BLOCK TS 5535
PAGE J 68
GROUP J

AIR CONDITIONING - HEATER CONTROLS - LHD

ILL	PART NO	DESCRIPTION	QTY	REMARKS
1	MTC5573	Heater Controls Assembly	1	
2	AEU1205	Switch-Fan Speed	1	
3	RTC7414	Vacuum Switch	1	See Note(1)
	RTC7443	Vacuum Switch	1	See Note(2)
4	RTC7414	Vacuum Switch	1	See Note(1)
	RTC7451	Vacuum Switch	1	See Note(2)
5	RTC7444	Control Cable-Long	1	See Note(1)
	RTC7445	Control Cable-Short	1	See Note(2)
6	RTC7448	Harness-Air Con	1	
7	RTC7447	Vacuum Harness	1	See Note(1)
	RTC7446	Vacuum Harness	1	See Note(2)
8	AEU1198	Knob	4	
	RTC7449	Jumper Thermostat	1	See Note(1)

NOTE(1): Phase 1 Air Con-Early Vehicles.
NOTE(2): Phase 2 Air Con-Late Vehicles.

TS5535

LAND ROVER PARTS LTD

MODEL LR110 - UP TO AUGUST 1986
BLOCK TS 5536
PAGE J 70
GROUP J

AIR CONDITIONING - PLENUM CHAMBER - LHD

ILL	PART NO	DESCRIPTION	QTY	REMARKS
1	MTC5557	Plenum Chamber	1	)
2	MTC5568	Hose-Long-To End Finisher	1	)
3	MTC6680	Closing Panel Assembly	1	)See Note(1)
4	AEU4002	+Vacuum Motor	1	)
5	AB606021	Drive Screw	22	)
	367078	Spacer-Plenum Chamber to Toebox	A/R	)

NOTE(1): Phase 1 Air Con-Early Vehicles.

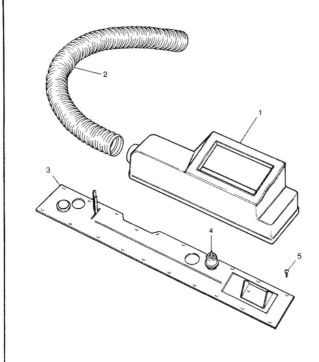

TS5536

 LAND ROVER PARTS LTD

MODEL LR110 - UP TO AUGUST 1986
BLOCK TS 5537
PAGE J 72
GROUP J

AIR CONDITIONING - PLENUM CHAMBER - LHD

ILL	PART NO	DESCRIPTION	QTY	REMARKS
1	RTC7408	Plenum Chamber	1	)
2	RTC7462	Seal-Centre Outlet	1	)
3	RTC7463	Seal-Passenger Outlet	1	)See Note(1)
4	RTC7464	Seal-Plenum Inlet	1	)
5	RTC7409	Hose-Short-To End Finisher	1	)
6	RTC7415	Closing Panel Assembly	1	)
7	AEU4002	+Vacuum Motor	1	)
8	AB606021	Drive Screw	22	)
	367078	Spacer-Plenum Chamber to Toebox	A/R	)

NOTE(1): Phase 2 Air Con-Early Vehicles.

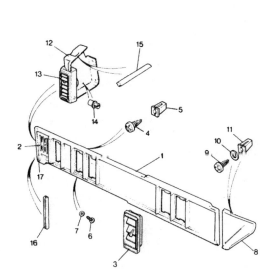

TS5537

MODEL LR110 - UP TO AUGUST 1986
BLOCK TS 5538
PAGE J 74
GROUP J

AIR CONDITIONING - FACIA PANEL - LHD

ILL	PART NO	DESCRIPTION	QTY	REMARKS
1	MTC5555	FACIA PANEL	1	See Note(1)
	RTC7450	FACIA PANEL	1	See Note(2)
2	AEU4000	+Instruction Plate	1	
3	AEU4001	+Louvre	5	
4	AC608065	Drive Screw-Facia to Front Plate	2	
5	ACU5431	Lokut Nut	2	
6	AB608051	Drive Screw-Facia to Front Plate	2	
7	WC105001	Plain Washer	2	
8	MTC5581	Finisher-Facia to Grab Handle	1	
9	AW606124	Drive Screw-Facia to Front Plate	1	
10	WA104004	Plain Washer	1	
11	ACU5431	Lokut Nut	1	
12	MTC5661	End Finisher-Narrow	1	See Note(1)
	RTC7410	END FINISHER-WIDE	1	See Note(2)
13	RTC7411	+Louvre	1	
14	79086	Rokut Rivet-End Finisher to Cowl	1	
15	MTC7516	Filler Piece-End Finisher to Crash Pad	1	
16	RTC7465	Trim-Facia Panel to Cowl	1	
17	RTC7412	PUSH BUTTON SWITCH	1	
	RTC7413	+Bulb	1	

NOTE(1): Phase 1 Air Con-Early Vehicles.
NOTE(2): Phase 2 Air Con-Late Vehicles.

TS5538

MODEL LR110 - UP TO AUGUST 1986
BLOCK TS 5539
PAGE J 80
GROUP J

AIR CONDITIONING - EVAPORATOR ASSEMBLY - LHD

ILL	PART NO	DESCRIPTION	QTY REMARKS
1	MUC1663	EVAPORATOR ASSEMBLY	1
2	MUC6050	+Heater Core	1
3	MUC6037	+Expansion Valve	1
4	MUC6038	+Extension Tube	1
5	MUC6042	+Thermostat	1
6	MUC4375	+Vacuum Switch	1
7	MUC1682	+Adaptor-Blower Assembly	1
8	MUC6040	+Seal	1
9	MUC6053	+Blower Wheel	1
10	MUC6054	+Spacer	1
11	MUC6055	+Locknut	1
12	MUC1675	+Blower Motor	1
13	MUC6052	+Seal	1
14	MUC6056	+Blower Harness	1
15	RTC7470	+Clamp	1
16	MUC4860	Seal	1

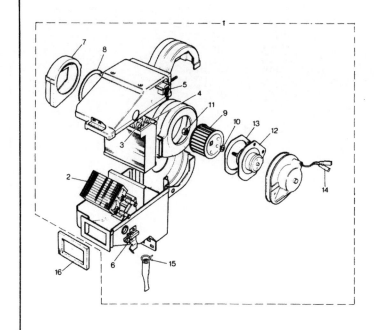

TS5639

LAND ROVER PARTS LTD

438

MODEL LR110 - UP TO AUGUST 1986
BLOCK TS 5540
PAGE J 82
GROUP J

AIR CONDITIONING - FRESH AIR DUCT - RHD

ILL	PART NO	DESCRIPTION	QTY REMARKS
1	MUC1668	Fresh Air Duct	1
2	MUC4884	Vacuum Motor	1
3	RTC7467	Vacuum Motor	1
4	MUC4883	Seal-to Wing Top	1
5	MUC4886	Seal-to Evaporator	1
6	MUC4888	Seal-to Dash	1
7	RTC7470	Clamp	1

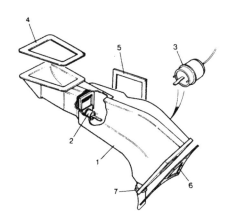

TS5540

LAND ROVER PARTS LTD

439

MODEL LR110 - UP TO AUGUST 1986
BLOCK TS 5541
PAGE J 84
GROUP J

AIR CONDITIONING - FLUID SYSTEM - RHD

ILL	PART NO	DESCRIPTION	QTY	REMARKS
1	MUC4875	Hose-Suction	1	
2	AEU3055	Valve-Service	1	
3	MUC4874	Seal	1	
4	MUC4872	Hose-Liquid	1	
5	RTC7457	Fitting-Aeroquip	2	
6	RTC7452	Ring-Rotolock	2	
7	MUC4358	Adaptor-R4 Comp/Rotolock	1	
	AEU1628	'O' Ring	2	
	AEU1626	'O' Ring	1	
	AEU1627	'O' Ring	1	
	AEU3056	'O' Ring	3	

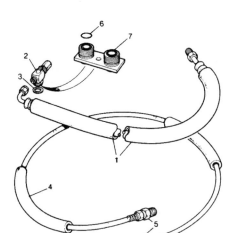

TS5541

440

MODEL LR110 - UP TO AUGUST 1986
BLOCK TS 5542
PAGE J 86
GROUP J

AIR CONDITIONING - VACUUM PIPES AND RESERVOIR - RHD

ILL	PART NO	DESCRIPTION	QTY	REMARKS
1	MUC1679	Vacuum Reservoir	1	
2	MUC4878	Vacuum Hose-30" x 0.109375"	1	
3		Vacuum Hose-5" x 0.109375"	1	)Use MUC4878
4		Vacuum Hose-20" x 0.109375"	1	)
5	MUC4455	Vacuum Tee	2	
6	MUC4866	Vacuum Hose-10" x 0.21875"	1	
7		Vacuum Hose-10" x 0.109375"	1	)Use MUC4878
8		Vacuum Hose-1" x 0.109375"	1	)
9	MUC4865	Vacuum Tee	1	
10	MUC1671	Vacuum Harness	1	
11	MUC4871	Vacuum Harness	1	

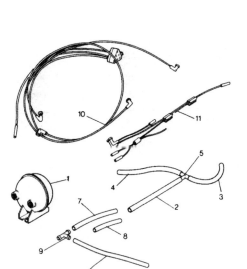

TS5542

441

MODEL LR110 - UP TO AUGUST 1986
BLOCK TS 5543
PAGE J 88
GROUP J

AIR CONDITIONING - ELECTRICAL PARTS - RHD

ILL	PART NO	DESCRIPTION	QTY	REMARKS
1	AEU1747	Resistor	1	
2	RTC7454	Relay	1	
3	MUC1676	Relay Harness	1	
4	MUC1678	Solenoid-Vacuum	1	
5	MUC1672	Main Harness	1	
6	MUC1677	Lighting Harness	1	

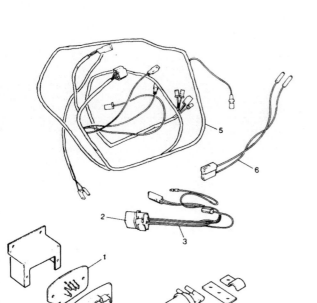

TS5543

LAND ROVER PARTS LTD

MODEL LR110 - UP TO AUGUST 1986
BLOCK TS 5544
PAGE J 90
GROUP J

AIR CONDITIONING - PLENUM AND DEFROSTERS - RHD

ILL	PART NO	DESCRIPTION	QTY	REMARKS
1	MUC1665	Plenum Chamber	1	
2	AEU4002	+Vacuum Motor	2	
3	MUC6021	+Seal	1	
4	MUC4882	Seal-Right Hand Duct	1	
5	MUC4881	Seal-Left Hand Duct	1	
6	MUC4891	Adaptor-Defroster	1	
7	MUC1673	Defroster Duct-LH	1	
8	MUC4892	Hose	1	
9	MUC1674	Defroster Duct-RH	1	
10	AB606021L	Drive Screw	22	
11	MUC3695	Insulation Pad	1	

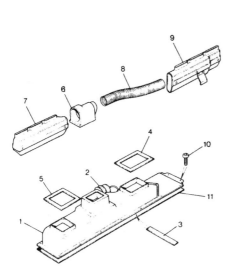

TS5544

 LAND ROVER PARTS LTD

MODEL LR110 - UP TO AUGUST 1986
BLOCK TS 5545
PAGE J 92
GROUP J

AIR CONDITIONING - FACIA PANEL ASSEMBLY - RHD

ILL	PART NO	DESCRIPTION	QTY	REMARKS
1	MUC1667	FACIA PANEL ASSEMBLY	1	
2	AEU4002	+Vacuum Motor	2	
3	MUC1666	+Control Head	1	
4	MUC6011	+Knob	1	
5	MUC6012	+Switch-Clutch	1	
6	MUC6013	+Switch-Fresh Air	1	
7	573289	+Bulb-Control Panel	1	
8	MUC4880	Louvre	4	
9	MUC1669	DUCT ASSEMBLY-RIGHT HAND SIDE	1	
10	RTC7411	+Louvre	1	
11	MUC4895	+Hose	1	
12	MUC1670	Closing Trim-Handle	1	
13	MUC1680	Bowden Cable	1	
14	RTC7465	Trim-Facia Panel to Cowl	1	

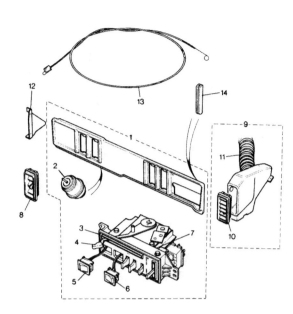

TS5545

MASTER INDEX

GROUP K

ELECTRICAL

MODEL LR110 - UP TO AUGUST 1986
BLOCK VS 3759
PAGE K 2
GROUP K

ENGINE ELECTRICS - 2.25 PETROL - DISTRIBUTOR

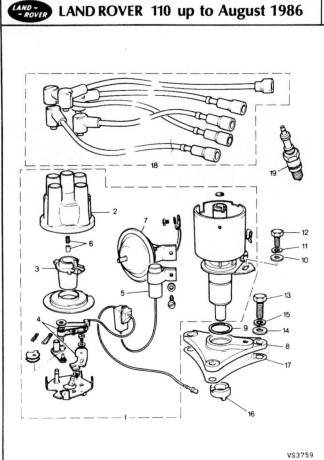

ILL	PART NO	DESCRIPTION	QTY	REMARKS
1	ERC8520	DISTRIBUTOR	1	
2	RTC3278	+Cap	1	)
3	RTC3614	+Rotor Arm	1	)
4	RTC3282	+Contact Set	1	)For Use With
5	RTC3474	+Condenser	1	)Lucas
6	RTC315	+Brush Set	1	)Distributor
7	AEU1034	+Vacuum Unit	1	)
2	RTC4932	+Cap	1	)
3	RTC4933	+Rotor Arm	1	)For Use With
4	RTC4934	+Contact Set	1	)Ducellier
5	RTC4935	+Condenser	1	)Distributor
7	AEU1684	+Vacuum Unit	1	)
	RTC4936	+Clamping Plate	1	)
8	549610	Adaptor-Distributor to Block	1	
9	52278	Washer Cork	1	
10	WB106041L	Washer-Dist to Adaptor	1	
11	WM600041L	Spring Washer-Dist to Adaptor	1	
12	253205	Screw UNC x 0.562" - Dist to Adaptor	1	
13	SH108251L	Screw UNF x 0.875"-Adaptor to Block	3	
14	WA108051L	Washer	3	
15	WL108001L	Spring Washer	3	
16	549611	Drive Coupling	1	
17	247212	Joint Washer	1	
18	ERC3256	Ignition Lead Set	1	
19	RTC3570	Spark Plug	4	8:1 CR
	RTC3569	Spark Plug	4	7:1 CR

VS3759

MODEL LR110 - UP TO AUGUST 1986
BLOCK VS 3759A
PAGE K 2.02
GROUP K

ENGINE ELECTRICS - 2.5 PETROL - DISTRIBUTOR

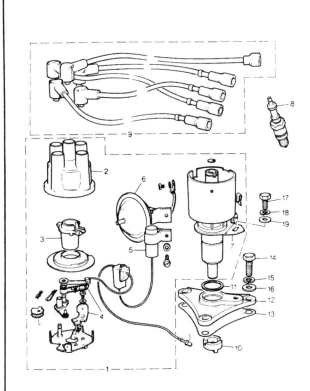

ILL	PART NO	DESCRIPTION	QTY	REMARKS
1	ETC5835	DISTRIBUTOR	1	
2	RTC3278	+Cap	1	
3	RTC3614	+Rotor Arm	1	
4	RTC5946	+Contact Set	1	Note(1)
	RTC5947	+Contact Set	1	Note(2) Alternatives
5	RTC3474	+Capacitor	1	
6	AEU1034	+Vacuum Unit	1	
7	245003	+Clamping Plate	1	
8	RTC3812	Sparking Plug	4	
9	ERC3256	Ignition Lead Set	1	
10	549611	Drive Coupling	1	
11	52278	Washer-Cork	1	
12	ETC4466	Adaptor	1	
13	247212	Joint Washer	1	
14	SH108201L	Screw	3	
15	WL108001L	Washer-Spring	3	
16	WA108051L	Washer	3	
17	SH106161L	Screw	1	
18	WL106001L	Washer-Spring	1	
19	WB106041L	Washer	1	

NOTE(1)   Sliding Contact Type
           Replace at 24000 Miles (40000 Kms)
           or 2 Years

NOTE(2)   Fixed Contact Type
           Replace at 12000 Miles (20000 Kms)
           or 1 Year

VS3759A

MODEL LR110 - UP TO AUGUST 1986
BLOCK 6RE 159
PAGE K 4
GROUP K

ENGINE ELECTRICS - 3.5 PETROL - DISTRIBUTOR
ENGINES PREFIX 14G,15G AND 17G

ILL	PART NO	DESCRIPTION	QTY	REMARKS
1	ERC4536	DISTRIBUTOR	1	Engine 15G
	ERC5745	DISTRIBUTOR	1	Engine 14G
	ERC7131	DISTRIBUTOR	1	Engine 17G
2	RTC3197	+Cover	1	
3	RTC3618	+Rotor Arm	1	
4	RTC3286	+Contact Set	1	Sliding Type
	608158	+Contact Set	1	Fixed Type
5	RTC3472	+Condenser	1	
6	608197	+Lead-Low Tension	1	
7	AAU8452	+Vacuum Unit	1	Engine 15G
	AEU1422	+Vacuum Unit	1	Engine 14G
	608266	+Vacuum Unit	1	Engine 17G
8	603446	O Ring	1	See Note(1)
9	ERC1353	Coupling	1	
10	613857	Clamp-Distributor to Timing Cover	1	
11	SH506121L	Screw-Clamp	1	
12	ETC6484	Kit-HT Leads	1	
13	RTC3570	Spark Plug	8	
14	603672	Retainer-HT Leads	1	
	603673	Retainer-HT Leads	4	
15	602953	Pin	1	

NOTE(1): Part of Engine Gasket/Seals Kit RTC2104

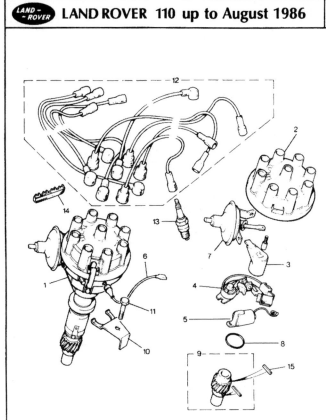

6RE159

448

MODEL LR110 - UP TO AUGUST 1986
BLOCK TS 5765
PAGE K 4.02
GROUP K

ENGINE ELECTRICS - 3.5 PETROL - DISTRIBUTOR
ENGINES 19G,20G,21G AND 22G

ILL	PART NO	DESCRIPTION	QTY	REMARKS
1	ETC4715	DISTRIBUTOR	1	Engine 22G
	ETC4717	DISTRIBUTOR	1	Engine 20G
	ETC5090	DISTRIBUTOR	1	Engine 19G
	ETC5354	DISTRIBUTOR	1	Engine 21G
6	608266	+Vacuum Unit	1	Engine 22G
6	RTC3201	+Vacuum Unit	1	Engine 20G
6	AAU8452	+Vacuum Unit	1	Engine 19G and 21G
2	RTC3197	Distributor Cap	1	
3	RTC3199	Rotor Arm	1	
4	RTC3200	Insulation Cover	1	
5	RTC3198	Pick Up and Base Plate	1	
7	603446	'O' Ring	1	
8	ERC1353	Coupling Assembly	1	
9	613857	Clamp-Distributor to Cover	1	
10	SH605121L	Screw-Clamp	1	
11	ETC6484	Kit-H.T. Leads	1	
12	RTC3570	Spark Plug	8	
	602672	Retainer-H.T. Leads	1	
	602673	Retainer-H.T. Leads	4	
13	602953	Pin	1	

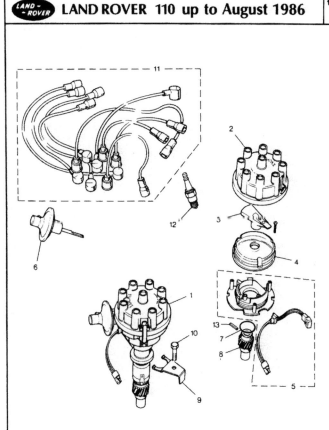

TS5765

449

MODEL LR110 - UP TO AUGUST 1986
BLOCK TS 5765
PAGE K 4.04
GROUP K

ENGINE ELECTRICS 3.5 PETROL - DISTRIBUTOR (SU CARBURETTERS)

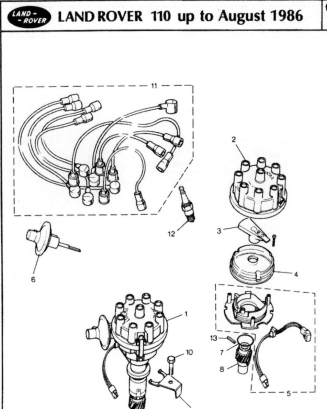

ILL	PART NO	DESCRIPTION	QTY	REMARKS
1	ETC6586	DISTRIBUTOR	1	)Upto Engine
2	RTC3197	+Cover	1	)Number
3	RTC3199	+Rotor Arm	1	)20G 01607A
4	RTC3200	+Insulating Cover	1	)24G 00235A
5	RTC3198	+Pick Up and Base Plate	1	)
6	RTC3201	+Vacuum Unit	1	)
1	ETC6976	DISTRIBUTOR	1	)From Engine
	RTC5089	+Module	1	)Number
2	RTC3197	+Cover	1	)20G 01608A
3	RTC3199	+Rotor Arm	1	)24G 00236A
4	RTC5091	+Insulation Cover	1	)
5	RTC5090	+Pick Up and Base Plate	1	)
6	RTC5092	+Vacuum Unit	1	)
7	603446	'O' Ring	1	
8	ERC1353	Gear and Coupling	1	
9	613857	Clamp-Distributor to Timing Cover	1	
10	SH506121L	Screw-Clamp	1	
11	ETC6484	Kit-H.T. Leads	1	
12	RTC3570	Spark Plug	8	
	603672	Retainer-H.T. Leads	1	
	603673	Retainer-H.T. Leads	4	
13	602953	Pin	1	

TS5765

450

MODEL LR110 - UP TO AUGUST 1986
BLOCK VS 4053
PAGE K 6
GROUP K

ENGINE ELECTRICS - IGNITION COIL AND BALLAST RESISTOR

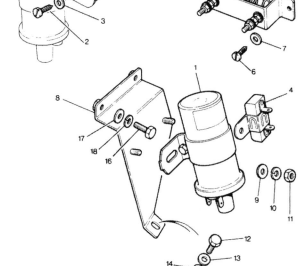

ILL	PART NO	DESCRIPTION	QTY	REMARKS
1	RTC5629	Ignition Coil	1	)4 Cylinder)Petrol
	573038	Ignition Coil	1	V8 Petrol
2	72628	Screw-Coil Fixing	2	)4 Cylinder
3	WJ106007	Plain Washer	2	)Petrol
4	134176	Ballast Resistor	1	V8 Petrol
5	PRC1716	Ballast Resistor	1	)
6	72628	Screw-Resistor Fixing	2	)See Note(1)
7	WA106041L	Washer-Resistor Fixing	2	)
8	PRC3131	Mounting Plate-Coil	1	)
9	WA106047L	Plain Washer-Coil to Plate	2	)
10	WL106007L	Spring Washer-Coil to Plate	2	)
11	NH106047	Nut-Coil to Plate	2	)
12	SH106167	Screw-Plate to Wheelarch	1	)
13	WA106047L	Plain Washer	1	)V8 Petrol
14	WL106007L	Spring Washer	1	)
15	NH106047	Nut	1	)
16	SE106167	Screw-Plate to Wing Top	2	)
17	WA106047L	Plain Washer	2	)
18	WL106007L	Spring Washer	2	)

NOTE(1):   2.25 Diesel-Not required for 2.5 Diesel

VS4053

451

MODEL LR110 - UP TO AUGUST 1986
BLOCK TS 5523
PAGE K 6.02
GROUP K

ENGINE ELECTRICS - IGNITION COIL - ELECTRONIC IGNITION - V8

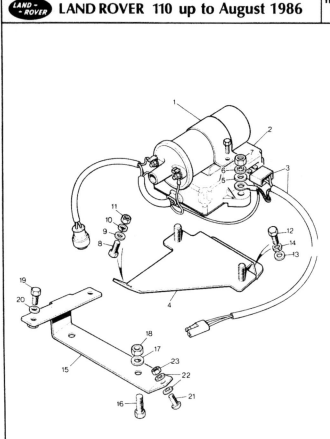

ILL	PART NO	DESCRIPTION		QTY	REMARKS
1	RTC5628	Ignition Coil		1	
2	RTC3188	Ignition Module		1	)To:Note(1)
3	PRC4503	Lead-Distributor to Module		1	)
	PRC6141	Link Lead-Coil		1	)From:Note(2)
	PRC6144	Link Lead-Coil		1	)
4	PRC4951	Mounting Bracket		1	To:Note(1)
	PRC3131	Mounting Bracket		1	From:Note(2)
5	WA108051L	Plain Washer		2	
6	WF108001L	Spring Washer		2	
7	NH108041L	Nut		2	
8	SH106167	Screw		1	
9	WA106047L	Plain Washer		1	
10	WL106047	Spring Washer		1	
11	NH106047	Nut		1	
12	SE106167	Screw		2	
13	WA106047L	Plain Washer		2	
14	WL106007L	Spring Washer		2	
15	MUC4212	Mounting Bracket)		1	To:Note(1)
	PRC6133	Mounting Bracket)		1	From:Note(2)
16	SH108251L	Screw)		2	
17	WA108051L	Plain Washer)		2	
18	NH108041L	Nut)Air Con		2	
19	SH106161L	Screw)RHD		1	
20	WA106041L	Plain Washer)		1	
21	SE106161L	Screw)		1	
22	WA106041L	Plain Washer)		2	
23	NH106041L	Nut)		1	

NOTE(1): Eng. No. 20G 01805A, 24G 00235A

NOTE(2): Eng. No. 20G 01806A, 24G 00236A

TS5523

LAND ROVER PARTS LTD

452

MODEL LR110 - UP TO AUGUST 1986
BLOCK VS 3983A
PAGE K 8
GROUP K

ENGINE ELECTRICS 2.25 PETROL/DIESEL - ALTERNATOR - EXCEPT AIR CON

ILL	PART NO	DESCRIPTION	QTY	REMARKS
1	AEU2506	ALTERNATOR-115/34	1	)Note(1))No Longer)Available use)RTC5083E
2	AEU2507	+Cover	1	
3	AEU3076	+Regulator	1	
1	PRC4287	ALTERNATOR-115/45	1	)Note(2))No Longer)Available Use)RTC5083E
2	AEU2507	+Cover	1	
3	AEU3076	+Regulator	1	
1	AEU2505	ALTERNATOR-115/45	1	)Note(3))No longer)Available Use)RTC5088E
2	AEU1814	+Cover	1	
3	AEU2464L	+Regulator	1	
4	BAU1825	+Rectifier	1	
5	BAU2193	+Slip Ring	1	
6	BAU2195	+Brush Box	1	
7	RTC3215	+Brush Set	1	
8	RTC4607	Surge Protection Diode	1	
9	568788	Pulley	1	
	ERC8986	Pulley	1	Split Charge
10	18G8619L	Kit-Bearing-Drive End	1	
11	AEU1532	Kit-Slip Ring & Bearing	1	
12	C37222L	Fan	1	
	AEU1706	Kit-Screw	1	
	AEU1710	Kit-Sundry Parts	1	
	AEU1942	Kit-Spacer	1	
1	PRC6366	ALTERNATOR-A127/45	1	)No Longer)Available Use)RTC5682N
	RTC5670	+Regulator & Brush Box	1	
	RTC5684	+Rectifier	1	
	RTC5926	+Bearing-Slip Ring End	1	
	RTC5687	+Bracket & Bearing-Drive End	1	
	RTC5925	+Kit-Through Bolts	1	
	RTC5685	Fan	1	
	RTC5686	Pulley	1	
	RTC5689	Spacer-Pulley	1	

NOTE(1): Petrol Engines Upto 11H05639C, All Diesel Engines
NOTE(2): Petrol Engines From 11H05640C
NOTE(3): High Output-Split Charge

VS3983A

LAND ROVER PARTS LTD

453

MODEL LR110 - UP TO AUGUST 1986
BLOCK VS 3983A
PAGE K 8.02
GROUP K

ENGINE - ELECTRICS 2.5 DIESEL - ALTERNATOR ASSEMBLY

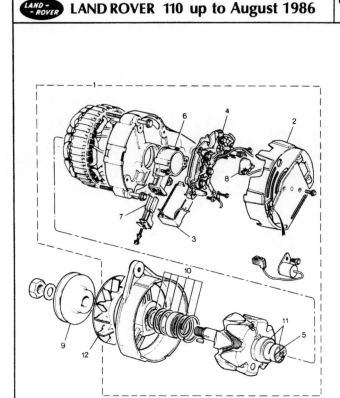

ILL	PART NO	DESCRIPTION	QTY	REMARKS
1	AEU2506	ALTERNATOR A115/34	1	)Upto 12J05496C)No Longer)Available Use)RTC5083E
	PRC4287	ALTERNATOR A115/45	1	)From 12J05497C)No Longer)Available)Use)RTC5083E
2	AEU2507	+Cover	1	
3	AEU3076	+Regulator	1	
4	BAU1825	+Rectifier	1	
5	BAU2193	+Slip Ring	1	
6	BAU2195	+Brush Box	1	
7	RTC3290	+Brush Set	1	Upto 12J05496C)
	RTC3215	+Brush Set	1	From 12J05497C)*
8	RTC4607	+Surge Protection Diode	1	
9	568788	Pulley	1	
10	18G8619L	Kit-Bearing-Drive End	1	
11	AEU1532	Kit-Slip Ring and Bearing	1	
12	C37222L	Fan	1	
	AEU1706	Kit-Screw	1	
	AEU1710	Kit-Sundry Parts	1	
	AEU1942	Kit-Spacer	1	
1	PRC6366	ALTERNATOR-A127/45	1	)No Longer)Available Use)RTC5682N
	RTC5670	+Regulator & Brush Box	1	
	RTC5684	+Rectifier	1	
	RTC5926	+Bearing-Slip Ring End	1	
	RTC5687	+Bracket & Bearing-Drive End	1	
	RTC5925	+Kit-Through Bolts	1	
	RTC5685	Fan	1	
	RTC5686	Pulley	1	
	RTC5689	Spacer-Pulley	1	

VS3983A

MODEL LR110 - UP TO AUGUST 1986
BLOCK VS 3983B
PAGE K 8.04
GROUP K

ENGINE ELECTRICS - 2.5 PETROL - ALTERNATOR

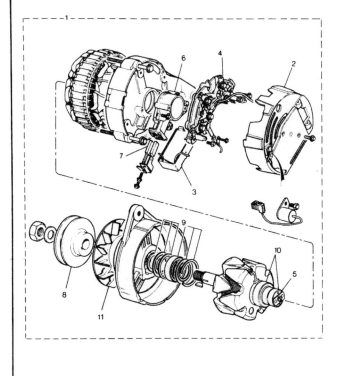

ILL	PART NO	DESCRIPTION	QTY	REMARKS
1	PRC4287	ALTERNATOR-A115/45	1	)No Longer)Available Use)RTC5083E
2	AEU2507	+Cover	1	
3	AEU3076	+Regulator	1	
4	BAU1825	+Rectifier	1	
5	BAU2193	+Slip Ring	1	
6	BAU2195	+Brush Box	1	
7	RTC3215	+Brush Set	1	
8	568788	Pulley	1	
9	18G8619L	Kit-Bearing-Drive End	1	
10	AEU1532	Kit-Slip Ring and Bearing	1	
11	C37222L	Fan	1	
	AEU1706	Kit-Screws	1	
	AEU1710	Kit-Sundry Parts	1	
	AEU1942	Kit-Spacer	1	
1	PRC6366	ALTERNATOR-A127/45	1	)No Longer)Available Use)RTC5682N
	RTC5670	+Regulator & Brush Box	1	
	RTC5684	+Rectifier	1	
	RTC5926	+Bearing-Slip Ring	1	
	RTC5687	+Bracket & Bearing-Drive End	1	
	RTC5925	+kit-Through Bolts	1	
	RTC5685	Fan	1	
	RTC5686	Pulley	1	
	RTC5689	Spacer-Pulley	1	

VS3983B

MODEL LR110 - UP TO AUGUST 1986
BLOCK VS 3160
PAGE K 10
GROUP K

ENGINE ELECTRICS - 4 CYLINDER - ALTERNATOR - AIR CONDITIONING
                              AND HIGH OUTPUT OPTIONS

ILL	PART NO	DESCRIPTION	QTY	REMARKS
1	PRC2668	ALTERNATOR-A133/65	1	)No Longer)Available Use)RTC5218E
2	AEU1725	+Cover	1	
3	AEU3076	+Regulator	1	
4	AEU1527	+Rectifier	1	
7	RTC3292	+Brush Set	1	
9	RTC4607	+Surge Protection Device	1	
5	AEU1726	Bearing Kit-Drive End	1	
6	AEU1532	Bearing Kit-Slip Ring End	1	
8	AEU1710	Kit-Sundry Parts	1	
	ERC8987	Nut-Special	1	
11	ERC8986	Pulley	1	
12	AEU1616	Suppression Capacitor	1	
	AEU1706	Kit-Screw	1	
	AEU1708	Kit-Spacer	1	
	AEU1709	Kit-Terminal	1	
10	ADU4928L	Fan	1	

VS3160

MODEL LR110 - UP TO AUGUST 1986
BLOCK VS 3886A
PAGE K 12
GROUP K

ENGINE ELECTRICS - ALTERNATOR - 'A' SERIES - 3.5 LITRE V8 PETROL

ILL	PART NO	DESCRIPTION	QTY	REMARKS
1	PRC2677	ALTERNATOR A115/45	1	)Note(1))No Longer)Available Use)RTC5086E
2	AEU1814	+Cover End	1	
3	AEU2464L	+Regulator	1	
4	BAU1825	+Rectifier	1	
5	18G8619L	+Kit-Bearing-Front Bearing	1	
6	AEU1532	+Kit-Bearing & Slip Ring	1	
	BAU2193L	+Slip Ring	2	
	BAU2195L	+Brush Box	1	
7	RTC3215	+Brush Set	1	
8	AEU1710	+Kit-Sundry Parts	1	
	AEU1706	+Kit-Screws	1	
	AEU1942	+Kit-Spacer	1	
9	RTC4607	+Surge Protection Diode	1	
1	PRC4288	ALTERNATOR A115/45	1	)Note(2))No longer)Available Use)RTC5085E
2	AEU2507	+Cover	1	
3	AEU3076	+Regulator	1	
4	BAU1825	+Rectifier	1	
5	18G8619L	+Bearing Kit-Drive End	1	
6	AEU1532	+Bearing Kit-Slip Ring End	1	
	BAU2193	+Slip Ring	2	
	BAU2195	+Brush Box	1	
7	RTC3215	+Brush Set	1	
8	AEU1710	Kit-Sundry Parts	1	
	AEU1706	Kit-Screw	1	
	AEU1942	Kit-Spacer	1	
10	C37222L	Fan	1	
11	602505	Pulley	1	
12	AEU1616	Capacitor	1	

NOTE(1): - Except Air Con and Split Charge
            Battery Sensed Up To Engine Numbers
            14G01446, 15G02240, 17G00182.

NOTE(2): - 'IND' Sensed From Engine Numbers
            14G01447, 15G02241, 17G00183

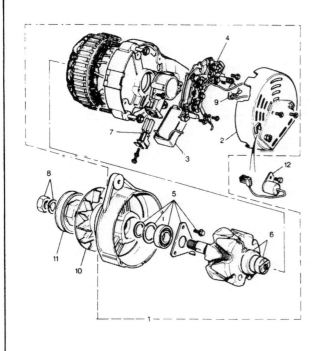

VS3886A

MODEL LR110 - UP TO AUGUST 1986
BLOCK VS 3160A
PAGE K 14
GROUP K

ENGINE ELECTRICS - ALTERNATOR 'A' SERIES - 3.5 LITRE V8 PETROL

ILL	PART NO	DESCRIPTION	QTY	REMARKS
1	PRC2669	ALTERNATOR A133/65	1	)Note(1))No Longer)Available Use)RTC5087E
	PRC2668	ALTERNATOR A133/65	1	)Note(2))No Longer)Available Use)RTC5218E
2	AEU1725	+Cover End	1	
3	AEU3076	+Regulator	1	
4	AEU1527	+Rectifier	1	
5	AEU1726	+Kit-Blanking-Front Bearing	1	
6	AEU1532	+Kit-Rear Bearing & Slip Ring	1	
7	RTC3292	+Brush Set	1	
8	AEU1710	+Kit-Sundry Parts	1	
	AEU1706	+Kit-Screws	1	
	AEU1708	+Kit-Spacers	1	
	AEU1709	+Kit-Terminals	1	
9	RTC4607	+Surge Protection Device	1	
10	ADU4928L	Fan	1	
11	ERC3345	Pulley	1	Note(1)
	ERC8851	Pulley	1	Note(2)
12	AEU1616	Capacitor	1	

NOTE(1): Split Charge System

NOTE(2): Air Con & Air Con with Power Steering

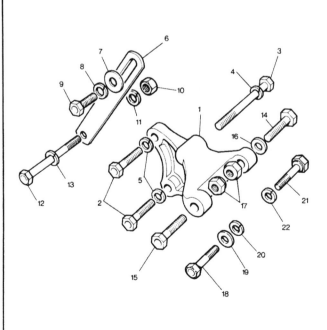

VS3160A

LAND ROVER PARTS LTD

MODEL LR110 - UP TO AUGUST 1986
BLOCK VS 4104
PAGE K 16
GROUP K

ENGINE ELECTRICS 2.25 PETROL - ALTERNATOR FIXINGS

ILL	PART NO	DESCRIPTION	QTY	REMARKS
1	574855	Bracket-Alternator (Suffix A & B Only)	1	)
1	ETC4357	Bracket-Alternator (Suffix C Onwards)	1	)
2	SH108301L	Screw-Bracket to Block	2	)
3	BH605261L	Bolt-Bracket to)Suffix Block)A & B Only	1	)Except
4	WM600051L	Spring Washer) Bracket to Block)	1	)Air Con
3	BH108161L	Bolt-Bracket to)Suffix C Block)Onwards	1	)
4	WL108001L	Spring Washer-) Bracket to Block)	1	)
5	WL108001L	Spring Washer	2	)
6	ERC5139	Adjusting Link	1	)
6	ERC6683	Adjusting Link	1	Air Con and Split Charge.
7	2266L	Washer-Link to Alternator	1	
8	WL108001L	Spring Washer-Link to Alternator	1	
9	SH108251L	Screw-Link to Alternator	1	
10	NH605041L	Nut-Link to Front Cover	1	)Air Con Only.
11	WM600051L	Spring Washer-Link to Front Cover	1	)
12	BH108201L	Bolt-Link to Block	1	)Except Air)Con
13	WL108001L	Spring Washer-Link to Block	1	
14	BH108081L	Bolt-UNF x 1.5" Alternator to Bracket	1	)
15	BH108091L	Bolt-UNF x 1.875" Alternator to Bracket	1	)Except P.A.S.
16	WC108051L	Washer-Alternator to Bracket	1	)
17	NY108041L	Nut-Nyloc-Alternator to Brkt	2	)
18	SH108351L	Screw-Alternator to Bracket	1	)
19	WC108051L	Washer-Alternator to Bracket	1	)
20	WL108001L	Spring Washer-Alternator to Bracket	1	)P.A.S. Only
21	SH108401L	Screw Alternator to Bracket Rear	1	)
22	WL108001L	Spring Washer-Alternator to Bracket	1	)

VS4104

LAND ROVER PARTS LTD

MODEL LR110 - UP TO AUGUST 1986
BLOCK VS 4104A
PAGE K 16.02
GROUP K

ENGINE ELECTRICS - 2.5 PETROL - ALTERNATOR FIXINGS

ILL	PART NO	DESCRIPTION	QTY	REMARKS
1	ETC4357	Bracket-Alternator	1	
2	SH108301L	Screw-Bracket to Block	2	
3	WL108001L	Spring Washer-Bracket to Block	2	
4	BH108161L	Bolt-Bracket to Block	1	
5	WL108001L	Spring Washer-Bracket to Block	1	
6	ERC5139	Adjusting Link	1	
7	2266L	Washer-Link to Alternator	1	
8	WL108001L	Spring Washer-Link to Alternator	1	
9	SH108251L	Screw-Link to Alternator	1	
10	BH108201L	Bolt-Link to Block	1	
11	WL108001L	Spring Washer-Link to Block	1	
12	BH108081L	Bolt-Alternator to Bracket	1	
13	BH108091L	Bolt-Alternator to Bracket	1	
14	WC108051L	Washer-Alternator to Bracket	1	
15	NY108041L	Nyloc Nut-Alternator to Bracket	2	

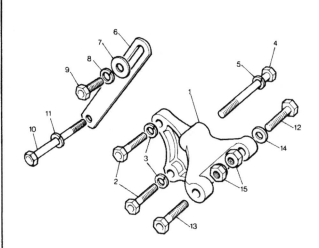

VS4104A

460

MODEL LR 110 - UP TO AUGUST 1986
BLOCK 1RE 246
PAGE K 18
GROUP K

ENGINE ELECTRICS 2.25 DIESEL - ALTERNATOR MOUNTING

ILL	PART NO	DESCRIPTION	QTY	REMARKS
1	574855	Bracket-Mounting	1	Suffix A & B Only
1	ETC4357	Bracket-Mounting	1	Suffix C Onward
2	BH605261L	Bolt-Bracket to Block	1	Suffix A & B Only
2	BH108161L	Bolt-Bracket to Block	1	Suffix C Onward
3	SH108301L	Screw-Bracket to Block	2	
4	WM600051L	Spring Washer-Bracket to Block	1	Suffix A & B Only
4	WL108001L	Spring Washer-Bracket to Block	1	Suffix C Onward
5	WL108001L	Spring Washer-Bracket to Block	2	
6	ERC5139	Link-Adjusting	1	
7	SH108201L	Screw-Link to Alternator	1	
8	WL108001L	Spring Washer	1	
9	2266L	Washer	1	
10	BH108201L	Bolt-Link to Block	1	
11	WL108001L	Spring Washer	1	
12	BH108181L	Bolt-Alternator to Bracket	1	
13	BH108091L	Bolt-Alternator to Bracket	1	
14	WC108051L	Washer	1	
15	NY108041L	Nut-Nyloc	2	

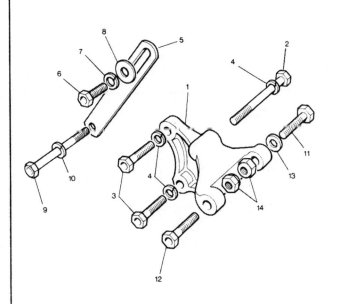

1RE246

461

MODEL LR110 - UP TO AUGUST 1986
BLOCK 1RE 246
PAGE K 18.02
GROUP K

ENGINE ELECTRICS 2.5 DIESEL - ALTERNATOR MOUNTING

ILL	PART NO	DESCRIPTION	QTY	REMARKS
1	ETC4357	Bracket-Mounting	1	
2	BH108161L	Bolt-Bracket to Block	1	
3	SH110301L	Bolt-Bracket to Block	2	
4	WL108001L	Washer-Spring-Bracket to Block	1	
5	WL108001L	Washer-Spring-Bracket to Block	2	
6	ERC5139	Link-Adjusting	1	Except Air Con
6	ERC6683	Link-Adjusting	1	Air Con Only *
7	SH108201L	Screw-Link to Alternator	1	
8	WL108001L	Washer Spring	1	
9	2266L	Washer	1	
10	ERC8964	Bolt-Link to Block	1	
11	WL108001L	Washer Spring	1	
12	BH108081L	Bolt-Bracket to Block	1	
13	BH108091L	Bolt-Bracket to Block	1	
16	ERC7974	Spacer	1	
14	WC108051L	Washer	1	
15	NY108041L	Nyloc Nut	2	

* Not Required with A127 Type Alternator

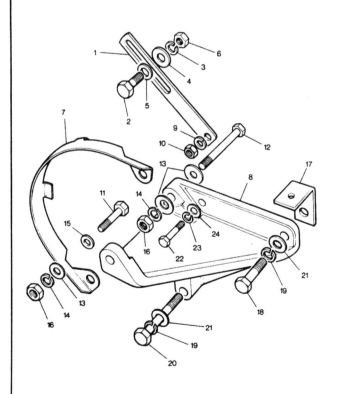

1RE246

LAND ROVER PARTS LTD

462

MODEL LR110 - UP TO AUGUST 1986
BLOCK N 554
PAGE K 20
GROUP K

ENGINE ELECTRICS - ALTERNATOR BRACKETS - EXCEPT AIR CONDITIONING
3.5 LITRE V8 PETROL

ILL	PART NO	DESCRIPTION	QTY	REMARKS
1	614939	Adjusting Link	1	
2	SH108351L	Screw-M8x3mm-Link/Alternator	1	
3	WM600051L	Spring Washer	1	
4	2217L	Plain Washer	1	
5	2266L	Plain Washer	1	*
	4868L	Plain Washer	1	**
6	NH108041L	Nut-M8	1	
7	613244	Fan Guard	1	*
	ETC7390	Fan Guard	1	**
8	611022	Bracket	1	
9	WM600051L	Spring Washer-Link to Stud Timing Cover	1	
10	NT605041L	Locknut	1	
11	BH605121L	Bolt Alternator/Bracket	1	*
	BH605131L	Bolt	1	**
12	BH605201L	Bolt Rear	1	
13	WA108051L	Plain Washer	3	
14	WM600051L	Spring Washer	2	
15	2266L	Plain Washer	1	*
	4868L	Plain Washer	1	**
16	NH605041L	Nut	2	
17	613620	Clip-Support Bracket	1	
18	BH506111L	Bolt-Bracket/Head	1	
19	WM600061L	Spring Washer	2	
20	BH506201L	Bolt	1	
21	3036L	Plain Washer	1	
22	BH505111L	Bolt	1	
23	WM600051L	Spring Washer	1	
24	WA108051L	Plain Washer	1	

* Use With A115 Or A133 Type Alternator

** Use With A127 Type Alternator

N554

LAND ROVER PARTS LTD

463

MODEL LR110 - UP TO AUGUST 1986
BLOCK VS 3876
PAGE K 22
GROUP K

ENGINE ELECTRICS - ALTERNATOR MOUNTING BRACKETS WITH AIR
CONDITIONING 3.5 LITRE V8 PETROL

ILL	PART NO	DESCRIPTION	QTY	REMARKS
1	ERC7548	Adjusting Link	1	
2	SH108351L	Bolt-M8 x 35mm Link to Support Bracket	1	
3	4866L	Washer-Plain	1	
4	WM600051L	Washer-Spring	1	
5	NH108041L	Nut	1	
6	BH605111L	Bolt-Adjusting Link to Pump	1	
7	WL108001L	Washer-Spring	1	
8	ERC6547	Bracket-Support-Alternator	1	
9	ERC6538	Mounting Bracket-LH Alternator	1	
10	SH506071L	Screw-Mounting Bracket Alternator	1	
11	WM600061L	Washer-Spring	1	
12	SA506081L	Screw	1	
13	90613442	Fan Guard	1	Also Split Charge
14	SH108251L	Screw-M8 x 25mm Alternator to Mounting Bracket	1	
15	4594L	Washer-Plain	1	
16	WM600051L	Washer-Spring	1	
17	BH108081L	Bolt-Frontlug M8 x 40mm	1	
18	WA108051L	Washer-Plain	2	
19	WM600051L	Washer-Spring	1	
20	NH108041L	Nut-M8	1	
21	BH108091L	Bolt-Rearlug M8 x 45mm	1	
22	WA108051L	Washer-Plain	2	
23	WM600051L	Washer-Spring	1	
24	NH108041L	Nut-M8	1	
25	602200	Bolt-Double Ended-Alternator Mounting Bracket to Cyl Head	1	
26	WM600061L	Washer-Spring	1	
27	NH604041L	Nut	1	

VS3876

LAND ROVER PARTS LTD

MODEL LR110 - UP TO AUGUST 1986
BLOCK VS 4236
PAGE K 24
GROUP K

ENGINE ELECTRICS - 4 CYLINDER PETROL- STARTER MOTOR

ILL	PART NO	DESCRIPTION	QTY	REMARKS
1	RTC5233E	STARTER MOTOR 2M100	1	
2	RTC5967	+Brush Set	1	
3	520455	+Pivot Pin	1	
4	AEU2501	+Solenoid	1	
5	AEU2502	+Drive Assembly	1	
6	608352	Kit-Bush	1	
7	WL110001L	Spring Washer-Fixing Starter	2	
8	NH110041L	Nut-Fixing Starter Motor	2	
9	ETC4133	Heat Shield Assembly	1	
10	ERC8722	Bolt-Shield to Ex Manifold	2	
13	608395	Kit-Retention	1	
14	90608178	Kit-Sundry Parts	1	

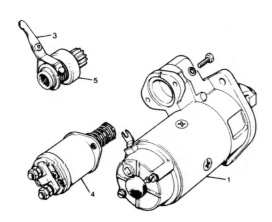
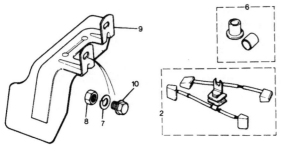

VS4236

LAND ROVER PARTS LTD

MODEL LR110 - UP TO AUGUST 1986
BLOCK VS 4076
PAGE K 26
GROUP K

ENGINE ELECTRICS 2.25 DIESEL - STARTER MOTOR

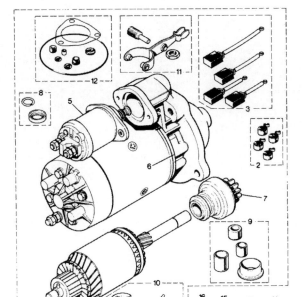

ILL	PART NO	DESCRIPTION	QTY	REMARKS
1	PRC3032	Starter Motor 2M113	1	NLA-Use RTC5249N
2	27H5932L	+Brush Spring	1	
3	270225	+Brush Kit	1	
4	607754	+Armature	1	No Longer Serviced
5	AEU1649	+Solenoid	1	
6	607747	+Bracket Assembly	1	
7	AEU2792	+Drive Assembly	1	
8	AEU2500	+Kit-Retention	1	
9	608304	+Kit-Bush	1	
10	37H6171L	+Kit-Brake	1	
11	AEU1613	+Kit-Engaging Lever	1	
12	37H7618L	+Kit-Sealing	1	
13	SH110301L	Screw-Starter to Flywheel Hsg	1	
14	NH110041L	Nut	2	
15	WL110001L	Spring Washer	3	
16	BH110091L	Bolt	1	

VS4076

LAND ROVER PARTS LTD

MODEL LR110 - UP TO AUGUST 1986
BLOCK VS 4076
PAGE K 26.02
GROUP K

ENGINE ELECTRICS - 2.5 DIESEL - STARTER MOTOR - LUCAS

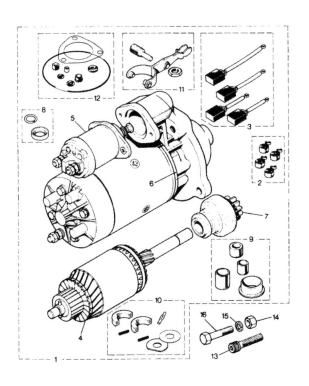

ILL	PART NO	DESCRIPTION	QTY	REMARKS
1	RTC5249N	STARTER MOTOR	1	
2	27H5932L	+Brush Spring	1	
3	AEU4151	+Brush Kit	1	
4	AEU4146	+Armature	1	No Longer Serviced
5	AEU1649	+Solenoid	1	
6	AEU4147	+Bracket Assembly	1	
7	AEU2792	+Drive Assembly	1	
8	AEU4148	+Kit-Retention	1	
9	AEU4149	+Kit-Bush	1	
10	37H6171L	+Kit-Brake	1	
11	AEU1613	+Kit-Engaging Lever	1	
12	37H7618L	+Kit-Sealing	1	
	AEU4150	+Kit-Sundry Parts	1	
		++Insulating Bush		
		++Washers		
		++Shaft Pin		
		++Dowel		
		++Bolts-Fixing Solenoid		
		++Screws		
		++Nuts		
		++Jump Rings		
		++Thrust Collars		
		++Insulation Piece		
13	SH110301L	Screw-Starter to Flywheel Hsg	1	
14	NH11004lL	Nut	2	
15	WL110001L	Washer-Spring	3	
16	BH110091L	Bolt	4	

VS4076

LAND ROVER PARTS LTD

MODEL LR110 - UP TO AUGUST 1986
BLOCK TS 5947
PAGE K 26.04
GROUP K

ENGINE ELECTRICS - 2.5 DIESEL - STARTER MOTOR - PARIS - RHONE

ILL	PART NO	DESCRIPTION	QTY	REMARKS
1	PRC5109	STARTER MOTOR	1	
2	RTC4981	+Inductor with Brush Holder	1	
3	RTC4982	+Pinion Drive Assembly	1	
4	RTC4979	+Shift Lever Assembly	1	
5	RTC4978	+Solenoid	1	
6	RTC4980	+Repair Kit	1	
7	RTC4983	+Gasket Kit	1	
	PRC5538	Earth Cable-Starter to Engine	1	
	SH110301L	Screw-Starter to Flywheel Hsg	1	
	NH110041L	Nut-Starter to Flywheel Hsg	2	
	WL110001L	Spring Washer-Starter to Flywheel Housing	3	
	BH110091L	Bolt-Starter to Flywheel Hsg	4	

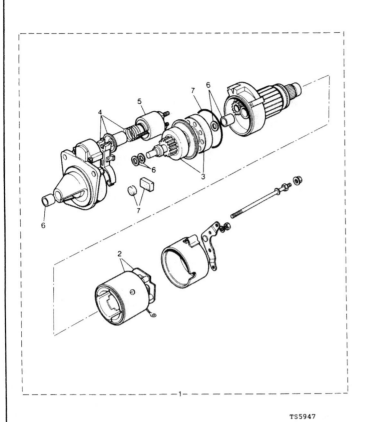

TS5947

MODEL LR110 - UP TO AUGUST 1986
BLOCK 3RE 452A
PAGE K 28
GROUP K

ENGINE ELECTRICS - STARTER MOTOR - 3.5 LITRE - V8 PETROL

ILL	PART NO	DESCRIPTION	QTY	REMARKS
1	RTC5228E	STARTER MOTOR - 3M100	1	
2	RTC837	+Solenoid	1	
3	RTC836	+Kit-Seals	1	
4	RTC830	+Kit-Brushes	1	
5	RTC1323	+Lever-Solenoid	1	
6	RTC834	+Pinion	1	
7	608352	+Bush Kit	1	
8	RTC839	+Kit-Thru Bolt	1	
10	RTC831	+End Cover	1	
11	SS506121L	Screw-Starter/Block	2	
12	WM600061L	Spring Washer	2	
13	WA110061L	Plain Washer	2	
	90608178	Sundry Parts Kit	1	

3RE452A

MODEL LR110 - UP TO AUGUST 1986
BLOCK VS 4062A
PAGE K 28.02
GROUP K

ELECTRICAL - HEADLAMPS

ILL	PART NO	DESCRIPTION	QTY	REMARKS
1	AEU1355	HEADLAMP-RHS	2	
	27H8207L	HEADLAMP-LHS	2	
2	RTC3682	+Light Unit-RHS	2	
	RTC3683	+Light Unit-LHS	2	
	BAU2144	HEADLAMP-QH-RHS	2	)
	AEU1742	HEADLAMP-QH-LHS	2	)Optional
	RTC4615	+Light Unit-QH-RHS	2	)
	PRC5252	+Light Unit-QH-LHS	2	)
3	156206	Cover-Sealing-Bulb-QH	2	
4	515218	Rim Light Unit	2	
5	27H6481L	Seating Rim-Light Unit	2	
6	531586	Gasket-Headlamp	2	
7	600226	Adaptor and Cable	2	
8	AB606022L	Screw	6	
9	BHM7058L	Trimmer Screw Kit	2	
10	589783	Bulb-QH	2	
	PRC2167	Bulb-Yellow-QH	2	
11	78348	Screw)	6	
12	WM702001L	Washer)Headlamp to Body	6	
13	HN2005L	Nut)	6	

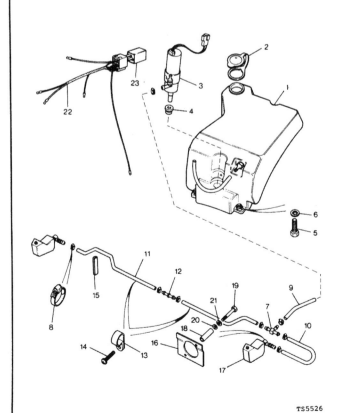

VS 4062A

MODEL LR110 - UP TO AUGUST 1986
BLOCK TS 5526
PAGE K 30
GROUP K

ELECTRICAL - HEADLAMP WASH - EXCEPT AIR CON

ILL	PART NO	DESCRIPTION	QTY	REMARKS
1	PRC3300	Reservoir	1	
2	PRC2854	Cap-Reservoir	1	
3	ADU6409L	Pump	1	
4	ADU6418L	Grommet-Pump	1	
5	78210	Screw-Fixing Reservoir	3	
6	WF600041L	Shakeproof Washer	3	
7	EAM5549L	'T' Piece	1	
8	CJ600041L	Hose Clip	8	
9	PRC3231	Tube-Pump to 'T' Piece	1	
10	PRC3232	Tube-'T' Piece to LH Jet	1	
11	PRC5127	Tube-'T' Piece to Connector	1	
	PRC5127	Tube-Connector to RH Jet	1	
12	PRC3030	Connector	1	
13	C34950L	Clip	2	
14	AB606051L	Screw-Clip Fixing	2	
	WA104001L	Plain Washer	2	
15	DRC1530	Edge Finisher	2	
16	MRC8564	Stiffener Plate	2	
17	PRC2291	Jet and Valve Housing Assembly	2	
18	PRC3250	Spacer Tube-Jet to Panel	4	
19	BH106131L	Bolt-Housing to Body	4	
20	WA106041L	Plain Washer	4	
21	WL106001L	Spring Washer	4	
22	PRC5141	Cable Assembly	1	
23	ADU1784L	Delay Unit	1	

TS5526

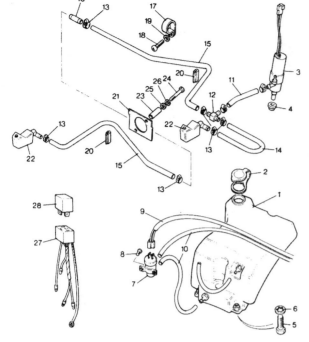

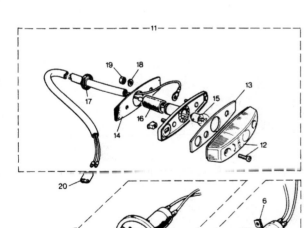

TS5528

MODEL LR110 - UP TO AUGUST 1986
BLOCK TS 5528
PAGE K 30.02
GROUP K

ELECTRICAL - HEADLAMP WASH - WINDSCREEN WASH - AIR CON

ILL	PART NO	DESCRIPTION	QTY	REMARKS
1	PRC3780	RESERVOIR	1	
2	PRC2854	+Cap-Reservoir	1	
3	ADU6409L	Pump	1	
4	ADU6418L	Grommet-Pump	1	
5	78210	Screw-Fixing Reservoir	3	
6	WF600041L	Washer	3	
7	PRC3369	Pump	1	)
8	AB606051L	Screw	2	)Windscreen
9	PRC3794	Cable Assembly	1	)Wash
10	RTC3650	Tubing	A/R	)
11	PRC3231	Tube-Pump to 'T' Piece	1	
12	EAM5549L	'T' Piece	1	
13	CJ600041L	Hose-Clip	8	
14	PRC3232	Tube-'T' Piece to LH Jet	1	
15	PRC5127	Tube-'T' Piece to Connector	1	
	PRC5127	Tube-Connector to RH Jet	1	
16	PRC3030	Connector	1	
17	C34950L	Clip	2	
18	AB606051L	Screw-Clip Fixing	2	
19	WA104001L	Plain Washer	2	
20	DRC1530	Edge Finisher	2	
21	MRC8564	Stiffener Plate	1	
22	PRC2291	Jet & Valve Housing Assembly	2	
23	PRC3250	Spacer Tube-Jet to Panel	4	
24	BH106131L	Bolt-Housing to Body	4	
25	WA106041L	Plain Washer	4	
26	WL106001L	Spring Washer	4	
27	PRC5141	Cable Assembly	1	
28	ADU1784L	Delay Unit	1	

LAND ROVER PARTS LTD

VS4061

MODEL LR110 - UP TO AUGUST 1986
BLOCK VS 4061
PAGE K 32
GROUP K

ELECTRICAL - FRONT SIDE & INDICATOR LAMPS

ILL	PART NO	DESCRIPTION	QTY	REMARKS
1	RTC5012	SIDELAMP-FRONT	2	
2	589284	+Lens	2	
3	570822	+Bulb	2	
4	608004	+Screw and Washer	4	
5	AB606041L	Screw-Lamp to Body	12	
6	AK606021L	Spring Nut-Lamp to Body	12	
7	RTC5013	INDICATOR LAMP-FRONT	2	
8	589285	+Lens	2	
9	264591	+Bulb	2	
10	608004	+Screw and Washer	4	
11	589143	SIDE REPEATER LAMP	2	Optional
12	27H2403L	+Lens Assembly	2	No Longer Available
13	608311	+Gasket	2	
14	608312	+Gasket	2	
15	570822	+Bulb	2	
16	515060	+Grommet	2	No Longer Available
17	233243	+Grommet	2	
18	WM704001L	+Spring Washer	4	
19	257203	+Nut	4	
20	BHA4460	Connector	2	

LAND ROVER PARTS LTD

MODEL LR110 - UP TO AUGUST 1986
BLOCK VS 4058
PAGE K 34
GROUP K

ELECTRICAL - STOP-TAIL AND REAR INDICATOR LAMPS

ILL	PART NO	DESCRIPTION	QTY	REMARKS
1	RTC5523	STOP-TAIL LAMP	2	
2	RTC210	+Lens	2	
3	264590	+Bulb	2	
4	77932	Screw-Lamp to Body	12	
	608004	Screw and Washer	4	
5	RTC5524	INDICATOR LAMP	2	
6	589202	+Lens	2	
7	264591	+Bulb	2	
8	AEU1652	NUMBER PLATE LAMP	1	
9	570822	+Bulb	1	
10	345597	Plinth-Lamp	1	
	PRC3588	Plinth-Lamp	1	HCPU
	257302	Screw	2	
	WL105001L	Spring Washer	2	
11	589026	Cable-No Plate Lamp	1	
	PRC3617	Cable-No Plate Lamp	1	HCPU
12	PRC2516	Rear Fog Lamp	1	
	PRC3299	Reverse Lamp	1	Optional
	RTC4183	+Lens-Red-Rear Fog Lamp	1	
	RTC4184	+Lens-Clear-Reverse Lamp	1	
	RTC4185	+Screw-Lens Fixing	2	
13	264591	+Bulb	1	
14	WA105001L	Plain Washer	2	
15	WL105001L	Spring Washer	2	
16	NH105041L	Nut	2	
17	PRC2876	Cable Assembly-4 Cylinder	1	
	PRC2032	Cable Assembly V8	1	Upto VIN 232762
	PRC4473	Cable Assembly V8	1	From VIN 232763
18	573246	Cable Tie	2	4 Cylinder
19	PRC2911	Switch-Reverse Lamp	1	4 Cylinder
	22A1613L	Locknut-Reverse Lamp Switch	1	4 Cylinder
	PRC1039	Switch-Reverse Lamp	1	V8

VS4058

LAND ROVER PARTS LTD

MODEL LR110 - UP TO AUGUST 1986
BLOCK VS 4267
PAGE K 34.02
GROUP K

ELECTRICAL - REAR REFLECTORS

ILL	PART NO	DESCRIPTION	QTY	REMARKS
1	551595	Reflector	2	)To VIN
2	WM702001L	Washer	2	)222353
3	RTC608	Nut	2	)
4	589877	Reflector) HCPU	2	)To VIN
5	AB606031L	Screw)	4	)222353
4	MUC1715	Reflector)See Note(1)	2	)From VIN
5	AB608041L	Screw)	2	)222354

NOTE(1): From 1st Vehicle Australia.

VS4267

LAND ROVER PARTS LTD

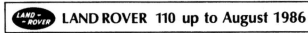
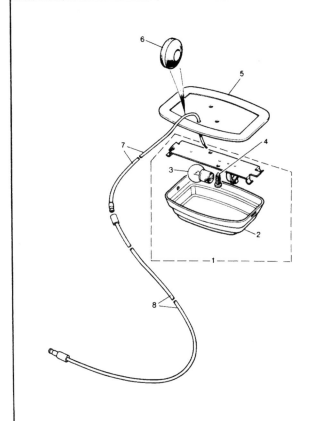

MODEL LR110 - UP TO AUGUST 1986
BLOCK VS 4020
PAGE K 36
GROUP K

ELECTRICAL - INTERIOR LAMP

ILL	PART NO	DESCRIPTION	QTY	REMARKS
1	265295	Interior Lamp Assy	1	
2	320608	+Lens	1	
3	264591	+Bulb	1	
4	AB606041L	Screw	2	
5	334111	Pad-Roof Lamp	1	
6	312856	Grommet	1	
7	PRC2964	Lead-Light to Roof Connection	1	
8	PRC3813	Lead-Switch to Roof Connection	1	

VS4020

LAND ROVER PARTS LTD

476

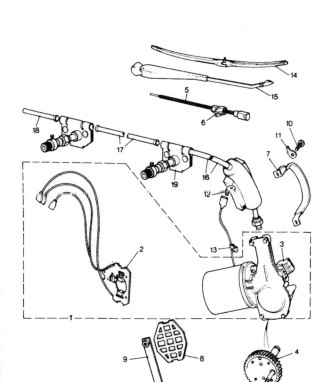

MODEL LR110 - UP TO AUGUST 1986
BLOCK VS 4059
PAGE K 38
GROUP K

ELECTRICAL - WINDSCREEN WIPERS

ILL	PART NO	DESCRIPTION	QTY	REMARKS
1	RTC3867	WINDSCREEN WIPER MOTOR	1	
2	RTC198	+Brush Set	1	
3	520160	+Park Switch	1	
4	608092	Gear-Wiper Motor	1	Note(1)
	517646	Gear-Wiper Motor	1	Note(2)
5	37H5208L	Rack	1	
6	37H3694L	Ferrule	1	
7	BHA4790L	Strap Assembly	1	
8	150844	Pad	1	
9	MTC2607	Nut Plate Assembly	1	
10	SE106161L	Screw	2	
11	505205	Lucar Blade-Wiper Earth	1	
12	90555649	Lucar Blade-Wiper Earth	1	)Pick-Up
13	570351	Cable Clip	1	)
14	PRC2422	Wiper Blade-Spigot Type	2	Note(1)
	PRC4278	Wiper Blade-Hook Type	2	Note(2)
15	PRC3649	Wiper Arm-RHS)Spigot Type	2	)Note(1)
	PRC3650	Wiper Arm-LHS)	2	)
	PRC4276	Wiper Arm-RHS)Hook Type	2	)Note(2)
	PRC4277	Wiper Arm-LHS)	2	)
16	PRC3671	Tube-Motor to Wheelbox-RHS	1	
	PRC3672	Tube-Motor to Wheelbox-LHS	1	
17	PRC2471	Tube-Wheelbox to Wheelbox	1	
18	575047	Tube-Wheelbox End	1	
19	PRC6283	Wheelbox Assembly	2	
	RTC4480	Splined Drum Wiper-Wheelbox	2	
	MUC3933	Cover-Wiper Pinch Bolt	2	Germany

NOTE(1): Spigot Type Arms & Blades To Be Used With
          608092 Wiper Motor Gear.

NOTE(2): Hook Type Arms & Blades To Be Used With
          517646 Wiper Motor Gear.

VS4059

LAND ROVER PARTS LTD

477

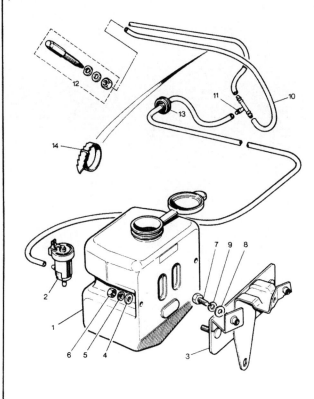

MODEL LR110 - UP TO AUGUST 1986
BLOCK VS 4023A
PAGE K 40
GROUP K

ELECTRICAL - WINDSCREEN WASH-EXCEPT AIR CON

ILL	PART NO	DESCRIPTION		QTY	REMARKS
1	PRC3340	Screenwash Bottle		1	
2	ADU3905	Screenwash Pump		1	
3	PRC3978	Mounting Bracket-RH		1	
	PRC3977	Mounting Bracket-LH		1	
4	WC106047	Plain Washer	) Bottle to	2	
5	WL106007L	Spring Washer	) Mounting	2	
6	NH106047	Nut	) Bracket	2	
7	SE106127	Screw	) Mounting	1	
8	WA106047L	Plain Washer	) Bracket to	1	
9	WL106047	Spring Washer	) Wing Top	1	
10	RTC3650	Tubing		A/R	
11	C15644L	T Piece		1	
12	PRC2437	Screenwash Jet		2	
13	555711	Grommet		1	
14	240429	Cleat		3	

VS4023A

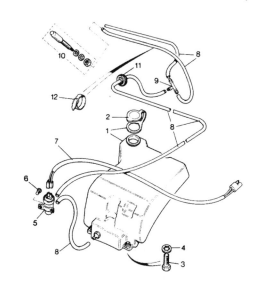

MODEL LR110 - UP TO AUGUST 1986
BLOCK TS 5527
PAGE K 40.02
GROUP K

ELECTRICAL - WINDSCREEN WASH - AIR CON

ILL	PART NO	DESCRIPTION	QTY	REMARKS
1	PRC3786	SCREENWASH BOTTLE	1	
2	PRC2854	+Cap-Bottle	1	
3	78210	Screw	3	
4	WF600041L	Shakeproof Washer	3	
5	PRC3369	Screenwash Pump	1	
6	AB606051L	Screw	2	
7	PRC3794	Cable Assembly	1	
8	RTC3650	Tubing	A/R	
9	C15644	T Piece	1	
10	PRC2437	Screenwash Jet	2	
11	555711	Grommet	1	
12	240429	Cable Cleat	3	

TS5527

MODEL LR110 - UP TO AUGUST 1986
BLOCK VS 4054
PAGE K 42
GROUP K

ELECTRICAL - INSTRUMENT PANEL AND COWL

ILL	PART NO	DESCRIPTION	QTY	REMARKS
1	MTC2808	Cowl-Instrument Panel	1	
	MUC3023	Cowl-Instrument panel-LHS	1	Air Con
2	AZ610081	Drive Screw	5	)
3	AFU1218L	Plain Washer	5	)Cowl to Upper
4	WL105001L	Spring Washer	5	)Crash Rail
	WF702108	Lockwasher	5	)
5	CZA4705L	Lokut Nut	5	)
6	MTC2810	Base Stiffener-Panel Cowl	1	RHS
	MTC2811	Base Stiffener-Panel Cowl	1	LHS
	MUC7598	Base Stiffener-Panel Cowl	1	RHS See Note(1)
	MUC7599	Base Stiffener-Panel Cowl	1	LHS See Note(1)
	CZH3287	Plug-Switch Aperture	1	
7	AB608044L	Screw	4	)
	AFU2636	Sems Drive Screw-LHS	4	)Air Con
8	WF703084	Shakeproof Washer	4	)Cowl to Base
9	AJ608031	Spring Nut	4	)Stiffener
10	MTC5458	Instrument Panel-RHS	1	
	MTC5459	Instrument Panel-LHS	1	
11	AD606044L	Screw	2	)Instrument
12	WK606214L	Cup Washer	2	)Panel Upper
13	AJ606041	Spring Nut	2	)to Cowl
14	AB606044L	Screw	2	)Instrument
15	WF704064	Shakeproof Washer	2	)Panel Lower
16	AJ606041	Spring Nut	2	)to Cowl

NOTE(1): With Aperture For Fuel Changeover Switch.

VS4054

LAND ROVER PARTS LTD

MODEL LR110 - UP TO AUGUST 1986
BLOCK VS 4019
PAGE K 44
GROUP K

ELECTRICAL - INSTRUMENTS

ILL	PART NO	DESCRIPTION	QTY	REMARKS
1	PRC4655	Speedometer-MPH	1	
	PRC4429	Speedometer-KPH	1	
		Speedometer Cable		Two-Piece
2	PRC5567	-Upper) RHS - 4 CYL	1	)Upto VIN
3	PRC5663	-Lower)	1	)266613
	PRC5567	-Upper) RHS - V8	1	)Upto VIN
	PRC5664	-Lower)	1	)267907
	PRC5567	-Upper) LHS	1	)Upto VIN
	PRC5662	-Lower)	1	)267696
		Speedometer Cable		One-Piece
	PRC6022	-RHS-4 Cyl	1	From VIN 266614
	PRC6023	-RHS-V8	1	From VIN 267908
	PRC6021	-LHS	1	From VIN 267697
	RTC5063	Locking Ring	1	
4	PRC7979	Support Bracket-RHS	1	)4 Cylinder
5	PRC2980	Support Bracket-RHS	1	)
	PRC3678	Bracket-Transfer Box	1	V8
	PRC3833	Bracket-Toebox	1	LHS
6	PRC3180	Clip-Speedometer Cable	2	
7	PRC3025	Double Clip-LHS	2	
	PRC3025	Double Clip-Air Cleaner	2	)V8
		Bracket		)
8	PRC3105	Water Temperature Gauge	1	
9	PRC3107	Fuel Gauge	1	
10	MRC8225	Blanking Plug-Clock Aperture	1	
11	PRC3108	Battery Condition Gauge	1	
12	PRC4504	Warning Lamp Module	1	
	PRC4928	Warning Lamp Module	1	See Note(1)
13	AEU2722	+Bulb Holder	13	
14	AEU2723	+Bulb Holder	1	
15	RTC3635	+Bulb-12V	9	
16	AEU2724	+Bulb-6V	1	2.25 Diesel
17	AEU2721	+Printed Circuit	1	

NOTE(1): Fitted To Vehicles With Heated Rear Window.

VS4019

LAND ROVER PARTS LTD

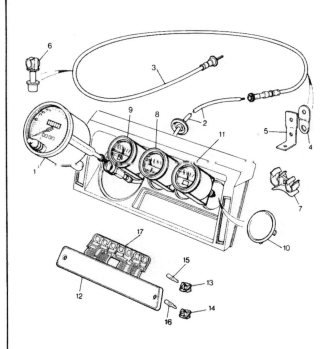

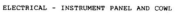

MODEL LR110 - UP TO AUGUST 1986
BLOCK VS 4098
PAGE K 44.02
GROUP K

ELECTRICAL - INSTRUMENTS CONTINUED

ILL	PART NO	DESCRIPTION	QTY	REMARKS
1	PRC2970	Clock	1	
2	PRC3116	Oil Pressure Gauge	1	4 Cylinder
	PRC3122	Oil Pressure Gauge	1	8 Cylinder
	PRC3115	Oil Temperature Gauge	1	
4	346786	Cover-Instruments	1	
5	AB606034	Drive Screw	2	
6	RTC3745	Lokut Nut	2	
7	SP105204	Screw	2	
8	WC105007	Plain Washer	2	
9	WL105004	Lock Washer	2	
10	NH105041L	Nut	2	

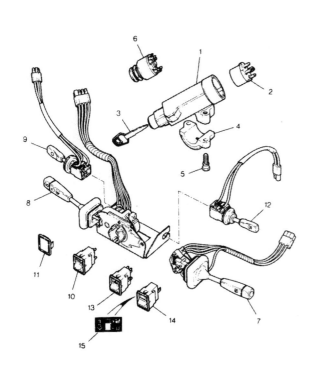

VS4098

482

MODEL LR110 - UP TO AUGUST 1986
BLOCK VS 4052A
PAGE K 46
GROUP K

ELECTRICAL - SWITCHES

ILL	PART NO	DESCRIPTION	QTY	REMARKS
1	NRC3907	STEERING COLUMN LOCK-PETROL	1	)
	NRC3908	STEERING COLUMN LOCK-DIESEL	1	)
2	579085	+Ignition Switch-Petrol	1	)
	PRC2735	+Heater/Start Switch-Diesel	1	)Optional Fitment
3	AAU8276	Key Blank-Range RO 1001-2000	1	)
4	NRC7422	Clamp	1	)
5	51K4001L	Shear Bolt	2	)
6	551508	Ignition Switch-Petrol	1	
	PRC2734	Heater/Start Switch-Diesel	1	
7	PRC3900	Wash Wipe Switch	1	
8	PRC3875	Indicator-Horn-Dipswitch	1	
9	PRC3430	Master Light Switch	1	
10	PRC2497	Panel-Interior Light Switch	1	
11	CZH3827L	Plug-Switch Aperture	3	
12	PRC3432	Switch-Rear Fog Lamp	1	)Optional
13	PRC2278	Switch-Hazard Warning	1	)
14	C38637	Switch-Fuel Changeover	1	
15	PRC5537	Label-Changeover Switch	1	

VS4052A

483

MODEL LR110 - UP TO AUGUST 1986
BLOCK TS 5207
PAGE K 46.02
GROUP K

ELECTRICAL - CIGAR LIGHTER-REAR WASH & HEATED REAR WINDOW

ILL	PART NO	DESCRIPTION	QTY	REMARKS
1	PRC4524	CIGAR LIGHTER	1	
2	DRC8398	+Popout Unit	1	
3	RTC3635	+Bulb	1	
4	PRC4576	Harness	1	
5	PRC3737	Fuse Box	1	
6	RTC4502	Fuse	1	
7	SE105121L	Screw	1	
8	WF105121	Shakeproof Washer	1	
9	PRC4449	Rear Wash Wipe Switch	1	
10	PRC4454	Knob-Wash Wipe Switch	1	
11	PRC4438	Harness	1	
12		Facia Plate		
	MUC1583	Cigar Lighter/Wash Wipe RH	1	
	MUC1584	Cigar Lighter/Wash Wipe LH	1	
	MUC1367	Wash Wipe-LH	1	
	MUC1368	Wash Wipe-RH	1	
	MUC2165	Cigar Lighter	1	
13	SP105204	Screw	2	
14	WC105004L	Plain Washer	2	
15	WL105004	Spring Washer	2	
16	NH105041L	Nut	2	
17	PRC4433	Switch-Heated Rear Window	1	
18	DRC1820	Relay	1	

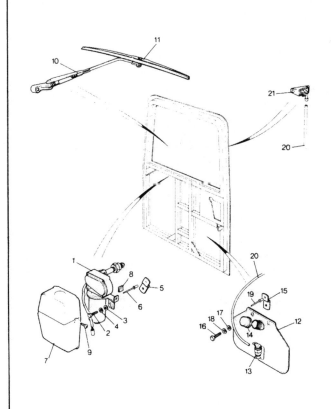

TS5207

MODEL LR110 - UP TO AUGUST 1986
BLOCK TS 5205
PAGE K 46.04
GROUP K

ELECTRICAL - REAR WASH WIPE

ILL	PART NO	DESCRIPTION	QTY	REMARKS
1	PRC4612	Wiper Motor Assembly	1	
2	SR106251L	Screw	1	
3	WA106041L	Plain Washer	1	
4	WL106001L	Spring Washer	1	
5	MUC1286	Mounting Bracket	1	
6	RA610167	Rivet	1	
7	PRC4613	Cover-Wiper Motor	1	
8	AK608141L	Spire Nut	2	
9	AA608044	Screw	2	
10	PRC4230	Rear Wiper Arm	1	
11	PRC3423	Rear Wiper Blade	1	
	PRC4624	Rear Wiper Blade	1	Germany
12	PRC4436	WASHER BAG AND PUMP	1	
13	ADU3905	+Pump	1	
14	RTC3175	+Cap Washer Bag	1	
15	MUC1287	Mounting Bracket	2	
16	SH106201L	Screw	2	
17	WJ106001L	Plain Washer	2	
18	WL106001L	Spring Washer	2	
19	RA610167	Rivet	2	
10	RTC3650	Tubing	A/R	
21	EAM9332	Washer Jet	1	

TS5205

MODEL LR110 - UP TO AUGUST 1986
BLOCK TS 5206
PAGE K 46.06
GROUP K

ELECTRICAL - REAR WASH WIPE AND HEATED REAR WINDOW

ILL	PART NO	DESCRIPTION	QTY	REMARKS
1	PRC4591	Harness	1	
2	BMK1714	Grommet	1	
3	PRC4471	Convoluted Grommet	1	
4	MTC9914	Mounting Bracket	1	
5	MTC9915	Cover-Mounting Bracket	1	
6	AA606044L	Screw	2	
7	AK606011L	Spire Nut	2	
8	AB610041L	Screw	1	
9	WA105001L	Plain Washer	1	
10	3H822L	Grommet-Lower	1	
11	27H5311	Grommet-Upper	1	

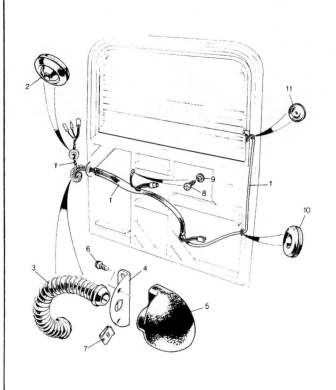

TS5206

LAND ROVER PARTS LTD

486

MODEL LR110 - UP TO AUGUST 1986
BLOCK TS 5517
PAGE K 48.02
GROUP K

ELECTRICAL - CHASSIS HARNESS

ILL	PART NO	DESCRIPTION	QTY	REMARKS
1	PRC3209	Chassis Harness	1	)Upto VIN 243342
	PRC4590	Chassis Harness-Note(1)	1	)
	PRC4970	Chassis Harness	1	)From VIN 243343
	PRC4993	Chassis Harness-Note(1)	1	)Note(2)
2	589452	Grommet	1	
3	AAU3686	Cable Strap	2	
4	C39377L	P Clip	1	
5	SE105121L	Screw	1	
6	WJ105001L	Plain Washer	1	
7	WL105001L	Spring Washer	1	
8	NH105041L	Nut	1	
9	PRC3368	Harness-Tank Unit	1	)
10	PRC3997	Harness-Twin Fuel Tanks	1	)Upto VIN 243342
	PRC4840	Harness-Twin Tanks-Twin Pumps	1	)
	PRC5544	Harness-Rear Tank-Diesel	1	)From VIN
	PRC5602	Harness-Rear Tank-Petrol	1	)243343 Note(2)
	RTC6545	Connector	1	) To Convert
				) PRC5602 Where
				) Necessary
	PRC5603	Harness-Twin Tanks-Diesel	1	)From VIN
	PRC5600	Harness-Twin Tanks-Petrol	1	)243343 Note(2)
	RTC6545	Connector	1	) To Convert
				) PRC5600 Where
				) Necessary
11	DRC1820	Relay	4	4 Cylinder
12	AFU1090L	Cable Clip	3	
13	PRC3537	Clip-Rear Crossmember	1	No Longer Available
14	570753	Flange Finisher	2	
15	269257	Grommet	1	
16	SE105121L	Screw	2	
17	WM702001L	Spring Washer	2	
18	WA105001L	Plain Washer	2	
19	NH105041L	Nut	2	
20	C393771L	Cable Strap	1	
21	SE105121L	Screw	2	
22	WJ105001L	Plain Washer	2	
23	WL105001L	Spring Washer	2	
24	NH105041L	Nut	2	

NOTE(1): Vehicles Fitted With Rear Wash Wipe
          & Heated Rear Window.

NOTE(2): Introduction of In Tank Fuel Pumps.

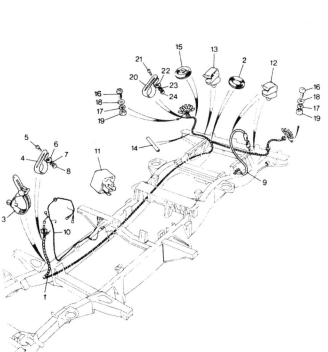

TS5517

LAND ROVER PARTS LTD

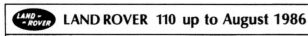
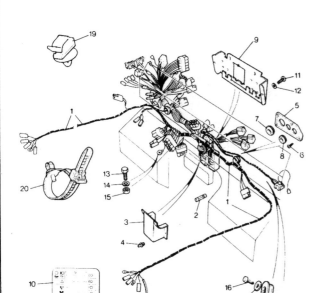

MODEL LR110 - UP TO AUGUST 1986
BLOCK TS 5174
PAGE K 50.02
GROUP K

ELECTRICAL - MAIN HARNESS

ILL	PART NO	DESCRIPTION	QTY	REMARKS
1		MAIN HARNESS-Note(1)		
	PRC3363	-2.25 Petrol	1	
	PRC5319	-2.5 & V8 Petrol	1	
	PRC3362	-2.25 Diesel	1	
	PRC3969	-2.5 Diesel	1	
	PRC5336	-Diesel	1	Note(2)
2	RTC4482	Fuse-5 Amp	2	
	RTC4500	Fuse-10 Amp	1	
	RTC4502	Fuse-15 Amp	6	
	RTC4505	Fuse-25 Amp	1	
	RTC4510	Fuse-35 Amp	1	Air Con
3	PRC3037	Cover-Harness-Dash Centre	1	
4	BRC8089	Rivet-Cover to Dash	4	
5	PRC1333	Bulkhead Grommet Plate	1	
6	78153	Drive Screw	8	
7	338024	Sealing Ring	1	
	338023	Sealing Ring	2	
9	PRC2443	Mounting Panel Fusebox & Relays	1	
10	PRC3389	Label-Fuse Identification	1	
11	SE106121L	Screw	2	
12	WF600041L	Washer-Shakeproof	2	
13	SH106121L	Screw	1	
14	WL106001L	Washer-Spring	1	
15	NH106041L	Nut	1	
16	78417	Drive Screw	1	
17	4034L	Washer-Plain	1	
18	C39377L	P Clip	1	
19	AFU1090L	Clip	A/R	
20	AAU3686	Cable Strap	A/R	
	PRC5123	Cable Assy-Running Light	1	Note(3)

NOTE(1): Fusebox Is Part Of Main Harness
          And Is Not Serviced Separately

NOTE(2): Norway, Finland, Germany, Jan 85 On.

NOTE(3): Norway, Jan 85 On.

TS5174

MODEL LR110 - UP TO AUGUST 1986
BLOCK TS 5175
PAGE K 50.04
GROUP K

ELECTRICAL - ENGINE HARNESS

ILL	PART NO	DESCRIPTION	QTY	REMARKS
1	PRC4019	Engine Harness-4 Cylinder	1	)To Eng No.)11H05638C)& 12J05496C
	PRC4785	Engine Harness-4 Cylinder	1	)From Eng No.)11H05639C)& 12J05497C
	PRC4020	Engine Harness-45 Amp Alternator-4 Cyl Option	1	
	PRC4021	Engine Harness-65 Amp Alternator-4 Cyl Option	1	
	PRC4096	Engine Harness-4 Cyl Air Con	1	
	PRC3979	Engine Harness-V8	1	To VIN232762
	PRC4952	Engine Harness-V8	1	)From VIN232763)To VIN 243342
	PRC3980	Engine Harness 65 Amp Alternator-V8 Option	1	)To VIN232762)
	PRC4953	Engine Harness-V8 Split Charge	1	)From VIN232763)To vin 243342
	PRC4097	Engine Harness-V8 Air Con	1	To VIN232762
	PRC4954	Engine Harness-V8 Air Con	1	)From VIN232763)To VIN 243342
2	PRC3839	Support Bracket-Pump Lead	1	V8
3	568680	Cable Clip	1	)4 Cylinder
	AFU1090L	Cable Clip	4	)
4	RTC3772	Cable Cleat	2	
5	PRC1794	Support Bracket-Cable	1	V8
6	PRC4376	Lead-Coil to Fuel Shut Off Solenoid	1	)4 Cylinder)Petrol
7	PRC3702	Clip	1	)
8	PRC3494	Mounting Plate-Clip	1	)
	PRC4994	Engine Harness-V8	1	)From VIN 243343
	PRC4995	Engine Harness-V8 Split Charge	1	)Note(1))
	PRC4996	Engine Harness-V8 Air Con	1	)

NOTE(1): Introduction Of In Tank Fuel Pumps.

TS5175

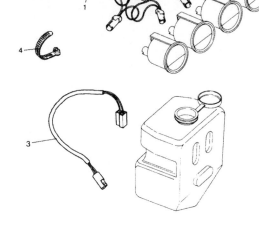

```
MODEL LR110 - UP TO AUGUST 1986
BLOCK TS 5176
PAGE K 52.02
GROUP K

ELECTRICAL - HARNESS CONTINUED
```

ILL	PART NO	DESCRIPTION	QTY	REMARKS
1	PRC7326	Harness-Instruments	1	
	RTC6164	+Bulb	4	
2	PRC4460	Harness-Additional Instruments	1	
3	PRC3101	Harness-Main to Washer Pump	1	
4	C45099L	Cable Cleat	4	
5	573289	Bulb	A/R	
6	PRC3095	Harness-Main to PDWA Switch	1	
	PRC5316	Cable Assy-Fuel Shut Off	1	)
	DRC1820	Relay	1	)Germany
	AB608031L	Screw	1	)
	WA105001L	Plain Washer	1	)

TS5176

LAND ROVER PARTS LTD

```
MODEL LR110 - UP TO AUGUST 1986
BLOCK TS 6328
PAGE K 54.02
GROUP K

ELECTRICAL - SPLIT CHARGE FACILITY
```

ILL	PART NO	DESCRIPTION	QTY	REMARKS
1	PRC4021	Engine Harness-4 Cyl	1	
	PRC3980	Engine Harness-V8	1	Upto VIN 232762
	PRC4953	Engine Harness-V8	1	From VIN 232763
2	PRC4092	Diode	1	
3	SH108201L	Screw-Diode Mounting	2	
4	WA108001	Plain Washer	2	
5	WL108001L	Spring Washer	2	
6	NH108041L	Nut	2	
7	PRC4082	Lead-Terminal Post to Diode	1	V8
	PRC4083	Lead-Terminal Post to Diode	1	4 Cylinder
8	PRC4084	Lead-Diode to Battery	1	
9	PRC4085	Lead-Diode to Terminal Box	1	
10	531604	Terminal Mounting Bracket	1	
11	532736	Terminal B+	1	
12	525569	Terminal B-	1	
13	AR608031L	Drive Screw	6	
14	WE703081	Shakeproof Washer	6	
15	SE106201L	Screw-Earth	1	
16	WL106001L	Spring Washer	1	
17	NH106041L	Nut	1	
18	C22257L	TERMINAL POST ASSY	1	
19	565847	+Insulation Bush	1	
20	3830L	+Plain Washer	2	
21	575014	+Spring Washer	2	
22	90575015	+Nut	2	
23	PRC2978	Terminal Post Bracket	1	V8
24	PRC3247	Terminal Post Bracket	1	4 Cylinder
25	SH106161L	Screw-Fixing Bracket	2	)
26	WA106041L	Plain Washer	2	)4 Cylinder
27	WL106001L	Spring Washer	2	)RHS
28	NH106041L	Nut	2	)
29	PRC3180	Clip	1	
30	13H9157	Double Clip	5	V8
	13H9157	Double Clip	3	4 Cylinder

TS6328

LAND ROVER PARTS LTD

MODEL LR110 - UP TO AUGUST 1986
BLOCK TS 6540
PAGE K 56
GROUP K

ELECTRICAL - HORN - FLASHER UNIT - RELAYS

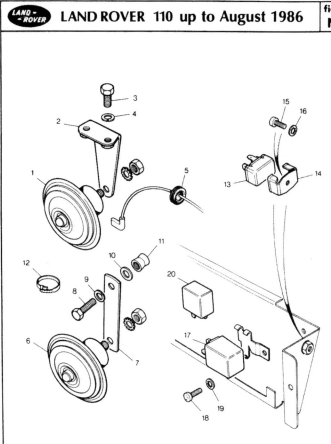

ILL	PART NO	DESCRIPTION	QTY	REMARKS
1	PRC2057	Horn	1	
2	PRC1984	Mounting Bracket	1	
3	SH106141L	Screw	2	
4	WL106001L	Spring Washer	2	
5	233244	Grommet	1	
6	PRC2057	Horn	1	)
7	PRC4456	Mounting Bracket	2	)Additional
8	SH108251L	Screw)Mounting	1	)Horn For
9	WL108001L	Spring Washer)Bracket to	1	)Middle East
10	4868L	Spacer Washer)Chassis	1	)
11	NN108021	Nutsert)Crossmember	1	)
12	C43640	Cable Cleat	3	)
13	RTC3562	Flasher Unit	1	
14	567959	Mounting Clip	1	
15	SE105101L	Screw	1	
16	WF105001L	Shakeproof Washer	1	
17	PRC2239	Hazard Flasher Unit	1	)Optional
18	SE106121L	Screw	1	)
19	WF106001L	Shakeproof Washer	1	)
20	DRC1820	Relay-Brake System Check	1	
	DRC1820	Relay-Starter	1	)Petrol Engine
				)Vehicles Only
	DRC1820	Relay-Fuel Changeover	2	Optional
	DRC1820	Relay	4	)
	SE105101L	Screw	2	)Norway
	WA105001L	Plain Washer	4	)Jan 1985
	WL105001L	Spring Washer	2	)Onwards
	NH105041L	Nut	2	)

TS 6540

LAND ROVER PARTS LTD

MODEL LR110 - UP TO AUGUST 1986
BLOCK TS 6382
PAGE K 56.02
GROUP K

ELECTRICAL - AIR CONDITIONING - ELECTRICS

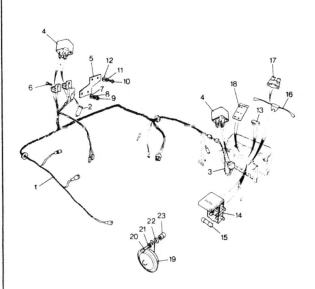

ILL	PART NO	DESCRIPTION	QTY	REMARKS
1	PRC4208	Cable Assembly-Main Fans	1	
2	AAU5034	+Diode	1	
3	PRC3905	Cable-Relay Extension	1	
4	DRC1820	Relay-Blower Fan	1	
	DRC1820	Relay-Condenser Fan	1	
	DRC1820	Relay-Comp.Clutch	1	
5	PRC3738	Bracket-Relay Connectors	1	
6	SE105121L	Screw	2	)Relay
7	WA105001L	Plain Washer	2	)Connectors
8	WL105001L	Spring Washer	2	)to Bracket
9	NM105011	Nut	2	)
10	SE105121L	Screw	2	)
11	WA105001L	Plain Washer	2	)Bracket
12	WL105001L	Spring Washer	2	)to Wing
13	DRC1530	Edge Finisher	A/R	
14	PRC3737	Fusebox	1	
15	RTC4510	Fuse 35A-Condenser Fans	1	
	RTC4500	Fuse 10A-Clutch	1	
16	PRC4311	Inline Fuse Assembly	1	
17	RTC4507	+Fuse	1	
18	PRC4306	Label	1	
19	PRC4321	Horn	1	
	PRC3948	Mounting Bracket	1	
20	SH106161L	Screw	1	
21	WA106001L	Spring Washer	1	
22	WA106001L	Plain Washer	1	
23	NH106041L	Nut	1	

TS6382

LAND ROVER PARTS LTD

MODEL LR110 - UP TO AUGUST 1986
BLOCK VS 4241
PAGE K 56.04
GROUP K

ELECTRICAL - RADIO AERIAL AND SPEAKERS

ILL	PART NO	DESCRIPTION	QTY	REMARKS
1	PRC4327	Radio Aerial Assembly	1	
2	PRC4305	Radio Speaker Assembly	2	
3	AD606074L	Screw	8	
4	WA104004L	Washer	8	
5	PRC4309	Harness	1	
	PRC4595	Radio Fitting Kit	1	

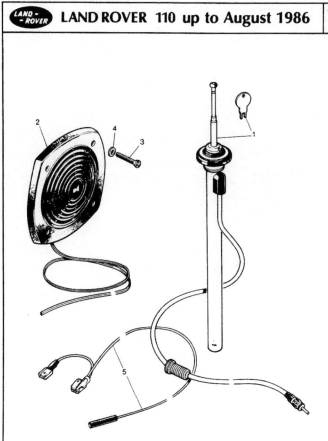

VS4241

LAND ROVER PARTS LTD

494

MODEL LR110 - UP TO AUGUST 1986
BLOCK VS 4060
PAGE K 58
GROUP K

ELECTRICAL - BATTERY

ILL	PART NO	DESCRIPTION	QTY	REMARKS
	RTC5892	Battery-11 Plate-Wet	1	)Petrol
	RTC5892DC	Battery-11 Plate-Dry	1	)
	RTC4598	Battery-14 Plate-Wet	1	)Diesel
	RTC4598DC	Battery-14 Plate-Dry	1	)From Oct 84
	RTC4599	Battery-15 Plate-Wet	1	)Diesel
	RTC4599DC	Battery-15 Plate-Dry	1	)To Oct 84
2	NRC5338	Battery Cover	1	Petrol
	NRC5387	Battery Cover	1	Diesel
3	MTC6302	Battery Spacer-Petrol	1	
	NRC9630	Battery Spacer-Diesel	1	From Vin 222578
4	MRC7132	Bolt-Battery Clamping	2	Upto VIN 222577
	MUC3201	Bolt-Battery Clamping	1	)From VIN 222578
	MRC7132	Bolt-Battery Clamping	1	)
5	AFU1271	Washer	2	)Alternatives
	WA106041L	Washer-Plain	2	)
6	AFU1272	Wing Nut	2	)Alternatives
	NH106041L	Nut	4	)
		Cable-Battery		
7	PRC1860	Positive-4 Cyl Petrol	1	
	PRC2230	Positive-V8	1	
	PRC4332	Positive-Diesel	1	Upto VIN 222577
	PRC4616	Positive-Diesel	1	From VIN 222578
8	PRC1859	Negative-Petrol	1	
	PRC4333	Negative-Diesel	1	Upto VIN 222577
	PRC4617	Negative-Diesel	1	From VIN 222578
9	PRC2015	Cable-Starter to Earth	1	Diesel
10	PRC3625	Cable-Engine Earth	1	
11	SH108251L	Setscrew	2	
12	WA108051L	Washer-Plain	2	
13	WL108001L	Washer-Lock	2	
14	NH108041L	Nut	2	

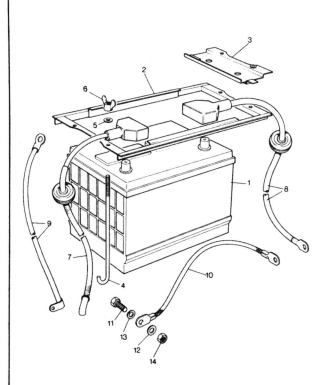

VS4060

LAND ROVER PARTS LTD

495

GROUP L

CHASSIS AND BODY

MASTER INDEX

MODEL LR110 - UP TO AUGUST 1986
BLOCK VS 4065A
PAGE L 2
GROUP L

CHASSIS

ILL	PART NO	DESCRIPTION	QTY	REMARKS
1		CHASSIS FRAME		
	NTC2768	2.25 Litre	1	)NOTE(1)
	NRC8459	V8	1	)
	NRC9564	2.5 Litre	1	)
	NTC2768	4 Cylinder	1	)NOTE(2)
	NTC2769	V8	1	)
2	NRC8421	Rear Crossmember	1	Upto VIN272317
	NTC1725	Rear Crossmember	1	)
3	NRC9749	Support Bracket-Tailboard Hinge	2	)
4	MRC5757	Nut Plate	2	)From
5	SH108201L	Screw	4	)VIN272318
6	WC108051L	Plain Washer	4	)
	RTC3354	Fitting Kit-Rear Crossmember	1	
7	NRC7436	Toe Box Support-RH	1	
	NRC7435	Toe Box Support-LH	1	
8	NRC7131	Packing Piece-Toe Box	6	
9	AFU1499	Screw	4	
10	WA108051L	Plain Washer	16	
11	WL108001L	Spring Washer	8	
12	NH108041L	Nut	6	
13	BH108201L	Bolt	4	
14	WC108051L	Plain Washer	4	
15	NRC7164	Bridge Plate-LH	1	
	NRC7165	Bridge Plate-RH	1	
16	NH108041L	Nut	4	
17	3898	Plain Washer	4	
18	NRC5528	Detachable Crossmember	1	
19	BH110201L	Bolt	4	
20	SH110251L	Screw	4	
21	WC110061L	Plain Washer	12	
22	WL110001L	Spring Washer	8	
23	NRC5485	'D' Washer	4	
24	NH110041L	Nut	8	
25	NRC6935	Grommet-Jacking Bracket	2	

NOTE(1): Up To VIN243977 RHS, VIN244542 LHS
NOTE(2): From VIN243978 RHS, VIN244543 LHS

VS 4065A

LAND ROVER PARTS LTD

MODEL LR110 - UP TO AUGUST 1986
BLOCK VS 4066
PAGE L 4
GROUP L

CHASSIS

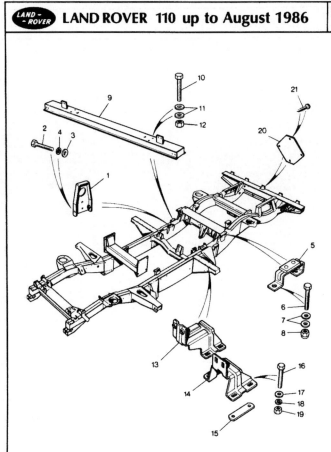

ILL	PART NO	DESCRIPTION	QTY	REMARKS
1	NRC8641	No.1 Body Floor Support Brkt	2	)
2	SH106201	Screw	6	)
3	WA106041L	Plain Washer	6	)
4	WL106001	Spring Washer	6	)Pick Up.
5	NRC5478	No.2 Body Floor Support Brkt	2	)
6	SH108251L	Screw	4	)
7	WA108051L	Plain Washer	4	)
8	NY108041L	Nut	4	)
9	NRC4171	Crossmember Body Mounting	1	)
10	SH108701	Screw	4	)Station Wagon
11	WA108051L	Plain Washer	8	)
12	NY108041L	Nut	4	)
13	NRC7053	Body Mounting Bracket	4	Pick Up.
	NRC7053	Body Mounting Bracket-Outer	2	)Chassis Cab
	NRC6951	Body Mounting Bracket-Inner	2	)
14	NRC5665	Body Mounting Bracket	4	Station Wagon.
15	NRC4693	Spreader Plate	8	
16	SH106201	Screw	16	
17	WC106041	Plain Washer	16	
18	WL106041	Spring Washer	16	
19	NH106041L	Nut	16	
20	NRC4966	Blanking Plate	1	
21	SL106121	Taptite Screw	4	

VS4066

LAND ROVER PARTS LTD

498

MODEL LR110 - UP TO AUGUST 1986
BLOCK VS 3908
PAGE L 4.02
GROUP L

BODY - FRONT BUMPER, BUMPERETTE, UNDER RIDER BAR AND LIFTING RING

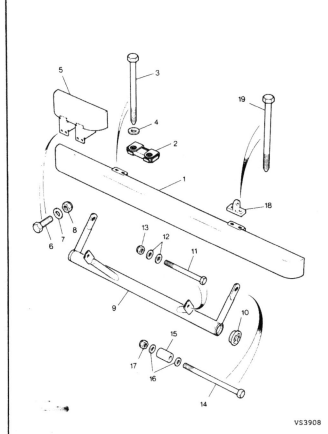

ILL	PART NO	DESCRIPTION	QTY	REMARKS
1	NRC9211	Bumper-Front	1	
2	NRC6994	Tapping Block	2	
3	AFU1386	Bolt	4	
4	WA110061L	Washer-Plain	4	
5	NRC4733	Bumperette-Front	2	)
6	SH110251L	Screw	16	) Optional
7	WA110061L	Washer-Plain	16	)
8	NY110041L	Nyloc Nut	16	)
9	NRC7009	Under-Rider Protection Bar	1	)
10	NRC5886	Blanking Plug	2	)
11	BH110241L	Bolt	2	)
12	WA110061L	Washer-Plain	4	)
13	NY110041L	Nut-Nyloc	2	)Optional
14	253952	Bolt	2	)
15	NRC5627	Spacer	1	)
16	WC112081	Washer-Plain	2	)
	2222	Washer-Plain	2	)
17	252164	Locknut	2	)
18	559882	Lifting and Towing Ring	2	)Optional
19	AFU1387	Bolt	4	)
	NRC7571	Protection Cover-Front Bumper	4	)Germany
	NRC7439	Protection Pad-Front Bumper	2	)
	78248	Rivet	8	)

VS3908

LAND ROVER PARTS LTD

499

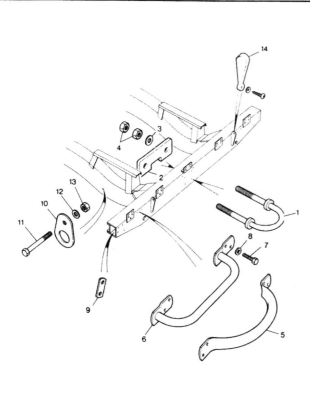

MODEL LR110 - UP TO AUGUST 1986
BLOCK TS 5198
PAGE L 4.04
GROUP L

BODY - RECOVERY RING, LIFTING HANDLE

ILL	PART NO	DESCRIPTION	QTY	REMARKS
1	NRC5396	Recovery Ring	1	
2	562756	Distance Piece	1	
3	4233	Washer	2	
4	NH116041L	Nut	4	
5	300816	Lifting Handle	2	)
6	NRC5606	Lifting Handle-RH	1	)Alternatives
	NRC5607	Lifting Handle-LH	1	)
7	SH108161L	Screw	8	
	SE108161L	Screw	8	Germany
8	WA108051L	Washer-Plain	8	
9	NRC5804	Nut Plate	4	
10	90577509	Recovery and Lashing Ring	4	Front and Rear
11	BH110241L	Bolt-Front Ring	2	
	BH110221L	Bolt-Rear Ring	2	
12	217245	Washer-Plain	4	
13	NY110041L	Nut-Nyloc	4	
14	NRC7425	Protective Cover-Tailboard Hinge	2	Germany

TS5198

 **LAND ROVER PARTS LTD**

MODEL LR110 - UP TO AUGUST 1986
BLOCK TS 5130
PAGE L 4.06
GROUP L

BODY - REAR BUMPERETTES, LIFTING RINGS

ILL	PART NO	DESCRIPTION	QTY	REMARKS
1	NRC4708	Bumperette-RH	1	
	NRC4709	Bumperette-LH	1	
2	BH110141L	Bolt	8	
3	WA110061L	Washer-Plain	8	
4	WL110001L	Washer-Spring	8	
5	NY110041L	Nut	8	
6	NRC4853	Lifting Ring	2	
7	NRC4854	Backing Plate	2	
8	BH110181L	Bolt	4	
9	WA110061L	Washer-Plain	4	
10	WL110001L	Washer-Spring	4	
11	NY110041L	Nut	4	

TS5130

 **LAND ROVER PARTS LTD**

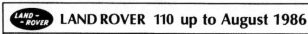
MODEL LR110 - UP TO AUGUST 1986
BLOCK TS 5138
PAGE L 6
GROUP L

BODY - RADIATOR GRILLE

ILL	PART NO	DESCRIPTION	QTY	REMARKS
		RADIATOR GRILLE PANEL		
1	MTC4837	Standard	1	
	MTC1810	When Oil Cooler Fitted	1	
	MUC6112	Air Con	1	
2	MRC9544	Seal-When Oil Cooler Fitted	1	
3	AB606057	Drive Screw	4	
4	WC105007	Plain Washer	4	
5	RTC3745	Lokut Nut	4	
6	SH108201L	Screw	2	
7	WL108001L	Spring Washer	2	
8	WA108051L	Plain Washer	2	
9	NJ108061L	Nut Retainer	2	
	MTC6332	Mounting Bracket-Grille Panel	2	)
		Side		)
	AB614065L	Drive Screw	2	)Air Con
	WL106005L	Spring Washer	2	)
	WA106045	Plain Washer	2	)
	AK612011L	Spring Nut	2	)

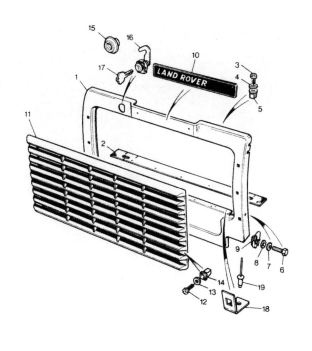

TS5138

LAND ROVER PARTS LTD

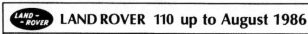
MODEL LR110 - UP TO AUGUST 1986
BLOCK TS 5138
PAGE L 6.02
GROUP L

BODY - RADIATOR GRILLE

ILL	PART NO	DESCRIPTION	QTY	REMARKS
		FRONT NAMEPLATE		
10	MTC9838	Self Adhesive	1	Note(3)
11	MTC3862	Grille	1	
12	AB614085	Screw)	8	
13	WA106045	Plain Washer) Except	8	
	WL106005L	Spring Washer) Air Con	2	
14	CZK3164	Lokut Nut)	8	
	SE105161L	Screw)	4	
	WC105001L	Plain Washer) Air Con	4	
	WF105001L	Shakeproof Washer)	4	
15	338023	Plug	1	
16		BONNET LOCK KIT		
	RTC3023	Except Air Con	1	)
	RTC3036	Air Con	1	)Note(2)
		Barrel and Keys	A/R	)
17		Key Blank	A/R	)
18	MTC6827	Mounting Bracket	2	)Note(1)
19	RA610183	Rivet	2	)
	MTC5603	Catch Lever and Hook) Air	1	
	AFU1350	Monobolt) Con	2	

NOTES:
(1): Not Required When Chaff Guard Fitted
(2): Refer to 'Barrel and Key Sets'
(3): Upto 1984 Facelift.
     For 1984 Facelift-Refer to 'Nametapes and Bodytapes'.

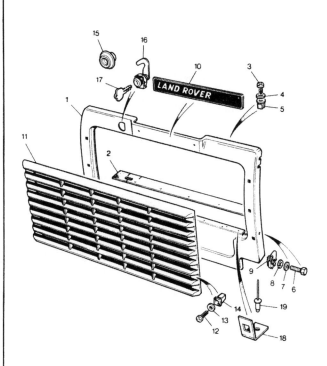

TS5138

LAND ROVER PARTS LTD

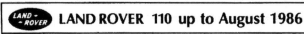

MODEL LR 110 - UP TO AUGUST 1986
BLOCK TS 5201
PAGE L 6.10
GROUP L

BODY - CHAFF GUARD/HAND GUARD

ILL	PART NO	DESCRIPTION	QTY	REMARKS
1	MTC4007	Chaff Guard-Except Air Con	1	
	MTC4220	Hand Guard-Air Con	1	
2	MTC4829	Seal	1	
3	MTC4826	Clamp Strip	1	
4	RA612253L	Rivet	7	
5	WA105001L	Plain Washer	2	

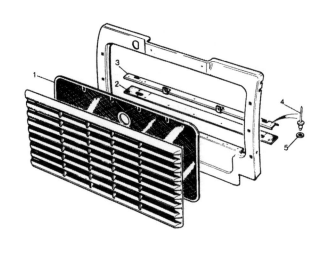

TS5201

 LAND ROVER PARTS LTD

MODEL LR110 - UP TO AUGUST 1986
BLOCK VS 3793
PAGE L 8
GROUP L

BODY - GRILLE TOP PANEL AND BRACE

ILL	PART NO	DESCRIPTION	QTY	REMARKS
1	MTC7170	Grille Top Panel-Standard	1	
	MTC7170	Grille Top Panel-Air Con	1	
2	SH108201L	Screw	4	
3	WL108001L	Spring Washer	4	
4	WA108051L	Plain Washer	4	
5	MTC3982	Cross Brace Tube-RH	1	
6	MTC3983	Cross Brace Tube-LH	1	
7	MRC6977	Bonnet Catch	1	
	MTC4932	Bonnet Catch-Air Con	1	
8	MRC6978	Washer Plate	1	
	MTC7140	Washer Plate-Air Con	1	
	NH106045	Nut (Washer Plate)-Air Con	2	
9	AFU1203	Screw	2	
10	AFU1080	Plain Washer	2	
11	WL106001L	Spring Washer	2	
12	SH108201L	Screw	2	
13	WA108051L	Plain Washer	2	
14	WL108001L	Spring Washer	2	
15	NH108041L	Nut	2	
	NY108041L	Nyloc Nut-Air Con	2	

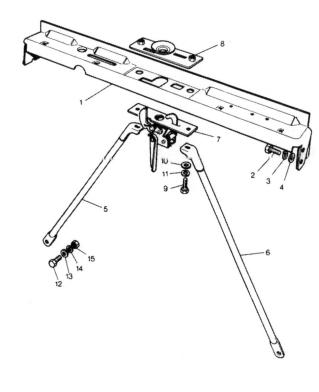

VS3793

 LAND ROVER PARTS LTD

MODEL LR110 - UP TO AUGUST 1986
BLOCK VS 3805
PAGE L 10
GROUP L

BODY - RADIATOR BAFFLE PLATE

ILL	PART NO	DESCRIPTION	QTY	REMARKS
	MRC9393	Baffle Plate RH	1	)
1	MRC9394	Baffle Plate LH	1	)
2	MRC8269	Backing Plate	2	)
3	MRC8047	Seal	2	)Except
4	RA612183	Rivet	8	)4 Cyl Diesel
5	SH106161	Screw	4	)and V8
6	WM106001	Spring Washer	4	)
7	WA106041L	Plain Washer	4	)
8	NH106041L	Nut	4	)
9	235113	Grommet-LH Side	1	)

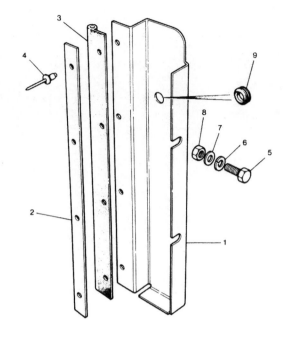

VS3805

LAND ROVER PARTS LTD

506

MODEL LR110 - UP TO AUGUST 1986
BLOCK VS 3794
PAGE L 12
GROUP L

BODY - BONNET

ILL	PART NO	DESCRIPTION	QTY	REMARKS
1	RTC6213	Bonnet	1	
2	MRC9244	Hinge	2	
3	SF106161	Screw	6	
4	WB106041	Plain Washer	6	
5	WL106001L	Spring Washer	6	
6	NH106041L	Nut	6	
7	346849	Bush	2	
8	MRC5016	Buffer-Bonnet Stop	4	
9	SE105141	Screw	8	
10	WA105001	Plain Washer	16	
11	NY105041	Nyloc Nut	8	
12	MRC9995	Bonnet Striker Pin	1	
13	MRC4501	Staple	1	)Note(1)
14	78248	Rivet	2	)

NOTE(1): Required When Bonnet Lock Fitted.

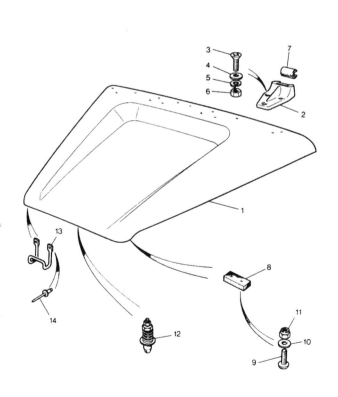

VS3794

LAND ROVER PARTS LTD

507

MODEL LR110 - UP TO AUGUST 1986
BLOCK VS 3795
PAGE L 14
GROUP L

BODY - BONNET PROP

ILL	PART NO	DESCRIPTION	QTY	REMARKS
1	MUC4208	Bonnet Prop Link Assembly	1	
2	336535	Pivot Pin	1	
3	ADU3430	Retainer Clip	1	
4	WS108001L	Spring Washer	1	
5	AFU1104	Plain Washer	1	
6	PS104127	Split Pin	1	
7	MTC2220	Bonnet Prop	1	
8	WS600061	Spring Washer	1	
9	WA110061L	Plain Washer	1	
10	PS106161	Split Pin	1	
11	MRC7623	Clip	1	
12	SP104101	Screw	1	
13	WL104001L	Spring Washer	1	
14	NH104041L	Nut	1	

VS3795

508

MODEL LR 110 - UP TO AUGUST 1986
BLOCK VS 3796
PAGE L 16
GROUP L

BODY - SPARE WHEEL MOUNTING ON BONNET - TYPE A

ILL	PART NO	DESCRIPTION	QTY	REMARKS
1	MTC3594	Plate	1	
2	RA612183	Rivet	11	
3	MTC4570	Reinforcement	2	
4	RA612183	Rivet	4	
5	MRC4619	Buffer	4	
6	WB108051L	Plain Washer	4	
7	NY108041L	Nyloc Nut	4	
8	MTC3598	Clamping Plate	1	
9	SH105161L	Screw	3	
10	WA105001L	Plain Washer	6	
11	WL105001L	Spring Washer	3	
12	NH105041L	Nut	3	
13	MRC5063	Retainer	1	
14	MRC4473	Bolt	2	
15	WD112081L	Plain Washer	2	

VS3796

509

MODEL LR110 - UP TO AUGUST 1986
BLOCK TS 5764
PAGE L 16.10
GROUP L

BODY - SPARE WHEEL MOUNTING ON BONNET - TYPE B

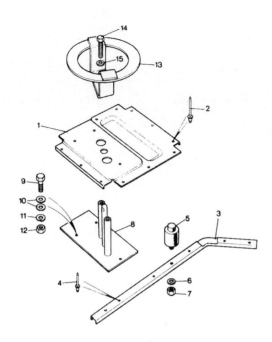

ILL	PART NO	DESCRIPTION	QTY	REMARKS
1	MUC2443	Plate	1	
2	RA612183	Rivet	11	
3	MUC6418	Reinforcement Channel-RH	1	
	MUC6419	Reinforcement Channel-LH	1	
4	RA612183	Rivet	10	
5	MRC4619	Buffer	4	
6	WB108051L	Plain Washer	4	
7	NY108041L	Nyloc Nut	4	
8	MUC2442	Clamping Plate	1	
9	SH105161L	Screw	3	
10	WA105001L	Plain Washer	6	
11	WL105001L	Spring Washer	3	
12	NH105041L	Nut	3	
13	MUC2440	Retainer	1	
14	MRC4473	Bolt	2	
15	WD112081L	Plain Washer	2	

TS5764

 LAND ROVER PARTS LTD

510

MODEL LR110 - UP TO AUGUST 1986
BLOCK VS 4254
PAGE L 18
GROUP L

BODY - FRONT WINGS

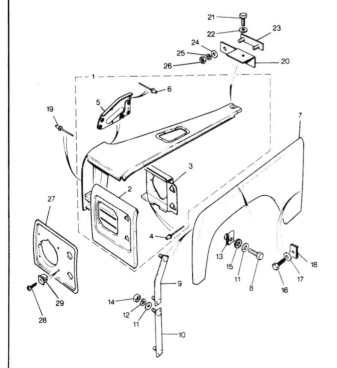

ILL	PART NO	DESCRIPTION	QTY	REMARKS
1	RTC6232	FRONT WING SPOTWELD ASSY RH	1	
	RTC6231	FRONT WING SPOTWELD ASSY LH	1	
	RTC6233	FRONT WING SPOTWELD ASSY LH	1	Air Con RHD
2	RTC6214	+Nose Panel RH	1	
	RTC6215	+Nose Panel LH	1	
	AM604051L	+Acme Screw)Nose Panel	6	
	3900L	+Plain Washer)to Wing Top	6	
	79246	+Spring Nut)	6	
3	MTC2062	+Headlamp Mounting Panel RH	1	
	MTC2063	+Headlamp Mounting Panel LH	1	
4	78248	+Rivet	8	
5	MRC6051	+Tie Plate RH	1	
	MRC6052	+Tie Plate LH	1	
6	78248	+Rivet	8	
7	RTC6235	Outer Panel RH	1	
	RTC6236	Outer Panel LH	1	
8	AM604051L	Acme Screw	22	
11	3900L	Plain Washer	22	
	79246	Spire Nut	20	
13	AH614011L	Spring Nut	2	
15	MUC9339	Fibre Washer	4	
8	SH106161L	Screw	14	)
9	MTC7435	Bolt Plate Upper	2	)
10	MTC7436	Bolt Plate Lower	2	) Note(1)
11	WA106041L	Plain Washer	22	)
12	WL106001L	Spring Washer	22	)
13	NJ106061L	Nut Retainer	14	)
14	NH106041L	Nut	8	)

NOTE(1): For Earlier Condition Front Wings Only
         Not Required For The Front Wings Listed Above.

VS4254

 LAND ROVER PARTS LTD

511

MODEL LR110 - UP TO AUGUST 1986
BLOCK VS 4254
PAGE L 18.02
GROUP L

BODY - FRONT WINGS - CONTINUED

ILL	PART NO	DESCRIPTION	QTY	REMARKS
16	AM605061	Acme Bolt	8	
17	WC108051L	Plain Washer	8	
18	78393	Spire Nut	8	
19	RU612373L	Rivet-Wing Support to Radiator Closing Panel	8	
	MTC2136	Fixing Bracket RH	1	
20	MRC8926	Fixing Bracket LH	1	
21	GG106167	Screw	2	
22	AAU9036	Plain Washer	2	
23	MTC2704	Fixing Plate	2	
24	RTC609	Plain Washer	4	
25	WM106001L	Spring Washer	4	
26	NH106041L	Nut	4	
27	MTC7769	Finisher-Headlamp Surround LH	1	
	MTC7770	Finisher-Headlamp Surround RH	1	
28	AB608044L	Drive Screw	12	
	AW606084	Self Drilling Screw	4	
29	79051	Expansion Nut	12	
	MUC3590	Wing Support Assembly-RHD	1	)Air Con
	MUC3601	Cleat-Wing Support	1	)

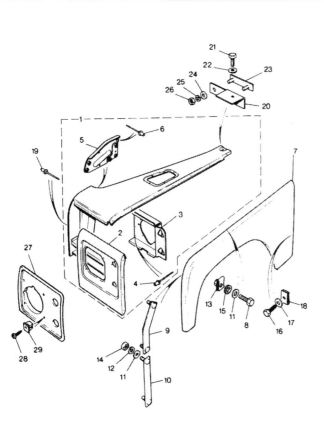

VS4254

LAND ROVER PARTS LTD

512

MODEL LR110 - UP TO AUGUST 1986
BLOCK VS 3798A
PAGE L 20
GROUP L

BODY - FRONT WINGS - CONTINUED

ILL	PART NO	DESCRIPTION	QTY	REMARKS
	MTC5120	Wheelarch RH	1	
1	MTC5119	Wheelarch LH	1	
	MTC7253	Wheelarch RH-Air Con LHD	1	
	MUC3094	Wheelarch LH-Air Con RHD	1	
2	AB614061L	Drivescrew	8	
3	AFU1069	Plain Washer	8	
4	RTC3744	Lokut Nut	8	
	MRC9735	Stay RH-RHD	1	
5	MRC9734	Stay LH-LHD	1	
6	SH106161L	Screw	4	
7	WA106041L	Plain Washer	4	
8	WL106001L	Spring Washer	4	
9	NH106041L	Nut	2	
10	NN106021	Blind Anchor Nut	2	
11	MRC9520	Cover-Front Suspension	2	
12	AR608021L	Screw	12	
13	SH108251L	Screw	4	
	SH108501L	Screw	2	
14	AFU1079	Plain Washer	12	
15	WM600051L	Spring Washer	6	
16	NH108041L	Nut	6	
17	MRC4037	Shim	12	

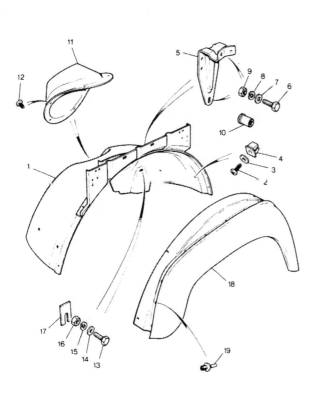

VS3798A

513

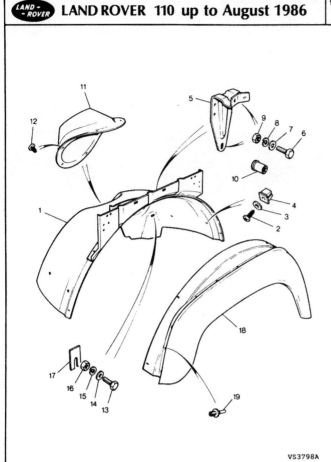

MODEL LR110 - UP TO AUGUST 1986
BLOCK VS 3798A
PAGE L 20.02
GROUP L

BODY - FRONT WINGS - CONTINUED

ILL	PART NO	DESCRIPTION	QTY	REMARKS
18		EYEBROW MOULDING - FRONT WING LH		
	MRC9377	Natural Black	1	
	MTC6875AA	Arizona Tan	1	
	MTC6875AE	Russet	1	
	MTC6875AF	Sand	1	
	MTC6875AV	Roan Brown	1	
	MTC6875CC	Masai Red	1	
	MTC6875CL	Venetian Red	1	
	MTC6875HC	Bronze Green	1	
	MTC6875HD	Light Green	1	
	MTC6875HN	Trident Green	1	
	MTC6875JC	Marine Blue	1	
	MTC6875JP	Stratos Blue	1	
	MTC6875LB	Mid Grey	1	
	MTC6875LN	Slate Grey	1	
	MTC6875NJ	Limestone	1	
	MTC6875NM	Ivory	1	
		EYEBROW MOULDING - FRONT WING RH		
	MRC9378	Natural Black	1	
	MTC6874AA	Arizona Tan	1	
	MTC6874AE	Russet	1	
	MTC6874AF	Sand	1	
	MTC6874AV	Roan Brown	1	
	MTC6874CC	Masai Red	1	
	MTC6874CL	Venetian Red	1	
	MTC6874HC	Bronze Green	1	
	MTC6874HD	Light Green	1	
	MTC6874HN	Trident Green	1	
	MTC6874JC	Marine Blue	1	
	MTC6874JP	Stratos Blue	1	
	MTC6874LB	Mid Grey	1	
	MTC6874LN	Slate Grey	1	
	MTC6874NJ	Limestone	1	
	MTC6874NM	Ivory	1	
19	AFU1075	Plastic Rivet	32	

VS3798A

LAND ROVER PARTS LTD

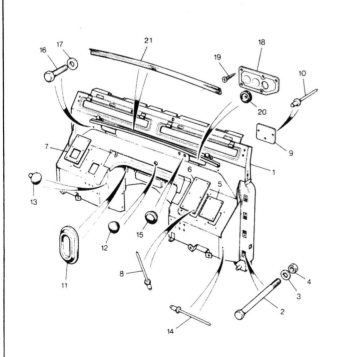

MODEL LR110 - UP TO AUGUST 1986
BLOCK TS 5137
PAGE L 22
GROUP L

BODY - DASH ASSEMBLY

ILL	PART NO	DESCRIPTION	QTY	REMARKS
1	RTC6267	Dash Assembly-RHD	1	)Except Air Con
	RTC6268	Dash Assembly-LHD	1	)
	MUC6686	Dash Assembly-RHD	1	)Air Con
	MUC9345	Dash Assembly-LHD	1	)
	MTC8444	Dash Assembly	1	Germany
2	MRC9420	Tie Bolt-M12 x 180mm	2	
3	WA112081L	Plain Washer	8	
4	NH112041L	Nut	2	
5	346981	Cover Plate-Pedal Hole	1	)
6	346599	Cover Plate-Pedal Hole	1	)Where Required
7	346598	Cover Plate-Pedal Hole	1	)
8	78248	Rivet	12	
9	395617	Blanking Plate-Heater Hole	1	
10	RA608123	Rivet	3	
11	MTC1650	Plug	2	
12	MRC1300	Plug	2	
	DRC1666	Grommet	1	
13	338015	Plug-Toe Box	1	
14	79106	Rivet-Toe Box	2	
15	332647	Buffer for Bonnet	2	
16	SX108251	Bolt-Dash to Strg Support	4	
17	WA108051L	Plain Washer	10	
	ATU1005L	Supersert	2	)Alternatives
	NN108021	Nutsert	2	)
18	PRC1333	Grommet Plate	2	
19	AB610051L	Drive Screw	8	
20	338023	Plug	2	
	BD155888L	Plug	1	
21	MWC2567	Seal-Drain Channel on Dash	1	
	MUC6905	Plate-Steering Column Aperture	1	
	RU608123L	Rivet	3	

TS5137

LAND ROVER PARTS LTD

MODEL LR110 - UP TO AUGUST 1986
BLOCK VS 3800
PAGE L 24
GROUP L

BODY - DASH VENTILATOR - EXCEPT AIR CON

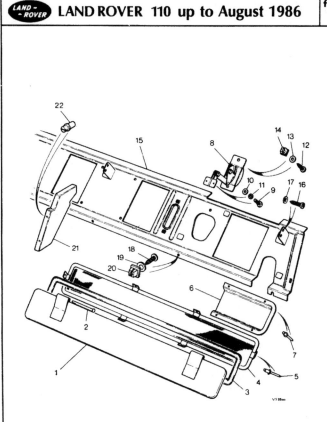

ILL	PART NO	DESCRIPTION	QTY	REMARKS
1	RTC6212	Ventilator Lid RH	1	)
	RTC6211	Ventilator Lid LH	1	)
2	334121	Hinge Pin	4	)Except Germany
3	MUC4299	Sealing Rubber	2	)
4	395185	Flyscreen	2	)
5	RA610123	Rivet	12	)
6	MTC2799	Splash Panel-LH Vent	1	
7	RA610123	Rivet	4	
8	346576	Ventilator Control	2	
9	SH105121L	Screw	4	)Except Germany
10	WC105001L	Plain Washer	4	)
11	WL105001L	Spring Washer	4	)
12	AB608041L	Screw	4	
13	AFU1257	Plain Washer	4	
14	RTC3745	Lokut Nut	4	
15	MTC4144	Front Plate RHD	1	
	MTC4145	Front Plate LHD	1	
16	AB608041L	Screw	6	
17	WA105001L	Plain Washer	6	
18	AB608054L	Screw	5	
19	WA104004L	Plain Washer	5	
20	RTC3745	Lokut Nut	5	
21	346941	Air Flow Divider Panel	1	)Except Germany
22	79106	Rivet	2	)

VS3800

LAND ROVER PARTS LTD

MODEL LR 110 - UP TO AUGUST 1986
BLOCK TS 5530
PAGE L 24.10
GROUP L

BODY - DASH VENTILATOR - AIR CON

ILL	PART NO	DESCRIPTION	QTY	REMARKS
1	MTC6109	Dash Ventilator Finisher	2	
2	MTC6015	Sealing Washer	6	
3	WA104001L	Plain Washer	6	
4	WW104001	Wave Washer	6	
5	NH104041L	Nut	6	
6	MUC3498	Front Plate-RHD	1	
	MUC1027	Front Plate-LHD	1	
7	AFU2636	Sems Drivescrew-Front Plate to Crash Rail-LHD	2	

TS5530

LAND ROVER PARTS LTD

MODEL LR110 - UP TO AUGUST 1986
BLOCK VS 3801A
PAGE L 26
GROUP L

BODY - WINDSCREEN

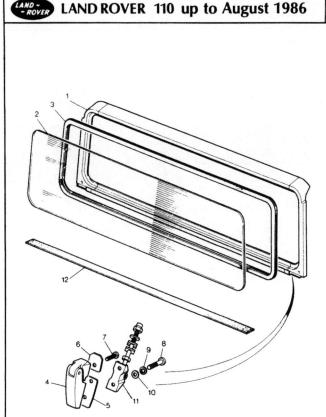

ILL	PART NO	DESCRIPTION	QTY	REMARKS
1	MUC2594	Windscreen Frame	1	
2	MTC3452	Glass-Laminated Tint	1	
	MTC2864	Glass-Laminated Clear	1	
	MTC2863	Glass-Toughened Clear	1	
3	MUC3733	Glazing Rubber	1	
4	MUC3531	Hinge LH	1	
	MUC3530	Hinge RH	1	
5	MTC3693	Gasket LH	1	)Upto
	MTC3692	Gasket RH	1	)VIN 239822
	MUC7903	Gasket	2	From VIN 239823
6	MTC3694	Gasket	2	Upto VIN 239822
	MUC7904	Gasket	2	From VIN 239823
7	SE110401	Screw	2	
	MUC3906	Nylon Washer	2	
8	SS108404	Screw	4	
9	WF108004L	Shakeproof Washer	4	
10	WA108051L	Plain Washer	4	
11	MTC4400	Clamp	2	
12	MUC6660	Seal-Dash to Windscreen	1	

VS3801A

LAND ROVER PARTS LTD

MODEL LR110 - UP TO AUGUST 1986
BLOCK VS 3802B
PAGE L 28
GROUP L

BODY - DIAPHRAGM AND TUNNEL PANELS

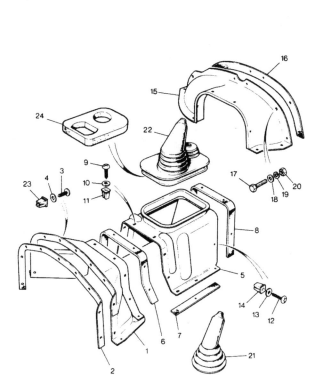

ILL	PART NO	DESCRIPTION	QTY	REMARKS
1	MTC2252	Diaphragm Panel-4 Cyl	1	
	MRC5378	Diaphragm Panel-V8 4 Speed	1	
	MUC4163	Diaphragm Panel-V8 5 Speed	1	
2	MRC8626	Seal	1	V8
3	AB614061L	Drive Screw	9	
4	MRC5527	Plain Washer	9	
5	MTC4095	Tunnel Panel-4 Cyl	1	
	MRC8173	Tunnel Panel-V8 4 Speed	1	
	MUC4319	Tunnel Panel-V8 5 Speed	1	
6	MTC6798	Seal-Front-Tunnel Panel-4 Cyl	1	
	MRC3609	Seal-Front-Tunnel Panel-V8 4 Speed	1	
	MUC1237	Seal-Front-Tunnel Panel-V8 5 Speed	1	
7	MTC6798	Seal-Side-Tunnel Panel-4 Cyl	2	
	MRC3611	Seal-Side-Tunnel Panel-V8 4 Speed	2	
	MUC1237	Seal-Side-Tunnel Panel-V8 5 Speed	2	
8	MTC6798	Seal-Rear-Tunnel Panel-4 Cyl	1	
	MRC3610	Seal-Rear-Tunnel Panel-V8 4 Speed	1	
	MUC1237	Seal-Rear-Tunnel Panel-V8 5 Speed	1	
9	AB614061L	Drive Screw	6	)
10	MRC5527	Plain Washer	6	)4 Cyl
11	RTC3744	Lokut Nut	6	)
	AB614061L	Drive Screw	4	)
	MRC5527	Plain Washer	4	)V8
	RTC3744	Lokut Nut	4	)
12	AB614061L	Drive Screw	6	)
13	MRC5527	Plain Washer	6	)4 Cyl
14	RTC3744	Lokut Nut	6	)

VS3802B

LAND ROVER PARTS LTD

MODEL LR110 - UP TO AUGUST 1986
BLOCK VS 3802B
PAGE L 28.02
GROUP L

BODY - DIAPHRAGM AND TUNNEL PANELS

ILL	PART NO	DESCRIPTION	QTY	REMARKS
15	MRC7411	Transfer Case Cover	1	)
16	MRC8626	Seal	1	)
17	SH106201L	Screw	2	)V8
18	WA106041L	Plain Washer	4	)
19	WL106001L	Spring Washer	2	)
20	NH106041L	Nut	2	)
	SH108201L	Screw	1	)
	WL108001L	Spring Washer	1	)V8 RHD
	NH108041L	Nut	1	)
	SH108201L	Screw	2	)
	WL108001L	Spring Washer	2	)V8 LHD
	NH108041L	Nut	2	)
21	MRC4857	Gaiter-Gear Lever	1	V8-4 Speed
22	MTC6392	Gaiter-Gear Lever/Transfer Lever	1	)4 Cyl-RHD)
	MTC6391	Gaiter-Gear Lever/Transfer Lever	1	)4 Cyl-LHD
	MUC4303	Gaiter-Gear Lever/Transfer Lever	1	)V8-5 Speed)
	AFU4173	Cable Tie-Gaiter to Tunnel	1	)
23	RTC3744	Lokut Nut	9	
24	MTC6872	Insulation Pad-4 Cyl	1	
	MUC4027	Insulation Pad-V8 5 Speed	1	

VS3802B

520

MODEL LR110 - UP TO AUGUST 1986
BLOCK VS 3803
PAGE L 30
GROUP L

BODY - FLOOR PLATES

ILL	PART NO	DESCRIPTION	QTY	REMARKS
1	MRC9720	Front Floor Plate RH-4 Cyl	1	
2	MTC2248	Front Floor Plate LH-4 Cyl	1	
	MRC3574	Front Floor Plate RH-V8 4 Speed	1	
	MRC6138	Front Floor Plate LH-V8 4 Speed	1	
	MUC1228	Front Floor Plate RH-V8 5 Speed	1	
	MUC1227	Front Floor Plate LH-V8 5 Speed	1	
3	AB614061L	Drive Screw	13	)
4	MRC5527	Plain Washer	13	) 4 Cyl
5	RTC3744	Lokut Nut	13	)
	AB614061L	Drive Screw	12	)
	MRC5527	Plain Washer	12	)V8
	RTC3744	Lokut Nut	12	)
6	320045	Acme Bolt	5	)
7	MRC5527	Plain Washer	5	)4 Cyl
8	79246	Spire Nut	5	)
	79048	Acme Bolt	1	)
	320045	Acme Bolt	5	)V8
	MRC5527	Plain Washer	6	)
	79246	Spire Nut	6	)
9	MRC8626	Seal RH Sill to Toebox	1	)
10	MRC8626	Seal LH Sill to Toebox	1	)V8
11	MRC8626	Seal RH Heelboard to Floor Plate	1	))
12	MRC8626	Seal LH Heelboard to Floor Plate	1	)

VS3803

521

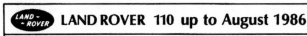

MODEL LR110 - UP TO AUGUST 1986
BLOCK VS 3804A
PAGE L 32
GROUP L

BODY - SEATBASE

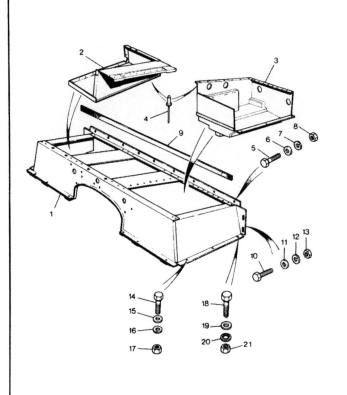

ILL	PART NO	DESCRIPTION	QTY	REMARKS
1		SEATBASE ASSEMBLY		
	MTC6339	-V8 4 SPEED	1	NOTE(1)
	MTC6340	-4 CYL	1	NOTE(1)
	MUC6166	-V8 5 SPEED	1	NOTE(1)
	MRC9663	-V8 4 SPEED	1	NOTE(2)
	RTC6218	-4 Cyl	1	NOTE(2)
	MUC6167	-V8 5 SPEED	1	NOTE(2)
	MTC8142	-V8 4 SPEED	1	NOTE(3)
2	MTC6305	+Tool Locker	1	
3	MRC9664	+Battery Tray	1	
4	78248	+Rivet Fixing Tool Locker	25	
	78248	+Rivet Fixing Battery Tray	28	
	MTC4684	+Nut Plate	4	Part of MTC8142
5	SH106201L	Screw	9	)
6	MRC5525	Plain Washer	9	)
	WA108051L	Plain Washer	9	)Pick-Up
7	WL106001L	Spring Washer	9	)
8	NH106041L	Nut	9	)
9	MRC8626	Seal	1	V8 Only
10	SH106161L	Bolt	4	)
11	WA106041L	Plain Washer	4	)
12	WM106001L	Spring Washer	4	)
	SH106161L	Bolt	4	)
	WC106041L	Plain Washer	4	)
	WM106001L	Spring Washer	4	)
13	NH106041L	Nut	4	)Station Wagon
14	SH106201L	Bolt	6	)
15	WA106045	Plain Washer	12	)
16	WM106001L	Spring Washer	6	)
17	NH106041L	Nut	6	)
18	SH106201L	Bolt	2	)
19	AFU1080	Plain Washer	4	)
20	WF600051L	Shakeproof Washer	2	)
21	NH106041L	Nut	2	)

NOTE(1)   Includes Tool Locker and Battery Tray

NOTE(2)   Includes Battery Tray Only-For Vehicles
           With Additional Fuel Tank

NOTE(3)   No Tool Locker and No Battery Tray
           For Vehicles With 10/15 Gallon Fuel Tanks

VS3804A

 LAND ROVER PARTS LTD

MODEL LR110 - UP TO AUGUST 1986
BLOCK TS 5121
PAGE L 34
GROUP L

BODY - SEATBASE FITTINGS

ILL	PART NO	DESCRIPTION	QTY	REMARKS
1	MUC1412	Extension Panel RH	1	
2	MUC1412	Extension Panel LH	1	
3	MUC4502	Locker Cover LH (Battery Access)	1	
4	MRC8136	Locating Angle-Lid	1	
	SH106201L	Screw	2	
	MRC5525	Plain Washer	2	
	NH106041L	Nut	2	
5	MRC8388	Overcentre Catch	1	
6	RU608123L	Rivet	2	
7	MTC4215	Centre Locker Cover-V8	1	
	MTC4197	Centre Locker Cover-V8	1	Note(1)
	MTC4216	Centre Locker Cover-4 Cyl	1	
	MTC4196	Centre Locker Cover-4 Cyl	1	Note(2)
8	AB610051L	Drive Screw	4	
9	WC106041L	Plain Washer	4	
10	53K3039L	Spire Nut	4	
	AB610051L	Drive Screw	4	)
	4034L	Plain Washer	4	)Note(1)
	78237	Spire Nut	4	)
	AB610051L	Drive Screw	6	)
	WC106041L	Plain Washer	6	)Note(2)
	53K3039L	Spire Nut	6	)

NOTE(1):   When Centre Console Fitted - V8

NOTE(2):   When Centre Console Fitted - 4 Cylinder

TS5121

LAND ROVER PARTS LTD

MODEL LR 110 - UP TO AUGUST 1986
BLOCK TS 5121
PAGE L 34.02
GROUP L

BODY - SEATBASE FITTINGS - CONTINUED

ILL	PART NO	DESCRIPTION	QTY	REMARKS
11	MTC2203	Cover Plate RHD-4 Cyl	1	
	MTC2202	Cover Plate LHD-4 Cyl	1	
	MRC8456	Cover Plate-LHD-V8 4 Speed	1	
	MRC8457	Cover Plate-RHD-V8 4 Speed	1	
	MUC1234	Cover Plate RHD-V8 5 Speed	1	
	MUC1233	Cover Plate LHD-V8 5 Speed	1	
12	78248	Rivet-Cover Plate to Heelboard	4	
13	MUC4496	Locker Cover RH (Tool Compartment Access).	1	Note(1)
	MUC4499	Locker Cover RH (Fuel Tank Access).	1	Note(2)
	MRC8136	Locating Angle	1	
	SH106201L	Screw	2	
	MRC5525	Plain Washer	2	
	NH106041L	Nut	2	
14	MRC8388	Overcentre Catch	1	
15	RU608123L	Rivet	2	
16	MRC3613	Seal-Transfer Lever	1	V8-4 Speed
	MRC5509	Bolt-Plate	1	
	RB613109	Bifurcated Rivet	1	
	392107	Sound Deading Pads-On Underside of Seatbase Lids	3	
	338015	Blanking Plug-For ¼"Diameter Hole-Redundant Safety Harness Holes in Seatbase	4	
	338028	Blanking Plug-For 2"Diameter Hole Seatbase Toolbox Compartment	1	
	338017	Blanking Plug-For 9/16" Diameter Hole-Redundant Holes in Seatbase	6	

NOTE(1):   Vehicles Without Extra Fuel Tank

NOTE(2):   Vehicles With Extra Fuel Tank

TS5121

LAND ROVER PARTS LTD

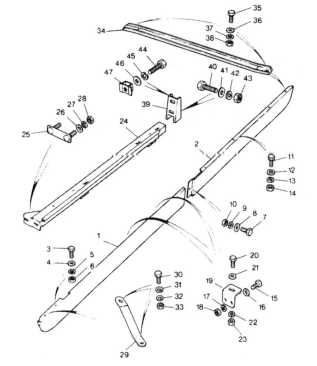

MODEL LR 110 - UP TO AUGUST 1986
BLOCK VS 3811
PAGE L 36
GROUP L

BODY - SILL PANELS - PICK UP

ILL	PART NO	DESCRIPTION	QTY	REMARKS
1	RTC6205	Sill Panel Front RH	1	
	RTC6206	Sill Panel Front LH	1	
2	MRC5049	Sill Panel Rear RH	1	
	MRC5050	Sill Panel Rear LH	1	
	337812	Sill Panel Rear RH	1	)Chassis
	337813	Sill Panel Rear LH	1	)Cab Vehicles
3	SH106161L	Bolt	4	
4	MRC5525	Plain Washer	8	
5	WL106001L	Spring Washer	4	
6	NH106041L	Nut	4	
7	SH106161L	Bolt	2	
8	RTC609	Plain Washer	4	
9	WM106001L	Spring Washer	2	
10	NH106041L	Nut	2	
11	SH106161L	Bolt	14	
12	RTC609	Plain Washer	12	
13	WM106001L	Spring Washer	6	
14	NH106041L	Nut	14	
15	SH106161L	Bolt	4	
16	RTC609	Plain Washer	8	
17	WM106001L	Spring Washer	4	
18	NH106041L	Nut	4	
19	MRC9438	Bracket	4	
20	SH106201L	Bolt	4	
21	AFU1069	Plain Washer	8	
22	WL106001L	Spring Washer	4	
23	NH106041L	Nut	4	

VS3811

LAND ROVER PARTS LTD

MODEL LR110 - UP TO AUGUST 1986
BLOCK VS 3811
PAGE L 36.02
GROUP L

BODY - SILL PANELS - PICK UP - CONTINUED

ILL	PART NO	DESCRIPTION	QTY	REMARKS
24	MWC1086	Sill Channel RH	1	
	MWC1087	Sill Channel LH	1	
25	MRC2481	Bolt Plate	2	
26	RTC601	Plain Washer	4	
27	WM600051L	Spring Washer	4	
28	NH605041L	Nut	4	
29	MRC5153	Front Stay	2	
30	SH106161L	Bolt	4	
31	WA106041L	Plain Washer	4	
32	WL106001L	Spring Washer	4	
33	NH106041L	Nut	4	
34	MRC6019	Centre Stay	2	
35	SH106161L	Bolt	4	
36	WA106041L	Plain Washer	4	
37	WL106001L	Spring Washer	4	
38	NH106041L	Nut	4	
39	347346	Mounting Bracket	2	
40	SH108201L	Screw	4	
41	RTC610	Plain Washer	8	
42	WL108001L	Spring Washer	4	
43	NH108041L	Nut	4	
44	SH106201L	Screw	4	
45	WL106001L	Spring Washer	4	
46	MRC5528	Plain Washer	4	
47	NK106081	Grip Nut	4	

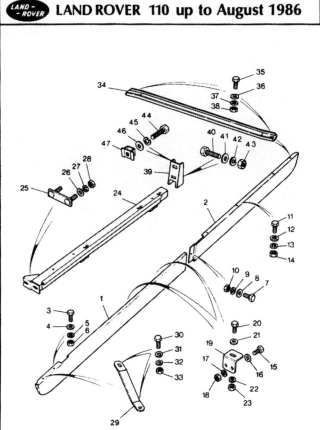

VS3811

LAND ROVER PARTS LTD

526

MODEL LR110 - UP TO AUGUST 1986
BLOCK VS 3812
PAGE L 38
GROUP L

BODY - SILL PANELS - STATION WAGON

ILL	PART NO	DESCRIPTION	QTY	REMARKS
1	RTC6205	Sill Panel Front RH	1	
	RTC6206	Sill Panel Front LH	1	
2	RTC6209	Sill Panel Rear RH	1	
	RTC6210	Sill Panel Rear LH	1	
3	SH106161L	Bolt	4	
4	MRC5525	Plain Washer	8	
5	WL106001L	Spring Washer	8	
6	NH106041L	Nut	4	
7	SH106161L	Bolt	2	
8	RTC609	Plain Washer	4	
9	WM106001L	Spring Washer	2	
10	NH106041L	Nut	2	
11	SH106161L	Bolt	4	
12	RTC609	Plain Washer	4	
13	WM106001L	Spring Washer	4	
14	NH106041L	Nut	4	
15	MRC9438	Bracket	6	
16	SH106201L	Bolt	6	
17	RTC609	Plain Washer	12	
18	WM106001L	Spring Washer	6	
19	NH106041L	Nut	6	
20	SH106161L	Bolt	4	
21	RTC609	Plain Washer	8	
22	WM106001L	Spring Washer	4	
23	NH106041L	Nut	4	

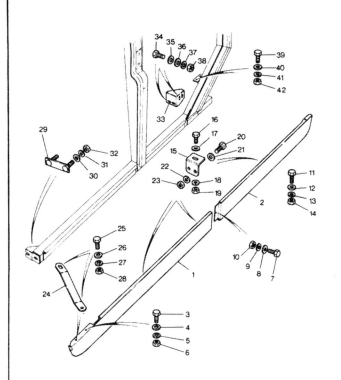

VS3812

LAND ROVER PARTS LTD

527

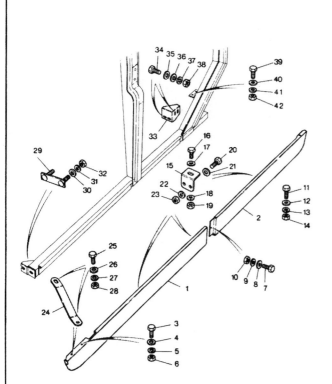

MODEL LR110 - UP TO AUGUST 1986
BLOCK VS 3812
PAGE L 38.02
GROUP L

BODY - SILL PANELS - STATION WAGON - CONTINUED

ILL	PART NO	DESCRIPTION	QTY	REMARKS
24	MRC5153	Front Stay	2	
25	SH106161	Bolt	4	
26	WA106041L	Plain Washer	4	
27	WL106001L	Spring Washer	4	
28	NH106041L	Nut	4	
29	MRC5765	Bolt Plate	2	
30	RTC610	Plain Washer	4	
31	WM600051L	Spring Washer	4	
32	NH108041L	Nut	4	
33	MRC6359	Bracket RH	1	
	MRC6360	Bracket LH	1	
34	SX108251L	Bolt	8	
35	WP185	Plain Washer	2	
36	RTC601	Plain Washer	16	
37	WM600051L	Spring Washer	8	
38	NH108041L	Nut	8	
39	SH108161	Bolt	4	
40	WC108051L	Plain Washer	4	
	RTC613	Plain Washer	4	
41	WM600051L	Spring Washer	4	
42	NH108041L	Nut	4	
	MUC9110	Nut Plate-M8	4	

VS3812

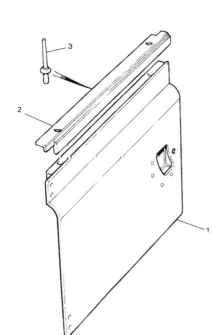

MODEL LR110 - UP TO AUGUST 1986
BLOCK VS 3813
PAGE L 40
GROUP L

BODY - FRONT DOOR - CLINCHED ASSEMBLY

ILL	PART NO	DESCRIPTION	QTY	REMARKS
1	RTC6287	Front Door Clinched RH	1	
	RTC6288	Front Door Clinched LH	1	
2	RRC5034	Top Capping RH	1	)Note(1)
	RRC5035	Top Capping LH	1	)
3	78248	Rivet	6	)

NOTE(1): Galvanised & Treated - Suitable For Painting
If Required.

VS3813

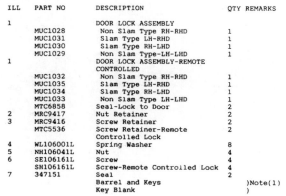

MODEL LR110 - UP TO AUGUST 1986
BLOCK VS 3814B
PAGE L 42
GROUP L

BODY - FRONT DOOR - LOCKS AND STRIKER

ILL	PART NO	DESCRIPTION	QTY	REMARKS
1		DOOR LOCK ASSEMBLY		
	MUC1028	Non Slam Type RH-RHD	1	
	MUC1031	Slam Type LH-RHD	1	
	MUC1030	Slam Type RH-LHD	1	
	MUC1029	Non Slam Type-LH-LHD	1	
1		DOOR LOCK ASSEMBLY-REMOTE CONTROLLED		
	MUC1032	Non Slam Type RH-RHD	1	
	MUC1035	Slam Type LH-RHD	1	
	MUC1034	Slam Type RH-LHD	1	
	MUC1033	Non Slam Type LH-LHD	1	
	MTC6858	Seal-Lock to Door	2	
2	MRC9417	Nut Retainer	2	
3	MRC9416	Screw Retainer	2	
	MTC5536	Screw Retainer-Remote Controlled Lock	2	
4	WL106001L	Spring Washer	8	
5	NH106041L	Nut	4	
6	SE106161L	Screw	4	
	SH106161L	Screw-Remote Controlled Lock	4	
7	347151	Seal	2	
		Barrel and Keys		)Note(1)
		Key Blank		)

NOTE(1):   Refer to 'Barrel & Key Sets'

VS3814B

530

MODEL LR110 - UP TO AUGUST 1986
BLOCK VS 3814B
PAGE L 42.02
GROUP L

BODY - FRONT DOOR - LOCKS AND STRIKER

ILL	PART NO	DESCRIPTION	QTY	REMARKS
10	MRC8444	Striker RH	1	
	MRC8445	Striker LH	1	
11	SH106201	Bolt	4	
12	WL106001L	Spring Washer	4	
13	AFU1259	Plain Washer	4	
14	MRC9431	Nut Plate	2	
15	MWC1736	Bracket-Striker Support RH	1	)
	MWC1737	Bracket-Striker Support LH	1	)
16	SH106161	Screw	4	)Except
17	AFU1259	Plain Washer	8	)Station Wagon
18	WL106001L	Spring Washer	4	)
19	NH106041L	Nut	4	)
20	MRC9006	Shroud RH	1	
	MRC9007	Shroud LH	1	

VS3814B

531

MODEL LR110 - UP TO AUGUST 1986
BLOCK VS 3934A
PAGE L 42.04
GROUP L

BODY - FRONT DOOR - REMOTE CONTROL HANDLE

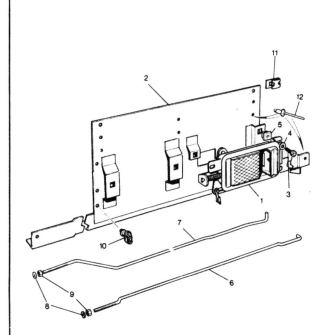

ILL	PART NO	DESCRIPTION	QTY	REMARKS
1	MUC1216	Remote Control Handle-RH	1	
	MUC1217	Remote Control Handle-LH	1	
2	MTC6606	Support Plate-RH	1	
	MTC6607	Support Plate-LH	1	
3	AB610051L	Screw	6	
4	WA105001L	Plain Washer	6	
5	ADU3775	Lokut Nut	6	
6	MTC6008	Link Rod-RH	1	
	MTC6009	Link Rod-LH	1	
7	MTC6010	Link Catch-RH	1	
	MTC6011	Link Catch-LH	1	
8	WA104001L	Plain Washer	8	
9	NH104041L	Nut	16	
10	79127	Pipe Clip	2	
11	AJ608021	Spring Nut	4	
12	RA612156L	Rivet	10	

VS3934A

LAND ROVER PARTS LTD

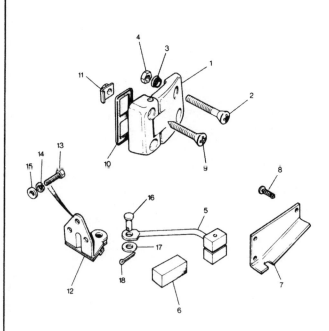
MODEL LR110 - UP TO AUGUST 1986
BLOCK 2RE 243
PAGE L 44
GROUP L

BODY - FRONT DOOR - HINGES AND DOORCHECK

ILL	PART NO	DESCRIPTION	QTY	REMARKS
		HINGE		
1	MRC3037	Upper RH	1	
	MRC3038	Upper LH	1	
	347362	Lower RH	1	
	347363	Lower LH	1	
2	MRC2762	Screw-Hinges to Doors	8	
3	MRC1980	Nylon Washer	8	
4	NH605041L	Nut	8	
5	395538	Check Strap Rod	2	
6	395481	Buffer	2	
7	346927	Retainer RH	1	
	346928	Retainer LH	1	
8	AB606031	Screw	6	
9	GD110401	Screw-Hinges to Dash	8	
10	347369	Seating Washer	4	
11	MRC2178	Nut Retainer	8	
12	346878	Retaining Bracket	2	
13	SH106201	Bolt	4	
14	W1106001L	Spring Washer	4	
15	WA106041L	Plain Washer	4	
16	PC108241	Clevis Pin	2	
17	WA108051L	Plain Washer	2	
18	PS103101	Split Pin	2	

2RE243

LAND ROVER PARTS LTD

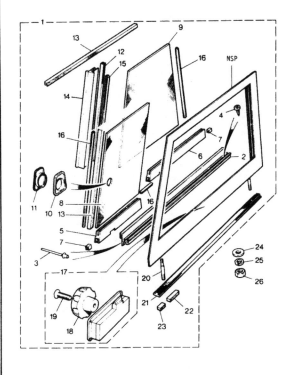

MODEL LR110 - UP TO AUGUST 1986
BLOCK TS 5119
PAGE L 46
GROUP L

BODY - FRONT DOOR - SIDESCREEN - 5MM GLASS

ILL	PART NO	DESCRIPTION	QTY	REMARKS
1		SIDESCREEN ASSEMBLY		
	MTC8840	WITH CLEAR GLASS RH	1	NLA-Note(1)
	MTC8841	WITH CLEAR GLASS LH	1	NLA-Note(2)
	MTC6202	WITH TINTED GLASS RH	1	NLA
	MTC6203	WITH TINTED GLASS LH	1	
2	MTC6206	+Removable Rail RH	1	
	MTC6207	+Removable Rail LH	1	
	MUC3746	+Draught Seal-Front	2	
	MUC3746	+Draught Seal-Rear	2	
3	AFU2637	+Rivet-Fixing Rail	4	
4	AB606031L	+Screw-Fixing Rail	8	
5	MTC6208	+Slide Rail-Outer RH	1	
	MTC6209	+Slide Rail-Outer LH	1	
6	MTC6210	+Slide Rail-Inner RH	1	
	MTC6211	+Slide Rail-Inner LH	1	
7	MTC6221	+Runner Block	6	
8	MTC6266	+Glass-Outer Clear	2	
	MTC6212	+Glass-Outer Tinted	2	
9	MTC6267	+Glass-Inner Clear	2	
	MTC6213	+Glass-Inner Tinted	2	
10	MTC6277	+Finger-Pull-Outer RH	1	
	MTC6279	+Finger-Pull-Outer LH	1	
11	MTC6276	+Finger-Pull-Inner RH	1	
	MTC6278	+Finger-Pull-Inner LH	1	

NOTE(1):   Use MWC4746 - 4mm Glass

NOTE(2):   Use MWC4747 - 4mm Glass

TS5119

 LAND ROVER PARTS LTD

MODEL LR110 - UP TO AUGUST 1986
BLOCK TS 5119
PAGE L 46.02
GROUP L

BODY - FRONT DOOR - SIDESCREEN

ILL	PART NO	DESCRIPTION	QTY	REMARKS
12	MTC7617	+Glazing Rubber-Draught Rail	2	
	MTC7616	+Glazing Rubber-Inner/Outer Slide Rail	4	
13	MTC7622	+Glazing Felt-Front/Rear Vertical	4	
	MTC7622	+Glazing Felt-Inner/Outer Top	4	
	MTC7622	+Glazing Felt-Inner/Outer Slide Rail	4	
14	MTC6214	+Draught Rail RH	1	
	MTC6215	+Draught Rail LH	1	
15	MTC6222	+Weatherseal Rubber	2	
16	MTC7611	+Infill Rubber-Front/Rear Vertical	4	
	MTC7611	+Infill Rubber-Outer Slide Rail	2	
17	RRC4878	+Window Catch RH	1	
	RRC4879	+Window Catch LH	1	
18	MTC6304	++Knob	2	
19	ADU1221L	++Screw	2	
20	MTC6223	+Stud	4	
21	MTC6224	+Seal	2	
22	MTC7549	+Pad-Long	8	
23	MTC7550	+Pad-Short	4	
24	WC110061L	Plain Washer	4	
25	WL110001L	Spring Washer	4	
26	NH110041L	Nut	4	

TS5119

LAND ROVER PARTS LTD

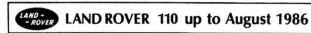

MODEL LR110 - UP TO AUGUST 1986
BLOCK VS 3936
PAGE L 46.06
GROUP L

BODY - SEALS - FRONT DOOR

ILL	PART NO	DESCRIPTION	QTY	REMARKS
1	MWC1080	Seal-Front Door-RH	1	
	MWC1081	Seal-Front Door-LH	1	
2	MTC8932	Seal Retainer-RH	1	
	MTC8931	Seal Retainer-LH	1	
3	SE105161L	Screw	10	
4	AFU1256	Plain Washer	10	
5	WL105001L	Spring Washer	10	
6	NH105041L	Nut	10	
7	MWC6130	Sill Seal	2	
8	78248	Rivet	18	

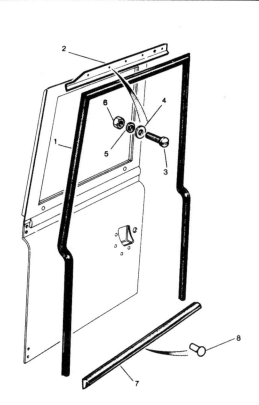

VS3936

LAND ROVER PARTS LTD

536

MODEL LR 110 - UP TO AUGUST 1986
BLOCK TS 5260
PAGE L 46.10
GROUP L

BODY - FRONT DOORS - WIND UP WINDOWS - 1984 FACELIFT

ILL	PART NO	DESCRIPTION	QTY	REMARKS
1	MUC3010	Front Door Clinched Assy RH	1	
	MUC3011	Front Door Clinched Assy LH	1	
2	201235	Filler-Rear Corner	2	
3	201647	Filler-Front Corner	2	
4	MUC1651	Filler-Vertical	2	
5	MUC1652	Filler-Top	2	
6	MUC1730	Filler-Sloping RH	1	
	MUC1731	Filler-Sloping LH	1	
7	MTC8473	Waist Seal Inner	2	
8	MTC8474	Waist Seal Outer	2	
9	MUC3928	Waist Capping RH	1	
	MUC3929	Waist Capping LH	1	
10	MUC3186	Fixing Clip	10	
11	AJU1136L	Snapsac	10	
12	MUC2074	Inner Panel RH	1	
	MUC2075	Inner Panel LH	1	
13	SH106101L	Screw	10	
14	WA106041L	Plain Washer	10	
	MUC4316	Water Curtain	2	
	MTC9180	Sound Deadening Pad	2	
	307220	Rubber Plug (Door Bottom)	4	
	MUC3848	Plug-Lock Pocket in Door	2	

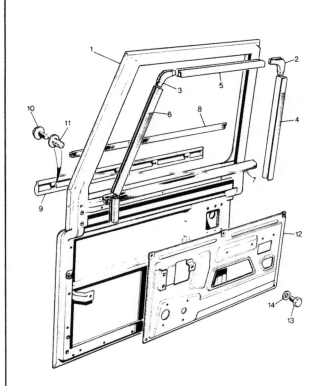

TS5260

LAND ROVER PARTS LTD

537

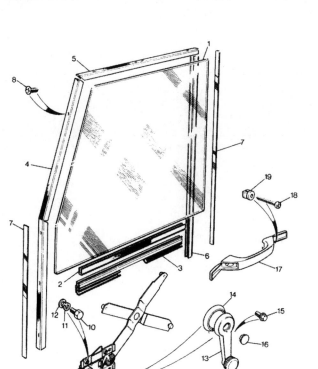

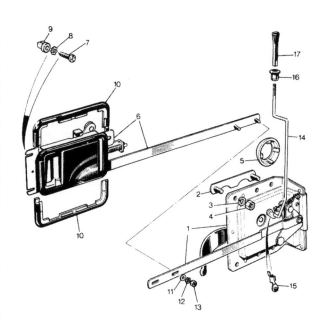

MODEL LR110 - UP TO AUGUST 1986
BLOCK TS 5261
PAGE L 46.12
GROUP L

BODY - FRONT DOORS - WIND UP WINDOWS - 1984 FACELIFT

ILL	PART NO	DESCRIPTION	QTY	REMARKS
1	MTC7825	Glass-Clear	2	
	MTC7826	Glass-Tinted	2	
2	MUC1713	Glazing Rubber-Lift Channel	2	
3	MTC8477	Channel-Window Lift	2	
4	MUC4071	Channel-Vertical Front	2	
5	MTC8468	Channel-Top	2	
6	MUC4072	Channel-Vertical-Rear	2	
7	MUC4073	Shim-Channel Adjustment	A/R	
8	AC606031L	Drive Screw	22	
	AC606041L	Drive Screw	4	
9	MUC3024	Window Regulator RH	1	
	MUC3025	Window Regulator LH	1	
10	SH106101L	Screw	8	
11	WL106001L	Spring Washer	8	
12	WA106001	Plain Washer	8	
13	RTC3939PA	Regulator Handle	2	
14	RTC3935PA	Escutcheon	2	
15	ADU5727L	Powerlok Screw	2	
16	RTC3940PA	Cover-Regulator Handle	2	
17	YGA451L	Door Pull	2	
18	AB610081L	Screw	4	
19	CZK3264L	Lokut Nut	4	

TS5261

LAND ROVER PARTS LTD

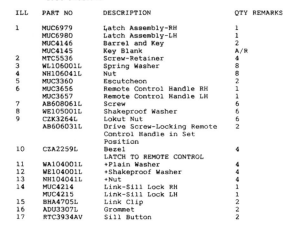

MODEL LR110 - UP TO AUGUST 1986
BLOCK TS 5262
PAGE L 46.14
GROUP L

BODY - FRONT DOORS - WIND UP WINDOWS - LOCKS, REMOTE CONTROL, LINKS - 1984 FACELIFT

ILL	PART NO	DESCRIPTION	QTY	REMARKS
1	MUC6979	Latch Assembly-RH	1	
	MUC6980	Latch Assembly-LH	1	
	MUC4146	Barrel and Key	2	
	MUC4145	Key Blank	A/R	
2	MTC5536	Screw-Retainer	4	
3	WL106001L	Spring Washer	8	
4	NH106041L	Nut	8	
5	MUC3360	Escutcheon	2	
6	MUC3656	Remote Control Handle RH	1	
	MUC3657	Remote Control Handle LH	1	
7	AB608061L	Screw	6	
8	WE105001L	Shakeproof Washer	6	
9	CZK3264L	Lokut Nut	6	
	AB606031L	Drive Screw-Locking Remote Control Handle in Set Position	2	
10	CZA2259L	Bezel	4	
		LATCH TO REMOTE CONTROL		
11	WA104001L	+Plain Washer	4	
12	WE104001L	+Shakeproof Washer	4	
13	NH104041L	+Nut	4	
14	MUC4214	Link-Sill Lock RH	1	
	MUC4215	Link-Sill Lock LH	1	
15	BHA4705L	Link Clip	2	
16	ADU3307L	Grommet	2	
17	RTC3934AV	Sill Button	2	

TS5262

LAND ROVER PARTS LTD

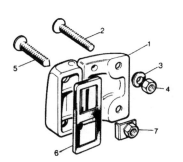

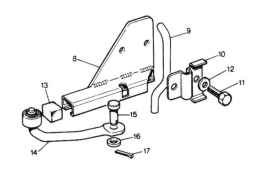

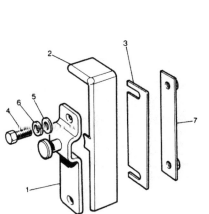

TS5263

LAND ROVER PARTS LTD

```
MODEL LR110 - UP TO AUGUST 1986
BLOCK TS 5263
PAGE L 46.16
GROUP L

BODY - FRONT DOORS - WIND UP WINDOWS - HINGES, CHECKSTRAP -
        1984 FACELIFT
```

ILL	PART NO	DESCRIPTION	QTY	REMARKS
1	MRC3037	Hinge Assembly-Upper RH	1	
	MRC3038	Hinge Assembly-Upper LH	1	
	347362	Hinge Assembly-Lower RH	1	
	347363	Hinge Assembly-Lower LH	1	
2	MRC2762	Screw-Hinge to Door	8	
	MWC1899	Screw-Hinge to Door	8	)Alternative
	MWC1898	Packer	4	)Fixings
3	MRC1980	Nylon Washer	8	
4	NH605041L	Nut	8	
5	79221	Screw-Hinge to Body	8	
6	347369	Seating Washer	4	
7	MRC2178	J-Nut	8	
8	MUC6164	Checkstrap Channel RH	1	
	MUC6163	Checkstrap Channel LH	1	
9	MUC6158	Torsion Bar RH	1	
	MUC6159	Torsion Bar LH	1	
10	MUC6157	Pivot Bracket	2	
11	SH106301L	Screw	4	
12	WA106041L	Plain Washer	4	
13	MWC5759	Rubber Buffer	2	
14	MUC1888	Checkstrap Link RH	1	
	MUC1889	Checkstrap Link LH	1	
15	306564	Clevis Pin	2	
16	WA108051L	Plain Washer	2	
17	2393	Split Pin	2	

540

```
MODEL LR110 - UP TO AUGUST 1986
BLOCK TS 5264
PAGE L 46.18
GROUP L

BODY - FRONT DOORS - WIND UP WINDOWS - STRIKER SHROUD - 1984 FACELIFT
```

ILL	PART NO	DESCRIPTION	QTY	REMARKS
1	MUC2959	Striker	2	
2	MUC4202	Shroud RH	1	
	MUC4203	Shroud LH	1	
3	MUC3038	Shim 0.7mm	A/R	
	MUC3039	Shim 1.2mm	A/R	
4	SH108201L	Screw	4	
5	WA108051L	Plain Washer	4	
6	WL108001L	Spring Washer	4	
7	MUC2961	Nut Plate	2	
	332484	Striker Support Bracket RH	1	)
	332485	Striker Support Bracket LH	1	)
	SH106161L	Screw	4	)
	WL106001L	Spring Washer	4	)
	AFU1259	Plain Washer	4	)Pick Up
	MUC1365	Nut Plate	2	)
	MUC1049	Stud Plate	2	)
	AFU1257	Plain Washer	4	)
	WL106001L	Spring Washer	4	)
	NH106041L	Nut	4	)

TS5264

LAND ROVER PARTS LTD

541

MODEL LR110 - UP TO AUGUST 1986
BLOCK VS 3935
PAGE L 48.02
GROUP L

BODY - REAR SIDE DOOR FRAME AND SEALS - STATION WAGON

ILL	PART NO	DESCRIPTION	QTY	REMARKS
1	MUC9126	Door Frame-RH	1	
	MUC9127	Door Frame-LH	1	
2	MWC1082	Seal-Rear Side Door-RH	1	
	MWC1083	Seal-Rear Side Door-LH	1	
3	MTC8928	Seal Retainer-RH	1	
	MTC8927	Seal Retainer-LH	1	
4	SE105161L	Screw	8	
5	AFU1256	Plain Washer	8	
6	WL105001L	Spring Washer	8	
7	NH105041L	Nut	8	
8	MWC1866	Sill Seal-RH	1	
	MWC1867	Sill Seal-LH	1	
9	RT612283	Rivet	8	

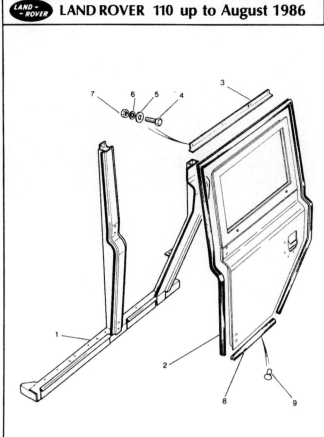

VS3935

LAND ROVER PARTS LTD

MODEL LR110 - UP TO AUGUST 1986
BLOCK VS 3940
PAGE L 50
GROUP L

BODY - REAR SIDE DOOR

ILL	PART NO	DESCRIPTION	QTY	REMARKS
1	MTC3230	Rear Side Door Clinched Assy RH	1	
	MTC3231	Rear Side Door Clinched Assy LH	1	
2	MTC3362	Waist Capping-RH	1	
	MTC3363	Waist Capping-LH	1	
3	78248	Rivet	10	

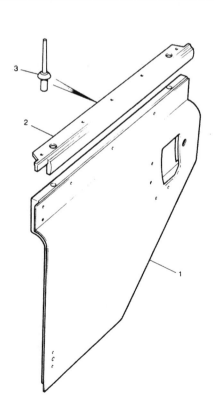

VS3940

LAND ROVER PARTS LTD

MODEL LR110 - UP TO AUGUST 1986
BLOCK VS 3875A
PAGE L 52
GROUP L

BODY - DOOR LOCKS - REAR SIDE DOOR

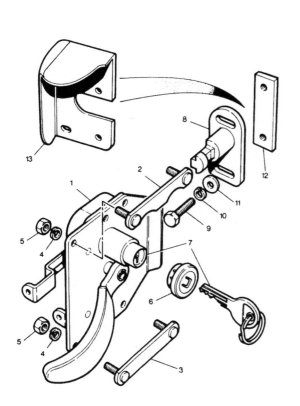

ILL	PART NO	DESCRIPTION	QTY	REMARKS
1		DOOR LOCK ASSEMBLY		
	MUC1030	Slam Type-RH	1	
	MUC1031	Slam Type-LH	1	
		DOOR LOCK ASSEMBLY-REMOTE CONTROLLED		
	MUC1034	Slam Type-RH	1	
	MUC1035	Slam Type-LH	1	
	MTC6858	Seal-Lock to Door	2	
2	MRC9416	Screw Retainer-Upper	2	
	MRC9605	Screw Retainer-Lower	2	
3	MTC5552	Screw Retainer-Lower Remote Controlled Lock	2	
4	WL106001L	Spring Washer	8	
5	NH106041L	Nut	8	
6	347151	Seal	2	
7		Barrel & Keys for Door Lock		)Note(1)
		Key Blank		)
8	MRC8444	Striker-RH	1	
	MRC8445	Striker-LH	1	
9	SH106201L	Screw	4	
10	AFU1259	Plain Washer	4	
11	WL106001L	Spring Washer	4	
12	MRC9431	Nut Plate	2	
13	MRC9006	Shroud-RH	1	
	MRC9007	Shroud-LH	1	

NOTE(1):   Refer to 'Barrel & Key Sets'.

VS3875A

LAND ROVER PARTS LTD

544

MODEL LR110 - UP TO AUGUST 1986
BLOCK VS 3955A
PAGE L 52.02
GROUP L

BODY - REMOTE CONTROL HANDLE - REAR SIDE DOOR

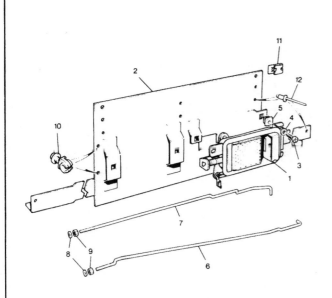

ILL	PART NO	DESCRIPTION	QTY	REMARKS
1	MUC1216	Remote Control Handle-RH	1	
	MUC1217	Remote Control Handle-LH	1	
2	MTC6608	Support Plate-RH	1	
	MTC6609	Support Plate-LH	1	
3	AB610051L	Screw	6	
4	WA105001L	Plain-Washer	6	
5	ADU3775L	Lokut Nut	6	
6	MTC6104	Link Rod-RH	1	
	MTC6105	Link Rod-LH	1	
7	MTC6106	Link Catch-RH	1	
	MTC6107	Link Catch-LH	1	
8	WA104001L	Plain-Washer	8	
9	NH104041L	Nut	8	
10	CRC1250L	Pipe Clip	4	
11	AJ608021	Spring Nut	4	
12	RA612156L	Rivet	10	

VS3955A

LAND ROVER PARTS LTD

545

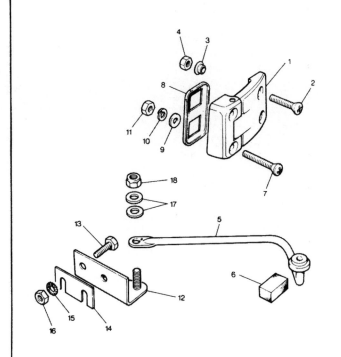

MODEL LR110 - UP TO AUGUST 1986
BLOCK VS 3995
PAGE L 54
GROUP L

BODY - HINGES, CHECKSTRAP - REAR SIDE DOOR

ILL	PART NO	DESCRIPTION	QTY	REMARKS
1	347362	Hinge RH	2	
	347363	Hinge LH	2	
2	MRC2762	Screw-Hinges to Doors	8	
	MWC1899	Screw-Hinges to Door	8	)Alternative
	MWC1898	Packer	4	)Fixings
3	MRC1980	Nylon Washer	8	
4	NH605041L	Nut	8	
5	333041	Check Strap Rod RH	1	
	333204	Check Strap Rod LH	1	
6	306295	Rubber Buffer	4	
7	AFU1036	Screw-Hinge to 'BC' Post	4	
8	347369	Seating Washer	4	
9	WC108051L	Plain Washer	8	)Upto VIN
10	WL108001L	Spring Washer	8	)263231
11	NH108041L	Nut	8	)
	MUC9110	Nut Plate	4	From VIN 263232
	MRC4753	Check Bracket-RH	1	
12	MRC4754	Check Bracket-LH	1	
13	SH108251L	Bolt	4	
14	305232	Shim	4	
15	WF108001L	Shakeproof Washer	4	
16	NH108041L	Nut	4	
17	AFU1262	Plain Washer	4	
18	NY106041L	Nyloc Nut	2	

VS3995

LAND ROVER PARTS LTD

546

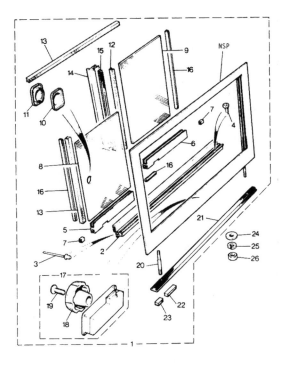

MODEL LR110 - UP TO AUGUST 1986
BLOCK TS 5120
PAGE L 54.02
GROUP L

BODY - REAR SIDE DOOR - SIDESCREEN

ILL	PART NO	DESCRIPTION	QTY	REMARKS
1		SIDESCREEN ASSEMBLY		
	MTC6284	WITH CLEAR GLASS-RH	1	
	MTC6285	WITH CLEAR GLASS-LH	1	
	MTC8846	WITH TINTED GLASS-RH	1	
	MTC8847	WITH TINTED GLASS-LH	1	
2	MTC6248	+Removable Rail-RH	1	
	MTC6249	+Removable Rail-LH	1	
3	AFU2637	+Rivet-Fixing Rail	4	
4	AB606031L	+Screw-Fixing Rail	8	
5	MTC6250	+Slide Rail Outer	2	
6	MTC6251	+Slide Rail Inner	2	
7	MTC6221	+Runner Block	20	
		+WINDOW GLASS		
8	MTC6258	Outer Clear	2	
	MTC6254	Outer Tinted	2	
9	MTC6259	Inner Clear	2	
	MTC6255	Inner Tinted	2	
10	MTC6281	+Finger Pull-Outer	2	
11	MTC6280	+Finger Pull-Inner	2	
12		+GLAZING RUBBER		
	MTC7617	Draught Rail	2	
	MTC7616	Inner/Outer Slide Rail	4	
13		+GLAZING FELT		
	MTC7622	Rear Vertical	2	
	MTC7622	Inner/Outer Top	4	
	MTC7622	Inner/Outer Slide Rail	4	
14	MTC6256	+Draught Rail	2	
15	MTC6222	+Weatherseal Rubber	2	
16		+INFILL RUBBER		
	MTC7611	Front/Rear Vertical	4	
	MTC7611	Inner/Outer Slide Rail	4	
	RRC4878	+Window Catch RH	1	
17	MUC1983	+Window Catch LH	1	
18	MTC6304	++Knob for Catch	2	
19	ADU1221L	++Screw	2	
20	MTC6223	+Stud	4	
21	MTC6224	+Seal	2	
22	MTC7549	+Pad-Long	4	
23	MTC7550	+Pad-Short	4	
24	WA110061L	Plain Washer	4	
25	WL110001L	Spring Washer	4	
26	NH110041L	Nut	4	

TS5120

LAND ROVER PARTS LTD

547

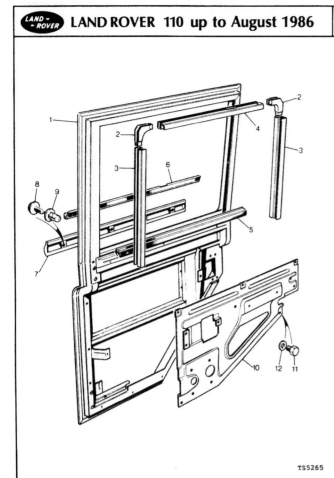

MODEL LR110 - UP TO AUGUST 1986
BLOCK TS 5265
PAGE L 54.10
GROUP L

BODY - REAR SIDE DOORS - WIND UP WINDOWS - 1984 FACELIFT

ILL	PART NO	DESCRIPTION	QTY	REMARKS
1	MUC3012	Rear Side Door Clinched Assy RH	1	
	MUC3013	Rear Side Door Clinched Assy LH	1	
2	201235	Filler-Corner	4	
3	MUC1651	Filler-Vertical	4	
4	MTC8788	Filler-Top RH	1	
	MTC8789	Filler-Top LH	1	
5	MUC1322	Waist Seal-Inner RH	1	
	MUC1323	Waist Seal-Inner LH	1	
6	MUC1604	Waist Seal-Outer RH	1	
	MUC1605	Waist Seal-Outer LH	1	
7	MUC3930	Waist Capping RH	1	
	MUC3931	Waist Capping LH	1	
8	MUC3186	Fixing Clip	10	
9	AJU1136L	Snapsac	10	
10	MUC2936	Inner Panel RH	1	
	MUC2937	Inner Panel LH	1	
11	SH106101L	Screw	10	
12	WA106041L	Plain Washer	10	
	MUC4317	Water Curtain	2	
	392743	Sound Deadening Pad	2	
	307220	Rubber Plug (Door Bottom)	4	
	MUC3848	Plug-Lock Pocket in Door	4	
	MUC6785	Deflector Panel LH (Above Lock)	1	
	MUC6786	Deflector Panel RH (Above Lock)	1	

TS5265

LAND ROVER PARTS LTD

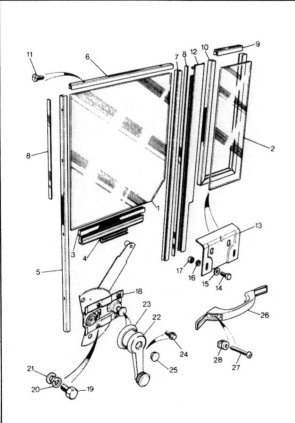

MODEL LR110 - UP TO AUGUST 1986
BLOCK TS 5266
PAGE L 54.12
GROUP L

BODY - REAR SIDE DOORS - WIND UP WINDOWS - 1984 FACELIFT

ILL	PART NO	DESCRIPTION	QTY	REMARKS
		GLASS		
1	MTC7828	Wind Up Window-Clear	2	
	MTC7829	Wind Up Window-Tinted	2	
2	MTC8460	Rear Qtr Window-Clear	2	
	MTC8461	Rear Qtr Window-Tinted	2	
3	MUC1714	Glazing Rubber-Lift Channel	2	
		CHANNEL-WIND UP WINDOW		
4	MTC8478	Window Lift	2	
5	MUC4072	Vertical Front	2	
6	MTC8471	Top	2	
7	MTC8472	Vertical-Rear	2	
8	MUC4073	Shim-Channel Adjustment	A/R	
		CHANNEL-REAR QTR WINDOW		
9	MTC8790	Top	2	
10	MTC8791	Lower	2	
11	AC606031L	Drive Screw	16	
	AC606041L	Drive Screw	2	
12	MUC3492	Division Channel RH	1	
	MUC3493	Division Channel LH	1	
13	MUC3200	Bracket-Rear Qtr Retention	2	
14	SH104101L	Screw	4	
15	WA104001L	Plain Washer	4	
16	WE104001L	Shakeproof Washer	4	
17	NH104041L	Nut	4	

VS5266

LAND ROVER PARTS LTD

MODEL LR110 - UP TO AUGUST 1986
BLOCK TS 5266
PAGE L 54.14
GROUP L

BODY - REAR SIDE DOORS - WIND UP WINDOWS
                            - 1984 FACELIFT

ILL	PART NO	DESCRIPTION	QTY	REMARKS
18	MUC3026	Window Regulator RH	1	
	MUC3027	Window Regulator LH	1	
19	SH106101L	Screw	8	
20	WL106001L	Spring Washer	8	
21	WA106001	Plain Washer	8	
22	RTC3939PA	Regulator Handle	2	
23	RTC3935PA	Escutcheon	2	
24	ADU5727L	Powerlok Screw	2	
25	RTC3940PA	Cover-Regulator Handle	2	
26	YGA451L	Door Pull	2	
27	AB610081L	Screw	4	
28	CZK3264L	Lokut Nut	4	

TS5266

550

MODEL LR110 - UP TO AUGUST 1986
BLOCK TS 5268
PAGE L 54.16
GROUP L

BODY - REAR SIDE DOORS - WIND UP WINDOWS - 1984 FACELIFT
                            - LATCH - REMOTE CONTROL HANDLE - LINKS

ILL	PART NO	DESCRIPTION	QTY	REMARKS
1	MUC6986	Latch Assembly RH	1	
	MUC6987	Latch Assembly LH	1	
2	MTC5536	Screw Retainer Upper	2	
3	MRC9605	Screw Retainer Lower	2	
4	WL106001L	Spring Washer	8	
5	NH106041L	Nut	8	
6	MUC3658	Remote Control Handle RH	1	
	MUC3659	Remote Control Handle LH	1	
7	AB608061L	Screw	6	
8	WE106001L	Shakeproof Washer	6	
9	CZK3264L	Lokut Nut	6	
10	CZA2259L	Bezel	4	
	AB606031L	Drivescrew-Locking Remote	2	
		Control Handle in Position		
		LATCH TO REMOTE CONTROL		
11	WA1040011	+Plain Washer	4	
12	WE104001L	+Shakeproof Washer	4	
13	NH104041L	+Nut	4	
14	MUC3191	Link-Lock	2	
15	BHA4705L	Link Clip	2	
16	DZA1435L	Bellcrank Lever	4	
17	MUC3190	Link-Intermediate	2	
18	DRC1697	Clip	2	
19	MUC4216	Link-Sill RH	1	
	MUC4217	Link-Sill LH	1	
20	ADU3307L	Grommet	2	
21	RTC3934AV	Sill Button	2	

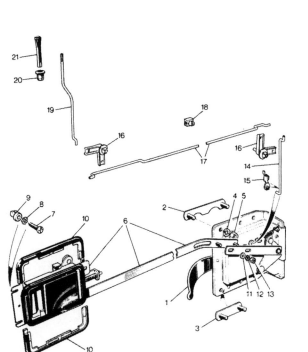

TS5268

MODEL LR110 - UP TO AUGUST 1986
BLOCK TS 5269A
PAGE L 54.18
GROUP L

BODY - REAR SIDE DOORS - WIND UP WINDOWS - 1984 FACELIFT
 - HINGES - DOORCHECK

ILL	PART NO	DESCRIPTION	QTY	REMARKS
1	347362	Hinge RH	2	
	347363	Hinge LH	2	
2	MRC2762	Screw-Hinge to Door	8	
	MWC1899	Screw-Hinge to Door	8	)Alternative
	MWC1898	Packer	4	)Fixings
3	MRC1980	Nylon Washer	8	
4	NH605041L	Nut	8	
5	AFU1036	Screw-Hinge to Body	8	
6	347369	Seating Washer	4	
7	WC108051L	Plain Washer	8	
8	WL108001L	Spring Washer	8	
9	NH108041L	Nut	8	
10	MUC1961	Bolt Plate	2	
11	MUC6158	Torsion Bar RH	1	
	MUC6159	Torsion Bar LH	1	
12	MUC6157	Pivot Bracket	2	
13	WA106041L	Plain Washer	4	
14	NH106041L	Nut	4	
15	306295	Rubber Buffer	2	
16	MWC1838	Checkstrap Link RH	1	
	MWC1837	Checkstrap Link LH	1	
17	AFU1262	Plain Washer	4	
18	NY106041L	Nyloc Nut	2	
19	MUC3090	Waterdam RH	1	
	MUC9377	Waterdam LH	1	
20	MUC3394	Sems Drive Screw	2	
21	MRC4753	Check Bracket RH	1	
	MRC4754	Check Bracket LH	1	
22	SH108251L	Screw	4	
23	305232	Shim	4	
24	WF108001L	Shakeproof Washer	4	
25	NH108041L	Nut	4	

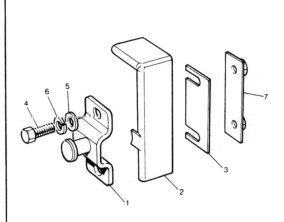

TS5269A

LAND ROVER PARTS LTD

MODEL LR110 - UP TO AUGUST 1986
BLOCK TS 5270
PAGE L 54.20
GROUP L

BODY - REAR SIDE DOORS - WIND UP WINDOWS - 1984 FACELIFT
 - STRIKER - SHROUD

ILL	PART NO	DESCRIPTION	QTY	REMARKS
1	MUC2963	Striker	2	
2	MUC2908	Shroud RH	1	
	MUC4205	Shroud LH	1	
3	MUC3040	Shim 0.7mm Thick	A/R	
	MUC3041	Shim 1.2mm Thick	A/R	
4	SH108201L	Screw	4	
5	WA108051L	Plain Washer	4	
6	WL108001L	Spring Washer	4	
7	MUC2965	Nut Plate	2	

TS5270

LAND ROVER PARTS LTD

MODEL LR110 - UP TO AUGUST 1986
BLOCK VS 3817
PAGE L 56
GROUP L

BODY - STIRRUP STEP - FRONT AND REAR SIDE DOORS

ILL	PART NO	DESCRIPTION	QTY	REMARKS
1	MTC2138	Step	1	
2	SE108251	Bolt	2	
3	WC108051L	Plain Washer	2	
4	WL108001L	Spring Washer	2	
5	NH108041L	Nut	2	
6	MTC2548	Finisher	1	Germany

NOTE: Quantities Shown Are For One Step Only

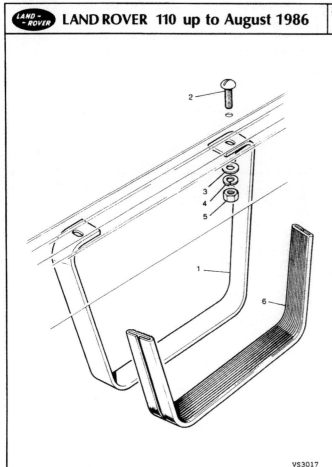

VS3017

LAND ROVER PARTS LTD

MODEL LR110 - UP TO AUGUST 1986
BLOCK VS 3816
PAGE L 58
GROUP L

BODY - FOLDING STEP - FRONT & REAR SIDE DOORS
     - EXCEPT GERMANY - NOTE(1)

ILL	PART NO	DESCRIPTION	QTY	REMARKS
1	MTC7466	STEP COMPLETE ASSEMBLY	1	
2	MTC3021	+Step	1	
3	MTC3076	+Rubber Tread	1	
4	RT612253	+Rivet	4	
5	WA105001L	+Plain Washer	4	
6	MTC3018	+Support	1	To 189413
	MTC7465	+Support	1	From 189414
7	MTC1233	+Spring	1	
8	MTC1241	+Special Bolt	2	To 189413 (NLA)
	MTC7464	+Special Bolt	2	From 189414
9	WB114001L	+Plain Washer	2	
10	NY108041L	+Nyloc Nut	2	
11	MXC1624	Brace-Front Step RH/LH Side	1	Note(2)
	MXC1624	Brace-Front Step LH Side	1	)Note(3)
	MUC3571	Brace-Front Step-RH Side	1	)
	MXC1624	Brace-Rear Step	1	
12	SH108251L	Screw	2	
13	WA108051L	Plain Washer	2	
14	NY108041L	Nyloc Nut	2	
15	SH108251L	Screw	1	
16	WL108001L	Spring Washer	1	
17	WC108051L	Packing Washer	A/R	
18	NN108021	Anchor Nut	1	
19	SE108201	Screw	1	
20	NY108041L	Nyloc Nut	1	

NOTE(1):   Quantities Shown Are For One Step Only

NOTE(2):   Vehicles Without Additional Fuel Tank

NOTE(3):   Vehicles With Additional Fuel Tank

LAND ROVER PARTS LTD

VS3816

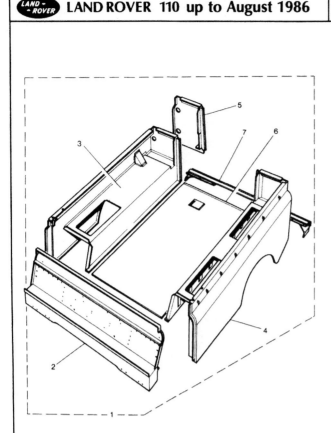

MODEL LR110 - UP TO AUGUST 1986
BLOCK VS 3868
PAGE L 60
GROUP L

BODY - REAR BODY LOWER - PICK UP

ILL	PART NO	DESCRIPTION	QTY	REMARKS
1	MUC3958	REAR BODY LOWER ASSEMBLY	1	Note(1)
	MUC3971	REAR BODY LOWER ASSEMBLY	1	Note(2)
	MUC9142	REAR BODY LOWER ASSEMBLY	1	Note(3)
2	RTC6246	+Front Panel	1	Note(1)
	MTC2285	+Front Panel	1	Note(2)
	MTC2285	+Front Panel	1	Note(3)
3	MUC3304	+Bodyside & Wheelarch-RH	1	Note(1)
	MUC3310	+Bodyside & Wheelarch-RH	1	Note(2)
	MUC9136	+Bodyside & Wheelarch-RH	1	Note(3)
	MUC3963	+Bodyside & Wheelarch-LH	1	
4	MUC3302	++Bodyside Panel-RH	1	Note(1)
	MUC3309	++Bodyside Panel-RH	1	Note(2)
	MUC3324	++Bodyside Panel-RH	1	Note(3)
	MUC3303	++Bodyside Panel-LH	1	
5	MTC7980	++Rear End Panel-RH	1	
	MTC7981	++Rear End Panel-LH	1	
6	330617	+Floor Plate	1	
7	MTC1039	+Rear Mounting Angle	1	
	78248	+Rivet	A/R	
	RU612373L	+Rivet	A/R	

NOTE(1): Rear Fuel Filler

NOTE(2): Front And Rear Fuel Filler

NOTE(3): Front Fuel Filler

VS3868

MODEL LR110 - UP TO AUGUST 1986
BLOCK VS 3867D
PAGE L 62
GROUP L

BODY - REAR BODY LOWER - PICK UP

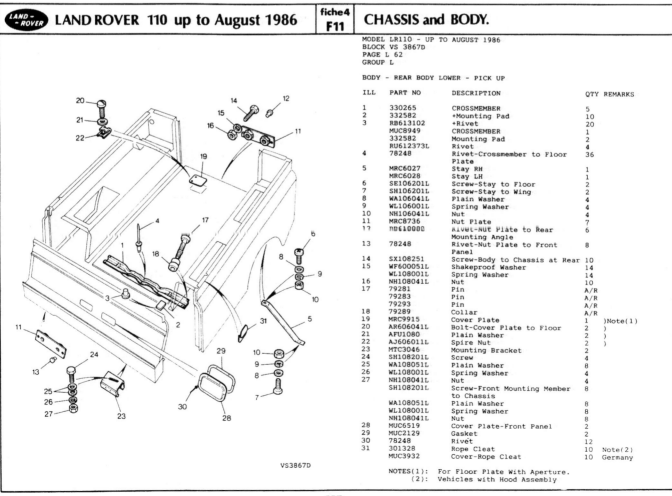

ILL	PART NO	DESCRIPTION	QTY	REMARKS
1	330265	CROSSMEMBER	5	
2	332582	+Mounting Pad	10	
3	RB613102	+Rivet	20	
	MUC8949	CROSSMEMBER	1	
	332582	Mounting Pad	2	
	RU612373L	Rivet	4	
4	78248	Rivet-Crossmember to Floor Plate	36	
5	MRC6027	Stay RH	1	
	MRC6028	Stay LH	1	
6	SE106201L	Screw-Stay to Floor	2	
7	SH106201L	Screw-Stay to Wing	2	
8	WA106041L	Plain Washer	4	
9	WL106001L	Spring Washer	4	
10	NH106041L	Nut	4	
11	MRC8736	Nut Plate	7	
12	RB610000	Rivet-Nut Plate to Rear Mounting Angle	6	
13	78248	Rivet-Nut Plate to Front Panel	8	
14	SX108251	Screw-Body to Chassis at Rear	10	
15	WF600051L	Shakeproof Washer	14	
	WL108001L	Spring Washer	14	
16	NH108041L	Nut	10	
17	79281	Pin	A/R	
	79283	Pin	A/R	
	79293	Pin	A/R	
18	79289	Collar	A/R	
19	MRC9915	Cover Plate	1	)Note(1)
20	AR606041L	Bolt-Cover Plate to Floor	2	)
21	AFU1080	Plain Washer	2	)
22	AJ606011L	Spire Nut	2	)
23	MTC3046	Mounting Bracket	2	
24	SH108201L	Screw	4	
25	WA108051L	Plain Washer	8	
26	WL108001L	Spring Washer	4	
27	NH108041L	Nut	4	
	SH108201L	Screw-Front Mounting Member to Chassis	8	
	WA108051L	Plain Washer	8	
	WL108001L	Spring Washer	8	
	NH108041L	Nut	8	
28	MUC6519	Cover Plate-Front Panel	2	
29	MUC2129	Gasket	2	
30	78248	Rivet	12	
31	301328	Rope Cleat	10	Note(2)
	MUC3932	Cover-Rope Cleat	10	Germany

NOTES(1): For Floor Plate With Aperture.
   (2): Vehicles with Hood Assembly

VS3867D

MODEL LR110 - UP TO AUGUST 1986
BLOCK TS 5133
PAGE L 64
GROUP L

BODY - REAR BODY LOWER - PICK UP

ILL	PART NO	DESCRIPTION	QTY	REMARKS
1	330602	Spare Wheel Housing	1	
2	78248	Rivet	14	
3	330616	Cover Plate-Wheelarch	1	
4	78248	Rivet	16	
5	MRC9627	Locker Lid Complete	1	
6	MRC8388	Overcentre Catch	1	
7	RA608236L	Rivet	2	
8	MRC9632	Hook for Overcentre Catch	1	
9	RA608236L	Rivet	2	
10	330366	Cover Plate-Side Filler	1	Note(1)
	MUC9158	Cover Plate-Side Filler	1	Note(2)
11	RU612373L	Rivet	9	
12	347553	Bracket-Squab Buffer	6	
13	RA612373L	Rivet-Bracket to Capping	24	

NOTE(1): Galvanised - Not Suitable For Painting

NOTE(2): Galvanised & Treated - Suitable For
         Painting If Required

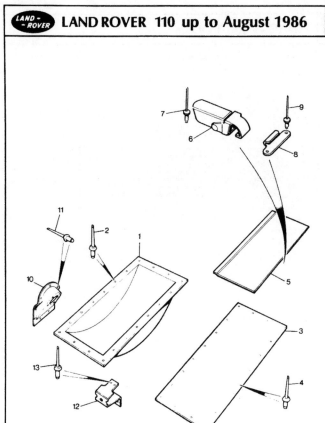

TS5133

LAND ROVER
PARTS LTD

558

MODEL LR110 - UP TO AUGUST 1986
BLOCK TS 5178
PAGE L 66
GROUP L

BODY - REAR BODY LOWER - PICK UP

ILL	PART NO	DESCRIPTION	QTY	REMARKS
1	MRC4846	Pivot Bracket Spare Wheel	1	
2	SH108201	Bolt-Bracket to Capping	2	
3	WC108051L	Plain Washer	2	
4	WL108001L	Spring Washer	2	
5	MRC5757	Nut Plate	1	
6	347866	Tie Bar	1	
7	BH106081L	Bolt-Tie Bar to Pivot Bracket	1	
8	WC106041L	Plain Washer	2	
9	WS106001	Spring Washer	2	
10	NY106041L	Nut	1	
11	303847	Clamp	1	
12	AFU1265	Plain Washer	1	
13	WL110001L	Spring Washer	1	
14	250053	Wing Nut	1	
15	332672	BRACKET-RUBBING STRIP	2	
16	332674	+Rubbing Strip	2	
17	78248	+Rivet	4	
18	78248	Rivet-Bracket to Capping	4	

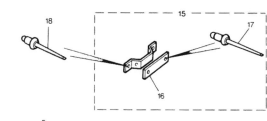

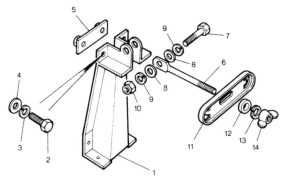

TS5178

LAND ROVER
PARTS LTD

559

MODEL LR110 - UP TO AUGUST 1986
BLOCK TS 5179
PAGE L 66.10
GROUP L

BODY - REAR BODY LOWER - PICK UP

ILL	PART NO	DESCRIPTION	QTY	REMARKS
1	MRC2244	Cover Panel RH-Rear Lamps	1	
	MRC2245	Cover Panel LH-Rear Lamps	1	
2	SP105121	Screw	4	
3	WC105001L	Plain Washer	4	
4	WL105001L	Spring Washer	4	
5	NM105011	Nut	4	
6	AB608031L	Drive Screw	4	
7	WC105001L	Plain Washer	4	
8	308206	Tread Plate-Front Panel	1	
9	330717	Tread Plate-Front Panel	4	
10	330615	Tread Plate-Floor	3	
	330615	Tread Plate-Wheelarch	2	
11	78248	Rivet-Fixing Tread Plates	88	

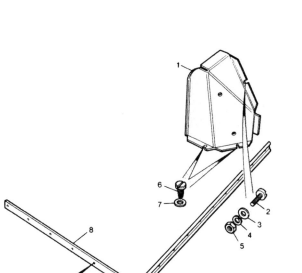

TS5179

 **LAND ROVER PARTS LTD**

MODEL LR110 - UP TO AUGUST 1986
BLOCK VS 3865A
PAGE L 68
GROUP L

BODY - REAR BODY LOWER - PICK UP

ILL	PART NO	DESCRIPTION	QTY	REMARKS
1	MWC2120	Top Capping RH	1	)Note(2)
2	MUC8727	Top Capping LH	1	)
3	78248	Rivet	38	
	RU612373L	Rivet	16	
		Rear Corner Capping		
4	MUC8710	RH-Note(2)	1	
5	MUC8711	LH-Note(2)	1	
6	RA612373L	Rivet	12	
	78248	Rivet	4	
	SH106201L	Screw)	2	)
	WA106001L	Plain Washer) Corner Capping	4	)Hard Top
	WL106001L	Spring Washer) to Body	2	)Vehicles
	NH106041L	Nut)	2	)
7		Rear Corner Bracket Inner		
	MRC2237	With Cotter RH-Note(1)(3)	1	
	MRC2238	With Cotter LH-Note(1)(3)(5)	1	Use MUC8731
	330237	Less Cotter RH-Note(1)(4)(5)	1	Use MUC9154
	330238	Less Cotter LH-Note(1)(4)	1	
	MUC8730	Pierced RH (Separate Cotter)	1	)Note(2) & (3)
	MUC8731	Pierced LH (Separate Cotter)	1	)
	MUC9154	Plain RH	1	)Note(2) & (4)
	MUC9155	Plain LH	1	)
8	RU612373L	Rivet	6	
	78248	Rivet	4	
9	MUC8748	Antiluce Cotter	2	Note(2) & (3)
10	WA112081L	Plain Washer	2	)Note(3)
11	NY112041L	Nyloc Nut	2	)
12	MUC8716	Protection Angle RH	1	)Note(2)
13	MUC8717	Protection Angle LH	1	)
14	78248	Rivet	22	
15	330245	Capping-Front Panel	1	Note(1)
	MUC8735	Capping-Front Panel	1	Note(2)
16	RA612373L	Rivet	39	
	MTC8334	Cover-Lower End	2	)
	RU608313L	Rivet	2	)Germany

NOTE(1): Galvanised - Not Suitable For Painting
NOTE(2): Galvanised & Treated - Suitable For Painting If Required
NOTE(3): Vehicles With Tailboard
NOTE(4): Vehicles With Rear End Door
NOTE(5): No Longer Available

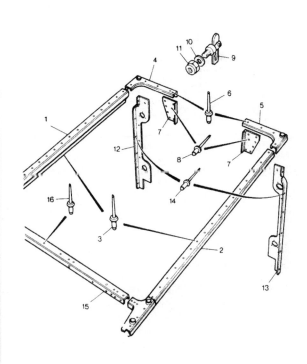

VS3865A

LAND ROVER PARTS LTD

MODEL LR110 - UP TO AUGUST 1986
BLOCK VS 3937B
PAGE L 70
GROUP L

BODY - REAR BODY LOWER - PICK UP

ILL	PART NO	DESCRIPTION	QTY	REMARKS
1	302825	Bracket-Tailboard Chain	2	)
2	SH106161L	Bolt	4	)
3	AFU1259	Plain Washer	4	)
4	WL106001L	Spring Washer	4	)Note(1)
5	NH106041L	Nut	4	)
6	MTC1827	Tailboard Chain	2	)
7	302828	Clevis Pin	2	)
8	3958L	Split Pin	2	)
9	330422	Sleeve	4	)
10	MUC8759	Bracket-Tailboard Cable	2	)
11	SH106161L	Screw	4	)
12	WL106001L	Spring Washer	4	)Note(2)
13	NH106041L	Nut	4	)
14	MTC4188	Tailboard Cable	2	)
15	SH108251L	Screw	2	)
16	WA108051L	Plain Washer	2	)
17	NH108041L	Nut	2	)
18	MTC4164	Seal RH	1	
	MTC4165	Seal LH	1	
19	332146	Buffer-Tailboard	2	
20	SP104121	Screw	2	
21	NH104001L	Plain Washer	2	
22	NH104041L	Nut	2	
23	MTC4460	Nameplate 'Land Rover'	1	)Note(3)
24	RA612373L	Rivet	2	)
25	330145	Protection Strip-Floor	1	
26	AB606041L	Drive Screw	7	

NOTE(1): Chain Retained Tailboard

NOTE(2): Cable Retained Tailboard

NOTE(3): Upto 1984 Facelift
          For 1984 Facelift-Refer to 'Nameplates & Bodytapes'

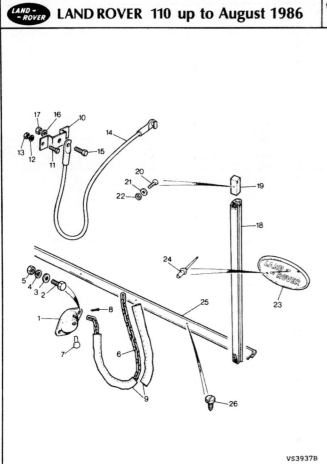

VS3937B

LAND ROVER PARTS LTD

MODEL LR110 - UP TO AUGUST 1986
BLOCK VS 3861
PAGE L 72
GROUP L

BODY - REAR BODY LOWER - STATION WAGON

ILL	PART NO	DESCRIPTION	QTY	REMARKS
1	MTC7889	REAR BODY LOWER ASSEMBLY	1	
2	MTC7886	+Bodyside & Wheelarch-RH	1	
	MUC3977	+Bodyside & Wheelarch-LH	1	
	RTC6291	++Bodyside Panel-RH	1	
3	MRC5071	++Bodyside Panel-LH	1	
4	MTC7980	++Rear End Panel-RH	1	
	MTC7981	++Rear End Panel-LH	1	
5	MTC8433	+Rear Floor	1	
6	MTC1039	+Rear Mounting Angle	1	
	78248	+Rivet	A/R	
	RU612373L	+Rivet	A/R	

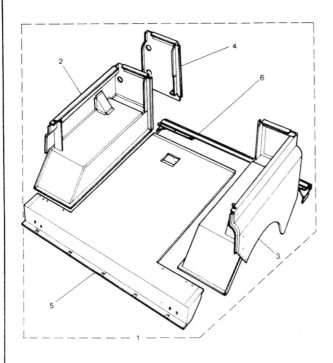

VS3861

LAND ROVER PARTS LTD

MODEL LR110 - UP TO AUGUST 1986
BLOCK VS 3862B
PAGE L 74
GROUP L

BODY - REAR BODY LOWER - STATION WAGON

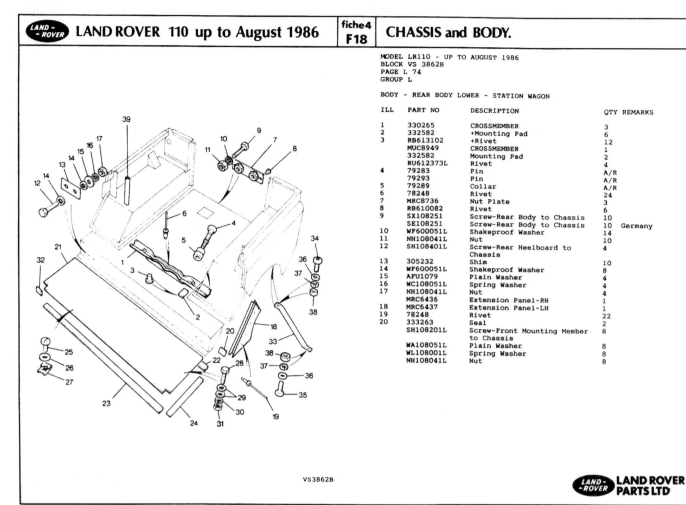

ILL	PART NO	DESCRIPTION	QTY	REMARKS
1	330265	CROSSMEMBER	3	
2	332582	+Mounting Pad	6	
3	RB613102	+Rivet	12	
	MUC8949	CROSSMEMBER	1	
	332582	Mounting Pad	2	
	RU612373L	Rivet	4	
4	79283	Pin	A/R	
	79293	Pin	A/R	
5	79289	Collar	A/R	
6	78248	Rivet	24	
7	MRC8736	Nut Plate	3	
8	RB610082	Rivet	6	
9	SX108251	Screw-Rear Body to Chassis	10	
	SE108251	Screw-Rear Body to Chassis	10	Germany
10	WF600051L	Shakeproof Washer	14	
11	NH108041L	Nut	10	
12	SH108401L	Screw-Rear Heelboard to Chassis	4	
13	305232	Shim	10	
14	WF600051L	Shakeproof Washer	8	
15	AFU1079	Plain Washer	4	
16	WC108051L	Spring Washer	4	
17	NH108041L	Nut	4	
	MRC6436	Extension Panel-RH	1	
18	MRC6437	Extension Panel-LH	1	
19	78248	Rivet	22	
20	333263	Seal	2	
	SH108201L	Screw-Front Mounting Member to Chassis	8	
	WA108051L	Plain Washer	8	
	WL108001L	Spring Washer	8	
	NH108041L	Nut	8	

VS3862B

LAND ROVER PARTS LTD

564

MODEL LR110 - UP TO AUGUST 1986
BLOCK VS 3862B
PAGE L 74.02
GROUP L

BODY - REAR BODY LOWER - STATION WAGON

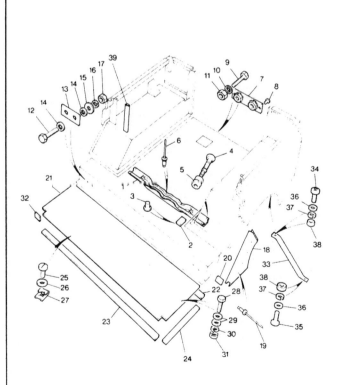

ILL	PART NO	DESCRIPTION	QTY	REMARKS
21	RTC6270	Intermediate Floor	1	
22	MRC8626	Seal-Floor to Toe Panel	1	
23	MRC8626	Seal-Floor to Heelboard	1	
24	MRC8626	Seal-Floor to Sill	2	
25	320045	Bolt-Floor to Heelboard and Toe Panel	6	
26	AFU1069	Plain Washer	6	)
	MRC5527	Plain Washer	6	)Alternatives
27	79246	Spire Nut	6	
28	SH106201L	Screw-Floor to Sill	6	
29	AFU1080	Plain Washer	12	)
	MRC5527	Plain Washer	12	)Alternatives
30	WM106001L	Spring Washer	6	
31	NH106041L	Nut	6	
32	333745	Seal	1	
33	MRC6027	Stay RH	1	
	MRC6028	Stay LH	1	
34	SE106201L	Screw-Stay to Floor	2	
35	SH106201L	Screw-Stay to Wing	2	
36	WA106041L	Plain Washer	4	
37	WL106001L	Spring Washer	4	
38	NH106041L	Nut	4	
39	MTC7513	Edging Strip-'D' Post Waist Stiffener	A/R	Germany

VS3862B

565

MODEL LR110 - UP TO AUGUST 1986
BLOCK TS 5134
PAGE L 76
GROUP L

BODY - REAR BODY LOWER - STATION WAGON

ILL	PART NO	DESCRIPTION	QTY	REMARKS
1	MRC2244	Cover Panel-RH-Rear Lamps	1	
	MRC2245	Cover Panel-LH-Rear Lamps	1	
2	SP105121	Screw-Fixing Cover Panel	4	
3	WC105001L	Plain Washer	4	
4	WL105001L	Spring Washer	4	
5	NM105011	Nut	4	
6	AB608031L	Drive Screw	4	
7	WC105001L	Plain Washer	4	
8	MRC9915	Cover Plate-Floor	1	)
9	AR606041L	Bolt-Fixing Cover Plate	2	)Note(1)
10	AFU1080	Plain Washer	2	)
11	AJ606011L	Spire Nut	2	)
12	MRC9627	Locker Lid Assembly	1	
13	MRC8388	Overcentre Catch	1	
14	RA608236L	Rivet-Catch to Locker Lid	2	
15	MRC9632	Hook for Overcentre Catch	1	
16	RA608236L	Rivet-Hook to Wheelarch	2	
17	MTC4460	Nameplate 'Land Rover'	1	)
18	306407	Nameplate 'Station Wagon'	1	)Note(2)
19	RA612373L	Rivet-Fixing Nameplates	4	)

NOTES:
(1): For Floor Plate With Aperture
(2): Up to 1984 Facelift
For 1984 Facelift Onwards-Refer to 'Nametapes & Bodytapes'

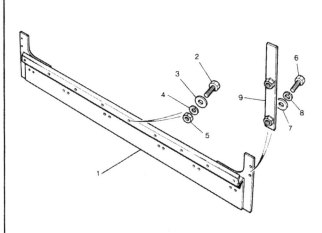

TS5134

LAND ROVER PARTS LTD

MODEL LR110 - UP TO AUGUST 1986
BLOCK VS 3863
PAGE L 78
GROUP L

BODY - REAR BODY LOWER - STATION WAGON

ILL	PART NO	DESCRIPTION	QTY	REMARKS
1	395413	Toe Panel-Gusset Bracket	1	
2	SH106201	Bolt-Toe Panel to Seatbase	2	
	SH106161	Bolt	7	
3	RTC609	Plain Washer	9	
4	WM600051L	Spring Washer	9	
5	NH106041L	Nut	9	
6	SH106161	Bolt	4	
7	WC106041L	Plain Washer	4	
8	WM106001	Spring Washer	4	
9	MRC9388	Nut Plate	2	

VS3863

LAND ROVER PARTS LTD

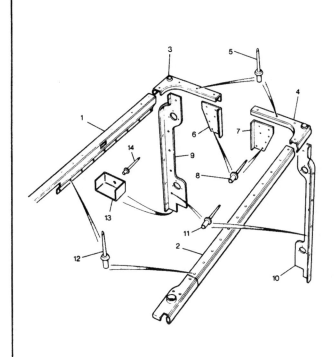

MODEL LR110 - UP TO AUGUST 1986
BLOCK VS 3864A
PAGE L 80
GROUP L

BODY - REAR BODY LOWER - STATION WAGON

ILL	PART NO	DESCRIPTION	QTY	REMARKS
1	MTC6074	Top Capping RH	1	)Note(1)
2	MTC6075	Top Capping LH	1	)
	MUC9152	Top Capping RH	1	)Note(2)
	MUC9153	Top Capping LH	1	)
		Rear Corner Capping		
3	333266	RH-Note(1)	1	
4	333267	LH-Note(1)(3)	1	Use MUC8711
	MUC8710	RH-Note(2)	1	
	MUC8711	LH Note(2)	1	
5	RA612373L	Rivet	12	
	78248	Rivet	4	
	SH106201L	Screw)	2	
	WA106001L	Plain Washer) Corner Capping	2	
	WL106001L	Spring Washer) to Body	2	
	NH106041L	Nut)	2	
		Rear Corner Bracket Inner		
6	330237	RH-Note(1)(3)	1	Use MUC9154
7	330238	LH-Note(1)	1	
	MUC9154	RH Note(2)	1	
	MUC9155	LH Note(2)	1	
8	78248	Rivet	6	
		Protection Angle		
9	MTC2134	RH-Note(1)	1	
10	MTC2135	LH-Note(1)(3)	1	Use MUC8717
	MUC8716	RH-Note(2)	1	
	MUC8717	LH-Note(2)	1	
11	78248	Rivet	24	
12	78248	Rivet-Fixing Top Capping	32	
13	MTC8334	Cover-Lower End	2	)Germany
14	RU608313L	Rivet	2	)

NOTE(1):   Galvanised - Not Suitable For Painting

NOTE(2):   Galvanised & Treated - Suitable for Painting
           if Required

NOTE(3):   No Longer Available

VS3864A

 **LAND ROVER PARTS LTD**

568

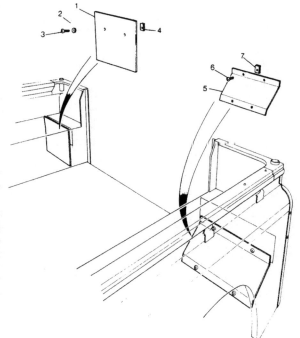

MODEL LR110 - UP TO AUGUST 1986
BLOCK TS 5177
PAGE L 82
GROUP L

BODY - REAR BODY LOWER - REAR LAMPS PROTECTION

ILL	PART NO	DESCRIPTION	QTY	REMARKS
1	MTC7861	Mudshield-Rear Lamps	1	
2	AFU1218L	Plain Washer	2	
3	AR610051L	Screw-Mudshield to RH Wheelarch Box	2	
4	AK610021L	Spire Nut	2	
5	MRC8094	Protection Plate-Rear Lamps	1	
6	AR610051L	Screw-Protection Plate to Inside of Tool Locker	4	
7	AK610021L	Spire Nut	4	

TS5177

 **LAND ROVER PARTS LTD**

569

MODEL LR110 - UP TO AUGUST 1986
BLOCK VS 3894
PAGE L 84
GROUP L

BODY - REAR BODY LOWER - EYEBROWS

ILL	PART NO	DESCRIPTION	QTY	REMARKS
1		EYEBROW MOULDING-REAR WING		
	MRC8420	Natural Black	2	
	MTC6873AA	Arizona Tan	2	
	MTC6873AE	Russet	2	
	MTC6873AF	Sand	2	
	MTC6873AV	Roan Brown	2	
	MTC6873CC	Masai Red	2	
	MTC6873CL	Venetian Red	2	
	MTC6873HC	Bronze Green	2	
	MTC6873HD	Light Green	2	
	MTC6873HN	Trident Green	2	
	MTC6873JC	Marine Blue	2	
	MTC6873JP	Stratos Blue	2	
	MTC6873LB	Mid Grey	2	
	MTC6873LN	Slate Grey	2	
	MTC6873NJ	Limestone	2	
	MTC6873NM	Ivory	2	
2	AFU1075	Plastic Rivet	24	

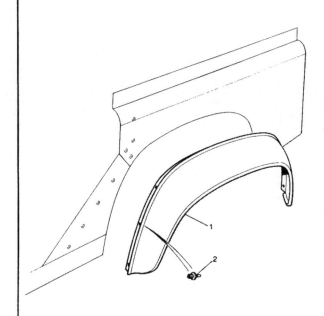

VS3894

LAND ROVER PARTS LTD

MODEL LR110 - UP TO AUGUST 1986
BLOCK TS 5293
PAGE L 84.10
GROUP L

BODY - HIGH CAPACITY PICK UP

ILL	PART NO	DESCRIPTION	QTY	REMARKS
1	MTC3902	REAR BODY ASSEMBLY	1	

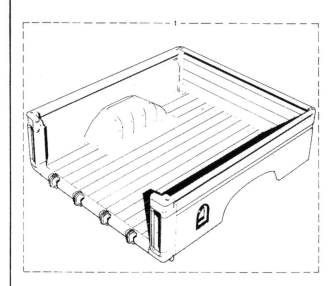

TS5293

LAND ROVER PARTS LTD

MODEL LR110 - UP TO AUGUST 1986
BLOCK TS 5294
PAGE L 84.12
GROUP L

BODY - HIGH CAPACITY PICK UP

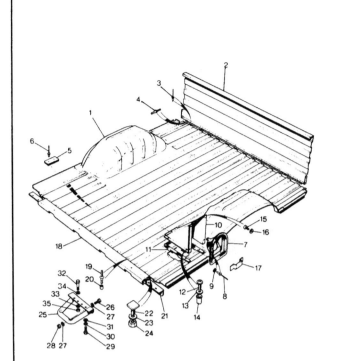

ILL	PART NO	DESCRIPTION	QTY	REMARKS
1	MTC3538	Floor	1	
2	MTC1409	Bulkhead	1	
3	RU612183	Rivet	15	
4	ACU3777	Monobolt	16	
5	MTC1595	Mounting Pad	12	
6	RJ612433	Rivet	24	
7	MTC3569	Cowl-Fuel Filler	1	
8	RA612373L	Rivet	4	
9	WA105001L	Plain Washer	4	
10	MTC1461	Cover	1	
11	MTC1462	Seal	1	
12	SE106161L	Screw-Cover to Floor	4	
13	WA106041L	Plain Washer	4	
14	MR106300	Rivnut	4	
15	AR606031L	Screw-Cover to Bodyside	5	
16	WA104001L	Plain Washer	5	
17	MTC1485	Spacer	2	No Longer Serviced
18	MTC3521	Rear Crossmember	1	
19	AAU6919	Avdelok Bolt	12	
20	AAU6774	Collar	12	
21	MTC4156	Reinforcing Angle	1	
22	MTC3558	Tee Bolt	4	
23	WA108051L	Plain Washer	4	
24	NH108041L	Nut	4	
25	MTC3126	Rear Bump Stop-RH	1	
	MTC3127	Rear Bump Stop-LH	1	
26	SH108251L	Screw-Bump Stop to Angle	4	
27	WA108051L	Plain Washer	8	
28	NH108041L	Nut	4	
29	SH108251L	Screw-Bump Stop to Body Pillar	2	
30	WL108001L	Spring Washer	2	
31	WA108051L	Plain Washer	2	
32	BH108121L	Bolt-Bump Stop to Body	2	
33	WL108001L	Spring Washer	2	
34	WA108051L	Plain Washer	2	
35	NH108041L	Nut	2	

TS5294

MODEL LR110 - UP TO AUGUST 1986
BLOCK TS 5296
PAGE L 84.16
GROUP L

BODY - HIGH CAPACITY PICK UP

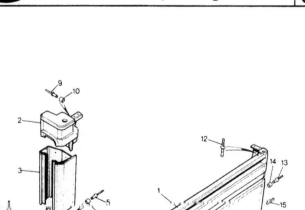

ILL	PART NO	DESCRIPTION	QTY	REMARKS
1	MTC3906	BODYSIDE ASSEMBLY RH	1	
	MTC3907	BODYSIDE ASSEMBLY LH	1	
2	MTC5038	+Rear Upper Pillar Casting RH	1	
	MTC5039	+Rear Upper Pillar Casting LH	1	
3	MTC1479	+Rear Pillar	2	
4	MTC1481	+Rear Lower Pillar Bracket RH	1	
	MTC1482	+Rear Lower Pillar Bracket LH	1	
5	ACU3530	+Avdelok Bolt	16	
6	AAU6774	+Collar	16	
7	ACU1161	+Avdelok Bolt	12	
8	AAU6774	+Collar	12	
9	ACU3530	+Avdelok Bolt	4	
10	AAU6774	+Collar	4	
11	ACU1762	+Monobolt	4	
12	ACU1762	Monobolt	4	
13	ACU2063	Avdelok Bolt	2	
	AAU8182	Avdelok Bolt	6	
14	AAU6774	Collar	8	
15	ACU3777	Monobolt	6	
	AFU1841	Monobolt	2	
16	RU612183	Rivet	8	
17	ACU3777	Monobolt	22	
18	ACU1161	Avdelok Bolt	58	
19	AAU6774	Collar	58	
20	ACU1762	Monobolt	4	
21	AAU6920	Avdelok Bolt	4	
22	AAU6774	Collar	4	
23	3H822L	Grommet	2	

TS5296

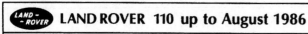
MODEL LR110 - UP TO AUGUST 1987
BLOCK TS 5297
PAGE L 84.18
GROUP L

BODY - HIGH CAPACITY PICK UP

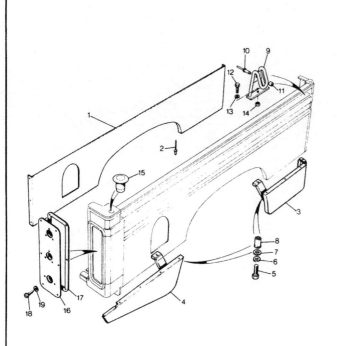

ILL	PART NO	DESCRIPTION	QTY	REMARKS
1	MTC3533	Inner Panel RH	1	
	MTC3534	Inner Panel LH	1	
2	RU612183	Rivet	58	
3	MTC7480	Front Valance Panel RH	1	
	MTC7481	Front Valance Panel LH	1	
4	MTC7482	Rear Valance Panel RH	1	
	MTC7483	Rear Valance Panel LH	1	
5	SH106201L	Screw	20	
6	WL106001L	Spring Washer	20	
7	WA106041L	Plain Washer	20	
8	NN106021	Anchor Nut	20	
9	MTC1439	Lashing Cleat	6	
10	ACU3530	Avdelok Bolt	6	
11	AAU6774	Collar	6	
12	SH106141L	Screw	6	
13	WL106001L	Spring Washer	6	
14	NH106041L	Nut	6	
15	MTC1594	Plug	2	
16	MTC3350	Mounting Plate-Rear Lamps	2	Note(1)
	MTC3350	Mounting Plate-Rear Lamps	1	Note(2) & (3)
	MTC3515	Mounting Plate-Rear Lamps	1	Note(2) & (3)
	MTC3515	Mounting Plate-Rear Lamps	2	Note(4)
17	MTC1448	Seal	2	
18	AR610051L	Screw	12	
19	WA105001L	Plain Washer	12	
	MTC7511	Corner Capping LH-Rear Valance	1	))Germany
	MTC7512	Corner Capping RH-Rear Valance	1	))

NOTES:

(1):   No Fog Lamp/No Reverse Lamp
(2):   Rear Fog Lamp Only
(3):   Reverse Lamp Only
(4):   Rear Fog Lamp and Reverse Lamp

TS5297

LAND ROVER PARTS LTD

574

MODEL LR110 - UP TO AUGUST 1986
BLOCK TS 5299
PAGE L 84.22
GROUP L

BODY - HIGH CAPACITY PICK UP - SPARE WHEEL MOUNTING

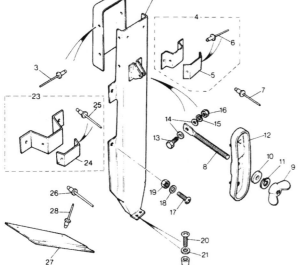

ILL	PART NO	DESCRIPTION	QTY	REMARKS
1	MTC1584	Spare Wheel Mounting Bracket	1	
2	MTC1416	Cover	1	
3	RA608177L	Rivet	4	
4	MTC1423	Rubbing Bracket	1	
5	MTC1490	+Rubbing Strip	1	
6	RA612347L	+Rivet	2	
7	RA608177L	Rivet	2	
8	302933	Tie Bar	1	
9	302934	Wing Nut	1	
10	3982L	Spacer	1	
11	WM600061L	Spring Washer	1	
12	303847	Clamp	1	
13	BH604081	Bolt	1	
14	3842	Plain Washer	2	
15	WS600041L	Spring Washer	1	
16	NY604041L	Nut	1	
17	SE106161L	Screw	4	
18	WA106041L	Plain Washer	8	
19	NY106041L	Nut	4	
20	SE106161L	Screw	1	
21	WA106041L	Plain Washer	1	
22	MR106300	Riv Nut	1	
23	332672	Rubbing Bracket-Bodyside	2	
24	332674	+Rubbing Strip	2	
25	78248	+Rivet	4	
26	RU612503	Rivet	4	
27	MTC1592	Wearing Plate	1	
28	RU612183	Rivet	4	

TS5299

LAND ROVER PARTS LTD

MODEL LR110 - UP TO AUGUST 1986
BLOCK TS 5300
PAGE L 84.24
GROUP L

BODY - HIGH CAPACITY PICK UP - BODY MOUNTINGS

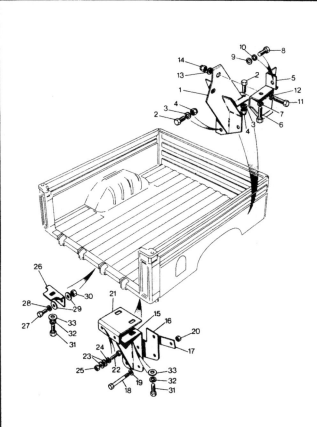

ILL	PART NO	DESCRIPTION	QTY	REMARKS
1	MTC3481	Front Mounting Bracket RH	1	
	MTC3482	Front Mounting Bracket LH	1	
2	SH110251L	Screw-Bracket to Chassis	6	
3	WA110061L	Plain Washer	6	
4	NY110041L	Nyloc Nut	6	
5	MTC3486	Front Anchor Bracket	2	
6	SH110301L	Screw-Anchor to Body	2	
7	WL110001L	Spring Washer	2	
8	SH110251L	Screw-Anchor to Body	2	
9	WA110061L	Plain Washer	2	
10	WL110001L	Spring Washer	2	
11	SH110251L	Screw-Anchor to Mounting Bracket	4	
12	WL110001L	Spring Washer	4	
13	WA110061L	Plain Washer	4	
14	NY110041L	Nyloc Nut	4	
15	MTC4992	Rear Mounting Bracket-RH	1	
	MTC4993	Rear Mounting Bracket-LH	1	
16	MTC5086	Packing Piece	2	
17	MTC6154	Backing Plate	4	
18	BH108141L	Bolt-Brackets to Chassis	8	
19	WA108051L	Plain Washer	8	
20	NH108041L	Nut	8	
21	MTC4002	Mounting Bracket-Outer	2	
22	SH108201L	Screw-Brackets to Body	4	
23	WA108051L	Plain Washer	8	
24	WL108001L	Spring Washer	4	
25	NH108041L	Nut	4	
26	MTC4003	Mounting Bracket-Inner	3	
27	SH108201L	Screw-Brackets to Chassis	6	
28	WL108001L	Spring Washer	6	
29	WA108051L	Plain Washer	6	
30	NH108041L	Nut	6	
31	SH110301L	Screw-Brackets to Body	7	
32	WL110001L	Spring Washer	7	
33	WA110061L	Plain Washer	7	

TS5300

 **LAND ROVER PARTS LTD**

MODEL LR110 - UP TO AUGUST 1986
BLOCK VS 3895B
PAGE L 86
GROUP L

BODY - REAR BODY UPPER - STATION WAGON - UP TO 1984 FACELIFT

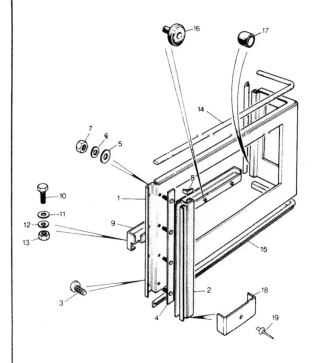

ILL	PART NO	DESCRIPTION	QTY	REMARKS
		BODYSIDE DESPATCH ASSEMBLY WITH REAR END WINDOW AND WITH INTEGRAL SLIDING WINDOW		
	MTC5420	With Clear Glass RH	1	NLA Use MTC5410
	MTC5421	With Clear Glass LH	1	NLA Use MTC5411
	MTC5422	With Tinted Glass RH	1	
	MTC5423	With Tinted Glass LH	1	NLA Use MTC5411
1		BODYSIDE DESPATCH PANEL WITH APERTURES FOR REAR END & SIDE WINDOWS		
	MTC5410	RH	1	
	MTC5411	LH	1	
2	MTC5394	Finisher & Seal Retainer-RH	1	
	MTC5395	Finisher & Seal Retainer-LH	1	
3	78832	Screw Retainer to Pillar	6	
4	332065	Stud Plate-2BA	2	
5	4034L	Plain Washer	8	
6	WM702001L	Spring Washer	8	
7	RTC608	Nut	8	
8	332215	Seal-Door Pillar-Upper and Lower	4	
9	336764	Drain Channel	2	
10	255206	Bolt	4	
11	WA106041L	Plain Washer	4	
12	WM600041L	Spring Washer	4	
13	NH604041L	Nut	4	
14	334612	Seal-Bodyside Upper-RH	1	
	334613	Seal-Bodyside Upper-LH	1	
15	333487	Seal-Bodyside Lower	2	
16	MUC1426	Bung-Drain Tube	8	)
17	MTC7407	Cover for Screw Heads	6	)Germany
18	MTC8333	'D' Post Finisher	2	)
19	RU608313L	Rivet	2	)

VS3895B

 **LAND ROVER PARTS LTD**

MODEL LR110 - UP TO AUGUST 1986
BLOCK VS 3960A
PAGE L 86.02
GROUP L

BODY - REAR BODY UPPER - STATION WAGON - UP TO 1984 FACELIFT

ILL	PART NO	DESCRIPTION	QTY	REMARKS
1	MTC5314	Sliding Light-Clear	4	
	MTC5315	Sliding Light-Tinted	4	
2	332230	Seal-Sliding Light	2	
3	330661	Channel for Seal	2	
4	336454	Channel-Side	4	
5	348396	Channel-Top	2	
6	332216	Packing Strip-Top Channel	4	
7	348394	Channel-Bottom Inner	2	
8	348393	Channel-Bottom Outer	2	
9	AC606041L	Drive Screw-Fixing Channels	52	
10	330848	Runner for Catch	4	
11	78248	Rivet Fixing Runner	16	
12	332324	Catch-Front	2	
	332325	Catch-Rear	2	
13	78401	Screw-Fixing Rear Catch	2	
	78402	Screw-Fixing Front Catch	2	
14	340391	Washer	12	
15	332329	Tapped Plate	4	
16	MTC3476	Glass-Rear End Window-Clear	2	
	MTC5034	Glass-Rear End Window-Tinted	2	
17	306287	Glazing Strip-Rear End Window	2	
18	306289	Filler Strip-Rear End Window	2	
19	MTC6631	Bung-Sliding Window Rail Upper	8	)Germany)

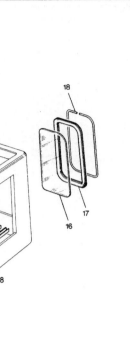

VS3960A

MODEL LR110 - UP TO AUGUST 1986
BLOCK TS 5052B
PAGE L 86.10
GROUP L

BODY - REAR BODY UPPER - STATION WAGON - 1984 FACELIFT

ILL	PART NO	DESCRIPTION	QTY	REMARKS
		BODYSIDE DESPATCH ASSEMBLY WITH REAR END WINDOW AND SLIDING SIDE WINDOW ASSEMBLY		
	MUC3536	-With Clear Glass RH	1	NLA Use RTC6253
	MUC3537	-With Clear Glass LH	1	NLA Use MUC1533
	MUC3538	-With Tinted Glass RH	1	NLA Use RTC6253
	MUC3539	-With Tinted Glass LH	1	NLA Use MUC1533
	MUC6182	-With Tinted Glass RH Australia	1	NLA Use RTC6253
	MUC6181	-With Tinted Glass LH Australia	1	NLA Use MUC1533
1		BODYSIDE DESPATCH PANEL WITH APERTURES FOR REAR END AND SIDE WINDOWS		
	RTC6253	RH	1	
	MUC1533	LH	1	
2	MTC5394	Finisher/Seal Retainer RH	1	
	MTC5395	Finisher/Seal Retainer LH	1	
3	78832	Screw	6	
4	AFU1080	Plain Washer	6	
5	MUC3566	Stud Plate-M5	2	
6	WA105001L	Plain Washer	8	
7	WL105001L	Spring Washer	8	
8	NM105011	Nut	8	
	332065	Stud Plate-2BA	2	)
	4034L	Plain Washer	8	)Alternative
	WM702001L	Spring Washer	8	)Fixings
	RTC608	Nut	8	)
9	332215	Seal-Door Pillar Upper and Lower	4	
10	334612	Seal-Bodyside Upper RH	1	
	334613	Seal-Bodyside Upper LH	1	
11	333487	Seal-Bodyside Lower	2	

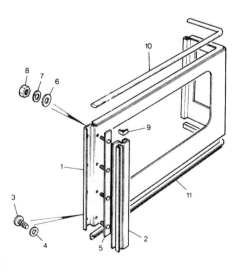

TS5052B

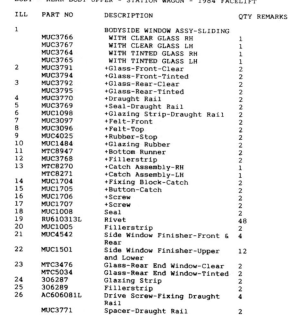

```
MODEL LR110 - UP TO AUGUST 1986
BLOCK TS 6150
PAGE L 86.12
GROUP L
```

BODY - REAR BODY UPPER - STATION WAGON - 1984 FACELIFT

ILL	PART NO	DESCRIPTION	QTY	REMARKS
1		BODYSIDE WINDOW ASSY-SLIDING		
	MUC3766	WITH CLEAR GLASS RH	1	
	MUC3767	WITH CLEAR GLASS LH	1	
	MUC3764	WITH TINTED GLASS RH	1	
	MUC3765	WITH TINTED GLASS LH	1	
2	MUC3791	+Glass-Front-Clear	2	
	MUC3794	+Glass-Front-Tinted	2	
3	MUC3792	+Glass-Rear-Clear	2	
	MUC3795	+Glass-Rear-Tinted	2	
4	MUC3770	+Draught Rail	2	
5	MUC3769	+Seal-Draught Rail	2	
6	MUC1098	+Glazing Strip-Draught Rail	2	
7	MUC3097	+Felt-Front	2	
8	MUC3096	+Felt-Top	2	
9	MUC4025	+Rubber-Stop	2	
10	MUC1484	+Glazing Rubber	2	
11	MTC8947	+Bottom Runner	2	
12	MUC3768	+Fillerstrip	2	
13	MTC8270	+Catch Assembly-RH	1	
	MTC8271	+Catch Assembly-LH	1	
14	MUC1704	+Fixing Block-Catch	2	
15	MUC1705	+Button-Catch	2	
16	MUC1706	+Screw	2	
17	MUC1707	+Screw	2	
18	MUC1008	Seal	2	
19	RU610313L	Rivet	48	
20	MUC1005	Fillerstrip	2	
21	MUC4542	Side Window Finisher-Front & Rear	4	
22	MUC1501	Side Window Finisher-Upper and Lower	12	
23	MTC3476	Glass-Rear End Window-Clear	2	
	MTC5034	Glass-Rear End Window-Tinted	2	
24	306287	Glazing Strip	2	
25	306289	Fillerstrip	2	
26	AC606081L	Drive Screw-Fixing Draught Rail	4	
	MUC3771	Spacer-Draught Rail	2	

TS6150

```
MODEL LR110 - UP TO AUGUST 1986
BLOCK VS 3897
PAGE L 86.20
GROUP L
```

BODY - MOUNTINGS - BODYSIDE UPPER - STATION WAGON

ILL	PART NO	DESCRIPTION	QTY	REMARKS
1	338554	Mounting Angle-Front Pillar	2	
2	SH108161L	Screw	4	
3	WL108001L	Spring Washer	4	
4	WC108051L	Plain Washer	4	
5	MUC1324	Nut Plate-Metric Thread	2	
6	332201	Support Bracket-Body Sides	2	
7	SH106201L	Screw	4	
8	AFU1080	Plain Washer	6	
9	WL106001L	Spring Washer	4	
10	NH106041L	Nut	4	
11	338550	Rubber Buffer	2	
12	338552	Support Bracket-Body Rear	2	
13	338550	Rubber Buffer	2	
14	SH106161L	Screw-Bracket to Bodyside	4	
15	AFU1135	Plain Washer	4	)Alternatives
	MRC5525	Plain Washer	4	)
16	WL106001L	Spring Washer	4	
17	NH106041L	Nut	4	
18	SH108301L	Screw-Bracket to Tailboard Corner	2	
19	WC108051L	Plain Washer	4	
20	WL108001L	Spring Washer	2	
21	NH108041L	Nut	2	
22	MRC9833	Mounting Stud	4	
23	338553	Rubber Buffer	4	
24	332293	Special Washer	4	
25	WC108051L	Plain Washer	4	
26	WL108001L	Spring Washer	8	
27	NH108041L	Nut	8	

VS3897

MODEL LR110 - UP TO AUGUST 1986
BLOCK VS 3959
PAGE L 88
GROUP L

BODY - REAR BODY UPPER - HARD TOP

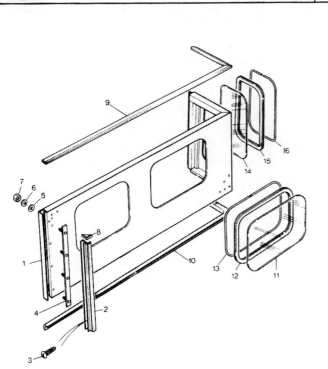

ILL	PART NO	DESCRIPTION	QTY	REMARKS
		BODYSIDE DESPATCH ASSEMBLY		
		WITH REAR END WINDOW		
	MTC5416	-WITH FIXED SIDE WINDOW RH	1	NLA Use MTC4411
	MTC5417	-WITH FIXED SIDE WINDOW LH	1	NLA Use MTC4412
	MTC5396	-WITHOUT SIDE WINDOWS RH	1	NLA Use RTC6220
	MTC5397	-WITHOUT SIDE WINDOWS LH	1	NLA Use RTC6221
1		+BODYSIDE DESPATCH PANEL		
	MTC4411	RH	1	)Note(1)
	MTC4412	LH	1	)
	RTC6220	RH	1	)Note(2)
	RTC6221	LH	1	)
2	MTC5394	+Finisher & Seal Retainer RH	1	
	MTC5395	+Finisher & Seal Retainer LH	1	
3	78832	+Screw-Retainer to Pillar	6	
	AFU1080	+Plain Washer	6	
4	332065	+Stud Plate-2BA	2	)
5	4034L	+Plain Washer	8	)
6	WM702001L	+Spring Washer	8	)
7	RTC608	+Nut	8	)Alternatives
	MUC3566	+Stud Plate-M5	2	)
	WA105001L	+Plain Washer	8	)
	WL105001L	+Spring Washer	8	)
	NM105011	+Nut	8	)
8	332215	+Seal-Door Pillar Upper and	4	
		Lower		
9	334610	+Seal-Bodyside Upper RH	1	
	334611	+Seal-Bodyside Upper LH	1	
10	333490	+Seal-Bodyside Lower	2	
11	MTC5312	+Glass-Side Window	4	
12	302177	+Glazing Strip	4	
13	302178	+Filler Strip	4	
14	MTC3476	+Glass-Rear End Window	2	
15	306287	+Glazing Strip	2	
16	306289	+Filler Strip	2	
	MTC8333	'D' Post Finisher	2	)
	RU608313L	Rivet	2	)Germany
	MUC3810	Cover-Rear Body Horizontal	2	)
		Stiffener		

NOTE(1): With Apertures For Rear End & Side Windows

NOTE(2): With Apertures For Rear End Windows Only.

VS3959

LAND ROVER PARTS LTD

582

MODEL LR110 - UP TO AUGUST 1986
BLOCK VS 4110
PAGE L 88.20
GROUP L

BODY - MOUNTING - BODYSIDE UPPER - HARD TOP

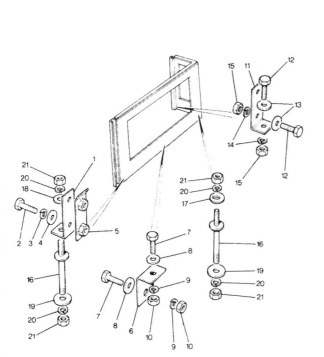

ILL	PART NO	DESCRIPTION	QTY	REMARKS
1	338554	Mounting Angle-Front Pillar	2	
2	SH108161L	Screw	4	
3	WL108001L	Spring Washer	4	
4	WC108051L	Plain Washer	4	
5	MUC1324	Nut Plate-Metric Thread	2	
6	332201	Support Bracket-Bodysides	4	
7	SH106201L	Screw	8	
8	MRC5527	Plain Washer	16	
9	WL106001L	Spring Washer	8	
10	NH106041L	Nut	8	
11	338552	Support Bracket-Body Rear	2	
12	SH106161L	Screw	6	
13	MRC5525	Plain Washer	8	
14	WL106001L	Spring Washer	6	
15	NH106041L	Nut	6	
16	338741	Mounting Stud-UNF Thread	4	)Alternatives
	MRC9833	Mounting Stud-Metric Thread	4	)
17	332293	Special Washer	2	
18	3830L	Plain Washer	2	)
19	WP185L	Plain Washer	4	)Use with
20	WM600051L	Spring Washer	8	)338741
21	NH605041L	Nut	8	)
	332293	Special Washer	4	)
	WC108051L	Plain Washer	4	)Use with
	WL108001L	Spring Washer	8	)MRC9833
	NH108041L	Nut	8	)

VS4110

LAND ROVER PARTS LTD

583

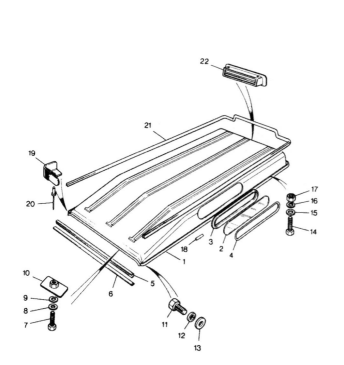

MODEL LR110 - UP TO AUGUST 1986
BLOCK TS 5494A
PAGE L 90.04
GROUP L

BODY - ROOF - STATION WAGON

ILL	PART NO	DESCRIPTION	QTY	REMARKS
1	RTC5587	Roof	1	
	MWC2884	Roof	1	Note(1)
2	MTC3474	Sidelight Glass	2	
3	302177	Weatherstrip	2	
4	302178	Filler Strip	2	
5	MTC4994	Seal-Inner	1	
6	MTC6568	Seal-Outer	1	
	MUC6400	Seal-Corner	2	
7	SH106161L	Screw	6	
8	WA106041L	Plain Washer	6	
9	WL106001L	Spring Washer	6	
10	MTC3203	Nut Plate	6	
11	SH106161L	Screw	2	
12	WA106041L	Plain Washer	2	
13	WL106001L	Spring Washer	2	
14	SH106201L	Screw	24	
15	WA106041L	Plain Washer	24	
16	WL106001L	Spring Washer	24	
17	NH106041L	Nut	24	
18	334615	Seal-'BC' Post	2	
19	MTC8332	Corner Capping-RH	1	)
	MTC8331	Corner Capping-LH	1	)Germany
20	RU608313L	Rivet	2	)
21	MTC7513	Edging Strip-Cantrail	A/R	)
22	MWC3141	Roof Ventilator-Black	2	

NOTE(1): With Ventilator Apertures In Rear End.

TS 5494A

 **LAND ROVER PARTS LTD**

584

MODEL LR110 - UP TO AUGUST 1986
BLOCK TS 5495
PAGE L 90.06
GROUP L

BODY - ROOF - HARD TOP

ILL	PART NO	DESCRIPTION	QTY	REMARKS
1	MWC6699	Roof	1	Note(2)
2	MTC4994	Seal-Inner	1	
3	MTC6568	Seal-Outer	1	
	MUC6400	Seal-Corner	2	
4	SH106161L	Screw	6	
5	WA106041L	Plain Washer	6	
6	WL106001L	Spring Washer	6	
7	MTC3203	Nut Plate	6	
8	SH106161L	Screw	2	
9	WA106041L	Plain Washer	2	
10	WL106001L	Spring Washer	2	
11	SH106201L	Screw	28	
12	WA106041L	Plain Washer	28	
13	WL106001L	Spring Washer	28	
14	NH106041L	Nut	28	
15	334068	Hinge Mounting Bracket-RH	1	)
	334069	Hinge Mounting Bracket-LH	1	)
16	MTC1697	Spacer	2	)Note(1)
17	78248	Rivet	4	)
18	RU612373L	Rivet	4	)
19	MWC3141	Roof Ventilator-Black	2	
	MTC7513	Edging Strip-Cantrail	A/R	)
	MTC8331	Corner Capping LH	1	)
	MTC8332	Corner Capping RH	1	)Germany
	RU608313L	Drivescrew	2	)
	MUC3809	Cover-Bracket/Cantrail	2	)
	MUC3882	Cover-Cantrail RH	1	)
	MUC3883	Cover-Cantrail LH	1	)

NOTE(1): Required When Rear Lid Fitted

TS5495/A

 **LAND ROVER PARTS LTD**

585

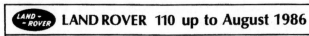

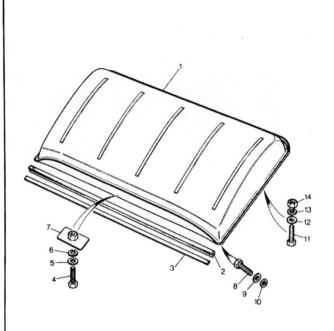

MODEL LR110 - UP TO AUGUST 1986
BLOCK TS 5241
PAGE L 90.08
GROUP L

BODY - ROOF - TRUCK CAB

1	MWC6055	Roof	1
2	MTC4994	Seal-Inner	1
3	MTC6568	Seal-Outer	1
	MUC6400	Seal-Corner	2
4	SH106161L	Screw	6
5	WA106041L	Plain Washer	6
6	WL106001L	Spring Washer	6
7	MTC3203	Nut Plate	6
8	SH106161L	Screw	2
9	WA106041L	Plain Washer	2
10	WL106001L	Spring Washer	2
11	SH106201L	Screw	8
12	WA106041L	Plain Washer	12
13	WL106001L	Spring Washer	12
14	NH106041L	Nut	12
	MTC7513	Edging Strip-Cantrail	A/R)
	MTC8331	Corner Capping LH	1)Germany
	MTC8332	Corner Capping RH	1)
	RU608313L	Rivet	2)

TS5241

LAND ROVER PARTS LTD

MODEL LR110 - UP TO AUGUST 1986
BLOCK VS 4162
PAGE L 90.10
GROUP L

BODY - REAR PANEL - TRUCK CAB

ILL	PART NO	DESCRIPTION	QTY REMARKS
	MTC5198	CAB REAR PANEL COMPLETE ASSY	1
1	RTC6222	+Rear Panel	1
2	MTC3461	+Quarter Light RH	1
	MTC3462	+Quarter Light LH	1
3	330790	+Weatherstrip	2
4	330791	+Fillerstrip	2
5	MTC5197	+Rear Window	1
6	MTC6544	++Sliding Glass	2
7	AEU2805	++Catch Assembly-LH	1
	AEU2806	++Catch Assembly-RH	1
8	MTC6233	+Seal	1
9	MTC6232	+Finisher	1
10	AS604044	+Screw	18
11	334614	+Seal	1
12	333486	+Seal	1
	MTC7513	Edging Strip Finisher-Top Corner Flanges of Rear Panel Assembly	A/R

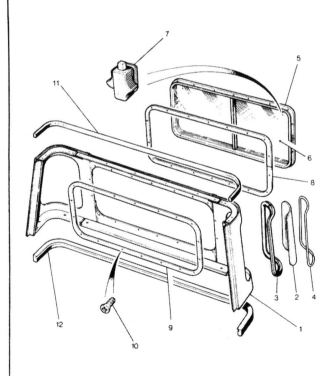

VS4162

LAND ROVER PARTS LTD

MODEL LR110 - UP TO AUGUST 1986
BLOCK VS 4164
PAGE L 90.12
GROUP L

BODY - REAR PANEL FIXINGS - TRUCK CAB

ILL	PART NO	DESCRIPTION	QTY	REMARKS
1	336577	Mounting Bracket	4	
2	SH106251L	Screw	8	
3	WL106001L	Spring Washer	8	
4	NH106041L	Nut	8	
5	SH607091L	Screw	4	
6	WM600071L	Spring Washer	4	
7	4580	Plain Washer	4	
8	330762	Mounting Stud-5/16" UNF	2	
9	WP185L	Plain Washer	4	
10	3829	Plain Washer	6	
11	WM600051L	Spring Washer	4	
12	NH605041L	Nut	4	
	MUC8928	Mounting Stud-M8	2	)
	WP185L	Plain Washer	4	)Alternative
	WC112081L	Plain Washer	6	)Fixings
	WL108001L	Spring Washer	4	)
	NH108041L	Nut	4	)

VS4164

LAND ROVER PARTS LTD

588

MODEL LR110 - UP TO AUGUST 1986
BLOCK VS 4163B
PAGE L 90.14
GROUP L

BODY - BASE ASSEMBLY - TRUCK CAB

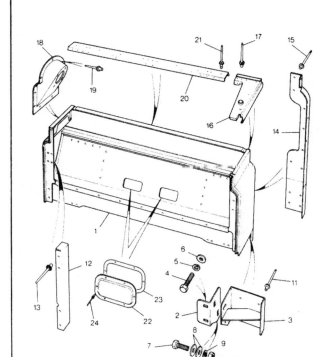

ILL	PART NO	DESCRIPTION	QTY	REMARKS
1	MUC3318	Cab Base	1	Note(1)
	MUC3340	Cab Base	1	Note(2)
2	MTC2106	Mounting Angle RH	1	
	MTC2107	Mounting Angle LH	1	
3	MTC2224	Reinforcing Angle RH	1	
	MTC2225	Reinforcing Angle LH	1	
4	SH106161L	Screw-Angle to Chassis	4	
5	WL106001L	Spring Washer	4	
6	WA106041L	Plain Washer	4	
7	SH106161L	Screw-Mounting Angle to	4	
		Reinforcing Angle		
8	MRC5527	Plain Washer	8	
9	WL106001L	Spring Washer	4	
10	NH106041L	Nut	4	
11	78248	Rivet-Reinforcing Angle to	8	
		Base		
12	MWC1820	Stiffener-Door Pillar RH	1	
	MWC1821	Stiffener-Door Pillar LH	1	
13	AFU1350	Monobolt	4	
14	MUC8756	Corner Protection Angle-LH	1	)Note(4)
	MUC8755	Corner Protection Angle-RH	1	)
	MTC4076	Corner Protection Angle-RH	1	Note(1)(3)
	MUC9551	Corner Protection Angle-RH	1	Note(1)(4)
15	78248	Rivet	26	
16	MTC5193	Corner Capping LH-Note(3)	1	
	MTC5194	Corner Capping RH-Note(3) (5)	1	Use MUC8732
	MUC8733	Corner Capping LH-Note(4)	1	
	MUC8732	Corner Capping RH-Note(4)	1	
17	78248	Rivet	8	
18	330366	Cowl-Side Fuel Filler	1	Note(1)(3)
	MUC9158	Cowl-Side Fuel Filler	1	Note(1)(4)
19	78248	Rivet	9	Note(1)
20	330245	Capping-Bulkhead	1	Note(3)
	MUC8735	Capping-Bulkhead	1	Note(4)
21	RU612373L	Rivet	39	
22	MUC6519	Cover Plate-Cab Base	2	
23	MWC2129	Gasket	2	
24	78248	Rivet	12	

NOTE(1): Vehicles With Additional Fuel Tank
NOTE(2): Vehicles Without Additional Fuel Tank
NOTE(3): Galvanised-Not Suitable For Painting
NOTE(4): Galvanised & Treated-Suitable For Painting
NOTE(5): No Longer Available

VS4163B

LAND ROVER PARTS LTD

589

MODEL LR110 - UP TO AUGUST 1986
BLOCK TS 5813
PAGE L 92
GROUP L

BODY - TAILBOARD - LOWER HINGED

ILL	PART NO	DESCRIPTION	QTY	REMARKS
1	320604	TAILBOARD ASSEMBLY	1	Note(1)
	MUC8736	TAILBOARD ASSEMBLY	1	Note(2)
2	345915	+Reinforcing Panel	1	Note(1)
	MUC8737	+Reinforcing Panel	1	Note(2)
3	78248	+Rivet	17	
	RR612063	+Rivet	8	
4	MUC8740	+Hinge-RH	1	
5	MUC8741	+Hinge-LH	1	
6	BH106111L	+Bolt	4	
7	MRC5528	+Plain Washer	10	
8	WL106001L	+Spring Washer	4	
9	NH106041L	+Nut	4	
10	MUC8746	+Locking Plate	2	
11	332445	+Hook-RH	1	Note(1)
	332446	+Hook-LH	1	Note(1)
12	MUC8738	+Bracket RH	1	Note(2)
	MUC8739	+Bracket LH	1	Note(2)
13	BH106111L	+Bolt	4	
14	WL106001L	+Spring Washer	4	
15	NH106041L	+Nut	4	
16	303975	+Seal	1	
17	78321	+Rivet	8	
18	WS600091	Spring Washer	1	
19	WA600091L	Plain Washer	1	
20	PS612080	Split Pin	1	

NOTE(1): Chain Retained Tailboard

NOTE(2): Cable Retained Tailboard

TS5813

590

MODEL LR110 - UP TO AUGUST 1986
BLOCK VS 4286
PAGE L 92.10
GROUP L

BODY - TAILBOARD - SIDE HINGED

ILL	PART NO	DESCRIPTION	QTY	REMARKS
1	MUC8707	Tailboard	1	
2	346341	Hinge	2	
3	257450	Capped Turret Nut	2	
4	WA106041L	Plain Washer	2	
5	SE108061	Screw-Hinges to Tailboard	4	
6	WC108051L	Plain Washer	1	
7	WA108051L	Plain Washer	2	
8	WL108001L	Spring Washer	4	
9	NH108041L	Nut	4	
10	MRC8440	Lock	1	
		Barrel & Keys		)Note(1)
		Key Blank		)
11	SE106201L	Screw	4	
12	WA106041L	Plain Washer	10	
13	WL106001L	Spring Washer	4	
14	NH106041L	Nut	4	
15	SE106501L	Screw-Redundant Holes	5	
16	WA106041L	Plain Washer	10	
17	WL106001L	Spring Washer	5	
18	NH106041L	Nut	5	
19	79086	Rokut Rivet-Redundant Hole	1	
20	303975	Sealing Rubber	1	
21	RT612283	Rivet	8	
22	MTC7523	Cleat	1	
23	398776	Check Strap	1	

NOTE(1): Refer to 'Barrel & Key Sets'

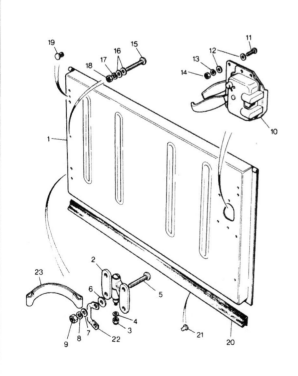

VS4286

591

MODEL LR110 - UP TO AUGUST 1986
BLOCK VS 4289
PAGE L 92.12
GROUP L

BODY - TAILBOARD - SIDE HINGED

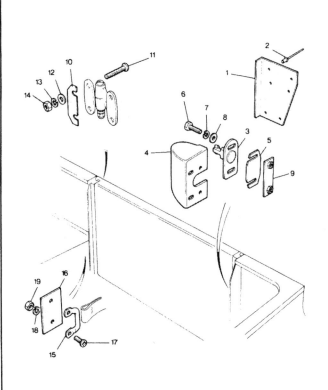

ILL	PART NO	DESCRIPTION	QTY	REMARKS
		REAR CORNER BRACKET		
1	330237	RH Note(1) (3)	1	Use MUC9154
	330238	LH Note(1)	1	
	MUC9154	RH Note(2)	1	
	MUC9155	LH Note(2)	1	
2	78248	Rivet	5	
3	MRC8444	Striker	1	
4	MRC9006	Shroud	1	
5	347594	Shim	A/R	
6	SH106351	Screw	2	
7	WL106001L	Spring Washer	2	
8	WA106041L	Plain Washer	2	
9	MRC9431	Nut Plate	1	
10	395463	Cover Plate-Upper Hinge	1	
11	SE108251	Screw-Hinges to Body	4	
12	WA108051L	Plain Washer	4	
13	WL108001L	Spring Washer	4	
14	NH108041L	Nut	4	
15	MTC7523	Cleat	1	
16	MTC7525	Spreader Plate	1	
17	SE108201	Screw	2	
18	WL108001L	Spring Washer	2	
19	NH108041L	Nut	2	

NOTE(1): Galvanised-Not suitable for Painting

NOTE(2): Galvanised & Treated-Suitable for Painting
if required

NOTE(3): No Longer Available

VS4289

LAND ROVER PARTS LTD

592

MODEL LR110 - UP TO AUGUST 1986
BLOCK TS 5303
PAGE L 92.14
GROUP L

BODY - TAILGATE - HIGH CAPACITY PICK UP

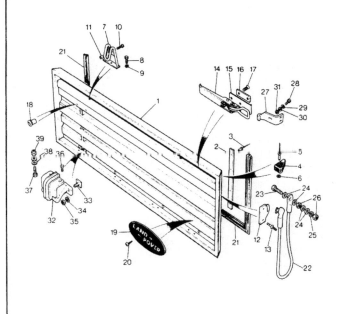

ILL	PART NO	DESCRIPTION	QTY	REMARKS
1	MTC3908	Tailgate	1	
2	MTC3139	Wearing Strip	5	
3	RU608183L	Rivet	20	
4	MTC1531	Buffer Stop	2	
5	RJ608603	Rivet	2	
6	WA103001L	Plain Washer	2	
7	MTC1439	Lashing Cleat	2	
8	SH106201L	Screw	2	
9	WL106001L	Spring Washer	2	
10	ACU3530	Rivet	2	
11	AAU6774	Collar	2	
12	MTC4824	Bracket	2	
13	AFU1841	Monobolt	4	
14	MTC3917	Latch	2	
15	MTC4846	Rubbing Plate	1	
16	MTC4888	Spreader Plate	2	
17	SF108251	Screw	4	
18	AFU1876	Rivet Nut-(Number Plate Lamp)	2	
19	MTC4460	Nameplate	1	
20	AB606031L	Drivescrew	2	
21	MTC3923	Seal	1	
22	RRC5539	Retaining Cable	2	
23	SH108301L	Screw	2	
24	WA108051L	Plain Washer	8	
25	WL108001L	Spring Washer	2	
26	NH108041L	Nut	4	
27	MTC4844	Catch-RH	1	
	MTC4845	Catch-LH	1	
28	SH106251L	Screw	6	
29	WD106041	Plain Washer	6	
30	WL106001L	Spring Washer	6	
31	WD106041	Plain Washer-Adjustment	A/R	
32	MTC3556	Hinge	4	
33	MTC3557	Tee Bolt	8	
34	WA108051L	Plain Washer	8	
35	NH108041L	Nut	8	
36	SA106141	Screw	4	
37	SH108251L	Screw	8	
38	WA108051L	Plain Washer	16	
39	NY108041L	Nut	8	

TS5303

LAND ROVER PARTS LTD

593

MODEL LR110 - UP TO AUGUST 1986
BLOCK VS 3992
PAGE L 92.20
GROUP L

BODY - REAR LID ASSEMBLY

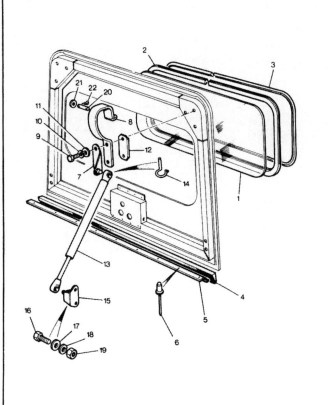

ILL	PART NO	DESCRIPTION	QTY	REMARKS
	MTC5381	REAR LID COMPLETE ASSEMBLY	1	
1	MTC3475	+Glass	1	
2	302177	+Weatherstrip	1	
3	302178	+Fillerstrip	1	
4	MTC4326	+Bottom Seal	1	
5	332122	+Retainer	1	
6	78257	+Rivet	5	
7	MTC6057	+Bracket	1	
8	333468	+Leaf Hinge	2	
9	SH605071	+Bolt	4	
10	WM600051L	+Spring Washer	4	
11	3830	+Plain Washer	4	
12	332047	+Tapped Plate	2	
13	RTC2486	Gas Strut	1	
14	BRC2623	Safety Clip	2	
15	MTC6058	Bracket	1	
16	SH106161	Screw	2	
17	WA106041L	Plain Washer	2	
18	WL106001L	Spring Washer	2	
19	NH106041L	Nut	2	
20	302165	Hinge Pin	2	
21	RTC613	Plain Washer	4	
22	RTC614	Split Pin	4	

VS3992

LAND ROVER PARTS LTD

MODEL LR110 - UP TO AUGUST 1986
BLOCK VS 3976
PAGE L 92.22
GROUP L

BODY - REAR LID ASSEMBLY

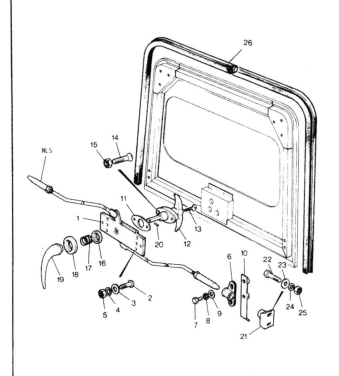

ILL	PART NO	DESCRIPTION	QTY	REMARKS
	MTC5381	REAR LID COMPLETE ASSEMBLY	1	
1	302164	+Lock	1	
2	77700	+Screw	4	
3	WC702101	+Plain Washer	4	
4	WM702001	+Spring Washer	4	
5	RTC608	+Nut	4	
6	332097	+Guide	2	
7	SH106201	+Screw	4	
8	WL106001L	+Spring Washer	4	
9	AFU1080	+Plain Washer	4	
10	MRC9616	+Nut Plate	2	
11	338423	+Escutcheon-Outer	1	
12	306461	+Locking Handle-Outer	1	
13	CD31709B	Key Blank	A/R	
14	78173	+Screw	2	
15	RTC608	+Nut	2	
16	320046	+Escutcheon-Inner	1	
17	313493	+Spring	1	
18	320047	+Cap	1	
19	302207	+Handle-Inner	1	
20	90302262	+Locking Pin	1	
21	332083	Socket-RH	1	
	332084	Socket-LH	1	
22	SH106201	Screw	4	
23	MRC5525	Plain Washer	4	
24	WL106001L	Spring Washer	4	
25	NH106041L	Nut	4	
26	MTC4166	Seal	1	

VS3976

LAND ROVER PARTS LTD

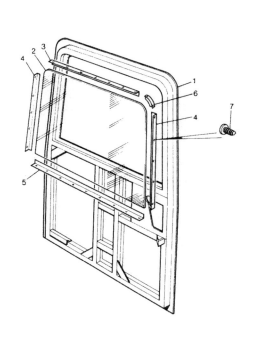

MODEL LR110 - UP TO AUGUST 1986
BLOCK VS 3900
PAGE L 94
GROUP L

BODY - REAR END DOOR

ILL	PART NO	DESCRIPTION	QTY	REMARKS
1		REAR END DOOR CLINCHED ASSY		
	RTC6247	With Pierced Panel	1	Note(1)
	RTC6248	With Plain Panel	1	Note(2)
	MUC4512	With Pierced Panel	1	Note(1)(3)
2	MTC3469	Window Glass-Clear	1	
	MTC3470	Window Glass-Sundym	1	
	MTC8951	Window Glass-Heated-Sundym	1	
3	78159	Glazing Strip	A/R	
	333034	Retainer-Top	1	
4	333033	Retainer-Sides	2	
5	333032	Retainer-Bottom	1	
6	333035	Retainer-Corners	2	
7	AB606031L	Drive Screw	30	
	MTC9807	Retaining Strip Washer Bag-LH	1	
	MTC9981	Retaining Strip Washer Bag-RH	1	
	RA612157L	Rivet	4	

NOTES:
(1): With Provision for Fitting Spare Wheel Carrier
(2): Without Provision for Fitting Spare Wheel Carrier
(3): Automatic Door Check with Manual Release

VS3900

LAND ROVER PARTS LTD

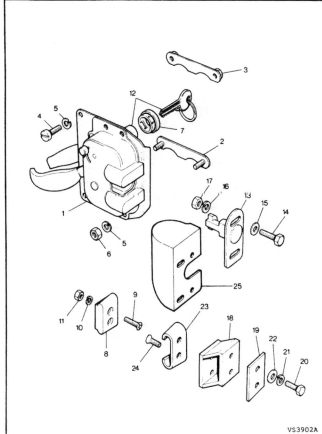

MODEL LR110 - UP TO AUGUST 1986
BLOCK VS 3902A
PAGE L 96
GROUP L

BODY - REAR END DOOR

ILL	PART NO	DESCRIPTION	QTY	REMARKS
1	MUC1030	Lock	1	
2	MRC9416	Screw Retainer	1	
3	MRC9417	Nut Retainer	1	
4	SE106161L	Screw	2	
5	WL106001L	Spring Washer	4	
6	NH106041L	Nut	2	
7	347151	Seal-Door Lock	1	
8	332942	Male Dovetail	1	
9	SA106251	Screw	2	
10	WL106001L	Spring Washer	2	
11	NH106041L	Nut	2	
12		Barrel & Keys		)Note(1)
		Key Blank		)
13	MRC8444	Striker	1	Station Wagon
	395094	Striker Plate	1	)Hard Top
	395078	Shim	1	)
14	SH106251L	Screw	2	
15	AFU1259	Plain Washer	2	Station Wagon
	MRC5525	Plain Washer	2	Hard Top
16	WL106001L	Spring Washer	2	
17	NH106041L	Nut	2	
18	MRC9619	Spacer	1	
19	305232	Shim	2	
20	SH106201L	Screw	2	
21	WL106001L	Spring Washer	2	
22	AFU1080	Plain Washer	2	
23	332147	Female Dovetail	1	
24	SA106161	Screw	2	
25	MRC9006	Shroud-Striker	1	
	MTC7155	Cover-Striker and Dovetail	1	Germany

NOTE(1): Refer to 'Barrel & Key Sets'

VS3902A

LAND ROVER PARTS LTD

MODEL LR110 - UP TO AUGUST 1986
BLOCK TS 5280
PAGE L 98
GROUP L

BODY - REAR END DOOR

ILL	PART NO	DESCRIPTION	QTY	REMARKS
1	333036	Hinge-Upper	1	
2	346341	Hinge-Centre	1	
	346341	Hinge-Lower	1	
3	257450	Capped Turret Nut	3	
4	SE108501	Screw-Hinges to Door	6	)
5	MRC1980	Nylon Washer	6	)Note(1)
6	NH108041L	Nut	6	)
	SE108501	Screw-Hinges to Door	4	)
	MRC1980	Nylon Washer	4	)Note(2)
	NH108041L	Nut	4	)
7	333041	Check Rod	1	)
8	306295	Rubber Buffer-Short	1	)Note(3)
	333445	Rubber Buffer-Long	1	)
9	SH108201L	Screw-Hinges to Body	6	Note(1)
	SE108251	Screw-Hinges to Body	6	Germany
10	WC108051L	Plain Washer	6	)Note(1)
11	WL108001L	Spring Washer	6	)
	SE108251	Screw-Hinges to Body	4	)
	3830L	Plain Washer	4	)Note(2)
	WM600051L	Spring Washer	4	)
12	NH108041L	Nut	4	Note(1)(2)
13	MTC1042	Nut Plate-Centre Hinge	1	Note(1)
14	BH106071	Bolt	1	)
15	AFU1262	Plain Washer	2	)
16	AFU1078	Plain Washer-Thick	1	)Note(3)
17	MRC5525	Plain Washer	1	)
18	WL106001L	Spring Washer	1	)
19	NH106041L	Nut	2	)
20	MTC6630	Nut-Cover	12	)Germany
	MUC3798	Nut-Cover	2	)

NOTES:
(1): Three Hinge Door
(2): Two Hinge Door
(3): Except Automatic Door Check with Manual Release

TS5280

MODEL LR110 - UP TO AUGUST 1986
BLOCK TS 5684
PAGE L 98.02
GROUP L

BODY - REAR END DOOR - AUTOMATIC DOOR CHECK WITH MANUAL RELEASE -
FROM VIN 242000

ILL	PART NO	DESCRIPTION	QTY	REMARKS
1	MUC4474	Release Lever	1	
2	MUC4486	Retainer	1	
3	RA608177L	Rivet	2	
4	MUC4481	Spring	1	
5	MUC4545	Rubber Buffer-Short	1	
6	MUC4471	Checkstrap Link	1	
7	MUC4544	Rubber Buffer-Long	1	
8	MUC4477	Mounting Bracket	1	
9	78248	Rivet	2	
10	346878	Retaining Bracket	1	
11	SH106201L	Screw	2	
12	WL106001L	Spring Washer	2	
13	306564	Clevis Pin	1	
14	349931	Plain Washer	1	
15	2393	Split Pin	1	

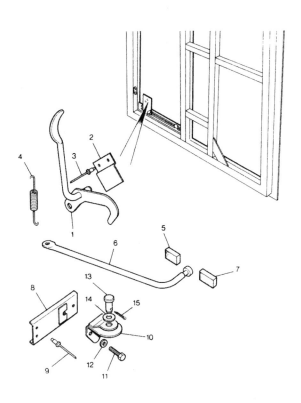

TS5684

MODEL LR110 - UP TO AUGUST 1986
BLOCK TS 5282
PAGE L 98.04
GROUP L

BODY - SPARE WHEEL CARRIER (REAR END DOOR) - UP TO 1984 FACELIFT

ILL	PART NO	DESCRIPTION	QTY	REMARKS
1	347441	Spare Wheel Carrier	1	
2	333446	Clamp Plate	1	
3	SE106251L	Screw	8	
4	WL106001L	Spring washer	8	
5	NH106041L	Nut	8	
6	MRC1210	U-Bolt	1	
7	NH112041L	Nut	4	
8	333439	Nave Plate-Circular	1	)Alternatives
	MTC6410	Nave Plate-Triangular	1	)
9	90577473	Wheel Nut	6	

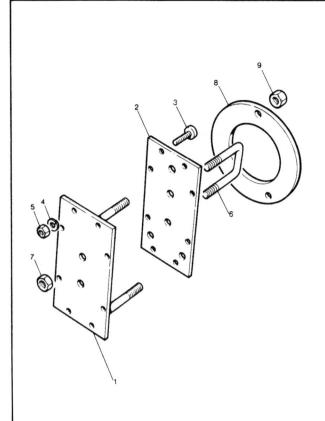

TS5282

LAND ROVER PARTS LTD

600

MODEL LR110 - UP TO AUGUST 1986
BLOCK TS 5279
PAGE L 98.06
GROUP L

BODY - SPARE WHEEL CARRIER (REAR END DOOR) - 1984 FACELIFT

ILL	PART NO	DESCRIPTION	QTY	REMARKS
1	MUC2366	Spare Wheel Carrier	1	
2	MUC2934	Clamp Plate	1	
3	SE106251	Screw	7	
4	WL106001L	Spring Washer	7	
5	NH106041L	Nut	7	
6	MUC2364	U-Bolt	1	
7	NH112041L	Nut	4	
8	MUC2368	Threaded Washer	3	)Alternatives
	MUC4546	Nut M16	3	)
9	90577473	Wheel Nut	3	

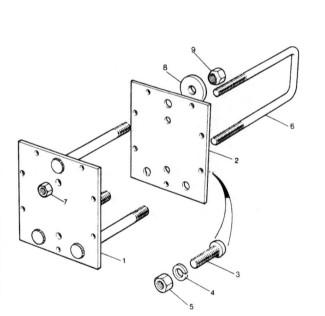

TS5279

LAND ROVER PARTS LTD

601

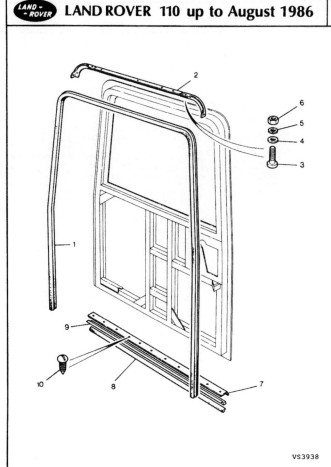

MODEL LR110 - UP TO AUGUST 1986
BLOCK VS 3938
PAGE L 98.10
GROUP L

BODY - SEALS - REAR END DOOR

ILL	PART NO	DESCRIPTION	QTY	REMARKS
1	MTC4111	Seal	1	
2	MTC4290	Seal Retainer	1	
3	SE105161	Screw	9	
4	AFU1256	Plain Washer	9	
5	WL105001	Spring Washer	9	
6	NH105041	Nut	9	
7	333203	Protection Strip	1	
8	332564	Seal	1	
9	332756	Seal Retainer	1	
10	AB606041L	Drive Screw	13	

VS3938

LAND ROVER PARTS LTD

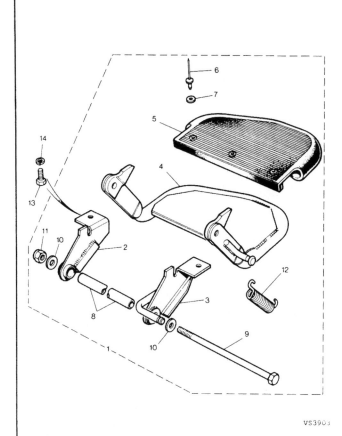

MODEL LR110 - UP TO AUGUST 1986
BLOCK VS 3903
PAGE L 100
GROUP L

BODY - FOLDING STEP - REAR END DOOR

ILL	PART NO	DESCRIPTION	QTY	REMARKS
1	MTC3084	Rear Step Assembly	1	
2	MTC3086	+Tube Retainer-RH	1	
3	MTC3087	+Tube Retainer-LH	1	
4	MTC3085	+Step	1	
5	MTC3091	++Mat	1	
6	RA612373L	++Rivet	7	
7	WA105001	++Plain Washer	7	
8	MTC3099	+Tube	1	
9	BH110521	+Bolt	1	
10	WC110061	+Plain Washer	2	
11	NY110041L	+Nyloc Nut	1	
12	MTC1233	+Spring	1	
13	SH110201	Screw-Step to Chassis	2	
14	WL110001L	Spring Washer	2	

VS3903

LAND ROVER PARTS LTD

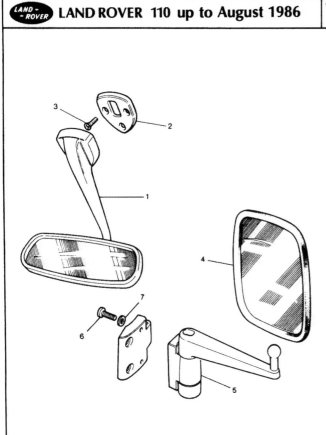

MODEL LR110 - UP TO AUGUST 1986
BLOCK VS 3904A
PAGE L 102
GROUP L

BODY - MIRRORS

ILL	PART NO	DESCRIPTION	QTY	REMARKS
1	MRC9564	Interior Mirror	1	
	MTC6376	Interior Mirror-Dipping	1	
2	372336	Base Plate	1	
3	SF104164	Screw	3	Vehicles with Trim
	SF104204L	Screw	3	Vehicles without Trim
4		EXTERIOR MIRROR HEAD		
	MTC5084	Convex Glass Type	2	
	MRC9747	Flat Glass Type	2	
	MUC3707	Flat Glass Type-RH	1	)Australia
	MUC3708	Flat Glass Type-LH	1	)
		+GLASS FOR MIRROR		
	RTC4341	Convex-For MTC5084	2	
	RTC4340	Flat-For MRC9747	2	
	RTC4342	Flat-For MUC3707/8	2	Australia
5		MIRROR ARM		
	MRC5083	For MTC5084	2	
	MRC4583	For MRC9747	2	
	MTC5083	For MUC3707/8	2	Australia
6	SE604071L	Screw	4	
7	MRC1979	Nylon Washer	4	

VS3904A

LAND ROVER PARTS LTD

604

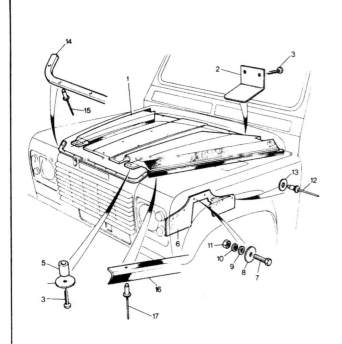

MODEL LR110 - UP TO AUGUST 1986
BLOCK VS 4045
PAGE L 110
GROUP L

BODY - HEAT AND SOUND INSULATION

ILL	PART NO	DESCRIPTION	QTY	REMARKS
1	MUC9850	Pad-Bonnet Insulation	1	
2	MTC4657	Bracket	2	
3	AR608061	Screw	13	
4	AFU1071	Washer	9	
5	AFU1497	Spacer	9	
6	MTC6324	Wheelarch Curtain	2	
7	SH106201L	Screw	4	
8	AFU1261	Washer-Plain	4	
9	WA106041L	Washer-Plain	4	
10	WL106001L	Washer-Spring	4	
11	NH106041L	Nut	4	
12	RA612346	Pop Rivet	8	
13	AFU1256	Washer-Plain	8	
14	MRC7104	Bonnet Finisher	1	
15	AFU1170	Rivet	9	
16	MTC6413	Seal-Bonnet Sides	2	
17	RU612373L	Rivet	16	

VS4045

LAND ROVER PARTS LTD

605

MODEL LR110 - UP TO AUGUST 1986
BLOCK VS 4078A
PAGE L 150
GROUP L

BODY - HOOD - FULL LENGTH

ILL	PART NO	DESCRIPTION	QTY	REMARKS
		HOOD ASSEMBLY		
1	MTC7031AG	Side Windows-Khaki Green	1	)
	MTC7031AE	Side Windows-Matt Sand	1	)Note(1)
	MTC7033AG	Plain Sides-Khaki Green	1	)
	MTC7033AE	Plain Sides-Matt Sand	1	)
	MTC7710AG	Side Windows-Khaki Green	1	)
	MTC7710AE	Side Windows-Matt Sand	1	)Note(2)
	MTC7711AG	Plain Sides-Khaki Green	1	)
	MTC7711AE	Plain Sides-Matt Sand	1	)
2	331249	+Suport and Staps		
		Khaki Green	1	)
3	90301332	+Strap-Side Curtain-Front	2	)Note(1)
		Khaki Green		
4	304797	+Rope Hook	2	
5	301343	+Washer Plate	2	
6	RF608041	+Rivet	6	Note(1)
	3547	+Rivet	6	Note(2)
7	MTC4314	+Sidelight	4	
8	MTC7193AG	+Rear Curtain-Khaki Green	1	
	MTC7193AE	+Rear Curtain-Matt Sand	1	
9	MTC4313	++Backlight	1	
10	331105	++Strap-Curtain to Body-	2	)No Longer
		Khaki Green		)Serviced
11	339935	++Strap-Curtain Retaining-	2	)Note(1)
		Khaki Green		)No Longer
				)Serviced
12	90301332	++Strap-Extention Flap-	2	)Note(1)
		Khaki Green		
13	331317	+Rope-Side Curtain	2	No Longer
				Serviced
	331221	+Rope-Rear Curtain	1	
	331222	+Rope-Hood Top and Sides	1	
14	301321	+Eyelet	A/R	No Longer
				Serviced
	301320	+Eyelet	A/R	No Longer
				Serviced
15	300953	+Buckle	A/R	
16	300954	+End Cap	A/R	
17	396800	+Eyelet	A/R	

NOTES(1): Up to VIN 224093
     (2): From VIN 224094

VS4078A

MODEL LR110 - UP TO AUGUST 1986
BLOCK VS 4079C
PAGE L 152
GROUP L

BODY - FRONT FITTINGS - FULL LENGTH HOOD

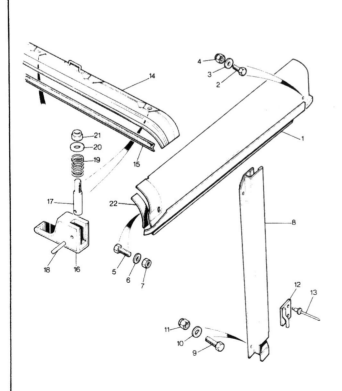

ILL	PART NO	DESCRIPTION	QTY	REMARKS
1	MTC6992	Top Drain Channel RH	1	)Note(1)
	MTC6993	Top Drain Channel LH	1	)
	MUC4042	Top Drain Channel RH	1	)Note(2)
	MUC4043	Top-Drain Channel LH	1	)
2	SH106201L	Screw	2	
3	AFU1080	Plain Washer	4	
4	NY106041L	Self Lock Nut	2	
5	SH106161L	Screw	2	
6	AFU1080	Plain Washer	4	
7	NY106041L	Self Lock Nut	2	
8	MTC5428	Side Drain Channel RH	1	
	MTC5429	Side Drain Channel LH	1	
9	SH106161L	Screw	4	
10	AFU1080	Plain Washer	8	
11	NY106041L	Self Lock Nut	4	
12	330578	Front Hook RH	1	
	330579	Front Hook LH	1	
13	78248	Rivet	4	
14	MTC6626	Header Rail	1	Note(1)
	MTC9773	Header Rail	1	Note(2)
15	MTC7252	Seal	1	
16	MTC4581	Handle	4	
17	MTC4583	Spindle	4	
18	PA106201	Spring Pin	4	
19	MTC4584	Spring	4	
20	WC106041L	Plain Washer	4	
21	NY106041L	Nyloc-Nut	4	
22	MTC7431	Seal	2	
	AFU4162	Hook-Top Drain Channel	4	)Note(2)
	MUC4538	Seal-Top Drain Channel to	2	)
		Hoodstick		)
	MUC4061	Strap-Hood to Header Rail	2	)

NOTES(1): Up to VIN 224093
     (2): From VIN 224094

VS4079C

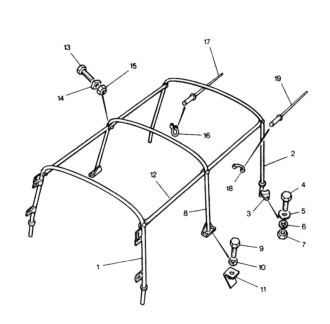

```
MODEL LR110 - UP TO AUGUST 1986
BLOCK VS 4080
PAGE L 154
GROUP L

BODY - HOODSTICKS - FULL LENGTH HOOD
```

ILL	PART NO	DESCRIPTION	QTY	REMARKS
1	330551	Front Hoodstick	1	Note(1)
	MUC4524	Front Hoodstick	1	Note(2)
2	330553	Rear Hoodstick	1	
3	304301	Clamp Arm	4	
4	SH108251L	Bolt	4	
5	WA108051L	Plain Washer	4	
6	WL108001L	Spring Washer	4	
7	NH108041L	Nut	4	
8	330699	Intermediate Hoodstick	1	
9	SR106201	Screw	4	
	MRC5527	Plain Washer	4	
10	WL106001L	Spring Washer	4	
11	MRC9603	Nut Plate	4	
12	330896	Tie Tube	4	
13	SA106451	Screw	6	
14	NS106011	Square Nut	6	
15	NY106041L	Self Lock Nut	6	
16	345699	Ropehook	2	
17	RR612103	Rivet	4	
18	395143	Staple	2	
19	RA612373L	Rivet	4	

```
NOTE(1):  Up To Vin 224093

NOTE(2):  From VIN 224094
```

VS4080

 **LAND ROVER PARTS LTD**

```
MODEL LR110 - UP TO AUGUST 1986
BLOCK VS 4081
PAGE L 160
GROUP L

BODY - HOOD - THREE QUARTER LENGTH - CAB FIXING
```

ILL	PART NO	DESCRIPTION	QTY	REMARKS
		HOOD ASSEMBLY		
1	MTC7200AG	SIDE WINDOWS-KHAKI GREEN	1	
	MTC7200AE	SIDE WINDOWS-MATT SAND	1	
	MTC7471AG	PLAIN SIDES-KHAKI GREEN	1	
	MTC7471AE	PLAIN SIDES-MATT SAND	1	
2	331249	+Support & Straps-Khaki Green	1	
3	304797	+Rope Hook	2	
4	301343	+Washer Plate	2	
5	RF608041	+Rivet	6	
6	MTC4314	+Sidelight	4	
7	MTC7193AG	+Rear Curtain-Khaki Green	1	
	MTC7193AE	+Rear Curtain-Matt Sand	1	
8	MTC4313	++Backlight	1	
9	331105	++Strap-Curtain to Body-Khaki Green	2	No Longer Serviced
10	339935	++Strap-Curtain Retaining-Khaki Green	2	No Longer Serviced
11	90301332	++Strap-Extension Flap-Khaki Green	2	
12	331221	+Rope-Rear Curtain	1	
	331222	+Rope-Hood Top and Sides	1	
13	301321	+Eyelet	A/R	) No Longer
	301320	+Eyelet	A/R	) Available
14	300953	+Buckle	A/R	
15	300954	+End Cap	A/R	
16	396800	+Eyelet	A/R	

VS4081

 **LAND ROVER PARTS LTD**

MODEL LR110 - UP TO AUGUST 1986
BLOCK VS 4082B
PAGE L 162
GROUP L

BODY - HOODSTICKS - THREE QUARTER LENGTH HOOD - CAB FIXING

ILL	PART NO	DESCRIPTION	QTY	REMARKS
1	330553	Front Hoodstick	1	
2	330553	Rear Hoodstick	1	
3	304301	Clamp Arm	4	
4	SH108251L	Bolt	4	
5	WA108051L	Plain Washer	4	
6	WL108001L	Spring Washer	4	
7	NH108041L	Nut	4	
8	330699	Intermediate Hoodstick	1	
9	SR106201	Screw	4	
10	WL106001L	Spring Washer	4	
11	MRC9603	Nut Plate	4	
12	330897	Front Tie Tube	2	
13	330896	Rear Tie Tube	2	
14	SA106201	Screw	6	
15	NS106011	Square Nut	6	
16	NY106041L	Self Lock Nut	6	
17	345699	Rope Hook-Rear	2	
18	RR612103	Rivet	4	
19	395143	Staple	2	
20	RA612373L	Rivet	4	
21	MTC7384	Frame-Hood Attachment	1	
22	RU612183	Rivet	12	
23	331673	Drain Channel RH	1	
24	331674	Drain Channel LH	1	
25	SE106201L	Screw	4	
26	AFU1080	Plain Washer	4	
27	WL106001L	Spring Washer	4	
28	NH106041L	Nut	4	

VS4082B

610

 **LAND ROVER 110 up to August 1986** | fiche4 I14 | **CHASSIS and BODY.**

MODEL LR110 - UP TO AUGUST 1986
BLOCK VS 4082B
PAGE L 164
GROUP L

BODY - HOODSTICKS - THREE QUARTER LENGTH HOOD - CAB FIXING

ILL	PART NO	DESCRIPTION	QTY	REMARKS
29	331675	Retaining Strip-Top	1	
30	331676	Retaining Strip-Sides	2	
31	348430	Stud	2	
32	SE105351L	Screw	2	
33	WA105001L	Plain Washer	2	
34	WL105001L	Spring Washer	2	
35	NM105011	Nut	2	
36	334245	Hook RH	1	
	334246	Hook LH	1	
37	330578	Front Hook RH	1	
	330579	Front Hook LH	1	
38	78248	Rivet	4	
39	MTC8145	Seal-Side	2	
40	MTC8146	Seal-Top	1	

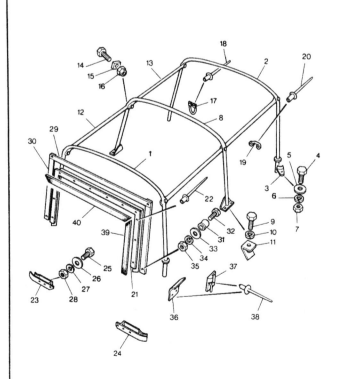

VS4082B

MODEL LR110 - UP TO AUGUST 1986
BLOCK VS 4083
PAGE L 170
GROUP L

BODY - HOOD - HIGH CAPACITY PICK UP

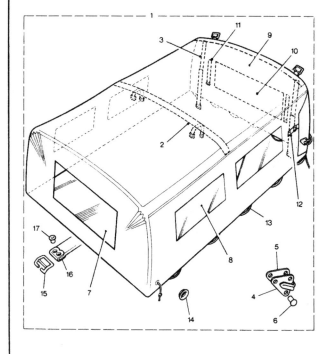

ILL	PART NO	DESCRIPTION	QTY	REMARKS
		HOOD ASSEMBLY		
1	MTC2575AG	SIDE WINDOWS-KHAKI GREEN	1	
	MTC2575AE	SIDE WINDOWS-MATT SAND	1	
	MTC2574AG	PLAIN SIDES-KHAKI GREEN	1	
	MTC2574AE	PLAIN SIDES-MATT SAND	1	
2	MTC4063	+Support and Straps-Centre-Khaki Green	1	No Longer Serviced
3	MTC4317	+Support and Straps-Rear-Khaki Green	1	
4	304797	+Rope Hook	4	
5	301343	+Washer Plate	4	
6	RF608041	+Rivet	12	
7	MTC4313	+Front Light	1	
8	MTC4314	+Side Light	4	
9	MTC4061AG	+Rear Curtain-Khaki Green	1	
	MTC4061AE	+Rear Curtain-Matt Sand	1	
10	MTC4313	++Back Light	1	
11	339935	++Strap-Retaining Rear Curtain-Khaki Green	2	No Longer Serviced
12	90301332	++Strap-Extension Flap-Khaki Green	2	
13	MTC4315	+Rope-Side Curtain	2	
	331221	+Rope-Rear Curtain	1	
	MTC4319	+Rope-Hood Top and Sides	1	
14	301321	+Eyelet	A/R	) No Longer
	301320	+Eyelet	A/R	) Serviced
15	300953	+Buckle	A/R	
16	300954	+End Cap	A/R	
17	396800	+Eyelet	A/R	
	MTC8376	Wearing Pad-Side Window Protection	1	

VS4083

612

MODEL LR110 - UP TO AUGUST 1986
BLOCK VS 4084
PAGE L 172
GROUP L

BODY - HOODSTICKS - HIGH CAPACITY PICK UP

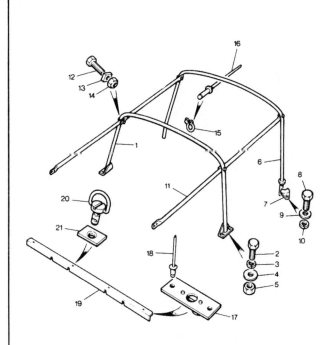

ILL	PART NO	DESCRIPTION	QTY	REMARKS
1	MTC4943	Intermediate Hoodstick	1	
2	SH106201	Screw	4	
3	WL106001L	Spring Washer	4	
4	WA106041L	Plain Washer	4	
5	NH106041L	Nut	4	
6	MTC4944	Rear Hoodstick	1	
7	304301	Clamp Arm	2	
8	SH108201L	Bolt	2	
9	WA108051L	Plain Washer	2	
10	WL108001L	Spring Washer	2	
11	MTC4945	Tie Tube	4	
12	SA106451	Screw	6	
13	NS106011	Square Nut	6	
14	NY106041L	Self Lock Nut	6	
15	045055	Rope Hook	2	
16	RU612373L	Rivet	4	
17	AFU2504	Spring Plate	4	
18	RJ610243	Rivet	8	
19	MTC4054	Front Retaining Angle	1	
20	AFU2503	Ring Head Stud	4	
21	AAU2367	Retainer	4	

VS4084

613

MODEL LR110 - UP TO AUGUST 1986
BLOCK TS 5304
PAGE L 174
GROUP L

BODY - LADDER RACK - HIGH CAPACITY PICK UP

ILL	PART NO	DESCRIPTION	QTY	REMARKS
1	MUC1086	LADDER RACK ASSEMBLY COMPLETE	1	
2	MTC4942	+Stop	2	
3	PC106641	+Clevis Pin	2	
4	WA106041L	+Plain Washer	2	
5	PS103121L	+Split Pin	2	
6	SH108301L	Screw	2	
7	WL108001L	Spring Washer	2	
8	WA108051L	Plain Washer	2	

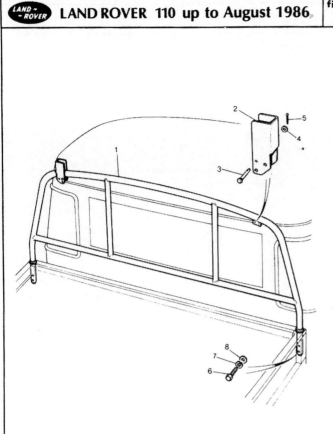

TS5304

MODEL LR110 - UP TO AUGUST 1986
BLOCK TS 5753
PAGE L 176
GROUP L

BODY - ROLL OVER BAR - HIGH CAPACITY PICK UP

ILL	PART NO	DESCRIPTION	QTY	REMARKS
1	RRC3264	Roll Over Bar	1	
2	BH110301L	Bolt	8	
3	WL110001L	Spring Washer	8	
4	WA110061L	Plain Washer	8	
5	MTC5519	Nut Plate	4	
6	BH110251	Bolt	4	
7	WL110001L	Spring Washer	4	
8	WA110061L	Plain Washer	4	
9	MTC5519	Nut-Plate	2	
10	RRC3584	Sliding Plate	2	
11	SA106161	Screw	4	
12	WA106041L	Plain Washer	8	
13	NY106041L	Nyloc Nut	4	
14	SD106401L	Screw-Sliding Plate to Hoodstick	4	
15	NS106011	Square Nut	4	
16	WA106041L	Plain Washer	4	
17	NY106041L	Nyloc Nut	4	

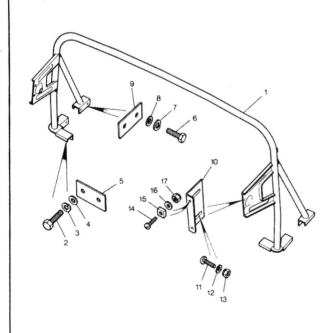

TS5753

MODEL LR110 - UP TO AUGUST 1986
BLOCK VS 4208
PAGE L 200
GROUP L

BODY - BODY TAPES AND BADGE - UP TO 1984 FACELIFT

ILL	PART NO	DESCRIPTION	QTY	REMARKS
		BODY TAPE		
1	MTC7142	Front Wing RH	1	
	MTC7143	Front Wing LH	1	
2	MTC7022	Front Door RH	1	
	MTC7023	Front Door LH	1	
3	MTC7144	Rear Side Door RH	1	
	MTC7145	Rear Side Door LH	1	
4	MTC7024	Rear Bodyside RH	1	
	MTC7025	Rear Bodyside LH	1	
5	MTC4719	Badge 'County'	2	

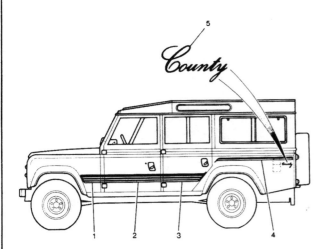

VS4208

616

MODEL LR110 - UP TO AUGUST 1986
BLOCK TS 5247
PAGE L 202
GROUP L

BODY - NAME TAPES AND BODY TAPES - 1984 FACELIFT

ILL	PART NO	DESCRIPTION	QTY	REMARKS
1	MUC2003	Front Name Tape	1	
2	MUC2002	Rear Name Tape	1	
3		FRONT WING TAPE		
	RTC6474	RH-Beige	1	
	MUC3170JU	RH-Blue	1	
	RTC6476	LH-Beige	1	
	MUC3171JU	LH-Blue	1	
4		FRONT DOOR TAPE		
	MUC3172AF	RH-Beige	1	
	MUC3172JU	RH-Blue	1	
	MUC3173AF	LH-Beige	1	
	MUC3173JU	LH-Blue	1	
5		REAR SIDE DOOR TAPE		
	MUC3176AF	RH-Beige	1	
	MUC3176JU	RH-Blue	1	
	MUC3177AF	LH-Beige	1	
	MUC3177JU	LH-Blue	1	
6		BODY SIDE TAPE		
	MUC3178AF	RH-Beige	1	
	MUC3178JU	RH-Blue	1	
	MUC3179AF	LH-Beige	1	
	MUC3179JU	LH-Blue	1	
7		LOGO-V8		
	MUC3373AF	Beige	2	
	MUC3373JU	Blue	2	

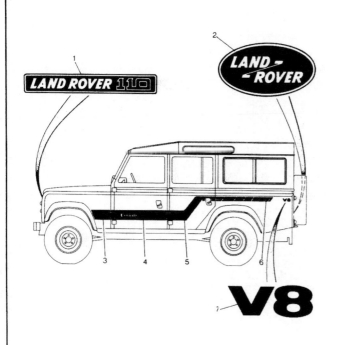

TS5247

617

MODEL LR110 - UP TO AUGUST 1986
BLOCK TS 5002
PAGE L 210
GROUP L

BODY - TOOL STOWAGE - BULKHEAD - PICK UP & TRUCK CAB

ILL	PART NO	DESCRIPTION	QTY REMARKS
1	367030	Bracket-Hand Pump	1
2	RU612123	Rivet	2
3	371144	Retaining Ring	1
4	MTC7449	Spring Clip-Hand Pump	1
5	RU612123	Rivet	1
6	367030	Bracket-Jack Base	1
7	RU612123	Rivet	2
8	371144	Retaining Ring	1
9	MTC1359	Strap-Side Lift Jack	2
10	AFU1256	Washer	2
11	RU612373L	Rivet	2
12	90508035	Spring Clip-Starting Handle	3
13	RU612123	Rivet	3
14	MTC7457	Anti Rattle Pad	A/R
15	367030	Bracket-Wheel Chock	1
16	78248	Rivet	2
17	371133	Retaining Ring	1

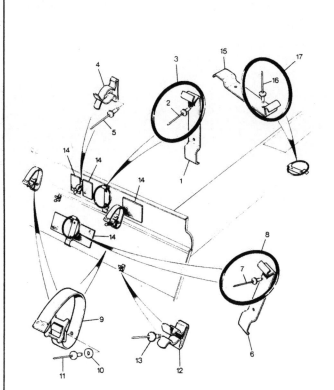

TS5002

LAND ROVER PARTS LTD

MODEL LR110 - UP TO AUGUST 1986
BLOCK TS 5003
PAGE L 212
GROUP L

BODY - TOOL STOWAGE - BULKHEAD - HIGH CAPACITY PICK UP

ILL	PART NO	DESCRIPTION	QTY REMARKS
1	367030	Bracket-Hand Pump	1
2	78248	Rivet	2
3	371144	Retaining Ring	1
4	MTC7449	Spring Clip-Hand Pump	1
5	78248	Rivet	1
6	367030	Bracket-Jack	1
7	78248	Rivet	2
8	371144	Retaining Ring	1
9	90508035	Spring Clip-Starting Handle & Jack Rods	7
10	78248	Rivet	7
11	MTC7457	Anti Rattle Pad	A/R
12	MTC1357	Bracket-Wheel Chock	1
13	78248	Rivet	2
14	371144	Retaining Ring	1

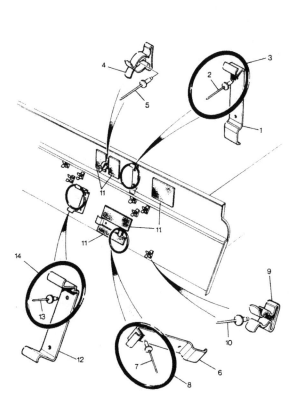

TS5003

LAND ROVER PARTS LTD

MODEL LR110 - UP TO AUGUST 1986
BLOCK TS 5004
PAGE L 214
GROUP L

BODY - TOOL STOWAGE - STATION WAGON

ILL	PART NO	DESCRIPTION	QTY	REMARKS
1	90508035	Spring Clip-Starting Handle	3	)
2	332376	Bracket	3	)10 Seater
3	78248	Rivet	9	)
4	90508035	Spring Clip-Starting Handle	3	)12 Seater
5	78248	Rivet	3	)
6	367030	Bracket-Hand Pump/Tool Roll	1	
7	78248	Rivet	2	
8	371144	Retaining Ring	1	

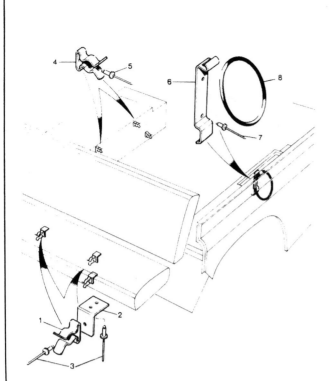

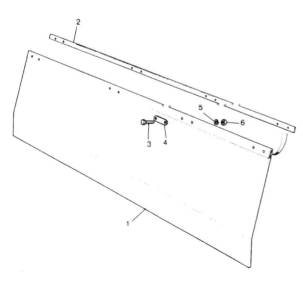

TS5004

620

MODEL LR110 - UP TO AUGUST 1986
BLOCK TS 5650
PAGE L 214.10
GROUP L

BODY - TOOL STOWAGE

ILL	PART NO	DESCRIPTION	QTY	REMARKS
1	MTC3165	Tool Curtain	1	)
2	MTC3166	Retaining Plate	1	)
3	SH106251L	Screw	8	)Germany
4	MTC4601	Washer Plate	4	)
5	WL106001L	Spring Washer	8	)
6	NH106041L	Nut	8	)

TS5650

LAND ROVER PARTS LTD

621

MODEL LR110 - UP TO AUGUST 1986
BLOCK VS 3869A
PAGE L 216
GROUP L

BODY - TOOL STOWAGE - STATION WAGON

ILL	PART NO	DESCRIPTION	QTY	REMARKS
1	MTC1357	Bracket-Jack Stowage	1	
2	MTC1356	Retention Ring	1	
3	MTC1359	Strap-Jack Stowage	2	
4	SH106201	Bolt	2	
5	WC106041L	Plain Washer	4	
6	MTC1355	Cup Washer	2	
7	WL106001L	Spring Washer	2	
8	NH106041L	Nut	2	

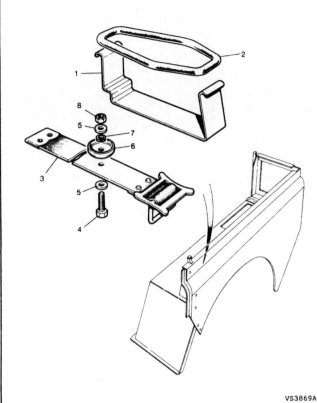

VS3869A

MODEL LR110 - UP TO AUGUST 1986
BLOCK VS 3604
PAGE L 218
GROUP L

BODY - TOOL STOWAGE - TAILBOARD

ILL	PART NO	DESCRIPTION	QTY	REMARKS
1	336344	Shovel Support Bracket	1	
2	336346	Tool Support Bracket	2	
3	336347	Pick Axe Support Bracket	1	
4	336348	Pick Axe Shaft Support	1	
5	336349	Pick Axe Shaft Stop Bracket	1	
6	RA612123L	Rivet	2	
7	336350	Pick Axe Support Bracket	1	
8	308792	Strap	4	
9	336345	Strap Plate	1	
10	336352	Pad	2	
11	WA105001L	Plain Washer	4	
12	337981	Pick Axe Support	1	
13	336351	Retaining Plate	1	
14	WL600081L	Spring Washer	1	
15	250055	Wing Nut	1	
16	BH108081L	Bolt	2	
17	WL108001L	Spring Washer	2	
18	NH108041L	Nut	2	
19	78248	Rivet-Brackets, Straps & Pads to Tailboard	18	

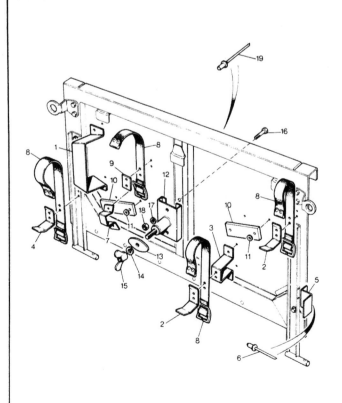

VS3604

MODEL LR110 - UP TO AUGUST 1986
BLOCK TS 5242
PAGE L 220
GROUP L

BODY - BARREL AND KEY SETS FOR LOCKS

ILL	PART NO	DESCRIPTION	QTY	REMARKS
1	RTC3022	1 Barrel & 2 Keys	1	
	MTC6503	2 Barrels & 2 Keys	1	
	MTC6504	3 Barrels & 2 Keys	1	
	MTC6505	4 Barrels & 2 Keys	1	
	MTC6506	5 Barrels & 2 Keys	1	
	MTC6507	6 Barrels & 2 Keys	1	
	MTC6508	7 Barrels & 2 Keys	1	) No Longer
	MTC6509	8 Barrels & 2 Keys	1	) Available
	CZK3438L	Key Blank	A/R	
	MUC4146	Barrel & Key-for Locks Fitted to Front Doors with Wind Up Windows	2	
	MUC4145	Key Blank	A/R	

TS5242

 **LAND ROVER PARTS LTD**

624

 **LAND ROVER PARTS LTD**

625

MODEL LR110 - UP TO AUGUST 1986
BLOCK VS 3930
PAGE M 2
GROUP M

FACIA - UPPER CRASH PAD

ILL	PART NO	DESCRIPTION	QTY	REMARKS
1	MTC5468	Upper Crash Pad	1	)Note(1)
	MUC1581	Upper Crash Pad-with Ashtray Aperture	1	
2	AB614064	Screw-Crash Pad to Dash	8	
3	WC106044L	Plain Washer	3	
4	CZK3164	Lokut Nut	3	
5	SE104124	Screw-Crash Pad to Front Plate-Main Earth	2	
6	WA104004L	Plain Washer	2	
7	WL104004	Spring Washer	2	
8	NH104044	Nut	2	
		Fixings-Crash Rail to Front Plate		
	WC105001L	Plain Washer	4	
	WM702001L	Spring Washer	2	
	NH105041L	Nut-Cover to Heater Duct	2	
	AB608051L	Screw	2	
	AK606031	Spring Nut	1	
	RTC3745	Lokut Nut	2	
	SE105121L	Screw	2	
9	MTC6040	Demister Outlet	2	
10	AB606064L	Drive Screw	4	
11	WA105001L	Plain Washer	4	
12	RTC3745	Lokut Nut	4	
13	MTC4572	End Closing Trim-RHD	1	)Except
	MTC4571	End Closing Trim-LHD	1	)Air Con
14	AD606044L	Screw	1	
15	RTC3745	Lokut Nut	1	
16	AB610124L	Screw	1	
17	AFU1248	Plain Washer	1	
18	RTC3744	Lokut Nut	1	

NOTE(1): No Longer Available - Use MUC1581

VS3930

LAND ROVER PARTS LTD

626

MODEL LR110 - UP TO AUGUST 1986
BLOCK VS 3930
PAGE M 4
GROUP M

FACIA - UPPER CRASH PAD

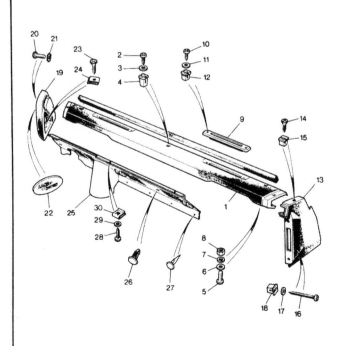

ILL	PART NO	DESCRIPTION	QTY	REMARKS
19	MTC6142	Grab Handle-RH-LHD	1	
	MTC6143	Grab Handle-LH-RHD	1	
20	SE105121L	Screw-Grab Handle to Crash Pad	1	
21	WF105001L	Starlock Washer	1	
22	MTC5851	Badge	1	
23	AC606104	Screw-Grap Handle to Heater Duct	1	
24	AK606031	Spring Nut	1	
25	MTC4617	Trim Panel-RHD	1	)Except
	MTC4618	Trim Panel-LHD	1	)Air Con
26	AFU1897	Drive Fastener-Trim Panel to Front Plate	2	
27	AFU2813	Drive Fastener-Trim Panel to Dash	6	
28	AB606044	Drive Screw-Trim Panel and Front Plate to Crash Pad	2	
29	WA104004L	Plain-Washer	2	
30	AJ606011L	Spring-Nut	2	
	AB608041L	Screw-Front Panel to Dash	6	
	WA105001L	Plain-Washer	6	

VS3930

LAND ROVER PARTS LTD

627

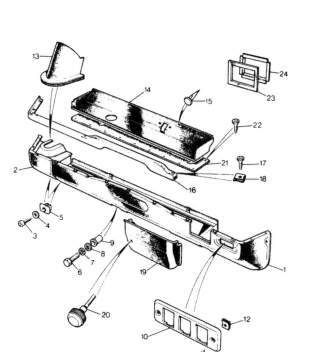

MODEL LR110 - UP TO AUGUST 1986
BLOCK TS 5649
PAGE M 6
GROUP M

FACIA - PARCEL TRAY AND HEATER DUCT

ILL	PART NO	DESCRIPTION	QTY	REMARKS
1		HEATER DUCT PADDED ASSEMBLY		
	MTC2826	RHD	1	)
	MTC2827	LHD	1	) Except
	MUC1384	RHD-Speaker Provision	1	) Air Con
	MUC1383	LHD-Speaker Provision	1	)
	MUC3249	RHD	1	)
	MUC1703	LHD	1	) Air Con
	MUC3244	RHD-Speaker Provision	1	)
	MUC1716	LHD-Speaker Provision	1	)
2		WIPER MOTOR COVER PADDED ASSEMBLY		
	MTC3523	RHD	1	
	MTC6080	LHD	1	
	MUC1701	RHD-Speaker Provision	1	
	MUC1382	LHD-Speaker Provision	1	
3	AB608054L	Screw	10	
4	AFU1248	Plain Washer	10	
5	AFU2692	Lokut Nut	10	
6	SH105201L	Screw	2	
7	WL105001L	Spring Washer	2	
8	WC105001L	Plain Washer	2	
9	NN105021L	Nutsert	2	
10	MTC2640	Switch Panel-RHD	1	
11	AD606041L	Screw	2	
12	AK606011L	Spring Nut	2	
13	MTC3705	Cover-Wiper Motor Drive	1	

TS5649

LAND ROVER PARTS LTD

628

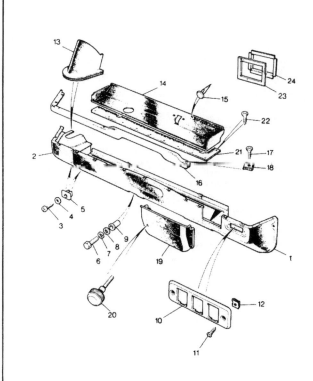

MODEL LR110 - UP TO AUGUST 1986
BLOCK TS 5649
PAGE M 6.02
GROUP M

FACIA - PARCEL TRAY AND HEATER DUCT

ILL	PART NO	DESCRIPTION	QTY	REMARKS
14	MRC7282	Parcel Tray-RHD	1	
	MRC7283	Parcel Tray-LHD	1	
15	AFU2813	Drive Fastener	5	)
	AB606044	Drive Screw	5	) Alternatives
	WA104004L	Plain Washer	5	)
16	MTC6166	Finisher-RHD	1	
	MTC6167	Finisher-LHD	1	
17	AC606064	Drive Screw	3	
18	AK606031	Spring Nut	3	
19	MRC9646	Fuse Box Cover	1	)4 Cyl & V8-4)Speed)No Longer)Available. Use)MUC7905
	MUC7905	Fuse Box Cover	1	V8 6 Speed
20	MTC9988	Screw	2	
21	MRC8584	Closing Panel and Insulation Pad Assembly-RHD	1	
	MRC8585	Closing Panel and Insulation Pad Assembly-LHD	1	
22	AB606041L	Drive Screw	22	
23	MTC6871	Seal-Heater Duct	1	Except Air Con
	MTC7400	Seal-Heater Duct	1	Air Con
24	MUC4801	Sealing Bezel-Heater Duct	1	Except Air Con

TS5649

LAND ROVER PARTS LTD

629

MODEL LR110 - UP TO AUGUST 1986
BLOCK TS 5009
PAGE M 6.20
GROUP M

FACIA - ASH TRAY - MOUNTED ON HEATER DUCT

ILL	PART NO	DESCRIPTION	QTY	REMARKS
1	RTC8071	Ashtray Kit Complete Assembly	1	

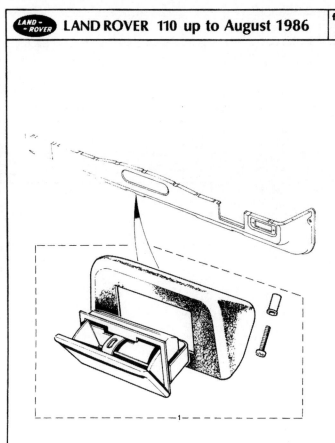

TS5009

MODEL LR110 - UP TO AUGUST 1986
BLOCK TS 5292
PAGE M 6.22
GROUP M

FACIA - ASH TRAY - MOUNTED IN UPPER CRASH PAD

ILL	PART NO	DESCRIPTION	QTY	REMARKS
1	DZA5097L	Ash Tray	1	
2	MUC1582	Retainer for Ash Tray	1	

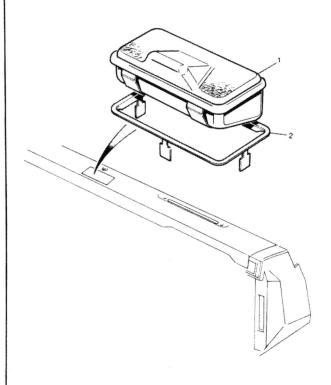

TS5292

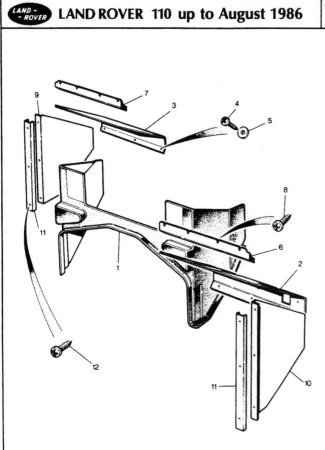

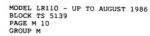

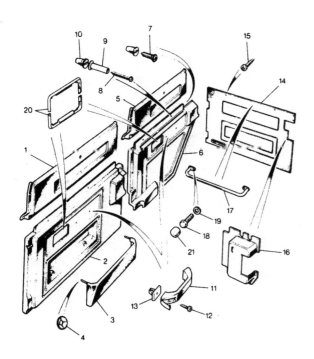

MODEL LR110 - UP TO AUGUST 1986
BLOCK VS 3929A
PAGE M 8
GROUP M

DASH TRIM

ILL	PART NO	DESCRIPTION	QTY	REMARKS
1		INSULATOR-DASH CENTRE		
	MTC4861	4 Cyl	1	
	MTC4863	V8-4 Speed	1	
	MTC1248	V8-5 Speed	1	
1		CARPET-DASH CENTRE		
	MUC1356	4 Cyl-Brushwood	1	
	MUC1342RD	V8-4 Speed-Brushwood	1	
	MUC1256RD	V8-5 Speed-Brushwood	1	
		TOE BOX TRIM		
2	MUC9167	RH-RHD	1	
3	MTC4866	LH-RHD-Except Air Con	1	
	MUC2210	LH-RHD-Air Con	1	
	MUC9168	RH-LHD-Except Air Con	1	
	MTC8360	RH-LHD-Air Con	1	
	MTC4865	LH-LHD	1	
	MTC8349	Baffle Toe Box Trim-Air Con	1	
4	AB606041L	Drive Screw	6	
5	WC104001L	Plain Washer	6	
6	MTC4916	Retainer-RH	1	
7	396416	Retainer-LH	1	
8	AB606031L	Drive Screw	6	
9	MRC5394	Cover Dash Side-LH	1	
10	MTC6820	Cover Dash Side-RH	1	
11	304716	Retainer	2	
12	AB606031L	Drive Screw	6	) Alternatives.
	AB606041L	Drive Screw	6	)

VS3929A

MODEL LR110 - UP TO AUGUST 1986
BLOCK TS 5139
PAGE M 10
GROUP M

DOOR TRIM - EXCEPT WIND UP WINDOWS

ILL	PART NO	DESCRIPTION	QTY	REMARKS
		Front Door Trim		
1	MTC9814	Upper-RH	1	
	MTC9815	Upper-LH	1	
2	MTC9824	Lower-RH	1	
	MTC9825	Lower-LH	1	
3	MTC3382	Front Door Pocket	2	
4	AFU2641	Push Nut Fastener	8	
		Rear Side Door Trim		
5	MTC9818	Upper RH	1	
	MTC9819	Upper LH	1	
6	MTC9826	Lower RH	1	
	MTC9827	Lower LH	1	
7	AFU2636	Sems Drive Screw	44	
8	AB608124	Drive Screw	8	
9	MTC9994	Spacer	8	
10	AFU1926	Captive Nut	52	
11	YGA451L	Door Pull	4	
12	AB610104L	Door Screw	8	
13	ADU3775L	Lokut Nut	8	
14	MTC4182	Rear End Door Trim-Note(1)	1	)Upto VIN
	MTC9801	Rear End Door Trim-Note(2)	1	)241999
	MUC4529	Rear End Door Trim-Note(1)	1	)From VIN
	MUC4528	Rear End Door Trim-Note(2)	1	)242000
15	AB606041L	Drive Screw	3	
16	MTC1710	Lock Cover	1	
17	MTC6456	Grab Handle	1	Note(1)
	MUC1402	Grab Handle	1	Note(2)
18	SH106204	Screw	2	
19	WL106004L	Spring Washer	2	
20	CZA2259L	Bezel-Remote Control Handle	8	
21	MTC6630	Cover For Grab Handle Screws	2	Germany

NOTE(1): Except Heated Window/Wash Wipe

NOTE(2): Heated Window/Wash Wipe

TS5139

MODEL LR110 - UP TO AUGUST 1986
BLOCK TS 5271
PAGE M 10.10
GROUP M

DOOR TRIM - WIND UP WINDOWS - 1984 FACELIFT

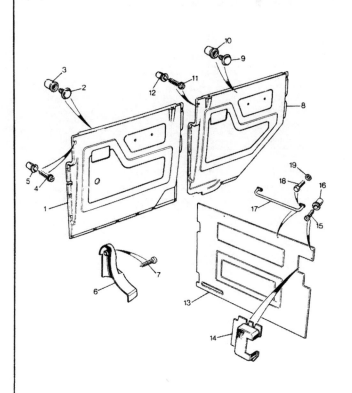

ILL	PART NO	DESCRIPTION	QTY	REMARKS
1	MTC8706	Front Door Trim RH	1	
	MTC8707	Front Door Trim LH	1	
	MUC3621	Foam Spacer	6	
2	AFU1075	Plastic Stud	4	
3	13H2475L	Stud Anchor	4	
4	MUC3394	Sems Drivescrew	26	
	MUC3395	Sems Drivescrew	2	
5	AFU1926	Captive Nut	28	
	AJU1136L	Snapsac	8	
6	MUC3036	Checkstrap Cover RH	1	
	MUC3037	Checkstrap Cover LH	1	
7	AB608064L	Drive Screw	2	
8	MTC8708	Rear Side Door Trim RH	1	
	MTC8709	Rear Side Door Trim LH	1	
	MUC3621	Foam Spacer	6	
9	AFU1075	Plastic Stud	4	
10	13H2475L	Stud Anchor	4	
11	MUC3394	Sems Drivescrew	24	
	MUC3395	Sems Drivescrew	2	
12	AFU1926	Captive Nut	22	
	AJU1136L	Snapsac	6	
13	MTC4182	Rear End Door Trim	1	Note(1)
	MTC9801	Rear End Door Trim	1	Note(2)
	MUC4529	Rear End Door Trim	1	Note(1)(3)
	MUC4528	Rear End Door Trim	1	Note(2)(3)
14	MTC1710	Lock Cover	1	
15	AB606041L	Drive Screw	4	Note(1)
	AFU2636	Drive Screw	4	
16	AFU1926	Captive Nut	3	
17	MTC6456	Grab Handle	1	Note(1)
	MUC1402	Grab Handle	1	Note(2)
18	SH106204	Screw	2	
19	WL106004L	Spring Washer	2	
	MUC4525	Arrow Label-Rear End Door Trim	1	Note(3)

NOTE(1): Except Heated Window/Wash Wipe
   (2): Heated Window/Wash Wipe
   (3): Automatic Door Check With Manual Release

TS5271

LAND ROVER PARTS LTD

MODEL LR110 - UP TO AUGUST 1986
BLOCK TS 5471
PAGE M 12
GROUP M

FRONT FLOOR TRIM - EXCEPT CARPETS

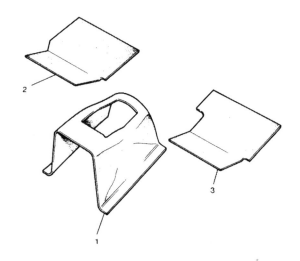

ILL	PART NO	DESCRIPTION	QTY	REMARKS
1		TUNNEL COVER		
	MUC1621	4 Cyl	1	
	MUC1616	V8-4 Speed	1	
	MUC1253	V8-5 Speed	1	
2		FRONT FLOOR COVER-RH		
	MUC2268	RHD-4 Cyl	1	
	MUC2270	LHD-4 Cyl	1	
	MUC2272	RHD-V8-4 Speed	1	
	MUC2274	LHD-V8-4 Speed	1	
	MUC1250	RHD-V8-5 Speed	1	
	MUC1254	LHD-V8-5 Speed	1	
3		FRONT FLOOR COVER-LH		
	MUC2269	RHD-4 Cyl	1	
	MUC2271	LHD-4 Cyl	1	
	MUC2273	RHD-V8-4 Speed	1	
	MUC2275	LHD-V8-4 Speed	1	
	MUC1249	RHD-V8-5 Speed	1	
	MUC1255	LHD-V8-5 Speed	1	

TS5471

LAND ROVER PARTS LTD

MODEL LR110 - UP TO AUGUST 1986
BLOCK TS 5472
PAGE M 12.02
GROUP M

SEATBASE TRIM - EXCEPT CARPETS

ILL	PART NO	DESCRIPTION	QTY	REMARKS
1		SEATBASE INSULATION-FRONT-RH		
	MUC2202	RHD-4 Cyl	1	
	MUC2206	RHD-4 Cyl-Note(1)	1	NLA-Use MXC1804PMA
	MTC8523	LHD-4 Cyl	1	
	MUC2205	LHD-4 Cyl-Note(1)	1	NLA-Use MXC1804PMA
	MUC2204	RHD-V8-4 Speed	1	
	MUC2207	RHD-V8-4 Speed	1	Note(1)
	MTC8502	LHD-V8-4 Speed	1	
	MUC2539	LHD-V8-4 Speed	1	Note(1)
	MUC1270	RHD-V8-5 Speed	1	NLA-Use MXC1806PMA
	MUC1272	RHD-V8-5 Speed-Note(1)	1	NLA-Use MXC1806PMA
	MUC1274	LHD-V8-5 Speed	1	NLA-Use MXC1806PMA
	MUC1273	LHD-V8-5 Speed-Note(1)	1	NLA-Use MXC1806PMA
2		SEATBASE INSULATION-FRONT-LH		
	MUC2201	RHD-4 Cyl	1	
	MTC8613	LHD-4 Cyl	1	
	MUC2203	RHD-V8-4 Speed	1	
	MTC8613	LHD-V8-4 Speed	1	
	MUC1271	RHD-V8-5 Speed	1	
	MUC1275	LHD-V8-5 Speed	1	NLA-Use MXC1806PMA
3		SEATBASE INSULATION-TOP		
	396950	RH	1	
	396951	LH	1	

NOTE(1): Vehicles with Additional Fuel Tank

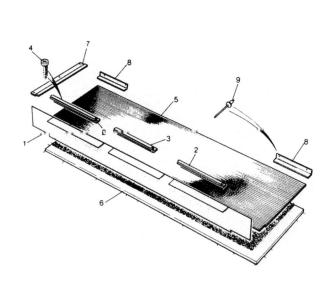

TS5472

MODEL LR110 - UP TO AUGUST 1986
BLOCK TS 5473A
PAGE M 12.04
GROUP M

INTERMEDIATE FLOOR TRIM - EXCEPT CARPETS

ILL	PART NO	DESCRIPTION	QTY	REMARKS
1	396540	Toe Panel Cover	1	
2	396541	Retainer-Outer	2	
3	396542	Retainer-Centre	1	
4	AB606041L	Drive Screw	6	
5	331481	Intermediate Floor Mat	1	
6	MUC1495	Intermediate Floor Felt	1	
7	MUC1699	Retainer-Side	2	
8	336780	Retainer RH	1	
	336781	Retainer LH	1	
9	78248	Rivet	4	

TS 5473A

MODEL LR110 - UP TO AUGUST 1986
BLOCK TS 5474
PAGE M 12.06
GROUP M

REAR FLOOR TRIM - EXCEPT CARPETS

1	331670	Rear Floor Mat	1
2	336780	Retainer RH	1
3	336781	Retainer LH	1
4	78248	Rivet	4

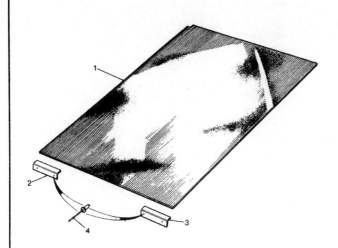

TS5474

 **LAND ROVER PARTS LTD**

638

MODEL LR110 - UP TO AUGUST 1986
BLOCK TS 5475
PAGE M 12.10
GROUP M

FRONT FLOOR TRIM - CARPETS

ILL	PART NO	DESCRIPTION	QTY	REMARKS
1		TUNNEL CARPET		
	MUC1361RD	4 Cyl-Brushwood	1	
	MUC1347RD	V8-4 Speed-Brushwood	1	
	MUC1257RD	V8-5 Speed-Brushwood	1	
2		TUNNEL FELT		
	MUC1499	4 Cyl	1	
	MUC1494	V8	1	
3		FRONT FLOOR CARPET-RH		
	MUC1358RD	RHD-4 Cyl-Brushwood	1	
	MUC1362RD	LHD-4 Cyl-Brushwood	1	
	MUC1344	RHD-V8 4 Speed-Brushwood	1	
	MUC1348RD	LHD-V8 4 Speed-Brushwood	1	
	MUC1258RD	RHD-V8 5 Speed-Brushwood	1	
	MUC1264RD	LHD-V8 5 Speed-Brushwood	1	
4		FRONT FLOOR CARPET-LH		
	MUC1357RD	RHD-4 Cyl-Brushwood	1	
	MUC1363RD	LHD-4 Cyl-Brushwood	1	
	MUC1343RD	RHD-V8 4 Speed-Brushwood	1	
	MUC1349RD	LHD-V8 4 Speed-Brushwood	1	
	MUC1259RD	RHD-V8 5 Speed-Brushwood	1	
	MUC1265RD	LHD-V8 5 Speed-Brushwood	1	
5		FRONT FLOOR FELT		
	MUC1498	RH-4 Cyl	1	
	MUC1497	LH-4 Cyl	1	
	MUC1492	RH-V8 4 Speed	1	
	MUC1493	LH-V8 4 Speed	1	
	MUC1268	RH-V8 5 Speed	1	
	MUC1269	LH-V8 5 Speed	1	
6	RTC3938AV	Drive Fastener	4	
7	13H2475L	Stud Anchor	4	

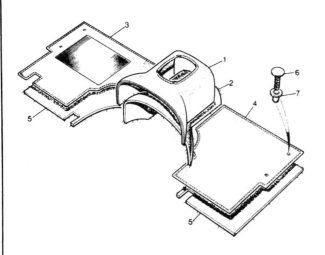

TS5475

 **LAND ROVER PARTS LTD**

639

MODEL LR110 - UP TO AUGUST 1986
BLOCK TS 5476
PAGE M 12.12
GROUP M

SEATBASE TRIM - CARPETS

ILL	PART NO	DESCRIPTION	QTY	REMARKS
1		SEATBASE CARPET-FRONT		
	MUC1360RD	RH-RHD-4 Cyl-Brushwood	1	
	MUC2160RD	RH-RHD-4 Cyl-Brushwood	1	Note(1)
	MUC1359RD	LH-RHD-4 Cyl-Brushwood	1	
	MUC1364RD	RH-LHD-4 Cyl-Brushwood	1	
	MUC2161RD	RH-LHD-4 Cyl-Brushwood	1	Note(1)
	MUC1365RD	LH-LHD-4 Cyl-Brushwood	1	
	MUC2012RD	RH-RHD-V8 4 Speed-Brushwood	1	
	MUC2162RD	RH-RHD-V8 4 Speed-Brushwood	1	Note(1)
	MUC2013RD	LH-RHD-V8 4 Speed-Brushwood	1	
	MUC1346RD	LHD-V8 4 Speed-Brushwood	1	
	MUC2163RD	LHD-V8 4 Speed-Brushwood	1	Note(1)
	MUC1260RD	RH-RHD-V8 5 Speed-Brushwood	1	
	MUC1260RD	RH-RHD-V8 5 Speed-Brushwood	1	Note(1)
	MUC1261RD	LH-RHD-V8 5 Speed-Brushwood	1	
	MUC1266RD	LHD-V8 5 Speed-Brushwood	1	
	MUC1266RD	LHD-V8 5 Speed-Brushwood	1	Note(1)
2	MUC1757	Seatbase Carpet-Top-Brushwood	1	
3	MUC1500	Retainer	2	
4	AB606054L	Drive Screw	6	
5	MTC9428	Tek Screw	16	
6	MTC9429	Cup Washer	16	

NOTE: (1) Vehicles with Additional Fuel Tank

 **LAND ROVER PARTS LTD**

MODEL LR110 - UP TO AUGUST 1986
BLOCK TS 5477
PAGE M 12.14
GTOUP M

INTERMEDIATE FLOOR TRIM - CARPETS

ILL	PART NO	DESCRIPTION	QTY	REMARKS
1	MUC6667RD	Toe Panel Carpet-Brushwood	1	
2	396541	Retainer-Outer	2	
3	396542	Retainer-Centre	1	
4	AB606041L	Drive Screw	6	
5	MUC1353RD	Intermediate Floor Carpet-Brushwood	1	
6	MUC1495	Intermediate Floor Felt	1	
7	RTC3938AV	Drive Fastener	4	
8	13H2475L	Stud Anchor	4	
9	MUC1756	Heelboard Carpet-Brushwood	1	Note(1)
	MUC1759	Heelboard Carpet-Brushwood	1	Note(2)
10	MTC9428	Tek Screw	12	
11	MTC9429	Cup Washer	12	

NOTE(1): 10 Seater Station Wagon
NOTE(2): 12 Seater Station Wagon

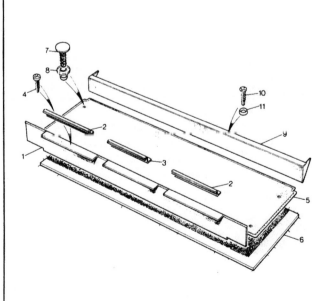

 **LAND ROVER PARTS LTD**

MODEL LR110 - UP TO AUGUST 1986
BLOCK VS 5478
PAGE M 12.16
GROUP M

REAR FLOOR TRIM - CARPETS

ILL	PART NO	DESCRIPTION	QTY	REMARKS
1	MUC4139RD	Rear Floor carpet-Brushwood	1	Note(1)
	MUC1758RD	Rear Floor Carpet-Brushwood	1	Note(2)

NOTE(1): 10 Seater Station Wagon
NOTE(2): 12 Seater Station Wagon

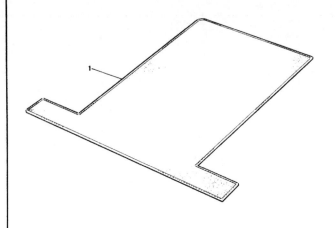

VS5478

MODEL LR110 - UP TO AUGUST 1986
BLOCK TS 5479
PAGE M12.20
GROUP M

ADDITIONAL FLOOR TRIM

ILL	PART NO	DESCRIPTION	QTY	REMARKS
1		ADDITIONAL FRONT MAT-RH		
	MUC2380	RHD-4 Cyl	1	
	MUC2382	LHD-4 Cyl	1	
	MUC2384	RHD-V8 4 Speed	1	
	MUC2386	LHD-V8 4 Speed	1	
	MUC4150	RHD-V8 5 Speed	1	
	MUC4152	LHD-V8 5 Speed	1	
2		ADDITIONAL FRONT MAT-LH		
	MUC2379	RHD-4 Cyl	1	
	MUC2381	LHD-4 Cyl	1	
	MUC2383	RHD-V8 4 Speed	1	
	MUC2385	LHD-V8 4 Speed	1	
	MUC4149	RHD-V8 5 Speed	1	
	MUC4153	LHD-V8 5 Speed	1	
3	331481	Additional Intermediate Floormat	1	
4	331670	Additional Rear Floor Mat	1	

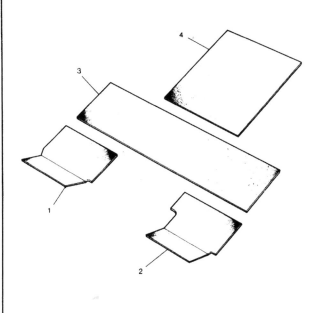

TS5479

MODEL LR110 - UP TO AUGUST 1986
BLOCK VS 4152B
PAGE M 14
GROUP M

TRIM - STATION WAGON

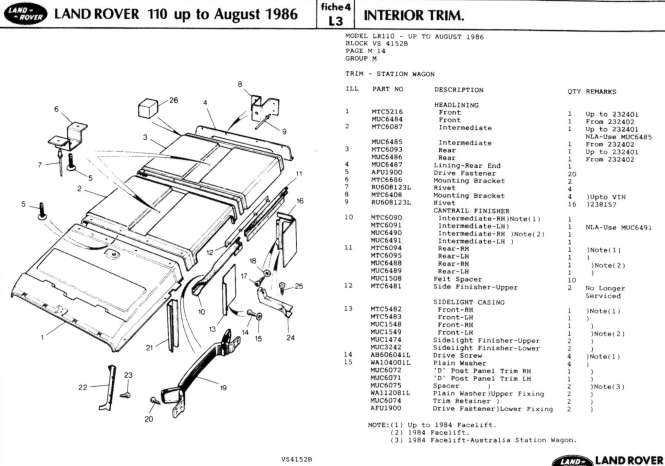

ILL	PART NO	DESCRIPTION	QTY	REMARKS
		HEADLINING		
1	MTC5216	Front	1	Up to 232401
	MUC6484	Front	1	From 232402
2	MTC6087	Intermediate	1	Up to 232401
				NLA-Use MUC6485
	MUC6485	Intermediate	1	From 232402
3	MTC6093	Rear	1	Up to 232401
	MUC6486	Rear	1	From 232402
4	MUC6487	Lining-Rear End	1	
5	AFU1900	Drive Fastener	20	
6	MTC6686	Mounting Bracket	2	
7	RU608123L	Rivet	4	
8	MTC6408	Mounting Bracket	4	)Upto VIN
9	RU608123L	Rivet	16	)238157
		CANTRAIL FINISHER		
10	MTC6090	Intermediate-RH)Note(1)	1	
	MTC6091	Intermediate-LH)	1	NLA-Use MUC6491
	MUC6490	Intermediate-RH)Note(2)	1	
	MUC6491	Intermediate-LH)	1	
11	MTC6094	Rear-RH	1	)Note(1)
	MTC6095	Rear-LH	1	)
	MUC6488	Rear-RH	1	)Note(2)
	MUC6489	Rear-LH	1	)
	MUC1508	Felt Spacer	10	
12	MTC6481	Side Finisher-Upper	2	No Longer
				Serviced
		SIDELIGHT CASING		
13	MTC5482	Front-RH	1	)Note(1)
	MTC5483	Front-LH	1	)
	MUC1548	Front-RH	1	)
	MUC1549	Front-LH	1	)Note(2)
	MUC1474	Sidelight Finisher-Upper	2	)
	MUC3242	Sidelight Finisher-Lower	2	)
14	AB606041L	Drive Screw	4	)Note(1)
15	WA104001L	Plain Washer	4	)
	MUC6072	'D' Post Panel Trim RH	1	)
	MUC6071	'D' Post Panel Trim LH	1	)
	MUC6075	Spacer)	2	)Note(3)
	WA112081L	Plain Washer)Upper Fixing	2	)
	MUC6074	Trim Retainer)	2	)
	AFU1900	Drive Fastener)Lower Fixing	2	)

NOTE:(1) Up to 1984 Facelift.
     (2) 1984 Facelift.
     (3) 1984 Facelift-Australia Station Wagon.

VS4152B

LAND ROVER PARTS LTD

MODEL LR110 - UP TO AUGUST 1986
BLOCK VS 4152B
PAGE M 14.02
GROUP M

TRIM - STATION WAGON

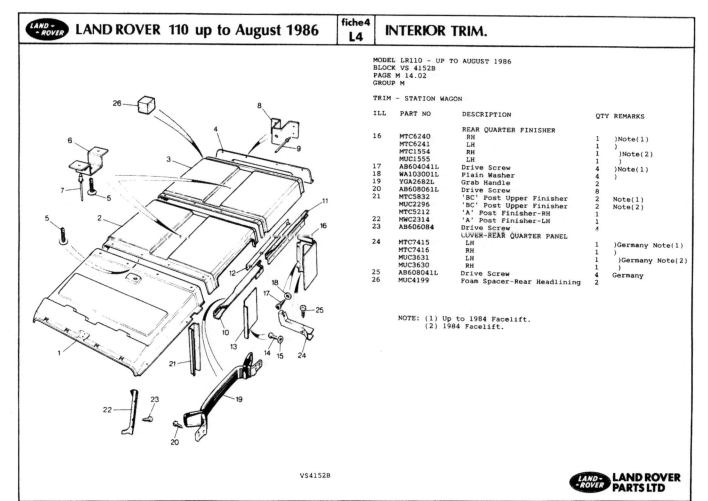

ILL	PART NO	DESCRIPTION	QTY	REMARKS
		REAR QUARTER FINISHER		
16	MTC6240	RH	1	)Note(1)
	MTC6241	LH	1	)
	MTC1554	RH	1	)Note(2)
	MUC1555	LH	1	)
17	AB604041L	Drive Screw	4	)Note(1)
18	WA103001L	Plain Washer	4	)
19	YGA2682L	Grab Handle	2	
20	AB608061L	Drive Screw	8	
21	MTC5832	'BC' Post Upper Finisher	2	Note(1)
	MUC2296	'BC' Post Upper Finisher	2	Note(2)
	MTC5212	'A' Post Finisher-RH	1	
22	MWC2314	'A' Post Finisher-LH	1	
23	AB606084	Drive Screw	4	
		COVER-REAR QUARTER PANEL		
24	MTC7415	LH	1	)Germany Note(1)
	MTC7416	RH	1	)
	MUC3631	LH	1	)Germany Note(2)
	MUC3630	RH	1	)
25	AB608041L	Drive Screw	4	Germany
26	MUC4199	Foam Spacer-Rear Headlining	2	

NOTE: (1) Up to 1984 Facelift.
      (2) 1984 Facelift.

VS4152B

LAND ROVER PARTS LTD

MODEL LR110 - UP TO AUGUST 1986
BLOCK VS 4256
PAGE M 14.10
GROUP M

TRIM - HARD TOP

ILL	PART NO	DESCRIPTION	QTY	REMARKS
1	MUC6651	Head Lining-Front	1	
2	AFU1900	Drive Fastener	8	
	MUC3630	Cover-Rear Quarter Panel RH	1	)
	MUC3631	Cover-Rear Quarter Panel LH	1	)
	AB608041L	Drive Screw	4	)Germany
	MUC3844	'B' Post Trim-RH	1	)
	MUC3845	'B' Post Trim-LH	1	)

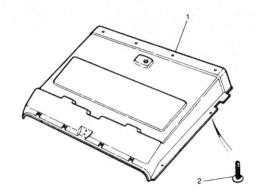

VS4256

LAND ROVER PARTS LTD

646

MODEL LR110 - UP TO AUGUST 1986
BLOCK VS 4132
PAGE M 16
GROUP M

TRIM - TRUCK CAB

ILL	PART NO	DESCRIPTION	QTY	REMARKS
1	MTC5206	Headlining	1	Up to VIN 232401
	MUC6496	Headlining	1	From VIN 232402
2	AFU1900	Drive Fastener	4	
	MTC5212	'A' Post Trim RH	1	
3	MWC2314	'A' Post Trim LH	1	
4	AB606084	Drive Screw	4	
	MUC6498	'B' Post Trim RH	1	
5	MTC5209	'B' Post Trim LH	1	Up to VIN 232401
	MUC6499	'B' Post Trim LH	1	From VIN 232402
	MUC6652	Rear Pillar Trim RH	1	
6	MUC6653	Rear Pillar Trim LH	1	
7	MUC6497	Rear Lower Trim	1	
8	AFU1900	Drive Fastener	7	
9	MTC5486	Mounting Bracket	7	
10	RA608176L	Rivet	14	

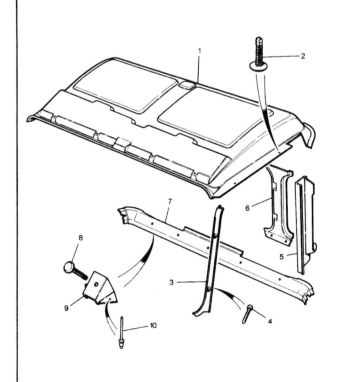

VS4132

LAND ROVER PARTS LTD

647

MODEL LR 110 - UP TO AUGUST 1986
BLOCK VS 3980
PAGE M 18
GROUP M

TRIM - SUN VISORS

ILL	PART NO	DESCRIPTION	QTY	REMARKS
1	MTC5698	Sun Visor RH	1	
2	MTC5699	Sun Visor LH	1	
3	SE106201L	Screw	4	Untrimmed Vehicles
	SE106251L	Screw	4	Trimmed Vehicles
4	WL106001L	Spring Washer	4	
5	WA106041L	Plain Washer	4	

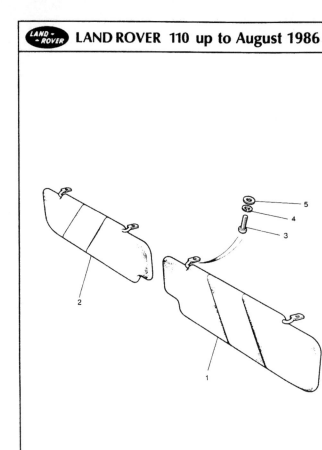

VS3980

LAND ROVER PARTS LTD

648

MODEL LR110 - UP TO AUGUST 1986
BLOCK VS 4153A
PAGE M 18.02
GROUP M

TRIM - CONSOLE UNIT

ILL	PART NO	DESCRIPTION	QTY	REMARKS
1	MTC7020	Console Unit	1	Note(1)
2	MTC4520	+Tray	1	
3	RTC3024	+Lock Kit	1	
4	AB606061L	+Screw-Fixing Lock	2	
5	CZK3438L	Key Blank	A/R	
6	SE106351L	Screw	4	
7	WA106041L	Plain Washer	4	
8	NN106021	Blind Anchor Nut	4	
9	AFU2501	Plug	4	

NOTE(1): No Longer Available-Use MUC6681-See Next Page

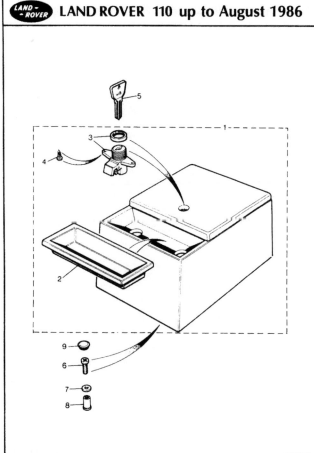

VS4153A

LAND ROVER PARTS LTD

649

MODEL LR110 - UP TO AUGUST 1986
BLOCK TS 5788
PAGE M 18.04
GROUP M

TRIM - CONSOLE ASSEMBLY

ILL	PART NO	DESCRIPTION	QTY	REMARKS
1	MUC6681	Console Assembly	1	
2	MUC6682	+Striker Plate	1	
3	MUC6452	+Latch	1	
4	MUC6453	+Lock,Barrel and Keys	1	
	BAU1849L	Key Blank	A/R	
5	SE106351L	Screw	4	
6	WA106041L	Plain Washer	4	
7	NN106021	Blind Anchor Nut	4	
8	AFU2501	Plug	4	

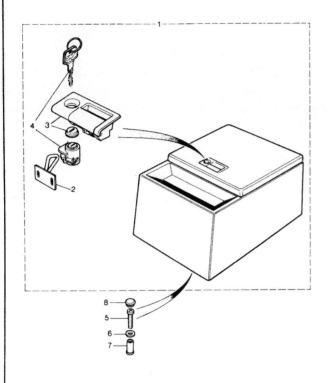

TS5788

LAND ROVER PARTS LTD

650

MODEL LR110 - UP TO AUGUST 1986
BLOCK VS 4172
PAGE M 20
GROUP M

FRONT SEATS - BASIC TYPE - PICK-UP - NOTE(1)

ILL	PART NO	DESCRIPTION	QTY	REMARKS
1	MUC1520	Front Squab-Driver	1	
	320698	Front Squab-Outer	1	
	MUC1488	Front Squab-Centre	1	
2	337873	+Interior-Driver Squab	1	
	337873	+Interior-Outer Squab	1	
	337880	+Interior-Centre Squab	1	
3	RTC3764	+Trim Clip	24	
4	346410	+Retainer Tube	3	
5	331273	+Strap-Outer Squab	1	
	331273	+Strap-Centre Squab	2	
6	AB610041L	+Drive Screw	3	
7	4034	+Plain Washer	3	
8	78237	+Spire Nut	3	
9	349931	+Plastic Washer-Driver Squab	4	
	349931	+Plastic Washer-Outer Squab	2	
	349931	+Plastic Washer-Centre Squab	2	
10	331709	+Bolt-Driver Squab	2	
11	RTC614	+Split Pin-Outer Squab	2	
	RTC614	+Split Pin-Centre Squab	2	
12	320699	Front Cushion-Driver	1	
	349967	Front Cushion-Outer	1	
	320726	Front Cushion-Centre	1	
13	337899	+Interior-Driver Cushion	1	
	337899	+Interior-Outer Cushion	1	
	337859	+Interior-Centre Cushion	1	
14	349943	+Protective Capping	12	
15	331973	Strap-Outer Cushion	1	
	331974	Strap-Centre Cushion	1	
16	RTC3755	Plastic Rivet	2	

NOTE(1):   Drivers Seat Only Adjustable

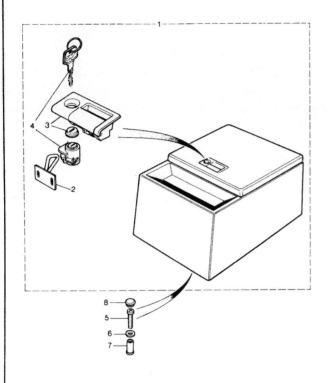

VS4172

LAND ROVER PARTS LTD

651

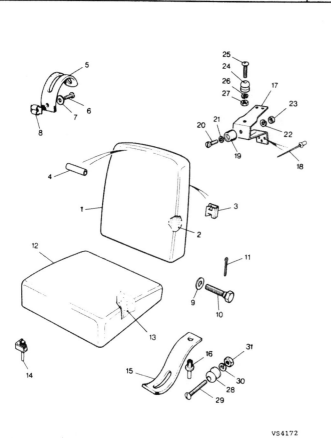

MODEL LR110 - UP TO AUGUST 1986
BLOCK VS 4172
PAGE M 20.02
GROUP M

FRONT SEATS - BASIC TYPE - PICK-UP - NOTE(1)

ILL	PART NO	DESCRIPTION	QTY	REMARKS
17	347553	Bracket-Squab Buffer	4	
18	RU612373L	Rivet	16	
19	304125	Buffer	4	
20	SE105251	Screw	4	
21	WC105001	Plain Washer	4	
22	WL105001	Spring Washer	4	
23	NH105041	Nut	4	
24	348430	Stud-Retaining Squab Strap	3	
25	SE105251	Screw	3	
26	WL105001	Spring Washer	3	
27	NH105041	Nut	3	
28	348430	Stud-Retaining Cushion Strap	2	
29	SE105251	Screw	2	
30	WL105001	Spring Washer	2	
31	NH105041	Nut	2	

NOTE(1):   Drivers Seat Only Adjustable

VS4172

MODEL LR110 - UP TO AUGUST 1986
BLOCK VS 4169
PAGE M 22
GROUP M

FRONT SEATS - BASIC TYPE - STATION WAGON - NOTE(1)

ILL	PART NO	DESCRIPTION	QTY	REMARKS
1	320708	Front Squab-Driver	1	
	320709	Front Squab-Outer	1	
	MUC1488	Front Squab-Centre	1	
2	337873	+Interior-Driver Squab	1	
	337873	+Interior-Outer Squab	1	
	337880	+Interior-Centre Squab	1	
3	RTC3764	+Trim Clip	24	
4	332355	+Strap-Outer Squab	2	
	332355	+Strap-Centre Squab	1	
5	339986	+Rubber Packing-Driver Squab	2	
	347869	+Rubber Packing-Outer Squab	2	
	347869	+Rubber Packing-Centre Squab	1	
6	AB610081	+Drive Screw-Driver Squab	2	
	AB610081	+Drive Screw-Outer Squab	4	
	AB610081	+Drive Screw-Centre Squab	2	
7	4034	+Plain Washer-Driver Squab	2	
	4034	+Plain Washer-Outer Squab	4	
	WC106041L	+Plain Washer-Centre Squab	2	
8	78237	+Spire Nut	8	
9	349931	+Plastic Washer-Driver Squab	4	
	349931	+Plastic Washer-Outer Squab	2	
	349931	+Plastic Washer-Centre Squab	2	
10	331709	+Bolt-Driver Squab	2	
11	RTC614	+Split Pin-Outer Squab	2	
	RTC614	+Split Pin-Centre Squab	2	

NOTE(1):   Drivers Seat Only Adjustable

VS4169

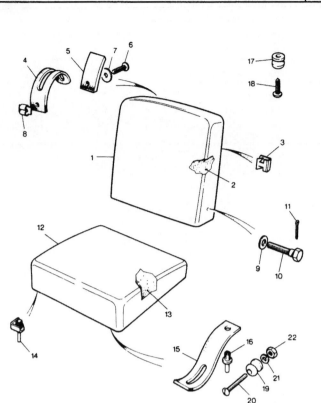

MODEL LR110 - UP TO AUGUST 1986
BLOCK VS 4169
PAGE M 22.02
GROUP M

FRONT SEATS - BASIC TYPE - STATION WAGON - NOTE(1)

ILL	PART NO	DESCRIPTION	QTY	REMARKS
12	320699	Front Cushion-Driver	1	
	349967	Front Cushion-Outer	1	
	320726	Front Cushion-Centre	1	
13	337899	+Interior-Driver Cushion	1	
	337899	+Interior-Outer Cushion	1	
	337859	+Interior-Centre Cushion	1	
14	349943	+Protective Capping	12	
15	331973	+Strap-Outer Cushion	1	
	331974	+Strap-Centre Cushion	1	
16	RTC3755	+Plastic Rivet	2	
17	348430	Stud-Retaining Squab Strap	3	
18	AB606081	Drive Screw	3	
19	348430	Stud-Retaining Cushion Strap	2	
20	SE105251	Screw	2	
21	WL105001	Spring Washer	2	
22	NH105041	Nut	2	

NOTE(1):   Drivers Seat Only Adjustable

VS4169

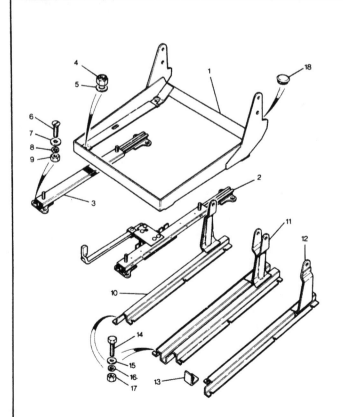

MODEL LR110 - UP TO AUGUST 1986
BLOCK VS 4246A
PAGE M 24
GROUP M

FRONT SEATS - SEAT SLIDES - NOTE(1)

ILL	PART NO	DESCRIPTION	QTY	REMARKS
1	349996	Adjustable Seat Frame	1	
2	MRC9492	Seat Slide RH with Control RHD	1	
	MRC9493	Seat Slide LH with Control LHD	1	
3	MRC9481	Seat Slide Plain	1	
4	NT108041L	Locknut	4	
5	WF108001L	Shakeproof Washer	4	
6	SA106201	Screw	8	
7	MRC5525	Plain Washer	8	
	MRC5526	Plain Washer	2	
8	WL106001L	Spring Washer	8	
9	NH106041L	Nut	8	
10	MTC1715	Seat Support Centre Single RHD	1	
	MTC1714	Seat Support Centre Single LHD	1	
11	MTC1718	Seat Support Centre-Double RHD	1	
	MTC1719	Seat Support Centre-Double LHD	1	
12	331008	Seat Support Outer-RHD	1	
	331007	Seat Support Outer-LHD	1	
13	331818	Retaining Bracket	2	
14	SH106201L	Screw	14	
15	MRC5525	Plain Washer	28	
16	WL106001L	Spring Washer	14	
17	NH106041L	Nut	14	
18	331083	Grommet Plug-Seat Frame	2	

NOTE(1)   Drivers Seat Only Adjustable

VS4246A

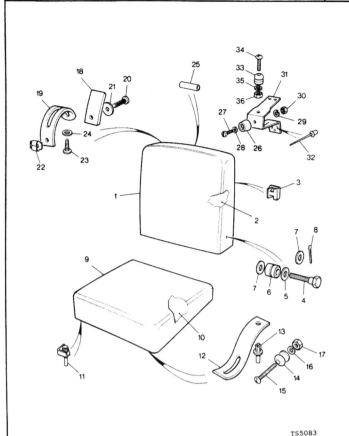

MODEL LR110 - UP TO AUGUST 1986
BLOCK TS 5083
PAGE M 26
GROUP M

FRONT SEATS - BASIC TYPE - PICK-UP AND STATION WAGON - NOTE(1)

ILL	PART NO	DESCRIPTION	QTY	REMARKS
1		FRONT SEAT SQUAB		
	MUC1520	Driver	1	
	MUC1520	Outer	1	
	MUC1488	Centre	1	
2		+Interior For Squab		
	337873	Driver/Outer	2	
	337880	Centre	1	
3	RTC3764	+Trim Clip	24	
4	331709	+Bolt-Driver/Outer	8	
5	WC108051L	+Plain Washer-Driver/Outer	8	
6	345213	+Rubber Washer-Driver/Outer	4	
7	349931	+Plastic Washer-Driver/Outer	4	
	349931	+Plastic Washer-Centre	2	
8	RTC614	+Split Pin-Centre	2	
	349997	Stop-Seat Squab	4	
	SP604061	Screw	4	
	WE600041L	Shakeproof Washer	4	
	349998	Protective Edging Strip-Seat Frame	4	
9		FRONT SEAT CUSHION		
	320699	Driver	1	
	320699	Outer	1	
	320726	Centre	1	
10		+Interior For Cushion		
	337899	Driver/Outer	2	
	337859	Centre	1	
11	349943	+Protective Capping	12	
12	331974	Strap-Centre Cushion	1	
13	RTC3755	Plastic Rivet	1	
14	348430	Stud	1	
15	SE105251	Screw	1	
16	WL105001	Spring Washer	1	
17	NH105041	Nut	1	

NOTE(1):   Driver and Outer Seats Adjustable

TS5083

LAND ROVER PARTS LTD

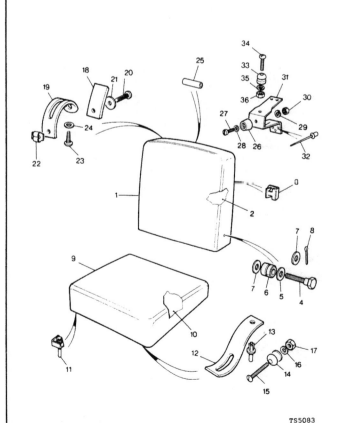

MODEL LR110 - UP TO AUGUST 1986
BLOCK TS 5083
PAGE M 28
GROUP M

FRONT SEATS - BASIC TYPE - PICK-UP AND STATION WAGON - NOTE(1)

ILL	PART NO	DESCRIPTION	QTY	REMARKS
18	339986	Rubber Packing-Driver/Outer Squab	4	)
20	AB610081	Screw	4	) Station
21	WJ105001	Plain Washer	4	) Wagon
22	78237	Spire Nut	4	)
18	347869	Rubber Packing-Centre Squab	1	)
19	332355	Strap	1	) Station
20	AB610061L	Screw	1	) Wagon
21	WJ105001	Plain Washer	2	)
22	78237	Spire Nut	2	)
23	AB606041L	Screw-Centre Squab Strap to Grab Rail	1	)
24	AFU1247	Plain Washer	1	) Station Wagon
19	331273	Strap-Centre Squab	2	)
20	AB610061L	Screw	2	)
21	WJ105001	Plain Washer	2	)
22	78237	Spire Nut	2	)
25	346410	Retainer Tube	3	) Pick-Up
26	304125	Buffer	2	)
27	SE105251	Screw	2	)
28	WC702101	Plain Washer	2	)
29	WE702101	Shakeproof Washer	2	)
30	NH105041	Nut	2	)
31	347553	Bracket-Squab Buffer	2	
32	RU612373L	Rivet	8	
33	348430	Stud	2	)
34	SE105251	Screw	2	) Pick-up
35	WL105001	Spring Washer	2	)
36	NH105041	Nut	2	)

NOTE(1):   Driver and Outer Seats Adjustable

TS5083

LAND ROVER PARTS LTD

MODEL LR110 - UP TO AUGUST 1986
BLOCK VS 4167
PAGE M 30
GROUP M

FRONT SEATS - DE-LUXE TYPE - PICK-UP - NOTE(1)

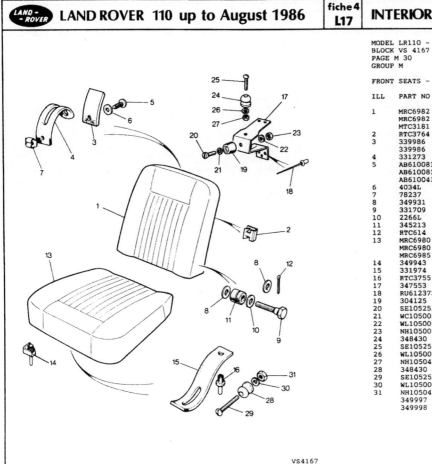

ILL	PART NO	DESCRIPTION	QTY	REMARKS
1	MRC6982	Front Squab-Driver	1	
	MRC6982	Front Squab-Outer	1	
	MTC3181	Front Squab-Centre	1	
2	RTC3764	+Trim Clip	24	
3	339986	+Rubber Packing-Driver Squab	2	
	339986	+Rubber Packing-Outer Squab	2	
4	331273	+Strap-Centre Squab	2	
5	AB610081L	+Drive Screw-Driver Squab	2	
	AB610081L	+Drive Screw-Outer Squab	2	
	AB610041L	+Drive Screw-Centre Squab	2	
6	4034L	+Plain Washer	6	
7	78237	+Spire Nut	6	
8	349931	+Plastic Washer	6	
9	331709	+Bolt-Driver/Outer Squabs	4	
10	2266L	+Plain Washer	8	
11	345213	+Rubber Washer	4	
12	RTC614	+Split Pin-Centre Squab	2	
13	MRC6980	Front Cushion-Driver	1	
	MRC6980	Front Cushion-Outer	1	
	MRC6985	Front Cushion-Centre	1	
14	349943	+Protective Capping	12	
15	331974	+Strap-Centre Cushion	1	
16	RTC3755	+Rivet	1	
17	347553	Bracket-Squab Buffer	2	
18	RU612373L	Rivet	8	
19	304125	Buffer	2	
20	SE105251L	Screw	2	
21	WC105001L	Plain Washer	2	
22	WL105001L	Spring Washer	2	
23	NH105001	Nut	2	
24	348430	Stud-Retaining Squab Strap	2	
25	SE105251L	Screw	2	
26	WL105001L	Spring Washer	2	
27	NH105041L	Nut	2	
28	348430	Stud-Retaining Cushion Strap	1	
29	SE105251L	Screw	1	
30	WL105001L	Spring Washer	1	
31	NH105041L	Nut	1	
	349997	Stop-Seat Squab	2	
	349998	Protective Edging Strip-Seat Frame	4	

VS4167

LAND ROVER PARTS LTD

MODEL LR110 - UP TO AUGUST 1986
BLOCK VS 4168
PAGE M 32
GROUP M

FRONT SEATS - DE-LUXE TYPE - STATION WAGON - NOTE (1)

ILL	PART NO	DESCRIPTION	QTY	REMARKS
1	MRC6982	Front Squab-Driver	1	
	MRC6982	Front Squab-Outer	1	
	MTC3182	Front Squab-Centre	1	
2	RTC3764	+Trim Clip-Driver Squab	8	
	RTC3764	+Trim Clip-Outer Squab	8	
	RTC3764	+Trim Clip-Centre Squab	16	
3	332355	+Strap-Centre Squab	1	
4	339986	+Rubber Packing-Driver Squab	2	
	339986	+Rubber Packing-Outer Squab	2	
	347869	+Rubber Packing-Centre Squab	1	
5	AB610081L	+Drive Screw-Driver Squab	2	
	AB610081L	+Drive Screw-Outer Squab	2	
	AB610061L	+Drive Screw-Centre Squab	2	
6	4034L	+Plain Washer-Driver Squab	2	
	4034L	+Plain Washer-Outer Squab	2	
	WC106041L	+Plain Washer-Centre Squab	2	
7	78237	+Spirenut	6	
8	349931	+Plastic Washer	6	
9	331709	+Bolt-Driver/Outer Squabs	4	
10	2266L	+Plain Washer	8	
11	345213	+Rubber Washer	2	
12	RTC614	+Split Pin-Centre Squab	2	
13	MRC6980	Front Cushion-Driver	1	
	MRC6980	Front Cushion-Outer	1	
	MRC6985	Front Cushion-Centre	1	
14	349943	+Protective Capping	12	
15	331974	+Strap-Centre Cushion	1	
16	RTC3755	+Rivet	1	
17	348430	Stud-Retaining Squab Strap	1	
18	AB606081L	Drive Screw	1	
19	RTC615	Plain Washer	1	
20	348430	Stud-Retaining Cushion Strap	1	
21	SE105251L	Screw	1	
22	WL105001L	Spring Washer	1	
23	NH105041L	Nut	1	
	349997	Stop-Seat Squab	2	
	349998	Protective Edging Strip-Seat Frame	4	

NOTE(1)   Driver and Outer Seats Adjustable

VS4168

LAND ROVER PARTS LTD

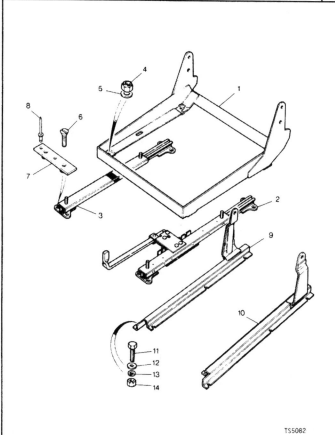

MODEL LR110 - UP TO AUGUST 1986
BLOCK TS 5082
PAGE M 34
GROUP M

FRONT SEATS - SEAT SLIDES - NOTE(1)

1	349996	Adjustable Seat Frame	2
2	MRC9492	Seat Slide RH with Control	1
	MRC9493	Seat Slide LH with Control	1
3	MRC9481	Seat Slide Plain	2
4	NT108041L	Lock Nut	8
5	WF108001L	Shakeproof Washer	8
6	SF106201L	Screw	16
7	MTC7631	Nut Plate	8
8	RU608253L	Rivet	16
9	MTC1714	Seat Support Centre Single RH	1
10	MTC1715	Seat Support Centre Single LH	1
11	SH106201L	Screw	6
12	MRC5525	Plain Washer	12
13	WL106001L	Spring Washer	6
14	NH106041L	Nut	6
	331083	Grommet Plug	2) Pick Up
	307220	Plug Redundant Hole	1)

NOTE(1):   Driver and Outer Seats Adjustable

TS5082

 **LAND ROVER PARTS LTD**

MODEL LR110 - UP TO AUGUST 1986
BLOCK TS 5081
PAGE M 36
GROUP M

FRONT SEATS - 'COUNTY' TYPE - OUTER

ILL	PART NO	DESCRIPTION	QTY	REMARKS
		FRONT SEAT ASSEMBLY COMPLETE OUTER		
	MTC1674RD	RH-Brushwood/Berber-Cloth	1	NLA-Use MUC8428RD
	MTC1670	RH-Black Vinyl	1	NLA-Use MWC3306
	MTC1675RD	LH-Brushwood/Berber-Cloth	1	NLA-Use MUC8429RD
	MTC1671	LH-Black Vinyl	1	NLA-Use MWC3307
1		+Front Squab		
	MTC1930RE	RH-Grey/Black-Cloth	1	
	MUC8448RD	RH-Brushwood/Berber Cloth	1	
	MWC3302	RH-Black Vinyl	1	
	MTC1931RE	LH-Grey/Black-Cloth	1	
	MUC8449RD	LH-Brushwood/Berber Cloth	1	
	MWC3303	LH-Black Vinyl	1	
2		++Cover		
	MTC1933RE	Grey/Black Cloth	2	No Longer Available
	MTC1933RD	Brushwood/Berber Cloth	2	
	MTC1923	Black Vinyl	2	
3	MTC1940AV	+Back Panel-Brushwood	2	
	MTC1940PB	+Back Panel-Black	2	
4	MTC9956	+Locking Trim	4	
5	RTC3106	+Knob-Recline Lever-Grey	2	
	RTC3105	+Knob-Recline Lever-Black	2	
6	RTC3108	+Mechanism Cover-LH	1	
	RTC3107	+Mechanism Cover-RH	1	

TS5081

LAND ROVER PARTS LTD

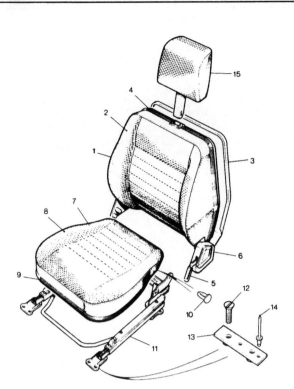

MODEL LR110 - UP TO AUGUST 1986
BLOCK TS 5081
PAGE M 36.02
GROUP M

FRONT SEATS - 'COUNTY' TYPE - OUTER

ILL	PART NO	DESCRIPTION	QTY	REMARKS
7		+Front Cushion		
	MTC1928RE	Grey/Black Cloth	2	
	MUC8780RD	Brushwood/Berber Cloth	2	
	MWC4535	Black Vinyl	2	
8		++Cover		
	MTC1932RE	Grey/Black Cloth	2	
	MTC1932RD	Brushwood/Berber Cloth	2	
	MWC4534	Black Vinyl	2	
9	MTC9967	++Locking Trim	2	
10	MTC9962	++Nail Trim	12	
	RTC4102	+Retaining Rod Assy	2	
11	MTC1938	+Sub Frame and Slide Assy	1	
12	SF106201L	Self Locking Screw	16	
13	MTC7631	Nut Plate	8	
14	RU608253L	Rivet	16	
15		HEADREST		
	MTC1929RE	Grey/Black Cloth	2	
	MWC1018RD	Brushwood-Berber Cloth	2	
	MWC1010	Black Vinyl	2	
	MWC4537	Stop Bracket-Seat Slide-RH Seat	2	

TS5081

662

MODEL LR110 - UP TO AUGUST 1986
BLOCK TS 5080
PAGE M 36.04
GROUP M

FRONT SEATS - 'COUNTY' TYPE - CENTRE

ILL	PART NO	DESCRIPTION	QTY	REMARKS
		FRONT SEAT ASSEMBLY COMPLETE-CENTRE		
	MTC1673RD	Brushwood/Berber Cloth	1	NLA-Use MUC8432RD
	MTC1672	Black Vinyl	1	
1		+FRONT SQUAB		
	MTC1948RE	Grey/Black Cloth	1	
	MTC1948RD	Brushwood/Berber Cloth	1	
	MUC8447	Black Vinyl	1	
2		++COVER		
	MTC1950RE	Grey/Black Cloth	1	
	MTC1950RD	Brushwood/Berber Cloth	1	
	MTC1944	Black Vinyl	1	
3	MTC1953AV	+Back Panel-Brushwood	1	
	MTC1953PB	+Back Panel-Black	1	
4	MTC9958	+Locking Trim	1	
5	MTC9962	+Nail Trim	2	
6		+FRONT CUSHION		
	MTC1947RE	Grey/Black Cloth	1	
	MUC8779RD	Brushwood/Berber Cloth	1	
	MWC4549	Black Vinyl	1	
7		++COVER		
	MTC1949RE	Grey/Black Cloth	1	
	MTC1949RD	Brushwood/Berber Cloth	1	
	MTC1943	Black Vinyl	1	
8	MTC9959	++Locking Trim	1	
9	MTC9962	++Nail Trim	4	
10	BH106071	Bolt-Front	2	
11	SF106201L	Screw-Rear	2	
12	MRC5525	Plain-Washer	4	
13	WL106001L	Spring Washer	4	
14	NH106041L	Nut	4	

TS5080

663

MODEL LR 110 – UP TO AUGUST 1986
BLOCK VS 3982
PAGE M 38
GROUP M

REAR SEATS – GRAB RAIL – STATION WAGON

ILL	PART NO	DESCRIPTION	QTY	REMARKS
1	333395	Grabrail	1	
2	SH108201L	Screw	4	
3	WC108051L	Plain Washer	4	
4	WL108001L	Spring Washer	4	

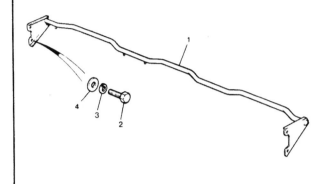

VS3982

664

MODEL LR 110 – UP TO AUGUST 1986
BLOCK VS 4266A
PAGE M 40
GROUP M

REAR SEATS – FORWARD FACING – TRANSVERSE BENCH TYPE

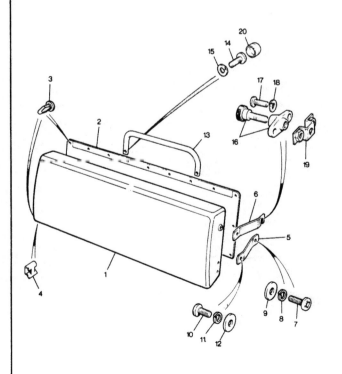

ILL	PART NO	DESCRIPTION	QTY	REMARKS
		REAR TRANSVERSE SEAT ASSY-		
	MTC6471	Black Vinyl	1	
	MTC6978RE	Grey/Black Cloth	1	
	MTC6978RD	Brushwood/Berber Cloth	1	
1	MTC1002	+Squab-Black Vinyl	1	
	MTC4486RE	+Squab-Grey/Black Cloth	1	
	MTC4486RD	+Squab-Brushwood/Berber Cloth	1	
2	396922	++Trimboard	1	
3	RTC3751	++Drive Fastener	15	
4	315264	++Trim Clip	6	
	315960	++Trim Clip	26	
5	MTC6539	+Front Support Link	2	
	MTC6754	+Support Link RH	1	
6	MTC6755	+Support Link LH	1	
7	SH108251	+Screw-Links to Squab	2	
8	WL108004	+Spring Washer	2	
9	WA108054L	+Plain Washer	2	
10	SE106204	+Screw-Link to Pillar	2	
11	WL106004L	Spring Washer	2	
12	WA106044	+Plain Washer	2	
13	MTC6457	+Grab Rail	1	
14	SE108254	+Screw	2	
15	WL108004	+Spring Washer	2	
16	MTC6756	Locking Plate and Screw Assembly	2	
17	255205	Screw	4	
18	WM600041L	Spring Washer	4	
19	334177	Nut Plate	2	
20	MTC6630	Cover	2	Germany

VS4266A

665

MODEL LR110 - UP TO AUGUST 1986
BLOCK VS 3986B
PAGE M 42
GROUP M

REAR SEATS - FORWARD FACING - TRANSVERSE BENCH TYPE

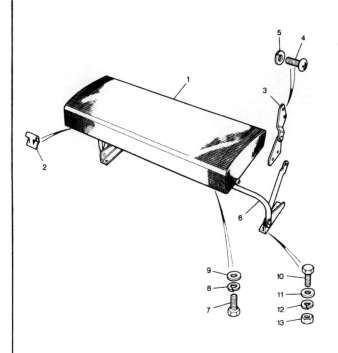

ILL	PART NO	DESCRIPTION	QTY	REMARKS
		REAR TRANSVERSE SEAT ASSY		
1	MTC1003	+Cushion-Black Vinyl	1	
	MTC4485RE	+Cushion-Grey/Black Cloth	1	
	MTC4485RD	+Cushion-Brushwood/Berber Cloth	1	
2	315264	++Trim Clip	6	
	315960	++Trim Clip	26	
3	MTC6466	+Hinge RH	1	
	MTC6467	+Hinge LH	1	
4	SE108164	+Screw	8	
5	WL108004	+Spring Washer	8	
6	MTC6470	+Support Tube	1	
7	BH108081L	+Bolt	2	
8	WL108001L	+Spring Washer	2	
9	WA108051L	+Plain Washer	2	
10	SE108204	Screw	4	
11	WL108004	Spring Washer	4	
12	WA108054L	Plain Washer	8	
13	NH108044	Nut	4	

VS3986B

LAND ROVER PARTS LTD

LR 110 - UP TO AUGUST 1986
BLOCK VS 4218
PAGE M 50
GROUP M

REAR SEATS - FORWARD FACING - INDIVIDUAL TYPE

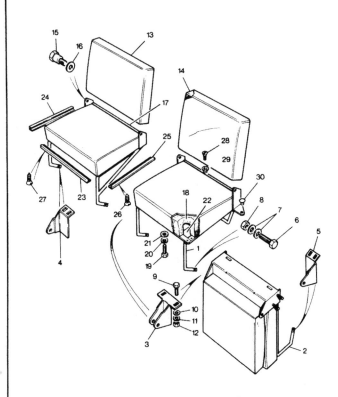

ILL	PART NO	DESCRIPTION	QTY	REMARKS
1	347343	Seat Frame-Centre	1	
2	347344	Seat Frame-Outer	2	
3	MTC6793	Bracket-Inner	2	
4	MTC6794	Bracket-Outer RH	1	
5	MTC6795	Bracket-Outer LH	1	
6	331709	Shouldered Bolt	6	
7	AFU1263	Plain Washer	12	
8	NH106041L	Nut	6	
9	SE106204	Screw	14	
10	WA106041L	Plain Washer	14	
11	WL106001L	Spring Washer	14	
12	NH106041L	Nut	14	
13	349514	Squab Assy-Black Vinyl	3	
	MTC4489RE	Squab Assy-Grey/Black Cloth	3	
	MTC4489RD	Squab Assy-Brushwood/Berber Cloth	3	
14	349529	+Interior-Squab	3	
15	331709	+Shouldered Bolt	6	
16	3830L	+Washer-Steel	6	
	349955	+Washer-Rubber	6	
	349931	+Washer-Plastic	6	
17	349515	Cushion Assy-Black Vinyl	3	
	MTC4483RE	Cushion Assy-Grey/Black Cloth	3	
	MTC4483RD	Cushion Assy-Brushwood/Berber Cloth	3	
18	349516	+Interior-Cushion	3	
19	BH604161L	Set Bolt	6	
20	WM600041L	Spring Washer	6	
21	3900L	Plain Washer	6	

VS4218

LAND ROVER PARTS LTD

MODEL LR110 - UP TO AUGUST 1986
BLOCK VS 4218
PAGE M 52
GROUP M

REAR SEATS - FORWARD FACING - INDIVIDUAL TYPE

ILL	PART NO	DESCRIPTION	QTY	REMARKS
22	306316	Seat Base Panel	3	
23	307418	Finisher-Front	3	
24	307419	Finisher-Side RH	3	
25	307420	Finisher-Side LH	3	
26	20138	Screw	6	
27	20147	Screw	12	
28	AF608081	Screw	6	
29	WK608311	Cup Washer	6	
30	301347	Plug	10	
	SH108201L	Screw-Redundant Holes in Floor	2	
	WL108001L	Spring Washer	2	
	WC108051L	Plain Washer	2	
	NH108041L	Nut	2	
	MRC1300	Plug	2	

VS4218

LAND ROVER PARTS LTD

668

MODEL LR110 - UP TO AUGUST 1986
BLOCK VS 4219
PAGE M 54
GROUP M

REAR SEATS - INDIVIDUAL TYPE - SEAT LOCKING MECHANISM

ILL	PART NO	DESCRIPTION	QTY	REMARKS
1	336294	Striker Plate	2	
2	SH106161	Screw	4	
3	MRC5525	Plain Washer	4	
4	WL106001L	Spring Washer	4	
5	NH106041L	Nut	4	
6	336288	Catch	2	
7	77869	Screw	8	
8	WC702101L	Plain Washer	8	
9	WM702001L	Spring Washer	8	
10	RTC608	Nut	8	
11	MTC6792	Support Bracket	2	
12	78248	Rivet	8	

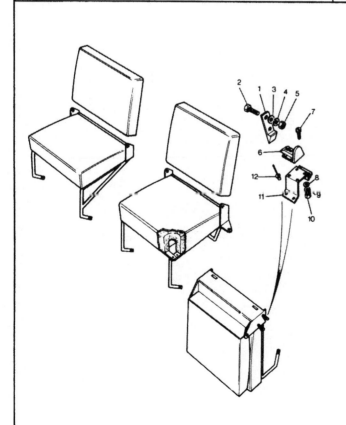

VS4219

LAND ROVER PARTS LTD

669

MODEL LR110 – UP TO AUGUST 1986
BLOCK VS 4220A
PAGE M 56
GROUP M

REAR SEATS - INDIVIDUAL TYPE - SQUAB LOCKING MECHANISM

ILL	PART NO	DESCRIPTION	QTY	REMARKS
1	347863	Nut Plate	3	
2	RA612156L	Rivet	6	
3	MRC4798	Shoulder Bolt	3	
4	347861	Squab Catch-RH	1	
	347861	Squab Catch-Centre	1	
	347862	Squab Catch-LH	1	
5	SE106161L	Screw	3	
6	AFU1080	Plain Washer	6	
7	NY106041L	Self Lock Nut	3	
8	79134	Screw-Catch Stop	3	
9	MTC6801	Spring	3	
10	MTC6802	Anchor Plate	3	
11	SH106204	Screw) Anchor Plate	1	
12	NH106044	Nut) to Centre Seat	1	

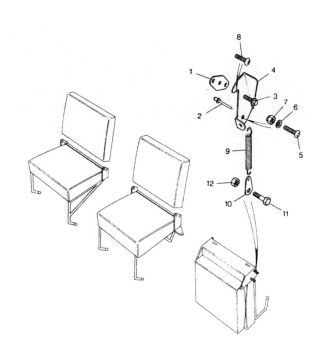

VS4220A

LAND ROVER PARTS LTD

MODEL LR110 - UP TO AUGUST 1986
BLOCK VS 4223A
PAGE M 60
GROUP M

REAR SEATS - INWARD FACING - TWO SEATER BENCH TYPE

ILL	PART NO	DESCRIPTION	QTY	REMARKS
1	MTC6448	Rear Seat Frame Assembly	1	
2	MTC6452	+Securing Clip RH	1	
	MTC6453	+Securing Clip LH	1	
3	SE106164	+Screw	4	
4	WL106004L	+Spring Washer	4	
5	NH106044	Nut	4	
6	302648	+Seat Strap	1	
7	301005	++Hook	1	
8	RU612373L	+Rivet	2	
9	WC702101L	+Plain Washer	2	
10	396739	Backrest Assy-Black Vinyl	1	
	MTC4488RE	Backrest Assy-Grey/Black Cloth	1	
	MTC4488RD	Backrest Assembly- Brushwood/Berber Cloth	1	
11	396696	+Pad	1	
12	301470	+Panel	1	
13	301476	+Retaining Rod	2	
14	SH106124	Screw-Backrest to Frame	5	
15	WL106004L	Spring Washer	5	
16	NH106044	Nut	5	

NOTE: Quantities Shown Are For One Seat Only

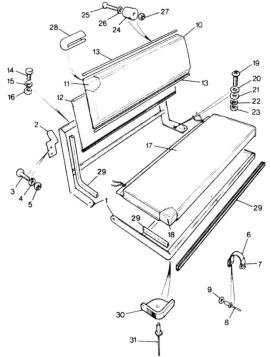

VS4223A

LAND ROVER PARTS LTD

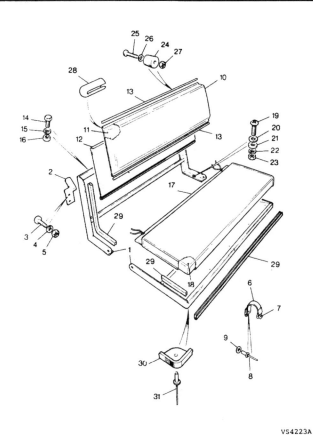

MODEL LR110 - UP TO AUGUST 1986
BLOCK VS 4223A
PAGE M 60.02
GROUP M

REAR SEATS - INWARD FACING - TWO SEATER BENCH TYPE

ILL	PART NO	DESCRIPTION	QTY	REMARKS
17	320674	Cushion Assembly-Black Vinyl	1	
	MTC4487RE	Cushion Assembly-Grey/Black Cloth	1	
	MTC4487RD	Cushion Assembly-Brushwood/ Berber Cloth	1	
18	331835	+Pad	1	
19	SE106201L	Screw	2	
20	MRC5528	Plain Washer	2	
21	AFU1070	Packing Washer	4	
22	WL106001L	Spring Washer	2	
23	NH106041L	Nut	2	
24	304125	Rubber Buffer	2	
25	SE105251L	Screw	2	
26	WA105001L	Plain Washer	2	
27	NH105041L	Nut	2	
28	MTC8335	Edge Cover	2	)
29	MTC7513	Edging Strip	A/R	)Germany
30	345683	Corner Finisher	2	)
31	RU608313L	Rivet	2	)

NOTE: Quantities Shown Are For One Seat Only

MODEL LR110 - UP TO AUGUST 1986
BLOCK VS 3991C
PAGE M 62
GROUP M

REAR SEATS - INWARD FACING - THREE SEATER BENCH TYPE

ILL	PART NO	DESCRIPTION	QTY	REMARKS
1	MTC6425	Rear Seat Frame	1	
2	334601	Retaining Bracket-Front	1	
3	333551	Retaining Bracket-Rear	1	
4	78248	Rivet	4	
5	BH108101L	Bolt)Seat Frame	2	
6	WL108001L	Spring Washer)to Wheelarch	2	
7	WC108051L	Plain Washer)Front	2	
8	MRC6845	Distance Piece)	2	
9	MRC6843	Stiffener)	1	
10	SH108201L	Screw)Seat Frame	2	
11	WC108051L	Plain Washer)to Wheelarch	2	
12	WL108001L	Spring Washer)Rear	2	
13	NH108041L	Nut)	2	
14	396698	Backrest-Black Vinyl	1	
	MTC4491RE	Backrest-Grey/Black Cloth	1	
	MTC4491RD	Backrest Brushwood/Berber Cloth	1	
15	396697	+Pad	1	
16	334532	+Panel	1	
17	334540	+Retaining Rod	2	
18	SH106124	Screw	6	
19	WL106004L	Spring Washer	6	
20	NH106044	Nut	6	
21	320719	Cushion-Black Vinyl	1	
	MTC4490RE	Cushion-Grey/Black Cloth	1	
	MWC2580RD	Cushion-Brushwood/Berber Cloth	1	
22	73198	Plug-Redundant Holes in Wheelarch	1	
23	MTC8335	Edge Cover	2	)
24	MTC7513	Edging Strip	A/R	)Germany
25	345683	Corner Finisher	2	)
26	RU608313L	Rivet	2	)

NOTE: Quantities Shown are for One Seat Only

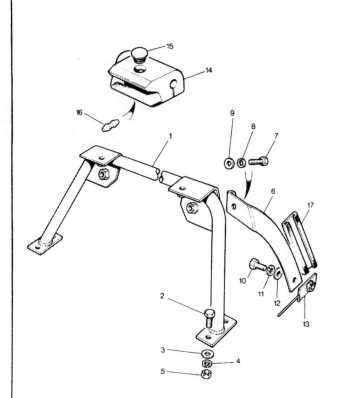

MODEL LR110 - UP TO AUGUST 1986
BLOCK VS 4087
PAGE M 80
GROUP M

SAFETY HARNESS ANCHORAGE - FRONT SEATS - ANCHOR RAIL - SOFT TOP

ILL	PART NO	DESCRIPTION	QTY	REMARKS
1	MRC7354	Anchor Rail	1	
2	SH108251L	Screw	4	
3	WA108051L	Plain Washer	4	
4	WL108001L	Spring Washer	4	
5	NH108041L	Nut	4	
6	MRC199	Tie Bar RH	1	
	MRC200	Tie Bar LH	1	
7	SH112251	Screw	2	
8	WL112001L	Spring Washer	2	
9	WA112081L	Plain Washer	2	
10	SH110201	Screw	2	
11	WL110001L	Spring Washer	2	
12	WA110061L	Plain Washer	2	
13	MRC7610	Nut Plate	2	
14	MRC8329	Finishing Cap RH	1	
	MRC8330	Finishing Cap LH	1	
15	MRC8389	Plug	4	
16	MRC8390	Fixing Lug	14	
17	MRC8392	Tie Bar Cover RH	1	
	MRC8393	Tie Bar Cover LH	1	

VS4087

LAND ROVER PARTS LTD

674

MODEL LR110 - UP TO AUGUST 1986
BLOCK VS 4086
PAGE M 82
GROUP M

SAFETY HARNESS ANCHORAGES - FRONT SEATS - HARNESS GUIDE - SOFT TOP

ILL	PART NO	DESCRIPTION	QTY	REMARKS
1	MRC7755	Guide	2	
2	345937	Guard Plate	2	
3	BH605101	Bolt	4	
4	WA108051L	Plain Washer	4	
5	WL600051	Spring Washer	4	
6	NH605041L	Nut	4	
7	MTC1631	Reinforcement Plate	2	
8	RU612373L	Rivet	8	
9	SH106201	Screw	8	
10	MRC5524	Plain Washer	8	
11	WL106001L	Spring Washer	8	
12	NH106041L	Nut	8	

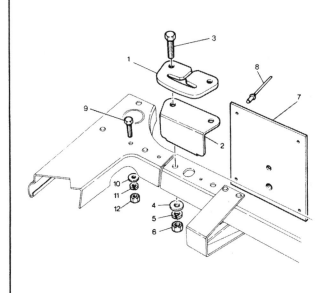

VS4086

LAND ROVER PARTS LTD

675

MODEL LR110 - UP TO AUGUST 1986
BLOCK VS 4088
PAGE M 84
GROUP M

SAFETY HARNESS ANCHORAGES - FRONT SEATS - SHOULDER ANCHORAGE - HARD TOP

ILL	PART NO	DESCRIPTION	QTY	REMARKS
1	395586	Mounting Bracket RH-Cantrail	1	
	395587	Mounting Bracket LH-Cantrail	1	
2	MRC7626	Bolt Plate	2	
3	WB106041L	Plain Washer	2	
4	WL106001L	Spring Washer	2	
5	NH106041L	Nut	2	

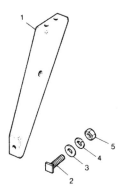

VS4088

676

MODEL LR110 - UP TO AUGUST 1986
BLOCK VS 4089
PAGE M 86
GROUP M

SAFETY HARNESS ANCHORAGES - FRONT SEATS - INERTIA REEL MOUNTING
                                        CHASSIS CAB AND HARDTOP

ILL	PART NO	DESCRIPTION	QTY	REMARKS
1	MTC4090	Mounting Bracket-Inertia Reel	2	
2	WC108051L	Plain Washer	4	
3	WL108001L	Spring Washer	4	
4	NH108041L	Nut	4	
5	MRC8524	Mounting Bracket-Bulkhead	2	
6	RA612347L	Rivet	4	
7	SH108251L	Screw	4	
8	WA108051L	Plain Washer	4	
9	WL108001L	Spring Washer	4	
10	NH108041L	Nut	4	

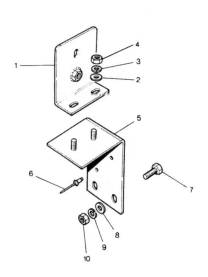

VS4089

677

MODEL LR110 - UP TO AUGUST 1986
BLOCK VS 4175
PAGE M 86.02
GROUP M

SAFETY HARNESS ANCHORAGES - FRONT SEATS - SEATBASE ANCHORAGE
STATION WAGON

ILL	PART NO	DESCRIPTION	QTY	REMARKS
1	345100	Sill Gusset RH	1	
	345101	Sill Gusset LH	1	
2	395249	Harness Bracket	2	
3	MRC4731	Nut Plate-Inertia Reel Mounting	2	
4	RU612373L	Rivet	2	

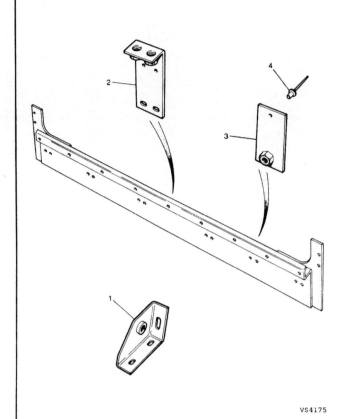

VS4175

LAND ROVER PARTS LTD

678

MODEL LR110 - UP TO AUGUST 1986
BLOCK VS 4090
PAGE M 88
GROUP M

SAFETY HARNESS ANCHORAGES - FRONT SEATS - SEATBASE ANCHORAGE
SOFT AND HARD TOP

ILL	PART NO	DESCRIPTION	QTY	REMARKS
1	395252	Harness Bracket	2	
2	MRC4885	Tie Bar RH	1	
	MRC4886	Tie Bar LH	1	
3	BH108071L	Bolt	4	
4	AFU1079	Plain Washer	6	
5	WL108001L	Spring Washer	4	
6	NH108041L	Nut	2	
7	SH108251L	Screw	2	
8	AFU1079	Plain Washer	4	
9	WL108001L	Spring Washer	2	
10	NH108041L	Nut	2	
11	345100	Sill Gusset RH	1	
	345101	Sill Gusset LH	1	

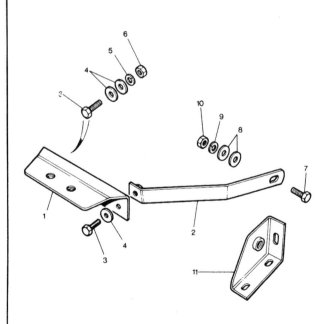

VS4090

LAND ROVER PARTS LTD

679

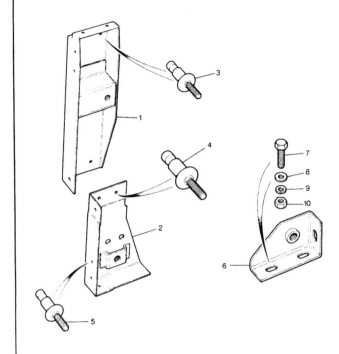

MODEL LR110 - UP TO AUGUST 1986
BLOCK VS 4166
PAGE M 90
GROUP M

SAFETY HARNESS ANCHORAGES - FRONT SEATS - SHOULDER AND SEATBASE
ANCHORAGES - TRUCK CAB

ILL	PART NO	DESCRIPTION	QTY	REMARKS
		SHOULDER ANCHORAGE		
1	MRC9361	Upper LH	1	
	MRC9362	Upper RH	1	
2	MRC9367	Lower LH	1	
	MRC9368	Lower RH	1	
3	AFU1298	Monobolt	12	
4	AFU1350	Monobolt	6	
5	AFU1298	Monobolt	12	
6	345100	Sill Gusset RH	1	
	345101	Sill Gusset LH	1	
7	SH106251L	Screw	2	
8	AFU1069	Plain Washer	2	
9	WL106001L	Spring Washer	2	
10	NH106041L	Nut	2	

VS4166

LAND ROVER PARTS LTD

680

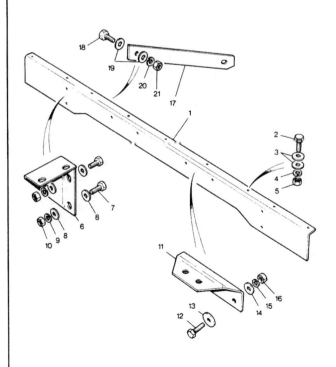

MODEL LR110 - UP TO AUGUST 1986
BLOCK VS 4165
PAGE M 92
GROUP M

SAFETY HARNESS ANCHORAGES - FRONT SEATS - ANCHORAGES ON BASE ASSY
TRUCK CAB

ILL	PART NO	DESCRIPTION	QTY	REMARKS
1	MTC3042	Reinforcing Angle-Cab Base	1	
2	SH108251L	Screw	9	
3	WC108051L	Plain Washer	18	
4	WL108001L	Spring Washer	9	
5	NH108041L	Nut	9	
6	MTC3051	Stiffener Bracket RH	1	
	MTC3052	Stiffener Bracket LH	1	
7	SH108251L	Screw-Upper	2	
	SH108301	Screw-Lower	2	
8	WC108051L	Plain Washer	8	
9	WL108001L	Spring Washer	4	
10	NH108041L	Nut	4	
11	395252	Harness Mounting Bracket	2	
12	SH108251L	Screw	4	
13	AFU1079	Plain Washer	4	
14	WC108051L	Plain Washer	4	
15	WL108001L	Spring Washer	4	
16	NH108041L	Nut	4	
17	MTC3032	Tie Bar	2	
18	SH108251L	Screw	4	
19	WC108051L	Plain Washer	8	
20	WL108001L	Spring Washer	4	
21	NH108041L	Nut	4	

VS4165

LAND ROVER PARTS LTD

681

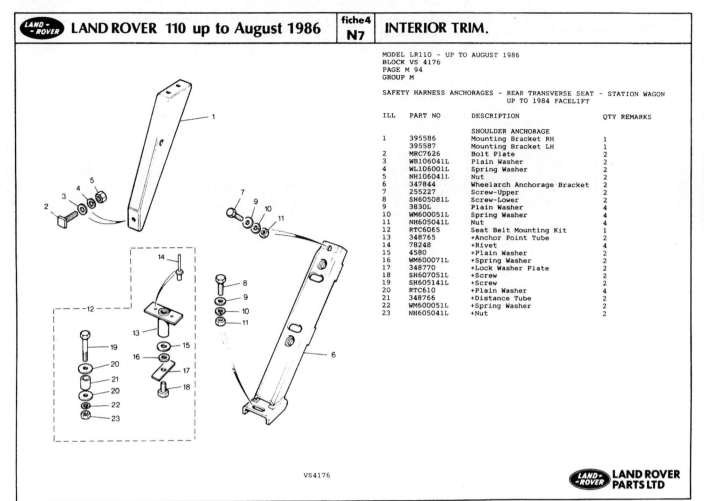

MODEL LR110 - UP TO AUGUST 1986
BLOCK VS 4176
PAGE M 94
GROUP M

SAFETY HARNESS ANCHORAGES - REAR TRANSVERSE SEAT - STATION WAGON
UP TO 1984 FACELIFT

ILL	PART NO	DESCRIPTION	QTY	REMARKS
		SHOULDER ANCHORAGE		
1	395586	Mounting Bracket RH	1	
	395587	Mounting Bracket LH	1	
2	MRC7626	Bolt Plate	2	
3	WB106041L	Plain Washer	2	
4	WL106001L	Spring Washer	2	
5	NH106041L	Nut	2	
6	347844	Wheelarch Anchorage Bracket	2	
7	255227	Screw-Upper	2	
8	SH605081L	Screw-Lower	2	
9	3830L	Plain Washer	4	
10	WM600051L	Spring Washer	4	
11	NH605041L	Nut	4	
12	RTC6065	Seat Belt Mounting Kit	1	
13	348765	+Anchor Point Tube	2	
14	78248	+Rivet	4	
15	4580	+Plain Washer	2	
16	WM600071L	+Spring Washer	2	
17	348770	+Lock Washer Plate	2	
18	SH607051L	+Screw	2	
19	SH605141L	+Screw	2	
20	RTC610	+Plain Washer	4	
21	348766	+Distance Tube	2	
22	WM600051L	+Spring Washer	2	
23	NH605041L	+Nut	2	

VS4176

LAND ROVER PARTS LTD

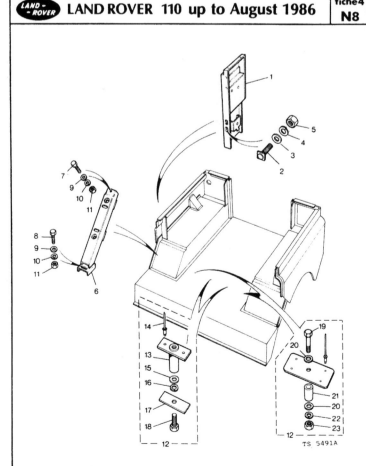

MODEL LR110 - UP TO AUGUST 1986
BLOCK TS 5491A
PAGE M 94.10
GROUP M

SAFETY HARNESS ANCHORAGES - REAR TRANVERSE SEAT - STATION WAGON
1984 FACELIFT

ILL	PART NO	DESCRIPTION	QTY	REMARKS
1	MUC1010	Shoulder Anchorage RH	1	
	MUC1011	Shoulder Anchorage LH	1	
2	MRC7626	Bolt Plate	2	
3	WB106041L	Plain Washer	2	
4	WL106001L	Spring Washer	2	
5	NH106041L	Nut	2	
6	347844	Wheelarch Anchorage Bracket	2	
7	255227	Screw-Upper	2	
8	SH605081L	Screw-Lower	2	
9	3830L	Plain Washer	4	
10	WM600051L	Spring Washer	4	
11	NH605041L	Nut	4	
12	RTC6065	Seat Belt Mounting Kit	1	
13	348765	+Anchor Point Tube	2	
14	78248	+Rivet	4	
15	4580	+Plain Washer	2	
16	WM600071L	+Spring Washer	2	
17	348770	+Lockwasher Plate	2	
18	SH607051L	+Screw	2	
19	SH605141L	+Screw	2	
20	RTC610	+Plain Washer	4	
21	348766	+Distance Tube	2	
22	WM600051L	+Spring Washer	2	
23	NH605041L	+Nut	2	

TS 5491A

LAND ROVER PARTS LTD

MODEL LR110 - UP TO AUGUST 1986
BLOCK TS 5333
PAGE M 96
GROUP M

SAFETY HARNESS ANCHORAGES - REAR INWARD FACING SEATS - STATION WAGON

ILL	PART NO	DESCRIPTION	QTY REMARKS
1	MTC6836	Wheelarch Stiffener-Front	2
2		Wheelarch Stiffener-Centre	
	MTC6834	LH	1
	MTC6835	RH	1
3	MRC1638	Wheelarch Stiffener-Rear	2
		Reinforcing Angle Bracket	
4	MTC6840	Front	2
5	MTC6839	Centre-RH Side	1
6	AFU1350	Monobolt	31
7	RA612156L	Blind Rivet	24
8	RA612236	Blind Rivet	8

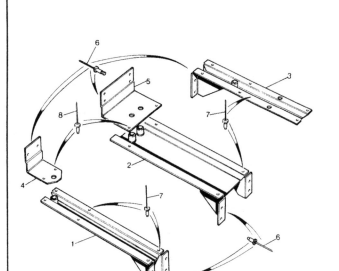

TS5333

LAND ROVER PARTS LTD

684

MODEL LR110 - UP TO AUGUST 1986
BLOCK VS 4180
PAGE M 100
GROUP M

SAFETY HARNESS - FRONT SEATS - STATIC TYPE - ALL VEHICLES

ILL	PART NO	DESCRIPTION	QTY REMARKS
1		Safety Harness-Static Type-	
		Outer Seat	
	MTC1614	RH	1
	MTC1615	LH	1

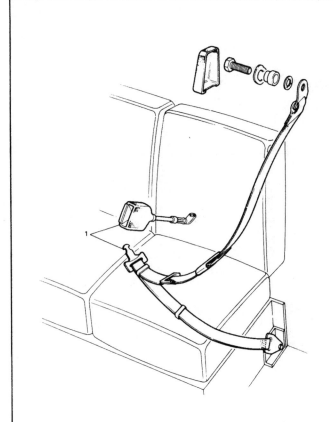

VS4180

LAND ROVER PARTS LTD

685

MODEL LR110 - UP TO AUGUST 1986
BLOCK VS 4185
PAGE M 102
GROUP M

SAFETY HARNESS - FRONT SEATS - VEHICLES WITH FULL LENGTH HOOD ONLY

ILL	PART NO	DESCRIPTION	QTY	REMARKS
1		Safety Harness-Inertia Type-Outer Seat		
	MTC1608	RH	1	
	MTC1609	LH	1	
	MTC7799	LH-With Audible Warning	1	Saudi Arabia
	AFU2875	Clip-Harness Restraint-On Seatbase	2	
	AB610054L	Drivescrew	4	

VS4185

LAND ROVER PARTS LTD

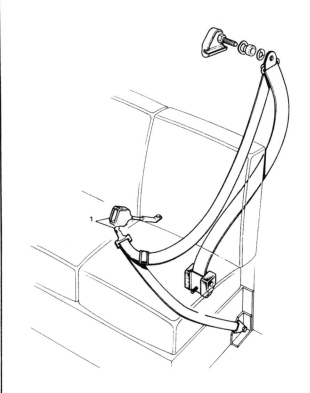

MODEL LR110 - UP TO AUGUST 1986
BLOCK VS 4184
PAGE M 104
GROUP M

SAFETY HARNESS - FRONT SEATS - ALL VEHICLES EXCEPT THOSE WITH FULL LENGTH HOOD

ILL	PART NO	DESCRIPTION	QTY	REMARKS
1		Safety Harness-Inertia Type-Outer Seat		
	MTC1606	RH	1	
	MTC1607	LH	1	
	MTC7798	LH-With Audible Warning	1	Saudi Arabia
	AFU2875	Harness Restraint Clip-on Seatbase	2	
	AB610054L	Drivescrew	4	

VS4184

MODEL LR110 - UP TO AUGUST 1986
BLOCK VS 4183
PAGE M 106
GROUP M

SAFETY HARNESS - FRONT SEATS - ALL VEHICLES

ILL	PART NO	DESCRIPTION	QTY	REMARKS
1	MXC5494	Safety Harness-Centre Seat Lap Strap	1	

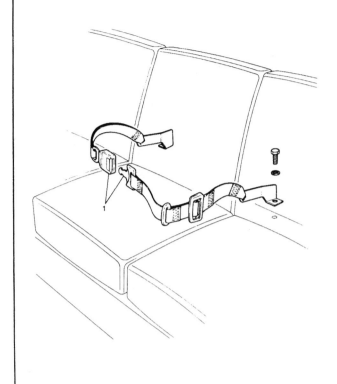

VS4183

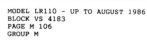

MODEL LR110 - UP TO AUGUST 1986
BLOCK VS 4182
PAGE M 108
GROUP M

SAFETY HARNESS - REAR FORWARD FACING SEATS

ILL	PART NO	DESCRIPTION	QTY	REMARKS
1	MRC7630	Safety Harness-Static Type- Outer Seats	2	

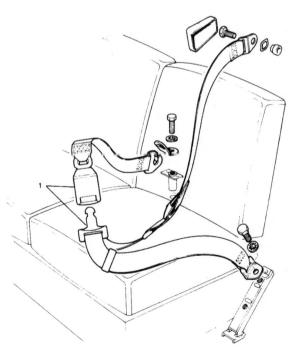

VS4182

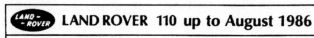
MODEL LR110 - UP TO AUGUST 1986
BLOCK VS 4181
PAGE M 110
GROUP M

SAFETY HARNESS - REAR FORWARD FACING SEATS

ILL	PART NO	DESCRIPTION	QTY	REMARKS
1	MRC7487	Safety Harness-Centre Seat Lap Strap	1	

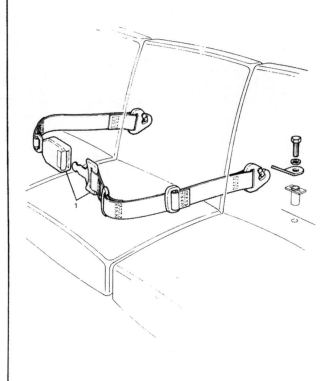

VS4181

LAND ROVER PARTS LTD

MODEL LR110 - UP TO AUGUST 1986
BLOCK VS 4255
PAGE M 112
GROUP M

SAFETY HARNESS - REAR INWARD FACING SEATS

ILL	PART NO	DESCRIPTION	QTY	REMARKS
1	MRC7696	Safety Harness-Lap Strap	4	

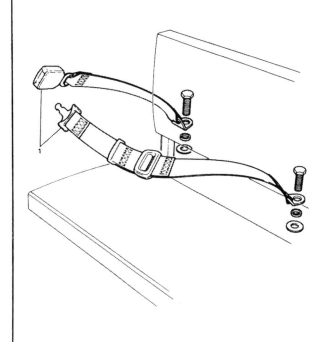

VS4255

LAND ROVER PARTS LTD

MASTER INDEX

GROUP N

MISCELLANEOUS AND OPTIONAL

LAND ROVER PARTS LTD

MODEL LR110 - UP TO AUGUST 1986
BLOCK VS 4064A
PAGE N 2
GROUP N

MISCELLANEOUS - TOOLS

ILL	PART NO	DESCRIPTION	QTY	REMARKS
1	NTC3296	Jack	1	
2	NRC6481	Ratchet Spanner	1	
3	NRC7455	Stowage Bag	1	
4	NTC3295	Jack	1	)H.C.P.U
5	543301	Handle-Wooden-Jack Shaft	1	)
6	592514	Jack Shaft-Handle Piece	1	)
7	592513	Jack Shaft-Jack Piece	1	)
8	219704	Tool Roll	1	
9	AFU1024	Combination Pliers	1	
10	NRC1081	Drainplug Wrench	1	
11	240836	Screwdriver and Feeler	1	Petrol

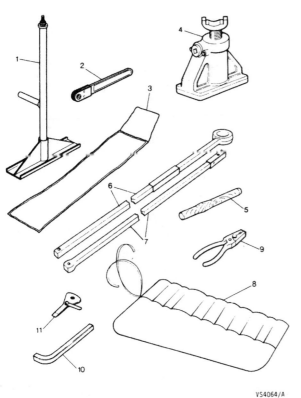

VS4064/A

LAND ROVER PARTS LTD

MODEL LR110 - UP TO AUGUST 1986
BLOCK VS 4063A
PAGE N 2.02
GROUP N

MISCELLANEOUS - TOOLS - CONTINUED

ILL	PART NO	DESCRIPTION	QTY	REMARKS
1	2705	Spanner 0.1875 x 0.25 BSF	1	
	230736	Spanner 0.3125 x 0.4375 BSF	1	
	276396	Spanner 0.50 x 0.4375 AF	1	
	277217	Spanner 0.6875 x 0.75 AF	1	
	AFU1004	Spanner 6mm x 8mm	1	
	AFU1005	Spanner 10mm x 12mm	1	
2	2707	Spanner-Adjustable	1	
3	AFU1003	Box Spanner 6mm	1	No Longer Available
4	MUC4275	Tommy Bar & Box Spanner	1	
5	276322	Box Spanner-Spark Plugs	1	)Petrol
6	276323	Extention-Spark Plug Spanner	1	)
7	549840	Spanner-DPA 0.3125 x 0.375	1	Diesel
8	562019	Tyre Pressure Gauge	1	
9	NRC6993	Screwdriver-Dual Purpose	1	
10	NRC1315	Wheelbrace	1	
11	218508	Starting Handle	1	4 Cylinder
	244384	Starting Handle	1	V8
12	523638	Tyre Pump	1	
13	11H5569L	Wheel Chock	1	
	MUC4291	Adjustable Pliers	1	

VS4063A

LAND ROVER PARTS LTD

MODEL LR110 - UP TO AUGUST 1986
BLOCK TS 5577
PAGE N 2.04
GROUP N

MISCELLANEOUS - PAINT

ILL	PART NO	DESCRIPTION	QTY	REMARKS
1		TOUCH UP PENCIL		
	RTC4027T	Arctic White	1	DFS
	RTC4032T	Masai Red	1	DFS
	RTC4033T	Russet	1	DFS
	RTC4035T	Venetian Red	1	DFS
	RTC4041T	Light Green	1	NLS
	RTC4042T	Bronze Green	1	DFS
	RTC4043T	Marine Blue	1	NLS
	RTC4044T	Limestone	1	NLS
	RTC4045T	Mid Grey	1	NLS
	RTC4046T	Sand	1	NLS
	RTC4047T	Trident Green	1	NLS
	RTC4048T	Roan Brown	1	NLS
	RTC4049T	Stratos Blue	1	DFS
	RTC4051T	Arizona Tan	1	DFS
	RTC4054T	Slate Grey	1	DFS
	RTC4058T	Ivory	1	DFS
	RTC4055T	White Primer	1	NLS
	RTC4056T	Grey Primer	1	NLS
	RTC4057T	Red Primer	1	NLS
2		AEROSOL		
	RTC4027A	Arctic White	1	DFS
	RTC4032A	Masai Red	1	DFS
	RTC4033A	Russet	1	DFS
	RTC4035A	Venetian Red	1	DFS
	RTC4041A	Light Green	1	DFS
	RTC4042A	Bronze Green	1	DFS
	RTC4043A	Marine Blue	1	DFS
	RTC4044A	Limestone	1	DFS
	RTC4045A	Mid Grey	1	DFS
	RTC4046A	Sand	1	DFS
	RTC4047A	Trident Green	1	DFS
	RTC4048A	Roan Brown	1	DFS
	RTC4049A	Stratos Blue	1	DFS
	RTC4051A	Arizona Tan	1	DFS
	RTC4054A	Slate Grey	1	DFS
	RTC4058A	Ivory	1	DFS
	RTC4055A	White Primer	1	DFS
	RTC4056A	Grey Primer	1	DFS
	RTC4057A	Red Primer	1	DFS
	Paint-1 Litre Cans		A/R	DFS See Introduction

DFS = 'Direct From Supplier' Item

NLS = No Longer Serviced.

FLAMMABLE HARMFUL
SPRAY PAINT WARNING
Harmful by inhalation
Harmful in contact with skin
Keep out of reach of children
Keep away from heat and sources of
ignition. When using, do not smoke
Do not breathe spray or swallow
In case of contact with skin or eyes rinse
immediately with plenty of water and seek
medical advice
Do not spray on a naked flame or any
incandescent material
Pressurised container
protect from sunlight and do not expose to
temperatures exceeding 50°C
Do not pierce or burn even after use

TS5577

LAND ROVER PARTS LTD

MODEL LR110 - UP TO AUGUST 1986
BLOCK VS 3911
PAGE N 4
GROUP N

OPTIONAL EQUIPMENT - TOWING PINTLE

ILL	PART NO	DESCRIPTION		QTY	REMARKS
1	535068	Towing Pintle		1	
2	NRC8323	Stiffener)		1	
3	BH110181L	Bolt	) Pintle to Cross	4	
4	NH110041L	Nut	) Member	8	
	BH110081L	Bolt	)	4	
	NH110041L	Nut	) Pintle to Drop Plate	8	

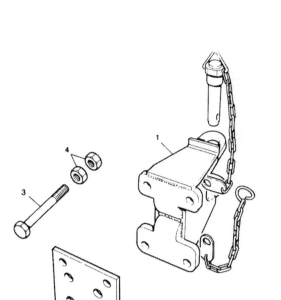

VS3911

696

MODEL LR110 - UP TO AUGUST 1986
BLOCK TS 5121
PAGE N 4.02
GROUP N

OPTIONAL EQUIPMENT - ROTATING TOWING PINTLE

ILL	PART NO	DESCRIPTION		QTY	REMARKS
1	NRC2051	Rotating Towing Pintle		1	
2	NRC8323	Stiffener		1	
3	BH112241	Bolt) Pintle to		4	
4	NH112041L	Nut) Crossmember		8	
5	BH112141L	Bolt) Pintle to		4	
6	NH112041L	Nut) Drop Plate		8	

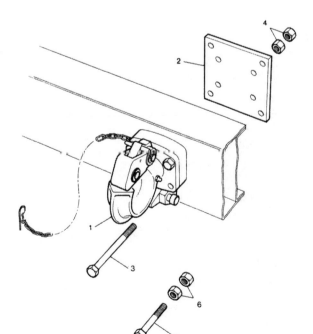

TS5121

697

MODEL LR110 - UP TO AUGUST 1986
BLOCK VS 3912
PAGE N 6
GROUP N

OPTIONAL EQUIPMENT - TOWING HOOK

ILL	PART NO	DESCRIPTION		QTY	REMARKS
1	246109	Towing Hook		1	No Longer Available
2	NRC8323	Stiffener)		1	
3	BH112201L	Bolt	) Towing Hook to	4	
4	WA112081	Washer	) Rear Crossmember	4	
5	NH112041	Nut	)	8	
	BH112101L	Bolt	) Towing Hook to	4	
	NH112041	Nut	) Drop Plate	8	

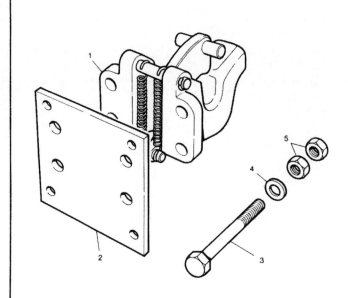

VS3912

LAND ROVER PARTS LTD

698

MODEL LR110 - UP TO AUGUST 1986
BLOCK VS 3910
PAGE N 8
GROUP N

OPTIONAL EQUIPMENT - TOWING JAW

ILL	PART NO	DESCRIPTION		QTY	REMARKS
1	559636	Towing Jaw		1	
2	562756	Distance Piece	)Towing Jaw	1	
3	BH116261	Bolt	)to Rear	2	
4	NY116041L	Nyloc Nut	)Crossmember	2	
5	BH116141	Bolt	) Towing Jaw to	2	
6	NY116041L	Nyloc Nut	) Attachment Bracket	4	

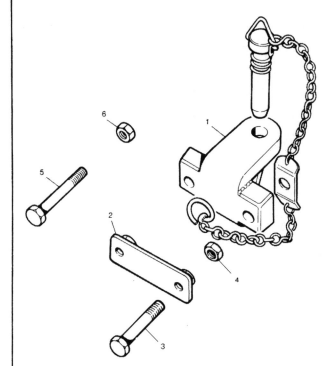

VS3910

LAND ROVER PARTS LTD

699

MODEL LR110 - UP TO AUGUST 1986
BLOCK VS 3905B
PAGE N 10
GROUP N

OPTIONAL EQUIPMENT - TOWING BRACKET AND TOWING BALL

ILL	PART NO	DESCRIPTION		QTY	REMARKS
1	NRC8208	Bracket-Towing Jaw		1	
2	NRC8210	Tie-Bar RH		1	
	NRC8211	Tie Bar LH		1	
3	BH110201L	Bolt	) Tie Bar to	2	
4	WA110061L	Washer-Plain	) Chassis	4	
5	WL110001	Washer-Spring	) Sidemember	2	
6	NY110041L	Nyloc Nut	)	2	
7	SH110301	Screw	) Tie Bar to	2	
8	WA110061L	Washer-Plain	) Bracket	4	
9	WL110001	Washer-Spring	)	2	
10	NY110041L	Nyloc Nut	)	2	
11	SH110251L	Screw	)	1	
12	WL110001	Washer-Spring	)	1	
13	WA110061L	Washer-Plain	) Bracket to	1	
14	BH110081L	Bolt	) Rear Cross-	2	
15	WA110061L	Washer-Plain	) Member	4	
16	WL110001	Washer-Spring	)	2	
17	NY110041L	Nyloc Nut	)	2	
18	568872	Towing Ball-50mm		1	Optional
19	BH116121L	Bolt	) Ball	2	
20	RTC625	Washer	) to Attachment	2	
21	NY116041L	Nyloc Nut	) Bracket	4	

VS3905B

700

MODEL LR110 - UP TO AUGUST 1986
BLOCK VS 4106
PAGE N 10.02
GROUP N

OPTIONAL EQUIPMENT - TOWING BRACKET AND TOWING BALL - HCPU

ILL	PART NO	DESCRIPTION		QTY	REMARKS
1	NRC7758	Extension Assembly		1	
2	BH110181	Bolt-Upper Fixing	)	2	
3	NRC7948	Plate	)	1	
4	NRC6324	Distance Washer	)Extention	2	
5	NY110041L	Nyloc Nut	)To	2	
6	BH116201	Bolt-Lower Fixing	)Rear	2	
7	NRC6636	Nut Plate	)Cross-	1	
8	4233	Washer	)Member	2	
9	NY116041L	Nyloc Nut	)	2	
10	NRC8208	Bracket-Towing Jaw		1	
11	SH110301	Screw	)	1	
12	WL110001	Spring Washer	)	1	
13	WA110041L	Plain Washer	) Bracket	1	
14	BH110071L	Bolt	) To	2	
15	WA110041L	Plain Washer	) Extention	4	
16	WL110001	Spring Washer	)	2	
17	NY110041L	Nyloc Nut	)	2	
18	NRC8229	Tie Bar LH		1	
	NRC8230	Tie Bar RH		1	
19	SH110301	Screw	)	2	
20	WA110041L	Plain Washer	) Tie Bar	4	
21	WL110001	Spring Washer	) To	2	
22	NY110041L	Nyloc Nut	) Bracket	2	
23	BH110201L	Bolt	)	2	
24	WA110041L	Plain Washer	) Tie Bar	4	
25	WL110001	Spring Washer	) To	2	
26	NY110041L	Nyloc Nut	) Chassis	2	
27	568872	Towing Ball-50mm		1	
28	BH116101	Bolt		2	
29	RTC625	Washer		2	
30	NY116041L	Nyloc Nut		2	

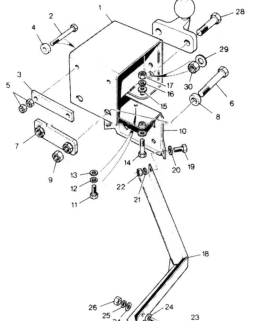

VS4106

701

MODEL LR110 - UP TO AUGUST 1986
BLOCK VS 3956A
PAGE N 12
GROUP N

OPTIONAL EQUIPMENT - TRAILER SOCKET 7 PIN - EXCEPT SWITZERLAND

ILL	PART NO	DESCRIPTION	QTY	REMARKS
1	579409	Trailer Socket-7 pin	1	
2	560553	Seal-Waterproof	1	
3	SE105351	Screw	3	
4	WL105001	Washer-Spring	3	
5	NH105041	Nut	3	
6	PRC2403	Cable Assembly	1	NOTE(1)
	PRC4209	Cable Assembly	1	NOTE(2)
	PRC3543	Cable Assembly-HC PU	1	NOTE(1)
	PRC3542	Cable Assembly-HC PU	1	NOTE(2)
7	PRC2439	Grommet	1	
8	NRC8048	Bracket	1	
9	SH106251	Screw-Fixing Bracket	2	
10	WA106041L	Washer-Plain	2	
11	WL106001	Washer-Lock	2	
12	NH106041L	Nut	2	
13	UNC6684	Cable Tie	2	

NOTES:
(1): UK and Europe
(2): Except UK and Europe

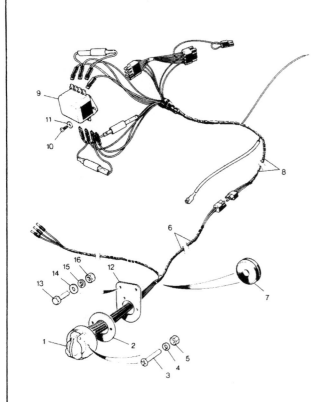

VS3956A

LAND ROVER PARTS LTD

MODEL LR110 - UP TO AUGUST 1986
BLOCK VS 4158
PAGE N 12.02
GROUP N

OPTIONAL EQUIPMENT - TRAILER SOCKER - 7 PIN - SWITZERLAND

ILL	PART NO	DESCRIPTION	QTY	REMARKS
1	579409	Trailer Socker - 7 Pin	1	
2	560553	Seal-Waterproof	1	
3	SE105351	Screw	3	
4	WL105001	Washer-Spring	3	
5	NH105041	Nut	3	
6	PRC4127	Cable	1	
	PRC4152	Cable	1	HC PU
7	PRC2439	Grommet	1	
8	PRC4151	Cable Assembly-Dash	1	
9	589598	Relay	1	
10	AB608031	Screw	2	
11	WA105001	Plain Washer	2	
12	NRC8048	Bracket	1	
13	SH106251	Screw-Fixing Bracket	2	
14	WA106041L	Washer-Plain	2	
15	WL106001	Washer-Lock	2	
16	NH106041L	Nut	2	

VS4158

LAND ROVER PARTS LTD

MODEL LR110 - UP TO AUGUST 1986
BLOCK TS 5140
PAGE N 14
GROUP N

OPTIONAL EQUIPMENT - MUD FLAPS - FRONT AND REAR

ILL	PART NO	DESCRIPTION	QTY	REMARKS
1	RTC4685	Mud-Flap-Front (Pair)	1	
2	MTC3874	Stiffener Bracket	2	
3	MTC3000	Mounting Bracket RH	1	
	MTC3001	Mounting Bracket LH	1	
4	SH106251L	Screw	6	
5	WA106041L	Washer-Plain	6	
6	WL106001L	Washer-Spring	6	
7	NH106041L	Nut	6	
8	SH106201L	Screw	4	
9	WL106001L	Washer-Spring	4	
10	WA106041L	Washer-Plain	4	
11	NN106021	Nutsert	4	
12	RTC4686	Mud Flap-Rear (Pair)	1	
13	MTC8358	Mounting Bracket RH	1	
	MTC8357	Mounting Bracket LH	1	
14	MTC8440	Extention Bracket RH	1	)H.C.P.U
	MTC8441	Extention Bracket LH	1	)
15	SH106161L	Screw	6	
16	WJ600041	Washer-Plain	6	
17	WC106041	Plain Washer	6	
18	WL106001L	Washer-Spring	6	
19	NH106041L	Nut	6	
20	SH106161L	Screw	2	
21	WL106001L	Washer-Spring	2	
22	WA106041L	Washer-Plain	2	
23	NN106001	Nutsert	2	
24	SH106161L	Screw	4	
25	WA106041L	Washer-Plain	8	
26	WL106001L	Washer-Spring	4	
27	NH106041L	Nut	4	
28	MTC7513	Edging Strip-Mudflap Bracket	A/R	Germany

TS5160

LAND ROVER PARTS LTD

MODEL LR110 - UP TO AUGUST 1986
BLOCK VS 4027
PAGE N 16
GROUP N

OPTIONAL EQUIPMENT - COVER - SPARE WHEEL

ILL	PART NO	DESCRIPTION	QTY	REMARKS
1	MRC7365	Cover-Spare Wheel	1	Optional
	MUC4161	Cover-Spare Wheel	1	Germany

VS4027

LAND ROVER PARTS LTD

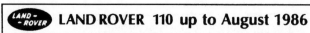
MODEL LR110 – UP TO AUGUST 1986
BLOCK TS 5006
PAGE N 16.02
GROUP N

OPTIONAL EQUIPMENT – COVER – SPARE WHEEL – GERMANY
                                          UP TO 1984 FACELIFT

ILL	PART NO	DESCRIPTION	QTY	REMARKS
1	395576	Spare Wheel Cover Assembly	1	
2	395579	+Retaining Strap	1	
3	301005	++Hook for Strap	2	
4	395577	+Cover Plate	1	
5	395578	+Edge Trim	1	
6	395143	+Staple	2	
7	79194	+Rivet-Staple to Cover Plate	4	
8	395580	+Knob for Cover Plate	1	

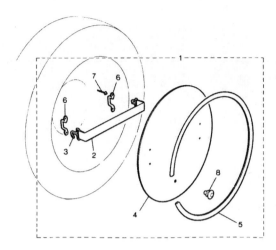

TS5006

LAND ROVER PARTS LTD

706

MODEL LR110 – UP TO AUGUST 1986
BLOCK VS 4029
PAGE N 18
GROUP N

OPTIONAL EQUIPMENT – FIRE EXTINGUISHER

ILL	PART NO	DESCRIPTION	QTY	REMARKS
1	MRC7350	Fire Extinguisher Complete With Bracket	1	
2	SF106161	Screw	2	
3	MM106301	Riv Nut	2	

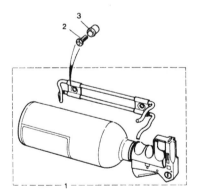

VS4029

LAND ROVER PARTS LTD

707

MODEL LR110 - UP TO AUGUST 1986
BLOCK VS 4091
PAGE N 20
GROUP N

OPTIONAL EQUIPMENT - WHEELGUARDS - STANDARD PICK UP

ILL	PART NO	DESCRIPTION	QTY	REMARKS
1	MRC7359	Wheelguard RH	1	
2	MRC7360	Wheelguard LH	1	
3	MRC7361	Seal RH	1	
4	MRC7362	Seal LH	1	
5	MRC8732	Stay for Wheelguard RH	1	
6	AB608041L	Screw-Wheelguard RH to Body	4	
7	AFU1218	Plain Washer	4	
8	RTC3745	Lokut Nut	4	
9	SH106161	Screw-Wheelguard RH to Stay	1	
10	WA106041L	Plain Washer	2	
11	WL106001	Spring Washer	1	
12	NH106041L	Nut	1	
13	AB608041L	Screw-Stay to Chassis	1	
14	AFU1218	Plain Washer	1	
15	RTC3745	Lokut Nut	1	
16	78248	Rivet-Wheelguard LH to Body	3	

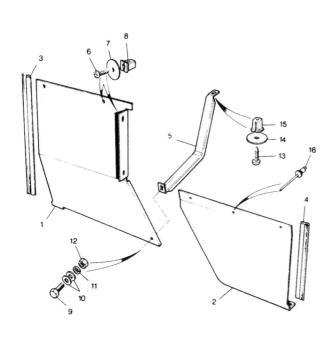

VS4091

LAND ROVER PARTS LTD

MODEL LR110 - UP TO AUGUST 1986
BLOCK VS 4092
PAGE N 22
GROUP N

OPTIONAL EQUIPMENT - WHEELGUARDS - HIGH CAPACITY PICK UP

ILL	PART NO	DESCRIPTION	QTY	REMARKS
1	MTC7041	Wheelguard Panel RH-Front	1	
	MTC7040	Wheelguard Panel RH-Rear	1	
2	MTC7040	Wheelguard Panel LH-Front	1	
	MTC7004	Wheelguard Panel LH-Rear	1	
3	RU612183	Rivet-Wheelguards to Body	8	
	78248	Rivet-Wheelguards to Body	8	

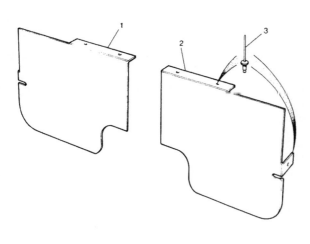

VS4092

LAND ROVER PARTS LTD

MODEL LR110 - UP TO AUGUST 1986
BLOCK VS 4157
PAGE N 24
GROUP N

OPTIONAL EQUIPMENT - CENTRE POWER TAKE OFF - 4 CYL

ILL	PART NO	DESCRIPTION	QTY	REMARKS
1	FRC5375	Centre Power Take Off Assy	1	
2	FRC5376	+Output Shaft	1	
3	FRC5381	+Sliding Dog	1	
4	FRC5379	+Selector Fork	1	
5	FRC7018	+Retaining Screw	1	
6	217325	+Bearing-Rear	1	
7	1643	+Ball-Detent	1	
8	NRC255	+Spring-Detent	1	
9	SH112201	+Screw-Detent	1	
10	FRC5380	+Selector Shaft	1	
11	FRC3477	+O Ring	1	
12	FRC5388	+Plate	1	
13	WL106001	+Spring Washer	2	
14	SH106141	+Screw	2	
15	576303	+Pivot Pin	1	
16	NH110041L	+Lock Nut	1	
17	WM600071	+Spring Washer	1	

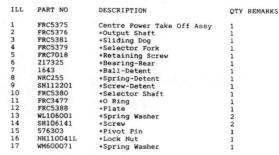

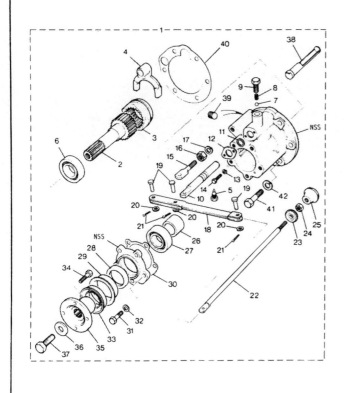

VS4157

LAND ROVER PARTS LTD

MODEL LR110 - UP TO AUGUST 1986
BLOCK VS 4157
PAGE N 26
GROUP N

OPTIONAL EQUIPMENT - CENTRE POWER TAKE OFF - 4 CYL

ILL	PART NO	DESCRIPTION	QTY	REMARKS
18	FRC5383	+Operating Lever	1	
19	PC106291	+Clevis Pin	3	
20	WA106041L	+Washer	3	
21	PS103121	+Split Pin	3	
22	FRC5391	+Operating Rod	1	
23	508571	+Grommet	1	
24	NT110041	+Locknut	1	
25	FRC3470	+Knob	1	
26	FRC5385	+Spacer	1	
27	214797	+Bearing-Front	1	
28	FRC5387	+Oil Seal	1	
29	236548	+Mudguard	1	
30	FRC5386	+Joint Washer	1	
31	SH108251L	+Screw	5	
32	WL108001L	+Spring Washer	5	
33	236074	+Mudshield	1	
34	509045	+Bolt	4	
35	FRC5378	+Coupling Flange	1	
36	571174	+Washer-Coupling Flange	1	
37	SH116301	+Screw-Flange to Shaft	1	
38	FRC6933	+Oil Catcher	1	
39	SK110101	+Grub Screw	1	
40	FRC5389	+Joint Washer	1	
41	FRC8029	+Bolt	6	
42	WL110001	+Spring Washer	6	

VS4157

LAND ROVER PARTS LTD

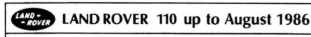

MODEL LR110 - UP TO AUGUST 1986
BLOCK VS 4161
PAGE N 28
GROUP N

OPTIONAL EQUIPMENT - CENTRE POWER TAKE OFF - V8

ILL	PART NO	DESCRIPTION	QTY	REMARKS
1	FRC3543	Centre Power Take Off Assy	1	
2	571809	+Output Shaft	1	
3	571810	+Sliding Dog	1	
4	571811	+Selector Fork	1	
5	571158	+Spring Pin	1	
6		+Housing	1	Not Serviced Separately
7	RTC3413	+Bearing	1	
8	571146	+Ball-Detent	1	
9	571439	+Spring-Detent	1	
10	SH112121	+Screw-Detent	1	
11	571812	+Shaft	1	
12	571609	+Plate	1	
13	571608	+Oil Seal	1	
14	WM106001	+Spring Washer	1	
15	SH106101	+Screw	1	
16	576303	+Pivot Pin	1	
17	NT110041	+Locknut	1	
18	WM110001	+Spring Washer	1	

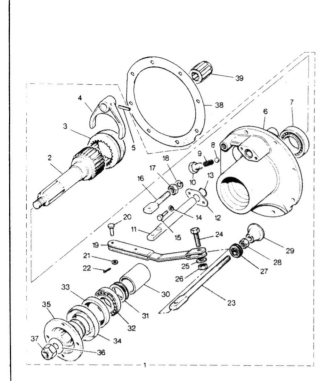

LAND ROVER PARTS LTD

MODEL LR110 - UP TO AUGUST 1986
BLOCK VS 4161
PAGE N 30
GROUP N

OPTIONAL EQUIPMENT - CENTRE POWER TAKE OFF - V8

ILL	PART NO	DESCRIPTION	QTY	REMARKS
19	FRC3553	+Operating Lever	1	
20	PC106291	+Clevis Pin	2	
21	WA106041L	+Plain Washer	2	
22	PS103121	+Split Pin	2	
23	FRC3544	+Operating Rod	1	
24	BH106061L	+Bolt	1	
25	WA106041L	+Plain Washer	1	
26	NY106041L	+Nyloc Nut	1	
27	508571	+Grommet	1	
28	NT110041	+Nut	1	
29	FRC3470	+Knob	1	
30	571813	+Spacer	1	
31	571619	+Shim-1.00mm	A/R	
	571623	+Shim-1.20mm	A/R	
	571627	+Shim-1.40mm	A/R	
	571633	+Shim-1.70mm	A/R	
32	RTC3398	+Bearing	1	
33	571607	+Oil Seal	1	
34	571177	+Mud Shield	1	
35	571954	+Flange	1	
36	571171	+Washer	1	
37	NY116041	+Nyloc Nut	1	
38	571846	Gasket	1	
39	571187	Needle Roller Bearing	1	

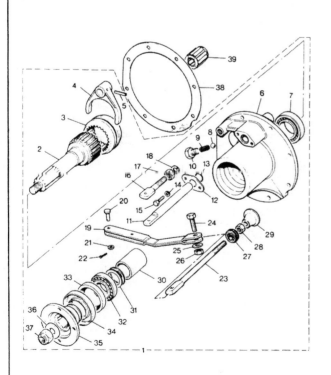

LAND ROVER PARTS LTD

MODEL LR110 - UP TO AUGUST 1986
BLOCK VS 4157
PAGE N 30.02
GROUP N

OPTIONAL EQUIPMENT - CENTRE POWER TAKE OFF - V8
5 SPEED GEARBOX

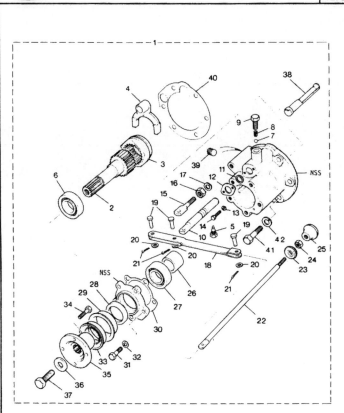

ILL	PART NO	DESCRIPTION	QTY	REMARKS
1	FRC8541	Centre Power Take Off Assy	1	
2	FRC5376	+Output Shaft	1	
3	FRC5381	+Sliding Dog	1	
4	FRC5379	+Selector Fork	1	
5	FRC7018	+Retaining Screw	1	
6	217325	+Bearing-Rear	1	
7	1643	+Ball-Detent	1	
8	NRC255	+Spring-Detent	1	
9	SH112201	+Screw-Detent	1	
10	FRC5380	+Selector Shaft	1	
11	FRC3477	+O Ring	1	
12	FRC5388	+Plate	1	
13	WC106001L	+Spring Washer	2	
14	SH106041	+Screw	2	
15	576303	+Pivot Pin	1	
16	NH110041L	+Locknut	1	
17	WM600071	+Spring Washer	1	

VS4157

 **LAND ROVER PARTS LTD**

MODEL LR110 - UP TO AUGUST 1986
BLOCK VS 4157
PAGE N 30.04
GROUP N

OPTIONAL EQUIPMENT - CENTRE POWER TAKE OFF - V8
5 SPEED GEARBOX

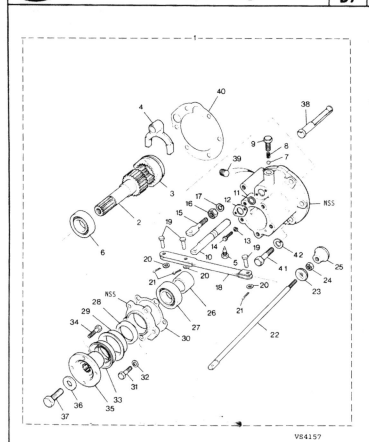

ILL	PART NO	DESCRIPTION	QTY	REMARKS
18	FRC5383	+Operating Lever	1	
19	PC106291	+Clevis Pin	3	
20	WA106041L	+Washer	3	
21	PS103121	+Split Pin	3	
22	FRC8538	+Operating Rod	1	
23	508571	+Grommet	1	
24	NT110041	+Locknut	1	
25	FRC3470	+Knob	1	
26	FRC5385	+Spacer	1	
27	214797	+Bearing-Front	1	
28	FRC5387	+Oil Seal	1	
29	236548	+Mudguard	1	
30	FRC5386	+Joint Washer	1	
31	SH108251L	+Screw	5	
32	WL108001L	+Spring Washer	5	
33	236074	+Mudshield	1	
34	509045	+Bolt	1	
35	FRC5378	+Coupling Flange	1	
36	571174	+Washer-Coupling Flange	1	
37	SH116301	+Screw-Flange to Shaft	1	
38	FRC6933	+Oil Catcher	1	
39	SK110101	+Grub Screw	1	
40	FRC5389	+Joint-Washer	1	
41	FRC8029	+Bolt	6	
42	WL110001	+Spring Washer	6	

VS4157

LAND ROVER PARTS LTD

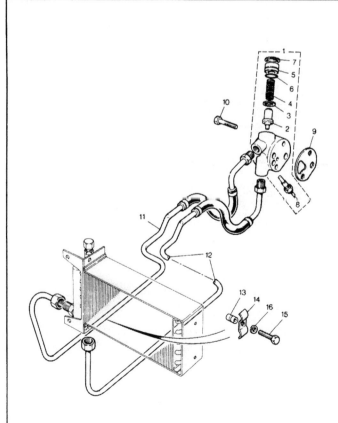

MODEL LR110 - UP TO AUGUST 1986
BLOCK VS 4145
PAGE N 32
GROUP N

OIL COOLER AND MOUNTING FRAME

ILL	PART NO	DESCRIPTION	QTY	REMARKS
1	NRC7741	Oil Cooler	1	
	NRC8201	Oil Cooler	1	V8 Air Con
2	NRC7458	Mounting Frame	1	)
3	SH106121L	Screw	2	)
4	SH106161L	Screw	2	)
5	WL106001L	Spring Washer	4	)Except
6	WA106041L	Plain Washer	2	)Aircon
7	NH106041L	Nut	2	)
8	NRC7459	'U' Bolt	4	)
9	WL106001L	Spring Washer	8	)
10	NH106041L	Nut	8	)
	SH106121L	Screw	2	)
	WL106001L	Spring Washer	4	)Air Con
	NH106041L	Nut	2	)

VS4145

LAND ROVER PARTS LTD

MODEL LR110 - UP TO AUGUST 1986
BLOCK VS 4147
PAGE N 34
GROUP N

OIL COOLER - ADAPTOR AND PIPES - 4 CYL

ILL	PART NO	DESCRIPTION	QTY	REMARKS
1	ERC7755	Adaptor Assembly	1	)
2	ERC5923	+Thermostat	1	)
3	ERC7756	+Joint Washer	1	)
4	ERC7757	+Spring	1	)
5	ERC5756	+Plug	1	)2.25 litre
6	ERC5757	+'O' Ring	1	)
7	CR110301	+Circlip	1	)
8	PRC2505	+Transmitter-Oil Temp	1	)
9	ERC7773	Joint Washer	1	)
10	ERC9499	Bolt-Filter and Adaptor to Block	2	)
11	NRC5820	Pipe Assembly-Feed	1	
	NRC8507	Pipe Assembly-Feed	1	2.5 Diesel
	NRC8196	Pipe Assembly-Feed 2.25 litre	1	)Air Con
	NRC8509	Pipe Assembly-Feed 2.5 litre	1	)
12	NRC5819	Pipe Assembly-Return	1	
	NRC5808	Pipe Assembly-Return	1	2.5 Diesel
	NRC8197	Pipe Assembly-Return 2.25 litre	1	)Air Con)
	NRC8510	Pipe Assembly-Return 2.5 litre	1	)
13	NN106011	Nutsert	1	
14	594637	Saddle Clip	1	
15	SH106161L	Screw	1	
16	WL106001L	Spring Washer	1	
	NRC8618	Pipe Coupling	2	

NOTE: For 2.5 Diesel Adaptor See Engine Section.

VS4147

LAND ROVER PARTS LTD

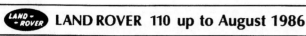
MODEL LR110 - UP TO AUGUST 1986
BLOCK VS 4146/A
PAGE N 36
GROUP N

OIL COOLER - ADAPTOR AND PIPES - V8

ILL	PART NO	DESCRIPTION	QTY	REMARKS
1	ERC6720	Bypass Adaptor Assembly	1	
2	ERC5923	+Thermostat	1	
3	TRS1114L	+O Ring	2	
4	ERC6722	Base Plate Assembly	1	
5	PA105101	+Spring Pin	1	
6	SH108301L	Screw	5	
7	ERC6890	Joint Washer	1	
8	ERC3724	Washer	1	
9	ERC3500	Tube Nut	1	
10	ERC6723	Joint Washer	1	
11	WA108051L	Plain Washer	5	
12	WL108001L	Spring Washer	5	
13	NH108041L	Nut	5	
14	NRC4162	Flexible Pipe Assembly	2	
15	NRC5824	Pipe Assembly-Feed	1	
	NRC8198	Pipe Assembly-Feed	1	Air Con
16	NRC5823	Pipe Assembly-Return	1	
	NRC8199	Pipe Assembly-Return	1	Air Con
17	NN106011	Nutsert	1	
18	594637	Saddle Clip	1	
19	SH106161L	Screw	1	
20	WL106001L	Spring Washer	1	

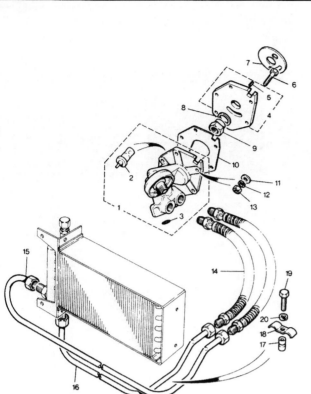

VS4146A

LAND ROVER PARTS LTD

MODEL LR110 - UP TO AUGUST 1986
BLOCK VS 4240
PAGE N 40
GROUP N

OPTIONAL EQUIPMENT - SEAT BELT AND OVERSPEED WARNING

ILL	PART NO	DESCRIPTION	QTY	REMARKS
1	PRC4301	Harness	1	
2	AAU5034	+Diode	1	
3	PRC4299	Buzzer	1	
4	PRC4304	Clip-Buzzer	1	
5	PRC4268	Overspeed Unit	1	
6	PRC4283	Speed Sensor	1	
7	PRC4298	Speedometer Cable-Upper	1	
8	PRC4282	Speedometer Cable-Lower	1	
9	C43640	Cable Tie	5	
10	AFU2879	Clip	2	

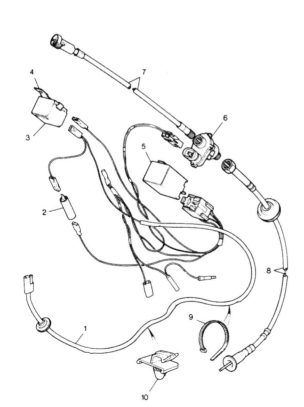

VS4240

LAND ROVER PARTS LTD

LR110 - UP TO AUGUST 1986
BLOCK TS 5007
PAGE N 42
GROUP N

OPTIONAL EQUIPMENT - LAMP GUARDS

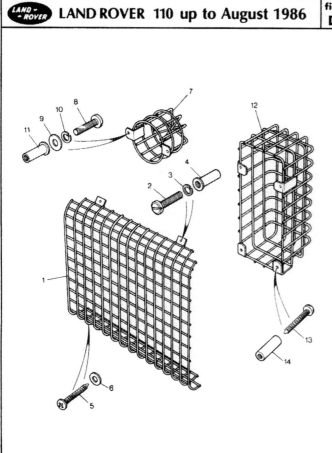

ILL	PART NO	DESCRIPTION	QTY	REMARKS
1	345985	Lamp Guard-Front	2	
2	78384	Screw)	4	
3	WL702001	Spring Washer)Upper Fixings	4	
4	AFU1876	Rivnut)	4	
5	AB608047	Screw)	4	
6	WC702101	Plain Washer)Lower Fixings	4	
7	RTC8064	Lamp Guard Kit-Rear	1	)
8	78384	+Screw	4	)
9	WC702101	+Plain Washer	4	)NOTE(1)
10	WL702001	+Spring Washer	4	)
11	AFU1876	+Rivnut	4	)
12	RTC8065	Lamp Guard Kit-Rear	1	)
13	AB608101	+Screw	8	)H.C.P.U
14	244009	+Spacer	8	)

NOTE(1):   Two Kits Required Per Vehicle-
            All Vehicles Except H.C.P.U

TS5007

LAND ROVER PARTS LTD

MODEL LR110 - UP TO AUGUST 1986
BLOCK N/A
PAGE N 50
GROUP N

OPTIONAL EQUIPMENT - 127 CREW CAB - UNIQUE PARTS

ILL	PART NO	DESCRIPTION	QTY	REMARKS
		GROUP E		
	RRC2303	Propshaft-Rear-V8	1	
	RRC2304	Propshaft-Rear-4 Cyl	1	
		GROUP G		
	RRC2479	Brake Pipe-PDWA to Rear	1	
		GROUP H		
	RRC2475	Fuel Pipe-Sedimentor to Pump	1	
	RRC2486	Fuel Spill Return Pipe	1	4 Cyl Petrol
	RRC2487	Fuel Pipe-Tank to Pump	1	V8
	RRC2488	Fuel Pipe-Spill Return	1	V8
	RRC2593	Hose Fuel Filler	1	HCPU
	RRC2644	Fuel Pipe-Tank to Pump	1	
	RRC2645	Fuel Spill Pipe-Rail to Tank	1	
	RRC2361	Exhaust Extension Pipe	1	
		GROUP K		
	RRC2480	Chassis Harness	1	
	RRC2579	Clamp Eye Assy-Battery	2	
	RRC2635	Battery Cable Assy-Positive	1	
	RRC2636	J-Bolt-Battery Clamp	2	
		GROUP L		
	RRC2403	Rear Body Assy	1	HCPU
	RRC2404	Bodyside Complete Assy RH	1	HCPU
	RRC2406	Bodyside Complete Assy LH	1	HCPU
	RRC2407	Floor Assy Complete	1	HCPU
	RRC2417	Front Valance Assy RH	1	HCPU
	RRC2420	Rear Side Door Clinched Assy RH	1	)Sidescreen)Type
	RRC2423	Rear Side Door Clinched Assy LH	1	))
	RRC2426	'BC' Post-Crew Cab-RH	1	
	RRC2427	'BC' Post-Crew Cab-LH	1	
	RRC2428	Floor Plate Assy-Rear Intermediate	1	
	RRC2432	Rear Seatbase Assy	1	
	RRC2436	Mounting Angle-Rear Body	3	
	RRC2437	Mounting Angle Assy-Rear Body RH	1	
	RRC2438	Mounting Angle Assy-Rear Body LH	1	
			1	
	RRC2439	Mounting Bracket Assy-Body Front	2	
	RRC2440	Body Mounting Bracket Assy	4	

LAND ROVER PARTS LTD

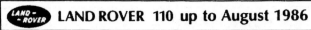
```
MODEL LR110 - UP TO AUGUST 1986
BLOCK TF
PAGE N 52
GROUP N

OPTIONAL EQUIPMENT - 127 CREW CAB - UNIQUE PARTS - CONTD

ILL    PART NO        DESCRIPTION                  QTY REMARKS

                      GROUP L - CONTINUED
       RRC2442        Sill Channel Bracket          2   Note(1)
       RRC2443        Rear Body Support Mounting     2
                      Pad
       RRC2445        Bodyside Inner Panel RH        1   HCPU
       RRC2447        Front Valance LH               1   HCPU
       RRC2473        Bodyside Inner Panel LH        1   HCPU
       RRC2463        Roof                           1
       RRC2481        Hood Assy-No Windows           1   HCPU
       RRC2491        Cab Base                       1
       RRC2497        Rear Cab Floor Support         1
       RRC2498        Seat Base                      1
       RRC2637        Bracket-Sill to Outrigger RH   1
       RRC2638        Bracket-Sill to Outrigger LH   1
       RRC2957        Panel-Gusset/Valance RH        1
       RRC2958        Panel-Gusset/Valance LH        1
       RRC2963        Hood Assy-With Side Windows     1
       RRC2974        Rear Sill Panel RH             1
       RRC2975        Rear Sill Panel LH             1
       RRC4422        Tie Bar-Hood Frame-Rear        2   )HCPU
                                                         )NLA-Note(2)
                      GROUP M
       RRC2409        Centre Headlining              1
       RRC2476        Rear Headlining                1
       RRC2477        Rubber Mat-Rear Cab Floor      1
       RRC2482        Trim Extension Rear Side Door 1   )Sidescreen
                      RH                                )Type Door
       RRC2483        Trim Extension Rear Side Door 1   )
                      LH                                )
       RRC2595        Cab Back Trim RH               1
       RRC2596        Cab Back Trim LH               1
       RRC2626        Trim Rear Door Cantrail RH     1
       RRC2629        Trim Rear Door Cantrail LH     1
       RRC2485        Truck Seat Assy-Slatted        2


NOTE(1):  Obsolete - Use RRC2637/8

NOTE(2):  Use 330896-Cut to Overall Length
          34". Flatten and Shape End
          Drill to 33" Hole Centres
```

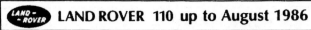
```
                    MASTER INDEX
```

PART NO	PAGE	PART NO	PAGE	PART NO	PAGE	PART NO	PAGE	PART NO	PAGE	PART NO	PAGE
10713	38	213961	122	2266L	658	236067	83	244488	25	247723	108
10713	62	213961	135	2266L	659	236072	263	244488	52	247726	340
10713	122	214228	328	22A1613L	189	236074	711	244488	76	247726	342
10802070	80	214229	328	22A1613L	206	236074	715	244488	105	247737	86
10802070	108	214795	221	22A1613L	251	236257	24	245003	447	247737	113
11009L	292	214797	711	22A1613L	474	236257	52	246109	698	247738	86
11011L	291	214797	715	22G1988L	177	236257	76	247040	31	247738	113
11011L	294	214995	24	22G1989L	177	236257	105	247040	57	247742	25
11015L	291	214995	76	230313	29	236548	711	247040	86	247742	52
11820L	316	216708	353	230313	55	236548	715	247040	113	247742	77
11987L	291	216962	190	230313	82	236632	263	247051	41	247755	20
11988L	291	216962	193	230313	110	2393	540	247051	65	247755	48
11H1781L	394	216962	207	230736	694	2393	599	247051	80	247755	72
11H5569L	694	216962	210	231190	385	239600	339	247051	108	247755	101
12H220L	340	216962	228	232037	32	239600	409	247121	32	247766	34
12H220L	342	216962	252	232038	215	239673	397	247121	87	247766	60
134176	451	216962	255	232039	37	240407	312	247127	20	247766	89
139082	164	216962	288	232039	93	240429	478	247127	48	247766	90
13H1515L	363	217245	290	232043	148	240429	479	247127	72	247766	141
13H2023L	174	217245	293	232043	149	240555	24	247127	101	247874	40
13H2475L	634	217245	296	232044	24	240555	76	247153	86	247874	64
13H2475L	639	217245	500	232044	52	240708	163	247153	113	247874	81
13H2475L	641	217325	226	232044	76	240836	693	247179	340	247874	109
13H7343L	414	217325	710	232044	105	243958	42	247179	342	247912	27
13H9157	491	217325	714	232046	36	243958	66	247212	340	247912	83
150844	477	217352	267	232046	61	243958	388	247212	446	247952	80
154503	355	217352	273	232046	91	243958	389	247212	447	247953	80
154545	139	217353	267	232046	117	243958	390	247554	33	247965	20
154545	141	217353	273	232046	118	243958	391	247554	59	247965	48
156206	470	218508	694	232046	119	243958	392	247554	92	247965	72
1643	710	219676	204	232046	120	243958	393	247554	121	247965	101
1643	714	219676	219	232538	343	243959	20	247555	33	250053	559
17H8764L	308	219676	249	233220	164	243959	26	247555	59	250055	623
18G8619L	453	219704	693	233243	473	243959	40	247555	92	250431	343
18G8619L	454	2204L	150	233244	492	243959	48	247555	121	250830	79
18G8619L	455	2215L	281	233326	27	243959	64	247583	74	250830	107
18G8619L	457	2217L	301	233326	83	243959	72	247583	103	250836	428
18G8951L	312	2217L	302	233328	27	243959	78	247606	87	252164	276
18G8953L	312	2217L	463	233328	83	243959	81	247607	86	252164	288
201235	537	2222	499	234124	27	243959	101	247614	31	252164	290
201235	548	2251L	259	234124	83	243959	106	247614	57	252164	293
20138	668	2265L	390	234532	275	243959	109	247624	32	252164	296
20147	668	2265L	391	234957	309	243967	136	247634	32	252164	499
201647	537	2265L	392	235113	506	243968	136	247665	25	252166	279
213700	20	2265L	393	235770	23	244009	720	247665	52	252513	131
213700	41	2266L	459	235770	51	244384	694	247665	76	252514	148
213700	65	2266L	460	235770	75	244487	25	247665	105	252516	142
213700	72	2266L	461	235770	104	244487	52	247683	80	252516	143
213961	38	2266L	462	236022	148	244487	76	247683	108	252623	151
213961	62	2266L	463	236067	27	244487	105	247723	80	253205	446

PART NO	PAGE	PART NO	PAGE	PART NO	PAGE	PART NO	PAGE	PART NO	PAGE	PART NO	PAGE
253942	338	2705	694	277388	27	302177	594	307419	668	330237	592
253948	280	2707	694	277388	83	302178	582	307420	668	330238	561
253952	276	272512	340	277956	31	302178	584	308206	560	330238	568
253952	499	272539	37	277956	57	302178	594	308792	623	330238	592
253963	288	272539	93	277956	86	302207	595	3101	391	330245	561
255205	665	272632	163	277956	113	302648	671	3101	392	330245	589
255206	577	272712	163	278109	24	302825	562	3101	393	330265	557
255227	682	272713	163	278109	76	302828	562	312856	476	330265	564
255227	683	272714	163	278166	163	302933	575	313493	595	330366	558
257011	233	272819	163	279648	41	302934	575	315264	665	330366	589
257011	395	273069	30	279648	65	3036L	151	315264	666	330422	562
257014	396	273069	32	279652	343	3036L	463	315960	665	330551	608
257017	132	273069	56	27H2403L	473	303847	559	315960	666	330553	608
257017	233	273069	58	27H5311	486	303847	575	320045	521	330553	610
257020	395	273069	85	27H5932L	466	303975	590	320045	565	330578	607
257064	148	273069	87	27H5932L	467	303975	591	320046	595	330578	611
257071	338	273069	112	27H6481L	470	304125	652	320047	595	330579	607
257123	395	273069	114	27H8207L	470	304125	657	320604	590	330579	611
257203	473	273069	340	2920	340	304125	658	320608	476	330602	558
257302	474	273069	342	293716	228	304125	672	320674	672	330615	560
257450	591	273111	24	2982	219	304301	608	320698	657	330616	558
257450	358	273070	720	2995	29	304301	610	320699	654	330617	556
261414	343	273521	340	2995	82	304301	613	320699	656	330661	670
261414	347	273521	342	2K8686L	164	304716	632	320699	657	330699	608
264024	278	273711	76	300816	500	304797	606	320708	653	330699	610
264590	474	274772	86	300953	606	304797	609	320709	653	330717	560
264591	473	274773	86	300953	609	304797	612	320719	673	330762	588
264591	474	274774	86	300953	612	3052	163	320726	654	330790	587
264591	476	274775	86	300954	606	305232	546	320726	656	330791	587
264767	164	275234	27	300954	609	305232	552	320726	657	330848	578
265169	22	275234	28	300954	612	305232	564	3259	263	330896	608
265175	22	275234	54	301005	671	305232	597	3261	288	330896	610
265175	50	275234	83	301005	706	306287	578	3261	296	330897	610
265295	476	275234	84	301320	606	306287	580	3261L	290	331007	655
266945	74	275565	362	301320	609	306287	582	3261L	293	331008	655
266945	103	275565	363	301320	612	306289	578	3290	131	331083	286
267451	27	275679	41	301321	606	306289	580	3290	155	331083	655
267451	83	275679	65	301321	609	306289	582	3290	156	331083	660
267604	148	275679	80	301321	612	306295	546	3290	214	331105	606
267837	391	275679	108	301328	557	306295	552	3290	219	331105	609
267837	392	276322	694	301343	606	306295	598	3290	236	331221	606
267837	393	276323	694	301343	609	306316	668	3290	266	331221	609
268292	30	276396	694	301343	612	306407	566	3291	266	331221	612
268293	30	276426	346	301347	668	306461	595	3292	168	331222	606
268887	32	276426	347	301470	671	306564	540	3292	218	331222	609
269257	487	276426	348	301476	671	306564	599	3292	237	331249	609
269783	163	276484	275	302164	595	307220	537	3292	244	331273	657
269889	37	277217	694	302165	594	307220	548	330145	562	331273	658
269889	93	277259	385	302177	582	307220	660	330237	561	331317	606
270225	466	277260	385	302177	584	307418	668	330237	568	331481	637

PART NO	PAGE	PART NO	PAGE	PART NO	PAGE	PART NO	PAGE	PART NO	PAGE	PART NO	PAGE
331481	643	332484	541	334613	579	338554	581	347151	597	348770	683
331670	638	332485	541	334614	587	338554	583	347343	667	349514	667
331670	643	332564	602	334615	584	338741	583	347344	667	349515	667
331673	610	332582	557	336288	669	339935	606	347346	526	349516	667
331674	610	332582	564	336294	669	339935	609	347362	533	349529	667
331675	611	332647	515	336344	623	339935	612	347362	540	349931	599
331676	611	332672	559	336345	623	339986	653	347362	546	349931	653
331709	653	332672	575	336346	623	339986	657	347362	552	349931	656
331709	656	332674	559	336347	623	339986	658	347363	533	349931	657
331709	657	332674	575	336348	623	339986	659	347363	540	349931	658
331709	658	332756	602	336349	623	340391	578	347363	546	349931	659
331709	659	332942	597	336350	623	345100	678	347363	552	349931	667
331709	667	333032	596	336351	623	345100	679	347369	540	349943	654
331818	655	333033	596	336352	623	345100	680	347369	546	349943	656
331835	672	333034	596	336454	578	345101	678	347369	552	349943	657
331973	654	333035	596	336535	508	345101	680	347441	600	349943	658
331973	657	333036	598	336577	588	345213	656	347553	558	349943	659
331974	654	333041	546	336764	577	345213	658	347553	652	349955	667
331974	656	333041	598	336780	637	345213	659	347553	657	349967	654
331974	657	333203	602	336780	638	345597	474	347553	658	349967	657
331974	658	333204	546	336781	637	345683	672	347586	414	349996	655
331974	659	333263	564	336781	638	345683	673	347594	592	349996	660
332047	594	333266	568	337812	525	345699	608	347641	347	349997	656
332065	577	333267	568	337813	525	345699	610	347844	682	349997	658
332065	579	333395	664	337859	654	345699	613	347844	683	349997	659
332065	582	333439	600	337859	656	345915	590	347861	670	349998	656
332083	595	333445	598	337859	657	345937	675	347862	670	349998	658
332084	595	333446	600	337873	653	345985	720	347863	670	349998	659
332097	595	333468	594	337873	656	346341	591	347866	559	3547	606
332122	594	333486	587	337873	657	346341	598	347869	653	367030	618
332146	562	333487	577	337880	653	346410	657	347869	657	367030	619
332147	597	333487	579	337880	656	346576	516	347869	659	367030	620
332201	581	333490	582	337880	657	346598	515	347939	414	367078	435
332201	583	333551	673	337899	654	346599	515	348393	578	367078	436
332215	577	333745	565	337899	656	346722	287	348394	578	371133	618
332215	579	334068	585	337899	657	346786	482	348396	578	371144	618
332215	582	334069	585	337981	623	346849	507	348430	611	371144	619
332216	578	334111	476	338015	515	346878	533	348430	652	371144	620
332230	578	334121	516	338017	524	346878	599	348430	654	372336	604
332293	581	334177	665	338023	488	346894	415	348430	656	3739	27
332293	583	334245	611	338023	503	346924	414	348430	657	3739	83
332324	578	334246	611	338023	515	346927	533	348430	658	3748	24
332325	578	334532	673	338024	488	346928	533	348430	659	3748	76
332329	578	334540	673	338028	524	346941	516	348747	287	37H3694L	477
332355	653	334601	673	338029	311	346976	415	348765	682	37H4558L	310
332355	657	334610	582	338423	595	346976	416	348765	683	37H5208L	477
332355	659	334611	582	338550	581	346941	515	348766	682	37H575L	363
332376	620	334612	577	338552	581	347151	530	348766	683	37H6171L	466
332445	590	334612	579	338552	583	347151	544	348770	682	37H6171L	467
332446	590	334613	577	338553	581					37H7618L	466

PART NO	PAGE	PART NO	PAGE	PART NO	PAGE	PART NO	PAGE	PART NO	PAGE	PART NO	PAGE
37H7618L	467	395830	416	4589L	36	504233	386	517706	364	530178	25
37H770	364	3958L	230	4589L	61	50446	163	517706	365	530178	52
37H770L	363	3958L	562	4589L	91	50446	311	517706	366	530178	105
37H7920	364	396416	632	4589L	118	504655	385	517706	378	530179	25
37H8119	364	396540	637	4589L	120	504656	385	517903	343	530179	52
37H8119L	363	396541	637	4589L	145	504657	385	517976	363	530179	105
3829	588	396541	641	4594	350	504673	385	518653	336	530476	64
3830	594	396542	637	4594L	111	504673	386	51K4001L	483	531586	470
3830L	491	396542	641	4594L	148	505205	477	520160	477	531604	491
3830L	583	396696	671	4594L	464	505244	385	520455	465	531689	398
3830L	598	396697	673	4866	426	506069	32	521452	395	531893	309
3830L	667	396698	673	4866L	464	50641	339	521453	395	532319	132
3830L	682	396739	671	4868L	463	506814	31	521453	396	532323	186
3830L	683	396800	606	4868L	492	506814	86	522745	25	532323	194
3842	575	396800	609	4905	288	507829	30	522745	52	532323	211
3890	391	396800	612	4905	290	507829	56	522745	77	532323	225
3890	392	396922	665	4905	293	507829	85	522745	105	532387	26
3890	393	396950	636	4905	296	507829	112	52278	446	532387	53
3898	497	396951	636	500201	164	508571	711	52278	447	532387	78
3900L	511	3972	392	500447	388	508571	713	522932	148	532387	106
3900L	667	3972	393	500447	389	508571	715	522932	343	532736	491
392107	524	3982L	575	500710	385	509045	226	522940	363	532943	176
392743	548	398776	591	500746	277	509045	275	522940	364	533358	217
392811	233	3H822L	486	500746	282	509045	711	523181	86	533358	219
395078	597	3H822L	573	501593	20	509045	715	523203	226	533765	193
395143	608	4034	653	501593	48	509510	347	523203	339	533765	210
395143	610	4034	657	501593	72	510267	383	523638	694	533765	229
395143	706	4034L	488	501593	101	510267	384	523765	210	533765	255
395185	516	4034L	523	502029	74	512206	31	523765	229	534790	333
395249	678	4034L	577	502116	155	512207	31	523765	255	534790	334
395252	679	4034L	579	502116	156	512646	328	524680	79	534790	335
395252	681	4034L	582	502116	157	512828	79	524765	41	534790	372
395294	597	4034L	658	50216	156	513171	66	524765	65	534797	372
395413	567	4034L	659	50216	157	513639	24	524765	79	534897	148
395463	592	4067	426	502473	30	513639	52	524765	107	535068	696
395481	533	4075L	141	502473	56	513639	76	524769	77	536373	300
395538	533	4095	116	502473	85	513641	24	525389	31	536382	300
395576	706	4233	500	502473	112	513641	76	525389	57	536577	20
395577	706	4233	701	502951	385	515060	473	525390	31	536577	26
395578	706	4421	142	502951	386	515218	470	525390	86	536577	72
395579	706	4421	143	503805	221	515291	32	525428	94	536577	78
395580	706	4478	301	503805	222	515466	310	525428	124	536577	101
395586	676	4478	302	503805	239	515467	310	525497	41	536577	106
395586	682	4478	428	503805	240	515468	310	525497	65	537229	37
395587	676	4580	588	503805	241	515470	310	525497	79	537229	93
395587	682	4580	682	504006	20	516951	336	525497	107	538038	34
395617	515	4580	683	504006	48	517646	477	525569	491	538038	60
395829	415	4581	301	504006	72	517689	363	527269	20	538038	89
395829	416	4581	302	504006	101	517689	364	527269	48	538038	90
395830	415	4581	428	504233	385	517706	363	527269	72	538038	115
								527269	101		
								528004	22		
								528004	50		

PART NO	PAGE	PART NO	PAGE	PART NO	PAGE	PART NO	PAGE	PART NO	PAGE	PART NO	PAGE
538039	34	543589	357	552818	277	564308	124	568689	107	571158	226
538039	60	543589	387	552818	282	564332	340	568788	453	571158	231
538039	89	543765	385	552819	278	564332	342	568788	454	571158	243
538039	90	543765	386	554602	31	564332E	340	568788	455	571158	712
538039	115	543767	385	554621	41	564332E	342	568858	297	571160	161
538131	23	543767	386	554621	65	564455	24	568872	700	571160	162
538131	51	543767	387	554880	301	564455	52	568872	701	571161	161
538131	75	543819	297	555711	478	564455	76	568883	163	571161	162
538131	104	546026	27	555711	479	564455	105	568895	163	571163	161
538132	23	546026	83	556239	216	564456	24	569006	392	571163	162
538132	51	546211	385	556633	227	564456	52	569006	393	571164	161
538132	75	546282	340	557523	27	564456	76	569291	311	571168	216
538132	104	546798	30	557523	28	564456	105	569522	285	571171	713
538133	23	546798	56	557523	54	564470	92	569701	163	571174	226
538133	51	546799	85	557523	83	564724	411	569714	312	571174	711
538133	75	546799	112	557523	84	564813	311	570351	477	571174	715
538133	104	546841	26	558168	79	564816	311	570753	487	571175	226
538134	23	546841	53	559625	383	564909	366	570822	473	571177	226
538134	51	546841	78	559636	699	565540	411	570822	474	571177	713
538134	75	546841	106	559882	499	565656	387	571043	230	571187	222
538134	104	548169	309	560553	702	565847	491	571043	243	571187	713
538890	398	549229	275	560553	703	566222	131	571059	216	571439	177
539706	264	549230	264	561195	262	566222	220	571062	221	571439	230
539707	263	549232	264	561196	262	566222	259	571063	222	571439	712
539718	263	549234	264	56140	156	566737	334	571064	222	571452	221
539720	263	549236	264	56140	157	566902	414	571065	222	571453	221
539722	263	549238	264	561699	224	567959	492	571066	221	571454	221
539724	263	549240	264	562019	694	568244	367	571067	221	571455	221
539745	263	549242	264	562481	394	568244	368	571090	221	571468	190
53K3039L	523	549244	264	562481	398	568333	23	571134	184	571468	193
541010	121	549246	264	562748	364	568333	51	571134	216	571468	207
541215	333	549248	264	562756	500	568333	75	571134	238	571468	210
541229	340	549250	264	562756	699	568335	80	571137	216	571468	228
542600	33	549252	264	562979	408	568431	156	571139	216	571468	252
542600	92	5494	163	563132	36	568431	157	571142	221	571468	255
542601	33	549473	267	563132	61	568550	30	571142	239	571536	193
542601	92	549473	268	563132	91	568550	56	571144	224	571536	201
542636	35	549473	273	563132	117	568550	85	571145	230	571536	229
542636	60	549610	446	563165	340	568550	112	571146	177	571536	246
542636	90	549611	446	563168	340	568664	94	571146	189	571607	713
542846	369	549611	447	563190	363	568680	274	571146	192	571608	712
542846	371	549702	41	563195	340	568680	339	571146	206	571609	712
542846	372	549702	65	563195	342	568680	489	571146	209	571619	712
542846	375	549840	694	564258	32	568686	41	571146	226	571623	713
542846	376	549909	24	564258	140	568686	65	571146	230	571627	713
542846	379	549909	76	564307	42	568687	41	571146	231	571633	713
542846	388	549911	134	564307	66	568687	65	571146	243	571665	193
543301	693	550732	164	564307	43	568688	79	571146	251	571665	194
543589	41	551508	483	564308	67	568688	107	571146	254	571665	210
543589	80	551595	475	564308	94	568689	79	571146	712	571665	211

PART NO	PAGE	PART NO	PAGE	PART NO	PAGE	PART NO	PAGE	PART NO	PAGE	PART NO	PAGE
571665	229	572166	401	575707	276	576843	219	591988	158	593983	231
571665	255	572166	402	575882	281	576973	309	592324	312	593991	230
571682	193	572166	403	576137	161	577458	339	592326	357	594018	221
571682	210	572166	404	576137	162	577458	387	592358	164	594019	221
571682	228	572166	405	576149	231	577548	356	592443	313	594020	221
571682	255	572167	400	576159	263	577548	357	592443	314	594021	221
571718	265	572167	401	576195	217	577548	358	592445	280	594022	221
571723	218	572167	402	576203	161	577548	359	592513	693	594023	221
571723	222	572167	403	576203	162	577549	356	592514	693	594024	221
571732	216	572167	404	576220	217	577643	164	592773	278	594029	228
571809	712	572167	405	576220	237	577703	281	593619	221	594087	215
571810	712	572168	400	576236	264	577846	132	593619	222	594091	161
571811	712	572168	401	576237	264	577898	297	593692	264	594134	215
571812	712	572168	402	576238	264	578023	349	593693	264	594176	161
571813	713	572168	403	576239	264	578293	378	593694	228	594244	224
571837	217	572168	404	576303	710	579085	483	593695	228	594290	186
571838	222	572168	405	576303	712	579409	702	593696	228	594290	225
571841	217	572312	407	576303	714	579409	703	593697	228	594291	222
571846	218	572389	386	576319	232	586440	140	593698	228	594292	221
571846	713	572535	365	576320	232	587405	42	593699	228	594320	217
571875	226	572535	366	576340	216	587405	43	593700	228	594337	226
571876	219	572839	356	576342	216	587405	66	593701	228	594338	228
571885	224	572839	357	576343	223	587405	67	593702	228	594346	227
571930	222	572839	369	576351	223	587517	42	593703	228	594389	224
571931	221	572839	371	576352	223	587684	369	593704	228	594493	264
571940	219	572839	385	576353	223	587684	371	593705	228	594594	339
571944	217	572839	387	576354	223	589026	474	593706	228	594594	351
571944	237	572994	349	576355	223	589202	474	593707	228	594594	352
571947	219	573038	451	576356	223	589254	339	593708	228	594594	398
571954	713	573246	474	576357	223	589284	473	593709	228	594594	419
571956	226	573256	339	576358	223	589285	473	593710	228	594637	422
571957	226	573289	444	576359	223	589452	487	593711	228	594637	717
571959	219	573289	490	576360	223	589598	703	593712	228	594637	718
571962	230	574469	35	576361	223	589783	470	593713	228	594753	343
571970	193	574469	60	576362	223	589806	274	593714	228	594753	385
571970	210	574469	90	576363	223	589877	475	593715	228	594753	386
571970	228	574654	94	576364	223	591227	237	593717	228	594753	387
571977	218	574654	124	576365	223	591231	158	593802	226	594946	288
571979	219	574658	32	576366	223	591279	275	593802	230	594946	290
571980	231	574855	459	576367	223	591290	217	593802	231	594946	293
571981	231	574855	461	576368	223	591320	230	593802	243	594946	296
571982	231	575014	491	576369	223	591345	226	593814	222	594947	288
571983	231	575047	477	576370	223	591394	216	593815	222	594947	290
571991	226	575548	314	576476	160	591394	238	593816	222	594947	293
572077	288	575579	277	576557	155	591519	242	593817	222	594947	296
572077	290	575615	280	576656	230	591562	232	593818	222	595119	220
572077	293	575616	280	576683	225	591603	219	593819	222	595199	297
572077	296	575628	280	576723	161	591891	225	593820	222	595478	219
572087	277	575651	220	576723	162	591900	225	593821	222	596490	43
572166	400			576779	231			593981	231	596490	67

PART NO	PAGE	PART NO	PAGE	PART NO	PAGE	PART NO	PAGE	PART NO	PAGE	PART NO	PAGE
597586	20	602201	141	603561	148	606553	292	608069	291	611212	302
597586	48	602212	131	603622	395	606561	292	608073	292	611213	301
597586	72	602236	150	603622	396	606563	291	608092	477	611213	302
597586	101	602289	79	603659	135	606564	291	608142	227	611213	428
597586	178	602289	107	603672	149	606566	291	608158	448	611215	301
598006	148	602289	138	603672	448	606567	292	608197	448	611215	302
598104	94	602388	141	603672	450	606661	139	608246	178	611215	428
599552	184	602411	134	603673	448	606666	266	608246	184	611323	160
599552	201	602505	457	603673	450	606688	308	608246	201	611324	160
599552	217	602512	140	603675	140	606731	161	608246	237	611351	360
599552	246	602545	132	603713	147	606733	161	608246	246	611379	301
599575	219	602582	144	603713	424	606754	234	608246	262	611409	131
599945	264	602587	134	603734	139	607163	271	608246	263	611440	301
600226	470	602609	133	603775	141	607165	272	608246	271	611440	302
600265	288	602634	339	603796	138	607166	272	608266	448	611440	428
600265	290	602672	449	603851	350	607167	272	608266	449	611514	136
600265	293	602673	449	603887	356	607168	272	608304	466	611786	149
600265	296	602910	136	603887	357	607169	272	608311	473	612064	335
600424	353	602912	136	603972	301	607173	271	608312	473	612320	395
600613	343	602913	136	603972	302	607177	272	608352	465	612326	142
601845	336	602953	448	605011	364	607178	272	608352	469	612326	143
602040	138	602953	449	605012	363	607179	272	608395	465	612435	339
602061	133	602953	450	605013	363	607180	272	608400	309	612505	333
602067	136	603031	138	605174	300	607181	271	610020	300	612505	334
602070	135	603127	140	605180	300	607182	271	610178	134	612689	151
602071	136	603143	131	605181	300	607183	271	610246	148	612710	135
602076	150	603184	140	605800	336	607185	271	610289	137	612898	131
602082	133	603224	148	605833	336	607187	272	610327	339	612980	135
602087	135	603224	149	605848	336	607188	272	610333	395	612989	134
602097	139	603237	395	606168	349	607189	272	610489	132	613087	144
602098	138	603277	148	606168	355	607190	272	610578	144	613244	463
602099	150	603301	134	606188	369	607191	272	610789	301	613402	360
602123	138	603330	360	606207	365	607197	272	610789	302	613514	333
602130	131	603376	360	606247	349	607357	271	610789	428	613514	334
602141	131	603378	139	606248	349	607567	295	610792	302	613540	427
602142	139	603428	144	606248	412	607747	466	610833	334	613601	354
602146	131	603431	369	606473	226	607754	466	610849	333	613602	146
602147	131	603431	371	606474	192	608000	292	611015	333	613620	463
602148	139	603431	372	606474	209	608000	295	611015	334	613671	134
602152	131	603431	375	606474	228	608004	473	611019	134	613718	360
602152	148	603431	376	606474	254	608004	474	611022	463	613805	349
602153	139	603431	379	606538	292	608064	292	611026	333	613805	355
602154	139	603431	388	606542	292	608065	291	611089	131	613857	448
602172	139	603441	148	606543	292	608065	294	611092	351	613857	449
602186	139	603446	448	606544	291	608066	291	611092	352	613857	450
602191	138	603446	449	606544	294	608066	294	611097	351	613910	397
602192	138	603446	450	606545	291	608067	291	611097	352	613915	343
602193	138	603521	136	606545	294	608067	294	611110	357	613915	397
602199	135	603535	134	606551	291	608068	291	611114	360	613916	397
602200	464	603554	138	606551	294	608068	294	611212	301	614037	136

LAND ROVER PARTS LTD

730

PART NO	PAGE	PART NO	PAGE	PART NO	PAGE	PART NO	PAGE	PART NO	PAGE	PART NO	PAGE
614088	138	7316	264	78248	623	79123	274	90508545	392	90575626	280
614089	138	73198	673	78248	637	79123	387	90508545	393	90575627	280
614188	137	77700	595	78248	638	79127	316	90511958	40	90575748	402
614202	136	77869	669	78248	669	79127	532	90511958	64	90575748	403
614443	151	77932	474	78248	673	79134	349	90511958	81	90575789	279
614538	396	77941	385	78248	682	79134	670	90512205	31	90575878	281
614555	333	77941	386	78248	683	79158	358	90512208	31	90575977	409
614555	334	78122	375	78248	708	79158	359	90513171	42	90576626	228
614585	132	78153	488	78248	709	79158	374	90513220	360	90576632	228
614617	312	78159	596	78257	594	79158	380	90513454	263	90576658	230
614617	355	78173	595	78321	590	79158	381	90516028	34	90577064	365
614670	147	78210	471	78348	470	79158	382	90516028	60	90577473	283
614718	427	78210	472	78384	720	79194	706	90516028	90	90577473	600
614743	302	78210	479	78393	512	79221	540	90517429	30	90577473	601
614866	353	78227	163	78401	578	79246	511	90517429	56	90577509	500
614866	354	78237	523	78402	578	79246	521	90517429	85	90577642	164
614891	333	78237	653	78417	488	79246	565	90517429	112	90577704	281
614891	334	78237	657	78593	140	79281	557	90517711	363	90600400	343
614891	338	78237	658	78704	349	79283	557	90518466	80	90600400	347
614891	353	78237	659	78782	141	79283	564	90518466	108	90602025	134
614891	354	78248	499	78832	577	79289	557	90519054	20	90602064	136
614892	353	78248	507	78832	579	79289	564	90519054	48	90602068	135
614939	463	78248	511	78832	582	79293	557	90519054	72	90602072	136
61K738	163	78248	515	78861	140	79293	564	90519054	101	90602202	141
61K738	311	78248	522	78862	132	810004	230	90519055	20	90602372	134
622324	219	78248	524	78862	140	850641	388	90519055	48	90606261	365
622324	233	78248	529	79048	521	850641	389	90519055	72	90606261	366
622324	244	78248	536	79051	512	8566L	23	90519055	101	90606262	365
622324	274	78248	543	79086	437	8566L	51	90519864	37	90606262	366
622388	230	78248	556	79086	591	8566L	75	90519864	93	90607170	272
622388	243	78248	557	79106	515	8566L	104	90555649	477	90608071	292
622538	222	78248	558	79106	516	8G7019L	310	90568054	149	90608178	465
624091	40	78248	559	79121	371	8G8600L	158	90571010	222	90608178	469
624091	64	78248	560	79121	372	8G8837L	164	90571030	230	90608545	271
624091	81	78248	561	79121	373	90217355	267	90571086	216	90610796	301
624091	109	78248	563	79121	375	90217355	273	90571086	237	90610796	302
625038	32	78248	564	79121	376	90217526	226	90571091	222	90610796	428
625038	140	78248	568	79121	379	90301332	606	90571104	169	90611014	333
6395L	34	78248	575	79121	380	90301332	609	90571104	217	90611014	334
6395L	60	78248	578	79122	358	90301332	612	90571104	218	90611112	360
6395L	89	78248	585	79122	359	90302262	595	90571104	237	90611439	301
6395L	90	78248	589	79122	371	90502209	24	90571105	216	90611504	150
6395L	115	78248	590	79122	372	90502209	52	90571106	216	90611812	138
6395L	160	78248	592	79122	373	90502209	76	90571451	221	90613049	425
6397	239	78248	599	79122	376	90502209	105	90575015	491	90613049	428
6860	274	78248	607	79122	379	90508035	618	90575511	402	90613442	464
6860L	394	78248	611	79122	380	90508035	619	90575511	403	90613913	397
72628	372	78248	618	79122	381	90508035	620	90575585	220	90614584	138
72628	374	78248	619	79122	382	90508545	390	90575585	259	90622240	228
72628	451	78248	620	79123	164	90508545	391	90575597	297	AA606044L	486

LAND ROVER PARTS LTD

731

PART NO	PAGE	PART NO	PAGE	PART NO	PAGE	PART NO	PAGE	PART NO	PAGE	PART NO	PAGE
AA608044	485	AB606021	436	AB608041L	416	AB614065L	502	ADU9081L	306	AEU1690	424
AAP810	413	AB606021L	32	AB608041L	475	AB614085	503	AEU1029	291	AEU1691	424
AAP811	413	AB606021L	89	AB608041L	516	ABU7142	300	AEU1034	446	AEU1694	423
AAP817	413	AB606021L	443	AB608041L	627	ABU7145	300	AEU1034	447	AEU1706	453
AAP876	414	AB606022L	470	AB608041L	645	AC606031L	538	AEU1044	312	AEU1706	454
AAP888	413	AB606031	533	AB608041L	646	AC606031L	549	AEU1045	312	AEU1706	455
AAP889	413	AB606031L	475	AB608041L	708	AC606041L	538	AEU1147	365	AEU1706	456
AAP890	414	AB606031L	534	AB608044L	480	AC606041L	549	AEU1192	424	AEU1706	457
AAU1053	397	AB606031L	539	AB608044L	512	AC606041L	578	AEU1198	434	AEU1706	458
AAU1700	315	AB606031L	547	AB608047	720	AC606041L	580	AEU1205	434	AEU1708	456
AAU1979	330	AB606031L	551	AB608051	437	AC606064	629	AEU1213	430	AEU1708	458
AAU1979	409	AB606031L	593	AB608051L	626	AC606081L	580	AEU1214	430	AEU1709	456
AAU1979	410	AB606031L	596	AB608054L	516	AC606104	627	AEU1248	292	AEU1709	458
AAU2304	193	AB606031L	632	AB608054L	628	AC608041L	412	AEU1248	295	AEU1710	453
AAU2304	194	AB606034	482	AB608061L	539	AC608065	437	AEU1355	470	AEU1710	454
AAU2304	210	AB606041L	473	AB608061L	551	ACU1161	573	AEU1356	292	AEU1710	455
AAU2304	211	AB606041L	476	AB608061L	645	ACU1762	573	AEU1357	292	AEU1710	456
AAU2304	229	AB606041L	562	AB608064L	634	ACU2063	573	AEU1358	291	AEU1710	457
AAU2304	255	AB606041L	602	AB608065	412	ACU3530	573	AEU1359	291	AEU1710	458
AAU2367	613	AB606041L	629	AB608101	720	ACU3530	574	AEU1422	448	AEU1725	456
AAU2825	271	AB606041L	632	AB608124	633	ACU3530	593	AEU1446	319	AEU1725	458
AAU2967	337	AB606041L	633	AB610031L	149	ACU3777	572	AEU1448	387	AEU1726	456
AAU3509	378	AB606041L	634	AB610031L	354	ACU3777	573	AEU1449	274	AEU1726	458
AAU3686	487	AB606041L	637	AB610031L	360	ACU5431	437	AEU1449	333	AEU1742	470
AAU3686	488	AB606041L	641	AB610041L	355	AD606041L	628	AEU1488	272	AEU1747	430
AAU5034	493	AB606041L	644	AB610041L	398	AD606044L	480	AEU1489	272	AEU1747	442
AAU5034	719	AB606041L	657	AB610041L	486	AD606044L	626	AEU1527	456	AEU1750	160
AAU6774	572	AB606044	627	AB610041L	657	AD606074L	494	AEU1527	458	AEU1775	423
AAU6774	573	AB606044	629	AB610041L	658	ADU1221L	535	AEU1532	453	AEU1776	423
AAU6774	574	AB606044L	480	AB610051L	515	ADU1221L	547	AEU1532	454	AEU1777	423
AAU6774	593	AB606051L	471	AB610051L	523	ADU1402L	148	AEU1532	455	AEU1778	423
AAU6919	572	AB606051L	472	AB610051L	532	ADU1784L	471	AEU1532	456	AEU1779	423
AAU6920	573	AB606051L	479	AB610051L	545	ADU1784L	472	AEU1532	457	AEU1780	423
AAU7219L	337	AB606054L	340	AB610054L	686	ADU2888L	318	AEU1532	458	AEU1782	423
AAU7604	336	AB606057	502	AB610054L	687	ADU3307L	539	AEU1613	466	AEU1784	423
AAU7899	336	AB606061L	34	AB610061L	653	ADU3307L	551	AEU1613	467	AEU1785	423
AAU7900	336	AB606061L	60	AB610061L	657	ADU3430	508	AEU1616	456	AEU1786	424
AAU7965	312	AB606061L	90	AB610061L	659	ADU3775	532	AEU1616	457	AEU1787	424
AAU8182	573	AB606061L	649	AB610081	653	ADU3775L	545	AEU1616	458	AEU1788	424
AAU8276	483	AB606064L	626	AB610081	657	ADU3775L	633	AEU1626	429	AEU1790	424
AAU8452	448	AB606081	654	AB610081L	538	ADU3905	478	AEU1626	440	AEU1791	424
AAU8452	449	AB606081L	659	AB610081L	550	ADU3905	485	AEU1627	429	AEU1792	424
AAU9036	512	AB606084	645	AB610081L	658	ADU4928L	456	AEU1627	440	AEU1814	453
AAU9902	363	AB606084	647	AB610081L	659	ADU4928L	458	AEU1628	440	AEU1814	457
AAU9902	364	AB608031	703	AB610104L	633	ADU5727L	538	AEU1649	466	AEU1848	336
AAU9903	363	AB608031L	490	AB610124L	626	ADU5727L	550	AEU1649	467	AEU1851	336
AAU9903	364	AB608031L	560	AB614061L	513	ADU6409L	471	AEU1652	474	AEU1880	309
AB600031	353	AB608031L	566	AB614061L	519	ADU6409L	472	AEU1684	446	AEU1891	312
AB604041L	645	AB608041L	398	AB614061L	521	ADU6418L	471	AEU1688	424	AEU1942	453
AB606021	435	AB608041L	415	AB614064	626	ADU6418L	472	AEU1689	424	AEU1942	454

LAND ROVER PARTS LTD

PART NO	PAGE	PART NO	PAGE	PART NO	PAGE	PART NO	PAGE	PART NO	PAGE	PART NO	PAGE
AEU1942	455	AEU2567	322	AEU2723	481	AEU4023	289	AFU1080	595	AFU1265	559
AEU1942	457	AEU2567	326	AEU2724	481	AEU4024	289	AFU1080	597	AFU1271	495
AEU2462	336	AEU2568	322	AEU2733	310	AEU4025	289	AFU1080	607	AFU1272	495
AEU2464L	453	AEU2568	326	AEU2734	310	AEU4026	289	AFU1080	610	AFU1298	680
AEU2464L	457	AEU2569	322	AEU2735	310	AEU4119	298	AFU1080	670	AFU1342L	339
AEU2496	309	AEU2569	326	AEU2736	310	AEU4146	467	AFU1085L	358	AFU1350	319
AEU2497	309	AEU2569	332	AEU2737	310	AEU4147	467	AFU1085L	359	AFU1350	503
AEU2498	309	AEU2570	332	AEU2738	310	AEU4148	467	AFU1090L	33	AFU1350	589
AEU2500	466	AEU2571	332	AEU2741	312	AEU4149	467	AFU1090L	35	AFU1350	680
AEU2501	465	AEU2572	322	AEU2760	362	AEU4150	467	AFU1090L	59	AFU1350	684
AEU2502	465	AEU2572	326	AEU2760	363	AEU4151	467	AFU1090L	60	AFU1386	499
AEU2505	453	AEU2573	332	AEU2761	288	AEU4858	331	AFU1090L	90	AFU1387	499
AEU2506	453	AEU2574	332	AEU2761	290	AF608081	668	AFU1090L	92	AFU1400	310
AEU2506	454	AEU2575	322	AEU2792	466	AFU1003	694	AFU1090L	116	AFU1497	605
AEU2507	453	AEU2575	326	AEU2792	467	AFU1004	694	AFU1090L	155	AFU1499	497
AEU2507	454	AEU2575	331	AEU2805	587	AFU1005	694	AFU1090L	487	AFU1841	573
AEU2507	455	AEU2577	322	AEU2806	587	AFU1008	387	AFU1090L	488	AFU1841	593
AEU2507	457	AEU2577	326	AEU3015	312	AFU1024	693	AFU1090L	489	AFU1848L	42
AEU2508	271	AEU2577	331	AEU3055	430	AFU1030	265	AFU1104	508	AFU1848L	67
AEU2515	271	AEU2578	321	AEU3055	440	AFU1031	308	AFU1172	605	AFU1848L	124
AEU2520	265	AEU2578	325	AEU3056	429	AFU1032	273	AFU1180	308	AFU1876	593
AEU2521	265	AEU2579	321	AEU3056	440	AFU1036	546	AFU1181	267	AFU1876	720
AEU2522	265	AEU2579	325	AEU3067	429	AFU1036	552	AFU1181	270	AFU1876L	107
AEU2536	271	AEU2579	332	AEU3068	429	AFU1069	513	AFU1203	505	AFU1882	73
AEU2537	308	AEU2580	321	AEU3076	453	AFU1069	525	AFU1217	316	AFU1882L	21
AEU2538	308	AEU2580	325	AEU3076	454	AFU1069	565	AFU1218	708	AFU1882L	49
AEU2539	308	AEU2580	331	AEU3076	455	AFU1069	680	AFU1218L	480	AFU1882L	102
AEU2557	324	AEU2581	321	AEU3076	456	AFU1070	672	AFU1218L	569	AFU1887L	102
AEU2557	327	AEU2581	325	AEU3076	457	AFU1071	605	AFU1234	265	AFU1887L	122
AEU2558	332	AEU2582	321	AEU3076	458	AFU1075	514	AFU1247	657	AFU1887L	123
AEU2560	322	AEU2582	325	AEU3077	336	AFU1075	570	AFU1248	626	AFU1890L	41
AEU2560	326	AEU2582	331	AEU3078	336	AFU1075	634	AFU1248	628	AFU1890L	65
AEU2560	332	AEU2583	321	AEU4000	437	AFU1077L	358	AFU1256	536	AFU1890L	80
AEU2561	322	AEU2583	325	AEU4001	437	AFU1077L	359	AFU1256	542	AFU1890L	108
AEU2561	326	AEU2583	331	AEU4002	432	AFU1077L	372	AFU1256	602	AFU1897	627
AEU2562	322	AEU2584	321	AEU4002	435	AFU1077L	373	AFU1256	605	AFU1900	644
AEU2562	326	AEU2584	325	AEU4002	436	AFU1077L	379	AFU1256	618	AFU1900	646
AEU2562	332	AEU2584	331	AEU4002	443	AFU1078	598	AFU1257	516	AFU1900	647
AEU2563	322	AEU2585	321	AEU4002	444	AFU1079	513	AFU1257	541	AFU1926	633
AEU2563	326	AEU2585	325	AEU4011	289	AFU1079	564	AFU1259	531	AFU1926	634
AEU2563	332	AEU2585	331	AEU4012	289	AFU1079	679	AFU1259	541	AFU2501	649
AEU2564	322	AEU2586	321	AEU4013	289	AFU1079	681	AFU1259	544	AFU2501	650
AEU2564	326	AEU2587	321	AEU4014	289	AFU1080	505	AFU1259	562	AFU2503	613
AEU2564	332	AEU2717	125	AEU4015	289	AFU1080	522	AFU1259	581	AFU2504	613
AEU2565	322	AEU2718	125	AEU4016	289	AFU1080	557	AFU1259	597	AFU2627	311
AEU2565	326	AEU2719L	125	AEU4017	289	AFU1080	565	AFU1261	605	AFU2636	480
AEU2565	331	AEU2720	125	AEU4018	289	AFU1080	566	AFU1262	546	AFU2636	517
AEU2566	322	AEU2721	481	AEU4019	289	AFU1080	579	AFU1262	552	AFU2636	633
AEU2566	326	AEU2722	481	AEU4020	289	AFU1080	581	AFU1262	598	AFU2636	634
AEU2566	331					AEU4021	289	AFU1080	582	AFU1263	667	AFU2637	534

LAND ROVER PARTS LTD

PART NO	PAGE	PART NO	PAGE	PART NO	PAGE	PART NO	PAGE	PART NO	PAGE	PART NO	PAGE
AFU2637	547	ARA1501L	388	BH106051L	120	BH108081L	95	BH108131L	401	BH108201L	459
AFU2641	633	ARA1501L	389	BH106051L	132	BH108081L	178	BH108141L	42	BH108201L	460
AFU2692	628	ARA1501L	390	BH106051L	181	BH108081L	400	BH108141L	43	BH108201L	461
AFU2778	400	ARA1501L	391	BH106051L	197	BH108081L	404	BH108141L	67	BH108201L	497
AFU2778	401	ARA1502L	388	BH106051L	256	BH108081L	405	BH108141L	576	BH108251L	285
AFU2779	400	ARA1502L	389	BH106061L	315	BH108081L	425	BH108151L	31	BH110071L	29
AFU2813	627	ARA1502L	390	BH106061L	316	BH108081L	459	BH108151L	34	BH110071L	55
AFU2813	629	ARA1502L	391	BH106061L	713	BH108081L	460	BH108151L	35	BH110071L	82
AFU2875	686	AS604044	587	BH106071	598	BH108081L	462	BH108151L	36	BH110071L	110
AFU2875	687	ATU1005L	515	BH106071	663	BH108081L	464	BH108151L	57	BH110071L	155
AFU2879	719	AUD2437L	395	BH106081L	559	BH108081L	623	BH108151L	60	BH110071L	184
AFU4162	607	AUD2437L	396	BH106091L	315	BH108081L	666	BH108151L	61	BH110071L	201
AFU4173	177	AUD4398	335	BH106111L	315	BH108091L	285	BH108151L	89	BH110071L	227
AFU4173	520	AUD4771L	335	BH106111L	590	BH108091L	316	BH108151L	90	BH110071L	246
AFU4214	297	AW606084	512	BH106131L	40	BH108091L	319	BH108151L	91	BH110071L	701
AH614011L	511	AW606124	437	BH106131L	64	BH108091L	402	BH108151L	95	BH110081L	184
AJ606011L	557	AZ610081	480	BH106131L	81	BH108091L	403	BH108151L	117	BH110081L	201
AJ606011L	566	B604151L	297	BH106131L	109	BH108091L	459	BH108151L	118	BH110081L	246
AJ606011L	627	BAU1689	244	BH106131L	471	BH108091L	460	BH108151L	119	BH110081L	696
AJ606041	480	BAU1825	453	BH106131L	472	BH108091L	461	BH108151L	120	BH110081L	700
AJ608021	532	BAU1825	454	BH106141L	368	BH108091L	462	BH108161L	36	BH110091L	156
AJ608021	545	BAU1825	455	BH106151L	40	BH108091L	464	BH108161L	61	BH110091L	157
AJ608031	480	BAU1825	457	BH106151L	64	BH108101L	34	BH108161L	91	BH110091L	184
AJ608041L	412	BAU1849L	650	BH106151L	81	BH108101L	35	BH108161L	117	BH110091L	201
AJU1136L	537	BAU2144	470	BH106151L	109	BH108101L	42	BH108161L	118	BH110091L	237
AJU1136L	548	BAU2193	453	BH108061L	27	BH108101L	60	BH108161L	119	BH110091L	246
AJU1136L	634	BAU2193	454	BH108061L	36	BH108101L	66	BH108161L	120	BH110091L	388
AK606011L	486	BAU2193	455	BH108061L	61	BH108101L	89	BH108161L	459	BH110091L	389
AK606011L	628	BAU2193	457	BH108061L	83	BH108101L	90	BH108161L	460	BH110091L	466
AK606021L	473	BAU2193L	457	BH108061L	91	BH108101L	169	BH108161L	461	BH110091L	467
AK606031	626	BAU2195	453	BH108061L	117	BH108101L	673	BH108161L	462	BH110091L	468
AK606031	627	BAU2195	454	BH108061L	118	BH108111L	36	BH108171L	36	BH110101L	237
AK606031	629	BAU2195	455	BH108061L	119	BH108111L	61	BH108171L	61	BH110101L	425
AK608141L	485	BAU2195	457	BH108061L	120	BH108111L	86	BH108171L	91	BH110121L	191
AK610021L	569	BAU2195L	457	BH108061L	158	BH108111L	91	BH108171L	117	BH110121L	208
AK612011L	502	BAU2325	95	BH108061L	164	BH108111L	113	BH108171L	118	BH110121L	227
AM604051L	511	BAU2326	95	BH108061L	177	BH108111L	115	BH108171L	119	BH110121L	237
AM605061	512	BAU4611	340	BH108061L	184	BH108111L	117	BH108171L	120	BH110121L	253
AR606031L	572	BAU4611L	341	BH108061L	187	BH108111L	181	BH108181L	187	BH110121L	297
AR606041L	557	BAU4865	289	BH108061L	201	BH108111L	187	BH108181L	204	BH110141L	501
AR606041L	566	BAU4870	289	BH108061L	204	BH108111L	197	BH108181L	249	BH110181	701
AR608021L	313	BAU4871	289	BH108061L	216	BH108111L	204	BH108181L	298	BH110181L	501
AR608021L	513	BD155888L	515	BH108061L	231	BH108111L	249	BH108181L	299	BH110181L	696
AR608031	286	BH106031	384	BH108061L	246	BH108111L	256	BH108181L	425	BH110201L	425
AR608031L	491	BH106051L	36	BH108061L	249	BH108121L	115	BH108181L	461	BH110201L	497
AR608041L	317	BH106051L	61	BH108061L	266	BH108121L	572	BH108201	212	BH110201L	700
AR608041L	318	BH106051L	91	BH108061L	364	BH108131L	35	BH108201L	35	BH110201L	701
AR608061	605	BH106051L	118	BH108061L	425	BH108131L	60	BH108201L	60	BH110221L	282
AR610051L	569	BH106051L	119	BH108071L	95	BH108131L	90	BH108201L	90	BH110221L	426
AR610051L	574	BH106051L	119	BH108071L	679	BH108131L	115	BH108201L	220	BH110221L	500

PART NO	PAGE	PART NO	PAGE	PART NO	PAGE	PART NO	PAGE	PART NO	PAGE	PART NO	PAGE
BH110241L	426	BH506201L	463	BX112201	296	CN100258	417	CRC1250	315	EAM9332	485
BH110241L	499	BH506441	151	C15644	479	CN100258	418	CRC1250	316	ERC1161	396
BH110241L	500	BH604081	575	C15644L	478	CN100258	419	CRC1250L	545	ERC1351	136
BH110251	615	BH604151L	297	C22257L	491	CN100258	421	CRC1487	315	ERC1353	448
BH110301L	615	BH604161L	667	C34950L	471	CN100258	422	CRC1487	316	ERC1353	449
BH110351	281	BH605101	675	C34950L	472	CN100304	419	CRC2015	285	ERC1353	450
BH110521	603	BH605101L	427	C36471L	313	CN100308	418	CRC2131	312	ERC1561	29
BH112091L	167	BH605111L	464	C37222L	453	CN100308	420	CRC2131	313	ERC1561	55
BH112101L	263	BH605121L	134	C37222L	454	CN100308	421	CRC2131	314	ERC1561	82
BH112101L	698	BH605121L	463	C37222L	455	CN100308	422	CRC2134	314	ERC1561	110
BH112121L	214	BH605131L	134	C37222L	457	CN100308L	352	CRC2135	313	ERC1637	139
BH112141L	236	BH605131L	463	C38637	483	CN100308L	361	CS600244	313	ERC2003	137
BH112141L	687	BH605201L	463	C393771L	487	CN100408	409	CS600244	314	ERC2042	338
BH112201L	698	BH605261L	459	C39377L	487	CN100408	410	CUD2399L	335	ERC210	138
BH112241	687	BH605261L	461	C39377L	488	CN100408L	36	CUD2785L	335	ERC211	138
BH114151	276	BH607161L	290	C435996L	323	CN100408L	61	CUD2788L	335	ERC2139	149
BH114161	276	BH607161L	293	C43640	492	CN100408L	91	CZA2259L	539	ERC2143	149
BH116101	701	BH607161L	296	C43640	719	CN100408L	117	CZA2259L	551	ERC2144	140
BH116121L	700	BH607381	288	C45099L	356	CN100408L	118	CZA2259L	633	ERC215	138
BH116141	699	BH608461	276	C45099L	490	CN100408L	119	CZA4705L	480	ERC2154	333
BH116161L	214	BH610281L	276	C457593	40	CN100408L	120	CZH3287	480	ERC2154	334
BH116201	701	BH610321L	279	C457593	81	CN100508	353	CZH3827L	483	ERC224	138
BH116261	699	BH612321	280	C457593	109	CN100508	354	CZK3164	503	ERC225	138
BH504101L	142	BHA4460	473	C457593	149	CN100508	385	CZK3164	626	ERC2254	41
BH504101L	143	BHA4705L	539	C457593L	64	CN100508	386	CZK3264L	538	ERC2254	65
BH504121L	301	BHA4705L	551	CA600404	347	CN100508	409	CZK3264L	539	ERC2254	108
BH504121L	302	BHA4790L	477	CA600424	350	CN100508	410	CZK3264L	550	ERC2297	148
BH504151L	142	BHM1079L	337	CA600424	354	CN100708L	374	CZK3264L	551	ERC2319	149
BH504151L	143	BHM7058L	470	CC600084L	369	CN100708L	380	CZK3438L	624	ERC2320	149
BH504151L	427	BHM7063L	161	CC600094L	369	CN100708L	381	CZK3438L	649	ERC2446	395
BH504161L	142	BHM7063L	162	CCN110L	264	CN100708L	382	CZK619	412	ERC2446	396
BH504161L	143	BLS108L	216	CCN260	222	CP105061	387	DRC1530	471	ERC256	148
BH505111L	339	BLS108L	221	CD31709B	595	CP105081	357	DRC1530	472	ERC2690	132
BH505111L	463	BLS108L	222	CJ600041L	471	CP105191	313	DRC1530	493	ERC2734	403
BH505121L	142	BLS108L	239	CJ600041L	472	CP106081	357	DRC1538	138	ERC2838	137
BH505121L	143	BLS108L	240	CJ600144L	149	CP106121	411	DRC1538	318	ERC2839	137
BH505201L	426	BLS108L	241	CJ600504L	345	CP108081L	359	DRC1666	515	ERC2866	32
BH505241L	141	BLS112L	175	CJ600504L	346	CR110301	717	DRC1697	551	ERC2869	33
BH505381L	142	BMK1714	486	CJ600504L	347	CR120061L	340	DRC1820	484	ERC2869	59
BH505381L	143	BMK1903	311	CJ600504L	348	CR120105L	175	DRC1820	487	ERC2920	138
BH505401L	142	BRC2623	594	CN100148L	32	CR120115L	329	DRC1820	490	ERC2973	132
BH505401L	143	BRC8089	488	CN100148L	58	CR120125L	192	DRC1820	492	ERC298	323
BH505441L	427	BT606101L	190	CN100208L	32	CR120171L	425	DRC1820	493	ERC298	330
BH506111L	426	BT606101L	207	CN100208L	58	CR120195L	298	DRC2479	136	ERC3101	151
BH506111L	463	BT606101L	252	CN100208L	306	CR120215L	182	DRC8398	484	ERC3163	395
BH506121L	150	BX11071L	266	CN100258	40	CR120215L	198	DZA1435L	551	ERC3179	140
BH506161L	150	BX110091L	280	CN100258	64	CR120215L	257	DZA5097L	631	ERC3256	446
BH506161L	214	BX110111L	280	CN100258	81	CR120335L	175	EAC32151	370	ERC3256	447
BH506165	163	BX112201	288	CN100258	109	CRC1226	148	EAM5549L	471	ERC3345	458
BH506165	164	BX112201	293	CN100258	343			EAM5549L	472	ERC3458	152

PART NO	PAGE	PART NO	PAGE	PART NO	PAGE	PART NO	PAGE	PART NO	PAGE	PART NO	PAGE
ERC3489	149	ERC4293	353	ERC5127	23	ERC5600	119	ERC5923	717	ERC6547	464
ERC3493	148	ERC4293	354	ERC5127	51	ERC5600	120	ERC5923	718	ERC6551	155
ERC3500	718	ERC4294	353	ERC5128	23	ERC5654	36	ERC5925	151	ERC6551	156
ERC3561	148	ERC4294	354	ERC5128	51	ERC5654	61	ERC5958	355	ERC6551	157
ERC3562	149	ERC4480	340	ERC5139	459	ERC5654	91	ERC6047	94	ERC6552	137
ERC3563	149	ERC4480	342	ERC5139	460	ERC5654	117	ERC6047	124	ERC6630	75
ERC3588	361	ERC4536	448	ERC5139	461	ERC5654	118	ERC6071	425	ERC6683	459
ERC3600	75	ERC4558	132	ERC5139	462	ERC5654	119	ERC6072	424	ERC6683	462
ERC3690	151	ERC4591	353	ERC5145	298	ERC5654	120	ERC614	140	ERC6691	42
ERC3690	152	ERC4591	354	ERC5146	298	ERC5654	140	ERC6200	32	ERC6720	718
ERC3699	151	ERC4644	20	ERC5151	425	ERC5655	36	ERC6200	58	ERC6722	718
ERC3724	718	ERC4644	48	ERC5152	425	ERC5655	61	ERC6329	334	ERC6723	718
ERC3729	148	ERC4644	72	ERC5155	425	ERC5655	91	ERC6330	334	ERC675	146
ERC3788	365	ERC4644	101	ERC5247	350	ERC5655	117	ERC6337	31	ERC675	147
ERC3884	353	ERC4650	23	ERC5247	351	ERC5655	118	ERC6337	57	ERC676	138
ERC3884	354	ERC4650	51	ERC5247	352	ERC5655	119	ERC6337	86	ERC6761	341
ERC3889	354	ERC4650	75	ERC5293	155	ERC5655	120	ERC6337	113	ERC6761E	341
ERC3890	353	ERC4650	104	ERC5314	40	ERC5681	340	ERC6341	31	ERC6821	41
ERC3890	354	ERC4658	155	ERC5314	64	ERC5705	143	ERC6341	57	ERC6821	65
ERC3891	353	ERC4658	156	ERC5314	81	ERC5707	145	ERC6341	86	ERC6821	80
ERC3891	354	ERC4658	157	ERC5349	23	ERC5708	36	ERC6341	113	ERC6821	108
ERC3892	349	ERC4670	360	ERC5349	51	ERC5708	61	ERC6362	334	ERC6859	75
ERC3893	349	ERC4672	23	ERC5361	34	ERC5708	91	ERC6363	334	ERC6859	104
ERC3896	349	ERC4672	75	ERC5361	60	ERC5708	118	ERC6364	333	ERC6860	75
ERC3897	349	ERC4672	104	ERC5386	425	ERC5708	120	ERC6365	333	ERC6860	104
ERC3899	350	ERC4820	148	ERC5387	425	ERC5708	145	ERC6380	41	ERC6861	75
ERC3899	353	ERC4877	134	ERC5400	350	ERC5709	36	ERC6380	65	ERC6861	104
ERC3915	351	ERC4878	134	ERC5400	353	ERC5709	61	ERC6399	353	ERC6869	34
ERC3915	352	ERC4879	134	ERC5400	354	ERC5709	91	ERC6408	155	ERC6869	60
ERC3930	360	ERC4880	134	ERC5453	350	ERC5709	118	ERC6432	155	ERC6878	351
ERC3931	360	ERC4949	139	ERC5462	134	ERC5709	120	ERC6432	156	ERC6878	352
ERC3946	349	ERC4989	151	ERC5475	29	ERC5709	145	ERC6432	157	ERC6878	361
ERC3954	349	ERC4995	20	ERC5475	55	ERC573	139	ERC6437	132	ERC6886	120
ERC3955	349	ERC4995	48	ERC5475	82	ERC5745	448	ERC6478	40	ERC6890	718
ERC3956	350	ERC4995	72	ERC5512	140	ERC5749	137	ERC6478	64	ERC6934	131
ERC3956	351	ERC4995	101	ERC5545	36	ERC5756	717	ERC6478	81	ERC6939	94
ERC3956	352	ERC4996	20	ERC5545	61	ERC5757	717	ERC6478	109	ERC6939	124
ERC3956	354	ERC4996	48	ERC5545	91	ERC5761	131	ERC6479	35	ERC6974	298
ERC3964	418	ERC4996	72	ERC5545	117	ERC5786	152	ERC6479	60	ERC6975	298
ERC3964	419	ERC4996	101	ERC5545	119	ERC5870	333	ERC6479	116	ERC6976	298
ERC3964	421	ERC5014	23	ERC5550	355	ERC5871	333	ERC6480	423	ERC6977	298
ERC3964	422	ERC5014	75	ERC5578	36	ERC5875	152	ERC6480	424	ERC6995	334
ERC3990	150	ERC5052	350	ERC5578	61	ERC5913	38	ERC6504	118	ERC6996	328
ERC4074	353	ERC5052	353	ERC5578	117	ERC5913	39	ERC6504	119	ERC6996	334
ERC416	134	ERC5052	354	ERC5578	119	ERC5913	62	ERC6517	95	ERC6997	334
ERC417	134	ERC5069	151	ERC5600	36	ERC5913	63	ERC6518	95	ERC7082	425
ERC4176	355	ERC5086	21	ERC5600	61	ERC5913	122	ERC6520	95	ERC7085	328
ERC4193	338	ERC5086	49	ERC5600	91	ERC5913	123	ERC6538	464	ERC7089	23
ERC4203	361	ERC5086	73	ERC5600	117	ERC5923	39	ERC6540	145	ERC7089	51
ERC4204	361	ERC5086	102	ERC5600	118	ERC5923	63	ERC6545	426	ERC7109	334
						ERC5923	123				

LAND ROVER PARTS LTD

PART NO	PAGE	PART NO	PAGE	PART NO	PAGE	PART NO	PAGE	PART NO	PAGE	PART NO	PAGE
ERC7110	334	ERC7756	717	ERC8460	66	ERC8964	34	ERC9071	66	ERC9468	35
ERC7131	448	ERC7757	717	ERC8505	349	ERC8964	35	ERC9073	33	ERC9468	60
ERC7144	353	ERC7763	111	ERC8520	446	ERC8964	60	ERC9073	92	ERC9468	90
ERC7144	354	ERC7766	341	ERC8536	408	ERC8964	90	ERC9073	121	ERC9476N	98
ERC7150	30	ERC7768	111	ERC8545	132	ERC8964	462	ERC9102	31	ERC9480	33
ERC7151	30	ERC7773	717	ERC8554	40	ERC8965	34	ERC9102	57	ERC9480	59
ERC7295	116	ERC7787	136	ERC8554	64	ERC8965	35	ERC9103	31	ERC9480	92
ERC7295	155	ERC7865	138	ERC8554	81	ERC8965	89	ERC9103	57	ERC9480	121
ERC7295	156	ERC7879	354	ERC8626	396	ERC8973	41	ERC9106	31	ERC9499	37
ERC7295	157	ERC7881	354	ERC8631	324	ERC8973	65	ERC9106	57	ERC9499	93
ERC7312	36	ERC7882	354	ERC8631	327	ERC8975	27	ERC9107	31	ERC9499	717
ERC7312	61	ERC7896	151	ERC8631	330	ERC8975	83	ERC9107	57	ERC9501	107
ERC7312	91	ERC7897	151	ERC8631	343	ERC8976	25	ERC9137	86	ERC9519	34
ERC7312	117	ERC7922	324	ERC8639	149	ERC8976	52	ERC9137	113	ERC9519	60
ERC7312	118	ERC7922	327	ERC8645	66	ERC8976	105	ERC9138	31	ERC9519	89
ERC7312	119	ERC7922	330	ERC86451	42	ERC8977	41	ERC9138	57	ERC9522	369
ERC7312	120	ERC7922	343	ERC865	428	ERC8977	80	ERC9199	116	ERC9525	369
ERC7313	36	ERC7929	137	ERC8663	79	ERC8980	26	ERC9201	116	ERC9526	369
ERC7313	61	ERC7940	25	ERC8663	107	ERC8980	53	ERC9213	339	ERC9528	34
ERC7313	91	ERC7940	52	ERC8712	43	ERC8980	78	ERC9220	32	ERC9528	60
ERC7321	151	ERC7940	76	ERC8712	67	ERC8980	106	ERC9220	58	ERC9528	90
ERC7513	340	ERC7940	105	ERC8722	67	ERC9006	457	ERC9220	97	ERC9504	367
ERC7329E	340	ERC7951	40	ERC8722	465	ERC8982	95	ERC9220	114	ERC9631	79
ERC7331	91	ERC7951	64	ERC8751	22	ERC8986	456	ERC9240	156	ERC9631	107
ERC7338	95	ERC7951	81	ERC8751	50	ERC8987	456	ERC9240	157	ERC9639	95
ERC7343	324	ERC7951	109	ERC8751	74	ERC9000	51	ERC9278	31	ERC9669	25
ERC7343	327	ERC7974	462	ERC8751	103	ERC9000	104	ERC9278	57	ERC9669	52
ERC7489	36	ERC7987	34	ERC8757	109	ERC9031	32	ERC9294	328	ERC9669	76
ERC7489	61	ERC7987	60	ERC8758	40	ERC9031	58	ERC9336	369	ERC9669	105
ERC7489	91	ERC7987	89	ERC8758	64	ERC9032	32	ERC9359	79	ERC9688	124
ERC7489	117	ERC7987	141	ERC8758	109	ERC9032	58	ERC9398	352	ERC9693	329
ERC7494	426	ERC8049	32	ERC8847	110	ERC9033	32	ERC9404	35	ERC9704	329
ERC7510	40	ERC8049	58	ERC8849	110	ERC9033	58	ERC9404	60	ERC9706	24
ERC7510	64	ERC8049	87	ERC8851	458	ERC9035	361	ERC9404	90	ERC9706	52
ERC7510	81	ERC8049	114	ERC8852	147	ERC9037	353	ERC9404	102	ERC9706	76
ERC7510	109	ERC8051	87	ERC8861	111	ERC9039	361	ERC9404	116	ERC9706	105
ERC7530	25	ERC8119	328	ERC8864	102	ERC9054	31	ERC9404	155	ERC9707	24
ERC7530	52	ERC8124	42	ERC8873	355	ERC9054	57	ERC9404	156	ERC9707	52
ERC7530	76	ERC8124	66	ERC8874	355	ERC9054	86	ERC9404	157	ERC9707	76
ERC7530	105	ERC8164	144	ERC8876	355	ERC9054	113	ERC9410	21	ERC9707	105
ERC7548	464	ERC8172	90	ERC8877	355	ERC9055	86	ERC9410	49	ERC9708	329
ERC758	428	ERC8408	25	ERC8890	61	ERC9055	113	ERC9410	73	ERC9713	321
ERC7611	151	ERC8408	52	ERC8906	339	ERC9056	86	ERC9410	102	ERC9727	92
ERC7629	361	ERC8408	76	ERC8907	339	ERC9056	113	ERC9432	80	ERC9728	87
ERC7630	361	ERC8408	105	ERC8938	36	ERC9059	86	ERC9432	108	ERC9728	114
ERC7631	361	ERC8410	321	ERC8938	61	ERC9059	113	ERC9448	41	ERC9738	85
ERC7642	64	ERC8447	298	ERC8938	91	ERC9060	86	ERC9448	65	ERC9738	112
ERC7673	340	ERC8450	80	ERC8964	34	ERC9060	113	ERC9448	80	ERC9765	104
ERC7744	395	ERC8450	108			ERC9069	42	ERC9448	108	ERC9808	340
ERC7755	717	ERC8460	42			ERC9069	66	ERC9467	35	ERC9819	116
						ERC9071	42				

LAND ROVER PARTS LTD

PART NO	PAGE	PART NO	PAGE	PART NO	PAGE	PART NO	PAGE	PART NO	PAGE	PART NO	PAGE
ERC9859	340	ETC4141	29	ETC4499	27	ETC4944	35	ETC5276	62	ETC5646	24
ERC9871	340	ETC4141	55	ETC4499	83	ETC4959	323	ETC5276	63	ETC5646	52
ERC9884	38	ETC4141	82	ETC4529	101	ETC4959	330	ETC5276	93	ETC5646	76
ERC9884	62	ETC4153	298	ETC4616	125	ETC4969	75	ETC5276	122	ETC5672	115
ERC9884	122	ETC4154	115	ETC4630	116	ETC4989	408	ETC5276	123	ETC5675	115
ERC9894	321	ETC4156	342	ETC4639	353	ETC4993	408	ETC5297	32	ETC5689	300
ERC9896	324	ETC4197	425	ETC4643	107	ETC4994	34	ETC5297	58	ETC5717	341
ERC9896	327	ETC4217	109	ETC4649	107	ETC4994	60	ETC5297	87	ETC5739	85
ERR244	377	ETC4218	116	ETC4670	110	ETC4994	89	ETC5297	114	ETC5739	112
ETC4006	397	ETC4218	425	ETC4677	343	ETC4995	35	ETC5305	325	ETC5780	156
ETC4014	110	ETC4246	30	ETC4678	343	ETC4995	60	ETC5306	325	ETC5780	157
ETC4020	340	ETC4246	56	ETC4686	343	ETC4995	90	ETC5312	94	ETC5783	299
ETC4021	38	ETC4246	85	ETC4697	102	ETC4996	116	ETC5312	124	ETC5792	299
ETC4021	39	ETC4246	112	ETC4706	105	ETC4999	369	ETC5330	66	ETC5815	299
ETC4021	62	ETC4266	95	ETC4709	41	ETC5021	369	ETC5331	124	ETC5835	447
ETC4021	63	ETC4267	95	ETC4709	65	ETC5027	369	ETC5337	401	ETC5866	30
ETC4021	122	ETC4272	298	ETC4709	79	ETC5027	370	ETC5340	381	ETC5866	56
ETC4021	123	ETC4276	136	ETC4709	107	ETC5040	43	ETC5340	382	ETC5900N	46
ETC4022	39	ETC4291	342	ETC4715	449	ETC5040	67	ETC5347	38	ETC5918	352
ETC4022	63	ETC4292	342	ETC4717	449	ETC5057	30	ETC5347	62	ETC5918	361
ETC4022	123	ETC4293	342	ETC4728	396	ETC5057	56	ETC5347	122	ETC5944	299
ETC4033	122	ETC4294	342	ETC4751	41	ETC5057	85	ETC5348	39	ETC5955	32
ETC4033	123	ETC4301	79	ETC4751	65	ETC5057	112	ETC5348	63	ETC5955	58
ETC4034	122	ETC4308	342	ETC4751	79	ETC5064	115	ETC5348	123	ETC5958	40
ETC4034	123	ETC4330	134	ETC4751	107	ETC5065	115	ETC5354	449	ETC5958	64
ETC4058	116	ETC4335	340	ETC4752	341	ETC5090	449	ETC5369	23	ETC5958	109
ETC4063	116	ETC4338	340	ETC4755	341	ETC5147	353	ETC5369	51	ETC5959	50
ETC4066	30	ETC4341	340	ETC4761	40	ETC5147	354	ETC5369	75	ETC5965	40
ETC4067	30	ETC4354	134	ETC4761	64	ETC5155	22	ETC5369	104	ETC5965	64
ETC4067	56	ETC4357	459	ETC4763	40	ETC5155	50	ETC5369	155	ETC5965	109
ETC4068	30	ETC4357	460	ETC4763	64	ETC5155	74	ETC5376	355	ETC5967	40
ETC4068	56	ETC4357	461	ETC4763	81	ETC5155	103	ETC5377	355	ETC5967	64
ETC4068	85	ETC4357	462	ETC4763	149	ETC5156	74	ETC5378	355	ETC5967	109
ETC4068	112	ETC4369	134	ETC4765	149	ETC5157	22	ETC5379	355	ETC5989	352
ETC4069	30	ETC4371	424	ETC4785	36	ETC5158	103	ETC5397	355	ETC5989	361
ETC4069	56	ETC4390	104	ETC4785	91	ETC5172	55	ETC5398	355	ETC5990	352
ETC4069	85	ETC4417	341	ETC4785	118	ETC5181	343	ETC5412	41	ETC5990	361
ETC4069	112	ETC4420	116	ETC4785	120	ETC5182	343	ETC5412	65	ETC5994	50
ETC4070	341	ETC4421	115	ETC4799	33	ETC5183	343	ETC5551	29	ETC6081	34
ETC4076	110	ETC4422	115	ETC4799	59	ETC5187	34	ETC5551	82	ETC6081	60
ETC4077	104	ETC4440	341	ETC4873	116	ETC5187	60	ETC5577	26	ETC6082	34
ETC4098	369	ETC4460	31	ETC4880	24	ETC5190	28	ETC5577	53	ETC6082	60
ETC4105	104	ETC4460	57	ETC4880	52	ETC5190	54	ETC5577	78	ETC6137	25
ETC4113	80	ETC4460	86	ETC4880	76	ETC5190	84	ETC5577	106	ETC6137	52
ETC4122	116	ETC4460	113	ETC4880	105	ETC5191	28	ETC5588	87	ETC6137	77
ETC4124	116	ETC4464	24	ETC4882	425	ETC5191	54	ETC5588	114	ETC6137	105
ETC4133	465	ETC4464	76	ETC4922	48	ETC5191	84	ETC5592	102	ETC6138	25
ETC4140	29	ETC4466	447	ETC4925	369	ETC5276	37	ETC5594	140	ETC6138	52
ETC4140	55	ETC4498	65	ETC4928	325	ETC5276	38	ETC5603	323	ETC6138	77
ETC4140	82	ETC4498	108	ETC4929	325	ETC5276	39	ETC5605	323	ETC6138	105

LAND ROVER PARTS LTD

PART NO	PAGE	PART NO	PAGE	PART NO	PAGE	PART NO	PAGE	PART NO	PAGE	PART NO	PAGE
ETC6139	25	ETC6634	151	ETC7553	145	FRC2241	226	FRC2479	240	FRC3132	273
ETC6139	52	ETC6675	341	ETC7554	36	FRC2256	226	FRC2481	162	FRC3133N	213
ETC6139	77	ETC6835	103	ETC7554	91	FRC2257	219	FRC2481	243	FRC3133R	213
ETC6139	105	ETC6849	137	ETC7554	118	FRC2258	226	FRC2482	184	FRC3136	273
ETC6142	25	ETC6850	137	ETC7554	120	FRC2273	233	FRC2482	201	FRC3146	244
ETC6142	52	ETC6901	378	ETC7708	48	FRC2274	233	FRC2482	237	FRC3147	273
ETC6142	77	ETC6902	378	ETC7708	101	FRC2275	233	FRC2482	246	FRC3162	193
ETC6142	105	ETC6903	378	ETC7714	130	FRC2301	239	FRC2487	244	FRC3162	210
ETC6155	370	ETC6912	352	ETC7788	80	FRC2301	240	FRC2488	239	FRC3162	229
ETC6156	370	ETC6924	114	ETC7788	108	FRC2309	237	FRC2488	240	FRC3162	255
ETC6243	370	ETC6929	66	ETC7867	26	FRC2310	267	FRC2528	162	FRC3166	237
ETC6249	352	ETC6976	450	ETC7867	53	FRC2317	186	FRC2542	237	FRC3196	186
ETC6278	41	ETC7012	352	ETC7867	78	FRC2334	239	FRC2554	239	FRC3205	267
ETC6278	65	ETC7054	24	ETC7867	106	FRC2334	240	FRC2555	239	FRC3234	310
ETC6290	135	ETC7054	52	ETC7915	148	FRC2349	265	FRC2556	239	FRC3282	243
ETC6350	331	ETC7054	76	ETC7934	23	FRC2361	238	FRC2577	243	FRC3286	193
ETC6394	155	ETC7054	105	ETC7934	51	FRC2365	169	FRC2578	242	FRC3286	210
ETC6438	87	ETC7061	396	ETC7934	75	FRC2365	179	FRC2583	244	FRC3286	229
ETC6438	114	ETC7122	335	ETC7934	104	FRC2365	185	FRC2587	244	FRC3286	255
ETC6439	32	ETC7123	335	ETC8445	128	FRC2365	194	FRC2612	244	FRC3310	193
ETC6439	58	ETC7127	335	ETC8620	107	FRC2365	202	FRC2622	244	FRC3310	210
ETC6471	138	ETC7128	29	ETC8633	139	FRC2365	211	FRC2623	244	FRC3310	229
ETC6474	361	ETC7128	55	ETC8658	139	FRC2365	237	FRC2626	237	FRC3310	255
ETC6484	448	ETC7128	82	ETC8829	51	FRC2365	247	FRC2626	244	FRC3319	242
ETC6484	449	ETC7128	110	ETC8829	104	FRC2368	243	FRC2644	265	FRC3326	158
ETC6484	450	ETC7135	41	ETC9077	298	FRC2370	237	FRC2648	244	FRC3327	158
ETC6496	300	ETC7135	65	ETC9077	299	FRC2370	243	FRC2671	155	FRC3355	219
ETC6510	41	ETC7135	80	FRC1032	242	FRC2381	243	FRC2718	231	FRC3416	158
ETC6510	65	ETC7135	108	FRC1034	242	FRC2390	243	FRC2719	231	FRC3417	158
ETC6510	80	ETC7188	351	FRC1035	242	FRC2402	161	FRC2858	214	FRC3470	711
ETC6510	108	ETC7188	352	FRC1185	221	FRC2402	162	FRC2859	215	FRC3470	713
ETC6531	102	ETC7189	351	FRC1193	263	FRC2445	239	FRC2883	266	FRC3470	715
ETC6532	102	ETC7189	352	FRC1195	263	FRC2446	239	FRC2884	266	FRC3477	710
ETC6538	151	ETC7193	351	FRC1197	263	FRC2447	239	FRC2885	266	FRC3477	714
ETC6549	352	ETC7195	352	FRC1199	263	FRC2448	239	FRC2886	266	FRC3481	243
ETC6549	361	ETC7199	351	FRC1201	263	FRC2449	239	FRC2889	265	FRC3500	225
ETC6550	352	ETC7199	352	FRC1203	263	FRC2454	273	FRC2894	266	FRC3502	310
ETC6550	361	ETC7201	351	FRC1336	222	FRC2455	273	FRC2897	266	FRC3507	225
ETC6579	352	ETC7201	352	FRC1337	221	FRC2457	241	FRC2906	266	FRC3508	219
ETC6581	352	ETC7203	30	FRC1339	221	FRC2464	190	FRC2916	266	FRC3509	228
ETC6586	450	ETC7203	56	FRC1343	221	FRC2464	193	FRC2933	264	FRC3511	266
ETC6589	128	ETC7203	85	FRC1344	222	FRC2464	194	FRC2963	225	FRC3515	218
ETC6599	38	ETC7203	112	FRC167	204	FRC2464	207	FRC2975	162	FRC3517	218
ETC6599	39	ETC7216	339	FRC167	219	FRC2464	210	FRC2980	275	FRC3517	222
ETC6599	62	ETC7336	156	FRC167	249	FRC2464	211	FRC3072	238	FRC3543	712
ETC6599	63	ETC7336	157	FRC168	187	FRC2464	252	FRC3073	237	FRC3544	713
ETC6599	122	ETC7345	141	FRC168	219	FRC2464	255	FRC3099	267	FRC3553	713
ETC6599	123	ETC7385	141	FRC1743	224	FRC2465	237	FRC3112	242	FRC3570	231
ETC6599	136	ETC7390	463	FRC1778	217	FRC2468	237	FRC3117	243	FRC3571	231
ETC6630	343	ETC7405	125	FRC2240	225	FRC2470	242	FRC3118	243	FRC3602	193

LAND ROVER PARTS LTD

PART NO	PAGE	PART NO	PAGE	PART NO	PAGE	PART NO	PAGE	PART NO	PAGE	PART NO	PAGE
FRC3602	210	FRC4339	170	FRC4572	230	FRC5235	173	FRC5409	194	FRC5458	209
FRC3602	255	FRC4341	170	FRC4586	263	FRC5243	172	FRC5409	201	FRC5458	254
FRC3642	223	FRC4343	170	FRC4714	239	FRC5244	172	FRC5409	211	FRC5459	192
FRC3643	223	FRC4345	170	FRC4718	274	FRC5245	172	FRC5409	246	FRC5460	192
FRC3644	223	FRC4347	170	FRC4719	274	FRC5246	172	FRC5413	184	FRC5461	192
FRC3645	223	FRC4349	170	FRC4754	232	FRC5247	172	FRC5413	194	FRC5465	192
FRC3646	223	FRC4351	170	FRC4755	232	FRC5253	172	FRC5413	201	FRC5468	189
FRC3647	223	FRC4353	170	FRC4799	275	FRC5255	158	FRC5413	211	FRC5468	205
FRC3648	223	FRC4355	170	FRC4803	162	FRC5279	172	FRC5413	246	FRC5468	250
FRC3649	223	FRC4357	170	FRC4808	26	FRC5280	172	FRC5415	184	FRC5469	189
FRC3650	223	FRC4359	170	FRC4808	53	FRC5284	173	FRC5415	201	FRC5469	205
FRC3651	223	FRC4361	170	FRC4808	78	FRC5286	173	FRC5415	246	FRC5469	250
FRC3652	223	FRC4363	170	FRC4808	106	FRC5288	173	FRC5416	184	FRC5473	189
FRC3653	223	FRC4365	170	FRC4808	184	FRC5290	173	FRC5416	194	FRC5473	194
FRC3654	223	FRC4367	170	FRC4808	194	FRC5292	173	FRC5416	201	FRC5473	206
FRC3655	223	FRC4369	170	FRC4808	201	FRC5294	173	FRC5416	211	FRC5473	211
FRC3656	223	FRC4377	267	FRC4808	211	FRC5296	173	FRC5416	246	FRC5473	251
FRC3657	223	FRC4377	273	FRC4808	217	FRC5298	173	FRC5419	184	FRC5478	181
FRC3658	223	FRC4434	175	FRC4808	246	FRC5300	173	FRC5419	194	FRC5478	197
FRC3659	223	FRC4435	175	FRC4810	169	FRC5302	173	FRC5419	211	FRC5478	256
FRC3660	223	FRC4449	169	FRC4810	179	FRC5305	171	FRC5420	186	FRC5479	182
FRC3725	266	FRC4489	178	FRC4810	217	FRC5306	237	FRC5421	192	FRC5479	194
FRC3731	237	FRC4489	179	FRC4810	218	FRC5317	241	FRC5428	185	FRC5479	198
FRC3732	242	FRC4490	177	FRC4810	237	FRC5318	230	FRC5428	202	FRC5479	211
FRC3795	242	FRC4490	179	FRC4835	217	FRC5370	219	FRC5428	247	FRC5479	257
FRC3806	242	FRC4493	169	FRC4835	219	FRC5375	710	FRC5435	192	FRC5480	182
FRC3890	265	FRC4494	169	FRC4838	266	FRC5376	710	FRC5436	192	FRC5480	198
FRC3891	265	FRC4494	241	FRC4839	266	FRC5376	714	FRC5438	193	FRC5480	257
FRC3896	240	FRC4499	182	FRC4840	266	FRC5378	711	FRC5438	210	FRC5482	181
FRC3897	240	FRC4499	183	FRC4841	266	FRC5378	715	FRC5438	255	FRC5483	181
FRC3898	239	FRC4499	198	FRC4845	171	FRC5379	710	FRC5439	190	FRC5486	181
FRC3898	240	FRC4499	199	FRC4856	170	FRC5379	714	FRC5439	207	FRC5486	194
FRC3987	242	FRC4499	200	FRC4873	170	FRC5380	710	FRC5439	252	FRC5486	197
FRC3988	267	FRC4499	257	FRC4873	179	FRC5380	714	FRC5440	188	FRC5486	211
FRC3988	268	FRC4499	258	FRC4875	238	FRC5381	710	FRC5440	205	FRC5486	256
FRC3988	273	FRC4501	169	FRC4882	176	FRC5381	714	FRC5440	250	FRC5494	186
FRC4062	244	FRC4501	179	FRC4890	175	FRC5383	711	FRC5442	190	FRC5498	188
FRC4142	265	FRC4505	183	FRC4905	176	FRC5383	715	FRC5442	207	FRC5500	188
FRC4206	265	FRC4505	199	FRC4940	175	FRC5385	711	FRC5442	252	FRC5562	189
FRC4282	169	FRC4505	258	FRC4946	174	FRC5385	715	FRC5446	193	FRC5562	192
FRC4307	262	FRC4509	182	FRC4947	174	FRC5386	711	FRC5446	210	FRC5562	206
FRC4319	267	FRC4509	194	FRC4951	175	FRC5386	715	FRC5446	255	FRC5562	209
FRC4320	267	FRC4509	198	FRC5076	182	FRC5387	711	FRC5449	188	FRC5562	251
FRC4321	172	FRC4509	211	FRC5076	198	FRC5387	715	FRC5449	205	FRC5562	254
FRC4327	170	FRC4509	257	FRC5076	257	FRC5388	710	FRC5449	250	FRC5564	185
FRC4329	170	FRC4565	182	FRC5095	174	FRC5388	714	FRC5450	193	FRC5564	202
FRC4331	170	FRC4565	194	FRC5162	174	FRC5389	711	FRC5450	210	FRC5564	247
FRC4333	170	FRC4565	198	FRC5180	158	FRC5389	715	FRC5450	255	FRC5566	275
FRC4335	170	FRC4565	211	FRC5186	174	FRC5391	711	FRC5454	186	FRC5574	182
FRC4337	170	FRC4565	257	FRC5204	263	FRC5409	184	FRC5458	192	FRC5574	198

LAND ROVER PARTS LTD

PART NO	PAGE	PART NO	PAGE	PART NO	PAGE	PART NO	PAGE	PART NO	PAGE	PART NO	PAGE
FRC5574	257	FRC5801	217	FRC6125	197	FRC6782	267	FRC7043	190	FRC7447	246
FRC5575	192	FRC5806	267	FRC6125	256	FRC6783	267	FRC7043	193	FRC7452	203
FRC5575	205	FRC5806	273	FRC6126	231	FRC6784	267	FRC7043	194	FRC7452	248
FRC5575	250	FRC5859	175	FRC6137	267	FRC6785	267	FRC7043	207	FRC7453	203
FRC5576	189	FRC5864	175	FRC6137	273	FRC6786	267	FRC7043	210	FRC7453	248
FRC5576	194	FRC5882	231	FRC6139	267	FRC6787	267	FRC7043	211	FRC7454	203
FRC5576	206	FRC5928R	166	FRC6141	273	FRC6788	267	FRC7043	252	FRC7454	248
FRC5576	211	FRC5931	221	FRC6145	168	FRC6789	267	FRC7043	255	FRC7457	209
FRC5576	251	FRC5931	222	FRC6243	275	FRC6790	267	FRC7064	168	FRC7457	254
FRC5594	184	FRC5978	240	FRC6244	169	FRC6861	186	FRC7064	179	FRC7487	182
FRC5594	201	FRC5998	183	FRC6246	169	FRC6865	187	FRC7104	218	FRC7487	198
FRC5594	246	FRC6000	183	FRC6249	271	FRC6872	181	FRC7145	171	FRC7493	178
FRC5595	184	FRC6000	199	FRC6284	225	FRC6872	197	FRC7155	177	FRC7499	191
FRC5595	201	FRC6000	200	FRC6285	225	FRC6872	256	FRC7158	177	FRC7499	208
FRC5595	246	FRC6030	189	FRC6286	225	FRC6873	181	FRC7160	177	FRC7499	253
FRC5596	177	FRC6030	205	FRC6287	225	FRC6873	197	FRC7192	176	FRC7569	191
FRC5597	230	FRC6030	250	FRC6288	225	FRC6873	256	FRC7194	175	FRC7575	174
FRC5598	230	FRC6066	183	FRC6306	182	FRC6933	711	FRC7195	175	FRC7602	174
FRC5600	230	FRC6066	199	FRC6306	194	FRC6933	715	FRC7201	308	FRC7652	189
FRC5602	241	FRC6069	189	FRC6306	198	FRC6943	184	FRC7202	308	FRC7686	189
FRC5603	241	FRC6098	192	FRC6306	211	FRC6943	201	FRC7214	174	FRC7713	168
FRC5604	241	FRC6103	187	FRC6306	244	FRC6943	244	FRC7229	274	FRC7740	227
FRC5605	241	FRC6103	194	FRC6306	257	FRC6950	168	FRC7230	274	FRC7745	227
FRC5606	241	FRC6103	204	FRC6316	177	FRC6956	191	FRC7257	273	FRC7752	239
FRC5607	241	FRC6103	211	FRC6317	178	FRC6956	227	FRC7313	178	FRC7752	240
FRC5608	241	FRC6103	249	FRC6318	177	FRC6956	253	FRC7315	183	FRC7752	241
FRC5609	241	FRC6104	187	FRC6375	167	FRC6958	191	FRC7315	199	FRC7753	241
FRC5610	241	FRC6104	204	FRC6402	308	FRC6958	227	FRC7325	183	FRC7754	243
FRC5611	241	FRC6104	249	FRC6403	308	FRC6958	253	FRC7325	199	FRC7757	240
FRC5612	241	FRC6105	187	FRC6468	231	FRC6960	191	FRC7325	258	FRC7761	240
FRC5613	241	FRC6105	194	FRC6537	202	FRC6960	227	FRC7326	192	FRC7763	240
FRC5614	241	FRC6105	204	FRC6539	202	FRC6960	253	FRC7329	308	FRC7764	239
FRC5615	241	FRC6105	211	FRC6541	202	FRC6962	191	FRC7330	175	FRC7766	243
FRC5618	230	FRC6105	249	FRC6543	202	FRC6962	227	FRC7332	175	FRC7767	243
FRC5629	217	FRC6106	187	FRC6545	202	FRC6962	253	FRC7333	175	FRC7769	243
FRC5648	230	FRC6106	204	FRC6547	202	FRC6964	191	FRC7334	175	FRC7810	203
FRC5656	233	FRC6106	249	FRC6549	202	FRC6964	227	FRC7335	175	FRC7810	248
FRC5661	263	FRC6109	189	FRC6551	202	FRC6964	253	FRC7362	178	FRC7852	239
FRC5668	184	FRC6109	205	FRC6573	178	FRC6968	191	FRC7414	177	FRC7860	178
FRC5668	201	FRC6109	250	FRC6578	184	FRC6968	208	FRC7426	203	FRC7869	181
FRC5668	246	FRC6110	189	FRC6593	182	FRC6968	227	FRC7427	209	FRC7870	181
FRC5674	226	FRC6110	206	FRC6595	182	FRC6968	253	FRC7434	209	FRC7871	188
FRC5674	237	FRC6110	251	FRC6595	198	FRC7018	175	FRC7434	254	FRC7871	205
FRC5678	172	FRC6117	182	FRC6595	257	FRC7018	192	FRC7437	203	FRC7871	250
FRC5679	172	FRC6117	198	FRC6631	160	FRC7018	209	FRC7437	248	FRC7884	248
FRC5681	192	FRC6117	257	FRC6670	172	FRC7018	254	FRC7439	203	FRC7885	254
FRC5688	263	FRC6121	190	FRC6674	208	FRC7018	710	FRC7439	248	FRC7886	177
FRC5690	263	FRC6121	207	FRC6674	253	FRC7018	714	FRC7441	209	FRC7904N	235
FRC5698	244	FRC6121	252	FRC6685	160	FRC7021	192	FRC7441	254	FRC7926	208
		FRC6125	181	FRC6751	219	FRC7026	184	FRC7447	201	FRC7926	253

LAND ROVER PARTS LTD

PART NO	PAGE	PART NO	PAGE	PART NO	PAGE	PART NO	PAGE	PART NO	PAGE	PART NO	PAGE
FRC7929	209	FRC8214	239	FRC8538	715	FRC9533	254	FRC9946	185	FTC738	205
FRC7929	254	FRC8215	238	FRC8540	273	FRC9546	209	FRC9946	202	FTC738	250
FRC7930	198	FRC8220	263	FRC8541	714	FRC9546	254	FRC9946	247	FTC740	188
FRC7930	257	FRC8221	267	FRC8544	206	FRC9547	176	FRC9948	185	FTC740	205
FRC7941	197	FRC8221	273	FRC8547	200	FRC9548	175	FRC9948	202	FTC740	250
FRC7941	256	FRC8222	273	FRC8548	198	FRC9549	209	FRC9948	247	FTC742	188
FRC7942	258	FRC8227	273	FRC8548	200	FRC9549	254	FRC9950	185	FTC742	205
FRC7944	180	FRC8232	171	FRC8555	273	FRC9555	197	FRC9950	202	FTC742	250
FRC7944	197	FRC8232	172	FRC8560	198	FRC9556	240	FRC9950	247	FTC744	188
FRC7944	256	FRC8246	174	FRC8560	257	FRC9562	169	FRC9952	185	FTC744	205
FRC7946	258	FRC8250	244	FRC8561	197	FRC9568	158	FRC9952	202	FTC744	250
FRC7948	206	FRC8270	243	FRC8573	156	FRC9568	161	FRC9952	247	FTC746	188
FRC7948	251	FRC8271	244	FRC8573	157	FRC9568	162	FRC9954	185	FTC746	205
FRC7970	209	FRC8285	174	FRC8574	156	FRC9620	238	FRC9954	202	FTC746	250
FRC7970	254	FRC8291	203	FRC8574	157	FRC9621	239	FRC9954	247	FTC748	188
FRC7998	187	FRC8291	248	FRC8700	267	FRC9812	173	FRC9956	185	FTC748	205
FRC7998	194	FRC8292	201	FRC8700	273	FRC9827	168	FRC9956	202	FTC748	250
FRC7998	204	FRC8292	246	FRC8722	178	FRC9845	208	FRC9956	247	FTC750	188
FRC7998	211	FRC8293	201	FRC8722	244	FRC9847	208	FRC9958	185	FTC750	205
FRC7998	249	FRC8293	246	FRC8724	177	FRC9849	208	FRC9958	202	FTC750	250
FRC8002	273	FRC8299	204	FRC8766	198	FRC9851	208	FRC9958	247	FTC752	188
FRC8025	177	FRC8299	249	FRC8767	200	FRC9853	208	FRC9960	185	FTC752	205
FRC8029	711	FRC8380	242	FRC8768	200	FRC9865	167	FRC9960	202	FTC752	250
FRC8029	715	FRC8382	174	FRC8769	200	FRC9928	185	FRC9960	247	FTC754	188
FRC8033	258	FRC8383	168	FRC8773	177	FRC9928	202	FRC9991	270	FTC754	205
FRC8041	206	FRC8383	174	FRC8777	239	FRC9928	247	FRC9995	270	FTC754	250
FRC8041	251	FRC8384	174	FRC8777	240	FRC9930	185	FTC148	156	FTC756	188
FRC8075	199	FRC8386	275	FRC8777	241	FRC9930	202	FTC148	157	FTC756	205
FRC8075	200	FRC8388	275	FRC8782	261	FRC9930	247	FTC159	155	FTC756	250
FRC8075	258	FRC8389	275	FRC8783	261	FRC9932	185	FTC160	160	FTC758	188
FRC8091	209	FRC8390	275	FRC8863	244	FRC9932	202	FTC503	178	FTC758	205
FRC8093	310	FRC8391	275	FRC8899	254	FRC9932	247	FTC726	188	FTC758	250
FRC8104	169	FRC8397	237	FRC8900	209	FRC9934	185	FTC726	205	FTC760	188
FRC8105	169	FRC8400	240	FRC8917	202	FRC9934	202	FTC726	250	FTC760	205
FRC8119	177	FRC8401	240	FRC8917	247	FRC9934	247	FTC728	188	FTC760	250
FRC8120	177	FRC8402	240	FRC9386	172	FRC9936	185	FTC728	205	FTC762	188
FRC8126	175	FRC8403	240	FRC9387	171	FRC9936	202	FTC728	250	FTC762	205
FRC8129	240	FRC8404	240	FRC9389	172	FRC9936	247	FTC730	188	FTC762	250
FRC8139	239	FRC8405	240	FRC9460	248	FRC9938	185	FTC730	205	FTC764	188
FRC8141	174	FRC8406	240	FRC9462	203	FRC9938	202	FTC730	250	FTC764	205
FRC8154	263	FRC8409	241	FRC9468N	245	FRC9938	247	FTC732	188	FTC764	250
FRC8176	241	FRC8421	242	FRC9469N	180	FRC9940	185	FTC732	205	FTC766	188
FRC8202	200	FRC8422	240	FRC9469N	196	FRC9940	202	FTC732	250	FTC766	205
FRC8203	198	FRC8452	243	FRC9513	209	FRC9940	247	FTC734	188	FTC766	250
FRC8204	200	FRC8454	243	FRC9513	254	FRC9942	185	FTC734	205	FTC768	188
FRC8208	240	FRC8455	243	FRC9525N	235	FRC9942	202	FTC734	250	FTC768	205
FRC8209	240	FRC8521	263	FRC9526	173	FRC9942	247	FTC736	188	FTC768	250
FRC8210	239	FRC8528	265	FRC9531	209	FRC9944	185	FTC736	205	FTC770	188
FRC8211	240	FRC8529	236	FRC9531	254	FRC9944	202	FTC736	250	FTC770	205
FRC8213	242	FRC8530	265	FRC9532	209	FRC9944	247	FTC738	188	FTC770	250

PART NO	PAGE	PART NO	PAGE	PART NO	PAGE	PART NO	PAGE	PART NO	PAGE	PART NO	PAGE
FTC772	188	MRC1980	546	MRC5153	526	MRC6980	658	MRC8444	531	MRC9438	527
FTC772	205	MRC1980	552	MRC5153	528	MRC6980	659	MRC8444	544	MRC9481	655
FTC772	250	MRC1980	598	MRC5378	519	MRC6982	658	MRC8444	592	MRC9481	660
FTC774	188	MRC199	674	MRC5394	632	MRC6982	659	MRC8444	597	MRC9492	655
FTC774	205	MRC200	674	MRC5509	524	MRC6985	658	MRC8445	531	MRC9492	660
FTC774	250	MRC2178	533	MRC5524	675	MRC6985	659	MRC8445	544	MRC9493	660
FTC776	188	MRC2178	540	MRC5525	522	MRC7104	605	MRC8456	524	MRC9520	513
FTC776	205	MRC2237	561	MRC5525	523	MRC7132	495	MRC8457	524	MRC9544	502
FTC776	250	MRC2238	561	MRC5525	524	MRC7279	416	MRC8524	677	MRC9564	604
GD110401	533	MRC2244	560	MRC5525	525	MRC7281	415	MRC8564	471	MRC9570	317
GG106167	512	MRC2244	566	MRC5525	527	MRC7281	416	MRC8564	472	MRC9570	318
GG106251L	287	MRC2245	560	MRC5525	581	MRC7282	629	MRC8584	629	MRC9571	317
GG108251L	287	MRC2245	566	MRC5525	583	MRC7283	629	MRC8585	629	MRC9603	608
GG108251L	311	MRC2481	526	MRC5525	595	MRC7350	707	MRC8626	519	MRC9603	610
GS108081L	238	MRC2762	533	MRC5525	597	MRC7354	674	MRC8626	520	MRC9605	544
GS110501	178	MRC2762	540	MRC5525	598	MRC7359	708	MRC8626	521	MRC9605	551
GS112141L	244	MRC2762	546	MRC5525	655	MRC7360	708	MRC8626	522	MRC9616	595
HN2005L	132	MRC2762	552	MRC5525	660	MRC7361	708	MRC8626	565	MRC9619	597
HN2005L	140	MRC3037	533	MRC5525	663	MRC7362	708	MRC8642	412	MRC9627	558
HN2005L	395	MRC3037	540	MRC5525	669	MRC7365	705	MRC8717	412	MRC9627	566
HN2005L	470	MRC3038	533	MRC5526	655	MRC7411	520	MRC8732	708	MRC9632	558
JS499L	336	MRC3038	540	MRC5527	519	MRC7610	674	MRC8736	557	MRC9632	566
JS657L	365	MRC3574	521	MRC5527	521	MRC7623	508	MRC8736	564	MRC9646	629
JS660L	365	MRC3609	519	MRC5527	565	MRC7626	676	MRC8926	512	MRC9663	522
JS660L	380	MRC3610	519	MRC5527	583	MRC7626	682	MRC9006	531	MRC9664	522
JZX1039	335	MRC3611	519	MRC5527	589	MRC7626	683	MRC9006	544	MRC9668	415
JZX1181L	335	MRC3613	524	MRC5527	608	MRC7630	689	MRC9006	592	MRC9669	415
JZX1303L	335	MRC4037	513	MRC5528	526	MRC7696	691	MRC9006	597	MRC9720	521
JZX1394L	335	MRC4473	509	MRC5528	590	MRC7755	675	MRC9007	531	MRC9734	513
KTP9024	407	MRC4473	510	MRC5528	672	MRC8047	506	MRC9007	544	MRC9735	513
LZX1505	335	MRC4501	507	MRC5695	357	MRC8094	569	MRC9244	507	MRC9747	604
LZX1540L	335	MRC4583	604	MRC5757	497	MRC8136	523	MRC9361	680	MRC9833	581
LZX1545L	335	MRC4619	509	MRC5757	559	MRC8136	524	MRC9362	680	MRC9833	583
LZX1600L	335	MRC4619	510	MRC5765	528	MRC8173	519	MRC9367	680	MRC9915	557
LZX1988L	335	MRC4731	678	MRC6019	526	MRC8225	481	MRC9368	680	MRC9915	566
LZX1989L	335	MRC4753	546	MRC6027	557	MRC8269	506	MRC9377	514	MRC9922	414
LZX2107L	335	MRC4753	552	MRC6027	565	MRC8329	674	MRC9378	514	MRC9938	412
ML106015	348	MRC4754	546	MRC6028	557	MRC8330	674	MRC9388	567	MRC9939	412
MM106301	707	MRC4754	552	MRC6028	565	MRC8377	412	MRC9393	506	MRC9940	412
MR106300	572	MRC4798	670	MRC6051	511	MRC8378	412	MRC9394	506	MRC9941	412
MR106300	575	MRC4846	559	MRC6052	511	MRC8388	523	MRC9416	530	MRC9995	507
MRC1210	600	MRC4857	520	MRC6138	521	MRC8388	524	MRC9416	544	MRC9998	412
MRC1300	515	MRC4885	679	MRC6359	528	MRC8388	558	MRC9416	597	MTC1002	665
MRC1300	668	MRC4886	679	MRC6360	528	MRC8388	566	MRC9417	530	MTC1003	666
MRC1525	415	MRC5016	507	MRC6437	564	MRC8389	674	MRC9417	597	MTC1039	556
MRC1525	416	MRC5049	525	MRC6843	673	MRC8390	674	MRC9420	515	MTC1039	563
MRC1638	684	MRC5050	525	MRC6845	673	MRC8392	674	MRC9431	531	MTC1042	598
MRC1979	604	MRC5063	509	MRC6977	505	MRC8393	674	MRC9431	544	MTC1078	287
MRC1980	533	MRC5071	563	MRC6978	505	MRC8420	570	MRC9431	592	MTC1233	555
MRC1980	540	MRC5083	604			MRC8440	591	MRC9438	525		

PART NO	PAGE	PART NO	PAGE	PART NO	PAGE	PART NO	PAGE	PART NO	PAGE	PART NO	PAGE
MTC1233	603	MTC1715	655	MTC2575AE	612	MTC3470	596	MTC4145	516	MTC4572	626
MTC1241	555	MTC1715	660	MTC2575AG	612	MTC3474	584	MTC4156	572	MTC4581	607
MTC1248	632	MTC1718	655	MTC2607	477	MTC3475	594	MTC4164	562	MTC4583	607
MTC1355	622	MTC1719	655	MTC2640	628	MTC3476	578	MTC4165	562	MTC4584	607
MTC1356	622	MTC1810	502	MTC2704	512	MTC3476	580	MTC4166	595	MTC4601	621
MTC1357	619	MTC1827	562	MTC2799	516	MTC3476	582	MTC4182	633	MTC4617	627
MTC1357	622	MTC1923	661	MTC2805	414	MTC3481	576	MTC4182	634	MTC4618	627
MTC1359	618	MTC1928RE	662	MTC2808	480	MTC3482	576	MTC4188	562	MTC4657	605
MTC1359	622	MTC1929RE	662	MTC2810	480	MTC3486	576	MTC4196	523	MTC4684	522
MTC1382	287	MTC1930RE	661	MTC2811	480	MTC3499	286	MTC4197	523	MTC4719	616
MTC1409	572	MTC1931RE	661	MTC2826	628	MTC3515	574	MTC4215	523	MTC4771	287
MTC1416	575	MTC1932RD	662	MTC2827	628	MTC3521	572	MTC4216	523	MTC4824	593
MTC1423	575	MTC1932RE	662	MTC2863	518	MTC3523	628	MTC4220	504	MTC4826	504
MTC1439	574	MTC1933RD	661	MTC2864	518	MTC3533	574	MTC4290	602	MTC4829	504
MTC1439	593	MTC1933RE	661	MTC3000	704	MTC3534	574	MTC4313	606	MTC4837	502
MTC1448	574	MTC1938	662	MTC3001	704	MTC3538	572	MTC4313	609	MTC4844	593
MTC1461	572	MTC1940AV	661	MTC3018	555	MTC3556	593	MTC4313	612	MTC4845	593
MTC1462	572	MTC1940PB	661	MTC3021	555	MTC3557	593	MTC4314	606	MTC4846	593
MTC1479	573	MTC1943	663	MTC3032	681	MTC3558	572	MTC4314	609	MTC4861	632
MTC1481	573	MTC1944	663	MTC3042	681	MTC3569	572	MTC4314	612	MTC4863	632
MTC1482	573	MTC1947RE	663	MTC3046	557	MTC3594	509	MTC4315	612	MTC4865	632
MTC1485	572	MTC1948RD	663	MTC3051	681	MTC3598	509	MTC4317	612	MTC4866	632
MTC1490	575	MTC1948RE	663	MTC3052	681	MTC3611	398	MTC4319	612	MTC4888	593
MTC1507	385	MTC1949RD	663	MTC3076	555	MTC3692	518	MTC4320	385	MTC4916	632
MTC1531	593	MTC1949RE	663	MTC3084	603	MTC3693	518	MTC4320	386	MTC4932	505
MTC1554	645	MTC1950RD	663	MTC3085	603	MTC3694	518	MTC4326	594	MTC4942	614
MTC1584	575	MTC1950RE	663	MTC3086	603	MTC3705	628	MTC4400	518	MTC4943	613
MTC1592	575	MTC1953AV	663	MTC3087	603	MTC3801	286	MTC4411	582	MTC4944	613
MTC1594	574	MTC1953PB	663	MTC3091	603	MTC3862	503	MTC4412	582	MTC4945	613
MTC1595	572	MTC2062	511	MTC3099	603	MTC3874	704	MTC4460	562	MTC4992	576
MTC1606	687	MTC2063	511	MTC3126	572	MTC3902	571	MTC4460	566	MTC4993	576
MTC1607	687	MTC2106	589	MTC3127	572	MTC3906	573	MTC4460	593	MTC4994	584
MTC1608	686	MTC2107	589	MTC3139	593	MTC3907	573	MTC4483RD	667	MTC4994	585
MTC1609	686	MTC2134	568	MTC3165	621	MTC3908	593	MTC4483RE	667	MTC4994	586
MTC1614	685	MTC2135	568	MTC3166	621	MTC3917	593	MTC4485RD	666	MTC5034	578
MTC1615	685	MTC2136	512	MTC3181	658	MTC3923	593	MTC4485RE	666	MTC5034	580
MTC1631	675	MTC2138	554	MTC3182	659	MTC3982	505	MTC4486RD	665	MTC5038	573
MTC1650	398	MTC2202	524	MTC3203	584	MTC3983	505	MTC4486RE	665	MTC5039	573
MTC1650	515	MTC2203	524	MTC3203	585	MTC4002	576	MTC4487RD	672	MTC5083	604
MTC1670	661	MTC2220	508	MTC3203	586	MTC4003	576	MTC4487RE	672	MTC5084	604
MTC1671	661	MTC2224	589	MTC3230	543	MTC4007	504	MTC4488RD	671	MTC5086	576
MTC1672	663	MTC2225	589	MTC3231	543	MTC4054	613	MTC4488RE	671	MTC5119	513
MTC1673RD	663	MTC2248	521	MTC3350	574	MTC4061AE	612	MTC4489RD	667	MTC5120	513
MTC1674RD	661	MTC2252	519	MTC3362	543	MTC4061AG	612	MTC4489RE	667	MTC5193	589
MTC1675RD	661	MTC2285	556	MTC3363	543	MTC4063	612	MTC4490RE	673	MTC5194	589
MTC1697	585	MTC2390	412	MTC3382	633	MTC4076	589	MTC4491RD	673	MTC5197	587
MTC1710	633	MTC2391	412	MTC3452	518	MTC4090	677	MTC4491RE	673	MTC5198	587
MTC1710	634	MTC2548	554	MTC3461	587	MTC4095	519	MTC4520	649	MTC5206	647
MTC1714	655	MTC2574AE	612	MTC3462	587	MTC4111	602	MTC4570	509	MTC5209	647
MTC1714	660	MTC2574AG	612	MTC3469	596	MTC4144	516	MTC4571	626	MTC5212	645

PART NO	PAGE	PART NO	PAGE	PART NO	PAGE	PART NO	PAGE	PART NO	PAGE	PART NO	PAGE
MTC5212	647	MTC6006	414	MTC6232	587	MTC6503	624	MTC6873HC	570	MTC7031AG	606
MTC5216	644	MTC6007	414	MTC6233	587	MTC6504	624	MTC6873HD	570	MTC7033AE	606
MTC5312	582	MTC6008	532	MTC6240	645	MTC6505	624	MTC6873HN	570	MTC7033AG	606
MTC5314	578	MTC6009	532	MTC6241	645	MTC6506	624	MTC6873JC	570	MTC7040	709
MTC5315	578	MTC6010	532	MTC6248	547	MTC6507	624	MTC6873JP	570	MTC7041	709
MTC5381	594	MTC6011	532	MTC6249	547	MTC6508	624	MTC6873LB	570	MTC7140	505
MTC5381	595	MTC6015	517	MTC6250	547	MTC6509	624	MTC6873LN	570	MTC7142	616
MTC5394	577	MTC6040	626	MTC6251	547	MTC6539	665	MTC6873NJ	570	MTC7143	616
MTC5394	579	MTC6057	594	MTC6254	547	MTC6544	587	MTC6873NM	570	MTC7144	616
MTC5394	582	MTC6058	594	MTC6255	547	MTC6568	584	MTC6874AA	514	MTC7145	616
MTC5395	577	MTC6074	568	MTC6256	547	MTC6568	585	MTC6874AE	514	MTC7155	597
MTC5395	579	MTC6075	568	MTC6258	547	MTC6568	586	MTC6874AF	514	MTC7170	505
MTC5395	582	MTC6080	628	MTC6259	547	MTC6606	532	MTC6874AV	514	MTC7193AE	606
MTC5396	582	MTC6087	644	MTC6266	534	MTC6607	532	MTC6874CC	514	MTC7193AE	609
MTC5397	582	MTC6090	644	MTC6267	534	MTC6608	545	MTC6874CL	514	MTC7193AG	606
MTC5410	577	MTC6091	644	MTC6276	534	MTC6609	545	MTC6874HC	514	MTC7193AG	609
MTC5411	577	MTC6093	644	MTC6277	534	MTC6626	607	MTC6874HD	514	MTC7200AE	609
MTC5416	582	MTC6094	644	MTC6278	534	MTC6630	598	MTC6874HN	514	MTC7200AG	609
MTC5417	582	MTC6095	644	MTC6279	534	MTC6630	633	MTC6874JC	514	MTC7252	607
MTC5420	577	MTC6104	545	MTC6280	547	MTC6630	665	MTC6874JP	514	MTC7253	513
MTC5421	577	MTC6105	545	MTC6281	547	MTC6631	578	MTC6874LB	514	MTC7384	610
MTC5422	577	MTC6106	545	MTC6284	547	MTC6680	435	MTC6874LN	514	MTC7400	629
MTC5423	577	MTC6107	545	MTC6285	547	MTC6686	644	MTC6874NJ	514	MTC7407	577
MTC5428	607	MTC6109	517	MTC6302	495	MTC6754	665	MTC6874NM	514	MTC7415	645
MTC5429	607	MTC6142	627	MTC6304	535	MTC6755	665	MTC6875AA	514	MTC7416	645
MTC5458	480	MTC6143	627	MTC6304	547	MTC6756	665	MTC6875AE	514	MTC7431	607
MTC5459	480	MTC6154	576	MTC6305	522	MTC6792	669	MTC6875AF	514	MTC7435	511
MTC5468	626	MTC6166	629	MTC6324	605	MTC6793	667	MTC6875AV	514	MTC7436	511
MTC5482	644	MTC6167	629	MTC6332	502	MTC6794	667	MTC6875CC	514	MTC7449	618
MTC5483	644	MTC6194	414	MTC6339	522	MTC6795	667	MTC6875CL	514	MTC7449	619
MTC5486	647	MTC6202	534	MTC6340	522	MTC6798	519	MTC6875HC	514	MTC7457	618
MTC5519	615	MTC6203	534	MTC6376	604	MTC6801	670	MTC6875HD	514	MTC7457	619
MTC5536	530	MTC6206	534	MTC6382	415	MTC6802	670	MTC6875HN	514	MTC7464	555
MTC5536	539	MTC6207	534	MTC6391	520	MTC6820	632	MTC6875JC	514	MTC7465	555
MTC5536	551	MTC6208	534	MTC6392	520	MTC6827	503	MTC6875JP	514	MTC7466	555
MTC5552	544	MTC6209	534	MTC6408	644	MTC6834	684	MTC6875LB	514	MTC7471AE	609
MTC5555	437	MTC6210	534	MTC6410	600	MTC6835	684	MTC6875LN	514	MTC7471AG	609
MTC5557	435	MTC6211	534	MTC6413	605	MTC6836	684	MTC6875NJ	514	MTC7480	574
MTC5559	430	MTC6212	534	MTC6425	673	MTC6839	684	MTC6875NM	514	MTC7481	574
MTC5561	437	MTC6213	534	MTC6448	671	MTC6840	684	MTC6978RD	665	MTC7482	574
MTC5568	435	MTC6214	535	MTC6452	671	MTC6858	530	MTC6978RE	665	MTC7483	574
MTC5571	432	MTC6215	535	MTC6453	671	MTC6858	544	MTC6992	607	MTC7511	574
MTC5573	434	MTC6221	534	MTC6456	633	MTC6871	629	MTC6993	607	MTC7512	574
MTC5578	416	MTC6221	547	MTC6456	634	MTC6872	520	MTC7004	709	MTC7513	348
MTC5581	437	MTC6222	535	MTC6457	547	MTC6873AA	570	MTC7020	649	MTC7513	565
MTC5603	503	MTC6222	547	MTC6466	666	MTC6873AE	570	MTC7022	616	MTC7513	584
MTC5698	648	MTC6223	535	MTC6467	666	MTC6873AF	570	MTC7023	616	MTC7513	585
MTC5699	648	MTC6223	547	MTC6470	666	MTC6873AV	570	MTC7024	616	MTC7513	586
MTC5832	645	MTC6224	535	MTC6471	665	MTC6873CC	570	MTC7025	616	MTC7513	587
MTC5851	627	MTC6224	547	MTC6481	644	MTC6873CL	570	MTC7031AE	606	MTC7513	672

PART NO	PAGE	PART NO	PAGE	PART NO	PAGE	PART NO	PAGE	PART NO	PAGE	PART NO	PAGE
MTC7513	673	MTC8332	584	MTC9428	340	MUC1216	532	MUC1361RD	639	MUC1660	433
MTC7513	704	MTC8332	585	MTC9428	641	MUC1216	545	MUC1362RD	639	MUC1661	430
MTC7516	437	MTC8332	586	MTC9429	340	MUC1217	532	MUC1363RD	639	MUC1663	438
MTC7523	591	MTC8333	577	MTC9429	641	MUC1217	545	MUC1364RD	340	MUC1665	443
MTC7523	592	MTC8333	582	MTC9773	607	MUC1227	521	MUC1365RD	340	MUC1666	444
MTC7525	592	MTC8334	561	MTC9801	633	MUC1228	521	MUC1367	484	MUC1667	444
MTC7549	535	MTC8334	568	MTC9801	634	MUC1233	524	MUC1368	484	MUC1668	439
MTC7549	547	MTC8335	672	MTC9814	633	MUC1234	524	MUC1382	628	MUC1669	444
MTC7550	535	MTC8335	673	MTC9815	633	MUC1237	519	MUC1383	628	MUC1670	444
MTC7550	547	MTC8349	632	MTC9818	633	MUC1249	635	MUC1384	628	MUC1671	441
MTC7611	535	MTC8357	704	MTC9819	633	MUC1250	635	MUC1402	633	MUC1672	442
MTC7611	547	MTC8358	704	MTC9824	633	MUC1253	635	MUC1402	634	MUC1673	443
MTC7616	535	MTC8360	632	MTC9825	633	MUC1254	635	MUC1412	523	MUC1674	443
MTC7616	547	MTC8376	612	MTC9826	633	MUC1255	635	MUC1426	577	MUC1675	438
MTC7617	535	MTC8433	563	MTC9827	633	MUC1256RD	632	MUC1474	644	MUC1676	442
MTC7617	547	MTC8440	704	MTC9838	503	MUC1257RD	639	MUC1484	580	MUC1677	442
MTC7622	535	MTC8441	704	MTC9914	486	MUC1258RD	639	MUC1488	653	MUC1678	442
MTC7622	547	MTC8444	515	MTC9915	486	MUC1259RD	639	MUC1488	656	MUC1679	441
MTC7631	660	MTC8460	549	MTC9956	661	MUC1260RD	340	MUC1488	657	MUC1680	444
MTC7631	662	MTC8461	549	MTC9958	663	MUC1261RD	340	MUC1492	639	MUC1682	438
MTC7651	412	MTC8468	538	MTC9959	663	MUC1264RD	639	MUC1493	639	MUC1699	637
MTC7652	412	MTC8471	549	MTC9962	662	MUC1265RD	639	MUC1494	639	MUC1701	628
MTC7710AE	606	MTC8472	549	MTC9962	663	MUC1266RD	340	MUC1495	637	MUC1703	628
MTC7710AG	606	MTC8473	537	MTC9967	662	MUC1268	639	MUC1495	641	MUC1704	580
MTC7711AE	606	MTC8474	537	MTC9968	629	MUC1269	639	MUC1497	639	MUC1705	580
MTC7711AG	606	MTC8477	538	MTC9981	596	MUC1270	636	MUC1498	639	MUC1706	580
MTC7737	414	MTC8478	549	MTC9994	633	MUC1271	636	MUC1499	639	MUC1707	580
MTC7769	512	MTC8500	429	MUC1005	580	MUC1272	636	MUC1500	340	MUC1713	538
MTC7770	512	MTC8502	636	MUC1008	580	MUC1273	636	MUC1501	580	MUC1714	549
MTC7798	687	MTC8523	636	MUC1010	683	MUC1274	636	MUC1508	644	MUC1715	475
MTC7799	686	MTC8613	636	MUC1011	683	MUC1275	636	MUC1520	656	MUC1716	628
MTC7825	538	MTC8706	634	MUC1027	517	MUC1286	485	MUC1520	657	MUC1730	537
MTC7826	538	MTC8707	634	MUC1028	530	MUC1287	485	MUC1533	579	MUC1731	537
MTC7828	549	MTC8708	634	MUC1029	530	MUC1322	548	MUC1548	644	MUC1756	641
MTC7829	549	MTC8709	634	MUC1030	530	MUC1323	548	MUC1549	644	MUC1757	340
MTC7861	569	MTC8788	548	MUC1030	544	MUC1324	581	MUC1555	645	MUC1758RD	642
MTC7886	563	MTC8789	548	MUC1030	597	MUC1324	583	MUC1581	626	MUC1759	641
MTC7889	563	MTC8790	549	MUC1031	530	MUC1342RD	632	MUC1582	631	MUC1888	540
MTC7980	556	MTC8791	549	MUC1031	544	MUC1343RD	639	MUC1583	484	MUC1889	540
MTC7980	563	MTC8840	534	MUC1032	530	MUC1344	639	MUC1584	484	MUC1961	552
MTC7981	556	MTC8841	534	MUC1033	530	MUC1346RD	340	MUC1604	548	MUC1983	547
MTC7981	563	MTC8846	547	MUC1034	530	MUC1347RD	639	MUC1605	548	MUC2002	617
MTC8142	522	MTC8847	547	MUC1034	544	MUC1348RD	639	MUC1616	635	MUC2003	617
MTC8145	611	MTC8927	542	MUC1035	530	MUC1349RD	639	MUC1621	635	MUC2012RD	340
MTC8146	611	MTC8928	542	MUC1035	544	MUC1353RD	641	MUC1651	537	MUC2013RD	340
MTC8270	580	MTC8931	536	MUC1049	541	MUC1356	632	MUC1651	548	MUC2074	537
MTC8271	580	MTC8932	536	MUC1086	614	MUC1357RD	639	MUC1652	537	MUC2075	537
MTC8331	584	MTC8947	580	MUC1098	580	MUC1358RD	639	MUC1657	433	MUC2129	557
MTC8331	585	MTC8951	596	MUC1139	416	MUC1359RD	340	MUC1658	433	MUC2160RD	340
MTC8331	586	MTC9180	537			MUC1360RD	340	MUC1659	433	MUC2161RD	340

LAND ROVER PARTS LTD

PART NO	PAGE	PART NO	PAGE	PART NO	PAGE	PART NO	PAGE	PART NO	PAGE	PART NO	PAGE
MUC2162RD	340	MUC3012	548	MUC3373AF	617	MUC3848	537	MUC4316	537	MUC6013	444
MUC2163RD	340	MUC3013	548	MUC3373JU	617	MUC3848	548	MUC4317	548	MUC6021	443
MUC2165	484	MUC3023	480	MUC3394	552	MUC3882	585	MUC4319	519	MUC6037	438
MUC2201	636	MUC3024	538	MUC3394	634	MUC3883	585	MUC4358	430	MUC6038	438
MUC2202	636	MUC3025	538	MUC3395	634	MUC3906	518	MUC4358	440	MUC6040	438
MUC2203	636	MUC3026	550	MUC3492	549	MUC3928	537	MUC4375	430	MUC6042	438
MUC2204	636	MUC3027	550	MUC3493	549	MUC3929	537	MUC4375	438	MUC6050	438
MUC2205	636	MUC3036	634	MUC3498	517	MUC3930	548	MUC4455	432	MUC6052	438
MUC2206	636	MUC3037	634	MUC3530	518	MUC3931	548	MUC4455	441	MUC6053	438
MUC2207	636	MUC3038	541	MUC3531	518	MUC3932	557	MUC4471	599	MUC6054	438
MUC2210	632	MUC3039	541	MUC3536	579	MUC3933	477	MUC4474	599	MUC6055	438
MUC2268	635	MUC3040	553	MUC3537	579	MUC3958	556	MUC4477	599	MUC6056	438
MUC2269	635	MUC3041	553	MUC3538	579	MUC3963	556	MUC4481	599	MUC6071	644
MUC2270	635	MUC3090	552	MUC3539	579	MUC3971	556	MUC4486	599	MUC6072	644
MUC2271	635	MUC3094	513	MUC3566	579	MUC3977	563	MUC4496	524	MUC6074	644
MUC2272	635	MUC3096	580	MUC3566	582	MUC4025	580	MUC4499	524	MUC6075	644
MUC2273	635	MUC3097	580	MUC3571	555	MUC4027	520	MUC4502	523	MUC6112	502
MUC2274	635	MUC3170JU	617	MUC3590	512	MUC4042	607	MUC4512	596	MUC6157	540
MUC2275	635	MUC3171JU	617	MUC3601	512	MUC4043	607	MUC4524	608	MUC6157	552
MUC2296	645	MUC3172AF	617	MUC3621	634	MUC4061	607	MUC4525	634	MUC6158	540
MUC2364	601	MUC3172JU	617	MUC3630	645	MUC4071	538	MUC4528	633	MUC6158	552
MUC2366	601	MUC3173AF	617	MUC3630	646	MUC4072	538	MUC4528	634	MUC6159	540
MUC2368	601	MUC3173JU	617	MUC3631	645	MUC4072	549	MUC4529	633	MUC6159	552
MUC2379	643	MUC3176AF	617	MUC3631	646	MUC4073	538	MUC4529	634	MUC6163	540
MUC2380	643	MUC3176JU	617	MUC3656	539	MUC4073	549	MUC4538	607	MUC6164	540
MUC2381	643	MUC3177AF	617	MUC3657	539	MUC4139RD	642	MUC4542	580	MUC6166	522
MUC2382	643	MUC3177JU	617	MUC3658	551	MUC4145	539	MUC4544	599	MUC6167	522
MUC2383	643	MUC3178AF	617	MUC3659	551	MUC4145	624	MUC4545	599	MUC6181	579
MUC2384	643	MUC3178JU	617	MUC3695	443	MUC4146	539	MUC4546	601	MUC6182	579
MUC2385	643	MUC3179AF	617	MUC3707	604	MUC4146	624	MUC4801	629	MUC6400	584
MUC2386	643	MUC3179JU	617	MUC3708	604	MUC4149	643	MUC4860	438	MUC6400	585
MUC2417	412	MUC3186	537	MUC3733	518	MUC4150	643	MUC4865	441	MUC6400	586
MUC2418	412	MUC3186	548	MUC3746	534	MUC4152	643	MUC4866	441	MUC6418	510
MUC2419	412	MUC3190	551	MUC3764	580	MUC4153	643	MUC4871	441	MUC6419	510
MUC2440	510	MUC3191	551	MUC3765	580	MUC4161	705	MUC4872	440	MUC6452	650
MUC2442	510	MUC3200	549	MUC3766	580	MUC4163	519	MUC4874	440	MUC6453	650
MUC2443	510	MUC3201	495	MUC3767	580	MUC4199	645	MUC4875	440	MUC6484	644
MUC2539	636	MUC3242	644	MUC3768	580	MUC4202	541	MUC4878	441	MUC6485	644
MUC2594	518	MUC3244	628	MUC3769	580	MUC4203	541	MUC4880	444	MUC6486	644
MUC2908	553	MUC3249	628	MUC3770	580	MUC4205	553	MUC4881	443	MUC6487	644
MUC2934	601	MUC3278	416	MUC3771	580	MUC4208	508	MUC4882	443	MUC6488	644
MUC2936	548	MUC3302	556	MUC3791	580	MUC4212	452	MUC4883	439	MUC6489	644
MUC2937	548	MUC3303	556	MUC3792	580	MUC4214	539	MUC4884	439	MUC6490	644
MUC2959	541	MUC3304	556	MUC3794	580	MUC4215	539	MUC4886	439	MUC6491	644
MUC2961	541	MUC3309	556	MUC3795	580	MUC4216	551	MUC4888	439	MUC6496	647
MUC2963	553	MUC3310	556	MUC3809	585	MUC4217	551	MUC4891	443	MUC6497	647
MUC2965	541	MUC3318	589	MUC3810	582	MUC4275	694	MUC4892	443	MUC6498	647
MUC2965	553	MUC3324	556	MUC3844	646	MUC4291	694	MUC4895	444	MUC6499	647
MUC3010	537	MUC3340	589	MUC3845	646	MUC4299	516	MUC6011	444	MUC6519	557
MUC3011	537	MUC3360	539			MUC4303	520	MUC6012	444	MUC6519	589

LAND ROVER PARTS LTD

PART NO	PAGE	PART NO	PAGE	PART NO	PAGE	PART NO	PAGE	PART NO	PAGE	PART NO	PAGE
MUC6651	646	MUC8755	589	MWC1899	540	NH105041	703	NH106041L	419	NH106041L	600
MUC6652	647	MUC8756	589	MWC1899	546	NH105041L	324	NH106041L	420	NH106041L	601
MUC6653	647	MUC8759	562	MWC1899	552	NH105041L	327	NH106041L	421	NH106041L	605
MUC6660	518	MUC8779RD	663	MWC2120	561	NH105041L	341	NH106041L	422	NH106041L	610
MUC6667RD	641	MUC8780RD	662	MWC2129	589	NH105041L	343	NH106041L	452	NH106041L	613
MUC6681	650	MUC8928	588	MWC2314	645	NH105041L	384	NH106041L	488	NH106041L	621
MUC6682	650	MUC8949	557	MWC2314	647	NH105041L	397	NH106041L	491	NH106041L	622
MUC6686	515	MUC8949	564	MWC2567	515	NH105041L	474	NH106041L	493	NH106041L	655
MUC6785	548	MUC9110	528	MWC2580RD	673	NH105041L	482	NH106041L	495	NH106041L	660
MUC6786	548	MUC9110	546	MWC2884	584	NH105041L	484	NH106041L	498	NH106041L	663
MUC6905	515	MUC9126	542	MWC3141	584	NH105041L	487	NH106041L	506	NH106041L	667
MUC6979	539	MUC9127	542	MWC3141	585	NH105041L	492	NH106041L	507	NH106041L	669
MUC6980	539	MUC9136	556	MWC3302	661	NH105041L	509	NH106041L	511	NH106041L	672
MUC6986	551	MUC9142	556	MWC3303	661	NH105041L	510	NH106041L	512	NH106041L	675
MUC6987	551	MUC9152	568	MWC4534	662	NH105041L	536	NH106041L	513	NH106041L	676
MUC7000	287	MUC9153	568	MWC4535	662	NH105041L	542	NH106041L	520	NH106041L	680
MUC7505	163	MUC9154	561	MWC4537	662	NH105041L	626	NH106041L	522	NH106041L	682
MUC7506	311	MUC9154	568	MWC4549	663	NH105041L	658	NH106041L	523	NH106041L	683
MUC7598	480	MUC9154	592	MWC5759	540	NH105041L	659	NH106041L	524	NH106041L	702
MUC7599	480	MUC9155	561	MWC6055	586	NH105041L	672	NH106041L	525	NH106041L	703
MUC7903	518	MUC9155	568	MWC6130	536	NH106041L	132	NH106041L	526	NH106041L	704
MUC7904	518	MUC9155	592	MWC6699	585	NH106041L	156	NH106041L	527	NH106041L	708
MUC7905	629	MUC9158	558	MXC1624	555	NH106041L	157	NH106041L	528	NH106041L	716
MUC8447	663	MUC9158	589	MXC5494	688	NH106041L	177	NH106041L	530	NH106044	670
MUC8448RD	661	MUC9167	632	NC112041	278	NH106041L	215	NH106041L	531	NH106044	671
MUC8449RD	661	MUC9168	632	NC112041L	297	NH106041L	236	NH106041L	539	NH106044	673
MUC8707	591	MUC9339	511	NH104041L	41	NH106041L	281	NH106041L	541	NH106047	505
MUC8710	561	MUC9345	515	NH104041L	80	NH106041L	305	NH106041L	544	NH106047	303
MUC8710	568	MUC9377	552	NH104041L	368	NH106041L	306	NH106041L	551	NH106047	411
MUC8711	561	MUC9551	589	NH104041L	382	NH106041L	308	NH106041L	552	NH106047	451
MUC8711	568	MUC9850	605	NH104041L	508	NH106041L	315	NH106041L	557	NH106047	452
MUC8716	561	MWC1010	662	NH104041L	517	NH106041L	316	NH106041L	561	NH106047	478
MUC8716	568	MWC1018RD	662	NH104041L	532	NH106041L	340	NH106041L	562	NH108041L	26
MUC8717	561	MWC1080	536	NH104041L	539	NH106041L	343	NH106041L	565	NH108041L	27
MUC8717	568	MWC1081	536	NH104041L	545	NH106041L	345	NH106041L	567	NH108041L	28
MUC8727	561	MWC1082	542	NH104041L	549	NH106041L	346	NH106041L	568	NH108041L	35
MUC8730	561	MWC1083	542	NH104041L	551	NH106041L	347	NH106041L	574	NH108041L	42
MUC8731	561	MWC1086	526	NH104041L	562	NH106041L	348	NH106041L	581	NH108041L	43
MUC8732	589	MWC1087	526	NH104044	626	NH106041L	357	NH106041L	583	NH108041L	53
MUC8733	589	MWC1736	531	NH105001	658	NH106041L	367	NH106041L	584	NH108041L	54
MUC8735	561	MWC1737	531	NH105041	286	NH106041L	368	NH106041L	585	NH108041L	60
MUC8735	589	MWC1820	589	NH105041	319	NH106041L	374	NH106041L	586	NH108041L	66
MUC8736	590	MWC1821	589	NH105041	383	NH106041L	380	NH106041L	588	NH108041L	67
MUC8737	590	MWC1837	552	NH105041	387	NH106041L	383	NH106041L	589	NH108041L	78
MUC8738	590	MWC1838	552	NH105041	602	NH106041L	384	NH106041L	590	NH108041L	83
MUC8739	590	MWC1866	542	NH105041	652	NH106041L	394	NH106041L	591	NH108041L	84
MUC8740	590	MWC1867	542	NH105041	654	NH106041L	409	NH106041L	594	NH108041L	90
MUC8741	590	MWC1898	540	NH105041	656	NH106041L	412	NH106041L	595	NH108041L	94
MUC8746	590	MWC1898	546	NH105041	657	NH106041L	417	NH106041L	597	NH108041L	102
MUC8748	561	MWC1898	552	NH105041	702	NH106041L	418	NH106041L	598	NH108041L	106

PART NO	PAGE	PART NO	PAGE	PART NO	PAGE	PART NO	PAGE	PART NO	PAGE	PART NO	PAGE
NH108041L	124	NH108041L	583	NH112041L	515	NK106081	285	NRC2383	409	NRC4708	501
NH108041L	200	NH108041L	588	NH112041L	600	NK106081	526	NRC2536	356	NRC4709	501
NH108041L	212	NH108041L	591	NH112041L	601	NM105011	493	NRC2536	357	NRC4733	499
NH108041L	216	NH108041L	592	NH112041L	687	NM105011	560	NRC2536	387	NRC4757	388
NH108041L	220	NH108041L	593	NH116041L	214	NM105011	566	NRC2538	387	NRC4757	389
NH108041L	276	NH108041L	598	NH116041L	500	NM105011	579	NRC255	710	NRC4759	388
NH108041L	278	NH108041L	608	NH604041L	163	NM105011	582	NRC255	714	NRC4765	390
NH108041L	279	NH108041L	610	NH604041L	328	NM105011	611	NRC2570	387	NRC4765	391
NH108041L	312	NH108041L	623	NH604041L	353	NN105011	357	NRC2572	387	NRC4765	392
NH108041L	317	NH108041L	668	NH604041L	354	NN105021L	628	NRC2652	356	NRC4765	393
NH108041L	318	NH108041L	673	NH604041L	367	NN106001	704	NRC2652	357	NRC4772	312
NH108041L	330	NH108041L	674	NH604041L	368	NN106011	281	NRC2652	387	NRC4775	312
NH108041L	340	NH108041L	677	NH604041L	464	NN106011	305	NRC2744	317	NRC4776	358
NH108041L	342	NH108041L	679	NH604041L	577	NN106011	306	NRC2744	318	NRC4776	359
NH108041L	346	NH108041L	681	NH605041L	134	NN106011	717	NRC2864	148	NRC4837	410
NH108041L	356	NH108041L	718	NH605041L	141	NN106011	718	NRC3301	132	NRC4839	407
NH108041L	364	NH108044	666	NH605041L	164	NN106021	383	NRC3314	131	NRC4842	410
NH108041L	390	NH110041L	21	NH605041L	277	NN106021	513	NRC3405	409	NRC4843	410
NH108041L	391	NH110041L	49	NH605041L	309	NN106021	574	NRC3406	408	NRC4844	410
NH108041L	392	NH110041L	73	NH605041L	333	NN106021	649	NRC3659	385	NRC4850	409
NH108041L	393	NH110041L	102	NH605041L	334	NN106021	650	NRC3659	387	NRC4852	409
NH108041L	400	NH110041L	155	NH605041L	339	NN106021	704	NRC3662	408	NRC4852	410
NH108041L	401	NH110041L	156	NH605041L	394	NN106021L	346	NRC3664	409	NRC4853	301
NH108041L	402	NH110041L	157	NH605041L	402	NN108021	287	NRC3753	385	NRC4854	501
NH108041L	403	NH110041L	168	NH605041L	403	NN108021	363	NRC3753	387	NRC4966	498
NH108041L	404	NH110041L	178	NH605041L	459	NN108021	492	NRC3848	375	NRC5088	319
NH108041L	405	NH110041L	184	NH605041L	463	NN108021	515	NRC3848	376	NRC5089	319
NH108041L	408	NH110041L	212	NH605041L	526	NN108021	555	NRC3907	483	NRC5104	319
NH108041L	409	NH110041L	237	NH605041L	533	NN108021L	412	NRC3908	483	NRC5110	319
NH108041L	425	NH110041L	274	NH605041L	540	NR604090	151	NRC3923	281	NRC5220	394
NH108041L	452	NH110041L	285	NH605041L	546	NR604090L	152	NRC3947	161	NRC5281	285
NH108041L	463	NH110041L	312	NH605041L	552	NRC1081	693	NRC3976	409	NRC5294	411
NH108041L	464	NH110041L	388	NH605041L	583	NRC1302	131	NRC3977	408	NRC5295	411
NH108041L	491	NH110041L	389	NH605041L	588	NRC1315	694	NRC4162	718	NRC5338	495
NH108041L	495	NH110041L	465	NH605041L	675	NRC1360	411	NRC4171	498	NRC5346	271
NH108041L	497	NH110041L	466	NH605041L	682	NRC2015	357	NRC4218	402	NRC5387	495
NH108041L	505	NH110041L	467	NH605041L	683	NRC2051	687	NRC4219	402	NRC5396	500
NH108041L	513	NH110041L	468	NH606041L	131	NRC2087	357	NRC4251	315	NRC5403	400
NH108041L	520	NH110041L	497	NH606041L	220	NRC2089	357	NRC4251	316	NRC5403	401
NH108041L	526	NH110041L	535	NH606041L	259	NRC2159	356	NRC4317	282	NRC5403	402
NH108041L	528	NH110041L	547	NH606041L	301	NRC2159	357	NRC4318	282	NRC5403	403
NH108041L	546	NH110041L	696	NH606041L	302	NRC2159	387	NRC4340	73	NRC5403	404
NH108041L	552	NH110041L	710	NH606041L	428	NRC2160	387	NRC4365	277	NRC5403	405
NH108041L	554	NH110041L	714	NH608061L	80	NRC2195	357	NRC4475	394	NRC5414	392
NH108041L	557	NH110041LD	131	NH608061L	108	NRC2211	164	NRC4514	276	NRC5414	393
NH108041L	562	NH110041LD	259	NH614041	290	NRC2214	356	NRC4515	276	NRC5415	358
NH108041L	564	NH110061	282	NH910011L	396	NRC2214	357	NRC4515	359	NRC5415	371
NH108041L	572	NH112041	698	NH910241L	396	NRC2214	387	NRC4516	276	NRC5415	372
NH108041L	576	NH112041L	214	NJ106061L	511	NRC223	339	NRC4665	311	NRC5415	373
NH108041L	581	NH112041L	341	NJ108061L	502	NRC2383	304	NRC4693	498	NRC5415	375

PART NO	PAGE	PART NO	PAGE	PART NO	PAGE	PART NO	PAGE	PART NO	PAGE	PART NO	PAGE
NRC5415	376	NRC6058	311	NRC6419	417	NRC6951	498	NRC7318	376	NRC7778	401
NRC5415	379	NRC6097	388	NRC6419	418	NRC6993	694	NRC7319	376	NRC7791	398
NRC5416	392	NRC6097	389	NRC6419	420	NRC6994	499	NRC7351	375	NRC7792	398
NRC5434	21	NRC6192	312	NRC6419	421	NRC7000	282	NRC7351	376	NRC7799	315
NRC5434	49	NRC62	388	NRC6420	417	NRC7009	499	NRC7357	313	NRC7801	315
NRC5434	73	NRC62	389	NRC6420	418	NRC7039	347	NRC7358	313	NRC7827	394
NRC5434	102	NRC62	390	NRC6421	417	NRC7040	390	NRC7372	364	NRC7835	286
NRC5478	498	NRC62	391	NRC6422	417	NRC7044	319	NRC7387	285	NRC7836	286
NRC5485	497	NRC62	392	NRC6430	408	NRC7050	281	NRC7422	483	NRC7842	404
NRC5494	394	NRC62	393	NRC6432	402	NRC7053	498	NRC7425	500	NRC7869	163
NRC5502	394	NRC6221	278	NRC6433	404	NRC7066	281	NRC7435	497	NRC7869	311
NRC5503	410	NRC6234	388	NRC6436	400	NRC7086	347	NRC7436	497	NRC7871	315
NRC5528	497	NRC6235	282	NRC6466	400	NRC7101	278	NRC7439	499	NRC7874	315
NRC5544	407	NRC6254	346	NRC6466	401	NRC7118	392	NRC7441	164	NRC7880	383
NRC5582	297	NRC6254	348	NRC6467	400	NRC7124	319	NRC7448	409	NRC7886	372
NRC5593	282	NRC6257	347	NRC6467	401	NRC7127	285	NRC7448	410	NRC7886	379
NRC5602	282	NRC6302	305	NRC6481	693	NRC7131	497	NRC7451	285	NRC7893	371
NRC5603	282	NRC6302	306	NRC6515	315	NRC7133	411	NRC7454	367	NRC7893	375
NRC5606	500	NRC6306	417	NRC6526	390	NRC7135	367	NRC7455	693	NRC7893	379
NRC5607	500	NRC6306	418	NRC6526	391	NRC7135	368	NRC7457	346	NRC7894	379
NRC5622	392	NRC6306	419	NRC6558	392	NRC7154	346	NRC7457	348	NRC7901	315
NRC5623	364	NRC6307	417	NRC6558	393	NRC7154	348	NRC7458	716	NRC7902	315
NRC5627	499	NRC6307	418	NRC6561	281	NRC7164	497	NRC7459	716	NRC7903	315
NRC5665	498	NRC6308	417	NRC6623	317	NRC7165	497	NRC7490	346	NRC7904	315
NRC5674	278	NRC6308	421	NRC6623	318	NRC7227	408	NRC7491	279	NRC7905	316
NRC5707	281	NRC6309	417	NRC6631	280	NRC7230	383	NRC7524	347	NRC7906	316
NRC5742	212	NRC6311	420	NRC6632	280	NRC7232	383	NRC7551	313	NRC7930	367
NRC5743	212	NRC6312	420	NRC6636	701	NRC7235	383	NRC7570	388	NRC7930	372
NRC5758	281	NRC6313	420	NRC6653	317	NRC7238	383	NRC7571	499	NRC7930	379
NRC5764	276	NRC6314	420	NRC6658	278	NRC7240	383	NRC7578PM	283	NRC7948	701
NRC5765	276	NRC6314	421	NRC6692	411	NRC7240	384	NRC7582	411	NRC7976	377
NRC5792	340	NRC6320	281	NRC6747	285	NRC7243	384	NRC7583	411	NRC7977	377
NRC5804	500	NRC6324	701	NRC6795	317	NRC7249	383	NRC7603	212	NRC7979	371
NRC5808	717	NRC6339	383	NRC6799	398	NRC7249	384	NRC7605	394	NRC7979	375
NRC5818	359	NRC6339	384	NRC6829	390	NRC7283	384	NRC7606	394	NRC7981	282
NRC5819	717	NRC6352	420	NRC6829	391	NRC7284	367	NRC7607	394	NRC7984	317
NRC5820	717	NRC6353	420	NRC6836	392	NRC7303	371	NRC7608	404	NRC7987	305
NRC5823	718	NRC6353	422	NRC6836	393	NRC7303	375	NRC7608	405	NRC7988	305
NRC5824	718	NRC6372	277	NRC6888	407	NRC7303	379	NRC7609	404	NRC8007	281
NRC5844	358	NRC6374	402	NRC6889	407	NRC7308	371	NRC7609	405	NRC8017	379
NRC5844	359	NRC6374	403	NRC6902	420	NRC7308	375	NRC7616	290	NRC8018	379
NRC5886	499	NRC6388	282	NRC6902	421	NRC7308	376	NRC7635	285	NRC8024	271
NRC5975	305	NRC6389	282	NRC6903	421	NRC7310	371	NRC7636	285	NRC8044	277
NRC5976	305	NRC6403	409	NRC6904	282	NRC7310	373	NRC7648	319	NRC8045	277
NRC5977	305	NRC6404	409	NRC6917	346	NRC7310	375	NRC7661	280	NRC8048	702
NRC5982	303	NRC6404	410	NRC6919	346	NRC7310	376	NRC7704	285	NRC8048	703
NRC5985	409	NRC6417	417	NRC6919	348	NRC7310	379	NRC7730	387	NRC8059	319
NRC6046	343	NRC6417	418	NRC6920	346	NRC7311	383	NRC7741	716	NRC8062	398
NRC6051	290	NRC6418	417	NRC6920	348	NRC7311	384	NRC7758	701	NRC8063	398
NRC6052	290	NRC6418	418	NRC6935	497	NRC7312	379	NRC7778	400	NRC8087	371

PART NO	PAGE	PART NO	PAGE	PART NO	PAGE	PART NO	PAGE	PART NO	PAGE	PART NO	PAGE
NRC8087	375	NRC8347	419	NRC9091	422	NRC9561	212	NT108041L	217	NTC1568	317
NRC8087	379	NRC8349	314	NRC9098	422	NRC9562	391	NT108041L	258	NTC1570	418
NRC8103	376	NRC8352	314	NRC9107	348	NRC9564	497	NT108041L	655	NTC1571	418
NRC8104	375	NRC8367	285	NRC9115	317	NRC9575	315	NT108041L	660	NTC1580	293
NRC8104	376	NRC8369	404	NRC9121	394	NRC9595	164	NT110041	711	NTC1581	293
NRC8107	371	NRC8375	281	NRC9123	317	NRC9620	373	NT110041	712	NTC1582	296
NRC8108	376	NRC8404	305	NRC9123	318	NRC9621	365	NT110041	713	NTC1583	296
NRC8111	371	NRC8404	306	NRC9137	400	NRC9621	366	NT110041	715	NTC1612	389
NRC8114	371	NRC8405	305	NRC9138	392	NRC9630	495	NT112041	265	NTC1643	319
NRC8116	394	NRC8405	306	NRC9138	393	NRC9668	416	NT112041L	394	NTC1650	345
NRC8117	394	NRC8408	305	NRC9169	311	NRC9669	416	NT605041L	142	NTC1664	400
NRC8196	717	NRC8408	306	NRC9183	311	NRC9678	393	NT605041L	143	NTC1681	306
NRC8197	717	NRC8413	343	NRC9211	499	NRC9710	409	NT605041L	463	NTC1682	306
NRC8198	718	NRC8421	497	NRC9217	163	NRC9711	285	NT605061L	31	NTC1683	306
NRC8199	718	NRC8459	497	NRC9224	311	NRC9713	263	NT605061L	86	NTC1684	306
NRC8201	716	NRC8462	376	NRC9233	311	NRC9722	400	NT607041L	164	NTC1685	306
NRC8204	212	NRC8502	398	NRC9238	345	NRC9722	402	NT608041L	277	NTC1686	306
NRC8206	398	NRC8503	398	NRC9246	274	NRC9722	403	NT614041	296	NTC1687	306
NRC8208	700	NRC8507	717	NRC9284	398	NRC9724	402	NT614041L	293	NTC1691	306
NRC8208	701	NRC8509	717	NRC9285	398	NRC9724	403	NTC1003	373	NTC1707	410
NRC8210	700	NRC8510	717	NRC9338	313	NRC9726	409	NTC1004	373	NTC1725	497
NRC8211	700	NRC8518	281	NRC9338	314	NRC9728	276	NTC1005	373	NTC1731	285
NRC8213	316	NRC8556	288	NRC9379	384	NRC9729	276	NTC1008	373	NTC1772	279
NRC8214	316	NRC8556	290	NRC9448	277	NRC9731	315	NTC1011	373	NTC1774	276
NRC8215	316	NRC8557	288	NRC9449	277	NRC9733	400	NTC1014	373	NTC1775	297
NRC8229	701	NRC8557	290	NRC9456	316	NRC9742	297	NTC1016	373	NTC1791	304
NRC8230	701	NRC8560	398	NRC9461	319	NRC9743	297	NTC1030	401	NTC1792	316
NRC8231	297	NRC8588	288	NRC9472	356	NRC9749	497	NTC1030	403	NTC1793K	401
NRC8232	297	NRC8589	288	NRC9492	305	NRC9770	374	NTC1043	368	NTC1794K	401
NRC8238	404	NRC8593	314	NRC9492	306	NRC9770	389	NTC1044	368	NTC1797	405
NRC8238	405	NRC8609	407	NRC9501	259	NRC9771	374	NTC1048	358	NTC1800K	405
NRC8245	419	NRC8618	717	NRC9507	358	NRC9771	389	NTC1077	311	NTC2017	389
NRC8247	419	NRC8620	422	NRC9508	356	NRC9772	374	NTC1088	422	NTC2029	410
NRC8248	419	NRC8626	398	NRC9515	388	NRC9786	374	NTC1089	422	NTC2036	400
NRC8286	305	NRC8627	398	NRC9526	372	NRC9786	380	NTC1090	422	NTC2064	381
NRC8287	305	NRC8629	314	NRC9536	372	NRC9812	384	NTC1091	384	NTC2069	374
NRC8290	305	NRC8641	498	NRC9540	372	NRC9862	359	NTC1112	163	NTC2069	380
NRC8291	305	NRC8683	345	NRC9543	391	NRC9863	359	NTC1133K	403	NTC2072	374
NRC8292	305	NRC8690	312	NRC9543	393	NRC9865	358	NTC1136K	403	NTC2073	374
NRC8323	687	NRC8707	420	NRC9551	303	NRC9865	359	NTC1144	384	NTC2073	380
NRC8323	696	NRC8721	315	NRC9552	303	NS106011	608	NTC1201	259	NTC2086	394
NRC8323	698	NRC8734	398	NRC9557	21	NS106011	610	NTC1212	421	NTC2087	394
NRC8329	164	NRC8885	163	NRC9557	49	NS106011	613	NTC1224	317	NTC2089	391
NRC8330	164	NRC8911	400	NRC9557	73	NS106011	615	NTC1384	398	NTC2093	382
NRC8332	398	NRC8955	345	NRC9557	102	NT108041L	31	NTC1385	398	NTC2096	374
NRC8333	398	NRC8962	345	NRC9560	21	NT108041L	57	NTC1532	317	NTC2096	380
NRC8346	418	NRC8966	400	NRC9560	49	NT108041L	86	NTC1532	318	NTC2097	382
NRC8346	419	NRC8984	348	NRC9560	73	NT108041L	113	NTC1557	317	NTC2099	393
NRC8346	421	NRC8987	345	NRC9560	102	NT108041L	199	NTC1563	318	NTC2110	393
NRC8346	422	NRC9035	316	NRC9560	212	NT108041L	200			NTC2120	380

PART NO	PAGE	PART NO	PAGE	PART NO	PAGE	PART NO	PAGE	PART NO	PAGE	PART NO	PAGE
NTC2122	380	NTC2879	382	NY108041L	111	NY116041L	226	PC108321L	182	PRC2734	483
NTC2156	389	NTC2880	382	NY108041L	143	NY116041L	699	PC108321L	183	PRC2735	483
NTC2157	375	NTC2914	386	NY108041L	164	NY116041L	700	PC108321L	198	PRC2854	471
NTC2157	376	NTC3295	693	NY108041L	183	NY116041L	701	PC108321L	199	PRC2854	472
NTC2179	375	NTC3296	693	NY108041L	199	NY120041	276	PC108321L	257	PRC2854	479
NTC2179	376	NTC3396	394	NY108041L	200	NY120041	279	PC108321L	258	PRC2876	474
NTC2180	391	NTC3455	383	NY108041L	206	NY120041L	190	PRC1039	226	PRC2911	189
NTC2223	374	NTC3457	383	NY108041L	209	NY120041L	193	PRC1039	237	PRC2911	206
NTC2224	374	NTC3543	409	NY108041L	226	NY120041L	207	PRC1039	474	PRC2911	251
NTC2224	380	NTC3686	398	NY108041L	251	NY120041L	210	PRC1333	488	PRC2911	474
NTC2225	381	NTC3687	398	NY108041L	254	NY120041L	228	PRC1333	515	PRC2964	476
NTC2225	382	NTC3692	380	NY108041L	258	NY120041L	252	PRC1716	451	PRC2970	482
NTC2227	381	NTC3793	339	NY108041L	285	NY120041L	255	PRC1794	489	PRC2978	491
NTC2229	386	NTC3794	339	NY108041L	316	NY604041L	297	PRC1859	495	PRC2979	481
NTC2263	381	NTC3866	374	NY108041L	341	NY604041L	575	PRC1860	495	PRC2980	481
NTC2263	382	NTC3867	374	NY108041L	362	NY606041L	263	PRC1984	492	PRC3025	481
NTC2269	386	NTC4165	306	NY108041L	388	NY607041	288	PRC2015	495	PRC3030	471
NTC2275	400	NTC4580	401	NY108041L	389	NY607041	288	PRC2032	474	PRC3030	472
NTC2275	401	NTC4586	401	NY108041L	390	NY607041L	290	PRC2057	492	PRC3032	466
NTC2278	400	NTC4609	407	NY108041L	391	NY607041L	293	PRC2167	470	PRC3037	488
NTC2278	401	NTC5002	407	NY108041L	459	NY607041L	296	PRC2230	495	PRC3095	490
NTC2292	339	NTC5171	407	NY108041L	460	NY608041L	277	PRC2239	492	PRC3098	392
NTC2333	393	NTC614041	288	NY108041L	461	NY608041L	280	PRC2278	483	PRC3098	393
NTC2334	393	NV605041L	362	NY108041L	462	NY608041L	282	PRC2291	471	PRC3101	490
NTC2337	386	NV605041L	363	NY108041L	498	NY610041	276	PRC2291	472	PRC3105	481
NTC2595	306	NV608041	277	NY108041L	505	NY612041	280	PRC2403	702	PRC3107	481
NTC2597	306	NV608041L	282	NY108041L	509	NZ606041L	275	PRC2437	478	PRC3108	481
NTC2655	386	NY105041	507	NY108041L	510	NZX8076L	335	PRC2437	479	PRC3115	482
NTC2676	386	NY105041L	181	NY108041L	555	PA105101	718	PRC2439	702	PRC3116	482
NTC2681	389	NY105041L	197	NY108041L	593	PA105101L	79	PRC2439	703	PRC3122	482
NTC2690	386	NY105041L	256	NY110041	279	PA105101L	107	PRC2443	488	PRC3131	451
NTC2699	386	NY106041	304	NY110041L	178	PA105161	394	PRC2471	477	PRC3131	452
NTC2701	405	NY106041L	193	NY110041L	244	PA106201	607	PRC2475	388	PRC3180	481
NTC2705	276	NY106041L	229	NY110041L	273	PA108361L	218	PRC2475	390	PRC3180	491
NTC2708	279	NY106041L	316	NY110041L	281	PA110260L	230	PRC2497	483	PRC3196	390
NTC2723	304	NY106041L	358	NY110041L	282	PA110300L	230	PRC2505	37	PRC3209	487
NTC2726	403	NY106041L	359	NY110041L	297	PA120751L	177	PRC2505	41	PRC3231	471
NTC2731	405	NY106041L	411	NY110041L	499	PA120801L	177	PRC2505	62	PRC3231	472
NTC2737	411	NY106041L	546	NY110041L	500	PC105401L	183	PRC2505	63	PRC3232	471
NTC2743	394	NY106041L	552	NY110041L	501	PC105401L	199	PRC2505	65	PRC3232	472
NTC2749	304	NY106041L	559	NY110041L	576	PC105401L	258	PRC2505	80	PRC3247	491
NTC2757	386	NY106041L	575	NY110041L	603	PC106291	711	PRC2505	108	PRC3250	491
NTC2768	497	NY106041L	607	NY110041L	700	PC106291	713	PRC2505	717	PRC3250	472
NTC2769	497	NY106041L	608	NY110041L	701	PC106291	715	PRC2506	149	PRC3268	388
NTC2837	389	NY106041L	610	NY110051L	280	PC106641	614	PRC2507	136	PRC3268	389
NTC2876	374	NY106041L	613	NY112041L	561	PC108241	533	PRC2516	474	PRC3299	474
NTC2876	380	NY106041L	615	NY114041	276	PC108291	317	PRC2668	456	PRC3300	471
NTC2876	381	NY106041L	670	NY116041	278	PC108291	318	PRC2668	458	PRC3340	478
NTC2876	382	NY106041L	713	NY116041	713	PC108291	319	PRC2669	458	PRC3343	365
NTC2878	382	NY108041L	95					PRC2677	457	PRC3353	318

PART NO	PAGE	PART NO	PAGE	PART NO	PAGE	PART NO	PAGE	PART NO	PAGE	PART NO	PAGE
PRC3359	149	PRC3969	488	PRC4333	495	PRC5141	472	PS103121	713	RA612373L	561
PRC3362	488	PRC3977	478	PRC4372	122	PRC5252	470	PS103121	715	RA612373L	562
PRC3363	488	PRC3978	478	PRC4372	123	PRC5316	490	PS103121L	206	RA612373L	566
PRC3366	40	PRC3979	489	PRC4376	323	PRC5319	488	PS103121L	243	RA612373L	568
PRC3366	64	PRC3980	489	PRC4376	489	PRC5336	488	PS103121L	614	RA612373L	572
PRC3366	81	PRC3980	491	PRC4429	481	PRC5537	483	PS104121L	182	RA612373L	603
PRC3366	109	PRC3997	487	PRC4430	149	PRC5538	468	PS104121L	257	RA612373L	608
PRC3368	487	PRC4019	489	PRC4433	484	PRC5543	382	PS104121L	258	RA612373L	610
PRC3369	472	PRC4020	489	PRC4436	485	PRC5544	487	PS104121L	317	RB610082	557
PRC3369	479	PRC4021	489	PRC4438	484	PRC5567	481	PS104121L	318	RB610082	564
PRC3389	488	PRC4021	491	PRC4442	318	PRC5600	487	PS104121L	319	RB613102	557
PRC3423	477	PRC4043	122	PRC4449	484	PRC5602	487	PS104127	508	RB613102	564
PRC3423	485	PRC4043	123	PRC4454	484	PRC5603	487	PS104127L	183	RB613109	524
PRC3430	483	PRC4044	62	PRC4456	492	PRC5662	481	PS104127L	198	RF608041	606
PRC3432	483	PRC4044	63	PRC4460	490	PRC5663	481	PS104127L	199	RF608041	609
PRC3494	323	PRC4082	491	PRC4471	486	PRC5664	481	PS104161	319	RF608041	612
PRC3494	489	PRC4083	491	PRC4473	474	PRC5852	389	PS105251	278	RJ608603	593
PRC3505	149	PRC4084	491	PRC4503	452	PRC5852	391	PS105321L	297	RJ610243	613
PRC3537	487	PRC4085	491	PRC4504	481	PRC5852	393	PS106161	508	RJ612433	572
PRC3541	40	PRC4092	491	PRC4524	484	PRC6021	481	PS106201	311	RKC5098L	172
PRC3541	64	PRC4096	489	PRC4576	484	PRC6022	491	PS606101L	139	RR612063	590
PRC3541	81	PRC4097	489	PRC4590	487	PRC6023	481	PS608101L	263	RR612103	608
PRC3541	109	PRC4127	703	PRC4591	486	PRC6133	452	PS608101L	280	RR612103	610
PRC3542	702	PRC4151	703	PRC4595	494	PRC6141	452	PS612080	590	RRC2303	721
PRC3543	702	PRC4152	703	PRC4612	485	PRC6144	452	RA608123	515	RRC2304	721
PRC3588	474	PRC4208	493	PRC4613	485	PRC6283	477	RA608177L	647	RRC2361	721
PRC3617	474	PRC4209	702	PRC4616	495	PRC6295	80	RA608177L	390	RRC2403	721
PRC3625	495	PRC4230	485	PRC4624	485	PRC6295	108	RA608177L	391	RRC2404	721
PRC3649	477	PRC4268	719	PRC4655	481	PRC6366	453	RA608177L	575	RRC2406	721
PRC3650	477	PRC4276	477	PRC4785	489	PRC6366	454	RA608177L	599	RRC2407	721
PRC3671	477	PRC4277	477	PRC4840	487	PRC6366	455	RA608236L	558	RRC2409	722
PRC3672	477	PRC4278	477	PRC4928	481	PRC6387	38	RA608236L	566	RRC2417	721
PRC3678	481	PRC4282	719	PRC4951	452	PRC6387	39	RA610123	516	RRC2420	721
PRC3702	323	PRC4283	719	PRC4952	489	PRC6387	62	RA610167	485	RRC2423	721
PRC3702	489	PRC4287	453	PRC4953	489	PRC6387	63	RA610183	503	RRC2426	721
PRC3737	484	PRC4287	454	PRC4953	491	PRC6387	122	RA612123L	623	RRC2427	721
PRC3737	493	PRC4287	455	PRC4954	489	PRC6387	123	RA612156L	532	RRC2428	721
PRC3738	493	PRC4288	457	PRC4970	487	PRC7018	391	RA612156L	545	RRC2432	721
PRC3780	472	PRC4297	311	PRC4972	389	PRC7019	393	RA612156L	670	RRC2436	721
PRC3786	479	PRC4298	719	PRC4975	391	PRC7020	389	RA612156L	684	RRC2437	721
PRC3794	472	PRC4299	719	PRC4993	487	PRC7204	136	RA612157L	596	RRC2438	721
PRC3794	479	PRC4301	719	PRC4994	489	PRC7326	490	RA612183	506	RRC2439	721
PRC3813	476	PRC4304	719	PRC4995	489	PS102081	398	RA612183	509	RRC2440	721
PRC3833	481	PRC4305	494	PRC4996	489	PS102081L	394	RA612183	510	RRC2442	722
PRC3839	489	PRC4306	493	PRC5109	468	PS103081L	394	RA612236	684	RRC2443	722
PRC3875	483	PRC4309	494	PRC5123	488	PS103101	533	RA612253L	504	RRC2445	722
PRC3900	483	PRC4311	493	PRC5127	471	PS103101L	183	RA612346	605	RRC2447	722
PRC3901	366	PRC4321	493	PRC5127	472	PS103101L	199	RA612347L	575	RRC2463	722
PRC3905	493	PRC4327	494	PRC5141	471	PS103101L	258	RA612347L	677	RRC2473	722
PRC3948	493	PRC4332	495			PS103121	711	RA612373L	558	RRC2475	721

PART NO	PAGE	PART NO	PAGE	PART NO	PAGE	PART NO	PAGE	PART NO	PAGE	PART NO	PAGE
RRC2476	722	RTC1323	469	RTC2916	96	RTC3175	485	RTC3413	712	RTC3664	327
RRC2477	722	RTC1481	337	RTC2918E	18	RTC3176	309	RTC3418	309	RTC3665	324
RRC2479	721	RTC1482L	337	RTC2918N	18	RTC3184	37	RTC3429	267	RTC3665	327
RRC2480	721	RTC1526	308	RTC2920	71	RTC3184	93	RTC3429	273	RTC3665	332
RRC2481	722	RTC1718	134	RTC2926	20	RTC3188	452	RTC3458	275	RTC3682	470
RRC2482	722	RTC171810	134	RTC2926	72	RTC3197	448	RTC3472	448	RTC3683	470
RRC2483	722	RTC171820	134	RTC294	291	RTC3197	449	RTC3474	446	RTC3725	355
RRC2485	722	RTC1730	22	RTC295	291	RTC3197	450	RTC3474	447	RTC3744	513
RRC2486	721	RTC1730	74	RTC297	291	RTC3198	449	RTC3479	349	RTC3744	519
RRC2487	721	RTC173010	22	RTC2972N	129	RTC3198	450	RTC3497	149	RTC3744	520
RRC2488	721	RTC173020	22	RTC2972R	129	RTC3199	449	RTC3499	361	RTC3744	521
RRC2491	722	RTC1956	181	RTC2973N	129	RTC3199	450	RTC3502	350	RTC3744	626
RRC2497	722	RTC1956	197	RTC2977N	70	RTC3200	449	RTC3502	353	RTC3745	482
RRC2498	722	RTC1956	256	RTC2977R	70	RTC3200	450	RTC3502	354	RTC3745	502
RRC2579	721	RTC198	477	RTC2978	19	RTC3201	449	RTC3511	267	RTC3745	516
RRC2593	721	RTC2057	169	RTC298	291	RTC3201	450	RTC3511	273	RTC3745	626
RRC2595	722	RTC2058	176	RTC299	291	RTC3215	453	RTC3511	348	RTC3745	708
RRC2596	722	RTC210	474	RTC2991	101	RTC3215	454	RTC3518	350	RTC3751	665
RRC2626	722	RTC2104	153	RTC2992	51	RTC3215	455	RTC3518	351	RTC3755	654
RRC2629	722	RTC2117	133	RTC2992	104	RTC3215	457	RTC3518	352	RTC3755	656
RRC2635	721	RTC211710	133	RTC299210	51	RTC3254	44	RTC3518	353	RTC3755	657
RRC2636	721	RTC211720	133	RTC299220	51	RTC3254	68	RTC3518	354	RTC3755	658
RRC2637	722	RTC2149	221	RTC2993	50	RTC3254	96	RTC3519	269	RTC3755	659
RRC2638	722	RTC2150	222	RTC2993	103	RTC3254	126	RTC3562	492	RTC3764	653
RRC2644	721	RTC218620	133	RTC299310	50	RTC327	300	RTC3566	335	RTC3764	656
RRC2645	721	RTC2186S	133	RTC300	291	RTC3278	446	RTC3569	446	RTC3764	657
RRC2957	722	RTC229520	133	RTC301	291	RTC3278	447	RTC3570	446	RTC3764	658
RRC2958	722	RTC2295S	133	RTC3022	386	RTC3282	446	RTC3570	448	RTC3764	659
RRC2963	722	RTC2348	140	RTC3022	624	RTC3286	448	RTC3570	449	RTC3772	35
RRC2974	722	RTC2349	140	RTC3023	503	RTC3290	454	RTC3570	450	RTC3772	60
RRC2975	722	RTC2372	130	RTC3024	649	RTC3292	456	RTC3607	411	RTC3772	90
RRC3264	615	RTC2408	133	RTC3033N	100	RTC3292	458	RTC3614	446	RTC3772	116
RRC3584	615	RTC240820	133	RTC3036	503	RTC3336	96	RTC3614	447	RTC3772	489
RRC3683	385	RTC2486	594	RTC3037	126	RTC3346	275	RTC3618	448	RTC3812	447
RRC3684	385	RTC2626	23	RTC3038	126	RTC3348	308	RTC3626	309	RTC3826	269
RRC4422	722	RTC2626	75	RTC304	292	RTC3354	497	RTC3627	309	RTC3833	53
RRC4878	535	RTC262610	23	RTC304	295	RTC3397	191	RTC3635	481	RTC3833	106
RRC4878	547	RTC262620	23	RTC305	292	RTC3397	208	RTC3635	484	RTC3867	477
RRC4879	535	RTC2726	264	RTC305320	103	RTC3397	227	RTC3644	36	RTC3889	179
RRC5034	529	RTC2762	292	RTC305340	103	RTC3397	253	RTC3644	61	RTC3890	194
RRC5035	529	RTC2825	23	RTC3053S	103	RTC3398	713	RTC3644	91	RTC3890	211
RRC5539	593	RTC2825	51	RTC3056	303	RTC3403	310	RTC3650	472	RTC3934AV	539
RRO2125L	407	RTC2825	75	RTC3058	303	RTC3406	190	RTC3650	478	RTC3934AV	551
RRO2126L	407	RTC2825	104	RTC306	292	RTC3406	193	RTC3650	479	RTC3935PA	538
RT612253	555	RTC2889	44	RTC307	291	RTC3406	207	RTC3650	485	RTC3935PA	550
RT612283	542	RTC2889	68	RTC3105	661	RTC3406	210	RTC3661	142	RTC3938AV	639
RT612283	591	RTC2890	44	RTC3106	661	RTC3406	228	RTC3663	324	RTC3938AV	641
RTC1139	271	RTC2890	68	RTC3107	661	RTC3406	252	RTC3663	327	RTC3939PA	538
RTC1148	392	RTC2913	153	RTC3108	661	RTC3406	255	RTC3663	332	RTC3939PA	550
RTC1148	393	RTC2914	173	RTC315	446	RTC3413	223	RTC3664	324	RTC3940PA	538

PART NO	PAGE	PART NO	PAGE	PART NO	PAGE	PART NO	PAGE	PART NO	PAGE	PART NO	PAGE
RTC3940PA	550	RTC418820	22	RTC4419	331	RTC4816	23	RTC5070	296	RTC5925	454
RTC3942	328	RTC418840	22	RTC4420	325	RTC4817	23	RTC5071	296	RTC5925	455
RTC3948	323	RTC4188S	22	RTC4420	331	RTC4817	51	RTC5072	296	RTC5926	453
RTC3949	323	RTC418920	50	RTC4421	325	RTC4825	306	RTC5073	296	RTC5926	454
RTC3962	303	RTC4189S	50	RTC4421	331	RTC4826	306	RTC5074	296	RTC5926	455
RTC3985	48	RTC419020	22	RTC4425	164	RTC4841	26	RTC5077	341	RTC5946	447
RTC4027A	695	RTC419040	22	RTC4472	297	RTC4841	53	RTC5089	450	RTC5947	447
RTC4027T	695	RTC4190S	22	RTC4477	136	RTC4841	78	RTC5090	450	RTC5967	465
RTC4032A	695	RTC419120	74	RTC4480	477	RTC4841	106	RTC5091	450	RTC5970	332
RTC4032T	695	RTC419140	74	RTC4482	488	RTC4849	331	RTC5092	450	RTC5978	414
RTC4033A	695	RTC4191S	74	RTC4485	298	RTC4850	322	RTC5228E	469	RTC601	526
RTC4033T	695	RTC419320	74	RTC4486	264	RTC4850	326	RTC5233E	465	RTC601	528
RTC4035A	695	RTC419340	74	RTC4488	272	RTC4850	331	RTC5249N	467	RTC6065	682
RTC4035T	695	RTC4193S	74	RTC4490	191	RTC4851	332	RTC5523	474	RTC6065	683
RTC4041A	695	RTC4198	288	RTC4490	208	RTC4852	331	RTC5524	474	RTC6072	335
RTC4041T	695	RTC4198	290	RTC4490	253	RTC4853	332	RTC5572	308	RTC608	385
RTC4042A	695	RTC4198	293	RTC4500	488	RTC4857	331	RTC5573	308	RTC608	386
RTC4042T	695	RTC4198	296	RTC4500	493	RTC4859	331	RTC5574	308	RTC608	475
RTC4043A	695	RTC4199	314	RTC4502	484	RTC4860	332	RTC5587	584	RTC608	577
RTC4043T	695	RTC4200	413	RTC4502	488	RTC4861	332	RTC5628	452	RTC608	579
RTC4044A	695	RTC4201	413	RTC4505	488	RTC4896	331	RTC5629	451	RTC608	582
RTC4044T	695	RTC4340	604	RTC4507	493	RTC4897	331	RTC5670	453	RTC608	595
RTC4045A	695	RTC4341	604	RTC4510	488	RTC4898	331	RTC5670	454	RTC608	669
RTC4045T	695	RTC4342	604	RTC4510	493	RTC4899	331	RTC5670	455	RTC6082N	166
RTC4046A	695	RTC4373	254	RTC4594	47	RTC4900	331	RTC5674	299	RTC609	141
RTC4046T	695	RTC437420	50	RTC4595N	46	RTC4901	331	RTC5675	299	RTC609	151
RTC4047A	695	RTC4374S	50	RTC4598	495	RTC4902	331	RTC5684	453	RTC609	152
RTC4047T	695	RTC4391	294	RTC4598DC	495	RTC4903	331	RTC5684	454	RTC609	328
RTC4048A	695	RTC4392	294	RTC4599	495	RTC4904	332	RTC5684	455	RTC609	512
RTC4048T	695	RTC4393	294	RTC4599DC	495	RTC4906	332	RTC5685	453	RTC609	525
RTC4049A	695	RTC4394	294	RTC4607	453	RTC4908	332	RTC5685	454	RTC609	527
RTC4049T	695	RTC4395	294	RTC4607	454	RTC4932	446	RTC5685	455	RTC609	567
RTC4051A	695	RTC4396	294	RTC4607	456	RTC4933	446	RTC5686	453	RTC610	163
RTC4051T	695	RTC4397	294	RTC4607	457	RTC4934	446	RTC5686	454	RTC610	412
RTC4054A	695	RTC4398	294	RTC4607	458	RTC4935	446	RTC5686	455	RTC610	526
RTC4054T	695	RTC4399	294	RTC4608N	129	RTC4936	446	RTC5687	453	RTC610	528
RTC4055A	695	RTC4400	294	RTC4615	470	RTC4978	468	RTC5687	454	RTC610	682
RTC4055T	695	RTC4401	294	RTC4637	277	RTC4979	468	RTC5687	455	RTC610	683
RTC4056A	695	RTC4402	295	RTC4638	282	RTC4980	468	RTC5689	453	RTC6110	291
RTC4056T	695	RTC4403	295	RTC4639	282	RTC4981	468	RTC5689	454	RTC6110	294
RTC4057A	695	RTC4404	295	RTC4685	704	RTC4982	468	RTC5689	455	RTC6115	131
RTC4057T	695	RTC4405	295	RTC4686	704	RTC4983	468	RTC5869	332	RTC6115	259
RTC4058A	695	RTC4406	295	RTC473320	103	RTC5001	308	RTC5869	297	RTC6129	289
RTC4058T	695	RTC4407	295	RTC4738	285	RTC5012	473	RTC5870	297	RTC613	152
RTC4059E	99	RTC4408	295	RTC4740	386	RTC5013	473	RTC5891	341	RTC613	528
RTC4059N	99	RTC4409	295	RTC4741	386	RTC5063	481	RTC5892	495	RTC613	594
RTC4102	662	RTC4410	295	RTC477820	103	RTC5064	209	RTC5892DC	495	RTC6130	289
RTC4183	474	RTC4411	292	RTC4778S	103	RTC5064	254	RTC5918	137	RTC614	594
RTC4184	474	RTC4411	295	RTC4815	23	RTC5068	296	RTC5919	137	RTC614	653
RTC4185	474	RTC4419	325	RTC4815	51	RTC5069	296	RTC5925	453	RTC614	656

PART NO	PAGE	PART NO	PAGE	PART NO	PAGE	PART NO	PAGE	PART NO	PAGE	PART NO	PAGE
RTC614	657	RTC6338	143	RTC7441	431	RTC836	469	RU612503	575	SE106121L	492
RTC614	658	RTC6396	293	RTC7442	431	RTC837	469	SA106141	593	SE106127	478
RTC614	659	RTC6397	293	RTC7443	434	RTC839	469	SA106161	597	SE106161	357
RTC615	659	RTC6398	296	RTC7444	434	RTC844	271	SA106161	615	SE106161L	452
RTC616	219	RTC6399	296	RTC7445	434	RTC845	271	SA106201	610	SE106161L	477
RTC6164	490	RTC6474	617	RTC7446	431	RU608123L	515	SA106201	655	SE106161L	530
RTC6167	105	RTC6476	617	RTC7446	434	RU608123L	523	SA106251	597	SE106161L	572
RTC6168	105	RTC6545	389	RTC7447	434	RU608123L	524	SA106451	608	SE106161L	575
RTC6180	363	RTC6545	391	RTC7448	434	RU608123L	644	SA106451	613	SE106161L	597
RTC6205	525	RTC6545	393	RTC7449	434	RU608183L	593	SA108161	309	SE106161L	670
RTC6205	527	RTC6545	487	RTC7450	437	RU608253L	660	SA108201L	310	SE106164	671
RTC6206	525	RTC7131	268	RTC7451	434	RU608253L	662	SA506081L	138	SE106167	451
RTC6206	527	RTC7132	268	RTC7452	430	RU608313L	561	SA506081L	464	SE106167	452
RTC6209	527	RTC7133	268	RTC7452	440	RU608313L	568	SB108201L	242	SE106201L	313
RTC6210	527	RTC7136	268	RTC7453	430	RU608313L	577	SD106401L	615	SE106201L	491
RTC6211	516	RTC7137	268	RTC7454	430	RU608313L	582	SE104121L	318	SE106201L	557
RTC6212	516	RTC7408	436	RTC7454	442	RU608313L	584	SE104124	626	SE106201L	565
RTC6213	507	RTC7409	436	RTC7455	430	RU608313L	585	SE105101L	492	SE106201L	591
RTC6214	511	RTC7410	437	RTC7456	430	RU608313L	586	SE105121L	389	SE106201L	610
RTC6215	511	RTC7411	437	RTC7457	430	RU608313L	672	SE105121L	391	SE106201L	648
RTC6218	522	RTC7411	444	RTC7457	440	RU608313L	673	SE105121L	393	SE106201L	672
RTC6220	582	RTC7412	437	RTC7458	430	RU610313L	580	SE105121L	484	SE106204	665
RTC6221	582	RTC7413	437	RTC7459	432	RU612123	618	SE105121L	487	SE106204	667
RTC6222	587	RTC7414	430	RTC7460	432	RU612183	385	SE105121L	493	SE106251	601
RTC6231	511	RTC7414	434	RTC7461	432	RU612183	572	SE105121L	626	SE106251L	600
RTC6232	511	RTC7415	436	RTC7462	436	RU612183	573	SE105121L	627	SE106251L	648
RTC6233	511	RTC7416	429	RTC7463	436	RU612183	574	SE105141	507	SE106351L	649
RTC6235	511	RTC7417	429	RTC7464	436	RU612183	575	SE105161	286	SE106351L	650
RTC6236	511	RTC7418	429	RTC7465	437	RU612183	610	SE105161	319	SE106501L	591
RTC6246	556	RTC7419	429	RTC7465	444	RU612183	709	SE105161	602	SE108061	591
RTC6247	596	RTC7420	429	RTC7467	432	RU612373L	512	SE105161L	414	SE108161L	500
RTC6248	596	RTC7421	429	RTC7467	439	RU612373L	556	SE105161L	503	SE108164	666
RTC625	700	RTC7422	429	RTC7468	431	RU612373L	557	SE105161L	536	SE108201	555
RTC625	701	RTC7423	429	RTC7469	431	RU612373L	558	SE105161L	542	SE108201	592
RTC6253	579	RTC7424	429	RTC7470	431	RU612373L	561	SE105201L	317	SE108204	666
RTC626	164	RTC7425	429	RTC7470	432	RU612373L	563	SE105201L	318	SE108251	554
RTC6267	515	RTC7426	429	RTC7470	438	RU612373L	564	SE105251	652	SE108251	564
RTC6268	515	RTC7427	429	RTC7470	439	RU612373L	585	SE105251	654	SE108251	592
RTC6270	565	RTC7428	429	RTC7471	430	RU612373L	589	SE105251	656	SE108251	598
RTC6287	529	RTC7429	429	RTC7472	430	RU612373L	605	SE105251	657	SE108254	665
RTC6288	529	RTC7430	429	RTC7473	430	RU612373L	613	SE105251L	658	SE108501	598
RTC6291	563	RTC7431	430	RTC7474	431	RU612373L	618	SE105251L	659	SE110401	518
RTC6331	117	RTC7432	430	RTC773	272	RU612373L	652	SE105251L	672	SE604071L	604
RTC6331	119	RTC7433	430	RTC8063	268	RU612373L	657	SE105351	702	SE808244	414
RTC6332	118	RTC7434	430	RTC8064	720	RU612373L	658	SE105351	703	SF104164	604
RTC6332	120	RTC7435	430	RTC8065	720	RU612373L	671	SE105351L	611	SF104204L	604
RTC6333	36	RTC7436	430	RTC8071	630	RU612373L	675	SE105401	286	SF106161	507
RTC6333	61	RTC7437	430	RTC830	469	RU612373L	678	SE106121L	116	SF106161	707
RTC6333	91	RTC7439	430	RTC831	469	RU612503	385	SE106121L	285	SF106201L	182
RTC6337	143	RTC7440	431	RTC834	469	RU612503	386	SE106121L	488	SF106201L	198

PART NO	PAGE	PART NO	PAGE	PART NO	PAGE	PART NO	PAGE	PART NO	PAGE	PART NO	PAGE
SF106201L	257	SH106121L	716	SH106161L	541	SH106201L	526	SH106451L	215	SH108201L	409
SF106201L	660	SH106124	671	SH106161L	562	SH106201L	527	SH108121L	353	SH108201L	447
SF106201L	662	SH106124	673	SH106161L	581	SH106201L	544	SH108141L	43	SH108201L	461
SF106201L	663	SH106141	383	SH106161L	583	SH106201L	557	SH108141L	67	SH108201L	462
SF108201L	226	SH106141	710	SH106161L	584	SH106201L	561	SH108141L	95	SH108201L	491
SF108251	593	SH106141L	38	SH106161L	585	SH106201L	565	SH108141L	298	SH108201L	497
SF108251L	184	SH106141L	39	SH106161L	586	SH106201L	568	SH108141L	299	SH108201L	502
SF108251L	201	SH106141L	62	SH106161L	589	SH106201L	574	SH108161	528	SH108201L	505
SF108251L	246	SH106141L	63	SH106161L	607	SH106201L	581	SH108161L	26	SH108201L	520
SG103084	414	SH106141L	122	SH106161L	704	SH106201L	583	SH108161L	36	SH108201L	526
SH104101L	549	SH106141L	123	SH106161L	716	SH106201L	584	SH108161L	53	SH108201L	541
SH104121L	41	SH106141L	346	SH106161L	717	SH106201L	585	SH108161L	60	SH108201L	553
SH104121L	92	SH106141L	358	SH106161L	718	SH106201L	586	SH108161L	61	SH108201L	557
SH104141L	368	SH106141L	359	SH106167	303	SH106201L	593	SH108161L	78	SH108201L	564
SH104201L	382	SH106141L	492	SH106167	451	SH106201L	597	SH108161L	92	SH108201L	576
SH105101	383	SH106141L	574	SH106167	452	SH106201L	599	SH108161L	106	SH108201L	598
SH105101L	384	SH106161	357	SH106201	498	SH106201L	605	SH108161L	116	SH108201L	613
SH105121	286	SH106161	506	SH106201	531	SH106201L	607	SH108161L	412	SH108201L	654
SH105121	357	SH106161	528	SH106201	533	SH106201L	655	SH108161L	500	SH108201L	668
SH105121	383	SH106161	531	SH106201	567	SH106201L	660	SH108161L	581	SH108201L	673
SH105121	387	SH106161	567	SH106201	595	SH106201L	704	SH108161L	583	SH108251L	25
SH105121L	116	SH106161	594	SH106201	613	SH106204	633	SH108201	364	SH108251L	26
SH105121L	384	SH106161	669	SH106201	622	SH106204	634	SH108201	559	SH108251L	33
SH105121L	516	SH106161	708	SH106201	675	SH106204	670	SH108201L	24	SH108251L	40
SH105161L	509	SH106161L	29	SH106201L	35	SH106207	411	SH108201L	25	SH108251L	52
SH105161L	510	SH106161L	55	SH106201L	60	SH106251	702	SH108201L	28	SH108251L	53
SH105201L	397	SH106161L	82	SH106201L	90	SH106251	703	SH108201L	33	SH108251L	64
SH105201L	628	SH106161L	95	SH106201L	116	SH106251L	215	SH108201L	35	SH108251L	75
SH106041	714	SH106161L	102	SH106201L	169	SH106251L	244	SH108201L	41	SH108251L	76
SH106101	712	SH106161L	110	SH106201L	177	SH106251L	304	SH108201L	43	SH108251L	78
SH106101L	161	SH106161L	176	SH106201L	181	SH106251L	316	SH108201L	52	SH108251L	80
SH106101L	162	SH106161L	177	SH106201L	197	SH106251L	417	SH108201L	54	SH108251L	81
SH106101L	537	SH106161L	216	SH106201L	256	SH106251L	418	SH108201L	59	SH108251L	92
SH106101L	538	SH106161L	305	SH106201L	281	SH106251L	588	SH108201L	60	SH108251L	95
SH106101L	548	SH106161L	306	SH106201L	298	SH106251L	593	SH108201L	65	SH108251L	104
SH106101L	550	SH106161L	340	SH106201L	299	SH106251L	597	SH108201L	67	SH108251L	105
SH106121	265	SH106161L	347	SH106201L	346	SH106251L	621	SH108201L	76	SH108251L	106
SH106121L	27	SH106161L	394	SH106201L	348	SH106251L	680	SH108201L	84	SH108251L	115
SH106121L	28	SH106161L	412	SH106201L	367	SH106251L	704	SH108201L	105	SH108251L	121
SH106121L	54	SH106161L	447	SH106201L	374	SH106301	281	SH108201L	108	SH108251L	158
SH106121L	80	SH106161L	452	SH106201L	380	SH106301	420	SH108201L	115	SH108251L	161
SH106121L	83	SH106161L	491	SH106201L	407	SH106301L	236	SH108201L	116	SH108251L	162
SH106121L	84	SH106161L	493	SH106201L	409	SH106301L	422	SH108201L	121	SH108251L	170
SH106121L	305	SH106161L	511	SH106201L	419	SH106301L	540	SH108201L	186	SH108251L	176
SH106121L	306	SH106161L	513	SH106201L	485	SH106351	592	SH108201L	203	SH108251L	178
SH106121L	308	SH106161L	522	SH106201L	520	SH106351L	224	SH108201L	248	SH108251L	181
SH106121L	343	SH106161L	525	SH106201L	522	SH106351L	358	SH108201L	400	SH108251L	183
SH106121L	345	SH106161L	526	SH106201L	523	SH106351L	359	SH108201L	401	SH108251L	187
SH106121L	367	SH106161L	527	SH106201L	524	SH106451	394	SH108201L	402	SH108251L	189
SH106121L	488	SH106161L	530	SH106201L	525	SH106451	394	SH108201L	403	SH108251L	197

PART NO	PAGE	PART NO	PAGE	PART NO	PAGE	PART NO	PAGE	PART NO	PAGE	PART NO	PAGE
SH108251L	199	SH108251L	677	SH110301	701	SH505061L	144	SH910241L	396	TE108041L	92
SH108251L	204	SH108251L	679	SH110301L	37	SH505071L	131	SK110101	711	TE108041L	106
SH108251L	206	SH108251L	681	SH110301L	38	SH505071L	301	SK110101	715	TE108041L	121
SH108251L	217	SH108251L	711	SH110301L	39	SH505071L	302	SL106121	498	TE108041L	143
SH108251L	218	SH108251L	715	SH110301L	62	SH505091L	141	SP104101	508	TE108051L	27
SH108251L	219	SH108254	665	SH110301L	63	SH505091L	149	SP104121	562	TE108051L	28
SH108251L	230	SH108301	681	SH110301L	93	SH506031	178	SP105121	383	TE108051L	41
SH108251L	231	SH108301L	42	SH110301L	122	SH506071L	138	SP105121	560	TE108051L	54
SH108251L	249	SH108301L	67	SH110301L	123	SH506071L	140	SP105121	566	TE108051L	65
SH108251L	251	SH108301L	218	SH110301L	155	SH506071L	301	SP105204	482	TE108051L	79
SH108251L	256	SH108301L	231	SH110301L	156	SH506071L	302	SP105204	484	TE108051L	83
SH108251L	258	SH108301L	243	SH110301L	157	SH506071L	428	SP108161L	231	TE108051L	84
SH108251L	276	SH108301L	298	SH110301L	184	SH506071L	464	SP604061	656	TE108051L	107
SH108251L	278	SH108301L	299	SH110301L	201	SH506081L	135	SR106201	608	TE108061L	73
SH108251L	279	SH108301L	363	SH110301L	246	SH506101L	151	SR106201	610	TE108061L	102
SH108251L	287	SH108301L	459	SH110301L	285	SH506121L	448	SR106251L	485	TE108061L	111
SH108251L	298	SH108301L	460	SH110301L	426	SH506121L	450	SS106201L	90 -	TE108071L	42
SH108251L	299	SH108301L	461	SH110301L	462	SH507091	131	SS108301L	125	TE108071L	79
SH108251L	317	SH108301L	581	SH110301L	466	SH604031L	132	SS108404	518	TE108071L	107
SH108251L	318	SH108301L	593	SH110301L	467	SH604031L	163	SS506121L	469	TE108081L	42
SH108251L	319	SH108301L	614	SH110301L	468	SH604041L	140	SU112101L	189	TE108081L	57
SH108251L	341	SH108301L	718	SH110301L	576	SH604051L	328	SU112101L	192	TE108081L	66
SH108251L	346	SH108351L	390	SH110351L	217	SH604061L	301	SU112101L	206	TE108111L	31
SH108251L	348	SH108351L	391	SH112121	712	SH604061L	302	SU112101L	209	TE108131L	42
SH108251L	356	SH108351L	459	SH112201	212	SH604081L	163	SU112101L	251	TE108131L	67
SH108251L	364	SH108351L	463	SH112201	710	SH605051L	152	SU112101L	254	TE110061L	155
SH108251L	390	SH108351L	464	SH112201	714	SH605061L	80	SX108201L	155	TE110061L	156
SH108251L	391	SH108401L	162	SH112251	674	SH605061L	301	SX108201L	156	TE110061L	157
SH108251L	392	SH108401L	238	SH112251L	21	SH605061L	302	SX108201L	157	TE112115L	217
SH108251L	393	SH108401L	298	SH112251L	49	SH605061L	428	SX108251	515	TE116155L	217
SH108251L	408	SH108401L	459	SH112251L	73	SH605071	420	SX108251	557	TE505105L	339
SH108251L	425	SH108401L	564	SH112251L	102	SH605071	594	SX108251	564	TE605211L	31
SH108251L	446	SH108501L	513	SH112251L	220	SH605071L	24	SX108251L	528	TKC1229	179
SH108251L	452	SH108701	498	SH112251L	259	SH605071L	76	SX108351L	243	TKC1229L	168
SH108251L	459	SH108701L	400	SH112301L	167	SH605081L	280	SX108701L	76	TKC1235	179
SH108251L	460	SH108701L	401	SH116301	711	SH605081L	301	SX110251	267	TKC1235L	168
SH108251L	464	SH108701L	402	SH116301	715	SH605081L	302	SY504072L	140	TKC1428L	174
SH108251L	492	SH108701L	403	SH406061	263	SH605081L	428	TD108091L	86	TKC290L	176
SH108251L	495	SH108701L	404	SH504041L	149	SH605081L	682	TD108091L	113	TKC4633L	174
SH108251L	498	SH108701L	405	SH504041L	215	SH605081L	683	TE106041L	156	TKC4635L	174
SH108251L	513	SH110161L	285	SH504041L	338	SH605121L	449	TE106041L	157	TKC4637L	174
SH108251L	546	SH110201	603	SH504041L	396	SH605141L	682	TE108031L	26	TKC4639L	174
SH108251L	552	SH110201	674	SH504051L	141	SH605141L	683	TE108031L	53	TKC4641L	174
SH108251L	555	SH110251L	282	SH504051L	144	SH606061L	160	TE108031L	78	TKC4643L	174
SH108251L	562	SH110251L	497	SH504051L	333	SH606061L	277	TE108031L	101	TKC4645L	174
SH108251L	572	SH110251L	499	SH504051L	395	SH606061L	319	TE108031L	106	TKC4647L	174
SH108251L	593	SH110251L	700	SH504051L	397	SH607051L	682	TE108041L	26	TKC4649L	174
SH108251L	608	SH110301	279	SH504061L	148	SH607051L	683	TE108041L	33	TKC4651L	174
SH108251L	610	SH110301	700	SH505041L	354	SH607081L	160	TE108041L	53	TKC4653L	174
SH108251L	674			SH505051	349	SH607091L	588	TE108041L	59	TKC4655L	174
								TE108041L	78		

PART NO	PAGE	PART NO	PAGE	PART NO	PAGE	PART NO	PAGE	PART NO	PAGE	PART NO	PAGE
TKC4657L	174	UTP1125	414	WA105001L	474	WA106041L	306	WA106041L	613	WA108051L	181
TKC4659L	174	UTP1126	414	WA105001L	486	WA106041L	308	WA106041L	614	WA108051L	182
TKC4661L	174	WA103001L	593	WA105001L	487	WA106041L	313	WA106041L	615	WA108051L	183
TKC4663L	174	WA103001L	645	WA105001L	490	WA106041L	316	WA106041L	648	WA108051L	184
TKC5779L	168	WA104001L	41	WA105001L	492	WA106041L	346	WA106041L	649	WA108051L	186
TKC6962L	171	WA104001L	80	WA105001L	493	WA106041L	347	WA106041L	650	WA108051L	187
TRS1013L	79	WA104001L	382	WA105001L	504	WA106041L	348	WA106041L	667	WA108051L	189
TRS1114L	79	WA104001L	471	WA105001L	509	WA106041L	367	WA106041L	702	WA108051L	198
TRS1114L	718	WA104001L	472	WA105001L	510	WA106041L	374	WA106041L	703	WA108051L	199
UKC1060	179	WA104001L	517	WA105001L	516	WA106041L	380	WA106041L	704	WA108051L	201
UKC1060L	170	WA104001L	532	WA105001L	532	WA106041L	394	WA106041L	708	WA108051L	203
UKC1689L	174	WA104001L	539	WA105001L	545	WA106041L	395	WA106041L	711	WA108051L	204
UKC1690L	174	WA104001L	545	WA105001L	555	WA106041L	396	WA106041L	713	WA108051L	206
UKC170L	168	WA104001L	549	WA105001L	572	WA106041L	397	WA106041L	715	WA108051L	209
UKC18L	174	WA104001L	572	WA105001L	574	WA106041L	409	WA106041L	716	WA108051L	212
UKC2089L	176	WA104001L	644	WA105001L	579	WA106041L	412	WA106044	665	WA108051L	220
UKC2089L	243	WA1040011	551	WA105001L	582	WA106041L	451	WA106045	502	WA108051L	230
UKC2105L	176	WA104004	437	WA105001L	611	WA106041L	452	WA106045	503	WA108051L	243
UKC2105L	243	WA104004L	494	WA105001L	623	WA106041L	471	WA106045	522	WA108051L	246
UKC24L	168	WA104004L	516	WA105001L	626	WA106041L	472	WA106047L	303	WA108051L	248
UKC24L	184	WA104004L	626	WA105001L	627	WA106041L	485	WA106047L	451	WA108051L	249
UKC25L	167	WA104004L	627	WA105001L	672	WA106041L	491	WA106047L	452	WA108051L	251
UKC2662L	174	WA104004L	629	WA105004L	414	WA106041L	495	WA106047L	478	WA108051L	254
UKC2738L	169	WA104041L	92	WA106001	538	WA106041L	498	WA106051L	102	WA108051L	257
UKC3058L	175	WA105001	286	WA106001L	550	WA106041L	506	WA108001	356	WA108051L	258
UKC3092	177	WA105001	357	WA106001L	265	WA106041L	511	WA108001	491	WA108051L	276
UKC30L	168	WA105001	383	WA106001L	384	WA106041L	513	WA108051L	25	WA108051L	278
UKC31L	171	WA105001	387	WA106001L	493	WA106041L	520	WA108051L	28	WA108051L	279
UKC31L	172	WA105001	415	WA106001L	561	WA106041L	522	WA108051L	35	WA108051L	287
UKC3530L	171	WA105001	416	WA106001L	568	WA106041L	526	WA108051L	42	WA108051L	299
UKC3530L	172	WA105001	507	WA106041L	38	WA106041L	528	WA108051L	43	WA108051L	311
UKC3531L	172	WA105001	603	WA106041L	39	WA106041L	533	WA108051L	52	WA108051L	316
UKC3660L	176	WA105001	703	WA106041L	62	WA106041L	537	WA108051L	54	WA108051L	317
UKC3794L	355	WA105001L	181	WA106041L	63	WA106041L	540	WA108051L	60	WA108051L	318
UKC3798L	355	WA105001L	183	WA106041L	116	WA106041L	548	WA108051L	66	WA108051L	319
UKC3799L	351	WA105001L	197	WA106041L	122	WA106041L	552	WA108051L	67	WA108051L	341
UKC3799L	352	WA105001L	199	WA106041L	123	WA106041L	557	WA108051L	76	WA108051L	343
UKC3802L	352	WA105001L	256	WA106041L	132	WA106041L	565	WA108051L	80	WA108051L	346
UKC3803	355	WA105001L	258	WA106041L	156	WA106041L	572	WA108051L	84	WA108051L	348
UKC3803L	339	WA105001L	317	WA106041L	157	WA106041L	574	WA108051L	94	WA108051L	363
UKC6683L	356	WA105001L	318	WA106041L	193	WA106041L	575	WA108051L	102	WA108051L	364
UKC73L	175	WA105001L	324	WA106041L	197	WA106041L	577	WA108051L	105	WA108051L	383
UKC75L	175	WA105001L	327	WA106041L	206	WA106041L	584	WA108051L	115	WA108051L	384
UKC8137L	139	WA105001L	341	WA106041L	229	WA106041L	585	WA108051L	121	WA108051L	388
UKC8677L	161	WA105001L	343	WA106041L	243	WA106041L	586	WA108051L	124	WA108051L	389
UKC8677L	162	WA105001L	384	WA106041L	256	WA106041L	589	WA108051L	141	WA108051L	390
UKC8L	171	WA105001L	389	WA106041L	287	WA106041L	591	WA108051L	142	WA108051L	391
ULC1796L	174	WA105001L	391	WA106041L	297	WA106041L	592	WA108051L	143	WA108051L	392
UNC6684	702	WA105001L	393	WA106041L	304	WA106041L	594	WA108051L	164	WA108051L	393
		WA105001L	414	WA106041L	305	WA106041L	605	WA108051L	170	WA108051L	395

PART NO	PAGE	PART NO	PAGE	PART NO	PAGE	PART NO	PAGE	PART NO	PAGE	PART NO	PAGE
WA108051L	396	WA110061L	212	WB600071L	329	WC108051L	528	WE106001L	551	WL104004	626
WA108051L	408	WA110061L	220	WC104001L	562	WC108051L	546	WE110001L	268	WL104041	368
WA108051L	409	WA110061L	244	WC104001L	632	WC108051L	552	WE600041L	656	WL105001	357
WA108051L	425	WA110061L	246	WC105001	437	WC108051L	554	WE600051L	80	WL105001	383
WA108051L	446	WA110061L	282	WC105001	652	WC108051L	555	WE600071L	164	WL105001	387
WA108051L	447	WA110061L	285	WC105001L	398	WC108051L	559	WE600081	285	WL105001	602
WA108051L	452	WA110061L	297	WC105001L	503	WC108051L	564	WE600101L	164	WL105001	652
WA108051L	463	WA110061L	425	WC105001L	516	WC108051L	581	WE702101	657	WL105001	654
WA108051L	464	WA110061L	426	WC105001L	560	WC108051L	583	WE703081	491	WL105001	656
WA108051L	495	WA110061L	469	WC105001L	566	WC108051L	591	WF104001L	318	WL105001	657
WA108051L	497	WA110061L	499	WC105001L	626	WC108051L	598	WF105001L	492	WL105001	702
WA108051L	498	WA110061L	501	WC105001L	628	WC108051L	656	WF105001L	503	WL105001	703
WA108051L	500	WA110061L	508	WC105001L	658	WC108051L	664	WF105001L	627	WL105001L	319
WA108051L	502	WA110061L	547	WC105004L	484	WC108051L	668	WF105121	484	WL105001L	384
WA108051L	505	WA110061L	576	WC105007	482	WC108051L	673	WF106001L	492	WL105001L	389
WA108051L	515	WA110061L	615	WC105007	502	WC108051L	677	WF108001L	452	WL105001L	391
WA108051L	518	WA110061L	674	WC106001L	714	WC108051L	681	WF108001L	546	WL105001L	393
WA108051L	522	WA110061L	700	WC106041	704	WC110061	603	WF108001L	552	WL105001L	397
WA108051L	533	WA112081	698	WC106041L	142	WC110061L	21	WF108001L	655	WL105001L	474
WA108051L	540	WA112081L	167	WC106041L	143	WC110061L	49	WF108001L	660	WL105001L	480
WA108051L	541	WA112081L	288	WC106041L	315	WC110061L	73	WF108004L	518	WL105001L	487
WA108051L	553	WA112081L	293	WC106041L	316	WC110061L	102	WF110001L	315	WL105001L	492
WA108051L	555	WA112081L	296	WC106041L	407	WC110061L	280	WF110001L	316	WL105001L	493
WA108051L	557	WA112081L	311	WC106041L	522	WC110061L	282	WF112001L	394	WL105001L	509
WA108051L	562	WA112081L	394	WC106041L	523	WC110061L	497	WF116001L	319	WL105001L	510
WA108051L	564	WA112081L	515	WC106041L	559	WC110061L	535	WF600041L	471	WL105001L	516
WA108051L	572	WA112081L	561	WC106041L	567	WC110061LD	131	WF600041L	472	WL105001L	536
WA108051L	576	WA112081L	644	WC106041L	607	WC110061LD	259	WF600041L	479	WL105001L	542
WA108051L	591	WA112081L	674	WC106041L	622	WC112081	278	WF600041L	488	WL105001L	560
WA108051L	592	WA120001	279	WC106041L	653	WC112081	499	WF600051L	522	WL105001L	566
WA108051L	593	WA600071	288	WC106041L	659	WC112081L	276	WF600051L	557	WL105001L	579
WA108051L	608	WA600071L	290	WC106044L	626	WC112081L	297	WF600051L	564	WL105001L	582
WA108051L	610	WA600091L	590	WC106047	411	WC112081L	401	WF600071L	164	WL105001L	611
WA108051L	613	WA702101L	116	WC106047	478	WC112081L	588	WF702101L	233	WL105001L	628
WA108051L	614	WA702101L	132	WC108001	356	WC116101	278	WF702108	480	WL105001L	658
WA108051L	666	WA702101L	140	WC108051L	95	WC702101	386	WF703084	480	WL105001L	659
WA108051L	674	WA702101L	338	WC108051L	102	WC702101	595	WF704064	480	WL105004	482
WA108051L	675	WA702101L	395	WC108051L	285	WC702101	657	WJ105001	657	WL105004	484
WA108051L	677	WA702101L	396	WC108051L	390	WC702101	720	WJ105001L	487	WL105001L	474
WA108051L	718	WB106041	507	WC108051L	391	WC702101L	385	WJ106001L	372	WL106001	265
WA108054L	665	WB106041L	140	WC108051L	392	WC702101L	669	WJ106001L	374	WL106001	357
WA108054L	666	WB106041L	446	WC108051L	393	WC702101L	671	WJ106001L	485	WL106001	383
WA110041L	701	WB106041L	447	WC108051L	425	WD106041	593	WJ106007	451	WL106001	420
WA110061L	155	WB106041L	676	WC108051L	459	WD110061L	131	WJ110001	297	WL106001	498
WA110061L	156	WB106041L	682	WC108051L	460	WD112081L	509	WJ600041	704	WL106001	702
WA110061L	157	WB106041L	683	WC108051L	461	WD112081L	510	WK606214L	480	WL106001	703
WA110061L	168	WB108051L	116	WC108051L	462	WE104001L	539	WK608311	668	WL106001	708
WA110061L	178	WB108051L	509	WC108051L	497	WE104001L	549	WL104001L	92	WL106001	710
WA110061L	184	WB108051L	510	WC108051L	512	WE104001L	551	WL104001L	382	WL106001L	35
WA110061L	201	WB114001L	555			WE105001L	539	WL104001L	508	WL106001L	36

PART NO	PAGE	PART NO	PAGE	PART NO	PAGE	PART NO	PAGE	PART NO	PAGE	PART NO	PAGE
WL106001L	40	WL106001L	422	WL106001L	605	WL108001L	42	WL108001L	220	WL108001L	505
WL106001L	60	WL106001L	447	WL106001L	608	WL108001L	43	WL108001L	238	WL108001L	520
WL106001L	61	WL106001L	471	WL106001L	610	WL108001L	52	WL108001L	256	WL108001L	526
WL106001L	64	WL106001L	472	WL106001L	613	WL108001L	53	WL108001L	266	WL108001L	541
WL106001L	81	WL106001L	485	WL106001L	621	WL108001L	57	WL108001L	276	WL108001L	546
WL106001L	90	WL106001L	488	WL106001L	622	WL108001L	59	WL108001L	278	WL108001L	552
WL106001L	91	WL106001L	491	WL106001L	648	WL108001L	60	WL108001L	279	WL108001L	553
WL106001L	109	WL106001L	492	WL106001L	655	WL108001L	61	WL108001L	287	WL108001L	554
WL106001L	110	WL106001L	505	WL106001L	660	WL108001L	64	WL108001L	298	WL108001L	555
WL106001L	117	WL106001L	507	WL106001L	663	WL108001L	65	WL108001L	299	WL108001L	557
WL106001L	118	WL106001L	511	WL106001L	667	WL108001L	66	WL108001L	311	WL108001L	559
WL106001L	119	WL106001L	513	WL106001L	669	WL108001L	75	WL108001L	312	WL108001L	564
WL106001L	120	WL106001L	520	WL106001L	672	WL108001L	76	WL108001L	317	WL108001L	572
WL106001L	125	WL106001L	522	WL106001L	675	WL108001L	78	WL108001L	318	WL108001L	576
WL106001L	132	WL106001L	525	WL106001L	676	WL108001L	80	WL108001L	319	WL108001L	581
WL106001L	156	WL106001L	526	WL106001L	680	WL108001L	81	WL108001L	330	WL108001L	583
WL106001L	157	WL106001L	527	WL106001L	682	WL108001L	83	WL108001L	340	WL108001L	588
WL106001L	161	WL106001L	528	WL106001L	683	WL108001L	86	WL108001L	342	WL108001L	591
WL106001L	169	WL106001L	530	WL106001L	704	WL108001L	89	WL108001L	346	WL108001L	592
WL106001L	176	WL106001L	531	WL106001L	716	WL108001L	90	WL108001L	348	WL108001L	593
WL106001L	181	WL106001L	538	WL106001L	717	WL108001L	91	WL108001L	352	WL108001L	608
WL106001L	244	WL106001L	539	WL106001L	718	WL108001L	252	WL108001L	354	WL108001L	610
WL106001L	281	WL106001L	541	WL106004L	633	WL108001L	92	WL108001L	363	WL108001L	613
WL106001L	287	WL106001L	544	WL106004L	634	WL108001L	94	WL108001L	364	WL108001L	614
WL106001L	298	WL106001L	550	WL106004L	665	WL108001L	104	WL108001L	390	WL108001L	623
WL106001L	299	WL106001L	551	WL106004L	671	WL108001L	105	WL108001L	391	WL108001L	664
WL106001L	305	WL106001L	557	WL106004L	673	WL108001L	106	WL108001L	392	WL108001L	666
WL106001L	306	WL106001L	561	WL106005L	502	WL108001L	108	WL108001L	393	WL108001L	668
WL106001L	308	WL106001L	562	WL106005L	503	WL108001L	113	WL108001L	400	WL108001L	673
WL106001L	313	WL106001L	565	WL106061L	303	WL108001L	116	WL108001L	401	WL108001L	674
WL106001L	315	WL106001L	568	WL106007L	411	WL108001L	117	WL108001L	402	WL108001L	677
WL106001L	340	WL106001L	574	WL106007L	451	WL108001L	118	WL108001L	403	WL108001L	679
WL106001L	343	WL106001L	581	WL106007L	452	WL108001L	119	WL108001L	404	WL108001L	681
WL106001L	345	WL106001L	583	WL106007L	478	WL108001L	120	WL108001L	405	WL108001L	711
WL106001L	346	WL106001L	584	WL106041	498	WL108001L	121	WL108001L	408	WL108001L	715
WL106001L	347	WL106001L	585	WL106041L	316	WL108001L	124	WL108001L	409	WL108001L	718
WL106001L	348	WL106001L	586	WL106041L	368	WL108001L	155	WL108001L	412	WL108004	665
WL106001L	358	WL106001L	588	WL106047	452	WL108001L	156	WL108001L	425	WL108004	666
WL106001L	359	WL106001L	589	WL106047	478	WL108001L	157	WL108001L	446	WL110001	212
WL106001L	367	WL106001L	590	WL108001L	24	WL108001L	158	WL108001L	447	WL110001	266
WL106001L	374	WL106001L	591	WL108001L	25	WL108001L	161	WL108001L	459	WL110001	700
WL106001L	380	WL106001L	592	WL108001L	26	WL108001L	162	WL108001L	460	WL110001	701
WL106001L	384	WL106001L	593	WL108001L	27	WL108001L	169	WL108001L	461	WL110001	711
WL106001L	394	WL106001L	594	WL108001L	31	WL108001L	176	WL108001L	462	WL110001	715
WL106001L	407	WL106001L	595	WL108001L	33	WL108001L	177	WL108001L	464	WL110001L	21
WL106001L	412	WL106001L	597	WL108001L	34	WL108001L	178	WL108001L	491	WL110001L	37
WL106001L	417	WL106001L	598	WL108001L	35	WL108001L	181	WL108001L	492	WL110001L	38
WL106001L	418	WL106001L	599	WL108001L	36	WL108001L	197	WL108001L	495	WL110001L	39
WL106001L	419	WL106001L	600	WL108001L	40	WL108001L	212	WL108001L	497	WL110001L	49
WL106001L	421	WL106001L	601	WL108001L	41	WL108001L	219	WL108001L	502		

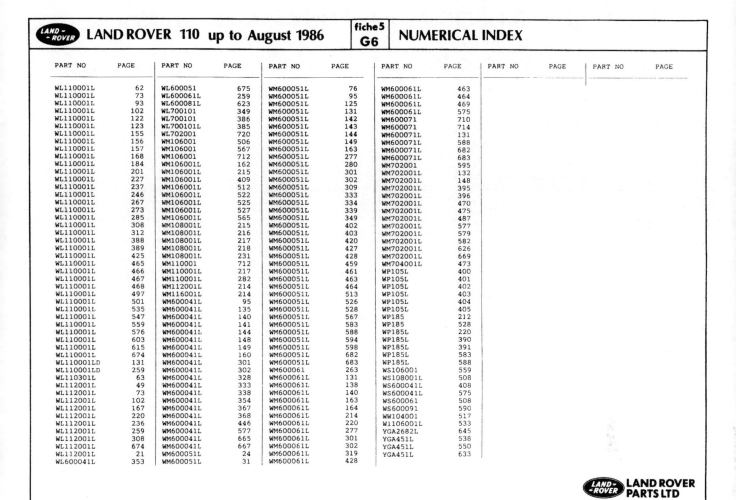

LAND ROVER PARTS LTD

Brooklands Books Ltd., PO Box 146, Cobham,
Surrey KT11 1LG, England Phone: (44) 1932 865051
E-mail: sales@brooklands-books.com   www.brooklandsbooks.com

ISBN: 9781855202887   Part No. RTC986CE   Ref: LR110PH   2T2/2146

LAND ROVER OFFICIAL FACTORY PUBLICATIONS

Land Rover Series 1 Workshop Manual	4291
Land Rover Series 1 1948-53 Parts Catalogue	4051
Land Rover Series 1 1954-58 Parts Catalogue	4107
Land Rover Series 1 Instruction Manual	4277
Land Rover Series 1 and II Diesel Instruction Manual	4343
Land Rover Series II and IIA Workshop Manual	AKM8159
Land Rover Series II and Early IIA Bonneted Control Parts Catalogue	605957
Land Rover Series IIA Bonneted Control Parts Catalogue	RTC9840CC
Land Rover Series IIA, III and 109 V8 Optional Equipment Parts Catalogue	RTC9842CE
Land Rover Series IIA/IIB Instruction Manual	LSM64IM
Land Rover Series 2A and 3 88 Parts Catalogue Supplement (USA Spec)	606494
Land Rover Series III Workshop Manual	AKM3648
Land Rover Series III Workshop Manual V8 Supplement (edn. 2)	AKM8022
Land Rover Series III 88, 109 and 109 V8 Parts Catalogue	RTC9841CE
Land Rover Series III Owners Manual 1971-1978	607324B
Land Rover Series III Owners Manual 1979-1985	AKM8155
Military Land Rover (Lightweight) Series III Parts Catalogue	61278
Military Land Rover Series III (L.W.B.) User Handbook	608179
Military Land Rover (Lightweight) Series III User Manual	608180
Land Rover 90/110 and Defender Workshop Manual 1983-1992	SLR621ENWM
Land Rover Defender Workshop Manual 1993-1995	LDAWMEN93
Land Rover Defender 300 Tdi and Supplements Workshop Manual 1996-1998	LRL0097ENGBB
Land Rover Defender Td5 Workshop Manual and Supplements 1999-2006	LRL0410BB
Land Rover Defender Electrical Manual Td5 1999-06 and 300Tdi 2002-2006	LRD5EHBB
Land Rover 110 Parts Catalogue 1983-1986	RTC9863CE
Land Rover Defender Parts Catalogue 1987-2006	STC9021CC
Land Rover 90 • 110 Handbook 1983-1990 MY	LSM0054
Land Rover Defender 90 • 110 • 130 Handbook 1991 MY - Feb. 1994	LHAHBEN93
Land Rover Defender 90 • 110 • 130 Handbook Mar. 1994 - 1998 MY	LRL0087ENG/2
Military Land Rover 90/110 All Variants (Excluding APV and SAS) User Manual	2320-D-122-201
Military Land Rover 90 and 110 2.5 Diesel Engine Versions User Handbook	SLR989WDHB
Military Land Rover Defender XD - Wolf Workshop Manual - 2320D128 -	302 522 523 524
Military Land Rover Defender XD - Wolf Parts Catalogue	2320D128711
Discovery Workshop Manual 1990-1994 (petrol 3.5, 3.9, Mpi and diesel 200 Tdi)	SJR900ENWM
Discovery Workshop Manual 1995-1998 (petrol 2.0 Mpi, 3.9, 4.0 V8 and diesel 300 Tdi)	LRL0079BB
Discovery Series II Workshop Manual 1999-2003 (petrol 4.0 V8 and diesel Td5 2.5)	VDR100090/6
Discovery Parts Catalogue 1989-1998 (2.0 Mpi, 3.5, 3.9 V8 and 200 Tdi and 300 Tdi)	RTC9947CF
Discovery Parts Catalogue 1999-2003 (petrol 4.0 V8 and diesel Td5 2.5)	STC9049CA
Discovery Owners Handbook 1990-1991 (petrol 3.5 V8 and diesel 200 Tdi)	SJR820ENHB90
Discovery Series II Handbook 1999-2004 MY (petrol 4.0 V8 and Td5 diesel)	LRL0459BB
Freelander Workshop Manual 1998-2000 (petrol 1.8 and diesel 2.0)	LRL0144
Freelander Workshop Manual 2001-2003 ON (petrol 1.8L, 2.5L and diesel Td4 2.0)	LRL0350ENG/4
Land Rover 101 1 Tonne Forward Control Workshop Manual	RTC9120
Land Rover 101 1 Tonne Forward Control Parts Catalogue	608294B
Land Rover 101 1 Tonne Forward Control User Manual	608239
Range Rover Workshop Manual 1970-1985 (petrol 3.5)	AKM3630
Range Rover Workshop Manual 1986-1989	SRR660ENWM &
(petrol 3.5 and diesel 2.4 Turbo VM)	LSM180WS4/2
Range Rover Workshop Manual 1990-1994	
(petrol 3.9, 4.2 and diesel 2.5 Turbo VM, 200 Tdi)	LHAWMENA02
Range Rover Workshop Manual 1995-2001 (petrol 4.0, 4.6 and BMW 2.5 diesel)	LRL0326ENGBB
Range Rover Workshop Manual 2002-2005 (BMW petrol 4.4 and BMW 3.0 diesel)	LRL0477
Range Rover Electrical Manual 2002-2005 UK version (petrol 4.4 and 3.0 diesel)	RR02KEMBB
Range Rover Electrical Manual 2002-2005 USA version (BMW petrol 4.4)	RR02AEMBB
Range Rover Parts Catalogue 1970-1985 (petrol 3.5)	RTC9846CH
Range Rover Parts Catalogue 1986-1991 (petrol 3.5, 3.9 and diesel 2.4 and 2.5 Turbo VM)	RTC9908CB
Range Rover Parts Catalogue 1992-1994 MY and 95 MY Classic	
(petrol 3.9, 4.2 and diesel 2.5 Turbo VM, 200 Tdi and 300 Tdi)	RTC9961CB
Range Rover Parts Catalogue 1995-2001 MY (petrol 4.0, 4.6 and BMW 2.5 diesel)	RTC9970CE
Range Rover Owners Handbook 1970-1980 (petrol 3.5)	606917
Range Rover Owners Handbook 1981-1982 (petrol 3.5)	AKM8139
Range Rover Owners Handbook 1983-1985 (petrol 3.5)	LSM0001HB
Range Rover Owners Handbook 1986-1987 (petrol 3.5 and diesel 2.4 Turbo VM)	LSM129HB

Engine Overhaul Manuals for Land Rover and Range Rover

300 Tdi Engine, R380 Manual Gearbox and LT230T Transfer Gearbox Overhaul Manuals	LRL003, 070 & 081
Petrol Engine V8 3.5, 3.9, 4.0, 4.2 and 4.6 Overhaul Manuals	LRL004 & 164
Land Rover/Range Rover Driving Techniques	LR369
Working in the Wild - Manual for Africa	SMR684MI
Winching in Safety - Complete guide to winching Land Rovers and Range Rovers	SMR699MI

Workshop Manual Owners Edition
Land Rover 2 / 2A / 3 Owners Workshop Manual 1959-1983
Land Rover 90, 110 and Defender Workshop Manual Owners Edition 1983-1995
Land Rover Discovery Workshop Manual Owners Edition 1990-1998

All titles available from Amazon or Land Rover specialists
Brooklands Books Ltd., P.O. Box 146, Cobham, Surrey, KT11 1LG, England, UK
Phone: +44 (0) 1932 865051   info@brooklands-books.com   www.brooklands-books.com

Printed in Great Britain
by Amazon

58464123R00214